About the Editors

Chuck Huff

is Associate Professor of Psychology at St. Olaf College. His research interests include status and gender effects in electronic interaction, the effects of social factors in computing education, and social factors in human-computer interaction. He has taught the course "Social Issues in Computing" at both St. Olaf College and Carnegie Mellon University. He has published research on gender and computing, on the social effects of electronic interaction, on the uses of computing in education, and on teaching about the social and ethical issues associated with computing. He is the Associate Editor for Psychology of *Social Science Computer Review*, Feature Article Editor of *Computers and Society*, and Chair of the Policy Board for the Academic Computing Center at St. Olaf College. Huff received his Ph.D. in Social Psychology from Princeton University in 1987 and was a post-doctoral fellow with the Committee for Social Science Research in Computing at Carnegie Mellon University.

Tom Finholt

is Assistant Professor of Organizational Psychology at the University of Michigan, Ann Arbor. His research interests include the impact of computer communication technology on information processing in organizations, occupational diseases associated with computer use, and the design of collaborative computing environments. Dr. Finholt's recent work has focused on the use of electronic databases by geographically peripheral members of organizations to overcome barriers of distance and time. He is currently involved in a five-year effort to design and assess the Upper Atmospheric Research Collaboratory (UARC), a National Science Foundation project to support remote collaboration among the community of space scientists using the Sondrestrom Upper Atmospheric Research Facility in Kangerlussuaq, Greenland. Dr. Finholt has published in the organizational and psychological literature, and has taught courses on computers and organizations at Carnegie Mellon University and the University of Michigan. Finholt earned his B.A. with High Honors from Swarthmore College, and his Ph.D. in Social and Decision Science from Carnegie Mellon University.

CONTENTS

PREFACE

The ACM and IEEE curriculum task force[1] has recognized the importance of understanding the social issues surrounding computing by requiring its consideration in the curriculum. Of course, most people are aware of some of the changes that the heralded "information age" has produced. Some people are put to work, others lose their jobs; some jobs are enhanced, others are deskilled; complex systems control sophisticated but critical life-support equipment; and questions about the meaning of ownership arise that we thought we had solved. Unfortunately, what many people hear about these problems is simplified popular reporting based on two customary sources.

The first is the cautionary tale (e.g., the boy who cried wolf). Tales with morals have a long history in civilization and there is certainly a place for these in the modern analysis of computing. The authors of many of the included readings will relate some cautionary tales. Nathaniel Rosenberg[2] and Frederick Brooks[3] both provide excellent collections of cautionary tales that should be read by any aspiring computer professional. The shortcoming of the cautionary tale, however, is evident in its telling: There is usually only one caution per tale and it takes a delicate balance of these cautions to even begin to represent the complexity of the social issues surrounding computing. But the popular press is not usually interested in a careful story and thus the news we receive is often incomplete.

More complete stories are offered by the various technophobes and technophiles who build a scenario of the future based on their particular premonition of the "new technology." These range from predictions of electronic sweatshops to electronic utopias.[4] These visions seem more comprehensive than the singular cautionary tale, but they are just as incomplete. Trends or data that do not fit the vision are discarded. Those that do fit are overgeneralized. Thus, though these visions seem more complete, close inspection reveals the cobwebs and cracks.

With a few exceptions,[5] these two approaches were the basis for most of the books when we began teaching courses in computers and society at

---

[1] Computing Curricula 1991: Report of the ACM/IEEE-CS Joint Curriculum Task Force, New York:ACM Press.

[2] Nathaniel Rosenberg (1991). *Programming as if People Mattered: Friendly Programs, Software Engineering, and Other Noble Delusions*. Princeton: Princeton University Press.

[3] Frederick Brooks (1975). *The Mythical Man-Month: Essays on Software Engineering*. Reading, MA: Addison Wesley.

[4] See Michael Benedikt (1991) Cyberspace: First Steps. Cambridge MA: MIT Press, for a utopian vision, and John Zerzan & Alice Carnes (Eds.) (1991) Questioning technology: Tool, toy, or tyrant? Philadelphia: New Society Publishers, for a distopic view.

[5] Joseph Weizenbaum (1976) *Computer Power and Human Reason*. (San Francisco, CA: W. H. Freeman and Company) is one, along with the classic by Norbert Weiner (1950) *The Human Use of Human Beings* (New York:Avon Books).

Carnegie Mellon University. There is now a much better selection. Several texts now look at the ethical bases for decisions made in computing,[6] and some provide a basic overview of the various controversies in the area.[7]

But as far as we can tell no reader systematically presents the research that has been done by social scientists on these questions. Sociologists, anthropologists, economists, political scientists, and psychologists have been engaged in asking questions about technology and society for over a decade now, and there is a collection of research on these topics that ought to inform the ethical and professional discussion.

What service can this approach provide a student of computer science? Any discussion of the ethical and social effects of computing will almost certainly be shot through with empirical questions. Does computing isolate students? Does the computerization of a job necessarily involve deskilling? Do patent and copyright law encourage innovation? Where do national databases get their data from, and how accurate is it? Does automation put people out of work? Why isn't technology being used well in our schools?

A quick perusal of the readings in this text will convince the reader that we cannot take for granted the standard answers to these questions. Besides which there are usually two, if not more, standard answers to be had. The real world is more sloppy, more complex, and more interesting and exciting that the standard answer(s) would lead us to believe. The technology we create is used by people with complex motivations. They are both managers and mothers, they care about money and friendship, and the technology they use is only one aspect of their world.

We hope that this text will introduce the student to social science readings that inform the debates about the uses of technology. That is, we hope to provide some light, in addition to the traditional heat that has surrounded these topics. Social science research does not (and perhaps cannot) definitively answer the empirical questions involved here. And even if it did, more basic questions of ethical choice would still remain. But the social science research provides an excellent place to begin understanding the nature of the issues. When one understands the social effects of a technology, the ethical questions may become more clear. What may become more clear is that the ethical questions are harder than we thought they were. This is a helpful realization—a little humility is good for us all.

Organization

We included selections because we found them to be (1) readable at an undergraduate level, (2) careful, empirical studies of how computing is actually used, and (3) current in their examination of a topic. There are of

---

[6]See David Ermann, Mary Williams, & Claudio Gutierrez (1990) *Computers, Ethics, and Society* (Oxford: Oxford University Press) for one example.

[7]See Charles Dunlop & Rob Kling (1991). *Computerization and Controversy* (Boston: Academic Press).

course, exceptions to all these rules, but we hope they will not be so grievous that the selection's point will be lost. In making our decisions, we tried to balance the various criteria against each other. For instance, some selections are more than eight years old, but they seemed to be the most readable. In no case have we included an older selection if more current work contradicted the basic story to be derived from the article. For some areas we had trouble identifying good empirical work and chose case studies or reviews of the issues that we thought would serve in their absence. In several instances, we have had to ask people well known for their work to contribute original articles.

In addition to the readings, we provide several helps to the student or nontechnical reader:

- Reading Questions to help orient the introductory level student in mastering the basic points of the articles
- Debatable discussion questions for class discussion or term papers
- A Practice section for each chapter to give students practical experience with, rather than merely academic review of, social and ethical aspects of computing

How to use this book

Feel free to skip around. The topics are not presented in any particular order of importance or difficulty. We do recommend that you read the first sections (Chapters 1, 2, and 3) early on since these contain some basic material that will help you in reading the other chapters. In addition, you might consider reading the concluding chapter on the design ethic both early in the class and at the end. But beyond that, let your personal interests be your guide.

Be skeptical. Empirical claims are easy to make, and much harder to prove. There are usually many more things in the world than are dreamt of in our philosophies. If an author makes a claim, be sure to find out what evidence there is to support it. We will try to help with this goal through the reading and discussion questions.

Beware of making excuses for your favorite technology. It is easy to say that your technology is so different from any of the research reviewed in this volume that we can learn nothing from the old work. This is the natural position of innovators and early adopters of technology. But remember that it is often not the technology that determines its use but the social organizations and people who adopt the technology. Blaming those who stupidly misuse or misunderstand your favorite technology may help you feel better, but it won't help you understand how people use technology.

Be empirical. Check your opinions about the various issues covered here against the realities in your organization. We have made some suggestions in almost every chapter about how you might do this.

An endeavor of this sort is never done without support. We are both grateful to Carnegie Mellon University's *Committee for Social Science Research in Computing* for providing an atmosphere in which we could explore these issues and work to investigate them. Sara Kiesler, Rob Kling, Lee Sproull, and Suzy Wiesband provided expert advice and willing consultation on the many decisions we had to make. Chuck Huff would like to thank the many students who helped in the formatting and preparation of this text, but particular thanks go to Debra Winter for her work on the glossary. Many thanks also go to Bruce Jawer for his work on the "Design Ethic" exercises. Bruce brought to this task and to our conversations on the book the useful perspective of the practicing programmer. Suzanne Riesman was unfailing in her attempts to secure permission for the articles we reprint here.

We would also like to thank the following reviewers for their many helpful comments and suggestions: Terrell Ward Bynum, Southern Connecticut State University; David Ermann, University of Delaware; Donald Gotterbarn, East Tennessee State University; Rob Kling, University of California, Irvine; C. Dianne Martin, George Washington University; and Keith Miller, The College of William and Mary.

Chuck Huff
Thomas Finholt

CHAPTER

1

PUTTING TECHNOLOGY IN ITS PLACE

Chuck Huff
St. Olaf College

Thomas Finholt
University of Michigan

When adaptation to a diet of bamboo required more flexibility in manipulation, pandas could not redesign their thumbs but had to make do with a makeshift substitute—an enlarged radial sesamoid bone of the wrist, the panda's false thumb. The sesamoid bone is a clumsy, suboptimal structure, but it works. Pathways of history (commitment of the true thumb to other roles during an irreversible past) impose such jury rigged solutions upon all creatures.

Stephen Jay Gould

In a delightful essay, Gould has described the standard computer keyboard as the "panda's thumb" of technology because it is a vestigial remnant of another time. This familiar and unassuming keyboard provides an excellent example of the ways that technology is embedded in society.

The current layout of the keyboard is a hangover from a time when typists had to be forced to type slowly to avoid jamming the machine. Current machines can outstrip the fastest typists, but we are still encumbered with a layout designed a hundred years ago.

In 1867 Christopher Latham Sholes designed the 52nd version of the "type writer"—with a keyboard that looked nothing like our current layout (see David, 1986, for a detailed history). Today it seems a cumbersome device, with the keyboard on top and the paper laid flat on a plate below the table. There is an obvious difficulty with this design—the typist could not see what he (at that time typists were mostly male) was doing. Of course, a skilled operator can overcome many of the defects of a tool, but it required

1

remembering where you were in a passage to be typed and typing slowly enough that the keys that struck the letters on the page would not jam. This latter skill required much practice and patience, since you could only tell when a jam had occurred by raising the carriage to look underneath it and seeing a long string of ooooooo's or whatever letter happened to be foremost when the keys jammed.

The machine was being marketed during the recession of the 1870s and businesses didn't want to hire highly trained workers for a still unproved machine that cost $125. What was needed was a design that would allow the untrained worker to type at the machine's speed.

Sholes began experimenting with the layout of the keyboard in an effort to make type writing on the machine slow enough that the machine could keep up. After many layouts based on trial and error, he found a layout that succeeded—the qwerty keyboard, named after the first six letters in the top row. If you think about which keys you use most, it soon becomes evident why the qwerty layout would slow a person down. The "e" is not in the middle row, and must be struck with the weaker fingers of the left hand. Other popular vowels (u, i, o) are also on the top row. The "a" must be struck with a weak finger of the left hand too. An optimal keyboard would have the letters "dhiatensor" in the middle row, since over 70 percent of the words in English can be spelled with these letters. Thus qwerty was a trial-and-error-based layout designed to minimize the defects of a machine that is today irrelevant.

Sholes, along with the promoter and underwriter of the machine, James Densmore, managed to sell the rights for the type writer to Remington (the renowned rifle manufacturer) in 1873. It was only one of many different type writers on the market, each with a different design and many with different keyboard layouts.

At the same time, several methods of training young women to type (remember the need for cheap labor?) were also in competition. Primers were published, and "technical" schools were set up to support the growing need for typists. Each of these schools usually specialized in a machine from a particular manufacturer and taught a distinct method of typing for the machine. Louis Taub, a proponent of the Caligraph—a competing machine, key layout, and typing method—challenged the leading Remington proponent to a heavily publicized typing match. This contest was celebrated as a match between the two machines as much as, if not more than, a match between the two typing methods.

The Caligraph typist's typing method involved using only two fingers on each hand—the argument being that these were the strongest fingers anyway. The Remington typist, using that school's method of four fingers on each hand, had memorized the layout of the keyboard and did not need to look at the keys while typing. The contest, of course, was a rout. The Remington touch-typist shamed the Caligraph typist, and the qwerty keyboard won the day.

Technical schools and "business" courses in public high schools quickly took up the touch-typing method—mostly using the Remington-based qwerty keyboard. These new cadres of typists were predominantly female—despite objections that women could not operate complicated machines well—and could be hired for lower wages than male office workers. As a consequence, it was cheaper for businesses to use a type writer that had a large base of inexpensive trained workers, and the qwerty standard prevailed. Other manufacturers of typewriters (now the generic name) changed their layout to the *de facto* qwerty standard.

Thus, the nontechnical, social surroundings determined the outcome of the supposedly technical issue of how best to design the keyboard. The influences included the needs of business, the tradition of designing machines for cheap labor, and the influx of women into the labor market. Better keyboards certainly exist. August Dvorak, a time & motion study devotee, has designed the best-known alternative. Navy studies in the 1940s made it clear that the change from qwerty to a more efficient keyboard would pay for itself within 10 days. But despite intermittent attempts to introduce a better layout (David, 1986), qwerty remains the standard.

MORAL: THE SOCIAL CONTEXT OF COMPUTING MATTERS

It was the social context of the qwerty keyboard that determined its acceptance and its dominance of the industry. This is all the more obvious because the qwerty standard is so inelegant and suboptimal. The layout is so bad we can only explain its dominance by social context.

The clarity of the point quickly fades when we talk about other technological artifacts. Since we are familiar with the technical issues of electronic mail, it is easy to think that *these* are what will determine its success. Faster transmission, better interfaces, more flexible standards, more reliable networks, etc., are what will *really* make electronic mail use take off. For some technologies, this may be true.: Some technologies have primarily succeeded because of their technical advantages (perhaps the integrated circuit).

But most computing technologies will fall in between. For this large majority of computing artifacts, then, it will be essential to understand *both* the technical issues *and* the social contexts before we can understand their successes. Some corollaries of this point follow.

The best machine does not always win

This is partly because we cannot today decide what "best" is for the next decade. The future adoption and use of a technology depend crucially upon more than that technology's current efficiency, ease of use, etc., And to understand how a technology is likely to be used, you need to understand more than the uses that were intended by the designer. Unless all the chips fall in the right place (see the example on telework in Chapter 9), a promising technology may be ignored. And if the chips do fall that way, a less efficient technology can supplant others (fax has been adopted much more rapidly than electronic mail).

It is hard to predict the technological future

No one at the time would have predicted that the "slow" keyboard would become the standard for a century. Technological innovation and change are so dependent upon the particular circumstances that surround the design, building, and implementation that only very short range and limited predictions can be made with any accuracy. The future you envision for the technology you design may be rosy, but there are more plants in the garden than you can control. Old predictions of the technological future are now being recycled as historical oddities (e.g., helicopters will become the primary mode of personal transportation—Willis, 1986). This does not mean that since it is so hard, any prediction is as good as any other. It does mean that any reasonable prediction should take into account the social context that will determine the outcome, and should include a healthy dose of modesty.

Careful analysis, done early, can sometimes save us from poor design

Historical "what-ifs" (e.g., if Kennedy hadn't been assassinated) are great fun, and it is tempting to speculate on what might have happened if the typing speed contest had allowed a fair comparison between keyboard layouts. But on the more practical level, a better analysis of keyboard efficiency—done early enough—might have saved a lot of money and sore fingers.

But the *timing* is essential. Paul David (1986) has shown that once a less efficient design gets the advantage of being the "standard" in the field, it is extremely difficult to supplant or even modify. We are then locked into decisions that we once thought were technically sound (and probably once were). It follows, then, that good designers need to be proficient in both technical matters and in matters of social context.

A CURRENT EXAMPLE: THE CYBERSPACE OFFICE

But perhaps a particular technology is so advanced and so different from the old, so rich, that it will quickly revolutionize those sectors of the economy in which it is used. This is the standard argument for the "revolutionary" character of a technology, and the logic proceeds in this manner: Technology X is such an advanced system that those who adopt it will have the competitive edge—they will become more productive, more flexible, and more profitable. This will drive others in that industry to adopt technology X, and it will quickly spread throughout the industry. This pattern of adoption is often represented in terms of a curve of adoption (see Figure 1-1).

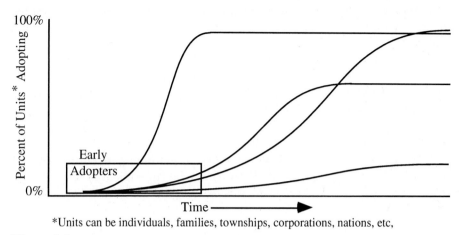

*Units can be individuals, families, townships, corporations, nations, etc,

Figure 1-1
Several typical adoption curves.

Familiar and traditionally cited examples of this kind of adoption curve are the typewriter, the telephone, the photocopy machine, facsimile transmission, and mainframe and desktop computers. These and other successful innovations have transformed the way we work, play, organize, and communicate.

These claims are indeed true, but this does not imply that social context will be absent from the success of any technology, or even that it is primarily the technical factors that account for the success of a particular product. To be successful, any technology must be developed by designers, supported by venture capital, built by manufacturers, sold by third parties, adopted by corporations, implemented by managers and technicians, used by people, and regulated by government. It is unlikely that the interests of all these groups will be the same. And the conflicting social influences created by these interests change more slowly than the technology. This means that an understanding of the social context that influenced the development and implementation of earlier, cruder, technologies can be useful in helping us understand the development of current technologies—not because the technologies are identical, but because the social contexts are likely to be similar.

Cyberspace Predictions

The hyperbole about cyberspace is a good exemplar of the usefulness of a socially literate analysis of technology. Virtual reality combined with advanced communications is supposed to transform our work, play, and communication patterns. Cyberspace is, according to Benedikt (1991), "a new and irresistible development in the elaboration of human culture and business under the sign of technology." It will transform the ways we think about what is and isn't real, the ways we communicate and collaborate with each other, and the ways we work and play. The volume Benedikt has edited contains a variety of euphoric visions about what cyberspace can or should do for us.

Pruitt & Barrett (1991) have participated in the design of virtual reality systems, and in an article in the book *Cyberspace*, share this dream of a transformed workplace. Here is an excerpt from their vision of the cyberspace workplace of the future:

> Cyberspace will free an individual from space and time constraints. An individual will be able to link up "physically" much the same way people link up via telephone today. Electronic commuting will become commonplace. . . Electronically nomadic, cyberspace workers will live wherever the electronic cyberspace infrastructure reaches . . .

Many similar claims were made in the 1970s for a similar technology, electronic communication. The easy and fast exchange of information in text, pictures and video, spreadsheets, etc., was supposed to transform the organizations of that time. Here are some claims from the chapter "The Electronic Cottage" of Toffler's book The *Third Wave* (1979):

> Many people will work at home part time and outside the home as well. Dispersed work centers will no doubt proliferate. Some people will work at home for months or years, then switch to an outside job, and then perhaps switch back again. Patterns of leadership and management will have to change. Small firms would undoubtedly spring up to contract for white collar tasks from larger firms and take on specialized responsibilities for organizing, training, and managing teams of homeworkers.

These visions sound remarkably similar. And it may be that both claims will turn out to be true. But given the similarity of the claims and the similarity of the technology, it would be useful to look at the actual effects that electronic communication has had on the workplace. Many scholars have been tracking the use of electronic communication in the workplace since the mid-'70s, and they have a mixed bag of success to report. (For more detail, see Chapter 9.) In short, electronic communication has been used in important and fascinating ways in many organizations, with good effect; but the effects have not taken the predicted form, nor have they been as pervasive as the technology prophets foretold.

The Actual Electronic Office

Early publicity about the potential of electronic communication and telecommuting led many corporations to run trial telecommuting programs (Olsen, 1987). In most of these pilot programs, the participants were highly skilled professionals whom companies compete to retain. The telecommuting aspect was considered a job "perk" that helped to increase the commitment of the workers. In those programs involving workers with less status (word processors, clerical work) the intention of the company was usually to reduce work hours and benefits, and thus to maintain productivity while reducing cost.

Many of these pilot programs were declared successes. But in most cases they were then terminated. The primary concerns that led to the waning of these telework programs were supervision and organizational culture. Even when productivity was unquestionably high, supervisors were worried that they could not closely oversee the work. Workers who were more tied to the day-to-day work of the corporation (e.g., accounting) were not allowed to participate in even the pilot programs (Olsen, 1987).

Most of the current teleworkers are "privileged professionals" who use telework to extend their workday, not to replace it. When clerical or other low status work is transferred to telework arrangements, it is usually the transferal of some easily routinized functions to regional work centers where office relations are replicated, with telecommunications used to maintain contact and supervision of upper-level management (Kraut, 1987). These regional work centers tend to be either in the suburbs or in southern and western towns where labor is less expensive and not unionized. Thus, for most workers, the grand predictions have not been realized. The obstacles are less the availability or richness of the technology than the social and organizational cultures of the corporations that could adopt telework.

But even if it does not fit the freewheeling vision of Toffler, electronic communication has clearly had an impact on how business is done. Most Fortune 500 companies use some version of electronic mail among their employees. Law enforcement at all levels now uses electronic mail. Many cities and other government organizations have extensive electronic mail connections, and electronic mail has made communication among scientists much easier and more productive.

The benefits of these electronic connections are well documented. Electronic mail connects people who are distant from each other in time and space, increasing productivity and enhancing commitment to organizations where it is used (Huff, Sproull, & Kiesler, 1989). It helps people form and maintain group and organizational commitments that they might otherwise miss (Finholt & Sproull, 1990). It helps people work in diverse groups more flexibly (Sproull & Kiesler, 1991).

But the offices in even the most networked places usually look like regular offices, and most people show up during normal office hours to do their work. Even in the face of explicit and varied attempts to change the structure of the traditional office (such as job redesign, flextime, participatory management, team approaches) office organization has remained substantially the same for almost a century (Kraut, 1987). The introduction of the telephone could have dispersed the workforce to their homes or to regional work centers, but it seems to have done the opposite. Managers moved away from the factories and gathered into office structures in the central city. Clerical work moved with them (Pool, 1977).

Advantages of the Traditional Office

The resilience of the traditional office and its resistance to attempts to restructure it come from many sources. Workers derive satisfaction from the social interaction they experience at work (Locke, 1976). This interaction provides a network of social support for both personal and work-related reasons (Thoite, 1983). Since office work is primarily face-to-face work, this social support is crucial in making things work smoothly. The traditional office also facilitates the socialization of new workers. It aids in the establishment and maintenance of informal communication networks, providing standards for dress, productivity, values, and cultural rules that would be difficult and awkward to include explicitly in electronic communication. The informal social network of the traditional office also provides other information about the structure of the organization (raises, hierarchy, procedures) that are difficult, if not embarrassing and ill advised, to explicitly list. And, of course, the traditional office aids in the supervision of workers and helps to structure their time.

For all these reasons, the traditional office is difficult to replicate electronically. And even if it were possible to replicate, the managers who make decisions about office structure would then have to be convinced that the change is for the better. As a result, electronic mail, the most basic form of electronic communication, has been integrated into the traditional office structure and has certainly added a great deal of value. But it has not changed the basic structure.

Will cyberspace fare better in revolutionizing the traditional office? In its best incarnations, it does provide more information and more "immediacy" than older forms of communication, but then it is also more obtrusive. It is more flexible and (under some circumstances) more engrossing. It is also more expensive. And it will face obstacles similar to those electronic communication faced. Predictions about its likely effects will have to take these socially based constraints into account. You can still remain wildly optimistic about cyberspace if you imagine the rest of the world is just like you, and wants the cool stuff you want. Much technology has been designed with this assumption (Borenstein, 1991; Huff & Cooper, 1987; Shneiderman, 1992). But, of course, the assumption is wrong.

The success of cyberspace in the next 10 or 20 years is likely to be similar to that of electronic communication: a lot of change in some places, some change in more places, not much change in most places. Admittedly, some things may need to change before cyberspace takes off. Communications speed and quality may need to be increased. The cyberspace office may have to wait until the majority of information in the traditional office is available online and until the majority of coworkers can (and will) use E-mail. In addition, communications costs may need to fall and the costs of computing in the office may have to be reduced as well. It is also possible that more of the work done in the traditional office will have to be made suitable for completion electronically. Even the visionaries are aware of the difficulties that lie in wait for the cyberspace office (Pruitt & Barrett, 1991). But these difficulties, combined with the advantages of the traditional office, may transform the vision of the cyberspace corporation into a more mundane—but more productive and more flexible—office.

The standard curve for the adoption of any innovation looks like the one pictured in Figure 1. At first only a few "early adopters" use the innovation. Then as more people or companies adopt it, the innovation becomes more widespread in the culture until the adoption rate "turns the corner" and takes off. Finally, with adoption by all those who are likely to find the innovation useful, the rate of adoption levels off. The adoption curves for television, the telephone, the VCR, and the home computer all look like this (though the rate for the telephone was much slower and home computers seem to have leveled off at about 20 percent of the population).

An important thing to recognize about this curve is that at the beginning, the innovation curve of a failure looks a lot like the curve of a slow but hampered success. So it is difficult to tell, at the beginning, whether an innovation will succeed or what form it will take when it does succeed. The "cautionary tale" we have related here about the adoption of electronic mail is a case in point. Electronic mail was an unforeseen outcome of the networks designed for the Defense Department (Sproull & Kiesler, 1991), and when it finally took shape, many people misunderstood or overgeneralized the impact it would have on the world of work. The factors that influenced its success and that shaped its impact were only partly technical. And those who predicted its future based on its technical promise alone were soon reminded of the social influences that shaped its evolution.

APPROACHING THIS TEXT

All the issues you will confront in this text have this complexity in common. If you are sure about the right answers to the questions, it probably means you have not thought carefully enough. Careful thought will not unfailingly provide the correct answer. There are no algorithms adequate to the task of predicting human behavior. But rules of thumb, cautionary tales, careful observation, and thoughtful analysis about how humans use technology can help you design better products and implement them in a way that will best assure their success.

Levels of Analysis

There are a broad range of issues you will be facing in this book. Some are large-scale issues, like the question of whether the government's use of pattern matching to detect fraud is a violation of civil rights. Others are relatively small in scale: What are some ways of minimizing the barriers to the handicapped in the design of systems? Some are primarily ethical questions: What are the designer's obligations to the users of a system? Others are primarily empirical questions: Do patent laws encourage innovation? A quick look at these questions makes it evident that there are no "pure" large- or small-scale or ethical versus empirical questions. Issues of "rights" enter into patent law, and access for handicapped individuals is now mandated by federal law.

The chapters in the book are not organized to deal with these "question types," partly because they are all important in any consideration of technology. Each of these types of questions, the empirical and ethical, the large-and the small-scale, are intertwined such that answers to one lead to questions about the other. For instance, in the use of computers in schools, all levels appear. What kinds of access should rural and poor schools have to international networks? What local issues help or hinder the implementation of technology in the curriculum? Does computer-aided instruction really help learning? Whose learning? To answer any of these questions requires answering large- and small-scale ethical and empirical questions.

Take, for instance, the question of equity in access to international networks. The current push for government funding of the National Research and Education Network (NREN) is based on the idea that a high-speed national computing network is a common good (like interstate highways) that should be provided by the agency most common to us all, the U.S. government (see the article by Cisler in Chapter 11). This is clearly large-scale. But the equity issue (e.g., should access to the NREN for poor schools be subsidized and by whom?) depends on small-scale questions: Can access to networks be shown to help educationally? And, of course, the issue of equity is an ethical issue (e.g., is equal access enough or should underprivileged schools get more subsidies than rich schools?). A primary skill in thinking about the social issues in computing will be determining what kind of question you are asking, since this implies the kind of answer you can expect.

We attempt to point these levels out by asking you to find them in the readings. The reading and discussion questions we provide are where some of the real work of understanding the social and ethical issues of computing will be done. Use these questions to take a close look at each of the readings. They not only focus on basic concepts and terminology but also provide hints on where the biases of the authors can be located in the text. We encourage you to be critical in your reading of these selections. Many of the authors have a well defined viewpoint (more crudely put, a bias). The assumptions and viewpoints of others may be less easy to identify. So when you read a selection, check the reading questions as you read, engage in discussion with friends or classmates, write a paper or take notes, pay attention to whose agenda is advanced by any claim. And make sure that the empirical claims made by authors are backed up with more than an example or two.

The Design Ethic

Possession of even the best information on social issues in technology will not relieve you of the responsibility to make choices. Life goes on whether you think carefully or not, and production schedules do not allow extended time for reflection, research, or experimentation. Computer professionals must make design, production, and implementation decisions in the face of the uncertainty that these issues produce.

This text is a chance to consider these issues with an eye toward how they will affect the work you are involved in as a professional. In Chapter 18 we present in detail an approach to these practical issues that emphasizes an awareness of the difficulties of designing computing systems for real people in real organizations. We call this approach a *design ethic*. The design ethic recognizes that for the computer professional committed to excellence, three areas of commitment are mutually supporting and must be intertwined: (a) commitment to designing and implementing a quality product, (b) awareness of ethical issues in design and implementation, and (c) concern about the social context that influences the use of a technology.

The emphasis on a quality product seems straightforward, and from it flow the other two points. This is because "quality" encompasses more than technical excellence. Technical excellence is required, and in itself is difficult to attain. But a narrow form of technical excellence can be attained without attention to the world in which the product will be used. Real quality requires more—it requires a commitment to designing a product that "fits" into the situations in which it will be regularly used. And this requires an understanding of those situations.

It is, then, an easy jump from commitment to a quality product to a concern for the social parameters that determine how a product is used. But once we become aware of how a product is used—become aware of the social and organizational issues that influence its use—we also become aware of the ethical dimension of the choices that confront us. Thus all three parts of the design ethic are mutually supporting.

As an example, consider the issue of the cyberspace office. A commitment to a quality cyberspace office product will require the technical expertise needed to design and implement a product that can be used in real organizations, not just the mythical "office of the future." It will have to take into account the variety of kinds of information that are exchanged in a real office, the variety of standards for that information, and the variety of purposes to which this information is put. It will need to be affordable by organizations wishing to purchase it, and powerful enough to be useful. These and other trade-offs are ones familiar to anyone who has participated in the design of hardware or software.

But in addition to these issues, the designer or implementer will need to take into account the ways that people work together in real organizations. For example, current software for collaborative groups assumes that people are always interested in cooperating, that they are not competitive, and that they will gladly make statements in an electronic medium that can be preserved and replicated for decades. (See Chapter 2 for a closer look at this issue.) These are clearly assumptions that will be wrong in a competitive sales office or a secretarial typing pool. High-quality technology will need to be aware of these differences in use if it is to succeed. An awareness of the social environment in which a proposed cyberspace product will be used is thus crucial to its success.

And once the designer becomes aware of the social milieu in which the cyberspace product is used, he or she will have to confront the ethical issues that this raises. As Allen argues in Chapter 2, groupware can all too easily become snoopware. To what extent is this electronic supervision ethical? If supervision is part of the job, how can it be made more ethical and less intrusive? Even by avoiding these questions we have made an ethical choice—to support the continuation of current practice.

Thus, we can do a better job designing a cyberspace office product for the real world if we consider quality design principles, are concerned about the organizational world in which our product will be used, and are aware of the ethical issues that become relevant when our product is put to use. Again, awareness of these issues will not solve the problems for you. You will still have to use your experience and judgment as the basis for making design and implementation decisions. But the design ethic may help you become aware of the wider context for your decision. The design ethic is not prescriptive, it does not require a particular kind of design or even design process. It does point out the variety of factors that should influence your design.

Practicing the Design Ethic

The design ethic explicitly requires that the actual practice of designing technological products should incorporate social and ethical concerns. Most courses on computing, even most internships, do not address these issues. For this reason, we have included in this text some exercises that will help you practice implementing the issues from each chapter. For example, in the chapter that addresses access, we ask you to survey several local labs for their accessibility to people with various handicaps. Having done this once, you might have a better appreciation both for how to do it later and for why it is important to consider.

We have several suggestions for you as you begin these exercises.

Be explicit in your plans. As you are preparing to do a practice exercise, make your plans explicit. For example, if you are surveying labs for accessibility, plan what you will measure (chair height, desk height, clearance in doors, availability of manuals, etc.). If you are going to do an interview, make sure you have the exact question wording, that you have not left out important questions, that you have plans for alternative questions and answers to questions your interviewee might ask, etc., Try to make your list as comprehensive and as detailed as possible. If you can, check your plan with a professional (your instructor, another faculty member, a local expert). This preparation is part of being professional in your approach to these issues.

Be alert for opportunity. It will almost always be the case that something unexpected will happen. Be ready for this, and be flexible in your reaction. Don't ignore opportunity because you have made extensive plans. If your plan was to look at accessibility by measuring desks, chairs, and monitor height in labs, allow yourself the opportunity to follow up when someone in the lab suggests another problem (e.g., remoteness of the facility).

Take careful notes. In the middle of an interview, it is easy to think that you will remember that favorite quote. In all likelihood, you won't. You will be doing the write-up two days later, and will have forgotten not only the quote but the setting of the interview, the tone of the interviewee, and the list of points they made. Take notes both during your project and afterward. Use the time immediately after an exercise to flesh out your sketchy notes, to make note of other items you should consider, and to consolidate things in a way that you can read your notes a week later and reconstruct everything that happened. Attention to detail will pay off.

Respect the rights of others. When your work involves talking to others or observing them or their work, *get their consent first.* If you use a sneaky cover story to do an interview and then ask embarrassing questions, you will ruin not only your project, but that of anyone else who might want to do a project with the group you have offended. So it is in your self-interest to get others' consent. It is also the right thing to do.

Make intrusions into others' lives and work minimal. For the purpose of this course, a short interview can probably be done in 20 minutes. To the extent that you keep your interview under that, respondents will be appreciative and willing to help again with later classes. Remember that you are benefiting from the opportunity to do this project—your interviewee usually gets no benefit. Be polite when interacting with others, and thank them for their time when you are done. Finally, if you do find out something that you think might be of interest, be sure to let those you interviewed or observed know.

You might want to read the design ethic chapter both early in your class and at the end. The early reading will allow you to get a feel for the issues before you begin some of the practice exercises, and the final reading will help you consolidate your experience in the class.

CONCLUSION

The real work in this text is yours. We provide some useful, even central, articles about the issues. We suggest topics that should concern you, and we even supply some opportunities for you to practice what you learn. We hope that as you sample readings and practice your understanding, you will come to the conclusion that the correct "place" for computers is in the real world—and that to understand computers you need to understand their social context.

REFERENCES

Benedikt, M. (ed.) (1991). *Cyberspace: First Steps.* Cambridge, MA: MIT Press.

Borenstein, N. S. (1991). *Programming as if People Mattered.* Princeton: Princeton University Press.

David, P. (1986). Understanding the economics of QWERTY: the necessity of history. In W. N. Paarker (ed.). *Economic History and the Modern Economist.* New York: Basil Blackwell.

Finholt, T. A., & Sproull, L. S. (1990). Electronic groups at work. *Organization Science, 1,* 41-64.

Gould, S. J. (1991). The panda's thumb of technology. In S. J. Gould, *Bully for Brontosaurus: Reflections in Natural History* (pp. 59-75). New York: Norton.

Huff, C. W., & Cooper, J. (1987). Sex bias in educational software: the effects of designers' stereotypes on the software they design. *Journal of Applied Social Psychology, 17,* 519-532.

Huff, C. W., Sproull, L., & Kiesler, S. (1989). Electronic communication and organizational commitment: Tracing the relationship in a city government. *Journal of Applied Social Psychology, 19,* 1371-1391.

Kraut, R. E.. (1987). Predicting the use of technology: the case of telework. In R. Kraut (ed.). *Technology and the Transformation of White Collar Work* (pp. 113-133). Hillsdale, NJ: Lawrence Erlbaum.

Locke, E. (1976). The nature and causes of job satisfaction. In M. Dunnette (ed.). *Handbook of Industrial and Organizational Psychology* (pp. 1297-1349). Chicago: Rand McNally College Publishing.

Olson, M. H. (1987). Telework: practical experience and future prospects. In R. Kraut (ed.). *Technology and the Transformation of White Collar Work* (pp. 135-152).Hillsdale, NJ: Lawrence Erlbaum.

Pool, I. (ed.) (1977). *The Social Impact of the Telephone.* Cambridge, MA: MIT Press.

Pruitt, S., & Barrett, T. (1991). Corporate virtual workspace. In M. Benedikt (ed.). *Cyberspace: First Steps* (pp. 383-409). Cambridge, MA: MIT Press.

Shneiderman, B. (1992). *Designing the User Interface.* Reading, MA: Addison-Wesley.

Sproull, L. S., & Kiesler, S. B. (1991). Computers, networks, and work. *Scientific American, 265(3),* 116-123.

Thoite, P. (1983). Multiple identities and psychological well-being: a reformulation and test of the social isolation hypothesis. *American Sociological Review, 48,* 174-187.

Toffler, A. (1979). *The Third Wave.* New York: Morrow.

Willis, C. (1986). Skyscraper utopias: visionary urbanism in the 1920s. In J. J. Corn (ed.). *Imagining Tomorrow: History, Technology, and the American Experience.* Cambridge, MA: MIT Press.

READING QUESTIONS

1) Why is the Panda's thumb a "makeshift substitute"? How might the Qwerty keyboard be regarded in the same way?
2) How did the Qwerty keyboard evolve? Why has it not been replaced with a more efficient one?
3) Why did the Caligraph lose the contest? Did it have anything to do with the technology itself?
4) How did "nontechnical, social surroundings" determine the outcome of the keyboard layout?
5) Why does Qwerty remain the standard today?
6) What morals can be drawn from this example?
7) Under what conditions is "this technology is different" not a good enough answer to support optimism when earlier technologies in an area have not succeeded?
8) How are Toffler's predictions like those of Pruitt and Barrett? What social constraints do both forecasters ignore?
9) What happened to the trial telework programs and why?
10) How have the actual uses of telecommunications differed from the predictions of Toffler?
11) Why does the contemporary office still look and function much like the office at the turn of the century?
12) Why does the curve of an innovation that is failing look like the curve of a slow success?
13) Why is it wrong to make predictions of future use based on technical promise alone?
14) What is the design ethic, and how is it based on a broad definition of "quality"?

DISCUSSION QUESTIONS

1) Use the information on office culture and cyberspace to discuss the changes that would take place, the fears that would arise, and the resistance that would occur if your school implemented cyberspace classrooms.
2) Why has fax been adopted more rapidly than electronic mail? Make sure to identify both technical and social issues that determined the response.

PRACTICING THE DESIGN ETHIC

1) Examine a particular common technological artifact at home or work (i.e., a telephone, a VCR, a television, an automobile, a fax machine). Work with two or three other people to determine what values or social preferences might have guided its design. How would your group design it differently today? What values are you using in your design? An alternative exercise might be to look at much older technologies (e.g., old radios, telephones, televisions, etc.).
2) You have been assigned to implement the Dvorak keyboard in your organization (e.g., on your campus or in your department). What would you have to do to make this adoption of the keyboard layout a success? Be sure to include specific points about training and assessment. Address the productivity and morale issues this change is likely to include. What economic and technical issues arise? Are any of these completely separable from social concerns?

CHAPTER

2

THE SOCIAL CONTEXT OF COMPUTING

How is the design of computing technology connected to social issues? The standard view of computer technology is that, hardware and software, it is a *technical* rather than a social artifact. Its design is constrained by mathematical and physical principles. Its implementation is directed by the logic of information flow. The nontechnical factors that do intrude are on the order of time and money constraints. The best approach to design then is, given a budget and a timeline, to use the physical, mathematical, and logical principles associated with computer science to produce a product, and then to give that product to the customer.

In this chapter, Rob Kling and Jonathon Allen—both computer scientists—take issue with this rationalist model of computer design. Kling argues that for many important computing applications, a mathematical and logical analysis is not enough. What must be added is an emphasis on *usability*—an analysis of how the computer system interacts with the organization into which it is placed. Systems designers who ignore the social context and focus only on the isolated computer system will find that their products may optimize something, but it will not be the performace of the organization that bought their system. Kling's answer is *Organizational Informatics*—the study of how computing and organizations interact.

In his critique of *groupware*, Allen provides a good example of an organizational informatics approach. Standard approaches to groupware, argues Allen, take a naive view of how these systems are likely to be used in the real world. And they do this at their peril. For example, groupware that assumes that all interaction is cooperative is doomed to failure if implemented in a competitive sales agency. To design better groupware, Allen suggests computer scientists pay attention to social psychological work on how groups in organizations actually interact. Doing this will produce software that is designed for real groups, and that will better facilitate their work.

17

ORGANIZATIONAL ANALYSIS IN COMPUTER SCIENCE[1]

Rob Kling
University of California at Irvine

Computer Science is being pressed on two sides to show broad utility for substantial research and educational support. For example, the High Performance Computing Act will provide almost two billion dollars for research and advanced development. Its advocates justified it with arguments that specific technologies, such as parallel computing and wideband nets, are necessary for social and economic development. In the US, Computer Science academic programs award well over 30,000 Bachelor of Science (BS) and almost 10,000 Master of Science (MS) degrees annually. Some of these students enter PhD programs and many work on projects which emphasize mathematical Computer Science. But many of these graduates also take computing jobs for which they are inadequately educated, such as helping to develop high performance computing applications to improve the performance of human organizations.

These dual pressures challenge leading Computer Scientists to broaden their conceptions of the discipline to include an understanding of key application domains, including computational science and commercial information systems. An important report that develops this line of analysis, "Computing the Future" (CTF) (Hartmanis and Lin, 1992), was recently issued by the Computer Science and Telecommunications Board of the U.S. National Research Council.

CTF is a welcome report that argues that academic Computer Scientists must acknowledge the driving forces behind the substantial Federal research support for the discipline. The explosive growth of computing and demand for CS in the last decade has been driven by a diverse array of applications and new modes of computing in diverse social settings. CTF takes a strong and useful position in encouraging all Computer Scientists to broaden our conceptions of the discipline and to examine computing in the context of interesting applications.

CTF's authors encourage Computer Scientists to envision new technologies in the social contexts in which they will be used. They identify numerous examples of computer applications in earth science, computational biology, medical care, electronic libraries and commercial computing that can provide significant value to people and their organizations. These assessments rest on concise and tacit analyses of the likely design,

---

[1] From Kling, R. (Mar-Jun, 1993) Organizational analysis in computer science. *The Information Society,* *9(2),* 71-87. Reprinted with permission.

implementation within organizations, and uses of these technologies. For example, CTF's stories of improved computational support for modelling are based on rational models of organizational behavior. They assume that professionals, scientists, and policy-makers use models to help improve their decisions. But what if organizations behave differently when they use models? For example suppose policy makers use models to help rationalize and legitimize decisions which are made without actual reference to the models?

One cannot discriminate between these divergent roles of modelling in human organizations based upon the intentions of researchers and system designers. The report tacitly requires that the CS community develop reliable knowledge, based on systematic research, to support effective analysis of the likely designs and uses of computerized systems. CTF tacitly requires an ability to teach such skills to CS practitioners and students. Without a disciplined skill in analyzing human organizations, Computer Scientists' claims about the usability and social value of specific technologies is mere opinion, and bears a significant risk of being misleading. Further, Computer Scientists who do not have refined social analytical skills sometimes conceive and promote technologies that are far less useful or more costly than they claim. Effective CS practitioners who "compute for the future" in organizations need some refined skills in organizational analysis to understand appropriate systems requirements and the conditions that transform high performance computing into high performance human organizations. Since CTF does not spell out these tacit implications, I'd like to explain them here.

BROADENING COMPUTER SCIENCE: FROM COMPUTABILITY TO USABILITY

The usability of systems and software is a key theme in the history of CS. We must develop theoretical foundations for the discipline that give the deepest insights into what makes systems usable for various people, groups and organizations. Traditional computer scientists commonly refer to mathematics as the theoretical foundations of CS. However, mathematical formulations give us limited insights into understanding why and when some computer systems are more usable than others.

Certain applications, such as supercomputing and computational science, are evolutionary extensions of traditional scientific computation, despite their new direction with rich graphical front ends for visualizing enormous mounds of data. But other, newer modes of computing, such as networking and microcomputing, change the distribution of applications. While they support traditional numerical computation, albeit in newer formats such as spreadsheets, they have also expanded the diversity of non-numerical computations. They make digitally represented text and graphics accessible to tens of millions of people.

These technological advances are not inconsistent with mathematical foundations in CS, such as Turing machine formulations. But the value of these formats for computation is not well conceptualized by the foundational mathematical models of computation. For example, text editing could be conceptualized as a mathematical function that transforms an initial text and a vector of incremental alterations into a revised text. Text formatting can be conceptualized as a complex function mapping text strings into spatial arrays. These kinds of formulations don't help us grasp why many people find "what you see is what you get" editors as much more intuitively appealing than a system that links line editors, command-driven formatting languages, and text compilers in series.

Nor do our foundational mathematical models provide useful ways of conceptualizing some key advances in even more traditional elements of computer systems such as operating systems and database systems. For example, certain mathematical models underlie the major families of database systems. But one can't rely on mathematics alone to assess how well networks, relations, or object-entities serve as representations for the data stored in an airline reservation system. While mathematical analysis can help optimize the efficiency of disk space in storing the data, they can't do much to help airlines understand the kinds of services that will make such systems most useful for reservationists, travel agents and even individual travellers. An airline reservation system in use is not simply a closed technical system. It is an open socio-technical system (Hewitt, 1986; Kling, 1992). Mathematical analysis can play a central role in some areas of CS, and an important role in many areas. But we cannot understand important aspects of usability if we limit ourselves to mathematical theories.

The growing emphasis of usability is one of the most dominant of the diverse trends in computing. The usability tradition has deep roots in CS, and has influenced the design of programming languages and operating systems for over 25 years. Specific topics in each of these areas also rest on mathematical analysis which Computer Scientists could point to as "the foundations" of the respective subdisciplines. But Computer Scientists envision many key advances as design conceptions rather than as mathematical theories. For example, integrated programming environments ease software development. But their conception and popularity have not been based on deeper formal foundations for programming languages. However, the growth of non-numerical applications for diverse professionals, including text processing, electronic mail, graphics, and multimedia, should place a premium on making computer systems relatively simple to use. Human Computer Interaction (HCI) is now considered a core subdiscipline of CS.

The integration of HCI into the core of CS requires us to expand our conception of the theoretical foundations of the discipline. While every computational interface is reducible to a Turing computation, the foundational mathematical models of CS do not (and could not) provide a sound theoretical basis for understanding why some interfaces are more effective for some groups of people than others. The theoretical foundations of effective computer interfaces must rest on sound theories of human behavior and their empirical manifestations (cf. Ehn, 1991, Grudin, 1989).

Interfaces also involve capabilities beyond the primary information processing features of a technology. They entail ways in which people learn about systems and ways to manage the diverse data sets that routinely arise in using many computerized systems (Kling, 1992). Understanding the diversity and character of these interfaces, that are required to make many systems usable, rests in understanding the way that people and groups organize their work and expertise with computing. Appropriate theories of the diverse interfaces that render many computer systems truly useful must rest, in part, on theories of work and organization. There is a growing realization, as networks tie users together at a rapidly rising rate, that usability cannot generally be determined without our considering how computer systems are shaped by and also alter interdependencies in groups and organizations. The newly-formed subdiscipline of Computer Supported Cooperative Work and newly-coined term "groupware" are responses to this realization (Greif, 1988; Galegher, Kraut and Egido, 1990).

BROADENING COMPUTER SCIENCE: FROM HIGH PERFORMANCE COMPUTING TO HIGH PEFORMANCE ORGANIZATIONS

The arguments of CTF go beyond a focus on usable interface designs to claims that computerized systems will improve the performance of organizations. The report argues that the US should invest close to a billion dollars a year in CS research because of the resulting economic and social gains. These are important claims, to which critics can seek systematic evidence. For example, one can investigate the claim that 20 years of major computing R&D and corporate investment in the US has helped provide proportionate economic and social value.

CTF is filled with numerous examples where computer-based systems provided value to people and organizations. The tough question is whether the overall productive value of these investments is worth the overall acquisition and operation costs. While it is conventional wisdom that computerization must improve productivity, a few researchers began to see systemic possibilities of counter-productive computerization in the early 1980s (King and Kraemer, 1981). In the last few years economists have found it hard to give unambiguously affirmative answers to this question. The issue has been termed "The Productivity Paradox," based on a comment attributed to Nobel laureate Robert Solow who remarked that "computers are showing up everywhere except in the [productivity] statistics (Dunlop and Kling, 1991a)."

Economists are still studying the conditions under which computerization contributes to organizational productivity, and how to measure it.[2] But even if computerization proves to be a productive investment, in the net, in most economic sectors, there is good reason to believe that many organizations get much less value from their computing investments than they could and should.

There is no automatic link between computerization and improved productivity. While many computer systems have been usable and useful, productivity gains require that their value exceed all of their costs.

There are numerous potential slips in translating high performance computing into cost-effective improvements in organizational performance. Some technologies are superb for well-trained experts, but are difficult for less experienced people or "casual users." Many technologies, such as networks and mail systems, often require extensive technical support, thus adding hidden costs (Kling, 1992).

Further, a significant body of empirical research shows that the social processes by which computer systems are introduced and organized makes a substantial difference in their value to people, groups and organizations (Lucas, 1981; Kraemer, et al. 1985; Orlikowski, 1992). Most seriously, not all presumably appropriate computer applications fit a person or group's work practices. While they may make sense in a simplified world, they can actually complicate or misdirect real work.

Group calendars are but one example of systems that can sound useful, but are often useless because they impose burdensome record keeping demands (Grudin, 1989). In contrast, electronic mail is one of the most popular applications in office support systems, even when other capabilities, like group calendars, are ignored (Bullen and Bennett, 1991). However, senders are most likely to share information with others when the system helps provide social feedback about the value of their efforts or they have special incentives (Sproull and Kiesler, 1991; Orlikowski, 1992). Careful attention to the social arrangements of work can help Computer Scientists improve some systems designs, or also appreciate which applications may not be effective unless work arrangements are changed when the system is introduced.

The uses and social value of most computerized systems can not be effectively ascertained from precise statements of their basic design principles and social purposes. They must be analyzed within the social contexts in which they will be used. Effective social analyses go beyond

---

[2] See Dunlop and Kling, 1991a for an accessible introduction to these debates. Economic statistics about national level productivity are inexact, and sometimes weak. Baily and Gordon (1988) examined the extent to which measurement problems account for the difficulties of seeing the positive computerization show up in the US national productivity statistics. They concluded that though measurements were inexact, and very poor in some sectors like banking, measurement errors were not the primary cause of difficulties.

accounting for formal tasks and purposes to include informal social behavior, available resources, and the interdependencies between key groups (Cotterman and Senn, 1992).

Many of the BS and MS graduates of CS departments find employment on projects where improved computing should enhance the performance of specific organizations or industries. Unfortunately, few of these CS graduates have developed an adequate conceptual basis for understanding when information systems will actually improve organizational performance. Consequently, many of them are prone to recommend systems-based solutions whose structure or implementation within organizations would be problematic.

ORGANIZATIONAL INFORMATICS[3]

Organizational Informatics denotes a field which studies the development and use of computerized information systems and communication systems in organizations. It includes studies of their conception, design, effective implementation within organizations, maintenance, use, organizational value, conditions that foster risks of failures, and their effects for people and an organization's clients. It is an intellectually rich and practical research area.

Organizational Informatics is a relatively new label. In Europe, the term Informatics is the name of many academic departments which combine both CS and Information Systems. In North America, Business Schools are the primary institutional home of Information Systems research and teaching. But this location is a mixed blessing. It brings IS research closer to organizational studies. But the institutional imperatives of business schools lead IS researchers to emphasize the development and use of systems in a narrow range of organizations -- businesses generally, and often service industry firms. It excludes information systems in important social sectors such as health care, military operations, air-traffic control, libraries, home uses, and so on. And Information Systems research tries to avoid messy issues which many practicing Computer Scientists encounter: developing requirements for effective systems and mitigating the major risks to people and organizations who depend upon them.

The emerging field of Organizational Informatics builds upon research conducted under rubrics like Information Systems and Information

---

[3] Organizational Informatics is a new term, and I have found that some people instantly like it while others are put off. I've experimented with alternative labels, like Organizational Computing, which has also resulted in strong and mixed reactions. Computing is a more common term than Informatics, but it's too narrow for some researchers. Informatics also can connote "information," which is an important part of this field. Sociological Computer Science would have the virtues of being a parallel construction of Mathematical Computer Science, but doesn't connote information either. I have not yet found a short distinctive label which characterizes the field and whose connotations are rapidly grasped by both outsiders and insiders.

Engineering. But it is more wide ranging than either of these fields are in practice.

Organizational Informatics Research

In the last 20 years a loosely organized community of some dozens of researchers have produced a notable body of systematic scientific research in Organizational Informatics. These studies examine a variety of topics, including:
- how system designers translate people's preferences into requirements;
- the functioning of software development teams in practice;
- the conditions that foster and impede the implementation of computerized systems within organizations;
- how people and organizations use systems in practice;
- the roles of computerized systems in altering work, group communication, power relationships, and organizational practices.

Researchers have extensively studied some of these topics, such as computerization and changing work, and summaries appear in synoptic review articles (Kling and Dunlop, in press). In contrast, researchers have recently begun to examine other topics, such software design (Winograd and Flores, 1986; Kyng and Greenbaum, 1991), and have recently begun to use careful empirical methods (e.g. Suchman, 1983; Bentley, et al, 1992; Fish, et al., 1993). I cannot summarize the key theories and rich findings of these diverse topics in a few paragraphs. But I would like to comment upon a few key aspects of this body of research.

Computer Systems Use in Social Worlds

Many studies contrast actual patterns of systems design, implementation, use or impacts with predictions made by Computer Scientists and professional commentators. A remarkable fraction of these accounts are infused with a hyper-rational and under-socialized view of people, computer systems, organizations and social life in general. Computer Scientists have found rule driven conceptions to be powerful ways to understand abstract domains like compilers. But many Computer Scientists extend them to be a tacit organizing frame for understanding whole computer systems, their developers, their users and others who live and work with them. Organizations are portrayed as generally cooperative systems with relatively simple and clear goals. Computer systems are portrayed as generally coherent and adequate for the tasks for which people use them. People are portrayed as generally obedient and cooperative participants in a highly structured system with numerous tacit rules to be obeyed, such as doing their jobs as they are formally described. Using data that is contained in computer systems, and treating it as information or knowledge, is a key element of these accounts. Further, computer systems are portrayed as powerful, and often central, agents of organizational change.

This Systems Rationalist perspective infuses many accounts of computer systems design, development, and use in diverse application domains, including CASE tools, instructional computing, models in support of public policy assessments, expert systems, groupware, supercomputing, and network communications (Kling, 1980; Kling, Scherson and Allen, 1992).

All conceptual perspectives are limited and simplify "reality." When Organizational Informatics researchers systematically examine the design practices in particular organizations, how specific groups develop computer systems, or how various people and groups use computerized systems, they find an enormous range of fascinating and important human behavior which lies outside the predictive frame of Systems Rationalism. Sometimes these behaviors are relatively minor in overall importance. But in many cases they are so significant as to lead Organizational Informatics researchers to radically reconceptualize the processes which shape and are shaped by computerization.

There are several alternative frames for reconceptualizing computerization as alternatives to Systems Rationalism. The alternatives reflect, in part, the paradigmatic diversity of the social sciences. But all of these reconceptions situate computer systems and organizations in richer social contexts and with more complex and multivalent social relations than does systems rationalism. Two different kinds of observations help anchor these abstractions.

Those who wish to understand the dynamics of model usage in public agencies must appreciate the institutional relationships which influence the organization's behavior. For example, to understand economic forecasting by the US Congress and the Executive branch's Office of Management and Budget, one must appreciate the institutional relations between Congress and the Executive branch. They are not well described by Systems Rationalist conceptions because they were designed to continually differ with each other in their perspectives and preferred policies. That is one meaning of "checks and balances" in the fundamental design of the US Federal Government. My colleagues, Ken Kraemer and John King, titled their book about Federal economic modelling, DataWars (Kraemer, et al., 1985). Even this title doesn't make much sense within a Systems Rationalist framework.

Modelling can be a form of intellectual exploration. It can also be a medium of communication, negotiation, and persuasion. The social relationships between modelers, people who use them and diverse actors in Federal policymaking made these socially mediated roles of models sometimes most important. In these situations, an alternative view of organizations as coalitions of interest groups was a more appropriate conceptualization. And within this coalitional view of organizations, a conception of econometric models as persuasion support systems rather than as decision support systems sometimes is most appropriate. Organizational Informatics researchers found that political views of organizations and systems developments within them apply to many private organizations as well as to explicitly political public agencies.

Another major idea to emerge from the broad body of Organizational Informatics research is that the social patterns which characterize the design, development, uses and consequences of computerized systems are dependent on the particular ecology of social relationships between participants. This idea may be summarized by saying that the processes and consequences of computerization are "context dependent." In practice, this means that the analyst must be careful in generalizing from one organizational setting to another. While data wars might characterize econometric modelling on Capitol Hill, we do not conclude that all computer modelling should be interpreted as persuasion support systems. In some settings, models are used to explore the effects of policy alternatives without immediate regard for their support as media for communication, negotiation or persuasion. At other times, the same model might be used (or abused with cooked data) as a medium of persuasion. The brief accounts of models for global warming in CTF fit a Systems Rationalist account. Their uses might appear much less "scientific" if they were studied within the actual policy processes within which they are typically used.

Repercussions for Systems Design

Even when computerized systems are used as media of intellectual exploration, Organizational Informatics researchers find that social relationships influence the ways that people use computerized systems. Christine Bullen and John Bennett (1991) studied 25 organizations that used groupware with diverse modules such as databases, group calendars, text annotating facilities and electronic mail. They found that the electronic mail modules were almost universally valued, while other system facilities were often unused.

In a recent study, Sharyn Ladner and Hope Tillman examined the use of the Internet by university and corporate librarians.

> While many of them found data access through databases and file transfer to be important services, they also reported that electronic mail was perhaps the most critical Internet feature for them. The participants in our study tell us something that we may have forgotten in our infatuation with the new forms of information made available through the Internet. And that is their need for community. To be sure, our respondents use the Internet to obtain information not available in any other format, to access databases that provide new efficiencies in their work, new ways of working. But their primary use is for communication. Special librarians tend to be isolated in the workplace—the only one in their subject specialty (in the case of academe), or the only librarian in their organization (in the case of a corporate library). Time and time again our respondents expressed

this need to talk to someone -- to learn what is going on in their profession, to bounce ideas off others, to obtain information from people, not machines. There are tremendous implications from the Internet technology in community formation -- the Internet may indeed provide a way to increase community among scholars, including librarians. The danger we face at this juncture in time, as we attach library resources to the Internet, is to focus all of our energies on the machine-based resources at the expense of our human-based resources, i.e., ourselves (Ladner and Tillman, 1992).

In these studies, Organizational Informatics researchers have developed a socially rich view of work with and around computing, of computing within a social world.

These studies have strong repercussions for the design of software. A good designer cannot assume that the majority of effort should go into the "computational centerpiece" of a system, while devoting minor efforts to supporting communication facilities. One of my colleagues designed a modelling system for managers in a major telephone company, after completing an extensive requirements analysis. However, as an afterthought, he added a simple mail system in a few days work. He was surprised to find that the people who used these systems regularly used his crude electronic mail system, while they often ignored interesting modelling capabilities. Such balances of attention also have significant repercussions. Many people need good mail systems, not just crude ones: systems which include facile editors, ease in exporting and importing files, and effective mail management (Kling and Covi, 1993).

Assessing people's preferences for systems' designs is an exercise in social inquiry. While rapid prototyping may help improve designs for some systems, it is less readily applicable to systems which are used by diverse groups at numerous locations. Computer scientists are beginning to develop more reliable methods of social inquiry to better understand which systems designs will be most useful (Bentley, et al. 1992; Kyng and Greenbaum, 1991). Fish and his colleagues (1993) recently reported the way that the explicit use of social theory helped them design more effective group meeting systems. Unfortunately, these newer methods are rarely taught to CS students. When computer specialists build an imbalanced system, it should not be a surprise when the resulting organizational value of their efforts is very suboptimal.

System Security and Reliability

In a simplified engineering model of computing, the reliability of products is assured through extensive testing in a development lab. The social world of technology is not perceived as shaping the reliability of systems, except through irascible human factors, such as "operator errors." An interesting and tragic illustration of the limitations of this view can be found in some recent studies of the causes of death and maiming by an electron accelerator which was designed to help cure cancer, the Therac-25 (Jacky, 1991, Leveson and Turner, 1992).[4]

The Therac-25 was designed and marketed in the mid 1980s by a Canadian firm AECL as an advanced medical technology. It featured complete software control over all major functions (supported by a DEC PDP-11), among other innovations. Previous machines included electro-mechanical interlocks to raise and lower radiation shields. Several thousand people were effectively treated with the Therac-25 each year. However, between 1985 and 1987 there were six known accidents in which several people died in the US. Others were seriously maimed or injured [3].

Both studies concur that there were subtle but important flaws in the design of the Therac-25's software and hardware. AECL's engineers tried to patch the existing hardware and (finally) software when they learned of some of the mishaps. But they treated each fix as the final repair.

Both studies show how the continuing series of mishaps was exacerbated by diverse organizational arrangements. Jacky claims that pressures for speedy work by radiological technicians coupled with an interface design that did not enhance important error messages was one of many causes of the accidents. Leveson and Turner differ in downplaying the working conditions of the Therac-25's operators and emphasize the flawed social system for communicating the seriousness of problems to Federal regulators and other hospitals. Both studies observe that it is unlikely for the best of companies to develop perfect error-free systems without high quality feedback from users. Their recommendations differ: Jacky discusses the licensing of system developers and the regulation of computerized medical systems to improve minimal standards of safety. Leveson and Turner propose extensive education and training of software engineers and more effective communication between manufacturers and their customers.

However, both studies indicate that an understanding of the safety of computer systems must go beyond the laboratory and extend into the organizational settings where it is used. In the case of the Therac-25, it required understanding a complex web of interorganizational relationships, as well as the technical design and operation of the equipment. Nancy Leveson (1992) points out that most major technological disasters in the last 20 years "involved serious organizational and management deficiencies." Hughes, Randall and Shapiro (1992:119) observe that no British civil collision in UK air space has been attributed to air traffic control failures. But their Mediator control system was failing regularly and had no backup during the period that they studied it. They observe that the reliability of the British air traffic

---

[4]Jacky's early study was based on published reports, while Leveson and Turner's more thorough study was based upon a significant body of original documents and interviews with some participants.

control system resides in totality of the relevant social and technical systems, rather than in a single component.

The need for this kind of organizational understanding is unfortunately slighted in the CS academic world today. CTF discusses only those aspects of computer system reliability which are amenable to understanding through laboratory-like studies (Hartmanis and Lin, 1992:110-111). But cases of safety critical systems, like the Therac-25 and British Air Traffic Control, indicate why some Computer Scientists must be willing to undertake (and teach) organizational analysis.

Worldviews and Surprises about Computerization

These few paragraphs barely sketch the highlights of a fertile and significant body of research about computer systems in use. Perhaps the most important simplification for traditional computer scientists is to appreciate how people and their organizations are situated in a social world and consequently compute within a social world. People act in relationship to others in various ways and concerns of belonging, status, resources, and power are often central. The web of people's relationships extend beyond various formally defined group and organizational boundaries (Kling and Scacchi, 1982; Kling, 1987; Kling, 1992). People construct their worlds, including the meanings and uses of information technologies, through their social interactions.

This view is, of course, not new to social scientists. On the other hand, there is no specific body of social theory which can easily be specialized for "the case of computing," and swiftly produce good theories for Organizational Informatics as trivial deductions. The best research in Organizational Informatics draws upon diverse theoretical and methodological approaches within the social sciences with a strong effort to select those which best explain diverse aspects of computerization.

ORGANIZATIONAL INFORMATICS WITHIN COMPUTER SCIENCE

CTF places dual responsibilities on Computer Scientists. One responsibility is to produce a significant body of applicable research. The other responsibility is to educate a significant fraction of CS students to be more effective in conceiving and implementing systems that will enhance organizational performance. It may be possible to organize research and instruction so as to decouple these responsibilities. For example, molecular biologists play only a small role in training doctors. However, CS departments act like an integrated Medical school and Biology department. They are the primary academic locations for training degreed computing specialists, and they conduct a diverse array of less applicable and more applicable research. In practice, the research interests of CS faculty shape the range of topics taught in CS departments, especially the 150 PhD granting departments. CS curricula mirror major areas of CS research and the topics which CS faculty understand through their own educations and subsequent research. As a consequence, CS courses are likely to avoid important CS topics which appear a bit foreign to the instructor.

An interesting example of this coupling can be illustrated by CTF, in a brief description of public-key encryption systems and digital signatures (Hartmanis and Lin, 1992:27). In the simple example, Bob and Alice can send messages reliably if each maintains a secret key. Nothing is said about the social complications of actually keeping keys secret. The practical problems are similar to those of managing passwords, although some operational details differ because the 100 digit keys may be stored on media like magstripe cards rather than paper. In real organizations, people lose or forget their password and can lose the media which store their keys. Also, some passwords can be shared by a group of with shifting membership, and the "secret key" can readily become semi-public. The main point is that the management of keys is a critical element of cryptographic security in practice. But Computer Scientists are prone to teach courses on cryptography as exercises in applied mathematics, such as number theory and Galois theory, and to skirt the vexing practical problems of making encryption a practical organizational activity.

Today, most of the 40,000 people who obtain BS and MS degrees in CS each year in the U.S. have no opportunities for systematic exposure to reliable knowledge about the best design strategies, common uses, effective implementation, and assessments of value of computing in a social world (Lewis, 1989). Yet a substantial fraction of these students go on to work for organizations attempting to produce or maintain systems that improve organizational performance without a good conceptual basis for their work. Consequently, many of them develop systems that underperform in organizational terms even when they are technically refined. They also recommend ineffective implementation procedures and are sometimes even counterproductive.

One defensible alternative to my position is that CS departments should not take on any form of organizational analysis. They should aggressively take a role akin to Biology departments rather than taking on any instructional or research roles like Medical schools. To be sincere, this position requires a high level of restraint by academic Computer Scientists. First and foremost, they should cease from talking about the uses, value or even problems of computerized systems that would be used in any organizational setting. Research proposals would be mute about any conceivable application of research results. Further, they should make effective efforts to insure that anyone who employs their graduates should be aware that they may have no special skills in understanding organizational computing. It would take an aggressive "truth in advertising" campaign to help make it clear that Computer Scientists have no effective methods for understanding computerization in the social world. Further, Computer Scientists would forsake their commitments to subfields like software engineering which tacitly deals with ways to support teams of systems developers to work effectively (Curtis, et al. 1988). Computer Scientists, in this view, would remove themselves from addressing organizational and human behavior, in the same way that molecular biologists are removed from professionally commenting on the practices of cardiologists and obstetricians. CTF argues that this view would be self-defeating. But it would be internally consistent and have a distinctive integrity.

In contrast, CS faculty are often reluctant to wholly embrace Organizational Informatics. But some CS subfields, such as software engineering, depend upon organizational analysis (Curtis, et al., 1988). Further, CS faculty do little to advertise the distinctive limitations in the analytical skills of our programs' graduates. Part of the dilemma develops because many CS faculty are ambivalent about systematic studies of human behavior. Applied mathematics and other modes of inquiry which seem to yield concise, crisp and concrete results are often the most cherished. As a consequence, those who conduct behaviorally oriented research in CS departments are often inappropriately marginalized. Their students and the discipline suffer as a result.

Between 1986 and 1989, the total number of BS and MS CS degrees awarded annually in the US declined from about 50,000 to approximately 40,000. The number of students majoring in CS rapidly declined at a time when computerization was becoming widespread in many fields. A significant fraction of the decline can be attributed to many students finding CS programs insular and indifferent to many exciting forms of computerization. The decline of military R&D in the U.S. can amplify these trends or stimulate a more cosmopolitan view in CS departments. The decline in military R&D is shifting the job market for new CS graduates towards a markedly more civilian orientation. This shift, along with the trend towards computing distributed into diverse work groups, is leading to more job opportunities for people with CS education who know Organizational Informatics.

The situation of CS departments has some parallels with Statistics departments. Statistics are widely used and taught in many academic disciplines. But Statistics departments have often maintained a monkish isolation from "applications." Consequently, the application of statistics thrives while Statistics departments have few students and modest resources. Might the status of Statistics indicate a future possibility for an insular approach to CS?

The best Organizational Informatics research in North America is conducted by faculty in the Information Systems departments in business schools and by scattered social scientists (cf. Boland and Hirschheim, 1987; Galegher, Kraut and Egido, 1990; Cotterman and Senn, 1992; Sproull and Kiesler, 1991). But Computer Scientists cannot effectively delegate the research and teaching of Organizational Informatics to business Schools or social science departments.

Like Computer Scientists, faculty in these other disciplines prefer to focus on their own self-defined issues. Computer Scientists are much more likely to ask questions with attention to fine grained technological nuances that influence designs. For example, the professional discussions of computer risks have been best developed through activities sponsored by the ACM's Special Interest Group on Software (SIGSOFT). They are outside the purview of business school faculty and, at best, only a few social scientists are interested in them. Generally, technology plays a minor role in social science theorizing. And when social scientists study technologies, they see a world of possibilities: energy technologies, transportation technologies, communication technologies (including television), medicinal drugs and devices, and so on. They see little reason to give computer-related information technologies a privileged role within this cornucopia. As a consequence, the few social scientists who take a keen interest in studying computerization are unfortunately placed in marginal positions within their own disciplines. Often they must link their studies to mainstream concerns as defined by the tastemakers of their own fields, and the resulting publications appear irrelevant to Computer Scientists.

Further, faculty in these other disciplines are not organized to effectively teach tens of thousands of CS students, students who are steeped in technology and usually very naive about organizations, about systems development and use in organizations. In North America there is no well developed institutional arrangement for educating students who can effectively take leadership roles in conceptualizing and developing complex organizational computing projects (Lewis, 1989).

CTF is permeated with interesting claims about the social value of recent and emerging computer-based technologies. While many of these observations should rest on an empirically grounded scientific footing, Computer Scientists have deprived themselves of access to such research. For example, the discussion of systems risks in the ACM rests on a large and varied collection of examples and anecdotes. But there is no significant research program to help better understand the conditions under which organizations are more likely to develop systems using the best risk-reducing practices. There is an interesting body of professional lore, but little scholarship to ground it.

Computer Scientists have virtually no scholarship to utilize in understanding when high performance networks, like the National Research and Education Network, will catalyze social value proportional to their costs. Consequently, many of the "obvious" claims about the value of various computing technologies that we Computer Scientists make are more akin to the lore of home remedies for curing illness. Some are valid, others are unfounded speculation. More seriously, the theoretical bases for recommending home medical remedies and new computer technologies can not advance without having sound research programs.

WHAT IS NEEDED

CTF sets the stage for developing Organizational Informatics as a strong subfield within Computer Science. CTF bases the expansion of the discipline on a rich array of applications in which many of the effective technologies must be conceived in relationship to plausible uses in order to provide attractive social value for multi-billion dollar public investments.

The CS community needs an institutionalized research capability to produce a reliable body of knowledge about the usability and value of computerized systems and the conditions under which computer systems improve organizational performance. In Western Europe there are research projects about Organizational Informatics in a few Computer Science departments and research funding through the EEC's Espirit program (Bubenko, 1992; Iivari, 1991; Kyng and Greenbaum, 1991). These new research and instructional programs in Western Europe give Organizational Informatics a significantly more effective place in CS education and research than it now has in North America.

The CS community in the U.S. has 30 years of experience in institutionalizing research programs, especially through the Defense Advanced Research Projects Agency and the National Science Foundation (NSF). There are many approaches, including establishing national centers, supporting individual investigator research grants, supporting short institutes to help train new investigators and supporting research workshops for ongoing research. All such programs aim to develop and sustain research fields with a combination of direct research funds, the education of future researchers, and the development of research infrastructure. They are all multimillion dollar efforts. Today, NSF devotes about $125K annually to Organizational Informatics as part of the Information Technology in Organizations program. This start is far short of the level of funding required to develop this field within CS.

The North American CS curricula must also include opportunities for students to learn the most reliable knowledge about the social dimensions of systems development and use (Denning, 1992). These opportunities, formed as courses, can provide varied levels of sophistication. The most elementary courses introduce students to some of the key topics in Organizational Informatics and the limitations of Systems Rationalism as an organizing frame (for example, Dunlop and Kling, 1991a). More advanced courses focus on specific topics, such as those I have listed above. They teach about substantive problems and theoretical approaches for analyzing them. While many of these approaches are anchored in the sociological theory of organizations, CS students usually won't grasp the importance of the theories without numerous computing examples to work with.[5] They also have trouble grasping the character of computing in organizations without guided opportunities for observing and analyzing computerization in practice. Consequently, some courses should offer opportunities for studying issues of computerization in actual organizations.

Fortunately, a few CS departments offer some courses in Organizational Informatics. In addition, some CS faculty who research and teach about human behavior in areas like Human-Computer Interaction and Software Engineering can help expand the range of research and instruction. Curricula would vary, but they should include diverse courses for students who seek basic exposure to Organizational Informatics and those seek more thorough instruction. Unfortunately, only a fraction of the CS departments in the US have faculty who study and teach about computing and human behavior.

While the study of Organizational Informatics builds upon both the traditional technological foundations of CS and the social sciences, the social sciences at most universities will not develop it as an effective foundational topic for CS. On specific campuses, CS faculty may be able to develop good instructional programs along with colleagues in social sciences or Schools of Management.

But delegating this inquiry to some other discipline does not provide a national scale solution for CS. Other disciplines will not do our important work for us. Mathematics departments may be willing to teach graph theory for CS students, but the analysis of algorithms would be a much weaker field if it could only be carried out within Mathematics departments. For similar reasons, it is time for academic Computer Science to embrace Organizational Informatics as a key area of research and instruction.

REFERENCES

Auvo. 1992. "Can Research and Education in the Field of Information Sciences Foresee the Future of Development?" in Lyytinen and Puuronen, 1992.

Baily, Martin Neal and Robert J. Gordon. 1988. "The Productivity Slowdown, Measurement Issues, and the Explosion of Computer Power." Brookings Papers on Economic Activity 2:347-431.

Bentley, Richard, Tom Rodden, Peter Sawyer, Ian Sommerville, John Hughes, David Randall and Dan Shapiro. 1992. "Ethnographically Informed Systems Design for Air Traffic Control." Proc. Conference on Computer-Supported Cooperative Work, Jon Turner and Robert Kraut (ed.) New York, ACM Press.

Boland, Richard and Rudy Hirschhiem (Ed). 1987. Critical Issues in Information Systems, New York: John Wiley.

Bullen, Christine and John Bennett. 1991. Groupware in Practice: An Interpretation of Work Experience" in Dunlop and Kling 1991b.

---

[5]One hears similar concerns about teaching mathematics to CS students. CS students are much more motivated to learn graph theory, for example, when they learn those aspects which best illuminate issues of computation and when their teaching includes some good computing examples.

Bubenko, Janis. 1992. "On the Evolution of Information Systems Modeling: A Scandinavian Perspective." in Lyytinen and Puuronen, 1992. Cotterman, William and James Senn (Eds). 1992. Challenges and Strategies for Research in Systems Development. New York: John Wiley.

Curtis, Bill, Herb Krasner and Niel Iscoe. 1988. "A Field Study of the Software Design Process for Large Systems," Communications of the ACM. 31(11):1268-1287.

Denning, Peter. 1991. "Computing, Applications, and Computational Science." Communications of the ACM. (October) 34(10):129-131.

Denning, Peter. 1992. "Educating a New Engineer" Communications of the ACM. (December) 35(12):83-97.

Dunlop, Charles and Rob Kling, 1991a. "Introduction to the Economic and Organizational Dimensions of Computerization." in Dunlop and Kling, 1991b. Dunlop, Charles and Rob Kling (Ed). 1991b. Computerization and Controversy: Value Conflicts and Social Choices. Boston: Academic Press.

Ehn, Pelle. 1991. "The Art and Science of Designing Computer Artifacts." in Dunlop and Kling, 1991.

Fish, Robert S., Robert E. Kraut, Robert W. Root, and Ronald E. Rice. "Video as a Technology for Informed Communication." Communications of the ACM,36(1)(January 1993):48-61.

Galegher, Jolene, Robert Kraut, and Carmen Egido (Ed.) 1990. Intellectual Teamwork: Social and Intellectual Foundations of Cooperative Work. Hillsdale, NJ: Lawrence Erlbaum.

Greif, Irene. ed. 1988. Computer Supported Cooperative Work: A Book of Readings. San Mateo, Ca: Morgan Kaufman.

Grudin, Jonathan. 1989. "Why Groupware Applications Fail: Problems in Design and Evaluation." Office: Technology and People. 4(3):245-264.

Hartmanis, Juris and Herbert Lin (Eds). 1992. Computing the Future: A Broader Agenda for Computer Science and Engineering. Washington, DC. National Academy Press. [Briefly summarized in Communications of the ACM,35(11) November 1992]

Hewitt, Carl. 1986. "Offices are Open Systems" ACM Transactions on Office Information Systems. 4(3)(July):271-287.

Hughes, John A., David Randall, and Dan Shapiro. 1992. "Faltering from Ethnography to Design." Proc. Conference on Computer- Supported Cooperative Work, Jon Turner and Robert Kraut (ed.) New York, ACM Press.

Iivari, J. 1991."A Paradigmatic Analysis of Contemporary Schools of IS Development." European J. Information Systems 1(4)(Dec): 249-272.

Jacky, Jonathan. 1991. "Safety-Critical Computing: Hazards, Practices, Standards, and Regulation" in Dunlop and Kling 1991b.

Jarvinen, Pertti. 1992. "On Research into the Individual and Computing Systems," in Lyytinen and Puuronen, 1992.

King, John L. and Kenneth L. Kraemer. 1981. "Cost as a Social Impact of Telecommunications and Other Information Technologies." In Mitchell Moss (Ed.) Telecommunications and Productivity, New York: Addison-Wesley.

Kling, Rob. 1987. "Defining the Boundaries of Computing Across Complex Organizations." Critical Issues in Information Systems. edited by Richard Boland and Rudy Hirschheim. London: John Wiley.

Kling, Rob. 1992. "Behind the Terminal: The Critical Role of Computing Infrastructure In Effective Information Systems' Development and Use." Chapter 10 in Challenges and Strategies for Research in Systems Development. edited by William Cotterman and James Senn. Pp. 153-201. New York: John Wiley.

Kling, Rob. 1993. "Computing for Our Future in a Social World" Communications of the ACM, 36(2)(February),

Kling, Rob and Charles Dunlop. 1993. "Controversies About Computerization and the Character of White Collar Worklife." The Information Society. 9(1) (Jan-Feb).

Kling, Rob and Lisa Covi. 1993. Review of Connections by Lee Sproull and Sara Kiesler. The Information Society, 9(1) (Jan-Feb, 1993).

Kling, Rob, Isaac Scherson, and Jonathan Allen. 1992. "Massively Parallel Computing and Information Capitalism" in A New Era of Computing. W. Daniel Hillis and James Bailey (Ed.).Cambridge, MA: The MIT Press.

Kling, Rob and Walt Scacchi. 1982. "The Web of Computing: Computing Technology as Social Organization", Advances in Computers. Vol. 21, Academic Press: New York.

Kraemer, Kenneth L., Dickhoven, Siegfried, Fallows-Tierney, Susan, and King, John L. 1985. Datawars: The Politics of Modeling in Federal Policymaking. New York: Columbia University Press.

Kyng, Morton and Joan Greenbaum. 1991. Design at Work: Cooperative Work of Computer Systems. Hillsdale, NJ.: Lawrence Erlbaum.

Ladner, Sharyn and Hope Tillman. 1992. "How Special Librarians Really Use the Internet: Summary of Findings and Implications for the Library of the Future" Canadian Library Journal, 49(3), 211-216.

Leveson, Nancy G. 1992. "High Pressure Steam Engines and Computer Software." Proc. International Conference on Software Engineering, Melbourne, Australia. (May).

Leveson, Nancy G. and Clark S. Turner. 1992. "An Investigation of the Therac-25 Accidents." Technical Report #92-108. Department of Information and Computer Science, University of California, Irvine.

Lewis, Philip M. 1989. "Information Systems as an Engineering Discipline." Communications of the ACM 32(9)(Sept):1045-1047.

Lucas, Henry C. 1981. Implementation : the Key to Successful Information Systems. New York: Columbia University Press.

Lyytinen, Kalle and Seppo Puuronen (Ed.) 1992. Computing in the Past, Present and Future: Issues and approaches in honor of the 25th anniversary of the Department of Computer Science and Information Systems. Jyvaskyla Finland, Dept. of CS and IS, University of Jyvaskyla.

Orlikowski, Wanda. 1992. "Learning from Notes: Organizational Issues in Groupware Implementation." Proc. Conference on Computer-Supported Cooperative Work, Jon Turner and Robert Kraut (Ed.) New York, ACM Press.

Poltrock, S.E. and Grudin, J., in press. Organizational Obstacles to Interface Design and Development: Two Participant Observer Studies. ACM Transactions on Computer and Human Interaction. Sarmanto,

Sproull, Lee and Sara Kiesler. 1991. Connections: New Ways of Working in the Networked Organization. Cambridge, Mass.: MIT Press.

Suchman, Lucy. 1983. "Office Procedure as Practical Action: Models of Work and System Design." ACM Transactions on Office Information Systems. 1(4)(October):320-328.

Winograd, Terry and Fernando Flores. 1986. Understanding Computers and Cognition. Norwood, NJ: Ablex Publishing.

Acknowledgements

This paper builds on ideas which I've developed over the last decade. But they have been deepened by some recent events, such as the CTF report. They were also sharpened through a lecture and followon discussion with colleagues at the University of Toronto, including Ron Baeker, Andy Clement, Kelley Gottlieb, and Marilyn Manteii. Rick Weingarten suggested that I write a brief position paper reflecting those ideas. At key points, Peter Denning and Peter Neumann provided helpful encouragement and sage advice. I also appreciate the efforts of numerous other friends and colleagues to help strengthen this paper through their comments and critical assistance. The paper is immeasurably stronger because of the prompt questions and suggestions that I received in response to an evolving manuscript from the following people: Mark Ackerman, Jonathon P. Allen, Bob Anderson, Lisa Covi, Brad Cox, Gordon Davis, Phillip Fites, Simson Garfinkel, Les Gasser, Sy Goodman, Beki Grinter, Jonathan Grudin, Pertti Jarvinen, John King, Heinz Klein, Trond Knudsen, Kenneth Kraemer, Sharyn Ladner, Nancy Leveson, Lars Matthiesen, Colin Potts, Paul Resnick, Larry Rosenberg, Tim Standish, John Tillquist, Carson Woo and Bill Wulf.

Published Materials about Computer Risks

Unfortunately, there is no single good book or comprehensive review article about the diverse risks of computerized systems to people and organizations, and ways to mitigate them. The Internet board, comp.risks, is the richest archive of diverse episodes and diverse discussions of their causes and cures. While its moderator, Peter Neumann, does a superb job of organizing discussions of specific topics each year and also creates periodic indices, there is no simple way to sift through the megabytes of accumulated comp.risks files.

Computerization and Controversy edited by Charles Dunlop and Rob Kling (1991) includes two major sections on "security and reliability" and "privacy and social control" which identify many key debates and reprint some key articles and book excerpts which reflect different positions. Another major source is a series of articles, "Inside Risks, which Peter Neumann edits for Communications of the ACM.

GROUPWARE AND SOCIAL REALITY[6]

Jonathon Allen
Department of Information & Computer Science
University of California at Irvine

GROUPWARE AND THE COOPERATIVE WORKPLACE

Much like spreadsheet programs for the personal computer, groupware is being positioned as the distinctive breakthrough product for the next great industry trend, networking. The challenge of developing effective groupware is forcing computer scientists to dive into the murky world of group behavior and social relations—definitely not a traditional strength of the discipline. Fortunately, a number of groupware researchers and developers have recognized the role of social scientific methods in the development and evaluation of groupware systems (Ellis, 1991; Grudin, 1988) rather than leave group design issues to their intuition. This explicit attempt to bridge the "social" and the "technical" has stirred the excitement of many social researchers of computing.

Bringing together these two ways of seeing the world, however, is not always easy. Groupware research in computer science takes place under the label of Computer Supported Cooperative Work (CSCW). Many commentators on the groupware scene have pointed out that the social reality of the workplace is not always cooperative and harmonious (Kling, 1991; Kyng, 1991). It can also be coercive, controlling, or manipulative, requiring constant negotiation between fundamentally different interests.

Why do these commentators feel the need to make this point over and over again? Possibly because of the technological visions in groupware papers and promotional videos[7] which appear to be, well, a bit naive in their view of social and organizational reality. For example, we see images of highly paid professionals in pleasant working environments happily putting video cameras in their offices and public meeting places for systems such as CAVECAT (Mantei et al, 1991), the Cruiser (Root, 1988), and the "ubiquitous computing" environment at Xerox PARC (Weiser, 1991). When these professionals are interrupted by requests from their colleagues watching them through the camera, they cheerfully stop what they are doing and respond to the request. Any thought of how these systems might work in a different organizational context (a typing pool, for instance, or a competitive sales office) is missing. As another kind of example, groupware users frankly and openly express themselves using structured communication and database

---

[6]From Jonathon Allen (1993). Groupware and Social Reality. *Computers and Society, 22,* 24-28. Reprinted with permission of the author.
[7] These examples are taken from videos shown at the 1989 SIGCHI conference.

tools such as gIBIS (Yakemovic and Conklin, 1990) knowing that the opinions they publicly express will be available years later to anyone who cares to look.

Are these somewhat idealistic visions merely advertising pitches, or are they symptomatic of the way groupware technologists view social reality? In this essay, my goal is to briefly compare the features of social reality that are studied by groupware researchers with those studied by social scientists concerned with group behavior. Do they see the same critical issues facing work groups, and share the same kind of understanding of their dynamics? I argue that, in many ways, they do not, and existing studies of work groups point to issues that will become crucial once groupware leaves the research labs for the reality of the workplace: the issue of snoopware (how will their tremendous potential for monitoring and selective history preservation be used in practice?), and the issue of groupware (how will they shift the boundaries of work group participation, to either make groups self-select into increasingly homogeneous subgroups or open to membership and participation from a much wider audience?). These crucial issues are almost impossible to study under the assumption of a cooperative workplace.

SOCIAL CONCERNS OF GROUPWARE RESEARCHERS

What do groupware designers consider the main problems facing work groups? Consider the typical groupware usage scenarios in their promotional videos and articles: workers need to find each other quickly, good ideas are repressed due to status differences, a lack of focus on important issues, and the need for unambiguous communication. These "social problems" involve relations between a few actors, and take place over a short time period. They emphasize group process inefficiency or bias as the main problems of concern.

Another kind of social problem is noted by developers worried about the political economy of groupware use; how much benefit do users of the system receive relative to the costs of using it? Gaining more than you lose with groupware use is the driver behind concerns for "seamless integration" with existing tools (Ishii and Miyaki, 1991), building a "critical mass" of users to make groupware participation worthwhile (Francik et al, 1991; Markus and Conolly, 1990), and generally finding a good "fit" that is minimally disruptive to existing work practices (Bullen and Bennett, 1990; Francik et al, 1991).

An emphasis on process efficiencies, costs, and benefits (as opposed to power relations, organizational context, and group development over time)[8] has led to a body of research that, when it is not simply anecdotal,

---

[8] Viewing group problems as apolitical, ahistorical inefficiencies, some have argued, is at least partially a product of the culture of groupware developers, who tend to be trained to see the world in terms of "rational models" and tend to work in professionally advantaged settings (see Grudin, 1991).

emphasizes controlled experiments. These small group studies manipulate group process variables such as anonymity, physical proximity, and the amount of structure imposed on the interaction process (see Kraemer and Pinsonneault, 1990 for a review of the literature). These variables are then associated with positive outcomes such as task focus, egalitarian promotion of ideas, and satisfaction with decision-making quality.

SOCIAL CONCERNS OF WORK GROUP RESEARCHERS

Social scientists who have studied group behavior, as a whole, have a different perspective on the most important features of group dynamics, the most important barriers to effective group behavior, and the importance of social context. A huge body of literature exists on group behavior (Bettelhausen, 1991 lists over 250 papers in the past five years). For our purposes, we will concentrate on the important work group research of Hackman (Hackman, 1991) and McGrath (McGrath, 1990) as examples of the valuable "groupware" insights to be gained from previous group behavior research.

Compare their view of some important groupware and group behavior issues—task focus, anonymity, and flexibility—to the concerns of groupware builders:

Task Focus

Task focus is often mentioned as a virtue of groupware, in particular for "meetingware" systems that support interaction at the same time and location (Waemer and Pinsonneault, 1990). Group members become distracted by outside interruptions and social pleasantries, or don't have a chance to participate in traditional meetings; this social problem is addressed in groupware by both increasing the amount of total participation (by simultaneous brainstorming, for example) and by focusing attention on an end product or decision through a structured process. Task focus increases the amount and quality of work, increasing productivity.

Studies of group behavior in field settings by researchers such as McGrath and Hackman describe group effectiveness as having three dimensions: outputs of the group (what we usually think of as productivity), viability of the group, and payoffs to the individual members for participating in the group. Work groups may churn out products or decisions, but if effort is not put into maintaining the group as a working social entity, and if group members do not receive rewards for participating in the group, "well documented" problems arise and groups begin to fall apart (McGrath, 1990). Fragmentation and avoidance of other group members when difficulties began to arise was one of the main problems Hackman found in the management groups he studied (Hackman, 1991). Socializing and "office politics", which could be seen as distracting from task focus and therefore something to be discouraged in groupware, could also be seen as essential for maintaining viable group relations and determining the payoffs that keep groups together.

Anonymity

An important social problem identified by groupware builders is how to help a group generate and evaluate ideas on the basis of merit, without regard to status. One particularly strong vision of anonymous interaction is the University of Arizona meetingware system (Nunamaker et al, 1991), where all communication in meetings takes place through terminals. Brainstorming, prioritizing, and voting on ideas is done without any names attached.

Hackman found, especially for management groups, that saying yes to the boss is much less of a problem than trying to get a group to "actively learn from their experiences" (Hackman, 1991). This ability to "actively learn", which he associated with successful management groups, was directly related to the amount of trust (and appropriate levels of heterogeneity) among group members. Trust within the group led to openness and better performance. Anonymous meetingware systems take a different approach, building openness through anonymity rather than trust. These two different versions of "active learning" could lead work groups down different paths in the reality of the workplace.

Flexibility

Popular management thinking in America today is celebrating the virtues of teamwork. In Hackman's study (Hackman, 1991), the great challenge facing groups working on the direct manufacture of a product was that their work would be understood in routinized "machine" terms, which are incompatible with the virtues of teams (adaptability, diversity, flexibility, and learning ability). For all kinds of work groups, Hackman found that there are many ways to achieve the same end results—a phenomenon he refers to as equifinality. Because groups inevitably develop and enact their own "version of reality", and evidence strongly suggests that there is no one best way of structuring groups, he argued that managers should concentrate on creating conditions that support effective teamwork rather than on "controlling" work groups.

Groupware systems sometimes embed social protocols that are not subject to (easy) change by the user. The Coordinator system (Flores et al, 1986) has been criticized for too strictly enforcing a model of conversations as commitments and requests. Systems such as gIBIS encode a rhetoric model of argumentation around issues and supporting/opposing statements (Yakemovic and Conklin, 1990). Importing a group interaction and structuring protocol from outside the group, and not giving the group the means or skills to adapt the protocol to their local needs, may prove to be needlessly constraining. Especially if groupware is imposed on all work group members as a way of avoiding "critical mass" problems, as some suggest (Ellison, 1989).

Flexibility is considered less important when the workplace is assumed to be homogeneous in its needs for social protocols and relatively free of conflict. McGrath has observed four stages of group activity: goal choice, means choice, political choice (conflict resolution), and execution (McGrath, 1989). He predicts that any group, or group protocol, that does not effectively support all four stages will hamper groups engaged in non-routine work. Problems could arise if groupware does not support disagreement over technical means and political choices, or support the expression of disagreement in a way that group participants think is fair. Ironically, means choice and political choice are not important for groups with highly routinized work. Groupware that emphasizes only cooperative behavior might be more appropriate for assigning tasks to clerical workers than for presumably more creative professionals and managers.

In sum, we see differences between the social reality of groupware builders and social researchers in the importance of the surrounding social and organizational context, the range of "reality construction" choices available to a group, and in definitions of effective behavior. Most important are the definitions of group effectiveness and group activity that broaden questions about the effectiveness of groupware beyond the microdynamics of the cubicle or meeting room.

TWO QUESTIONS TO BE ANSWERED

Groupware researchers have established a program of research based on what they consider are the important features of group dynamics. Unfortunately, by not taking advantage of the theories and insights of previous work group research, they risk missing crucial dynamics that might affect groupware use in the reality of the workplace much more strongly than anonymity or task focus. Previous work group research points to two issues that I believe will become crucial as groupware moves out of the labs and comes into contact with social and organizational reality:

Snoopware

Proponents of networked computing are touting the benefits of enhanced "visibility" and organizational "memory" (Zuboff, 1988; Scott Morton, 1991). Data collected and stored by information systems, the argument goes, will give users powerful insights into how organizations work, and how they can be improved (a process Zuboff calls "informating"). Of course, the value of this "visibility" is heavily dependent on the process which creates the information, how this information is allowed to be used, and how organizational procedures might be encoded into the system (see Orlikowski, 1991 for a definitely non-informating approach).

"Visibility" and organizational "memory" are also known by an older, less appealing name: monitoring. How will the tremendous monitoring potential of a groupware system that mediates most or all social interaction be tapped? The capability of monitoring the performance of managers and professionals, and not just clerical workers, is increasing (Kraemer and Danziger, 1990). We are now even hearing accounts of "killer" groupware with the discretion to shutdown computer systems and stop budgets if a group's performance is not up to par (Govoni, 1992). That groupware research would neglect these monitoring "'visibility" issues seems, to me, to reflect an incredible lack of interest in the social and organizational contexts groupware will actually be working in. The snoopware issue will bring questions of trust, "active learning", and definitions of group effectiveness to the forefront.

Groupware

How will groupware affect the boundaries of work group participation? One of Hackman's main results, alluded to earlier, was that effective groups should be neither too heterogeneous (so group members can understand each other and work together) nor too homogeneous (so that group members have something to learn from each other and can create alternatives). Given the choice of who to interact with, instead of being constrained by physical proximity, will people tend to self-select into stable, homogeneous groups with little outside contribution? Hackman also reported on the fragmentation and avoidance problem: can groupware users more easily avoid each other when problems arise?

Or, alternatively, in what settings will the more equal participation and egalitarianism we see in electronic communications (Perolle, 1991) encourage anyone to participate in the group's work, welcome or unwelcome? Will this participation be valuable, or will it simply frustrate those who are already overloaded with information (Falk, 1992)? Some good research has already been done on patterns of electronic communication for predefined groups with definite tasks (e.g., Finholt, Sproul, and Kiesler, 1990), but not for understanding how group membership choices will be made electronically.

A RESEARCH AGENDA

Groupware systems are just beginning to be adopted in real settings. As they are adopted, groupware research which measures the effects of easily controlled social protocol variables (such as anonymity) will be replaced by research that examines its actual effectiveness in the workplace. This research, out of necessity, will need to consider all aspects of group process and effectiveness, not simply decision-making quality. This research will have to come to grips with existing social and organizational reality, and how that social order will shape and be shaped by groupware. I have proposed what I believe will be two crucial issues for groupware as it makes its way into the reality of the workplace, the issues of snoopware and groupware. I welcome your comments and feedback.

REFERENCES

Bettenhausen, K, (1991). Five Years of Groups Research: What We Have Learned and What Needs to be Addressed. Journal of Managment, 17(2), 345-381.

Bullen, C., and J. Bennett, (1990). Learning From User Experience With Groupware. In Proceedings of CSCW '90, 291-302.

Ellis, C., S. Gibbs, and G. Rein, (1991). Groupware: Some Issues and Experiences. Communications of the ACM, 34(1), 38-58.

Ellison, C., (1989). Managing People and Projects. PC Computing, 71-74.

Falk,B.,(1992). ElectronicMail: The Medium IsThe Malaise. MicroTimes, January 1,1992.

Finholt, T., L.Sproull, and S.Kiesler, (1990). "Communication and Performance in Ad Hoc Task Groups," in J. Galegher , R. Kraut, C. Egido, (eds.), Intellectual Teamwork: Social and Technical Foundations of Cooperative Work. Lawrence Erlbaum Associates, Hillsdale, NJ.

Flores, F., M. Graves, B. Hartfield, and T. Winograd, (1988). Computer Systems and the Design of Organizational Interaction. ACM Transactions on Office Informaiton Systems, 6(2), 153-172.

Francik, E., S. Rudman, D. Cooper, and S. Levine, (1991). Putting Innovation to Work: Adoption Strategies for Multimedia Communication Systems. Communications of the ACM, 34(12),36-51.

Govoni, S., (1992). License to Kill.. Information Week, January 6,1992.

Grudin, J., (1988). Why CSCW Applications Fail: Problems in the Design and Evaluation of Organizational Interfaces. In Proceedings of CSCW '88, 85-93.

Grudin, J., (1991). CSCW Introduction. Communications of the ACM, 34(12), 30-35.

Hackman, J., (1990). Groups that work (and those that don't): Creating Conditions for Effective Teamwork. JosseyBass, San Francisco.

Ishii, H., and N. Miyake, (1991). Toward An Open Shared Workstation: Computer and Video Fusion Approach of TeamWorkStation. Communications of the ACM, 34(12), 36-51.

Kling, R., (1991). Cooperation, Coordination, and Control in Computer-Supported Work. Communications of the ACM, 34 (12) ,83-87.

Kraemer, K, and A. Pinsonneault, (1990). "Technology and Groups: Assessment of the Empirical Research," in J. Galegher, R. Kraut, C.Egido, (eds.), Intellectual Teamwork: Social and Technological Foundations of Cooperative Work Lawrence Eribaum Associates, Hillsdale, NJ..

Kraemer, K, and J. Danziger, (1990). The Impacts of Computer Technology on the Worklife of Information Workers. Social Science Computer Review, 8(4), 592-613.

Kyng, M., (1991). Designing for Cooperation: Cooperating in Design. Communications of the ACM, 34(12), 64-73.

Mantei, M., R. Baecher, A. Sellen, W. Buxton, T. Milligan, and B. Wellman, (1991). Experiences in the Use of a Media Space. In Proceedings of the 1991 CHI Conference, 203-207.

Markus, M., and T. Connolly, (1990). Why CSCW Applications Fail: Problems in the Adoption of Interdependent Work Tools. In Proceedings of CSCW '90, 371-380.

McGrath,J.,(1990). "Time Matters in Groups,"in J. Galegher, R.Kraut, C. Egido, (eds.), Intellectual Teamwork: Social and Technical Foundations of Cooperative Work: Lawrence Erlbaum Associates, Hillsale, NJ.

Nunamaker, J., A. Dennis, J. Valacich, D. Vogel, and J. George, (1991). Electronic Meeting Systems to Support Group Work.Communications of the ACM, 34(7), 40-61.

Orlikowski, W., (1991). Integrated Information Environment or Matrix of Control? The Contradictory Implications of Information Technology. MIT Sloan School Working Paper #3270-91-MSA

Perolle, J., (1991). Computer-Mediated Communications. Natonal Forum: The Phi Kappa Phi Journal, 71(3), 21-25.

Root, R., (1988). Design of a Multi-media Vehicle for Social Browsing. Proceedings of CSCW '88, 25-38.

Scott Morton, M., (1991). The Corporation of the 1990's: Information Tecnology and Organizational Transformation. Oxford University Press, New York.

Weiser,M., (1991). The Computer for the 21st Century. Scientific American, September 1991,94-104.

Yakemovic, K, and E. Conklin,, (1990). Report on a Development Project Use of an Issue-Based Information System. In Proceedings of CSCW '90,105-118.

Zuboff, S., (1988). In the Age of the Smart Machine: The Future of Work and Power. Basic Books, New York.

READING QUESTIONS

1) What is the difference between a persuasion support system and a decision support system? Could you tell by looking at just the software?

2) Why doesn't a vector analysis of the word processing task help us understand the preference for WYSIWYG editors?

3) What is the "productivity paradox"?

4) How can the addition of a useful computer application "actually complicate or misdirect real work"?

5) What is the "systems rationalist" perspective, and why does it fall short as an analysis of the use of computing in the real world?

6) Why did the extensive use of a "simple mail system" astonish the designer of the modeling system?

7) Why must "an understanding of the safety of computer systems go beyond the laboratory?"

8) How are CS departments like an integrated Medical school and Biology department?

9) Why does the current research on groupware emphasize controlled experiments?

10) Why is task focus considered a virtue of groupware, and what might be missing with this characterization?

11) Why does groupware focus on anonymity rather than trust as a way to help groups generate and evaluate ideas on the basis of merit? What might be wrong with this approach?

12) What are the four stages of group process and why is a groupware product at risk if it does not support all four?

13) How can groupware be easily turned into snoopware? Is this a problem?

14) What effects might groupware have on group membership over the long term?

DISCUSSION QUESTIONS

1) Look at the curriculum and syllabi from your program. To what extent are the uses of computers in the real world represented? How does this square with the statements your program makes about what it trains its students to do?

2) Review at least one CSCW product, and try to determine the underlying assumptions about actual group interaction that underlie its design.

3) What responsibility does a "decision support system" designer have to ensure that the software is not used as merely a "persuasion support system"? What responsibility does the designer of medical treatment technology have to ensure that the technology is used safely?

PRACTICING THE DESIGN ETHIC

1) Examine an existing system in your business or school that has been installed for at least six months. Make individual appointments to have a private 15 minute conversation with at least three people who worked both before and after the system was implemented. At least one of the people should be a "user" of the system rather than an administrator. Remember to consider the ethical issues involved in interviewing for a lab project (see Chapter 1).

After you start your interview, ask them to describe how work was done both before and after the system was installed. Also ask how the decision was made to make the change, and how the change was implemented. In the process of the discussion that ensues, try to clarify the following things:
   - Did the organization chart change?
   - Did the informal organization change?
   - Did they notice if they increased interactions with certain people and reduced interactions with others?
   - Who now makes decisions about the system or the work associated with the system?
   - Who benefits from the system, and in what ways?
   - What characteristics of the system produced these changes?

In writing up your report on these interviews, make sure to note differences in perception between your informants, and attempt to explain these differences. Identify those changes that you think are a result of the actual design of the system and those changes that are more a result of organizational decisions. Identify at least one alternative approach to the implementation of the system that could have been taken. Finally, give an estimate of how much of the system implementation and its effects was based on "technical" issues and how much was based on "organizational" issues.

2) Come up with a reasonably detailed design concept for software that your class could use in doing these exercises. It should allow communication and cooperative work among students, and between students and the instructor. It can involve E-mail, fax, video, etc. As you make decisions about the design (e.g., should the instructor be able to monitor progress?) keep track of the ethical and social issues decisions you must make. How will systems that make different ethical and social decisions differ?

CHAPTER
3

PROFESSIONAL ETHICS AND COMPUTER SCIENCE

How is the design of computing technology connected to ethics? We briefly introduced ethical concern as the third pillar of the design ethic in Chapter 1. This chapter explores in detail the connections between computing technology and ethical concern by focusing on the recently adopted Association for Computing Machinery's code of ethics and on a proposal for integrating ethical concerns into the engineering curriculum. These are both exercises in what philosophers might call "practical ethics." McLean calls this a focus on "doing the right thing" rather than thinking about ethical conundrums.

Anderson's article explores the history and character of the current ACM code of ethics. He emphasizes that the code of ethics is an expression of the values of a community—not a detailed or rigid specification of rules. One can clearly see the community in action in the section that documents the disagreements in the community that became evident as the code took form. We will explore many of these disagreements in later chapters in this book. One point to note now is that, in our attempts to make safe and ethical technology for society, "all we have to fall back on are people and their ethical standards."

McLean proposes a particular way of helping engineering students form their ethical standards. Since in his view engineering is "all about" ethical choices, we need to integrate the teaching and learning of those choices into the entire engineering curriculum. He provides an example of a engineering curriculum that takes ethical issues seriously at all levels and does not merely banish it to a single course or to "business ethics" courses. A crucial question that McLean attempts to answer in his article is: "Does this approach help to train better engineers?" We think he makes a good argument that the answer is "yes," even for a narrow "technical excellence" definition of "good engineer."

THE ACM CODE OF ETHICS:
HISTORY, PROCESS, AND IMPLICATIONS[1]

Ronald E. Anderson
University of Minnesota

COMPUTER RISKS AND THE NEED FOR ETHICS

Only 15 years ago it was rare to hear computer specialists say the word "risk." Now computer scientists often talk about risks and risk factors. For over a year the Communications of the ACM has published a monthly column called "Risks" by Peter Neumann, who has collected thousands of anecdotes of damage resulting from computer-related systems. In 1990 the National Research Council published a major study, *Computers at Risk* (Clark, 1990). In 1991 IEEE and ACM jointly released a model curriculum with a recommended topic on "risks and liabilities" (IEEE, 1991; topic SP2).

One major source of vulnerability is the pervasive installation of networks linking together millions of computers of all types. Despite passwords and other security devices, the Internet suffered four security breaches per day during 1992. While security systems can be improved, we remain dependent upon the ethical restraint of persons who have the capacity for widespread harm to computerized communication systems and their users.

A few years ago when computer "worms" and "viruses" first spread from microcomputer to microcomputer via user diskettes, the computing public awoke to still another vulnerability. Despite a new industry of antivirus software manufacturers, the risks persist. An organization in Eastern Europe has claimed to release a new computer virus every seven minutes, but as yet there is no system of international criminal justice that addresses such global threats (Hey, 1991).

On the horizon is yet another vulnerability. This risk derives from the digitization of all kinds of information, especially works of art and music. More and more sound and video material is being digitized, yet there are no techniques for tracing fraudulent alterations of these creations. Digitization combined with virtual reality, experiences where fantasy and reality are indistinguishable, could create entirely fabricated "events." Enforcement institutions can not keep pace with such rapid technological change. All we have to fall back on are people and their ethical standards.

The greatest hope we have for impeding the harm resulting from computer risks lies with society itself and its social institutions. The more serious the public views violations of computer laws and computer ethics, the fewer the future problems will be. But the general public is not likely to take

---

[1] This article was written expressly for inclusion in this text.

these problems seriously unless the professional societies and educational institutions take the lead. One of the main institutions that clarifies and monitors ethics in the workplace, and in society at large, is the professional association. But is computing a profession? This question will be directly addressed in the next section.

Computer ethics applies not just to computer professionals but to all who use computers or come into contact with their inputs and outputs, which means every one living in industrialized societies. The focus of the following sections is upon professional codes of ethics; nonetheless, many if not most of these ethical principles apply to those who don't consider themselves computer professionals.

PROFESSIONS AND ETHICS

Established professions and professionals have the following characteristics: requirements for specialized training including a college education; a professional association with definite membership criteria; a service orientation; an expectation of a fair degree of professional autonomy; and a code of ethics (Guy, 1985; Hatch, 1988; Pavalko, 1988). The specification of a code of ethics generally comes late in the emergence of a profession, but it is an essential attribute because of its moral commitment of service to the public.

Many computing specialists satisfy these criteria for professional status; however, some groups do not. For instance, most computer operators would be marginal professionals in that they do not have a great deal of specialized training, nor do they typically have a significant degree of professional autonomy in their work, and their service orientation is mainly to an employer rather than to the public.

While the computing community may not be an established profession, it possesses many of the characteristics of professional groups, and most importantly, it labels itself as a profession. People writing in the literature of the computing associations often refer to themselves as "computing professionals." But there are computing persons, e.g., students, who do not think of themselves as professionals. In this discussion the term "professional" is used loosely, but the important point is that codes of ethics are relevant to less established as well as established professionals.

Professional groups are both technical and moral communities because in order to be self-regulatory the members must set shared goals and specify appropriate ways to achieve them (Camenisch, 1983; Frankel, 1989). In order to specify these appropriate standards it is necessary to detail what types of behavior are ethically acceptable or not. Professional codes of ethics serve that function, and every major association of computing specialists has developed a code of ethics, with the exception of the Computer Professionals for Social Responsibility (CPSR). They rejected a code of ethics because it was seen as an excuse for avoiding personal and collective action (Chapman, 1990). Another major argument against ethical codes is more philosophical.

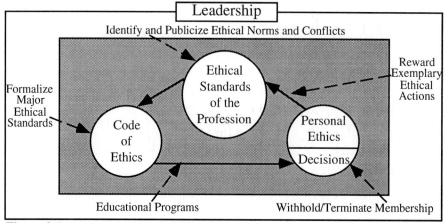

Figure 3-1

A Model of Leadership Opportunity in Professional Ethics.

Ladd (1980; 1982) argued that ethical codes are morally confusing, especially because they contradict the concept of the "autonomous professional."

When codes of professional ethics first emerged, they tended to be regulatory, if not authoritarian, in character. The obligations of members were explicitly stated so that there could be a basis for judging compliance and sanctioning noncompliance. The current trend in codes of professional ethics is away from formal enforcement, perhaps because of a growing appreciation for the role of social norms and socialization.

The new, normative model of professional ethics recognizes that a code of professional ethics is only a partial representation of the ethical standards of the members of the professional group (Parker, Swope, and Baker, 1990). But it is these norms that constitute the most critical driving force toward widespread, appropriate ethical behavior. The ethical performance of the group is the sum total of personal ethical decisions, which are based primarily upon one's socialization to the ethical standards of the profession, with the aid of a more formal code of ethics, as well as one's own broader moral development.

Within this new ethical framework, the most important actions of the leadership of a professional group are to identify and publicize ethical norms and conflicts, formalize these norms as imperatives of a code of ethics, and reward exemplary ethical actions by the members. These functions of ethical leadership are depicted in Figure 3-1 between the outer box and the inner box. The smaller box represents the normative, ethical system of the profession, and the larger box, the leadership of that professional group. Inside the smaller box are three circles that distinguish ethical standards (norms) from ethical codes and ethical decisions. Ethical standards, which most often are applied informally, appear within the largest circle to show their importance within the system. The leadership of a profession can most effectively guide this ethical system by formalizing and publicizing the ethical norms through maintaining a code of ethics. But educational programs and awards for meritorious ethical contributions are also important leadership activities. Enforcing these ethical standards by withholding or terminating the membership of violators may also be important, but most likely the significance of these sanctions is more symbolic than deterrent (Forester and Morrison, 1990).

The regulatory purpose of a code is accomplished to the degree that it deters unethical behavior. It is sometimes assumed that this cannot be fulfilled unless penalties are spelled out and an enforcement procedure has been installed. However, the code may be effective simply by suggesting an appropriate sanction for any given violation and by requiring professionals to report errant colleagues. In the latter case, each professional assumes a responsibility for upholding the group's integrity.

Frankel (1989) outlined the positive functions of a code of ethics and in so doing gave us several compelling arguments for them. His most important distinction is between codes that are primarily aspirational or educational and those that are primarily regulatory, that is, established to sanction violations. An aspirational or educational emphasis can be observed when the principles of a code are expressed in the language of ideals and guidelines for professionals to use in making decisions. Thus the code works toward the collective good even though it may be a mere distillation of collective experience and reflection. A benefit of an educationally oriented code is its contribution to the solidarity of the group by reinforcing professional identity and allegiance, as well as commonly held group values (Frankel, 1989).

Lastly and most importantly, the process of developing and maintaining a code of ethics benefits the professional group. Getting a large number of people attentive to ethical concerns and then organizing discussions around these issues can yield surprisingly greater sensitization to issues of ethics and the profession.

COMPARISONS OF CODES OF PROFESSIONAL ETHICS

In order to make these comparisons among ethical codes, we use as a standard the newly revised ACM (Association for Computing Machinery) Code of Ethics. The newly revised Code of Ethics and Professional Conduct appears as an appendix to this article. The Revised ACM Code is divided into four sections with the first section giving a set of general moral considerations, the second identifying additional ethical principles applying to computing professionals, the third pertaining to organizational leaders, and the final section dealing with issues of general compliance with the code. Table 3.1 shows these four groups; all 24 imperatives of the revised code are listed along the left margin.

Table 3.1

Correspondence of each of 24 Principles of the 1992 ACM Code of Ethics with Codes of other associations. An "x" means the ethical principle is explicitly stated in the code.

		ACM92	ACM72	ASIS	DPMA	ICCP	IEEE	IFIP	ISTE
1.	GENERAL MORAL IMPERATIVES								
1.1	Contribute to society	x	x	x	x		x	x	
1.2	Aviod harm to others	x	x		x	x	x	x	
1.3	Be honest and trustworthy	x	x	x	x	x	x	x	
1.4	Be fair and not discriminate	x	x	x			x	x	x
1.5	Honor property rights	x	x	x	x			x	x
1.6	Credit intellectual property	x	x		x		x		
1.7	Respect the privacy of others	x	x	x	x	x		x	x
1.8	Honor confidentiality	x	x	x	x	x			x
2.	MORE SPECIFIC PROFESSIONAL RESPONSIBILITIES								
2.1	Strive for quality in work	x							
2.2	Manitain professional competence	x	x		x	x	x	x	x
2.3	Respect law on professional work	x			x				
2.4	Facilitate professional review	x				x	x	x	
2.5	Evaluate impacts and risks	x	x		x				
2.6	Honor contracts and agreements	x	x	x	x				
2.7	Improve public understanding	x	x	x	x	x	x	x	
2.8	Access only when authorized	x							
3.	ORGANIZATIONAL LEADERSHIP IMPERATIVES								
3.1	Encourage social responsibility	x						x	
3.2	Manage to enhance quality of work	x						x	
3.3	Support proper computer uses	x						x	x
3.4	Ensure user input in design	x						x	
3.5	Protect dignity of users	x						x	
3.6	Create learning opportunities	x						x	x
4	COMPLIANCE WITH THE CODE								
4.1	Uphold and promote this code	x					x		
4.2	Treat violations as inconsistent with ACM membership	x							

Key:
ACM92:   Association for Computing Machinery (1992 code)
ACM72:   Association for Computing Machinery (1972 code)
ASIS: American Society for Information Science
DPMA: Data Processing Management Association
ICCP: Institute for Certification of Computer Professionals
IEEE: Institute for Electrical and Electronic Engineers
IFIP: International Federation for Information Processing
ISTE: International Society for Technology in Education

There is an important consideration embedded within this structure. The first section contains general moral imperatives that on the surface do not have anything to do with issues unique to computing. One purpose of incorporating these general moral imperatives is to implicitly demonstrate how specific professional issues are grounded in the general moral principles found in every ethical code. Too often the imperatives of an ethical code appear to be arbitrary rules rather than interpretations of how to apply general ethical principles (Luegenbiehl, 1992). One significance of this approach is that it demonstrates how individual members can apply the general moral principles to new problems or dilemmas. With a rapidly evolving technology that often raises new moral dilemmas, it is critical that the individual members be given the "tools" to make their own decisions in the face of novel ethical situations (Christensen, 1986).

The codes of ethics of six other computing associations were chosen for comparison with the revised ACM code. The associations, in the order they appear in Table 3.1, are the Association for Computing Machinery (ACM, 1973); the American Society for Information Science (Barnes, 1990); the Data Processing Management Association (Spiro, 1989); the Institute for Certification of Computer Professionals (ICCP, 1977); the Institute for Electrical and Electronic Engineers (IEEE, 1990); the International Federation for Information Processing (Sackman, 1991); and the International Society for Technology in Education (ISTE, 1987). For other comparisons of the codes of ethics of computer associations see Martin and Martin (1990) and Dunlop and Kling (1991).

It is noteworthy that we found only a few common ethical principles in every code. These include the general moral principle of honesty, the principles of privacy and confidentiality, the responsibility of maintaining professional competence, and the improvement of public understanding. The principles of honor for property rights, professional review, fairness and nondiscrimination, and crediting intellectual property were found in only half or fewer of the association codes.

Even more enlightening are those imperatives that have been neglected by most codes of professional ethics. These include the principle requiring authorized access to computer-communication systems and the one admonishing quality in one's work. In addition, almost all associations have ignored the organizational principles and the compliance issues outlined in sections 3 and 4 of the Code of Ethics.

ORGANIZATIONAL ETHICS

A glaring omission in professional codes of ethics is the specification of ethical responsibilities for organizations including employers and organizational decision makers. Codes of ethics of the computing associations share the same bias inherent in the codes of most engineering societies, as well as in business codes of ethics: emphasis on the need for loyalty to employer rather than on the obligations of employer to employee (Johnson, 1985; Johnson, 1989). The International Federation for Informatic Processing code has taken the lead in attempting to delineate the ethical responsibilities of organizations. Rather than follow the structure of their code, the ACM revision sought to retain a personalized approach to the statement of each imperative. That is, each imperative begins with the phrase "I will . . ." Each imperative in section three begins with the phrase "As an ACM member and an organization leader, I will . . ." Thus while the

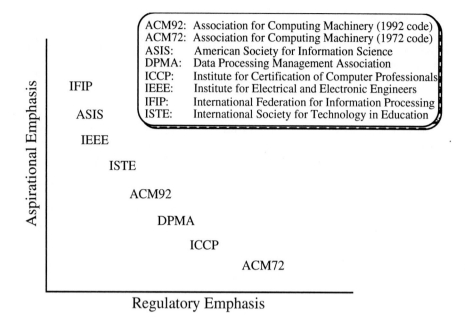

Figure 3-2
Comparison of Codes of Ethics by Degree of Aspiriational and Regulatory
Emphasis.

imperatives of the code are person-centric, those in the third section apply
specifically to organizations.

To compare the new ACM Code of Ethics to the codes of the six other
computing associations, these codes were placed on a grid with two axes:
degree of aspirational emphasis and emphasis on regulatory actions (Figure
3-2). The current ACM Code sits about midway between the extremes of
heavy emphasis on aspiration without regulation (top left), on the one hand,
and emphasis upon regulation with little priority given to aspirational
functions (lower right). The latter orientation characterizes the ICCP Code
and the early ACM Code, whereas the other type is best represented by the
IFIP, ASIS, and IEEE Codes of Ethics.

THE PROCESS OF DEVELOPING A CODE OF ETHICS

ACM's first code of ethics was adopted in 1972 (ACM, 1973) and was
retained unchanged for 20 years, except for minor wording refinements. In
1990, ACM's Special Interest Group on Computers and Society was
unusually busy. Not only did it hold the first conference on Computers and
the Quality of Life (CQL'90), but a proposal was submitted to the ACM SDF
(SIG Discretionary Fund). The Special Interest Group Board (SIGBOARD)
awarded funds for a task force to work on a draft revision of an ethical code.
The project was launched during CQL'90 with an all-day symposium on
computer ethics.

Ethical Disagreements:
 • Ethical relevance of environmental harm
 • Ethical relevance of "minor" violations of copyrights, leases, and other impositions on intellectual property
 • Mandate for nondiscrimination on the basis of sexual orientation
 • Ethical relevance of provacy and confidentiality safegaurds. E.g. When is confidentiality implied? When do violations constitute ethical problems? What personal information do individuals own and when is privacy deserved?
 • Ethical relevance and priority of quality in work and quality of life
 • Ethical obligations to follow existing law
 • Ethical requirements for extensive user input and impact assessment in system design
 • Ethical requirements for extensive peer review of one's professional work
 • Moral implications of unauthorized access to computer systems

Disagreements on the Role of Professional Codes:
 • Preference for stating ethics as ideals versus rules
 • Desire for generality versus specificity in ethical statements
 • View of the scope of ethics as broad or narrow
 • Inclusion of obligations of organizations and organizational members in codes of professional ethics
 • Voluntary or mandatory enforcement of professional ethics. E.g. What are the obligations to assist or report others conformance to ethical principles?
 • Penalties and disciplinary action for violations of ethical codes

Table 3.3
Some Points of Ethical Controversy in Computing.

During 1991 a series of open meetings on ethics were held in conjunction with the Computer Science Conference and the National Educational Computer Conference. Between these meetings the Task Force outlined plans and drafted statements of ethical principles. After several rounds of drafts, which were reviewed by the ACM Executive Committee as well as by members of the Task Force, a draft was accepted by the ACM Council for circulation to the ACM membership. In May 1992 the draft Code of Ethics was published in the Communications of the ACM (CACM), which is distributed to the 80,000 members of the association (ACM, 1992). Members of the association were asked to rate each item of the draft code and to provide any type of feedback desired. On the basis of the responses from members, revisions were made and proposed to the ACM Council. On October 16, 1992, a new Code of Ethics was officially adopted by the ACM Council.

The changes that were made between the published draft and the final Code of Ethics reveal a great deal about the ethical beliefs of computing professionals as well as the political realities of professional associations. Consequently, some of these details will be highlighted. As noted, when the draft was published in the CACM, members were invited to give feedback to the Task Force by way of a survey rating form or by other comments. The results of the survey feedback form show considerable support overall (Table 3.2). As shown in Table 3.2, the amount of support ranged mostly between 75 percent and 95 percent. The written comments offered numerous suggestions for improving or changing specific ethical principles or their interpretation. As can be seen in these statistical results, there was some serious concern over several items, especially those in the compliance section.

ETHICAL DISAGREEMENTS

The diverse comments on the Code reveal a number of important differences of ethical opinion that persist despite consensus on a solid ethical core. This section discusses these ethical controversies, and Table 3.3 summarizes the items with the greatest dissensus. The reader is reminded that the ACM "Code of Ethics" refers to the 24 imperatives preceded by a preamble; the "Guidelines" refers to the supplemental commentary on the Code.

Environmental Harm

The Guidelines on the first two imperatives ("Contribute to society" and "Avoid harm to others") of the Code of Ethics specify the natural environment as an ethical responsibility. Several members suggested that this was inappropriate, but others felt that the affirmation should be stronger and include prevention of harm.

Intellectual Property

The intellectual property imperatives (1.5 and 1.6) are probably the most controversial and complex, though essential, principles in the entire code. Principle 1.5 addresses unauthorized software duplication, which is rampant across the globe, but few computer professionals consider it sufficiently serious to "blow the whistle" on violators or to otherwise crusade against it. The principle depends upon a cultural definition of property not shared throughout the world, and even in the U.S.A. the definition is evolving and to some extent dependent upon forthcoming court cases. Furthermore, a growing community of activists continues to argue that contemporary notions of intellectual property are detrimental to innovation and progress. Copyrights, patents, and trade secrets, while preserving individual property rights, inhibit widespread sharing of ideas and resources and consequently conflict with the improvement of human well-being. Several critics questioned the relevance of "minor" impositions on intellectual property in the Code of Ethics. One argument was that many violations fall within the acceptable range of "fair use," analogous to the consensus on acceptable photo duplication of published, copyrighted materials. To add more balance, I proposed to the Task Force that the following sentence be added to the end of the 1.6 guideline: "Since the sharing of ideas and other intellectual property is generally beneficial, the professional should consider options that will maximize widespread dissemination." The Task Force voted me down.

Nondiscrimination

The Guidelines for imperative 1.4, which deals with discrimination, prohibit "discrimination on the basis of race, sex, religion, age, disability, national origin, or other such factors." Several members asked that "sexual orientation" be added to this list. I proposed this to the Task Force, but the amplification was voted down. I would not be surprised if it were added to the Code in the next revision process.

Privacy

Imperative 1.7 deals with privacy and 1.8 with confidentiality. The Guidelines of the Code of Ethics specify an obligation to protect data about individuals "from unauthorized access or accidental disclosure to inappropriate individuals." The Guidelines also specify that organizational leaders have obligations to "verify that systems are designed and implemented to protect personal privacy." The Guidelines delineate several types of action essential for protecting individual privacy. Several responses from persons outside the United States questioned the appropriateness of treating privacy as an ethical issue because neither the laws nor the norms in their counties supported this.

Quality

The draft Code, as well as the final Code, contains numerous references to quality. Principle 2.1 stipulates quality as a goal for professional work, and 3.2 stipulates enhancement of quality of life as a criterion for evaluating information systems. While those outside the United States strongly supported the emphasis on quality, some Americans felt uncomfortable with this link between ethics and quality.

Existing Law

Imperative 2.3 says that one should "know and respect existing laws pertaining to professional work." While most members appear to support this principle, a few expressed their opinion that if a law was seen as unethical, they should not be ethically required to comply with it. The Guidelines of the Code of Ethics state that members must obey laws "unless there is a compelling ethical basis not to do so." The Guidelines clarify this further by stating that compliance must be balanced with the statement that some laws are inappropriate and "must be challenged," but individuals must accept full responsibility for any violation of existing laws.

Peer Review

Some criticism was expressed over the emphasis of imperative 2.4 on professional review of one's work. Most of this criticism came from those employed by businesses where their work was not subject to peer review because of its proprietary nature. The Guidelines provide for such situations by stating that peer review is necessary "whenever appropriate."

System Design

Several of the principles in the new Code of Ethics mandate consideration of user needs in system design and call for attempts to assess the impact of these systems. While several of the comments criticized these principles, the majority of the comments were supportive.

Unauthorized Access

In the draft Code of Ethics, imperative 1.7 provided for access to computing systems "only when authorized to do so." This principle arose from the growing concern in the computing community over controlling the rising variety of "computer viruses" and other intrusions that have threatened computers and communications systems within the past few years. While a few persons questioned the specificity of this imperative, at least one person suggested that it be even broader. The principle was preserved but renumbered as 2.8 in the final Code of Ethics.

Role of Codes of Professional Ethics

Several objected strongly to the first section because the general ethical imperatives offered no delineation of the boundary between personal and professional ethics. Some argued that a professional code of ethics should not be used to legislate private, personal morality. These points of dissension were addressed by adding a paragraph to the preamble that explicitly stated the purpose of the Code.

Compliance

The most common criticisms of the Code were made about issues in the last section on compliance. In general, three kinds of complaints were made: One was that there was too much emphasis upon penalties and not enough on supporting and assisting those who attempted to comply with the Code; a second major complaint was that the statements in section 4.0 were either internally inconsistent or inconsistent with the preamble and its emphasis upon the Code as guidelines; finally, several indirectly criticized this section by pointing out how it is impossible to comply with principles that are expressed. It was noted that a complaint review process would be much more difficult if only statements of ideals were available as a basis for adjudication.

The original draft of the revised ACM Code included three compliance principles, but the final, adopted Code omitted the principle that promised particular sanctions for violations. This compromise was necessary to address the concerns of several ACM leaders who sought to avoid taking disciplinary action against violators of the Code. The new Code unquestionably preserves the discretionary rights of the individual professional to make ethical judgments.

The ACM Council is charged constitutionally with responsibility for enforcing a code of ethics. The existing ACM Policy and Procedures Guidelines spell out a procedure for reviewing any professional conduct complaints against members of the association. In addition, in conjunction with the old Code of Professional Conduct there was a committee charged with reviewing any "gross misconduct." Nonetheless, over a 20-year period ACM's complaint review process was never utilized.

In February 1993 the ACM Council voted to establish a new Committee on Professional Ethics, reporting directly to the Executive Committee. The Committee's charge is to (1) promote ethical conduct among computing professionals by publicizing the Code of Ethics and by offering suggested interpretations of the Code; (2) plan and review activities to educate the membership in ethical decision making on issues of professional conduct; and (3) review and recommend updates, as necessary, to the Code of Ethics and Professional Conduct and its Guidelines. Undoubtedly, the Committee also will struggle with issues on enforcement of the Code of Ethics and Professional Conduct.

Several ethical topics were not specifically interpreted in either the Code or the Guidelines. For instance, specific requirements of integrity for research in computing and computer science were not detailed. Nor were specific suggestions offered for maintaining professional competence. Other ethical issues, such as software copyright violation, were addressed but not with sufficient detail relative to their salience to the field of computing. These issues, as well as new issues not yet imagined, will confront the field of computing in the future. These should be among the tasks of the ACM leadership to address with future additions to the Guidelines.

USING THE ACM CODE OF ETHICS

To illustrate the practical use of a code of ethics such as the ACM Code of Ethics, two scenarios with ethical decision making are described next. Following the scenario are comments on relevant connections to the ACM Code of Ethics and its Guidelines. Several additional case studies with interpretations from the perspective of the ACM Code of Ethics can be found in Anderson et al. (1993).

SCENARIO 1.

John buys a new computer game that runs on his family's computer as well as on those at his school. Even though the diskette was "copy protected" and the label warned not to try to copy it, he discovered that he could copy it using a special copy program. John liked the game program and made copies for each of three of his friends. One of John's teachers overheard them talking about these copies and told them it was wrong to make such unauthorized copies. John replied: "We always make copies. If my friends buy a game, they give me a copy, and I'm expected to do the same for them. Besides no one has ever checked up on us."

The ACM Code of Ethics addresses questions of intellectual property in imperative 1.6, but 1.5 makes it imperative to honor copyrights, patents, trade secrets, and license agreements. These restrictions are grounded in the need to comply with existing laws (2.3), professional integrity, and respect for property.

Suppose John had installed the program on a network instead of making any diskette copies. Would that be an ethical violation? The answer almost always is yes. The only exception might be where access to the game required password entry and he did not give out the password to anyone. Even though it is generally desirable to share ideas and programs that you have written, using bootlegged software or violating the terms of a purchase or lease is unethical. These principles apply not only to professional computer specialists but to student members of the ACM and to computer users in general.

SCENARIO 2.

Nancy notices that her history instructor also buys books from the same store. Upon Nancy's request, the store clerk gives Nancy a computer listing of all the books her teacher has bought. When the history instructor finds out, she gets very angry and storms into the bookstore, saying, "You should not give the names of the books I buy to anybody. Nobody has the right to know what books I am reading."

In the Code of Ethics, principle 1.7 deals with privacy and 1.8 with confidentiality. The Guidelines of the Code stipulate one's obligation to protect data about individuals "from unauthorized access or accidental disclosure to inappropriate individuals." The Code also specifies that organizational leaders have obligations to "verify that systems are designed and implemented to protect personal privacy and enhance personal dignity" (3.5), and to assess the needs of all those affected by a system (3.4). In this scenario the bookstore should have had policies and procedures that protected the identity of its customers.

CONCLUSION

It is clear that our ethical responsibilities continue to increase as the potential for harm from a single unethical decision widens because of ever more powerful technologies (Kidder, 1992). Law enforcement cannot keep pace with such rapid technological change. It is impossible to write a completely definitive ethical code for computing because of the rapidly changing nature of the field. Although it is only part of the solution, creating and applying an effective code of ethics can be an extremely important process for computing professionals.

New technological risks and dilemmas cause us to rethink how to apply fundamental moral imperatives to our everyday lives. Thus, computing serves as a mirror for society to reflect upon its moral standards and ethical performance. The many ongoing ethical issues raised by the evolution of computing technology point to the significance of this reflective experience for society. We should not forget that ultimately our hope for survival in the face of computer-based risks depends largely on the ethical standards of individuals working with computers.

While the ethical controversies in computing may seem prominent, the ethical consensus is far more significant. Examining either the values of the "cyberspace freedom fighters" on the one hand or the "computer establishment" on the other, we find a remarkable degree of ethical consensus. The vast majority still deeply believe in integrity, fairness, human well-being, respect for privacy, professional responsibility, and even respect for intellectual property. We need to remember these solid areas of agreement while discussing or debating the controversial topics. We also should attempt to coordinate action on the divisive issues, such as intellectual property and privacy, that underlie specific ethical disagreements.

NOTES

Ronald E. Anderson was Chair of the Task Force for the Revision of the ACM Code of Ethics. The author acknowledges the important contributions of other members of the ACM Task Force for the Revision of the ACM Code of Ethics: Gerald Engel, Donald Gotterbarn, Grace C. Hertlein, Alex Hoffman, Bruce Jawer, Deborah G. Johnson, Doris K. Lidtke, Joyce Currie Little, Dianne Martin, Donn B. Parker, Judith A. Perrolle, and Richard S. Rosenberg.

REFERENCES

ACM (Association for Computing Machinery) (1973). Proposed ACM code of professional conduct. *Communications of the ACM, 16(4)*, 265-269.

ACM (Association for Computing Machinery) (1992). *ACM Code of Ethics and Professional Conduct.*

AMA (American Medical Association) (1989). *Current Opinions.* American Medical Association, 535 N. Dearborn St., Chicago IL 60610.

Anderson, Ronald E. et al. (1992). Using the new ACM Code of Ethics. *Communications of the ACM, 35(5)*, 94-99.

Barnes, Robert F. (1990). The making of an ethics code. *Bulletin of the American Society for Information Science* (August/September), 24-25.

Camenisch, Paul F. (1983). *Grounding Professional Ethics in a Pluralistic Society.* New York: Haven Publications.

Chapman, Gary (1990). *Presentation at the ACM/SIGCAS conference on Computers and the Quality of Life.* Washington, DC: The George Washington University.

Christensen, Kathleen E. (1986). Ethics of information technology. In G. Geiss and N. Viswanathan (eds),*The Human Edge: Information Technology and Helping People.* New York: Haworth Press.

Clark, D. (1990). *Computers at Risk: Safe Computing in the Information Age*, National Research Council. Washington, DC: National Academy Press.

Dunlop, Charles, & Kling, Rob (1991). Ethical perspectives and professional responsibilities. In Charles Dunlop and Rob Kling (eds.). *Computerization and Controversy* (pp. 654-664). Boston, MA: Academic Press, Inc.

Forester, Tom, & Morrison, P. (1990). *Computer Ethics: Cautionary Tales and Ethical Dilemmas in Computing*. Cambridge, MA: MIT Press.

Frankel, Mark S. (1989). Professional Codes: why, how, and with what impact? *Journal of Business Ethics, 8(2 & 3)*, 109-116.

Guy, Mary E. (1985). *Professionals in Organizations*. New York: Praeger Scientific.

Hatch, Nathan O. (1988). Introduction: The Professions in a Democratic Culture. In N. O. Hatch (ed.).*The Professions in American History,* Notre Dame, IN: Univ. of Notre Dame Press.

Hey, K. R. (1991). Techno-Wizards and Couch Potatoes. *Omni, 13(11)*, 51ff.

ICCP (Institute for Certification of Computer Programmers) (1977). *Code of Ethics.* ICCP, 2200 E. Devon Ave, #268, Des Plaines, IL 60018.

IEEE (Institute of Electrical and Electronics Engineers) (1990). *IEEE Code of Ethics.* IEEE, 345 East 47th St., New York, NY 10017-2394.

IEEE Computer Society Press (1991). *Computing Curricula 1991, Report of the ACM/IEEE-CS Joint Curriculum Task Force.* Los Alamitos, CA: IEEE Computer Society Press.

ISTE (International Society for Technology in Education) (1987). Code of ethical conduct for computer-using educators. *The Computing Teacher, 15(2),* 51-53.

Johnson, Deborah. 1985. *Computer Ethics*. Englewood Cliffs, NJ: Prentice Hall.

Johnson, Deborah (1989). The social responsibility of computer professionals. Unpublished paper. Rensselaer Polytechnic Institute, Troy, NY.

Johnson, Deborah (1991). *Ethical Issues in Engineering*. Englewood Cliffs, NJ: Prentice Hall.

Kidder, Rushworth M. (1992). Ethics: a matter of survival. *The Futurist* (March-April), 10-12.

Ladd, John (1980). The quest for a code of professional ethics: An intellectual and moral confusion. In Rosemary Chalk, Mark Frankel, and Sallie B. Chafer (eds.). *AAAS Professional Ethics Project: Professional Ethics Activities in the Scientific and Engineering Societies.* (pp. 154-159). Washington, DC: AAAS.

Ladd, John. (1982). Collective and individual moral responsibility in engineering. *IEEE Technology and Society Magazine, 1(2),* 3-10.

Luegenbiehl, Heinz C. (1992). Computer professionals: moral autonomy and a code of ethics. *Journal of Systems Software, 17,* 61-68.

Martin, C. Dianne, & Martin, David H. (1990). Comparison of ethics codes of computer professionals, *Social Science Computer Review, 9(1),* 96-108.

Parker, Donn, Swope, Susan, & Baker, Bruce (1990). *Ethical Conflicts in Information and Computer Science, Technology and Business.* Wellesley, MA: QED Information Sciences.

Pavalko, R. M. (1988). *Sociology of Occupations and Professions, 2d ed.* Itasca, IL: F. E. Peacock Publishers.

Sackman, Hal (1991). A prototype IFIP code of ethics based on participative international consensus. In Charles Dunlop and Rob Kling (eds.). *Computerization and Controversy,* (pp 698-703), Boston, MA: Academic Press, Inc.

Spiro, Bruce E. (1989). Ethics in the information age. *Information Executive, 2(4)*, 38-41.

APPENDIX

ACM Code of Ethics and Professional Conduct[2]

Preamble. Commitment to ethical professional conduct is expected of every member (voting members, associate members, and student members) of the Association for Computing Machinery (ACM).

This Code, consisting of 24 imperatives formulated as statements of personal responsibility, identifies the elements of such a commitment. It contains many, but not all, issues professionals are likely to face. Section 1 outlines fundamental ethical considerations, while Section 2 addresses additional, more specific considerations of professional conduct. Statements in Section 3 pertain more specifically to individuals who have a leadership role, whether in the workplace or in a volunteer capacity such as with organizations like ACM. Principles involving compliance with this Code are given in Section 4.

The Code shall be supplemented by a set of Guidelines, which provide explanation to assist members in dealing with the various issues contained in the Code. It is expected that the Guidelines will be changed more frequently than the Code.

The Code and its supplemented Guidelines are intended to serve as a basis for ethical decision making in the conduct of professional work. Secondarily, they may serve as a basis for judging the merit of a formal complaint pertaining to violation of professional ethical standards.

It should be noted that although computing is not mentioned in the imperatives of section 1.0, the Code is concerned with how these fundamental imperatives apply to one's conduct as a computing professional. These imperatives are expressed in a general form to emphasize that ethical principles which apply to computer ethics are derived from more general ethical principles.

It is understood that some words and phrases in a code of ethics are subject to varying interpretations, and that any ethical principle may conflict with other ethical principles in specific situations. Questions related to ethical conflicts can best be answered by thoughtful consideration of fundamental principles, rather than reliance on detailed regulations.

1. **General Moral Imperatives**. As an ACM member I will ...

    1.1 Contribute to society and human well-being.

    1.2 Avoid harm to others.

    1.3 Be honest and trustworthy.

    1.4 Be fair and take action not to discriminate.

    1.5 Honor property rights, including copyrights and patents.

    1.6 Give proper credit for intellectual property.

---

[2] Adopted by ACM Council, Oct. 16, 1992.

1.7 Respect the privacy of others.

1.8 Honor confidentiality.

2. **More Specific Professional Responsibilities**. As an ACM computing professional I will …

2.1 Strive to achieve the highest quality, effectiveness, and dignity in both the process and products of professional work.

2.2 Acquire and maintain professional competence.

2.3 Know and respect existing laws pertaining to professional work.

2.4 Accept and provide appropriate professional review.

2.5 Give comprehensive and thorough evaluations of computer systems and their impacts, including analysis of possible risks.

2.6 Honor contracts, agreements, and assigned responsibilities.

2.7 Improve public understanding of computing and its consequences.

2.8 Access computing and communication resources only when authorized to do so.

3. **Organizational Leadership Imperatives**. As an ACM member and an organizational leader, I will …

3.1 Articulate social responsibilities of members of an organizational unit and encourage full acceptance of those responsibilities.

3.2 Manage personnel and resources to design and build information systems that enhance the quality of working life.

3.3 Acknowledge and support proper and authorized uses of an organization's computing and communication resources.

3.4 Ensure that users and those who will be affected by a system have their needs clearly articulated during the assessment and design of requirements; later the system must be validated to meet requirements.

3.5 Articulate and support policies that protect the dignity of users and others affected by a computing system.

3.6 Create opportunities for members of the organization to learn the principles and limitations of computer systems.

4. **Compliance with the Code**. As an ACM member, I will …

4.1 Uphold and promote the principles of this Code.

4.2 Treat violations of this code as inconsistent with membership in the ACM.

GUIDELINES

1. **General Moral Imperatives.** As an ACM member I will …

1.1 Contribute to society and human well-being.

This principle concerning the quality of life of all people affirms an obligation to protect fundamental human rights and to respect the diversity of all cultures. An essential aim of computing professionals is to minimize negative consequences of computing systems, including threats to health and safety. When designing or implementing systems, computing professionals must attempt to ensure that the products of their efforts will be used in socially responsible ways, will meet social needs, and will avoid harmful effects to health and welfare.

In addition to a safe social environment, human well-being includes a safe natural environment. Therefore, computing professionals who design and develop systems must be alert to, and make others aware of, any potential damage to the local or global environment.

1.2 Avoid harm to others.

"Harm" means injury or negative consequences, such as undesirable loss of information, loss of property, property damage, or unwanted environmental impacts. This principle prohibits use of computing technology in ways that result in harm to any of the following: users, the general public, employees, employers. Harmful actions include intentional destruction or modification of files and programs leading to serious loss of resources or unnecessary expenditure of human resources such as the time and effort required to purge systems of "computer viruses."

Well-intended actions, including those that accomplish assigned duties, may lead to harm unexpectedly. In such an event the responsible person or persons are obligated to undo or mitigate the negative consequences as much as possible. One way to avoid unintentional harm is to carefully consider potential impacts on all those affected by decisions made during design and implementation.

To minimize the possibility of indirectly harming others, computing professionals must minimize malfunctions by following generally accepted standards for system design and testing. Furthermore, it is often necessary to assess the social consequences of systems to project the likelihood of any serious harm to others. If system features are misrepresented to users, coworkers, or supervisors, the individual computing professional is responsible for any resulting injury.

In the work environment the computing professional has the additional obligation to report any signs of system dangers that might result in serious personal or social damage. If one's superiors do not act to curtail or mitigate such dangers, it may be necessary to "blow the whistle" to help correct the problem or reduce the risk. However, capricious or misguided reporting of violations can, itself, be harmful. Before reporting violations, all relevant aspects of the incident must be thoroughly assessed. In particular, the assessment of risk and responsibility must be credible. It is suggested that advice be sought from other computing professionals. See principle 2.5 regarding thorough evaluations.

1.3 Be honest and trustworthy.

Honesty is an essential component of trust. Without trust an organization cannot function effectively. The honest computing professional will not make deliberately false or deceptive claims about a system or system design, but will instead provide full disclosure of all pertinent system limitations and problems.

A computer professional has a duty to be honest about his or her own qualifications, and about any circumstances that might lead to conflicts of interest.

Membership in volunteer organizations such as ACM may at times place individuals in situations where their statements or actions could be interpreted as carrying the "weight" of a larger group of professionals. An ACM member will exercise care to not misrepresent ACM or positions and policies of ACM or any ACM units.

1.4 Be fair and take action not to discriminate.

The values of equality, tolerance, respect for others, and the principles of equal justice govern this imperative. Discrimination on the basis of race, sex, religion, age, disability, national origin, or other such factors is an explicit violation of ACM policy and will not be tolerated.

Inequities between different groups of people may result from the use or misuse of information and technology. In a fair society, all individuals would have equal opportunity to participate in, or benefit from, the use of computer resources regardless of race, sex, religion, age, disability, national origin, or other such similar factors. However, these ideals do not justify unauthorized use of computer resources, nor do they provide an adequate basis for violation of any other ethical imperatives of this code.

1.5 Honor property rights including copyrights and patents.

Violation of copyrights, patents, trade secrets, and the terms of license agreements is prohibited by law in most circumstances. Even when software is not so protected, such violations are contrary to professional behavior. Copies of software should be made only with proper authorization. Unauthorized duplication of materials must not be condoned.

1.6 Give proper credit for intellectual property.

Computing professionals are obligated to protect the integrity of intellectual property. Specifically, one must not take credit for other's ideas or work, even in cases where the work has not been explicitly protected by copyright, patent, etc.

1.7 Respect the privacy of others.

Computing and communication technology enables the collection and exchange of personal information on a scale unprecedented in the history of civilization. Thus there is increased potential for violating the privacy of individuals and groups. It is the responsibility of professionals to maintain the privacy and integrity of data describing individuals. This includes taking precautions to ensure the accuracy of data, as well as protecting it from unauthorized access or accidental disclosure to inappropriate individuals. Furthermore, procedures must be established to allow individuals to review their records and correct inaccuracies.

This imperative implies that only the necessary amount of personal information be collected in a system, that retention and disposal periods for that information be clearly defined and enforced, and that personal information gathered for a specific purpose not be used for other purposes without consent of the individual(s). These principles apply to electronic communications, including electronic mail, and prohibit procedures that capture or monitor electronic user data, including messages, without the permission of users or bona fide authorization related to system operation and maintenance. User data observed during the normal duties of system operation and maintenance must be treated with strictest confidentiality, except in cases where it is evidence for the violation of law, organizational regulations, or this Code. In these cases, the nature or contents of that information must be disclosed only to proper authorities. (See 1.9.)

1.8 Honor confidentiality.

The principle of honesty extends to issues of confidentiality of information whenever one has made an explicit promise to honor confidentiality or, implicitly, when private information not directly related to the performance of one's duties becomes available. The ethical concern is to respect all obligations of confidentiality to employers, clients, and users unless discharged from such obligations by requirements of the law or other principles of this Code.

2. **More Specific Professional Responsibilities**. As an ACM computing professional I will …

2.1 Strive to achieve the highest quality, effectiveness, and dignity in both the process and products of professional work.

Excellence is perhaps the most important obligation of a professional. The computing professional must strive to achieve quality and to be cognizant of the serious negative consequences that may result from poor quality in a system.

2.2 Acquire and maintain professional competence.

Excellence depends on individuals who take responsibility for acquiring and maintaining professional competence. A professional must participate in setting standards for appropriate levels of competence, and strive to achieve those standards. Upgrading technical knowledge and competence can be achieved in several ways: doing independent study; attending seminars, conferences, or courses; and being involved in professional organizations.

2.3 Know and respect existing laws pertaining to professional work.

ACM members must obey existing local, state, province, national, and international laws unless there is a compelling ethical basis not to do so. Policies and procedures of the organizations in which one participates must also be obeyed. But compliance must be balanced with the recognition that sometimes existing laws and rules may be immoral or inappropriate and, therefore, must be challenged. Violation of a law or regulation may be ethical when that law or rule has inadequate moral basis or when it conflicts with another law judged to be more important. If one decides to violate a law or rule because it is viewed as unethical, or for any other reason, one must fully accept responsibility for one's actions and for the consequences.

2.4 Accept and provide appropriate professional review.

Quality professional work, especially in the computing profession, depends on professional reviewing and critiquing. Whenever appropriate, individual members should seek and utilize peer review as well as provide critical review of the work of others.

2.5 Give comprehensive and thorough evaluations of computer systems and their impacts, including analysis of possible risks.

Computer professionals must strive to be perceptive, thorough, and objective when evaluating, recommending, and presenting system descriptions and alternatives. Computer professionals are in a position of special trust, and therefore have a special responsibility to provide objective, credible evaluations to employers, clients, users, and the public. When providing evaluations the professional must also identify any relevant conflicts of interest, as stated in imperative 1.3.

As noted in the discussion of principle 1.2 on avoiding harm, any signs of danger from systems must be reported to those who have opportunity and/or responsibility to resolve them. See the guidelines for imperative 1.2 for more details concerning harm, including the reporting of professional violations.

2.6 Honor contracts, agreements, and assigned responsibilities.

Honoring one's commitments is a matter of integrity and honesty. For the computer professional this includes ensuring that system elements perform as intended. Also, when one contracts for work with another party, one has an obligation to keep that party properly informed about progress toward completing that work.

A computing professional has a responsibility to request a change in any assignment that he or she feels cannot be completed as defined. Only after serious consideration and with full disclosure of risks and concerns to the employer or client, should one accept the assignment. The major underlying principle here is the obligation to accept personal accountability for professional work. On some occasions other ethical principles may take greater priority.

A judgment that a specific assignment should not be performed may not be accepted. Having clearly identified one's concerns and reasons for that judgment, but failing to procure a change in that assignment, one may yet be obligated, by contract or by law, to proceed as directed. The computing professional's ethical judgment should be the final guide in deciding whether or not to proceed. Regardless of the decision, one must accept the responsibility for the consequences.

However, performing assignments "against one's own judgment" does not relieve the professional of responsibility for any negative consequences.

2.7 Improve public understanding of computing and its consequences.

Computing professionals have a responsibility to share technical knowledge with the public by encouraging understanding of computing, including the impacts of computer systems and their limitations. This imperative implies an obligation to counter any false views related to computing.

2.8 Access computing and communication resources only when authorized to do so.

Theft or destruction of tangible and electronic property is prohibited by imperative 1.2: "Avoid harm to others." Trespassing and unauthorized use of a computer or communication system are addressed by this imperative. Trespassing includes accessing communication networks and computer systems, or accounts and/or files associated with those systems, without explicit authorization to do so. Individuals and organizations have the right to restrict access to their systems so long as they do not violate the discrimination principle (see 1.4). No one should enter or use another's computer system, software, or data files without permission. One must always have appropriate approval before using system resources, including communication ports, file space, other system peripherals, and computer time.

3. **Organizational Leadership Imperatives**. As an ACM member and an organizational leader, I will …

Background Note: This section draws extensively from the draft IFIP Code of Ethics, especially its sections on organizational ethics and international concerns. The ethical obligations of organizations tend to be neglected in most codes of professional conduct, perhaps because these codes are written from the perspective of the individual member. This dilemma is addressed by stating these imperatives from the perspective of the organizational leader. In this context "leader" is viewed as any organizational member who has leadership or educational responsibilities. These imperatives generally may apply to organizations as well as their leaders. In this context "organizations" are corporations, government agencies, and other "employers," as well as volunteer professional organizations.

3.1 Articulate social responsibilities of members of an organizational unit and encourage full acceptance of those responsibilities.

Because organizations of all kinds have impacts on the public, they must accept responsibilities to society. Organizational procedures and attitudes oriented toward quality and the welfare of society will reduce harm to members of the public, thereby serving the public interest and fulfilling social responsibility. Therefore, organizational leaders must encourage full participation in meeting social responsibilities as well as quality performance.

3.2 Manage personnel and resources to design and build information systems that enhance the quality of working life.

Organizational leaders are responsible for ensuring that computer systems enhance, not degrade, the quality of working life. When implementing a computer system, organizations must consider the personal and professional development, physical safety, and human dignity of all workers. Appropriate human-computer ergonomic standards should be considered in system design and in the workplace.

3.3 Acknowledge and support proper and authorized uses of an
* organization's computing and communication resources.*

Because computer systems can become tools to harm as well as to benefit an organization, the leadership has the responsibility to clearly define appropriate and inappropriate uses of organizational computing resources. While the number and scope of such rules should be minimal, they should be fully enforced when established.

3.4 Ensure that users and those who will be affected by a system have their
* needs clearly articulated during the assessment and design of*
* requirements; later the system must be validated to meet requirements.*

Current system users, potential users, and other persons whose lives may be affected by a system must have their needs assessed and incorporated in the statement of requirements. System validation should ensure compliance with those requirements.

3.5 Articulate and support policies that protect the dignity of users and
* others affected by a computing system.*

Designing or implementing systems that deliberately or inadvertently demean individuals or groups is ethically unacceptable. Computer professionals who are in decision making positions should verify that systems are designed and implemented to protect personal privacy and enhance personal dignity.

3.6 Create opportunities for members of the organization to learn the
* principles and limitations of computer systems.*

This complements the imperative on public understanding (2.7). Educational opportunities are essential to facilitate optimal participation of all organizational members. Opportunities must be available to all members to help them improve their knowledge and skills in computing, including courses that familiarize them with the consequences and limitations of particular types of systems. In particular, professionals must be made aware of the dangers of building systems around oversimplified models, the improbability of anticipating and designing for every possible operating condition, and other issues related to the complexity of this profession.

4. **Compliance With The Code.** As an ACM member I will ...

4.1 Uphold and promote the principles of this Code.

The future of the computing profession depends on both technical and ethical excellence. Not only is it important for ACM computing professionals to adhere to the principles expressed in this Code, each member should encourage and support adherence by other members.

4.2 Treat violations of this code as inconsistent with membership in the ACM.

Adherence of professionals to a code of ethics is largely a voluntary matter. However, if a member does not follow this code by engaging in gross misconduct, membership in ACM may be terminated.

Note: This Code and the supplemental Guidelines were developed by the Task Force for the Revision of the ACM Code of Ethics and Professional Conduct: Ronald E. Anderson, Chair, Gerald Engel, Donald Gotterbarn, Grace C. Hertlein, Alex Hoffman, Bruce Jawer, Deborah G. Johnson, Doris K. Lidtke, Joyce Currie Little, Dianne Martin, Donn B. Parker, Judith A. Perrolle, and Richard S. Rosenberg. The Task Force was organized by ACM/SIGCAS and funding was provided by the ACM SIG Discretionary Fund. This Code and the supplemental Guidelines were adopted by the ACM Council on October 16, 1992.

INTEGRATING ETHICS AND DESIGN[3]

G. F. McLean
University of Victoria

At the college level, the subject of engineering ethics has traditionally been limited primarily to issues of public safety, taught by considering case studies alter the fact. Today, with increased interest in environmental issues and sustainable development, there is opportunity to reconsider the manner in which questions of ethics and social impact are introduced to engineering students. The range of issues for which society is willing to hold the engineering profession accountable is expanding; it follows that engineering educators should reexamine the issues and assumptions surrounding the technology to which students are exposed.

We need to find new ways in which the subject of ethics can be better integrated within the engineering curriculum. Here, a hierarchical model of ethics is developed based on the three levels of technical, professional, and social ethics. By considering methodologies of unstructured engineering design, we illustrate that the nature of the questioning demanded by the three levels of ethics is congruent with the nature of questioning demanded by the principals of good engineering design as described by most design methodologies. Questions encountered in the design process are really questions of ethics, leading naturally to the view that an emphasis on design education within the engineering curriculum will necessarily introduce broad ethical questioning as a normal part of good engineering. This is an improvement over the present situation in which questions of ethics are seen by students as somehow separate and distinct from the more pragmatic, technical aspects of engineering.

COMPLEMENTARY STUDIES

In Canada, within the last decade or so, there has been a new impetus to explicitly include aspects of engineering ethics within the undergraduate curriculum. The Canadian Council of Professional Engineers now requires that all engineers seeking professional status pass a written examination on the subject of law, ethics, and professional practice. This change put pressure on Canadian engineering schools to prepare students for the examination. As a result, many schools introduced courses on engineering law and ethics as non technical senior electives. Since then, the Canadian Engineering Accreditation Board, which regulates the professional engineering programs in Canadian universities, has adopted the requirement that at least half of one

---

[3]From G.F. McLean (Fall 1993). Integrating ethics and design, *IEEE Technology and Society Magazine,* 19-30. Copyright © 1993 IEEE. Reprinted with permission.

academic year (or the equivalent) of the curriculum be devoted to complementary studies:

A minimum of 0.5 years of studies in humanities, social sciences, arts, management, engineering economics and communications that complement the technical content of the curriculum. The curriculum must include studies in engineering economics and on the impact of technology on society, and on subject matter that deals with central issues, methodologies and thought processes of the humanities and social sciences.

Within this requirement, which equates to approximately six one-semester courses, explicit mention is made of two particular topics: small business economics and the social impact of technology on society. These "complementary study" requirements are also used up on other important subjects such as technical writing, or introductory psychology. What at first appears to be a generous allotment to the important subject of ethics and responsibility is often reduced to only one or two half-year courses,[4] providing at best a superficial overview of the area. In addition, the majority of these courses are included in the senior year, intended as a capstone on the curriculum recognizing that a certain level of maturity on the part of the student is required before these subjects can be properly comprehended.[5] Finally, there are few engineering professors who are actually involved in such courses, and those that are typically "specialized" in the field. More often, it is the case that these courses are delivered by part-time instructors who do not hold regular faculty positions.

The positioning of these courses within the curriculum, and the manner in which they are delivered to the students has the potential to send the wrong message to the students.

The presentation of a course on ethics or values requires students to question the fundamental premises of their technical identity. Thus, after having spent four years studying mathematics and sciences, it is unfair suddenly (and rapidly) to force them to question every assumption which has been slowly and gradually ingrained in them throughout the previous four years. In a sense, a senior course in ethics can induce intellectual vertigo on students. Therefore, at a time when the students are about to leave the educational system and begin practicing as engineers-in-training, they are

---

[4]The 1991/92 annual report of the CEAB acknowledges this limitation, recognizing that only about 5% of the total curriculum is devoted to social science and humanities courses. Courses on ethics and social impacts of technology are included in this group.

[5]Of 15 Canadian Engineering Schools surveyed, the vast majority refer to unpublished lists of courses which are appropriate for "complementary studies." Four of the 15 schools included an explicit course in a subject related to "technology and society" within the first year, the remainder listed courses associated with ethics under a variety of titles in the senior year of the program. A number of programs required courses on engineering law to be taken, particularly in civil engineering. Although the manner in which the complementary studies are offered varies, it is clear that the topic of "impact" or "ethics" is most often dealt with in a single, usually isolated, course offering.

confronted for the first time with fundamental questions *about* their careers. Nothing in their previous training will have prepared them for this.

The lack of involvement of engineering professors in "complementary studies" presents a double-edged problem. On one hand the implicit message sent to the students is that these courses are less critical, almost second class in nature. In other words, the mode by which the material is delivered suggests that its value is marginal. Conversely, this method of delivery perpetuates the "culture of expertise" [2] in which the student learns quickly that there are a class of people—philosophers, social critics, and advocates — who are "experts" in this field, and can be drawn up when needed. This expert mentality is accompanied with a similar view of engineering expertise as being generally irrelevant beyond the domain of purely technical issues. Either outlook perpetuated the view that the social impact of technology and the formal study of ethics are things better left to others. Finally, the delivery of an ethics curriculum as courses which are separate and distinctly different from the technical core may alienate the students from this field of questioning: good grades may be achieved, but are the students learning?

It should be pointed out that the amount of attention paid to ethics and complementary studies within the engineering curriculum in Canada has never been greater.[6] While we may speculate that students in previous eras were more concerned *as individuals* and thus were more aware of their ethical responsibilities, we have no evidence to support such a claim. Although explicit education in social impact of technology and engineering ethics is a major step forward, our concerns about alienation, vertigo and the adoption of an "expert" mentality regarding ethics suggests that ethics and social impact may be taught more successfully when integrated more completely into the engineering curriculum.

If the call for socially responsible engineering is to be taken seriously, then it behooves us all to reconsider the role of ethics and social impact within the curriculum. It is not so much that engineering graduates can successfully pass ethics examinations as in ensuring that they are aware of their responsibilities to society, and that they will practice their profession in an ethical manner. The challenge for the educator is, therefore, to ingrain the student with a sense of ethics and responsibility that is an integral part of the student's identity as a engineer. The consideration of ethics and social impact of technology should be a normal and expected part of engineering education and practice.

---

[6]A recent comparison of the engineering curriculum between 1916 and 1992 at one Canadian University shows marked similarity in content then and now. Based on this study, the conclusion is made that the concern for ethics and responsibility has only recently been shown explicit consideration in the curriculum. See Hyde [3].

ENGINEERING ETHICS

The very notion of a definition of "ethics" is problematic for the engineer, perhaps in much the same way that a working definition of an engineering concept such as "entropy" is difficult for a non technical person to grasp. If one looks at simple definitions, ethics can be viewed as a "set of moral principals or values," or "the discipline of dealing with good and bad and with moral duty or obligation." It is not necessary to venture too far beyond these superficial definitions before semantic difficulties arise: words, phrases and concepts which are foreign to the engineer. The problem with these definitions is that they require a pursuit of ethics as a *philosophical* study which the typical engineering student is by no means equipped to engage in. Certainly, a few isolated courses on the general issues of social impact and ethics do not equip a student to fully engage the subject. At the outset, then, even the very rudimentary definitions of ethics tend to bar the engineer from entry: while we would like to invite the student to explore the issues which are encompassed by ethical questioning, we find an edifice of intellect that is intimidating and exclusive. The task of defining ethics can force engineers to retreat, leaving this domain to philosophers.

In addition, a focus on ethics as concerning principally moral issues can lead many engineers to conclude that ethics is not associated with technology, but rather with the use of technology. This view can be used to sidestep the issues of ethics, based upon the idea that the technology can be regarded as a commodity like any other which is bought, sold, or traded. Therefore, "engineering ethics" may be regarded merely as a branch of "business ethics" which is concerned primarily with principals of correct behavior concerning relationships between buyer and seller,[7] thus dismissing the issues raised by the technology, and leaving consumers and users of the technology to address its moral and ethical implications. Implicit here is the idea that technology is value neutral, assemblies and systems which neither challenge nor influence the social, cultural, political or economic settings into which they are introduced. However, the value-neutrality of technology is a perspective that is challenged by most critics of technology, based largely upon the argument that any technological artifact implicitly embodies the values of its designers, and influences its use setting to adopt "machine" or "instrumental" values in evaluating performance or worth.[8] If we suspend

---

[7]Although academic treatments of engineering ethics usually recognise the broader implications of engineering ethics, it is a common perception among students that engineering ethics primarily involves good business relations.

[8]A good discussion of the question of the value-neutrality of technology can be found in Langdon Winner's essay "Do Artifacts have Politics'" [4]. The answer to the question *is technology value neutral?* is perhaps not as important as the recognition that the introduction of technology will undoubtedly introduce change beyond the realm of the simple technical. The nature of the changes introduced by new technology have been aptly described by Lewis Mumford [5] who described the nature of machine values (precision, economy, slickness, severity, and restriction to the essential) and their role in a new aesthetic

this view of neutrality, then the concern of the engineer must expand beyond the technical and necessarily include issues such as use, integration, acceptance, etc. These are largely non quantifiable aspects that are not easily incorporated into a technological mind set, but they are nonetheless critical factors influencing the success of a particular technology and, as we shall elaborate upon later, form essential questions for the good design of engineering products.

However difficult engineers may find the formal study of ethics, every engineer will encounter decisions which involve ethical issues for the most of their professional lives. Therefore, while ethics *as something to be studied* is foreign to the engineer, ethics *as something to be encountered* forms a large part of the engineer's practicing identity. This difficulty between study and practice has prompted us to consider a definition of ethics that can be comprehended by an engineering student and integrated into the curriculum of engineering education. We hope this definition can be a touchstone by which the engineer can delve deeper into ethical questioning when their societal role demands that they respond to important social questions. To this end, we adopt the simplistic notion of ethics as *doing the right thing*.[9]

THREE LEVELS OF ETHICS

Combining the idea that technology influences its setting (and that the acceptance of technology is an important part of "successful" technology) with the simple notion that ethics involves *doing the right thing* means that engineering ethics is concerned with far more than the business relationships implied in treating technology as a commodity. In fact, the scope of questioning involved in engineering ethics must now be expanded to include all aspects of engineering, from the actual technical design through to the consideration of the impact of the technology. Interestingly enough, this fact is recognized by the "codes of ethics" of may professional engineering organization which typically include statements about the need for technical virtuosity in the design and production of engineering products, moral behavior in an engineer's relationship with clients in the delivery of products, and the upholding and protection of the social good in the decision to develop

---

appreciation of industrial design. In a more recent work, Albert Borgmann [6] has described the general trend of changes introduced by technology with his description of the "device paradigm" describing the transition through technology, of the human-technological practices into the separation of a valued commodity and a machinery which is used to obtain or produce that commodity. In Borgmann's terms, the drive of technological development is toward maximizing the "availability" of the commodity, making it instantaneously accessible, ubiquitously available, safe. and easy to use. The drive of much engineering work toward optimal design in terms of quantifiable cost functions can be easily cast in the framework of either Mumford's "machine values" or Borgmann's "device paradigm."
[9] I recognize the difficulties arising from this definition from a philosophical perspective. What is "the right thing" anyway? Must ethics involve action? The purpose of the definition, however, is to provide a straightforward and accessible basis from which to consider the ways in which engineers encounter ethics. The correct definition of ethics and its placement within the larger discourse on moral reasoning is left to philosophers. See [7].

a particular technology or implement a particular project.[10] Codes of ethics outline principles of behavior intended to govern the activities of the practicing engineer. For example, the following excerpts describe the major sections of the Code of Ethics of the IEEE[10]:

> ...in recognition of the importance of our technologies in affecting the quality of life throughout the world, and in accepting a personal obligation to our profession, its members and the communities we serve ... [we] agree...

> ...to accept responsibility in making engineering decisions consistent with the safety, health, and welfare of the public...

> ...to avoid real or perceived conflicts of interest...

> ...to improve the understanding of technology...

> ...to undertake technological tasks for others only if qualified by training or experience...

There is an implicit recognition that the engineer's ethical commitment is broad and includes all of the engineer's professional activities. This provides an accessible starting point from which to consider the role of ethics within the engineering curriculum. As an all-encompassing commitment, ethics is not an aspect of engineering which can be categorized, like thermodynamics, solid state physics, or predicate logic. Rather, it is an aspect of engineering which permeates all aspects of the work. It is encountered, not adopted, and thus should be presented in this manner within the curriculum.

The nature of the ethical questioning required of practicing engineers can be divided into separate arenas concerning how best to build an engineering product,[11] how best to represent and deliver that product, and finally, how best to serve the social grouping into which the engineering product is delivered. This rough division of the scope of engineering ethics is extended into three distinct "levels" which focus upon technical ethics,

There is, undoubtedly, a continuum of questioning, but the division into three distinct levels is intended as a useful construction aimed at allowing engineers to see how much of their work is based upon ethical decisions. As discussed later in this paper, the ethical questioning implied by the three levels coincides remarkably well with the sort of non-quantitative

---

[10]The Codes of Ethics of various professional organizations have been reviewed by Unger [8]. A common frustration among practicing engineers, though, is that while the professional organizations reserve the right to discipline their members for obvious infractions, there is seldom any support for individual engineers who speak out against the wrong practices of their employers or colleagues. The phrase "whistle-blowing" has been coined to describe such action—the charge is made that the codes of ethics are largely meaningless until the professional organizations explicitly protect the interests of whistle-blowers.

[11]"Engineering products" in this context means the totality of what is done by engineers, so this includes "made things" which are designed and distributed, as well as "technical services" which are offered. Therefore, use of the word "product" to refer to the result of engineering should not be construed as limiting the discussion to the physical artifacts of engineering, but rather to the broader range of products, activities, and services which are created or offered by practicing engineers.

	Level 1: Technical Ethics	Level 2: Professional Ethics	Level 3: Social Ethics
Issues	Technical	Moral	Philosophical, Political
Questions	How?		Why?
Participants	Engineers	Managers, Engineers, Lawyers	Politicians

Table 3.4
A Hierarchy of Areas of Ethical Questions Encountered by Engineers.

questioning that ought to be included in engineering design, providing a natural link between the (artificially divided) concerns of "good engineering" and those of "good ethics." The three levels are arranged in a hierarchy based upon the scope of questions encountered, i.e., technical ethics is purely the domain of the engineer, professional ethics involves engineers interacting with other, potentially non technical groups, and social ethics primarily involves actors at the political or societal level. In traversing the three levels, we move from questions of "how?" through to questions of "why?," from narrow technical specification to broad questions regarding relevance and benefit, from issues for which the engineer is trained to issues for which engineering education provides no hint of preparation. The three levels, with a description of the nature of questioning, the actors involved and the roles assumed by individuals is shown schematically in Table 3.4.

Technical Ethics

Technical Ethics includes all manner of technical decisions and judgements concerning the selection and arrangement of component parts, choice of fabrication methods, inclusion of safety factors, etc. At this level, the engineer is most concerned with questions of function only, i.e., *how* do we produce an engineering product? The use of the word "ethic" to describe good technical practice may seem too grandiose, since correct technical practice is expected as a normal part of competent engineering. Making a distinction between "technical practice" and moral questioning *about* technical practice can tend to perpetuate the implicit idea that technology is value-neutral, allowing the engineer to make a false distinction between technical values[12] and social or moral values.

---

[12]The distinction between a technical value, implying some recognized standard of practice, in the creation of an engineering product and technological values which imply a set of values which may be adopted by a social group as a result of adopting technological mind-set is important. The technological values are discussed at length in Ellul's important work [11]. Technical values by contrast are discipline specific and best represented in various codes and standards which are voluntarily adopted by the engineering profession. There are an overwhelming number of standards defined by technical and governmental organizations worldwide as can be seen by surveying catalogues of recognized standards [12]-[14]. Such standards encapsulate the technical values of various technologies.

The scope of creative choice at the level of technical development is enormous and engineers make decisions daily which quite literally change the way a product or service will look. Whether it is the design of a structural member, laying out a circuit board, or developing an algorithm the engineer applies knowledge of "good practice" to achieve a result which not only works, but which adheres to the standard set out by the profession.

The dictates of technical ethics are best laid out in the various codes and standards of each technical discipline. The most obvious and familiar examples are the various building codes which are used to guarantee the quality of civil constructions, but equivalent standards exist for other disciplines. It is important to realize that these standards are not dictated by the limits of feasibility, or by some simply-defined criterion function. Instead, they represent a codification of the accumulated experience of the profession. Therefore, instead of regarding technical standards as cold, cast-in-stone dictates, they are better viewed as the codification of the collective wisdom or consensus of a group of professional "elders."[13]

The realm and impact of technical ethics tends to be limited to the eventual makeup of the engineering product under consideration. This is precisely why the "technical ethics" level of a hierarchy at first appears out of place: technical ethics is what engineering is all about. However there are examples of ethical questions raised at the technical level having profound impact upon a technology's acceptance at the social level. For instance, the emerging discipline of software testing raises a technical point which causes social acceptance of some technologies to be rejected. When large-scale software systems are developed, their testing is problematic. It is virtually impossible to foresee every possible situation that might be encountered by a large system, resulting in the dilemma that a system may operate correctly for normal scenarios (which occur frequently), while the operation of the system during abnormal (infrequent) events will remain largely unknown since the nature of the event cannot be predicted. Thus there is a problem at the *technical level* which has profound impact upon the *social* outcome of the application of a particular technology.[14]

---

[13]Standards are mostly regarded in terms of the protection they offer to users of technology, for example the standards set by the CSA or UL for consumer products, or the building codes used in house construction. Alternately, voluntary standards are set by those with a vested interest as a matter of convenience and efficiency, for example the adoption of standard sizing of components in bicycle manufacture. There is, however, another area in which standards are adopted to provide quality engineering products, with common interfaces to ensure correct operation in a competitive marketplace. a good example of this would be the RS-232C interface standard for serial data communication. This standard is based neither upon minimum cost, nor optimal performance, nor direct issues of safety, but rather upon a reasonable compromise between efficiency, performance, and feasibility that is deemed "good" by the technical community. Although technically suboptimal, the RS-232C interface standard is ubiquitous in the computer industry, adopted by all.

[14]Dr. David Parnas has presented a case in point, in which the licensing of a nuclear power-generating facility has been suspended due to issues concerning software testing and verification [15].

To summarize, at the level of technical ethics, the engineer acts in the comfortable role of technician, working within well defined parameters of operation. This is the role for which engineers have been trained, and this is the level of ethics which engineers understand: questions about implementation, cast in a purely technical framework, requiring the individual to act as a professional engineer only, remaining largely indifferent to the greater societal issues created or amplified by their technology.

Professional Ethics

"Professional Ethics" moves beyond the domain of technical questioning and into the level of interactions between cooperating or competing groups. These intersections emerge as the ideas and products of engineers are implemented and distributed, often embodying themselves in the form of business contracts (hence the usual association of this level of ethics with business ethics). Here the engineer is required to leave behind the relative comfort of technical decisions and is forced into the more subtle world of relationships.

The rules of correct behavior for professional ethics have been largely codified into standards of minimal performance in a manner similar to the level of technical ethics. For instance, contract law, patent law, conflict of interest guidelines, etc., are all important tools for ensuring correct behavior. Professional ethics seeks to determine how engineers should act when retained in a formal relationship with a client, supplier, or other engineering group. There is often a tendency to equate the entire domain of engineering ethics as a special case of business ethics concerned mostly with the interaction between groups buying and selling a particular type of commodity.[15] This fails to recognize that the products of engineering are not merely neutral commodities, but rather are systems which have a purpose and which influence values. To avoid this pitfall, it is worthwhile to consider ethical questioning at this level from the perspective of the technical rather than relational issues, by examining the effect of professional decisions upon the ability of the engineering product to function properly. An engineering product is not complete until it has been put into use. This means that the decisions made at this level should not be separated from the technical aspects of the engineering product but rather be viewed as equally important technical aspects. Certainly, if unethical decisions are made at this level (concerning the financing, economic realization, or relationships with suppliers, for example) then the overall success of the product is in jeopardy.

---

[15]What is labeled in this work as "professional ethics" is often considered to be the complete domain of engineering ethics. In Canada, applicants for professional registration are required to pass an examination on law and ethics, which is largely concentrated on the legal issues of contract law and liability. Our reference to the large literature on this subject is primarily pointing to this.

Therefore, even a well-conceived and beneficial product is totally dependent upon ethical behavior at the professional level. Questions at this level involve technical and economic aspects of the product, and require the engineer to be part technician, part manager.

Social Ethics

Finally, we come to the level of "Social Ethics." Here we must recall the statements in the codes of ethics which describe the responsibility of the engineer to maintain the public good, and to serve society with the products of engineering activity. Questions concerning cost versus benefit, serving the interests of a few versus the interests of many, and the use of public funds for engineering projects are among those addressed at this level. The expected role of the engineer is no longer clear, for unlike the lower levels of the hierarchy it is difficult to identify a set of standards, codes, or legal principals which encapsulate the norms of behavior here. Rather, decisions are now made through the nebulous media of public debate and political forum. The issues are complex and there is seldom a single, clear solution or decision presented. undoubtedly, decisions at this level have profound technical and legal implications and, conversely, the technical and legal ramifications of a project may constrain the social debate to some degree, which is good. However, there is in general no particular standard to which the engineer must adhere, making teaching and communicating this level of ethics particularly difficult.

A Total View of Ethics

Ascending the hierarchy of the three levels of ethics, we begin with technical ethics in which engineers act in a purely technical role, supported by the weight of the profession, their education and the codification of good behavior in the form of codes and standards. Here the engineer is not individual, but an ambassador of an important and highly skilled professional discipline. At the top of the hierarchy, the situation is completely opposite. The profession no longer contributes much of value, since the issues being discussed concern particular associations of technology, people, and places instead of technical questions which can be addressed in isolation from a social context. The engineer is thus regarded by the collective decision making group *as an individual*, seldom recognizing useful insights which may provide guidance or particular topics. This situation is, of course, lamentable, especially given the increasingly technological nature of our society. If engineers were equipped to deal with the issues of social ethics, there is little doubt that their contribution would be felt.

Issues of social ethics have, of course, been addressed by the technical community. For instance, research on the question of acceptable risk attempts to cast public discussions in a technical framework. However, instances in which the tools produced by the research have been used to aid decision making at the social level have, in the past, been few.[16]

Consider the design of a new product or device, such as new high-speed computers, personal stun guns, or the design of a bridge linking a small island community to the mainland (replacing traditional ferry service). In each case there is a clear technical challenge, with constraints on cost, power consumption, manufacturing methods, etc., that must be satisfied. At the level of technical ethics, each project poses challenges and demands that make the engineers responsible for the correct choices in designing the product. Next, there is the step of actually fabricating and distributing the products into use and again there are technical/economic questions which may be as broad as deciding if fabrication should be done within the local economy or by some offshore vendor at lower cost. But these first two levels of questioning are comparatively east to address given the technical and economic constraints that accompany any decision to proceed with a project. The really hard questions, and also the really important questions, are at the social level: *why are we doing this anyway?* Who is served by making computers faster, or by manufacturing stun guns, or by building the bridge? How will the pattern of crime and abuse be changed by stun guns? Will our new computer be used in a benevolent manner? How will the bridge alter the pattern of daily life for the island residents and business people? While narrow views of engineer would focus on the first level of ethics, and venture into the second occasionally, it can be argued that engineering ethics demands that these larger social questions be addressed *as a normal part of engineering activity.* This is not to say that the engineer should be prepared to solve all of society's problems, but rather to point out that engineering products do alter the fabric of life, and that engineers should at least recognize their obligation to become involved in public debate regarding the wisdom of these changes.

The simplified definition of ethics as "doing the right thing," and the subsequent dissection of the field of engineering into the realms of technical, professional, and social ethics has led to a view of engineering ethics which involves the engineer in a hierarchy of questioning that begins with the narrowly technical and ends with the broadly societal aspects of a technology. Therefore, the questions of ethics are pervasive in engineering, making the utility of one or two undergraduate courses questionable as an introduction to this broad field. The undergraduate engineering student must

---

[16]The field of Risk Research is in some ways burgeoning due to the potential economic advantage of reducing the cost associated with having made the "wrong decision." Risk Research is supported heavily by various insurance companies; as well as by large governmental interests. However, tools of risk research still evade use in a more normal setting of social decision making to which the practicing engineer may be exposed [16].

be given the opportunity to learn, not just the ideology of good ethics, but the manner in which these ideas interact and influence their technical practice.

Design Education

Within the context of engineering education, the content of what is learned by the student may be roughly divided into "material" and "process" knowledge. Material knowledge is communicated through typical teaching formats. It tends to be analytic, repeatable methods, or fact that can be formally communicated and examined in an objective fashion, including subjects such as basic mathematics, and physics, engineering sciences, and the "technology of the day" (i.e., microprocessor architecture, finite element analysis, or object oriented programming). Such material fits well within the traditional mold of engineering education because the material is well laid out, usually organized into textbooks, and can—above all—be presented in such a manner the "objective" examinations are possible.

"Process" knowledge, by contrast, tends to be far more difficult to communicate or examine. It refers to the range of methods and abilities which an engineering students acquires that, while not representing a repeatable scientific or mathematical fact, nonetheless represents a vital component of engineering education. Knowledge of "process" is acquired by students during the rigor of a program, through the experience gained in laboratories and through the lessons learned by applying the material knowledge to the solution of project oriented problems. Process knowledge is gained at the technical level by students choosing to apply their knowledge of engineering sciences, and is supported heavily by professional engineering organizations.[17] While the acquisition of process knowledge specific to technical disciplines forms an important complement to the material knowledge communicated in the classroom, it must be remembered that there are entire subjects which are properly included in the engineering curriculum that are based upon process knowledge alone. Subjects which communicate "process" knowledge are perhaps more ethereal in their content, more "subjective" and harder to communicate in a complete or rigorous fashion. It is also much more difficult for any individual instructor to claim expertise in such "process" oriented subjects as there simply is no single "correct" answer. Courses in engineering design fall into the category of communicating process knowledge and, as shall be elaborated in the following, provide a natural setting into which the issues of engineering ethics can be raised.

---

[17]Both the IEEE and the ASME support large scale competitions in which students are invited to submit design related to a very narrow technical function. For example, there is the IEEE Micro-mouse competition, or the various ASME vehicle competitions. These competitions allow students to acquire process knowledge specific to a particular area of technology, i.e., the design of circuits, the programming of microcontrollers, or the operation of engines and vehicles. Such competitions *do not*, however, encourage the students to engage in broader questioning *about* these technologies.

The traditional view of ethics as being an academic discipline unto itself leads naturally to its inclusion in the collection of subjects associated with communicating material knowledge to the student. While most certainly a *bona fide* branch of moral philosophy, the idea that engineering ethics is communicable as material knowledge is questionable. Presented as material knowledge, ethics becomes a dry and perhaps irrelevant element of the engineering curriculum. However, if presented as process knowledge, the subject becomes implicitly relevant through the context in which it is discussed. It becomes something that can be encountered, an essential part of *all* engineering. The range of questions posed by the three levels of ethical consideration is very closely linked to the information-gathering stages of the engineering design process, thus illustrating that "ethics" and "design" can be presented as process knowledge within the same framework.

What is meant by design education? In its broadest sense, design refers to a deliberate plan, pattern or mode of execution of an idea, as the following definition of engineering design suggests [17]:

Its (engineering's) central focus is design, an art entailing the exercise of ingenuity, imagination, skill, discipline, and knowledge based on experience.

Design, as practices by engineers, has both a material as well as a process component. In the material sense, design is often used to describe the process of optimization: given a problem which is expressed in quantitative terms, the activity of design is to find some point in the solution space which is deemed to be "optimal".[18] Whereas this view of design as material knowledge has produced a vast array of methods of finding optimal solutions in a mathematical space, it does not adequately represent the activities of engineers who engage in design that is *not* optimization. In the broader sense, engineering design takes place when a problem is identified and analysed, and when a technical solution is proposed, specified, and realized. Although the task of design is conceptually similar to that of optimization,[19] design as general problem solving does not dictate a precise procedure or repeatable mathematical technique to locate a desirable, feasible solution. Rather, design requires that general strategies for approaching problems be adopted, that methods of effectively synthesizing various technical skills be

---

[18]Optimization is an essential part of the modern engineering curriculum, the importance of which ought not be underestimated. However, it is important that design as optimization limits the scope of questioning engaged in by the engineer to the narrow technical field which can be describe quantitatively, Furthermore, the goal of such design is to maximize (minimize) some cost function. Cast in the hierarchy of ethics discussed in this work, design as optimization is limited in scope to the first level of technical ethics, with efficiency as its chief value.

[19]One potentially useful way of making the distinction between design as optimization and design as problem solving is to think of the degree of structure which has been imposed on the problem. Hence design problems which can be expressed in mathematical terms may be thought of as problems in "structured design," whereas design associated with general problem solving in a non-quantitative setting are problems in "unstructured design." Both types of design may produce useful engineering products, but structured design constitutes a narrower focus than unstructured design.

developed, and that as complete as possible an investigation of all of the ramifications of a problem being solved be explored.

It is interesting to note the prominence of process rather than material knowledge in design, most pointedly described by the use of the word synthesis in most definitions of engineering design. Since design methodology is not tied to any particular technology, it emphasizes process and must assume that the necessary material knowledge can be easily mastered. This is an inversion of the more typical relationship which teaches material knowledge and assumes that it is the process knowledge which will be easily mastered. The material knowledge component of the design process comes to light in the stages of feasibility analysis and refinement in which analytic techniques can be employed to solve particular aspects of the overall problem. Here lies the true domain of the bulk of the traditional engineering curriculum: given a relatively narrow technical specification the tools of engineering can be well employed to determine feasibility, analyze proposed methods and even optimize particular parameters of the proposal to produce the best possible performance. But in the overall design process, this constitutes less than one third of the total activity.

Both the Canadian Engineering Accreditation Board and the U.S. Accreditation Board for Engineering Technology now require that design not be included as a secondary aspect of engineering curriculum, but rather that "a meaningful, major design experience" be explicitly included [1], [18]. A series of articles by J. Dixon has reviewed the state of engineering design education in mechanical engineering, leading to strong recommendations concerning the need for more explicit design education and graduate programs in design [19]-[21]. In electrical engineering there is a similar move toward improving the quality of design education. For example, the new electrical engineering curriculum at Carnegie Mellon University emphasizes the importance of design as a "capstone experience" on the curriculum. As a final statement emphasizing the importance of the process aspects of design education within the engineering curriculum, Canada's National Committee of Deans of Engineering and Applied Science make the following recommendation in their 1992 report on the future of engineering in Canada [22]:

the students' competency in realistic design and problem solving must be improved. ... Increase the emphasis on design, unstructured problem solving,... in engineering programs.

This recognition of the need to explicitly include design activities within the curriculum provides a new opportunity for the integration of ethical questioning about technology to be integrated as a normal part of engineering activity. Design methodologies, such as those presented in [23]-[26] all emphasize the need for breadth, and for the consideration of the whole problem, not just particular technical aspects of it. One particularly comprehensive approach, presented by Roe, Soulis, and Handa [27] is based upon the ideas of general systems theory, and provides a view of design as an

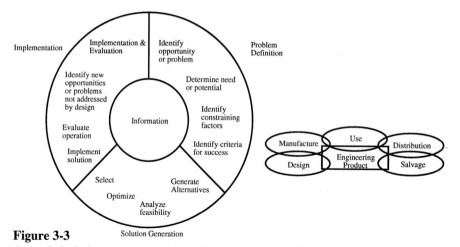

Figure 3-3

A morphological representation of the design process, adapted from [28].

iterative process which involves the steps of identifying the problem, producing a set of constraints and criteria for success, generating a set of feasible solutions, selecting and optimizing a solution and then implementing and evaluating the final solution, leading to either a revision of the overall problem being solved, or the generation of a set of sub-problems. This process is illustrated schematically in Figure 3-3. The methodology summarizes the approach taken by others, namely recognizing the holistic nature of good design, the need for information, the enormous amount of effort which must be spent in simply identifying the problem and its context, and in generating conceptual solutions. It is typical of what is communicated to students as a good process of design.

According to the design methodologies, comprehensive design dictates that an enormous amount of information be gathered concerning the "design problem." The scope of such information gathering is not limited to any particular technical aspect of the problem, but rather holds paramount the value of allowing the potential solution space to be as large as possible. Thus, the scope of information gathering and questioning about the problem being solved necessarily includes issues raised by potential solutions at the technical, professional, and social level.[20] Thus, questions of an "essentially ethical" nature begin to impinge on the process of "purely technical" design.

---

[20]The relationship between design and vested interest is an important one which has been studied [28],[29]. The term "participatory design" is used to describe design in which all parties who will be influenced by a particular design are involved in the information-gathering and decision-making process, thus ensuring that all manner of issues associated with a design problem are addressed [30]. Perhaps the most prominent criticism of engineering design which has not considered the full range of questioning raised by the technology has been generated by feminist critics of technology, who argue that much technology has been designed by men for use by women.

Viewing the product as a "system," the scope of investigation for information gathering can be compartmentalized into five "product environments," that is to say the product exists at several independent states during its lifetime. These environments refer to the design, manufacture, distribution, use and finally, disposal [27]. Until recently, engineering was concerned largely with the first three of these environments (particularly in the design of consumer goods), but now more consideration is given to such user issues as "ergonomics," and an increased sensitivity to issues associated with the disposal environment. Good design must consider the entire breadth of the problem under consideration, from initial stages of design to final destruction and salvage.

Combining such a broad design methodology with a view of a product as existing within the five environments, creates a large set of possibilities which must be explored in order to understand and effectively design a "good" engineering product. When an engineer engages in such a process, the issues which must be addressed concern the technical, professional, and social questions explored by a product. In short, *the process of information gathering demanded by good design methodologies demands nothing less than a complete inquiry into the ethical aspects of proposed products*. The questions posed by the three level hierarchy of engineering ethics demand that all five product environments be considered, and demand that both technical and social questions be raised within each environment. Thus, there is a congruence of interest between the concerns of engineering ethics and those of engineering design. Good design demands that ethics be encountered.

An engineering project is initiated, and a group of people are drawn together to form the "design team" based upon particular abilities presumed necessary for the completion of the project. How is the team organized? How much freedom or control of the project do they have? The project continues, leading to the fabrication of some physical products. Under what conditions is the product manufactured? How was the project financed? The made things are distributed and installed, to be pressed into service for their intended purpose. Do these things seriously change the pattern of people's lives? Are there hazards associated with their use? Finally, the project ends and the made things are taken out of service, now useless. What do we do with the junk? Overall, who derived benefit from the project, what were the consequences and for whom? Within every design environment we can devise questions which may appear to be orthogonal to the technical questions posed by engineers, but which are nonetheless vital for the correct functioning of the product.

INTEGRATING ETHICS AND DESIGN

Ethics, with design, must be included as a vital component of each students "process" education. This is not to say that it is an invisible part of the curriculum, but rather that these subjects ought not be presented within the regular lecture/assignment/exam framework of the material-knowledge curriculum. Two examples from personal experience illustrate this point. The first example details an experience from an introductory course in digital circuits and systems. After spending several months of the course developing the technical syllabus on digital components, combinatorial and sequential logic, one lecture was spent discussing design. Students were asked to design a safety interlock system for a large electro-mechanical press, under the assumption that such a safety interlock would reduce the chance of operator injury while using the press. The eventual design included component modules labeled "timer," "shut-out" "fault-detect," etc. The students were justifiably proud of developing a redundant system which would not operate unless multiple sensors produced the same output. Motivated by safety considerations, the design promised to function very well; i.e., it was technically ethical. In addition, the design was formulated *entirely* from components with which the students had gained expertise during the course, so it was based upon the technical experience (process knowledge) developed through the many component design laboratories which had by now been completed by the students. At this point in the exercise the instructor employed the same component modules, in a redundant fashion for another purpose, building a detonator for a bomb. Obviously, this latter application of the student-designed component modules raised ethical objections, providing a natural introduction to a discussion with the students on the capabilities they had learned, on the ability they had to choose the application toward which to apply their technology, and the responsibility they had to ensure that "good" uses for the technology would be found. By initially adopting the "neutral" approach to the design at the technical level, the exercise illustrated the nature of questioning which can and will arise at the social level. Unlike the technical design, which had been a harmonious exercise, the discussion at this point was heated, emotional, and often irrational. When questions of ethics and social impact were raised the students had no process knowledge to draw upon.

The second example is drawn from a course which is directly related to teaching process knowledge in the form of engineering design methodologies. The goal of the course is for small student teams to develop a working prototype solution to a "real world" problem. The expectation is that the students will make use of their technical knowledge of engineering sciences, but first they must take a very poorly defined problem and utilize a design methodology to transform the user specification of the problem into an appropriate set of technical specifications. In one particular offering of the course, students were required to solve some problems identified with hospital beds used in long term care facilities. The problem clearly required a physical modification to a frame supporting the bed, thus drawing upon material knowledge of the students. However, in determining the constraints of the problem, they were required to explore the larger impact of the bed itself as a component in the hospital system, in the life of the residents, in the life of the caregivers. Technically, the operation of the original bed was flawless, but it was too high for residents to transfer from the bed to a wheelchair independently. Hospital staff had experimented with lowering the bed (by removing wheels) to provide the correct transfer height but this made the bed too low for cleaning underneath, too low for care-givers to attend to residents while in the bed, and totally immobile, producing a hazard in the event of some emergency requiring evacuation of the residence. Along the way to determining feasible solutions, students spent time with residents, caregivers, janitorial staff, and management. They determined, for instance, that the dimensions of the mops used to clean the floors had been established and written into the collective bargaining agreement of the care-givers. They determined that this simple technical problem was causing a significant number of back injuries which in turn had a social cost in terms of compensation. They determined, finally, that the original bed had been designed very poorly given the concerns expressed by the various groups which came into contact with the beds. The design had been produced in an unethical manner and the technology was failing because of this. As a result of the exercise, a retrofit modification to the existing beds was designed by the students, prototyped and tested in the hospital, and is now being manufactured by a student-operated company. Throughout the process of the design the students have been exposed to the effects of an earlier poor design whose designer had not been concerned with anything beyond technical questions of economic fabrication.

The hospital bed experience changed the attitude of many of the students toward the "social" aspects of engineering design. Whereas many originally had a negative view toward the exercise (it was "soft" and not a very difficult technical problem),the vast majority completed the course recognizing the need for elaborate consultation with users and detailed consideration of the full scope (i.e., the three levels of ethics and the five environments) of design.

ESSENTIAL COMPONENT OF DESIGN EDUCATION

There are similarities between activities associated with engineering ethics and general "unstructured" engineering design. Two aspects of the design process can be directly linked to the process of ethical investigation. First, design will involve the identification of constraints and will identify criteria for successful performance. In other words, a good approach to design identifies ethical issues which must be addressed, the characteristics and bounds of solutions to those ethical questions, and behaviors which are deemed "unethical" by virtue of contradicting a constraint. Second, the design process based upon systems ideas demands that this ethical questioning be carried out over the totality of uses of each component. Whereas engineering ethics is casually thought to be limited to the level of professional interactions, the view of ethics presented here suggests that engineering is *all about* ethical questions, and has shown that formal approaches to engineering design methodologies induce such questions and require their solution.

Instead of teaching ethics in the sense of yet another course, adding to the material knowledge of the student, ethics should be incorporated into the curriculum as an essential component of design education. The benefit of this approach is not in enhancing students' material knowledge , but rather in enhancing their process knowledge. Such skills cannot be easily enumerated in a textbook, presented, and then examined. But such skills are nonetheless important and vital to any successful engineer.

The proposal, therefore, is to extend the definition of design to explicitly consider the three levels of ethics, and to infiltrate the curriculum with this formal approach to design. This will have the effect of eliminating the currently dominant view of ethics as a specialty subject outside of the domain of engineering, one which is esoteric and foreign. Instead, students will be taught, from the very beginning to the end of their engineering careers, that good ethics makes good design.

REFERENCES

[1] Canadian Council of Professional Engineers, "Canadian engineering accreditation board annual report," 401-116 Albert St. Ottawa Ontario, 1991.
[2] A. Pacey, *The Culture of Technology*, Cambridge, Mass: MIT Press, 1983.
[3] R. Hyde & G. McLean, "Alienated engineers: Part of the problem?" Presented at Meet. Canadian Sociological and Anthropological Assoc., Halifax, Nova Scotia, June 2-5, 1992.
[4] L. Winner, "Do artifacts have politics?" in *Technology and Politics*, M. Kraft and N. Vig, Eds. Duke Univ. Press.
[5] L. Mumford, *Art and Technics*. Columbia Univ. Press, 1952.
[6] A. Borgmann, Technology and the Character of Contemporary Life. Oxford Univ. Press, 1984.
[7] A. P. Iannone, Ed., *Contemporary Moral Controversies in Technology*. Oxford Univ. Press, 1987.
[8] S.H. Unger, *Controlling Technology: Ethics and the Responsible Engineer*. Holt, Rhinehart, and Winston, 1982.
[9] M.W. Martin and R. Schinzinger, *Ethics in Engineering*. New York, NY: McGraw-Hill, 1989.
[10] Institute of Electrical and Electronic Engineers, *IEEE Policy and Procedures Manual*. 345 East 47th Street, New York, NY, 1993.
[11] J. Ellul, *The Technological Society*. New York: Knopf, 1964.
[12] American National Standards Institute, *American National Standards 1992 Catalogue*, 1992.
[13] International Standards Organization, *ISO Catalogue*, Geneva, Switzerland, 1993.
[14] Standards Council of Canada, *Directory and Index of Standards*, Ottawa, Ont., 1992.
[15] D.L. Parnass, A.J. van Schouwen, and S.P. Kwan, "Evaluation and safety critical software," *Communications of the ACM*, vol 33, pp. 636-648, June 1990.
[16] N.C. Lind, Ed., *Proc. Symp. Risk in New Technologies*. Waterloo, Ont.: Univ. Waterloo Press, 1982.
[17] Canadian Academy of Engineering, "Engineering research in Canadian universities," Taskforce Rep., 130 Albert St., Suite 1414, Ottawa, Ont.: 1991.

[18] Carnegie Mellon University, "Designing a curriculum for the 90's" Currents, *Newsl. Elec. Computer Eng.*, 1992.
[19] J.R. Dixon, "Engineering design science: The state of education," *Mech. Eng.*, pp. 64-67, Feb. 1991.
[20] J.R. Dixon, "Engineering design science: New goals for engineering education," *Mech. Eng.*, pp. 56-62, Mar. 1991.
[21] J.R. Dixon, "Why we need doctoral program in design," *Mech. Eng.*, pp. 75-79, Feb. 1992.
[22] National Committee of Deans of Engineering and Applied Science, "The future of engineering in Canada," Taskforce Rep., 1992.
[23] N. Cross, *Engineering Design Methods*. New York: Wiley, 1989.
[24] M.J. French, *Conceptual Design for Engineers*. New York: Springer Verlag, 1989.
[25] S.H. Kim, *Essence of Creativity: A Guide to Tackling Difficult Problems*. Oxford University Press, 1990.
[26] J. Walton, *Engineering Design: From Art to Practice*. West, 1991.
[27] P.H. Roe, G.N. Soulis, and V.K. Handa, *The Discipline of Design*. Waterloo, Ont.: Univ. Waterloo, 1965.
[28] D. Noble, *The Forces of Production*. Cambridge Mass.: MIT Press, 1984.
[29] M. Cooley, *Architect or Bee?* Boston, MA: South End Press, 1980.
[30] V. Papanek, *Design for the Real World*. Chicago, IL: Acad. Chicago Pub., 1985.
[31] D. Mackenzie and J. Wacjman, *The Social Shaping of Technology*. Open Univ. Press, 1985.

READING QUESTIONS

1) Why does Anderson claim that "all we have to fall back on are people and their ethical standards"?
2) What is a profession? What computing specialists may not satisfy the criteria for being "professionals"?
3) What is the "normative model of professional ethics"?
4) According to this model, what is the job of leaders in a profession?
5) What are some of the positive functions of a code of ethics?
6) Why are general moral principles included in the ACM code of ethics?
7) What issues does the ACM code of ethics address that other codes do not?
8) Outline the process of the revision of the ACM code of ethics.
9) How much support did the draft version of the code of ethics receive from the members of ACM?
10) What topics produced disagreement? For each topic, outline the disagreement and the reasons each side uses.
11) Name several ways that the "generous allotment" of the curriculum to ethical issues in the Canadian system often reduced in importance?
12) Why are "engineering ethics" often consigned to "business ethics"? Why is this a mistake?
13) Why is ethics as "doing the right thing" simplistic? Why might this approach be useful for engineering ethics?
14) In what way are technical standards a form of technical ethics?
15) What are professional ethics about, and why are they not reducible to business ethics?
16) What are social ethics? Do you agree that this is the most difficult area?

17) How is the question "Why are we doing this anyway?" a normal part of engineering activity?
18) In what way is engineering ethics "process knowledge"?
19) Why does good design "require a complete inquiry into the ethical aspects of proposed products"?
20) Name several ways that engineering a hospital bed involves social and ethical issues.

DISCUSSION QUESTIONS

1) Identify those ethical disagreements among ACM members that seem to vary depending upon the country the members come from. How might cultural differences produce these disagreements? Can we make any claims about which side has a better approach, or must we just say "folks disagree on this one"?
2) Take the items of the code, and compare them to the topics in this book or your syllabus. Which items apply to which chapter or subject? Try also looking at the various courses in your curriculum to see where the items of the code might be relevant. Anything interesting?
3) McLean's approach suggests that ethical and social issues should be incorporated into every course in the curriculum. What are the advantages and disadvantages of this?

PRACTICING THE DESIGN ETHIC

1) Determine if your CS or MIS department has a code of conduct. Schedule a short interview with one of the professors (managers) in the CS/MIS department (a professor who has been in the department at least one year). In the process of interviewing the professor/manager determine the following:
    • Is there a formal ethical code of conduct for the department members?
    • If no, why not? Does the professor/manager agree with this policy and why?
    • If yes, is it "required reading" of all members (and students)of the department?
    • Is there an ethics board that periodically reviews and updates the code?
    How does the department's code of conduct compare to the ACM Code of Conduct described in this chapter? Using either the department's or ACM's code of conduct, what changes would you make to the code, and why? Do you believe that having an ethical code of conduct helps increase the technical professional's awareness of social issues and impacts? Do you believe this is important, and why?
2) Obtain three or more syllabi for courses in the computing or engineering curriculum at your institution or a nearby institution. Are social and ethical issues integrated into the schedule? Are there points in each syllabus that could support such integration? Take the catalogue description of the computing or engineering curriculum and attempt the same analysis. How drastic a change would integrating social and ethical issues produce?

CHAPTER

4

THE SOCIAL CONTEXT OF WORKPLACE HEALTH

The standard story of an industrial health problem usually has two actors: the victim and the villain. Usually, the villain carelessly exposes the victim to job-related hazards without any concern for their effect on the workforce. The real story is, not surprisingly, more complicated. The standard story makes some crucial assumptions: that it is always more profitable for the employer to ignore risks, that the cause of the health problem is straight-forward, that it is the greed of government and employers that makes them fail to recognize it, and that merely eliminating the identified health risks will solve the problem.

As you will see from the following two articles, all of these assumptions can be questioned. Kiesler and Finholt make the case that, though Repetitive Strain Injury is a real injury, its causes in the workplace remain obscure. RSI's symptoms, progress, prognosis, and epidemiology are embedded in a social context that must be understood to fully understand the nature of the injury and the steps needed to cure or prevent it.

Rowe presents the implementation of a program that addresses many of the aspects Kiesler and Finholt think important. Unless you read Kiesler and Finholt's analysis first, the program presented by Rowe appears to be overkill. But in the context of an informed understanding of RSI, Rowe's approach is measured and timely. And its practical effect is indisputable: reductions in the prevalence of injury and progress in rehabilitation from injuries that have occurred.

RSI is only one of the health hazards that have been associated with computing technology. Others have included eye strain, visual display unit radiation, muscle fatigue, and stress levels associated with work pacing. But the pattern of evidence these articles make evident is clear. The technology cannot be blamed as the simple or sole cause of the injury; understanding the social context is essential.

THE MYSTERY OF RSI[1,2]

Sara Kiesler
Carnegie Mellon University

Thomas Finholt
University of Michigan

A Day in My Life

Here I am—lost at 33.
Wondering where to go, wondering what to do
Totally ostracised by my peers—feeling hopeless,
As I tread the windmill of my life.
So many thoughts to express—where to start
Start with the pain—all encompassing so that I don't
know how to alleviate it—
To sit, to stand, to do something to make it go away.
Sometimes I feel like cutting. Yes cutting it off—
Being limbless, being nothing.
Take a pill—kill the pain
My independence, so valued, so wanted, has slipped away.
Nothing for me but carefulness.
Days stretching forever, unending.
Careful stretching my arms,
Careful putting on my clothes.
Careful turning a tap.
Careful drones on and on—infinite in my thoughts.
Wearing splints, spoiling my appearance

---

[1] From Kiesler, S., Finholt, T. (1988). The mystery of RSI. *American Psychologist* 43, 1004-15. Copyright 1988 by the American Psychological Association. Reprinted by permission.
[2] Preparation of this article was supported by a Research Scientist Development Award from the National Institute of Mental Health, Grant Number 5KO2 MH00533-04 to Sara Kiesler and by a National Science Foundation Graduate Fellowship to Tom Finholt. The authors wish to thank Julie Zatz for legal and historical research on compensation and Len Epstein and Robyn Dawes for information and advice on psycho-physiological illnesses. We are grateful to Australian, New Zealand, and Swedish colleagues who provided references, ideas, entry into computing environments, and in two instances, room and board. We especially thank Stephen Little, Olov Ostberg, librarians at the State Library of South Australia in Adelaide, and Barbara Single Bice and Malini Dias for archival research and interviews they did in our behalf. We thank Arlene Simon the executive secretary and administrator on our research projects, whose personal bout with carpal tunnel syndrome and interest in the Australian experience initially motivated this work. A further note is in order. Although we have done many research studies on social aspects of computing, we come to this particular topic as foreigners and outsiders. We apologize for any insensitivity we might convey as a result. We hope our naive perspective is useful, and we look forward to an Australian paper on the mystery of America's back problems. Correspondence concerning this article should be addressed to Sara Kiesler, Department of Social and Decision Sciences, Carnegie Mellon University, Pittsburgh, PA 15213.

'What's wrong, broken your wrist?'
Given up explaining—no one wants to know.
How I envy, jealous am I of people being able to eat without
pain.
To drive, to comb my daughter's hair—
To make love without pain.
—(An RSI sufferer; Mersina, 1985)

A computer-related health epidemic known as repetitive strain injury (RSI) is rampant in Australia and threatens to overwhelm the workers' compensation system. RSI is a label given to a variety of painful, debilitating conditions believed to be caused by rapid, repetitive movements of the hands or arms.[3] Traditionally, RSI affects manual laborers such as carpenters and meatcutters who make repeated movements with their arms and wrists in awkward positions. In Australia, the latest wave of RSI complaints is centered among female office workers who develop symptoms as a result of extensive typing at computer keyboards. Government, business, and labor have reacted vigorously to counter the spread of RSI. Every state in Australia has appointed blue-ribbon commissions to investigate the causes and possible solutions to the "RSI epidemic." In some places special work rules restrict the number of hours people may work at computer terminals to 3 to 5 hours a day. Firms are employing professionals to design equipment and run medical programs to counter the threat. Strangely, Australia is virtually alone in experiencing these RSI problems. In our analysis of this mysterious epidemic, we examine the nature of RSI and its known correlates in the human-computer design interface and context. Based on available evidence, we speculate as to the reasons for the emergence of RSI in Australia. We will argue that RSI is an extreme illustration of how the social context of work and technological change defines and determines the nature of occupational health problems.

THE NATURE OF RSI

At the outset, RSI is a real injury involving moderate to severe pain from working at a job. Some workers are awakened at night by the pain. Some lose their ability to grip objects normally and cannot perform even ordinary household chores. People with RSI are rarely malingering; frequently they are conscientious workers who resent losing time from their jobs (e.g., Ryan, 1986). If these workers try ignoring the pain and continue to work, they experience further deterioration (e.g., Brown & Dwyer, 1983). Despite the intensity of pain it causes, RSI involves soft tissue and cannot be measured

---

[3]More exactly, RSI appears most often in work involving (a) rapid, repetitive movements, as those of people operating keyboards, (b) less frequent but more forceful movements, as in electronics assembly work, and (c) static load, as in welding but also in keyboard operators who hold wrists and shoulders in the same position for long periods (Stone, 1983).

directly (Littlejohn, 1986). In a minority of cases, as in some outbreaks of carpal tunnel syndrome, RSI can be measured using indirect but objective physical indicators such as electromyography. But even in instances of clinically defined disease, the nature, causes, and appropriate treatments or preventions of RSI are controversial. For example, repetitive movements with the wrist in a flexed position are thought to cause or to exacerbate carpal tunnel syndrome (Armstrong, 1983). Yet in some organizations where considerable investments have been made in ergonomic equipment and task design to ensure that peoples' wrists are held properly, the incidence of carpal tunnel and other RSI syndromes has continued unabated or has even increased (e.g., National Occupational Health and Safety Commission [NOHSC], 1986, p. 44; see also Westgaard & Aaras, 1980). In discussing light assembly work in Australia, Welch (1972) stated that "the peak of tenosynovitis was reached in 1963—64; since then remedial steps have been taken in most factories and the incidence has decreased" (cited in NOHSC, 1986, p. 22). He was proven wrong, as the incidence greatly increased after his article was published. We shall return to the relationship between ergonomics and injury. Suffice it to reiterate at this point that even in the United States, where carpal tunnel, tenosynovitis, and related clinical diseases are considered rare but clinically well-defined, the mechanisms of injury are actually unclear. Causes of carpal tunnel in the medical literature range from fracture to arthritis to obesity to congenital defects to vitamin deficiency, as well as to repetitive movements (e.g., Armstrong & Chaffin, 1979a, 1 979b; Armstrong, Foulke, Joseph, & Goldstein, 1982; Cseuz, Thomas, Lambert, Love, & Lipscomb, 1966; Folkers, 1986; Frymoyer & Bland, 1973; Kendall, 1960). A common medical therapy for carpal tunnel in the United States is surgical "release." The surgery relieves pain but inexplicably fails to improve grip in many cases (e.g., Masear, Hayes, & Hyde, 1986). Many medical doctors in Australia believe that surgery may make the problem worse (e.g., Browne, Nolan, & Faithfull, 1984).

RSI as it is known in Australia arises in two forms. The minority of cases—in some accounts only 5%—consist of that cluster of medical injuries or diseases whose presence can be determined physiologically, such as carpal tunnel disease, epicondylytis, and tenosynovitis. Each of these is a clinical entity defined in the international medical literature. The name of the condition varies with the location of the tissues involved. For example, epicondylytis occurs at the elbow; in sports it is called "tennis elbow." Tenosynovitis occurs at the forearm or wrist, and it has been called "golfer's wrist." Carpal tunnel is thought to be a nerve block that occurs at the base of the palm of the hand between the thumb and little finger where the carpal ligament stretches between the two muscle groups. With excessive use, it is thought, the ligament tightens and depresses the median nerve into the carpal bones just underneath.

In the United States, these clinical problems occur in less than 1% of the population, but in certain jobs or activities, in some places, they have occurred in as much as 20% of people. Novice tennis players get tennis elbow from using their racquets incorrectly; violinists and windsurfers get carpal tunnel from overpracticing (e.g., Owen, 1985; Sword, 1986). Recently, some food processing plants have experienced what is for the United States very high rates of carpal tunnel; for example, in one meatpacking plant, 14.8% of the employees have carpal tunnel syndrome (Masear et al., 1986). It is instructive to read a description of conditions at such plants.

> Meatpackers work in extreme heat or refrigerated cold, often standing shoulder to shoulder wielding honed knives and power saws. Grease and blood make the floors and the tools slippery. The roar of the machines is constant. Occasionally, an overpowering stench from open bladders and stomachs fills the air. The workers cut themselves. They cut each other. They wear out their insides doing repetitive-motion jobs. They are sliced and crushed by machines.

> Tim Denherder and a partner share a wobbly hydraulic bench that travels up and down with them as they split 175 beef carcasses every hour. The beef chain moves 84% faster than it did in 1979. There are no breaks except when the chain stops. And it only stops for a 30-minute dinner break at noon, a 10-minute break in the morning, and a 10-minute break in the afternoon.

> At 28, [Tim] already has the hands of a packing house worker. They call what he has carpal tunnel syndrome, and he has had two operations for it. Long before the doctors were calling it a syndrome, the packing house workers knew about the hands. On the chain, workers say it is not unusual to see people forcing their fingers open in the morning and then forcing them back to grip the handle of a knife or saw for the day.

> Even after an operation, the weakness and pain often return. Already, Tim Denherder's grip is so weak he cannot pick up his children and carry them up to bed. At night, he feels as if something sharp is digging into his wrist. He cannot open his hands all the way, and though he is a strong man who has worked all his life, his handshake has the grip of a boy.

> "I think, what's going to happen to me 20 years from now when I can't do anything with my hands?" he said. "I'll be a cripple." He has looked for other work but no one will hire him, he said, because his hands are weak (Glaberson, 1987, Section 3, pp. 1,8).

The large majority of RSI cases involve much the same pain, tenderness, and weakness as described above but have no objective indications from radiological, vascular electrodiagnostic, pathological, or other physiological tests. This form of RSI resembles hysterical or "conversion" illnesses such as hysterical blindness or shell-shock (Lucire, 1981). Conversion illnesses have been documented in workplaces, but unlike RSI, they were observed to sweep through a single workplace and then quickly disappear. For example, in a dormitory of our own university a large number of students suddenly developed skin rashes and stomach cramps from what they believed to be a brown spider. The spider was never found, and the problem came and left within a few days. By contrast, RSI has emerged throughout Australia, in both factory and office environments. Most workers acquire RSI gradually, and many are afflicted for years. The breadth, incidence, and severity of RSI has surprised and perplexed managers and workers (NOHSC, 1986, p. 1). RSI has entered the workers' compensation arena to such an extent that in the March and June quarters of 1985 no federal public servant who applied for RSI compensation was refused (Spillane, 1986). In the hardest-hit Australian state, New South Wales, the number of RSI compensation cases increased 100% from 1979 to 1980 to 1,344 cases. By 1984 there were 2,865 cases (NOHSC, 1986). Suits have been entered, and settlements as high as $350,000 have been reached. Australian employers who are part of private insurance programs have encountered huge increases in compensation premiums—more than 2 billion Australian dollars in 1984 alone (Williams, 1985).

Although Australia's incidence of RSI in both factories and offices is extremely high by international standards, many experts claim the data reflect considerable *underreporting* of both frequency and severity of the problem (e.g., Ferguson, 1984; Walker, 1979). For instance, a study of women who assemble electronics equipment showed that when symptoms first appear most workers continue working because of financial reasons or because they fear getting sacked if they go off work sick. Eventually the swelling and pain becomes so extreme that they are simply incapable of working any more. (We have been told of instances where women were in such pain every day that they spent their break periods in tears.) The usual pattern is that they go off work on compensation and a large proportion are never able to work again. . . a large majority of people said they felt permanently crippled by their condition and have not been able to write a letter for 12 or 18 months, twisting a door knob causes pain, also peeling potatoes, etc.

In many cases the husband and children take over a large share of the wife's housework but when this goes on for months or years, strains in the family relationships appear. Particularly with the migrant women, they feel they are not fulfilling their role as a wife and mother (Walker 1979, pp. 20-21).

The biggest recent increases in RSI, and also the most public and professional controversy, center on office work by female keyboard operators and government clerks. In studies of various Australian industries, organizations, and states, the percentage of women doing keyboard work (data entry, typing, secretarial work) with diagnosed RSI ranges from about 10%, which is considered abnormally high in the United States, to more than 50% (e.g., Ryan, 1986; Ryan, Mullerworth, & Bampton, 1985; Spillane,

Table 4.1

Cases of RSI Reported in Western Australian Government Employment as of January 1985.

Category	No. of Operators	Reported Cases	%
Secretary stenographers	397	70	17.6
Typists	1,163	137	11.7
Clerk typists	838	60	7.1
Word processing operators	340	99	19.1
Data processing operators	379	84	22.1
Telephonists	172	6	3.4
Accounting machinists	72	7	9.7
Computer programmers	749	9	1.2
Clerks	1,190	40	3.3
Clerical assistants	193	9	4.6
Telex operators	49	—	—
Journalists	12	—	—
Hansard/court reporters	32	7	21.8
Other keyboard operators	938	32	3.4
Other affected personnel		29	
Total	6,524	560[a]	8.58

Note: From Report of the Repetitive Strain Injuries in the Western Australian Public Service Task Force by Western Australia Public Service Board, October 1985, Perth: Author. Other affected personnel include draftspersons, Public Works, Main Roads Department; forestry officers, Forests; library assistants, Health Department; dental therapists, Health Department; assayers, Perth Mint; technical assistants, State Energy Commission; technical officers, Agriculture protection Board; engineers, Main Roads Department; tradespeople, State Energy Commission; stamp duty assessors, State Taxation Department; and research officers, Metropolitan Transport Trust.

[a] Excludes "other affected personnel."

1986; Western Australia Public Service Board, 1985). In New South Wales, nearly half of all the new claims for workers' compensation by women in the first half of the 1980s were for RSI, and the incidence was increasing yearly. In Victoria, RSI accounted for 62.5% of all claims by women in 1985. Table 4.1 shows the results of a study of government workers in Western Australia, which indicates how RSI has entered the office in that state.

Computing in clerical jobs is highly correlated with RSI in Australia (see Table 4.1, for example). One explanation of the correlation is that computer workstations are not designed for human comfort and especially not for women's comfort. For example, the left pinky may be extended thousands of times a day for hitting control and shift keys (Baidya & Stevenson, 1982). People often ask why typewriters do not cause RSI. One answer is that typewriters were designed to be used by women; the inventor tested models on his own daughter. Typewriters elicit more wrist movement than do computer keyboards. As a result, less pressure is placed on the ulnar and median nerves. Typewriters require breaks to insert paper, change margins, adjust platens, and so on. Breaks reduce muscular fatigue, which has been implicated in repetitive strain injury (e.g., Hagberg, Michaelson, & Ortelius, 1982).[4]

The secondary effects on work practices caused by computing might be another reason for computing to cause RSI. Computer power allows management and workers to increase productivity using means that also increase monotony, muscle strain, and fatigue. For example, with the introduction of computer data entry and word processing, files are accessed through the computer rather than kept in filing cabinets. This makes it possible to cut the number of work breaks and increase the pace of work, and managers can monitor these activities automatically using the computer. When the Australian Taxation Office introduced computers in the 1970s, the organization progressively increased productivity by increasing the rate of data entry; by 1981, data processing clerks were required to make 14,000 keystrokes per hour. Compensation claims by these clerks also increased each year. A health study in 1981 showed that 37% of the clerks had muscular strain injuries in neck, shoulder, elbow, wrist, or hand, and 25% were off work on compensation (e.g., Australian Council of Trade Unions-Victorian Trades Hall Council [ACTU-VTHC], 1982). Unions asked for a 10,000 keystroke/hour rate. Government officials not only refused, but proposed an individual log-in procedure that would allow for exact individual monitoring of productivity. This response prompted employee work rate refusals, employer stand-downs, and finally strikes. An arbitrator entered an 11,000 keystroke/hour limit. Some unions accepted this; some refused. As the dispute continued, the Queensland Taxation Branch was offering operators bonuses to key at a higher rate of 12,000, while the unions were educating their members about the hazards of working at computer terminals (Quinlan, 1984b, pp. 162-163).

The emergence of RSI in women office workers in Australia represents a unique experience. For the first time, a prolonged occupational health epidemic has struck women in offices. For the first time, serious labor-management disputes have involved women's office work; such disputes have heretofore been associated mainly with factory and outdoor work. For the first time, occupational safety and health officials face a national health problem whose true nature, cause, prevention, and cure are murky. After more than 100 reports and studies, even the rate and incidence of RSI in Australia is unknown (see NOHSC, 1986). In one comparison in the 1970s, the data given by the government from insurance statistics and the data from the state department of industrial relations from employer reports matched

---

[4]Another answer is that typewriters do cause RSI, as do pencils, ball-points, and the traditional ink-dipped pen. In the first book on occupational diseases, published in 1713 in Latin, the physician, Ramazzini, (1713/1940), described how scribes' "incessant driving the pen over paper" caused intense fatigue and eventually, failure of grip. However, neither typing nor writing has been implicated in a national epidemic as computing has been in Australia.

exactly in only 6% of cases (Morrissey, 1985, p. 139)! Although it seems clear that the average rate in Australia is exceedingly high compared with that in other countries, within Australia the variability is enormous. Despite this ambiguity and this variation, several variables consistently show a correlation with RSI. Let us summarize the research on these variables, and then look at whether they can explain the overall phenomenon.

CORRELATES OF RSI

The first study of Australian workers with muscular problems was published by Ferguson (1971a).[5] Ferguson examined the medical records of 77 women whose job was to assemble electronics equipment and who had lost time from work from upper body and limb injuries over the previous 12 months. He found that the majority suffered poorly defined but real physical symptoms involving the upper arm. He proposed a number of possible causes, since identified by other researchers as variables correlated with RSI. These variables fall into three categories: (a) worker characteristics, (b) equipment design and training (ergonomics), and (c) work practices.

The individual characteristic that best predicts RSI is the sex of the worker. In the 1980s, women have accounted for two thirds of the RSI compensation cases in Australia, and the proportion has increased each year. In research on workers and health records, the reported female:male ratio for RSI rose from 2:1 to more than 10: 1. Unfortunately, nearly all the research consists of retrospective case studies, usually in one organization or industry. These studies look backward from health or compensation records or use questionnaires or interviews of workers who indicate they suffer from RSI. This research, at most, can suggest correlations and is not capable of identifying causes. Moreover, without proper comparison groups, even the correlations may be illusory. Take, for example, the following worker characteristics: small wrist size, pregnancy, oral contraceptives, menopause, and gynecological surgery, each of which has been found to be correlated with RSI. It has even been suggested these are causes of RSI and the reasons why women get RSI far more than do men (e.g., Sabour & Fadel, 1970). An equally plausible and more conservative hypothesis is that these individual factors have nothing to do with RSI. Pregnancy, menopause, oral contraceptives, and so on might be statistically correlated with RSI incidence only because these attributes are more characteristic of women than men. Women may acquire RSI more than men do for entirely different reasons.

---

[5] The first such study in England was published two decades earlier (Thompson, Plewes, & Shaw, 1951), yet most English people have never heard of RSI. Recently, an English journalist, Auberon Waugh, published a parody of the Australian epidemic in the prestigious *Spectator* entitled "Introducing Kangaroo's Paw, a Wonderful New Disease From Australia" (Waugh, 1986). In the article he said RSI is resistance to video display terminals that "has now spread to everything. Obviously, it is the disease England has been waiting for. I prophesy a tremendous future for this wankers' disease in Britain, as soon as a few more people learn about it. It will go through the country like a dose of salts" (p. 8).

In the main, the search for individual predictors of RSI independent of sex has been fruitless. Diseases such as arthritis and diabetes are found in RSI victims (e.g., Barnes & Currey, 1967). These diseases, as well as some RSI problems such as carpal tunnel, may have a genetic basis. They run in some families and can appear quite independently of repetitive jobs and activities (e.g., Arm- strong, 1983). But the incidence of known physical predispositions is so low as to be an unimportant predictor of the distribution of RSI. To our knowledge, no prospective study of families with and without the alleged predispositional attributes of RSI has been undertaken. Are there mental predispositions? Studies of "accident proneness," that is, a tendency of certain types of workers to experience injury, have identified such workers (e.g., Najman, 1978). These classifications are suspect because statistical artifacts explain the distribution of injuries rather well—multiple injuries are about as frequent in the population of workers as would be expected by chance (e.g., Lee & Wrench, 1982; Sampson, 1971). The probability of being injured once is nonzero, and for those injured once, the probability of being injured again is nonzero, and so on. Hence bad luck alone will result in the appearance of accident-proneness in some people.[6]

One cluster of worker characteristics we label "Job dissatisfaction" is reliably correlated with job injuries and sicknesses in many countries but is rarely mentioned in the Australian literature. The phenomenon of interest is that workers who are absent from work for long periods due to sickness or injury tend to report more insecurity and to consider their jobs more monotonous, stressful, and detrimental to health than workers who are not absent (e.g., Kvarnstrom, 1983a, 1983b). Some studies show that absenteeism from work injuries is positively related to strikes and labor action (see Quinlan, 1984a). The RSI literature in Australia states or implies that negative attitudes are an outcome, not a cause of RSI, and that sick and injured workers resent the situation that has caused them pain, loss of income, and in some cases, loss of esteem in their families and communities. Although this argument is convincing, it might also be true that dissatisfactions predispose workers to report RSI. An uncorroborated report reached one of the authors describing a study sponsored by American air traffic controllers to assess how perceptual vigilance and tracking tasks in their work led to job pressures that might account for their exceedingly high rates of hypertension. The researchers found that these tasks had no relation to controllers' hypertension; rather, unpleasant work organization and poor relations with supervisors were reliably associated with the disease. Hypertension is a psychophysiological condition thus named because the problem varies with both psychological and physical states. RSI might show a similar pattern. Unfortunately, no prospective research has been done to

---

[6]This is a slight oversimplification. The distribution of injured workers is not identical with the distribution of reported injuries.

examine the relative impact of attitudes of workers or managers on RSI. Studies of workers' *ongoing experience* in jobs, and not just of injured workers' perceptions and memories of job conditions, would help us to discriminate between predisposing and post hoc attitudinal factors in RSI. These studies should always involve comparisons across jobs and organizations to identify factors in the social context of work that may produce negative attitudes.[7]

Poor ergonomic design of equipment and tools is, in some studies, associated with RSI. Ergonomic factors have long been associated with occupational injury in industry in the United States, Japan, and Europe (Ostberg & Nilsson, 1985). In Australia, ill-designed equipment and inadequate operator training are thought to produce bad posture, fatigue, and awkward arm or body movements, and hence RSI (Mills & Sallans, 1984; South Australian Health Commission, 1984; but cf. Oxenburgh, 1984). Taking a cue from the Swedes and a new California standard for government offices, Australian unions such as the Australian Public Service Association and a number of private firms are establishing detailed workstation design principles. They would probably come as a shock to most U.S. managers. The standards include footrests for short operators; identical viewing distance for screen, source document, and keyboard; a 38° angle of viewing; a 90° screen angle; a 33 mm keyboard; and fully adjustable height and knee clearance of computer tables. Ergonomic standards have been difficult and costly to implement for Australians because Australia imports most of its computers, and Australians have no part in most design decisions. Furthermore, and more disheartening, during the 1980s when many organizations invested heavily in better ergonomics design, the rate of RSI increased. This replicates the experience of some of the Swedish experiments in "biotechnology and sociotechnology" at the Volvo and Saab automobile plants, that is, deterioration of the experienced working environment despite extensive investment in worker comfort. Table 4.2 provides an example of data from the Kalmar Volvo plant, a plant that has been cited worldwide for its advanced ergonomics and job designs.

A highly cited factor associated with RSI in Australia today is work practices. Many work practices are changing with automation to increase productivity. These include fewer staff, heavier workloads, more task specialization, faster pacing of work, fewer rest breaks, more overtime, more

---

[7] We recognize that researchers have much more difficulty finding sponsorship for research on social contexts than on physical and individual variables. Social context variables are very difficult to study, as they can produce illness through interactions of physical and mental states. Furthermore, social contexts are perceived as difficult or impossible to change. In one U.S. meatpacking plant, for instance, increasing overtime hours and work pace on the cutting lines is thought to be responsible for an increasing incidence of carpal tunnel syndrome. However, the medical experts have put their efforts into ergonomics and designing wrist supports, not to changing work requirements; they claim adjusting jobs is not feasible due to union seniority rules and the need to make a profit (see Masear et al., 1986, p. 226).

Table 4.2

Percentage of Blue Collar Workers Satisfied with the Working Environment in the Swedish Volvo Kalmar Plant in 1976 and 1983.

Feature of the working environment	Percentage of Satisfied Workers	
	1976[a] (N = 69)	1983[b] (N = 70)
Physical workload	83	67
Work postures	55	57
Noise	80	64
Lighting	86	79
Windows, outlook	71	74
Climate, air pollution	49	39
Chemical labelling, etc.	58	58
Personnel areas	71	63
Safety hazards	81	77
Company health services	96	67
Safety and health precautions	86	84
Workplace and environment	83	—
Working place	—	54

Note: Reprinted from "Emerging Technology and Stress" by O. Ostberg and C. Nilsson. In Job Stress and Blue Collar Work (p. 163) by C.L. Cooper and M.J. Smith (Eds.), 1985, New York: Wiley. Copyright 1985 by J. Wiley & Sons. Used by permission.

[a] Interview investigation reported by Gyllenhammar (1977).

[b] Questionnaire investigation reported by Aguren, Bredbacka, Hansson, Ihregren, and Karlson (1984).

shift work and nonstandard hours, and more piece work and bonus systems (e.g., Ryan, Mullerworth, & Pimble, 1984). These work practices can entail very prolonged rapid or forceful repetitive motions leading to fatigue and overuse of muscles. Normally, people self-correct overuse problems by resting or changing position when they feel physical discomfort; this explains why computer programmers, computer scientists, and journalists have a low incidence of RSI even when they use a computer keyboard 8, 10 or more hours in a day. However, in nonprofessional factory and office jobs, work requirements and incentives act as barriers to prevent people from taking these self-corrective measures. Although no research has yet demonstrated a causal effect of work practices on RSI, a study in Europe showed that workers in jobs entailing higher daily keystroke rates have more injuries (e.g., Laubli, 1982). Also, injuries among people who do repetitive work tend to decline during vacation months (Kivi, 1984).

One difficulty of interpreting the overuse hypothesis is that repetitive, unrelieved work co-occurs with otherwise unchallenging, dead-end, monotonous, low status, low paid work. Are people getting sick from doing the job or from having the job? Are they getting RSI from physical overload or from psychological underload? It has been argued that RSI occurs even when employees work too hard of their own volition, which supports the overuse hypothesis. In a study of the free break system in Japan, researchers found that most Japanese operators continued to work even when they were tired and that they developed more complaints than those in a fixed break system (Pulket & Kogi, 1984). The study seems to show how injury may result in jobs where workers determine their own pace, but this conclusion is unwarranted. It is not obvious that Japanese operators on the "free" break system are actually free; implicit social pressures to perform can produce more conformity than explicit pressures. In summary, the data indicate that work conditions are associated with RSI, but the mechanisms by which physical and social factors operate to produce injury are unknown.

The most effective method to illuminate the effects of worker characteristics, ergonomic factors, and work conditions on RSI would be to set up some experiments. For example, in places planning to introduce new computer systems, subunits could be randomly assigned to acquire these systems at different times. Equipment could be compared. Work rules and incentives could be systematically varied. Rehabilitative treatments could be assigned randomly to victims across jobs. To our knowledge, not a single true experiment in office working conditions has been conducted in Australia. In their absence, we can see how different rehabilitation strategies have taken effect. For example, if drugs alleviate pain, that suggests RSI is a true medical condition resulting from overuse. In Australia, the methods of reducing RSI include psychotropic, steroid, and other drugs; surgery; exercise; hypnosis; rest; immobilization by splints, gloves, casts, and bands; physiotherapy; and work modification. What is noticeable about this list is its length, which suggests either that RSI can be alleviated by anything or that nothing works. That the latter is more true is suggested by a questionnaire study of workers with RSI. When asked which of a list of treatments helped them most, the most frequent response was "none at all" followed by "rest" (Taylor, Gow, & Corbett, 1982). Hence the research on treatments tells us very little about the etiology of RSI.

THE AUSTRALIAN EXPERIENCE

The studies described above do not explain the following questions: (a) why RSI is epidemic in Australia and not in other countries; (b) why women are struck by RSI much more frequently than men, and why the ratios vary from 2:1 to more than 10:1 from study to study; (c) why women in offices are getting RSI, in some places more than women in assembly line jobs (e.g., Stone, 1983); (d) why office computers that are used worldwide are creating reports of RSI only in Australia; (e) why reported RSI has increased in this decade; (f) why the epidemic rages in some workplaces but not in other seemingly comparable workplaces; and (g) why rehabilitation has such poor prognosis.

The uniqueness of the Australian RSI phenomenon raises interesting questions. For example, why is Australia affected? Australian experts assume that RSI is a medical/biomechanical problem that exists everywhere, but is simply mislabeled in other countries (NOHSC, 1985, 1986). This does not seem to be the case. For example, although carpal tunnel syndrome is known in the United States, it is rare and is infrequently mentioned in conjunction with office work or computers. Australians have pointed to large numbers of "musculoskeletal" work injuries in the United States, but the large majority of these are back injuries from twisting, lifting, and using force (U.S. Department of Health and Human Services, 1984). Curiously, back injuries are rarely if ever mentioned in connection with RSI in Australia.[8] We believe RSI can be described as an international problem if all muscle, skeletal, overuse, and technology-related problems (e.g., vision impairments) are lumped together into one giant category. Even with that, the Australian statistics are exceedingly high in terms of number of jobs affected, incidence within jobs, and severity. For example, an Australian study recently identified 74 RSI sufferers in one Australian university in 1984, and followed up in 1985 on 101 sufferers. Many were secretaries; 91% used a computer terminal or word processor in their work. By contrast, a recent study of 109 clerical employees using workstations at the University of Michigan in the United States turned up no such health problem; indeed, the secretaries who had the highest work load complained the least, and the authors concluded that workstations were probably not an occupational stressor (Sutton & Rafaeli, 1987).

Surveys we have taken in our own university have failed to uncover RSI-like health problems from computing. In 1985, Hartman (1987) interviewed a random sample of 25 secretaries. They were asked, "Is there anything about computing that you don't like?" Twenty secretaries said "no." Of the 5 who answered affirmatively, 1 mentioned noise from the printers, 2 mentioned sitting for long periods, and 2 said eye strain. Nobody mentioned muscular strain or pains. Recently, we put a notice on one of the computer bulletin boards; the board reaches more than 2,000 faculty, staff and graduate students. The notice asked anyone who had suffered any injury or problem as a result of using a computer keyboard to send us computer mail. We received 13 answers, less than 1% of the population. The problems were described as follows: one person reported a small skin cancer, maybe from sitting in front of a CRT; one reported carpal tunnel from playing the viola; one reported back injury; this person read a book on RSI by an Australian journalist and said the problem should be taken more seriously by the U.S. medical profession; one mentioned "hacker's neck" which lasted three days and was

---

[8]The location of muscular-skeletal problems seems to move with the countries in which their victims reside. In Finland, for instance, only 4.3% of total "rheumatic" disorders from repetitive work involve the neck and back; the percentage is much higher in Sweden.

attributed to working with a keyboard on his lap for 10 hours a day; two mentioned that family members have carpal tunnel but do not use computers; one reported a pinched sciatic nerve from falling down the steps and said it was very painful to sit at work; one mentioned eyestrain; one cited a finger joint problem from hitting the keyboard in frustration; one reported carpal tunnel from typing a grant and being under tension, but problem has disappeared; and three mentioned pain in the left pinky from using a computer keyboard; one of these respondents explained that his machine has 11 keys operated with the left pinky. Together, the data on the university workplaces in the United States suggest, first, that acquiring a physical problem while computing has a nonzero probability, and second, that the incidence and severity is minimal compared to that in universities in Australia.

Hence RSI seems to be a health problem whose occurrence varies tremendously with location. What might be the reason? There is no evidence that Australian women and office workers have special bodily or genetic predispositions to RSI not true of women and office workers in other countries. At this time we cannot rule out a physical cause attributable to Australia such as meat in the diet, presence of snakes and crocodiles, or reverse torque of the Australian continent. A physical cause might be discovered in the future, just as occurred with a few other mysterious health problems. Gout is such a health problem. It is caused by genetically linked high uric acid level in the blood and was originally misattributed to ambitious and hyperactive personality types—behavior that turns out also to respond to uric acid. The bewitched girls whose bizarre behavior set off the Salem witch trials were probably victims of ergot poisoning, a convulsive disease caused by eating rye contaminated with the ergot fungus (Caporeal, 1976). These and other examples suggest that physical causes can arise from unexpected quarters. The epidemiological data, however, suggest that a simple physical cause of RSI in Australia is highly unlikely.

On the basis of all of the evidence, we speculate that the spread of RSI in Australia is indicative of a larger social problem. That is, RSI itself and the mounting claims payments associated with RSI are symptoms of a more fundamental difficulty that provokes complaints of RSI. We believe that this fundamental difficulty is rooted in dissatisfaction with the workplace that is revealed when new technology is introduced, and that this dissatisfaction is expressed in the form of "techno-illnesses," such as RSI.[9]

RSI cannot be studied in isolation. The context in which the complaints occur is as important as the complaints themselves. In Australia, that context is traditional offices converting to computer technologies. This conversion has occurred suddenly, with much greater rapidity and magnitude than in

---

[9]Spillane (1986), Littlejohn (1986), Quinlan (1984b), and Willis (1986) arrived at similar conclusions but did not speculate, as we do, why RSI has emerged in Australian offices exclusively.

other countries. Several things happen during this speedy transition. The most significant, we feel, is that the installation of new technology focuses attention on the way work is done. This process begins with disruptions caused by the arrival of computer systems. Workers must adapt to new technology that is complex and requires special training. They must learn new concepts and jargon. And they must adjust to higher expectations for output. In the process of adapting to this new world, workers reexamine the nature of their jobs. For example, even the most trivial task, such as typing a memo, must be rethought when done on the computer. Files must be opened, editors and formatters must be invoked, the text of the memo must be input, files must be saved, and finally, the file must be sent to a printer to produce the document. We believe that the result of this reexamination is that all aspects of the job are made more salient. In Australia, these jobs are not pleasant. Pool typists are given little autonomy, they are closely monitored, their earnings and status are low, and their physical work environment is uninteresting. Many secretaries spend 80% to 100% of their time on one task (Levick, 1986). They are not consulted about the nature of this specialization or about how their module might be coordinated with those of others (Magarey, 1985). Furthermore, many of these fragmented, unchallenging jobs are offered only as part-time work (see, e.g., Prerost, 1982; Red Fems, 1982). When job characteristics increase in saliency, these negative features become more visible to workers.

Introducing new technology also elicits rethinking among managers, who sometimes use the inevitable chaos as a cover to implement nontechnological changes in staffing, organization, and work procedures. This would tend to increase the amount of change employees experience, as well as the attributions of blame that are made to new technology.

A theoretical underlying psychological process can account for negative somatic effects when technological change is juxtaposed on a work setting. First, technological change focuses attention on negative aspects of work such as repetitive typing on a keyboard. Communications from co-workers, supervisors, and the outside world legitimate particular interpretations of the problem (Salancik & Pfeffer, 1978; see also Fordyce, 1979). Then, attention focused on the stressor interferes with habituation to it (Matthews, Scheier, Brunson, & Carducci, 1980). It is the slowed habituation brought on by heightened attention that causes unpredictable stressors such as low-flying aircraft to have more severe consequences than predictable stressors, and ambiguous therapies to result in more chronicity than clear ones (e.g., Fordyce, Brockway, Bergman, & Spengler, 1986). Physical unpredictability and ambiguous treatments draw attention to suffering. Technological change can do so also.

An expected outcome of this process might be that workers grow dissatisfied, but gradually accommodate themselves to their changed jobs. This assumes, however, that the workers do not have an alternative. In Australia workers do have an alternative. They can make RSI claims. This is only possible, though, because in Australia RSI has been socially legitimated. We maintain that this social legitimization has occurred through four mechanisms. First, there is historical precedent for RSI-like conditions on the job in Australia. Second, RSI has become a cause celebre of unions and feminist groups. Third, RSI has received official validation by the Australian medical establishment. Fourth, the Australian press has covered the RSI story in intense detail.

References to RSI-like ailments in Australia can be found as far back as the 19th century. In her famous book, *My Brilliant Career*, the teenager Miles Franklin wrote,

> Among the dairying fraternity little toddlers, ere they are big enough to hold a bucket, learn to milk. Thus their hands become inured to the motion, and it does not affect them. With us it was different. Being almost full grown when we started to milk, and then plunging heavily into the exercise, it had a painful effect upon us. Our hands and arms, as far as the elbows, swelled, so that our sleep at night was often disturbed by pain (Franklin, 1901/1986,p. 14).

In more modern times, RSI has affected telegraph operators. The constant keying of the signaling apparatus produced a condition that the operators called "glass arm" (Dargan, 1985). In railway journals, telegraph publications, and medical journals from the 19th century through the early 20th century, descriptions of telegraphist's cramp were quite common (e.g., Ferguson, 1971b; Thompson & Sinclair, 1912). Its symptoms resemble those associated with carpal tunnel syndrome: tingling in the fingers accompanied by weakness in the hand. Apparently, telegraph workers suffering from "glass arm" were eligible for settlements to cover treatment. The early incidence of RSI in Australia means that the condition was documented in the medical literature and the diagnostic characteristics were considered well known. Thus, when similar symptoms emerged in another generation of workers, in a completely different line of work, an explanation was available—complete with prescribed treatments and estimates of recovery time.

The key question is, however, why, suddenly in the 1980s, did RSI develop as an epidemic? Willis (1986) suggested, and we agree, that an important mechanism was the adoption of RSI as a cause by unions and feminist groups in Australia. The unions' behavior arises as a natural result of a strong trade union tradition of resistance in Australia. Further, the workers' health movement has been an important aspect of this resistance. Occupational health and safety have become labor relations issues in part because unemployment (previously low) reduced the ability of workers to leave unpleasant jobs. Also, the massive entry of Anglo-Saxon women into white-collar clerical positions using keyboard technologies meant that injuries could not be dismissed with racist stereotypes as easily as they were when similar injuries were incurred by migrant workers in industrial jobs.

Concurrently, feminist groups took up the cause of RSI as a symbol and natural consequence of the women's movement's outcry against deskilling and partial-work in the so called secondary labor market (Bevege, James, & Shute, 1982). Hence, RSI can be understood as a labor relations and political issue, a form of economic and political resistance to conditions of work or society, whose legal and medical disposition could lead to the expenditure of millions or even billions of dollars by business and government.

Not surprisingly, Australian medical experts have been called to testify on RSI. On the whole, these experts have come to agree, and have been disposed to make definitive statements about RSI (e.g., Browne, Nolan, & Faithfull, 1984; Stone, 1983). These pronouncements come despite the fact that RSI covers a range of conditions from carpal tunnel syndrome to tenosynovitis to ill-defined pain, all of which have overlapping symptoms but dramatically different implications in terms of worker impairment. Nonetheless, Australian doctors remain quite confident that they know RSI when they see it. This official medical position has led business and the government to take the RSI problem seriously. It is unlikely that the compensation system would include a category for RSI in the absence of some official recognition of the condition by physicians.

Historical precedent, political meaning, and official recognition would be irrelevant without some means for the public to find out about RSI. Thus, in Australia, the press has played a large role in popularizing RSI. Periodically, the media becomes absorbed with a particular story, and the story assumes a life of its own. Health problems are particularly likely candidates for this treatment. In the United States coverage of herpes, drug use, and AIDS can all be described by this pattern. In Australia, RSI has been a lead story off and on for the last five years. Sample headlines include, "The RSI Epidemic: Technology Spawns its Own Disease" (McIntosh, 1986); "Change of Diet Could Be Key to Relief of RSI Pain" (Smith, 1986); "Woman Claims Damage for RSI" (1986); "RSI—Control the Curse: Curb the Costs" (Galbraith, 1985); "RSI: Scientists Seek Solutions to Centuries-Old Health Problem" (1986); "Hi-tech Epidemic: Victims of a Bright New Technology That Maims" (O'Mara, 1984). This coverage, although sometimes at the level of grocery store tabloids, has served a very important function. It has taken the official pronouncements of the doctors and of the government on RSI and communicated it to a mass audience. In Australia RSI is a household concept. Everyone, particularly those in the vulnerable worker groups, is very aware of the alleged causes of RSI, its symptoms, and the fact that the government and businesses believe that RSI is a real disease.

Armed with this knowledge, Australian office workers have a legitimate ticket out of the pink ghetto. Workers in other countries, of course, have recourse to workers' compensation or litigation when they are injured on the job. As consciousness about health and well-being has increased worldwide, pressures to improve these systems, as well as to set work environment standards, have increased too (Ostberg & Nilsson, 1985). In 1972, New

Zealand introduced a no-fault insurance system that covers work injuries (Palmer, 1979). The same year, Finland passed an accident insurance act making it possible to compensate for pain in muscles and tendons contracted at work (Kivi, 1984). In 1977, Sweden passed a law requiring employers to establish working conditions adapted to the physical and psychical makeup of the worker. Recently in the United States, states have increased compensation award levels and expanded the types of injuries covered (Tinsley, 1986). Increased levels of compensation have led to increased injury claims and to stronger expectations that injury on the job deserves economic remediation (e.g., Kivi, 1984; Klar, 1983). Despite these changes, workers still have difficulty making claims for many injuries, such as damage they acquire gradually; in many U.S. states the limit is 2 years. Usually they must prove damage through clinical tests. And, most important, the medical doctors who certify work injuries must believe the work environment is dangerous. What marks Australia in this regard are three distinguishing factors: (a) RSI is considered an occupational injury even though the victim has worked on the job in a "normal" office environment months or years without developing it; (b) RSI is compensable with or without physical indications; and (c) certifying physicians believe office environments are dangerous.

We do not intend to suggest that RSI is a scam to promote the practice of medicine or that Australian workers use RSI claims to defraud their employers. We believe that they legitimately have symptoms of RSI. We speculate that if the work environment were better and if jobs were more satisfying, RSI complaints would not be as important. The epidemic in Australia ostensibly involves RSI, but we hypothesize that it is really related to bad work conditions and an unfulfilling work life. The ambiguous nature of RSI makes it the perfect candidate for many workers as they seek an approved exit from the computing pool while preserving benefits and some salary. In addition, the social status of women in Australia may be improving more slowly relative to technological change than in other technology-advanced countries. Managers who are technology optimists but hold traditional stereotypes of women may be contributing to a double bind of secretaries whereby the only way they can gain sympathy, if not respect, is to get injured.

If as we suspect, it is really the quality of work life that underlies the RSI dilemma, this implies that the present emphasis in RSI research is misdirected. That is, the nearly exclusive focus on biomechanical factors and individual-level variables will not illuminate the real problem, which might instead be embedded in the social structure of the workplace and the organization of work life in Australia. Attention should turn toward understanding what it is about the work that these RSI victims perform that causes them to escape the workplace with RSI. Several possibilities seem relevant. First, the work is unrewarding. There are few opportunities for advancement. Personal initiative is not encouraged. One of us visited a university in which clerks doing word processing were not permitted to use a spelling checker program and were reprimanded for altering the text, even to correct a spelling error. This approach to the organization of office tasks needs to be reformed. When workers acquire computing skills, they can become much more than mere typists. This increased sophistication should be encouraged and recognized by expanding job definitions. Pool word processors should have more access to learning computing skills and to promotion opportunities as they learn more about computing, for example, advancement to accounting departments if they become familiar with spreadsheets. Second, the introduction of new technology needs to be managed better. Too often computers in offices are approached as replacements for typewriters when they are actually more complex. This complexity needs to be handled through appropriate training and orientation. Firms frequently adopt a "sink-or-swim" approach to installing the technology. Instead, clerical workers should be teaching each other, and those who have special teaching abilities should be paid more. Finally, some aspects of office word processing cannot be improved. Typing other people's papers is not intrinsically interesting. Also, typing other people's papers is not as necessary in a computer environment. Therefore, businesses and other employers need to concentrate on improving those aspects of the work environment that can be easily manipulated, for example, providing a pleasant physical space to work in, including "social enclosures" that facilitate socializing, and enlarging jobs to encompass both administration and typing.

The obvious question is, Aren't these factors present in other places too? That is, certainly Australia does not have a monopoly on data entry clerks and pool word processing operators who are unhappy or bored with their work. The answer to this question is complex. Yes, life for low-level clerical and secretarial employees is hard everywhere. But this hardship, and particularly the reaction of secretarial employees outside Australia to new technology, is not expressed in the form of RSI complaints. However, there are analogous health issues. Each nation has its own set of new-technology health problems. In the United States, a major concern is with radiation from visual display terminals, or VDTs (e.g., Horton, 1984). This is a special preoccupation of the press and is also a concern of Congress, the Occupational Safety and Health Administration (OSHA), and other branches of the federal government. As with RSI, it is not hard to imagine that VDT ailments could reach epidemic proportions as computer technology proliferates. In Europe, the chief concern is with ergonomics, the physical arrangement of keyboards and screens to reduce eye and muscle strain. Entire institutes have been created by European governments to develop standards for construction of computer workstations (e.g., Ostberg, Moller, & Ahlstrom, 1986). In Japan, a curriculum in "robot medicine" has been established to counter stress and health problems caused by automation (Noro, 1984). Still another work- related problem is painter's syndrome, a form of brain damage diagnosed in the Scandinavian countries and acknowledged by the workers' compensation systems of these countries to occur in all painters exposed to paint solvents for seven years or more. In the United States, where this new syndrome is beginning to spread and to affect litigation, clinical neurologists do not agree on a physical basis. Some argue that variability across subtests of the Wechsler Adult Intelligence Scale-Revised (WAISR), across psychomotor and attention tests, or across emotional reactivity measures is evidence of neurotoxic damage. Some argue that the scores of appropriate control groups do not differ from the scores of painters and that psychologists have given a false syndrome legal respectability.[10] (See Cherry, Hutchins, Pace, & Waldron, 1985; Gregersen, Angelso, Nielsen, Norgaard, & Uldal, 1984; Gregersen, Klausen, & Elsnab, 1987; White & Feldman, 1987.)

These examples illustrate, we think, that it is not simply RSI that is significant, but the existence of socially legitimated work-related health problems. Once a socially valid health problem is created, it becomes an avenue and occasion for workers to express and reveal pain— and in some cases negative feelings about their jobs— without fear of reprisal. That is, an RSI problem in Australia or an eye strain problem in Sweden is likely to be taken seriously by superiors. To address these problems requires addressing both the underlying causes and the mechanisms through which injuries are expressed. We believe that this article describes some of the causes in a speculative fashion and suggests the direction research should take. We do not claim that RSI and other new-technology health issues are purely social in nature. Indeed, the evidence we have reviewed is not inconsistent with the view—strongly held by many laypeople and professionals—that socially conditioned illness always has a physiological basis and, ultimately, a physiological cure. But we feel that examining these problems from a social perspective provides valuable insight that is lost when these problems are regarded solely as individual medical/biomechanical problems.

Our analysis does not resolve the problem of how to categorize RSI as a health problem. RSI stands at the intersection of three traditional categories of illness: physical overuse injury, psychophysiological syndrome, and hysterical or conversion illness. Overuse injuries such as writer's cramp and tennis elbow can be measured physiologically, and they vary with physical changes such as rest and drug therapy. Psychophysiological syndromes such as asthma and hypertension can be measured physiologically, and they vary with physical changes and with social changes such as psychological treatment and leaving work. Conversion illnesses such as hysterical paralysis and shellshock cannot be measured physiologically, and they vary with social changes. RSI, falling somewhere in these categories, is a classic

---

[10]The authors wish to thank an anonymous reviewer for this information on painter's syndrome and for pointing us to the literature on this subject.

demonstration of some anomalies and inadequacies of the existing paradigm of clinical knowledge. It seems clear that the professional and public definition of an illness/injury such as RSI does not occur in a vacuum and that it is important to try to understand its social, organizational, economic, and political context. Research using a social perspective would improve our ability to discriminate among RSI problems and would lead to better understanding of schemes for classifying occupational illness.

REFERENCES

Aguren, S., Bredbacka, C., Hansson, R., Ihregren, K., & Karlson, K. G. (1984). *Volvo Kalmar revisited*. Stockholm, Sweden: Efficiency and Participation Council SAF-LO-PTK.

Armstrong, T. J. (1983). *Ergonomics guides: An ergonomics guide to carpal tunnel syndrome*. Cleveland, OH: American Industrial Hygiene Association.

Armstrong, T. J., & Chaffin, D. (1979a). Carpal tunnel syndrome and selected personal attributes. *Journal of Occupational Medicine, 21*, 481-486.

Armstrong, T. J., & Chaffin, D. (l979b). Some biomechanical aspects of the carpal tunnel. *Journal of Biomechanics, 12,.*567-570.

Armstrong, T. J., Foulke, J. A., Joseph, B. S., & Goldstein, S. A. (1982). Investigation of cumulative trauma disorders in a poultry processing plant. *American Industrial Hygiene Association, 43*, 103-116.

Australian Council of Trade Unions-Victorian Trades Hall Council. (1982). Health and safety unit. *Health and Safety Bulletin, 12*, 17-19.

Baidya, K. N., & Stevenson, M. G. (1982). *The cost to industry of tenosynovitis and related diseases associated with repetitive work*. Paper presented at the 52nd meeting of the ANZASS Congress, Macquarie University, Sydney, Australia.

Barnes, C., & Currey, H. (1967). Carpal tunnel syndrome on rheumatoid arthritis, a clinical and electrodiagnostic survey. *Annual of Rheumatic Disorders, 26*, 226-233.

Bevege, M., James, J., & Shute, C. (Eds.). (1982). *Worth her salt: Women at work in Australia*. Sydney, Australia: Hale & Iremonger.

Brown, M. C., & Dwyer, J. M. (1983). *Repetition strain injury: An approach to treatment and prevention*. Melbourne, Australia: Ergonomics Society of Australia and New Zealand.

Browne, C. D., Nolan, B. M., & Faithfull, D. K. (1984). Occupational repetition strain injur: s: Guidelines for diagnosis and treatment. *The Medical Journal of Australia, 140*, 329-332.

Caporael, L. R. (1976). Ergotism: The satan loosed in Salem? *Science, 192,*17-19.

Cherry, N., Hutchins, T. P., Pace, T., & Waldron, H. A. (1985). Neurobehavioural effects of repeated occupational exposure to toluene and paint solvents. *British Journal of Industrial Medicine, 42*, 291-300.

Cseuz, K. A., Thomas, J. E., Lambert, E. H., Love, J. G., & Lipscomb, P. R. (1966). Long-term results of operation for carpal tunnel syndrome. *Mayo Clinic Proceedings, 41*, 232-241,

Dargan, J. (1985). The railway telegraph. *Australian Railway Historical Society 36*, 49-71.

Ferguson, D. (1971a). Repetition injuries in process workers. *Medical Journal of Australia. 2*, 408-411.

Ferguson, D. (197lb). An Australian study of telegraphist's cramp. *British Journal of Medicine. 28*, 280-285.

Ferguson, D. (1984). The "new" industrial epidemic. *The Medical Journal of Australia, 2*, 318-319.

Folkers, K. (1986, April 21). Contemporary therapy with Vitamin B$_6$, Vitamin B$_2$, and Coenzyme Q$_{10}$. *Chemical and Engineering News*, pp. 27-30, 55-56.

Fordyce, W. E. (1979). Environmental factors in the genesis of low back pain. In J. Bonica, J. Liebeskind, & V. Albe-Fessard (Eds.), *Advances in pain research and therapy* (pp. 659-666). New York: Raven Press.

Fordyce, W. E., Brockway, J., Bergman, J., & Spengler, D. (1986). A control group comparison of behavioral versus traditional management methods in acute low back pain. *Journal of Behavioral Medicine, 5*, 127-140.

Franklin, M. (1986). *My brilliant career.* New South Wales, Australia: Angus & Robertson. (Original work published 1901)

Frymoyer, J. W., & Bland, J. (1973). Carpal tunnel syndrome in patients with myxedematous arthropathy. *Journal of Bone and Joint Surgery 55*, 78–81.

Galbraith, M. (1985, June). RSI—Control the curse: Curb the costs. The *Australian Secretary 10*(2), 10-I1.

Glaberson, W. (1987, June 14). Misery on the meatpacking line. *New York Times*, Section 3, pp. l, 8.

Gregersen, P., Angelso, B., Nielsen, T. E., Norgaard, B., & Uldal, C. (1984). Neurotoxic effects of organic solvents in exposed workers: An occupational, neuropsychological, and neurological investigation. *American Journal of Industrial Medicine, 5*, .201-225.

Gregersen, P., Klausen, H., & Elsnab, C. U. (1987). Chronic toxic encephalopathy in solvent.exposed painters in Denmark, 1976-1980 Clinical cases and social consequences after a 5-year follow-up. *American Journal of Industrial Medicine*, 11, 399-417.

Gyllenhammar, P. G. (1977). *People at work.* Reading, MA: Addison Wesley.

Hagbert, M., Michaelson, G., & Ortelius, A. (1982). Serum creatinine kinase as an indicator of local muscle strain in experimental and   occupational work. *International Archives of Occupational and Environmental Health.* 50,377-386.

Hartman, K. (1987). Secretaries and computers. In S. Kiesler & L. Sproull (Eds.), *Computing and change on campus* (pp. 114-130). New York: Cambridge University Press.

Horton, S. (1984, May). Computer hazards. *Playgirl*, pp. 90-92,97.

Kendall, D. (1960). Aetiology, diagnosis, and treatment of paraesthesiae in the hands. *British Medical Journal, 2*, 1633-1640.

Kivi, P. (1984). Rheumatic disorders of the upper limbs associated with repetitive occupational tasks in Finland in 1975-1979. *Scandinavian Journal of Rheumatology 13*, 101-107.

Klar, L. N. (1983). New Zealand's accident compensation scheme: A tort lawyer's perspective. *University of Toronto Law Journal, 80*, 80-107.

Kvsrnstrom, S. (1983a). Diseases of the musculo-skeletal system in an engineering eomtsny. *Scandinavian Journal of Rehabilitation Medicine Suppl., 8*, 61-70.

Kvarnstrom, S. (1983b). Occupational cervicobrachial disorders in an engineering company. *Scandinavian Journal of Rehabilitation Medicine, 8*, 77-100.

Laubli, T. (1982). *Cervicobrachial syndrome in visual display terminal operators.* Paper presented at the international workshop meeting of the Neck and Upper Limb Disorders Due to Repetitive Movements and Constrained Postures, Tokyo.

Lee, G., & Wrench, J. (1982). Piecework and industrial accidents: Two contemporary case studies. *Sociology 16*, 513-525.

Levick, P. (1986, May). *Occupational overuse disorders in a university.* Paper presented at the meeting of the Australian Physiotherapy As sociation Congress, Brisbane.

Littlejohn, G. (1986, May). Is repetitive strain injury a separate medical entity? In M. Wallace (Ed.), *Occupational pain (RSI): Proceedings of seminar "Occupational Pain (RSI)"* held at La Trobe University and Macquarie University Bundoora, Australia: Brain-Behaviour Institute.

Lucire, Y. (1981, November 21). *Neurosis in the workplace.* Paper presented at the RSI Medical Mythology Seminar, Sydney, Australia.

Magarey, S. (1985). Women and technological change. *Australian Feminist Studies. 1,* 91—103.

Masear, V. R., Hayes, J. M., & Hyde, A. G. (1986). An industrial cause of carpal tunnel syndrome. *Journal of Hand Surgery 11A,* 222-227.

Matthews, K. P., Scheier, M., Brunson, B. E., & Carducci, B. (1980). Attention, unpredictability, and reports of physical symptoms. *Journal of Personality and Social Psychology 38,* 525-537.

McIntosh, P. (1986, November 21). The RSI epidemic: Technology spawns its own disease. *The Age,* p. 17.

Mersina, (1985, August-October), A day in my life. *WR.I.S.T Newsletter* p. 19.

Mills, C. G., & Sallans, P. (1984). *Survey: Repetition injury syndrome. Telecom operators using screen-based equipment.* (Report to Telecom Occupational Health Service, Western Australia)

Morrissey, M. (1985). Technological change and occupational health. In S. Hill & R. Johnston (Eds.), *Future tense? Technology in Australia* (pp. 137-153), Queensland, Australia: University of Quecnsland Press.

Najman, J. (1978). A social epidemiology of accident deaths in Australia. *Control,* 3-17.

National Occupational Health and Safety Commission, Australia. (1985). *Interim report of the RSI committee.* Canberra, Australia: Australian Government Publishing Service.

National Occupational Health and Safety Commission, Australia. (1986). *Repetition strain injury: A report and model code of practice.* Canberra, Australia: Australian Government Publishing Service.

Noro, K. (1984). Educational and training in relationship between man and robot. In H. W. Hendrick & O. Brown (Eds.), *Human factors in organizational design and management* (pp. 441-445). Amsterdam: Elsevier.

O'Mara, N.(1 984, October 12-18). Hi-tech epidemic: Victims of a bright new technology that maims. *The National Times.* pp. 15-18.

Ostberg, O., Moller, L., & Ahlstrom, G. (1986). Ergonomie procurement guidelines for visual display units as a tool for progressive change. *Behaviour and Information Technology 5,* 71-80.

Ostberg, O., & Nilsson, C. (1985). Emerging technology and stress. In C. L, Cooper & M. J Smith (Eds.), *Job stress and blue collar work* (pp. 149-169). New York: Wiley,

Owen, E. R, (1985), Instrumental musicians and RSI. *Journal of Occupational Health and Safety Australia, 1,* 135-139.

Oxenburgh, M. (1984). *Musculo-skeletal injuries occurring in word processor operators.* Sydney, Australia: Ergonomics Society of Australia and New Zealand.

Palmer, G. (1979). *Compensation for incapacity: A study of law and social change in New Zealand and Australia.* Wellington, New Zealand: Oxford University Press,

Prerost, S. (1982). Technological change and women's employment in Australia. In M. Bevege, M. James, & C. Shute (Eds.), *Worth her salt: Women at work in Australia* (pp. 134-147). Sydney, Australia: Hale & lremonger.

Pulket, C., & Kogi, K. (1984). *Fatigue of visual display unit operators in the free break system.* Paper presented at the meeting of the Inter national Occupational Health Congress, Dublin.

Quinlan, M. (1984a). *The industrial relations of occupational health.* Queensland, Australia: Griffith University.

Quinlan, M. (1984b). Technological innovation and occupational health. In R. Lansbury & E. Davis (Eds.), *Technology, work and industrial relations* (pp. 153-176). Melbourne, Australia: Longman and Cheshire.

Ramazzini, B. (1940). *Diseases of workers* (W. C. Wright, Trans.). Chicago: University of Chicago Press. (Original work published 1713)

Red Fems. (1982). The implications of technological change for women workers in the public sector. In M. Bevege, M. James, & C. Shute (Eds.), *Worth her salt: Women at work in Australia* (pp. 148-162). Sydney, Australia: Hale & Iremonger.

RSI: Scientists seek solutions to centuries-old health problem. (1986, September 24). *University News (Queensland),* p. 3.

Ryan, G.A. (1986). *RSI: The clinical picture.* Bundoora, Australia: Brain Behaviour Institute.

Ryan, G.A., Mullerworth, J. H. M., & Bampton, M.(1 985). Repetition injury and the influence of the work environment. *Journal of Occupational Health and Safety Australia and New Zealand, 1,* 172.

Ryan, G.A., Mullerworth, J. H. M., & Pimble, J. (1984). *The prevalence ofrepetition strain injury in data process operators.* Sydney, Australia: Ergonomics Society of Australia & New Zealand.

Sabour, M., & Fadel, H. (1970). The carpal tunnel syndrome: A new complication ascribed to the "pill." *American Obstetrics and Gynecology, 107,* 1265-1267.

Salancik, G., & Pfeffer, J. (1978). A social information processing approach to job attitudes and task design. *Administrative Science Quarterly 23,* 224-253.

Sampson, A. (1971). The myth of accident-proneness. *Medical Journal ofAustralia,* 913-916.

Smith, G. E. (1986, February 4), Change of diet could be key to relief of RSI pain. *Sun Living* (Suppl.), p. Il.

South Australian Health Commission, Public Service Board, Public Service Association. (1984). *Preventing repetition strain injuries in keyboard operators.* Adelaide, Australia: Author.

Spillane, R. (1986), *RSI: Medical mythology.* Bundoora, Australia: Brain Behaviour Institute.

Stone, W, E. (1983). Repetitive strain injuries. *The Medical Journal of Australia, 2,* 616-618.

Sutton, R. I., & Rafael, A. (1987). Characteristics of work stations as potential occupational stressors. *Academy of Management Journal, 30,* 160-176.

Sword, R. (1986, June). Carpal tunnel syndrome. *Windsurf,* p. 24.

Taylor, R., Gow, C., & Corbett, S. (1982). Repetition injury in process workers. *Community Health Studies, 6,* 7-13.

Thompson, A. R., Plewes, L. W., & Shaw, E. G. (1951). Peritendinitis crepitans and simple tenosynovitis: A clinical study of 54 cases in industry. *British Journal of Industrial Medicine, 8,* 150-158.

Thompson, H. T., & Sinclair, J. (1912). Telegraphist's cramp. *Lancet,* 889-890, 941-944, 1008-1010.

Tinsley, L. C. (1986). Key workers' compensation laws enacted by states in 1985. *Monthly Labor Review, 109,* 61-66.

U.S. Department of Health and Human Services. (1984). *Program of the National Institute for Occupational Safety and Health: Program plan by program areas for FY 1984-1989* (DHAS NIOSH Publication No. 84-107). Atlanta, GA: National Institute for Occupational Safety and Health.

Walker, J. (1979). A crippling new epidemic in industry. *New Doctor,* 19-21.

Waugh, A. (1986, November 15). Introducing kangaroo's paw, a wonderful new disease from Australia. *The Spectator 8*, p. 8.

Welch, R. (1972). The causes of tenosynovitis in industry. *Industrial Medicine*, 14.

Western Australia Public Service Board. (1985, October). *Report of the repetitive strain injuries in the Western Australian Public Services Task Force*. Perth, Australia: Author.

Westgaard, R., & Aaras, A. (1980). *Static muscle load and illness among workers doing electromechanical assembly work*. Oslo, Norway: Institute of Work Physiology.

White, F. W., & Feldman, R. G. (1987). Neuropsychologlcal assessment of toxic encephalopathy. *American Journal of Industrial Medicine, 11*, 395-398.

Williams, P. (1985, August). Fighting a $400 million pain in the arm. *Today's Computers*, pp. 73-78.

Willis, E. (1986). Commentary: RSI as a social process. *Community Health Studies, 10*, 210-219.

Woman claims damage for RSI. (1986, February 2). *The Herald*, p. 7.

MANAGEMENT INVOLVEMENT: A KEY ELEMENT IN PREVENTING MUSCULOSKELETAL PROBLEMS IN VISUAL DISPLAY UNIT USERS IN AUSTRALIA[11]

Susan A. Rowe
Health Services, CSR Limited

The incidence of musculoskeletal symptoms reported among clerical workers using visual display units (VDU's) in Australia has risen steadily since 1981 (NOHSC 1985). In a large Sydney office complex a strategy has been developed to assist in the prevention of musculoskeletal symptoms, referred to as occupational over-use syndrome, also known as repetition strain injury.

The findings from a 3-year study of users reporting musculoskeletal symptoms to the occupational health centre, have formed the basis of evaluating and updating the strategy. Over 3 years there has been a significant reduction in the incidence of reporting musculoskeletal symptoms and time lost from work.

VDU GUIDELINES: COMPONENTS OF THE STRATEGY

The strategy, an integral part of the company's occupational health and safety programme, was supported by senior management. It consisted of five key elements:

(i) *Assessment of operators*: health-including assessment of vision and the musculoskeletal system; skills-capabilities assessed as part of the training process.

(ii) *Training:* operators-including instructions on technical VDU use, ergonomic aspects, posture and keying technique, health aspects and work organization; managers-emphasizing responsibility for preventing adverse health effects.

(iii) *Workstation*: design, environmental aspects, furniture and hardware in accordance with accepted ergonomic principles.

(iv) *Work organization*: jobs designed to provide variety and flexibility in tasks demand, work flow organized to avoid deadlines, rest and exercise pauses during continuous keyboard work.

(v) *Treatment and rehabilitation:* a working environment conducive to reporting health problems; prompt access to appropriate health professionals. Detailed guidelines for the implementation of the strategy were disseminated to managers and VDU users. Briefing sessions were run

[11]From Rowe, S.A. (1987). Management involvement: A key element in preventing musculoskeletal problems in visual display unit users in Australia. Special Issue: Musculoskeletal injuries in the workplace. *Ergonomics, 30,* 367-372. Reprinted by permission.

by members of the occupational health team to assist in the communication process.

CASE REVIEW I MARCH 1984

By March 1984, 45 VDU users had presented themselves at the occupational health centre reporting complaints. These included fatigue, discomfort, pain, tenderness and limitation of function in muscle and tendon groups in the upper limbs and neck. These symptoms or signs were referred to as occupational over-use syndrome as described by Browne *et al.* (1984). These cases were investigated and compared with a symptom-free control group in similar jobs. Investigation and comparison included assessment of each workstation and an analysis of the work-load. These findings are reported fully by Oxenburgh (1984).

The comparison between the controls and cases revealed no significant differences in age, years of service, performance rating and ergonomic factors including type of keyboard, height of desk and chair and lighting levels. The most significant finding was the difference in work-load. From the control group 72% spent less than 5 hours each day at the keyboard, while over 80% of the cases reported spending more than 5 hours each day at the keyboard.

The control strategy

Based on the findings of the case review, the control strategy was reassessed and revised. This included placing greater emphasis on the importance of work organization and work load. The VDU guidelines were reissued in a brochure and included the following comments regarding the organization of work:

Managers and operators should work together to establish systems of work which include:

- limiting continuous keyboard work to 40-50 min before changing for 10-15 min to other duties;
- managers having sufficient understanding of the task load;
- organizing work flow to avoid rush and unnecessary deadlines and hence stressful periods;
- work priorities organized by managers, especially where the operator receives work from more than one person, and communicating these priorities to all persons in the work group;
- avoiding unnecessary drafts of documents as editing has been a major source of strain;
- sharing work among operators in the same or adjacent groups to ensure a fair distribution of work-avoiding the 'private secretary' syndrome;
- avoiding job categories that keep people glued to a VDU, for example 'word processor operator' and 'data entry operator', and providing a variety of tasks;
- avoiding overloading the best workers.

Treatment and rehabilitation

Early, accurate assessment and involvement of appropriate health professionals was found to be necessary to enhance recovery. VDU users reporting to the health centre were assessed initially by the occupational health nurse using a standardized assessment format. All cases were also assessed by a medical practitioner. A team approach to treatment and rehabilitation was adopted and involved a range of health practitioners including nurses, doctors, physiotherapists, chiropractors and other medical specialists as indicated.

Our experience has shown that treatment should be simple, commenced promptly and aimed at: relieving physical discomfort and restoring full functioning; minimizing anxiety and muscle tension; correcting contributing factors.

Physical/psychosocial aspects included: promoting circulation, using intermittent cold packs, heat to neck muscles, perhaps gentle massage, low pulsed ultrasound, and non-aggravating exercise such as walking, jogging or a heated pool/spa; learning and practising relaxation techniques; resting the affected area, sometimes bandaging or light splinting, and modifying the activities of daily living; self-development and assertiveness training.

Workplace aspects included: checking workstation adjustment; reducing the work rate, varying the work tasks and incorporating adequate rest periods; avoiding tasks which may aggravate symptoms such as typing, stapling, hole punching, stamping, extended periods of writing, filing and photocopying; transferring to appropriate non-repetitive tasks if necessary; gradually returning to full work load.

Planning individualized programmes for a graduated return to normal work was essential. Through discussions between the person, their supervisor and occupational health advisers, a timetable for monitoring progress was established. Short and long term goals that could be regularly reviewed were set and, where appropriate, activities upgraded to meet these goals. Another important aspect of the programme was ensuring that the person and their supervisors clearly understood any work restrictions and physical limitations, and the appropriate actions to be taken should problems arise.

CASE REVIEW II (MARCH 1985)

By March 1985, an additional 40 people using VDUs had presented themselves at the occupational health centre reporting symptoms classified as over-use syndrome. A comparison was then made between the 45 cases reported up to March 1984 (group A) and the 40 cases reported between April 1984 and March 1985 (group B).

Several significant differences between the two groups were noted:
• the symptoms reported by group B were much less severe than group A;
• the number of clerical workers reporting symptoms had decreased but there was a rise in other groups, such as accountants and programmers;

- the total number of days lost for group A was 1527 days and for group B was 135 days; the mean number of days lost per person for group A was 34 but for group B was only 3 days;
- the total number of days on alternative and/or restricted work for group A was 4087 and for group B was 1258 days;
- the mean number of days on alternative and/or restricted work per person for group A was 91 but for group B only 32 days.

The Wilcoxon rank-sum test was used to determine the statistical significance between days lost from work for each group and days on alternative work for each group. There was a significant difference ($P < 0.01$) between group A and group B when testing days lost and alternative work, with group B results being better than group A in both categories. These results are reported fully by Oxenburgh *et al.* (1985).

The information gained from the case analysis again provided a basis for a further review of our control strategy. Indications were that the treatment and rehabilitation aspects of the programme were more successful, indicated by an improved recovery rate and reduced lost time. Group A had 44% fully fit (15 months after the end of the reporting period for this group) compared with 73% fully fit for group B (3 months after the end of the reporting period).

Treatment and rehabilitation patterns had changed, so that people were maintained at work on an appropriate alternative work programme rather than resting away from work. Some cases did not require medical intervention and were managed by the occupational health nurse in consultation with the person's manager.

It was found that psychosocial factors in the person's work and external environment significantly affected their response to pain, rehabilitation and ultimate return to full, productive work. Training in relaxation and assertive communication were important aspects of the rehabilitation programme.

Management briefing

To maintain a high level of management involvement, briefing sessions for managers were arranged following the case reviews. These sessions included; reviewing the incidence rate of over-use syndrome; identifying probable contributing factors including the interaction between the physical and psychosocial aspects; emphasizing the need for continued management support in rehabilitation, including the provision of meaningful and productive alternative work and job restructuring; identifying the need for management support for changes in VDU-user's training programmes and for further management action in areas of work balancing and priority setting; reviewing the cost to the company in worker's compensation, reduced productivity and human terms.

Table 4.3
Differences between groups at March 1986.

	Group A	Group B	Group C
People reporting symptoms	45	40	17
Total days lost	1627	225	5
Total days on alternative/ restrictive work	4532	2511	557

CASE REVIEW III (MARCH 1986)

By March 1986 a further 17 people using VDUs had reported symptoms classified as over-use syndrome. These 17 cases (group C) were compared with the cases in groups A and B. The findings have been summarized in Table 4.3. Since the March 1985 case review, some people in groups A and B continued to spend time away from work or on alternative work. These days have been added to the previous figures for each group.

The Wilcoxon rank-sum test was again used to confirm differences between the groups. There was a significant difference between groups B and C in lost time (P<0.0l), group C results being better than group B, with no significant difference in alternative work days. Similar conclusions could be drawn between groups A and C.

Over the 3 years of the study, there has also been an increase in the number of people who have fully recovered and resumed their original work tasks. This is shown in Table 4.4.

CONCLUSION

The information gained from the over-use syndrome case reviews provided a useful basis on which to evaluate the effectiveness of our control strategy. The findings confirm the value of a positive approach to prevention and rehabilitation in the workplace. Managers and workers using VDUs have been kept informed at review and training sessions about successful aspects of the strategy and about areas requiring more concerted effort.

There are no easy answers to managing these perplexing problems once

Table 4.4
Return to work results: all groups.[*]

	Group A		Group B		Group C	
	N	%	N	%	N	%
Fully fit for work	20	44	29	73	13	76
Fit but some restrictions[**]	22	49	10	25	2	12
Still on alternative work	3	17	1	25	2	12

[*] For those people who had left the company before 31 March 1986, their work status is recorded at their date of leaving.

[**] This means that at 31 March 1986 their capacity for keyboard work was less than 40 minutes in each hour.

they occur; continued efforts must be made toward prevention, particularly in relation to organization.

REFERENCES

Brown, C. D., Nolan. B. M., and Faithfull, D. K., 1984, Occupational repetition strain injuries. *Medical Journal of Australia*, 140, 329-332.
National Occupational Health and Safety Commission (NOHSC), 1985, Interim Report of the RSI Committee Australian Government Public Service, Canberra, Part I.
Oxenburgh, M. S., 1984, Musculoskeletal injuries occurring in word processor operators. *Proceedings of the 21st Annual Conference of the Ergonomics Society of Australia and New Zealand*. Sydney, pp. 137-143.
Oxenburgh, M. S., Rowe, S. A., and Douglas, D. B., 1985, Repetition strain injury in keyboard operators. *Journal of Occupational Health and Safety ANZ.* l, 106-112.

READING QUESTIONS

1) What do Kiesler and Finholt mean when they say: "RSI is an extreme example of how the social context of work ... defines and determines the nature of occupational health problems."?
2) What are the symptoms of RSI? What are the standard medical treatments?
3) What are the two forms of RSI that Kiesler and Finholt present?
4) What are the two reasons that computing might cause RSI in clerical jobs?
5) What single individual characteristic of workers is the best predictor of whether they will get RSI?
6) Why might the use of oral contraception be associated with RSI?
7) Why is "accident proneness" not a good explanation of RSI?
8) How might job dissatisfaction cause RSI?
9) What ergonomic problems are associated with RSI? Why do medical experts concentrate on these causes rather than other sorts of job adjustment (e.g., varied work tasks)?
10) What do Kiesler and Finholt mean by "Are people getting sick from doing the job or having the job?"?
11) Why might a system that allows breaks in jobs not be a good answer to RSI?
12) According to workers who have it, what are the two best treatments for RSI?
13) How is the introduction of computing into the office associated with stress and changes in job satisfaction? How might these changes be responsible for RSI complaints?
14) What mechanisms have legitimized RSI as a complaint for office workers?
15) What job changes do Kiesler and Finholt recommend to reduce RSI complaints among office workers?
16) "Once a socially valid health problem is created, it becomes an avenue and occasion for workers to express and reveal pain ... without fear of reprisal." Relate this to back injury, VDT-produced eye strain and RSI.
17) Which aspects of Rowe's control strategy for RSI are physical? Which are social or job structure related? Are there some that serve both functions?
18) Why would Rowe include self-development and assertiveness training in the program? How might this help?

DISCUSSION QUESTIONS

1) Kiesler and Finholt say: "People with RSI are rarely malingering" and also "the only way [women] can gain sympathy, if not respect, is to get injured." How can you reconcile these two statements?

2) Will treating RSI as partially caused by job structure and social context make it less legitimate as an illness? If so, how might this be a good result of this inquiry?

PRACTICING THE DESIGN ETHIC

1) Investigate your school's (company's) policy concerning work-related injuries. Work in teams and schedule short interviews with someone in the school/company's human resources department, computer department, and a department that uses the school/business's computer (for example, registrar's office or secretarial staff). Each member of the team should interview at least two people, and ensure that all three departments are covered. Try to include at least one manager and one nonmanager in your interviews. As the interviews proceed try to clarify the following:
   • What is the school/company's policy about work-related injury involving a computer?
   • Do they believe there are computer-related health issues such as RSI and EMF? Why or why not?
   • Do they consider these health issues important? Why or why not?
   • What kind of work do they do on the computer terminal, and how much do they use the terminal?
   • Have your interviewees noticed any difference in health problems after a new system was installed?

   After the interviews are complete, get together as a team and analyze the data. Determine the following things about the viewpoints regarding computer-related health issues:
   • Are there any patterns (similar/dissimilar viewpoints) among the departments?
   • Are there any differences in the reports from managers and nonmanagers?
   • Are there differences in viewpoints between the men and women you interviewed?
   • Are there differences in viewpoints among the departments? How do you account for this?

2) Visit a public computer lab at your school and observe (for at least an hour) the practices of those using the machines there. On the basis of your observations and the program suggested by Rowe, design a program to help minimize RSI-related injuries among those who use that lab.

Chapter 5

CRITICAL SYSTEMS

Most headlines and news stories that document technology-related tragedy finger a single culprit for the crime. This is usually a person involved in the immediate operation or maintenance of the technology in question. If only he had checked the pressure gauges more often, or if only she had been alert enough to follow the correct instructions, this would not have happened. This leads reformers to concentrate on firing the guilty as the solution to the problem.

In this chapter, both Reason and Parnas take issue with this approach to safety-critical technology. They find the culprit distributed throughout the system involved—including social, organizational, personnel, and technical factors in their analysis. Reason's analysis is based on extensive research in social, organizational, and cognitive psychology. Parnas's analysis is based on extensive experience in development of a particular kind of safety-critical system: weapons systems.

Reason's work is reprinted here in some detail. This is because the analysis he presents is not well known in computer science circles and deserves wider distribution. Second, the analysis exposes the myriad interconnections between the social and organizational factors and the technical factors in safety-critical systems. It makes it clear that computer scientists who want to promote safe systems need to be aware of the entire system, rather than just the single technical component for which they have responsibility.

In more concrete terms, Parnas makes this point too. Systems that work well in the lab, under what seem to be reasonable testing conditions, will fail in the rigors of battle. And if the system is being tested under battle conditions for the first time, it is sure to fail, since even excellent designers and testers cannot anticipate the complexities that arise in the confusion of battle. If systems must evolve in order to attain a reasonable level of reliability, then basing our defense on systems that cannot be tested seems a great risk. This is a specific example of Reason's more general point: Latent errors are difficult to discover in any system, and these are the real threats to system safety.

LATENT ERRORS AND SYSTEMS DISASTERS[1]

James Reason
University of Manchester

In considering the human contribution to systems disasters, it is important to distinguish two kinds of error: active error, whose effects are felt almost immediately, and latent error whose adverse consequences may lie dormant within the system for a long time, only becoming evident when they combine with other factors to breach the system's defences (see Rasmussen & Pedersen, 1984). In general, active errors are associated with the performance of the 'front-line' operators of a complex system: pilots, air traffic controllers, ships' officers, control room crews and the like. Latent errors, on the other hand, are most likely to be spawned by those whose activities are removed in both time and space from the direct control interface: designers, high-level decision makers, construction workers, managers and maintenance personnel.

Detailed analyses of recent accidents, most particularly those at Flixborough, Three Mile Island, Heysel Stadium, Bhopal, Chernobyl and Zeebrugge, as well as the Challenger disaster, have made it increasingly apparent that latent errors pose the greatest threat to the safety of a complex system. In the past, reliability analyses and accident investigations have focused primarily upon active operator errors and equipment failures. While operators can, and frequently do, make errors in their attempts to recover from an out-of-tolerance system state, many of the root causes of the emergency were usually present within the system long before these active errors were committed.

Rather than being the main instigators of an accident, operators tend to be the inheritors of system defects created by poor design, incorrect installation, faulty maintenance and bad management decisions. Their part is usually that of adding the final garnish to a lethal brew whose ingredients have already been long in the cooking.

There is a growing awareness within the human reliability community that attempts to discover and neutralise these latent failures will have a greater beneficial effect upon system safety than will localised efforts to minimise active errors. To date, much of the work of human factors specialists has been directed at improving the immediate human-system interface (i.e., the control room or cockpit). While this is undeniably an important enterprise, it only addresses a relatively small part of the total safety problem, being aimed primarily at reducing the 'active failure' tip of

---

[1] Chapter 7 from *Human Error* by James Reason, New York: Cambridge University Press, 1990. Copyright © Cambridge University Press. Reprinted by permission.

the causal iceberg. One thing that has been profitably learned over the past few years is that, in regard to safety issues, the term 'human factors' embraces a far wider range of individuals and activities than those associated with the front-line operation of a system. Indeed, a central theme of this chapter is that the more removed individuals are from these front-line activities (and, incidentally, from direct hazards), the greater is their potential danger to the system.

Other attempts to minimise errors have been purely reactive in nature, being concerned with eliminating the recurrence of particular active failures identified *post hoc* by accident investigators. Again, while it is sensible to learn as many remedial lessons as possible from past accidents, it must also be appreciated that such events are usually caused by the unique conjunction of several necessary but singly insufficient factors. Since the same mixture of causes is unlikely to recur, efforts to prevent the repetition of specific active errors will have only a limited impact on the safety of the system as a whole. At worst, they merely find better ways of securing a particular stable door once its occupant has bolted.

This chapter considers the contribution of latent errors to the catastrophic breakdown of a number of different complex systems. Since the notion of latent error is intimately bound up with the character of contemporary technology, I begin by summarising some of the significant changes that have occurred in the control of high-risk systems over the past few decades. I also consider some of the psychological problems associated with the supervisory control of complex systems.

1. TECHNOLOGICAL DEVELOPMENTS

Over the past 30 to 40 years, a technological revolution has occurred in the design and control of high-risk systems. This, in turn, has brought about radical (and still little understood) changes in the tasks that their human elements are called upon to perform. Some of the more important factors affecting human performance are outlined below.

1.1. SYSTEMS HAVE BECOME MORE AUTOMATED

One of the most remarkable developments of recent years has been the extent to which operators have become increasingly remote from the processes that they nominally control. Machines of growing complexity have come to intervene between the human and the physical task.

In the beginning, operators employed direct sensing and manipulation. They saw and touched what they controlled or produced. Then came the intervention of remote sensing and manipulation devices. Either the process was too dangerous or too sensitive to handle directly, or there was a need to extend human muscle power or the operator's unaided senses were insufficient to detect important physical changes.

But the most profound changes came with the advent of cheap computing power. Now the operator can be separated from the process by at least two

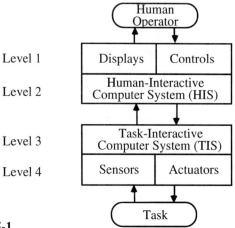

Figure 5-1
The basic elements of supervisory control (after Moray, 1986).

components of the control system. At the lowest level, there are task-interactive systems controlling the various detailed aspects of the operation. And intervening between the specialised task-interactive systems and the operators is the human-system interface, where the control system presents various selected pieces of information to the operators. This interface generally permits only a very prescribed degree of interaction between the human and the now remote process.

This is the situation termed supervisory control, defined by Sheridan and Hennessy (1984) as "initiating, monitoring, and adjusting processes in systems that are otherwise automatically controlled." The basic features of human supervisory control are shown in Figure 5-1.

According to Moray (1986), true supervisory control is achieved through four distinct levels. The lowest two levels comprise the task-interactive system (TIS). This exercises closed-loop control over the hardware components of the task (e.g., propellers, engines, pumps, switches, valves and heaters) through automatic subsystems (e.g., thermostats, autopilots, governors, preprogrammed robots and packaged subroutines). The TIS can trim the system to predetermined set points, but it is incapable of adjusting these set points or of initiating any kind of adaptive response. The TIS is controlled by the human- interactive system (HIS). This comprises the top two levels of the control hierarchy. The HIS is an 'intelligent' computer that intercedes between the human operator and the lower-level controllers. This is the distinctive feature of human supervisory control. The HIS communicates the state of the system to the operator through its displays. It also receives commands from the operator regarding new goals and set points. Its intelligence lies in the fact that it can use its stored knowledge to issue tactical commands to the TIS that will optimise various performance criteria.

Such a control system has brought about a radical transformation of the human-system relationship. As Moray (1986, pp. 404-405)) has pointed out:

There is a real sense in which the computer rather than the human becomes the central actor. For most of the time the computer will be making the decisions about control, and about what to tell or ask the operator. The latter may either pre-empt control or accept it when asked to do so by the computer. But normally, despite the fact that the human defines the goals for the computer, the latter is in control. The computer is the heart of the system.

We have thus traced a progression from where the human is the prime mover and the computer the slave to one in which the roles are very largely reversed. For most of the time, the operator's task is reduced to that of monitoring the system to ensure that it continues to function within normal limits. The advantages of such a system are obvious; the operator's workload is substantially reduced, and the HIS performs tasks that the human can specify but cannot actually do (see Moray, 1986, for a complete list of the advantages of supervisory control). However, the main reason for the human operator's continued presence is to use his still unique powers of knowledge-based reasoning to cope with system emergencies. And this, as will be discussed in Section 2, is a task peculiarly ill-suited to the particular strengths and weaknesses of human cognition.

1.2. SYSTEMS HAVE BECOME MORE COMPLEX AND MORE DANGEROUS

One of the accompaniments of the increasing computerisation has been that high-risk systems such as nuclear power plants and chemical process installations have become larger and more complex. This means that greater amounts of potentially hazardous materials are concentrated in single sites under the centralised control of fewer operators. Catastrophic breakdowns of these systems pose serious threats not only for those within the plant, but also for the neighbouring public. And, in the case of nuclear power plants and weapons systems, this risk extends far beyond the immediate locality.

Complexity can be described in relation to a number of features. Perrow (1984) has identified two relatively independent system characteristics that are particularly important: complexity of interaction and tightness of coupling.

Systems may be more or less linear in their structure. Relatively complex, nonlinear systems possess the following general features (adapted from Perrow, 1984):

(a) Components that are not linked together in a production sequence are in close proximity.

(b) Many common-mode connections (i.e., components whose failure can have multiple effects 'downstream') are present.

(c) There is only a limited possibility of isolating failed components.

(d) Due to the high degree of specialization, there is little chance of substituting or reassigning personnel. The same lack of interchange ability is also true for supplies and materials.

(e) There are unfamiliar or unintended feedback loops.

(f) There are many control parameters that could potentially interact.

(g) Certain information about the state of the system must be obtained indirectly, or inferred.

(h) There is only a limited understanding of some processes, particularly those involving transformations.

In addition, the elements of a system may be coupled either tightly or loosely. The characteristics of a tightly-coupled system are listed below (adapted from Perrow, 1984):

(a) Processing delays are unacceptable.

(b) Production sequences are relatively invariant.

(c) There are few ways of achieving a particular goal.

(d) Little slack is permissible in supplies, equipment and personnel.

(e) Buffers and redundancies are deliberately designed into the system.

It should be stressed that interactiveness and tightness of coupling are tendencies, not hard-and-fast properties. No one system is likely to possess all the characteristics of complexity outlined above. Nuclear power plants, nuclear weapons systems, chemical process plants and large passenger aircraft are examples of systems that possess both a high degree of interaction and tightness of coupling. Dams, power grids, rail and marine transport have tight coupling but linear interactions. Mining operations, research and development companies, universities, and multigoal public agencies (such as the Department of Health and Social Security in Britain) have loose coupling and complex interactions. Trade schools, assembly-line production and most manufacturing plants have loose coupling and linear interactions.

1.3. SYSTEMS HAVE MORE DEFENCES AGAINST FAILURE

Because of the increasing unacceptability of a catastrophic disaster, and because of the widespread availability of intelligent hardware, designers have sought to provide automatic safety devices (ASDs) sufficient to protect the system against all the known scenarios of breakdown. According to Perrow (1984, p. 43): "The more complicated or tightly coupled the plant, the more attention is paid to reducing the occasion for failures."

The design of a modem nuclear power station is based upon the philosophy of 'defence in depth'. In addition to a large number of 'back-up' subsystems, one line of defence is provided by ASDs: devices that, having sensed an out-of-tolerance condition, automatically 'trip' the reactor, and/or switch off the turbines and/or release excess pressure. Not only are they programmed to shut down various aspects of the process, they also call in automatic safety systems, such as the emergency core cooling system (ECCS) or safety injection (51), should there be the danger of a core melt. A further line of defence is provided by the containment a massive concrete structure that prevents the accidental release of radioactive material to the outside world in the event of a failure of the ASDs. If all of these defences fail, and dangerous materials are released to the exterior, then it is hoped that their harmful consequences would be minimised by the general (though not universal) practice of siting nuclear power stations in sparsely populated areas.

For a catastrophe to happen, therefore, a number of apparently unlikely events need to occur in combination during the accident sequence (see Rasmussen & Pedersen, 1984). First, the ASDs must fail to restore the disturbed system to a safe state. Second, the containment must fail !o prevent the release of toxic material to the exterior. But such disasters still happen. One of the most obvious reasons is that the safety systems themselves are prey to human error, particularly of the latent kind. We are thus faced with a paradox: those specialised systems designed solely to make the plant safe are also its points of greatest weakness.

1.4. SYSTEMS HAVE BECOME MORE OPAQUE

One of the consequences of the developments outlined above is that complex, tightly-coupled and highly defended systems have become increasingly opaque to the people who manage, maintain and operate them. This opacity has two aspects: not knowing what is happening and not understanding what the system can do.

As we have seen, automation has wrought a fundamental change in the roles people play within certain high-risk technologies. Instead of having 'hands on' contact with the process, people have been promoted "to higher-level supervisory tasks and to long-term maintenance and planning tasks" (Rasmussen, 1988). In all cases, these are far removed from the immediate processing. What direct information they have is filtered through the computer-based interface. And, as many accidents have demonstrated, they often cannot find what they need to know while, at the same time, being deluged with information they do not want nor know how to interpret. In simpler, more linear systems, it was always possible for an operator or manager to go out and inspect the process at first hand, to examine directly the quality of the product, to look at the leaky valve or to talk to the experienced man or woman on the job. But these alternatives are not available in chemical and nuclear plants where an unapproachable and only partially understood process is largely hidden within a maze of pipes, reinforced vessels and concrete bunkers.

There is also another important factor contributing to system opacity: the system's own defences. Rasmussen (1988, pp. 3-4) has called this 'the fallacy of defence in depth'.

> Another important implication of the very nature of the 'defence in depth' philosophy is that the system very often does not respond

actively to single faults. Consequently, many errors and faults made by the staff and maintenance personnel do not directly reveal themselves by functional response from the system. Humans can operate with an extremely high level of reliability in a dynamic environment when slips and mistakes have immediately visible effects and can be corrected. Survival when driving through Paris during rush hours depends on this fact.

Compare this to working in a system designed according to the 'defence in depth' principle, where several independent events have to coincide before the system responds by visible changes in behaviour. Violation of safety preconditions during work on the system will probably not result in an immediate functional response, and latent effects of erroneous acts can therefore be left in the system. When such errors are allowed to be present in a system over a longer period of time, the probability of coincidence of the multiple faults necessary for release of an accident is drastically increased. Analyses of major accidents typically show that the basic safety of the system has eroded due to latent errors. A more significant contribution to safety can be expected from efforts to decrease the duration of latent errors than from measures to decrease the basic frequency.

1.5. THE IRONIES OF AUTOMATION

Lisanne Bainbridge (1987) of University College London has expressed in an elegant and concise form many of the difficulties that lie at the heart of the relationship between humans and machines in advanced technological installations. She calls them 'the ironies of automation'.

Many systems designers view human operators as unreliable and inefficient and strive to supplant them with automated devices. There are two ironies here. The first is that designers' errors, as discussed later in this chapter, make a significant contribution to accidents and events. The second is that the same designer who seeks to eliminate human beings still leaves the operator "to do the tasks which the designer cannot think how to automate" (Bainbridge, 1987, p. 272).

In an automated plant, operators' are required to monitor that the automatic system is functioning properly. But it is well known that even highly motivated operators cannot maintain effective vigilance for anything more than quite short periods; thus, they are demonstrably ill-suited to carry out this residual task of monitoring for rare, abnormal events. In order to aid them, designers need to provide automatic alarm signals. But who decides when these automatic alarms have failed or been switched off?

Another operator task is to take over manual control when the automatic control system fails. Manual control is a highly skilled activity, and skills must be practised continuously in order to maintain them. Yet an automatic control system that fails only rarely denies operators the opportunity for practising these basic control skills. One of the consequences of automation, therefore, is that operators become de-skilled in precisely those activities that justify their marginalised existence. But when manual takeover is necessary something has usually gone wrong; it means that operators need to be more rather than less skilled in order to cope with these atypical conditions. Duncan (1987, p. 266) makes the same point: "The more reliable the plant, the less opportunity there will be for the operator to practise direct intervention, and the more difficult will be the demands of the remaining tasks requiring operator intervention."

These ironies also spill over into the area of training. Conscious of the difficulties facing operators in the high-workload, high-stress conditions of a plant emergency, designers, regulars and managers have sought to proceduralise operator actions. These frequently involve highly elaborate branching structures or algorithms designed to differentiate between a set of foreseeable faults. Some idea of what this means in practice can be gained from the following extract from the U.S. Nuclear Regulatory Commission's report on the serious loss of main and auxiliary feedwater accident at Toledo Edison's Davies-Besse plant in Ohio (NUREG, 1985). The extract describes the actions of the crew immediately following the reactor and turbine trips that occurred at 1.35 a.m. on 9 June 1985.

> The primary-side operator acted in accordance with the immediate post-trip action, specified in the emergency procedure that he had memorized.... The secondary-side operator heard the turbine stop valves slamming shut and knew the reactor had tripped. This 'thud' was heard by most of the equipment operators who also recognized its meaning and two of them headed for the control room. ... The shift supervisor joined the operator at the secondary-side control console and watched the rapid decrease of the steam generator levels. ... The assistant shift supervisor in the meantime opened the plant's looseleaf emergency procedure book (It is about two inches thick with tabs for quick reference...). As he read aloud the immediate actions specified, the reactor operators were responding in the affirmative. After phoning the shift technical advisor to come to the control room, the administrative assistant began writing down what the operators were saying, although they were speaking faster than she could write.

> [later] The assistant shift supervisor, meanwhile, continued reading aloud from the emergency procedure. He had reached the point in the supplementary actions that require verification that feedwater flow was available. However, there was no feedwater, not even from the Auxiliary Feedwater System (AFWS), a safety system designed to provide feedwater in the situation that existed. Given this condition, the procedure directs the operator to the section entitled, 'lack of

Heat Transfer'. He opened the procedure at the tab corresponding to this condition, but left the desk and the procedure at this point, to diagnose why the AFWS had failed. He performed a valve alignment verification and found that the isolation valve in each AFW train had closed. [Both valves had failed to reopen automatically.] He tried unsuccessfully to open the valves by the push buttons on the back panel. ... The AFW system had now suffered its third common-mode failure, thus increasing the number of malfunctions to seven within seven minutes after the reactor trip. ... At this point, things in the control room were hectic. The plant had lost all feedwater; reactor pressure and temperature were increasing; and a number of unexpected equipment problems had occurred. The seriousness of the situation was appreciated." [It should be added that despite the commission of a number of slips and mistakes, the plant was restored to a safe state within 15 minutes. This was a very good crew!]

This passage is worth quoting at length because it reveals what the reality of a serious nuclear power plant emergency is like. It also captures the moment when the pre-programmed procedures, like the plant, ran out of steam, forcing the operators to improvise in the face of what the industry calls a 'beyond design basis accident'. For our present purposes, however, it highlights a further irony of automation: that of drilling operators to follow written instructions and then putting them in a system to provide knowledge-based intelligence and remedial improvisation. Bainbridge (1987, p. 278) commented: "Perhaps the final irony is that it is the most successful automated systems, with rare need for manual intervention, which may need the greatest investment in operator training."

1.6. THE OPERATOR AS TEMPORAL COORDINATOR

French (Montmollin, 1984) and Belgian (De Keyser, Decortis, Housiaux & Van Daele, 1987) investigators have emphasised the importance of the temporal aspects of human supervisory control. One of the side effects of automation has been the proliferation of specialised working teams acting as satellites to the overall process. These include engineers, maintenance staff, control specialists and computer scientists. In many industrial settings, the task of orchestrating their various activities falls to the control room operator. De Keyser and her colleagues are currently documenting the errors of temporal judgement that can arise in these circumstances (De Keyser, 1988).

2. THE 'CATCH 22' OF HUMAN SUPERVISORY CONTROL

As indicated earlier, the main reason why humans are retained in systems that are primarily controlled by intelligent computers is to handle 'non-design' emergencies. In short, operators are there because system designers cannot foresee all possible scenarios of failure and hence are not able to provide automatic safety devices for every contingency.

In addition to their cosmetic value, human beings owe their inclusion in hazardous systems to their unique, knowledge-based ability to carry out 'on-line' problem solving in novel situations. Ironically, and notwithstanding the Apollo 13 astronauts and others demonstrating inspired improvisation, they are not especially good at it; at least not in the conditions that usually prevail during systems emergencies. One reason for this is that stressed human beings are strongly disposed to employ the effortless, parallel, preprogrammed operations of highly specialised, low-level processors and their associated heuristics. These stored routines are shaped by personal history and reflect the recurring patterns of past experience.

The first part of the catch is thus revealed: Why do we have operators in complex systems? To cope with emergencies. What will they actually use to deal with these problems? Stored routines based on previous interactions with a specific environment. What, for the most part, is their experience within the control room? Monitoring and occasionally tweaking the plant while it performs within safe operating limits. So how can they perform adequately when they are called upon to reenter the control loop? The evidence is that this task has become so alien and the system so complex that, on a significant number of occasions, they perform badly.

One apparent solution would be to spend a large part of an operator's shift time drilling him or her in the diagnostic and recovery lessons of previous system emergencies. And this brings us to the second part of the catch. It is in the nature of complex, tightly-coupled, highly interactive, opaque and partially understood systems to spring nasty surprises. Even if it were possible to build up — through simulations or gameplaying — an extensive repertoire of recovery routines within operating crews, there is no guarantee that they would be relevant, other than in a very general sense, to some future event. As case studies repeatedly show, accidents may begin in a conventional way, but they rarely proceed along predictable lines. Each incident is a truly novel event in which past experience counts for little and where the plant has to be recovered by a mixture of good luck and laborious, resource-limited, knowledge-based processing. Active errors are inevitable. Whereas in the more forgiving circumstances of everyday life, learning from one's mistakes is usually a beneficial process, in the control room of chemical or nuclear power plants, such educative experiences can have unacceptable consequences.

The point is this: human supervisory control was not conceived with humans in mind. It was a by-product of the microchip revolution. Indeed, if a group of human factors specialists sat down with the malign intent of conceiving an activity that was wholly ill-matched to the strengths and weaknesses of human cognition, they might well have come up with something not altogether different from what is currently demanded of nuclear and chemical plant operators. To put it simply: the active errors of stressed controllers are, in large part, the delayed effects of system design failures.

Table 5.1

The distribution of error types in 200 NPP incidents (from Rasmussen, 1980).

Breakdown of error types	
Absent-mindedness	3
Familiar association	6
Alertness low	10
Omission of funtionally isolated acts	68
Other omissions	17
Mistakes among alternatives	11
Strong expectation	10
Side effect(s) not considered	15
Latent conditions not considered	20
Manual variability, lack of precision	10
Spatial orientation weak	10
Other, unclassifiable	20
Total	200

Table 5.2

The distribution of omissions across tasks (from Rasmussen, 1980).

Omissions per task	
Monitoring and inspection	0
Supervisory control	2
Manual operation and control	5
Inventory control	8
Test and calibration	28
Repair and modification	35
Administrative task	1
Management, staff planning	1
Other (not mentioned)	5
Total	85

Table 5.3

The distribution of omissions across mental task phases (from Rasmussen, 1980).

Omissions per mental task	
Detection of demand	2
Observation/communication	2
Target: tactical system state	1
Procedure: plan, recall	77
Execution	3
Total	85

Perrow (1984, p. 9), having noted that between 60 and 80 per cent of systems accidents are attributed to 'operator error', went on to make the following telling comment: "But if, as we shall see time and time again, the operator is confronted by unexpected and usually mysterious interactions among failures, saying that he or she should have zigged instead of zagged is only possible after the fact. Before the accident no one could know what was going on and what should have been done."

3. MAINTENANCE-RELATED OMISSIONS

By their nature, it is generally difficult to quantify the contribution made by latent errors to systems failures. An interesting exception, however, are those committed during the maintenance of nuclear power plants. Two independent surveys (Rasmussen, 1980; INPO, 1984) indicate that simple omissions—the failure to carry out some of the actions necessary to achieve a desired goal—constitute the single largest category of human performance problems identified in the significant event reports logged by nuclear plants. Moreover, these omission errors appear to be most closely associated with maintenance-related tasks. Here, the term maintenance-related includes preventive and corrective maintenance, surveillance testing, removal and restoration of equipment, checking, supervision postmaintenance testing and modifications.

3.1. THE RASMUSSEN SURVEY

Drawing upon the Nuclear Power Experience compilation of significant event reports in NPPs, Rasmussen (1980) analysed 200 cases classified under the heading of 'Operational problems'. Omissions of functionally isolated acts accounted for 34 per cent of all the incidents, and a further 8.5 per cent involved other kinds of omission. The complete error distribution is shown in Table 5.1.

The 85 omission errors were further broken down according to (a) the kind of task involved, and (b) the type of mental activity implicated in the phase of the task at which the error occurred. These two analyses are shown in Tables 5.2 and 5.3.

Two aspects of these data are of particular importance. First, they reveal the significance of omission errors in test, calibration and maintenance activities. Second, the mental task analysis shows a close association between omissions and the planning and recalling of procedures. This point is further highlighted by the INPO root cause analysis discussed below.

3.2. THE INPO ROOT CAUSE ANALYSIS

The root causes of 87 significant events reported to the Institute of Nuclear Power Operations (INPO is the U.S nuclear industry's own organization, located in Atlanta, Georgia) in 1983 were analysed using the Root Cause Record Form. Of the 182 root causes identified, 80(44 per cent) were classified as human performance problems (see Figure 5-2).

The event descriptions provided were sufficient to allow omissions to be distinguished from other behavioural error forms. Forty-eight of the 80(60 per cent) human performance root causes were classified as involving either single or multiple omissions.

The following points are of interest: (a) Ninety-six per cent of the deficient procedures involved omissions (31.3 per cent of all human performance root causes). (b) Omissions were most frequently associated

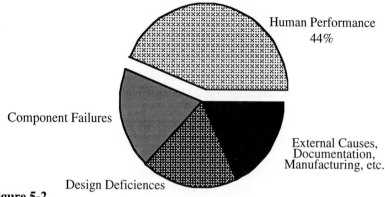

Figure 5-2
INPO analysis of the 182 root causes identified in 87 significant events occurring within nuclear power plants in 1983.

with maintenance-related activities: 64.5 per cent of the errors in this task category involved omitted acts. These made up a quarter of all human performance root causes, (c) Seventy-six per cent of the human errors in the operation task category were omissions, representing 20 per cent of all human performance root causes.

3.3. GENERAL CONCLUSIONS

Clearly, there are some differences between the Rasmussen and INPO analyses regarding the distribution of omissions over tasks. But these are more likely to reflect discrepancies in categorisation and emphasis than real changes in the pattern of NPP errors over time (the Rasmussen study sampled the period up to 1978; the INPO data related to 1983). Of greater importance, however, is that both studies highlighted maintenance-related activities as being the most productive source of event root causes and both identified omissions as the most prevalent error form. The former conclusion is further

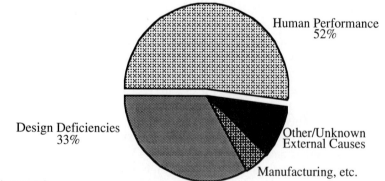

Figure 5-3
INPO analysis of the 387 root causes identified in 180 significant event reports in both 1983 and 1984.

supported by the more extensive NUMARC study (INPO, 1985a), while the latter is in close accord with the relative incidence of error types in everyday life (Reason & Mycielska, 1982; Reason, 1984a), where forgetting intentions was the most common form of lapse.

4. OPERATOR ERRORS

In a subsequent INPO report (INPO, 1985b), the classificatory scheme was modified in two ways: to eliminate 'component failure' (preferring to seek more assiduously for the cause of these failures), and to include 'construction and installation deficiencies' in the human performance category. This revised scheme was then applied to 180 significant event reports issued in both 1983 and 1984, in which a total of 387 root causes were identified. This analysis is summarised in Figure 5-3.

The human performance problems were further broken down into subcategories, as shown in Table 5.4. There are two important conclusions to be drawn from these data. First, at least 92 per cent of all root causes were manmade (see Figure 5-3). Second, only a relatively small proportion of the root causes were actually initiated by front-line personnel (i.e., failure to follow procedures). Most originated in either maintenance-related activities or in bad decisions taken within the organizational and managerial domains.

5. CASE STUDY ANALYSES OF LATENT ERRORS

This section attempts to show something of the nature and variety of latent errors through case study analyses of six major accidents: Three Mile Island, Bhopal, Challenger, Chernobyl, Zeebrugge, and the King's Cross underground fire. These events were not chosen because of the unusually critical part played by latent failures. Other disasters like Flixborough, Seveso, Aberfan, Summerland, Tenerife, Heysel Stadium and the Bradford and Piper Alpha fires would have demonstrated the significance of these dormant factors equally well. Three criteria influenced this particular selection: (a) all the events are comparatively recent so that their general nature will be familiar to the nontechnical reader, (b) they are all well

Table 5.4
Breakdown of human performance problems (from INPO, 1985b).

Human performance problems	
Deficient procedures or documentation	43%
Lack of knowledge or training	18%
Failure to follow procedures	16%
Deficient planning or scheduling	10%
Miscommunication	6%
Deficient supervision	3%
Policy problems	2%
Other	2%

documented, indeed many have been the subject of high-level governmental investigations, and (c) they cover a range of complex, high-risk systems.

In view of the diversity of the systems considered here, it is unlikely that any one reader will be conversant with all of their technical details. Accordingly, the major part of each case study will be presented in the form of a summary table indicating some of the major contributory latent failures—not all because, by their nature, many remain undiscovered. A latent failure in this context is defined as an error or violation that was committed at least one to two days before the start of the actual emergency and played a necessary (though not sufficient) role in causing the disaster. Accompanying each table will be a short description of the accident sequence and, where appropriate, some additional commentary on the general 'health' of the system.

As always in such analyses, there is the problem of defining the explanatory time frame. Any catastrophic event arises from the adverse conjunction of several distinct causal chains. If these are traced backwards in time, we encounter a combinatorial explosion of possible root causes, where the elimination of any one could have thwarted the accident sequence. There are no clear-cut rules for restricting such retrospective searches. Some historians, for example, trace the origins of the charge of the Light Brigade back to Cromwell's Major-Generals (see Woodham-Smith, 1953); others are content to begin at the outset of the Crimean campaign, still others start their stories on the morning of 24 October 1854.

In the present context, there are two obvious boundary conditions. The combined constraints of space, information and the reader's patience place severe limits on how far back in time we can go. Yet the immediate need to demonstrate the significance of antecedent events makes it essential to focus upon those human failures that were committed prior to the day of the actual catastrophe. As it turns out, these antecedent time frames vary in length from around 2 years for Three Mile Island to 9 years for the Challenger disaster, their precise extents being determined by the particular histories of each disaster and the available sources.

The point is that these starting points are fairly arbitrary ones. However, no particular significance is being placed on the quantities of latent and active errors; given their relative time scales, the former will always be more numerous than the latter. Rather, our purpose is to illustrate the insidious and often unforeseeable ways in which they combine to breach the system's defences at some critical moment.

5.1. THREE MILE ISLAND

At 0400 on 28 March 1979, one of the turbines stopped automatically (tripped) in Unit No. 2 of Metropolitan Edison's two pressurized water reactors (PWRs) on Three Mile Island (TMI) in the Susquehanna River, 10 miles south of Harrisburg (principal source: Kemeny, 1979). This was due to a maintenance crew attempting to renew resin for the special treatment of the plant's water. A cupful of water had leaked through a faulty seal in the condensate polisher system and had entered the plant's instrument air system. The moisture interrupted the air pressure applied to two valves on the two feedwater pumps, and 'told' them something was wrong (which was not actually the case in this particular subsystem). The feedwater pumps stopped automatically. This cut the water flow to the steam generator and tripped the turbine. But this automatic safety device was not sufficient to render the plant safe. Without the pumps, the heat of the primary cooling system (circulating around the core) could not be transferred to the cool water in the secondary (nonradioactive) system.

At this point, the emergency feedwater pumps came on automatically. They are designed to pull water from an emergency storage tank and run it through the secondary cooling system to compensate for the water that boils off once it is not circulating. However, the pipes from these emergency feedwater tanks were blocked by closed valves, erroneously left shut during maintenance two days earlier.

With no heat removal from the primary coolant, there was a rapid rise in core temperature and pressure. This triggered another automatic safety device: the reactor 'scrammed' (graphite control rods, 80 per cent silver, dropped into the core and absorb neutrons, stopping the chain reaction). But decaying radioactive materials still produce heat. This further increased temperature and pressure in the core. Such pressure is designed to be relieved automatically through a pilot-operated relief valve (PORV). When open, the PORV releases water from the core through a large pressurizer vessel and then into the sump below the containment. The PORV was supposed to flip open, relieve pressure and then close automatically. But on this occasion, still only about 13 seconds into the emergency, it stuck open. This meant that the primary cooling system had a hole in it through which radioactive water, under high pressure, was pouring into the containment area, and thence down into the basement.

The emergency lasted in excess of 16 hours and resulted in the release of small quantities of radioactive material into the atmosphere. No loss of life has been traced directly to this accident, but the cost to the operating companies and the insurers was in the region of one billion dollars. It also marked a watershed in the history of nuclear power in the United States, and its consequences with regard to public concern for the safety of nuclear power plants are still felt today. The principal events, operator errors and contributing latent failures are summarised in Case Study No. 1 (see Appendix).

The subsequent investigations revealed a wide range of sloppy management practices and poor operating procedures. Subsequent inspection of TMI-1 (the other unit on the site) revealed a long-term lack of maintenance. For example, "boron stalactites more than a foot long hung from the valves and stalagmites had built up from the floor" (Kemeny, 1979) in the TMI-1 containment building. Other discoveries included:

(a) The iodine filters were left in continuous use rather than being preserved to filter air in the event of radioactive contamination. Consequently, on the day of the accident, they possessed considerably less than their full filtering capacity.

(b) Sensitive areas of the plant were open to the public. On the day before the accident, as many as 750 people had access to the auxiliary building.

(c) When shifts changed, no mechanism existed for making a systematic check on the status of the plant. Similarly, maintenance personnel were assigned jobs at the beginning of their shift, but no subsequent check was made on their progress.

(d) A retrospective review of TMI-2's licensee event reports revealed repeated omissions, inadequate failure analyses and lack of corrective actions.

(e) Pipes and valves lacked suitable means of identification. Thus, 8 hours after the start of the accident, operators spent 10 minutes trying unsuccessfully to locate three decay heat valves in a high radiation field.

Was the state of TMI-2 unusual? Was this simply the "bad apple in the nuclear barrel" (Perrow, 1984)? The evidence suggests not. Some years earlier, Morris and Engelken (1973) had examined eight loss-of-coolant (LOCA) accidents that had occurred in six different boiling water reactors over a 2-year period when there were only 29 plants operating. They looked particularly at the cooccurrence of multiple failures. Each accident involved between two to four different types of failure. In half of them there were also violations of operating procedures, but they occurred in conjunction with two to five other failures. Nor were failures limited to plant personnel. Deficient valves were found in 20 plants supplied by 10 different manufacturers. As Perrow (1984) pointed out, it is from the concatenation of these relatively trivial events in nontrivial systems that accidents such as TMI-2 are born. Generating electric power from nuclear energy is a highly technical business; but it would be naive to suppose that NPPs are managed or operated by a special breed of supermen. They are no worse than those in other industries, but neither are they significantly better.

5.2. BHOPAL

On the night of 2-3 December 1984, a gas leak from a small pesticide plant, owned by a subsidiary of Union Carbide Corporation, devastated the central Indian city of Bhopal. It was the worst industrial disaster ever. At least 2,500 people were killed, and more than 200,000 were injured. Perhaps more than any other event, it revealed the hitherto largely unrealised dangers associated with the manufacture of highly toxic chemicals, in this case, methyl isocyanate (MIC).

The immediate cause of the discharge was an influx of water into an MIC storage tank. How it got there is a tangled story of botched maintenance, operator errors, improvised bypass pipes, failed safety systems, incompetent management, drought, agricultural economics and bad governmental decisions. It is too long to tell in detail here, though an inventory of the major latent failures is shown in Case Study No. 2 (see Appendix).

With such a terrible catastrophe, it is difficult to find unbiased sources. Union Carbide's own report (March, 1985) clearly has its own axe to grind, as also does the Morehouse and Subramanian account, published by the Council on International and Public Affairs (1986). Other, less comprehensive, though more balanced accounts have been written by Lihou and Lihou (1985) and Bellamy (1985). Still other accounts can be found in the general scientific press (e.g., New Scientist) and in the chemical journals throughout 1985.

5.3. CHALLENGER

Described in purely physical terms, the cause of the Space Shuttle Challenger disaster on the morning of 28 January 1986 was brutally simple. A rubbery seal, called an 0-ring, on one of the solid rocket boosters split shortly after lift-off, releasing a jet of ignited fuel that caused the entire rocket complex to explode, killing all seven astronauts. But how that item came to be there after a 9-year history of repeated erosion and faults is a complicated tale of incompetence, selective blindness, conflicting goals and reversed logic. The main protagonists were NASA's principal solid-rocket contractor, Morton Thiokol, and all levels of the NASA management. It is summarised in Case Study No. 3 (see Appendix).

More detailed accounts can be found in the Report of the Presidential Commission on the Space Shuttle Challenger Accident (June, 1986), and in an excellent article by Cooper (1987). A discussion of how these facts were obtained from reluctant and often devious sources has been given by Kerhli (1987), one of the presidential commission's principal investigators (his previous job had been prosecuting mafiosi).

5.4. CHERNOBYL

At 0124 on Saturday, 26 April 1986, two explosions blew off the 1000-tonne concrete cap sealing the Chernobyl-4 reactor, releasing molten core fragments into the immediate vicinity and fission products into the atmosphere. This was the worst accident in the history of commercial nuclear power generation. It has so far cost over 30 lives, contaminated some 400 square miles around the Ukrainian plant and significantly increased the risk of cancer deaths over a wide area of Scandinavia and Western Europe. It was an entirely man-made disaster.

The chain of events leading up to the accident together with the associated latent failures are shown in Case Study No. 4 (see Appendix). Other more detailed accounts of the accident can be found in the report of the USSR State Committee on the Utilization of Atomic Energy (1986), in

Nature (vol. 323, 1986), and in a report prepared for the Central Electricity Generating Board (CEGB) by Collier and Davies (1986).

In the immediate aftermath of the accident, the Western nuclear industry vigorously asserted that 'it couldn't happen here' (see Reason, 1987; Baker & Marshall, 1988; Reason, 1988). Whereas the Russian analysts highlighted human errors and violations as the principal cause, their Western counterparts, and especially Lord Marshall, head of the CEGB, preferred to blame the poor design of the Russian reactor and the inadequacy of the 'Soviet safety culture' — although the latter came to sound increasingly hollow after the Zeebrugge and King's Cross disasters.

Notwithstanding the obvious design defects of the RBMK reactor, it is clear from these latent failure analyses that the main ingredients for the Chernobyl disaster were not unique to the Soviet Union. There was a society committed to the generation of energy through large-scale nuclear power plants. There was a system that was hazardous, complex, tightly-coupled, opaque and operating outside normal conditions. There was a fallible management structure that was monolithic, remote and slow to respond, and for whom safety ranked low in the league of goals to be satisfied. There were operators who possessed only a limited understanding of the system they were controlling and in any case, were set a task that made dangerous violations inevitable.

5.5. ZEEBRUGGE

At 1805 on 6 March 1987, the 'roll-on/roll-off' passenger and freight ferry *Herald of Free Enterprise,* owned by Townsend Thoresen, sailed from the inner harbour at Zeebrugge en route to Dover with her bow doors open. As she passed the Outer Mole and increased speed, water came over the bow sill and flooded into the lower car deck (Deck G). At around 1827, the *Herald* capsized rapidly (in fewer than 2 minutes) and came to rest in shallow waters with her starboard side above the water. No fewer than 150 passengers and 38 crew lost their lives. Many others were injured. The chain of events and a limited inventory of the latent failures are shown in Case Study No. 5 (see Appendix). The single best source for more detailed information is the Department of Transport's report on the formal investigation, conducted by Mr. Justice Sheen, the Wreck Commissioner (published September 1987).

Mr. Justice Sheen's investigation was an interesting exception to the general tendency of postaccident inquiries to focus primarily upon active errors. It is worth quoting at some length from what he wrote about the management's part in this catastrophe (Sheen, 1987, p. 14):

> At first sight the faults which led to this disaster were the aforesaid errors of omission on the part of the Master, the Chief Officer and the assistant bosun, and also the failure by Captain Kirk to issue and enforce clear orders. But a full investigation into the circumstances of the disaster leads inexorably to the conclusion that the underlying

or cardinal faults lay higher up in the Company. The Board of Directors did not appreciate their responsibility for the safe management of their ships. They did not apply their minds to the question: What orders should be given to the safety of our ships? The directors did not have any proper comprehension of what their duties were. There appears to have been a lack of thought about the way in which the Herald ought to have been organised for the Dover/Zeebrugge run. All concerned in management, from the members of the Board of Directors down to the junior superintendents, were guilty of fault in that all must be regarded as sharing responsibility for the failure of management. From top to bottom the body corporate was infected with the disease of sloppiness.... The failure on the part of the shore management to give proper and clear directions was a contributory cause of the disaster.

5.6. KING'S CROSS

At 1925 on 18 November 1987, discarded smoker's material probably set light to highly inflammable rubbish that had been allowed to accumulate in the running tracks of an escalator. Twenty minutes later, jets of flame shot up the escalator shaft and hit the ceiling of the ticket hall in which those evacuated via the Piccadilly and Victoria line escalators were gathering. Although a number of active failures were committed by the station staff and the emergency services in the intervening period, the primary causes of the disaster were present long before the start of the fire. These latent failures are summarised in Case Study No. 6 (see Appendix).

In the subsequent investigation (Fennell, 1988), the inspector placed the responsibility for the disaster squarely with the managements of London Regional Transport and its operating company, London Underground. Three quotations will serve to convey the flavour of his judgement.

The Chairman of London Regional Transport.... told me that where as financial matters were strictly monitored, safety was not. ... In my view, he was mistaken as to his responsibility. (Fennell, 1988, p. 17)

It is clear from what I heard that London Underground was struggling to shake off the rather blinkered approach which had characterised its earlier history and was in the middle of what the Chairman and Managing Director described as a change of culture and style. But in spite of that change the management remained of the view that fires were inevitable in the oldest most extensive underground system in the world. In my view they were fundamentally in error in their approach. (Fennell, 1988, p. 17)

I have devoted a chapter to the management of safety because the principal lesson to be learned from this tragedy is the right approach to safety. (Fennell, 1988, p. 18)

6. DISTINGUISHING ERRORS AND VIOLATIONS

An important lesson to be learned from both the Chernobyl and Zeebrugge disasters is that the term 'error' does not capture all the ways in which human beings contribute to major accidents. An adequate framework for aberrant behaviours (literally 'a straying from the path') requires a distinction to be made between errors and violations. Both can be (and often are) present within the same action sequence, but they can also occur independently. One may err without committing a violation; a violation need not involve error.

Errors involve two distinct kinds of 'straying': the unwitting deviation of action from intention (slips and lapses) and the departure of planned actions from some satisfactory path towards a desired goal (mistakes). But this error classification, restricted as it is to individual information processing, offers only a partial account of the possible varieties of aberrant behaviour. What is missing is a further level of analysis acknowledging that, for the most part, humans do not plan and execute their actions in isolation, but within a regulated social milieu. While errors may be defined in relation to the cognitive processes of the individual, violations can only be described with regard to a social context in which behaviour is governed by operating procedures, codes of practice, rules and the like. For our purposes, violations can be defined as deliberate—but not necessarily reprehensible—deviations from those practices deemed necessary (by designers, managers and regulatory agencies) to maintain the safe operation of a potentially hazardous system.

The boundaries between errors and violations are by no means hard and fast, either conceptually or within a particular accident sequence. What is certain, however, is that dangerous aberrations cannot be studied exclusively within either the cognitive or the social psychological traditions; both need to be integrated within a single framework.

7. A PRELIMINARY CLASSIFICATION OF VIOLATIONS

7.1. THE BOUNDARY CATEGORIES

Violations may be committed for many reasons. One way of identifying the extremes of this range of possibilities is through the issue of intentionality. The first step is to ask: Was there a prior intention to commit this particular violation? If the answer is no, we can assign the violation to a category labelled erroneous or unintended violations. If the violation was deliberate, we need to know whether or not there was a prior intention to cause damage to the system. If there was, we can assign the violation to the general category of sabotage. Since the former category lies within the now well-defined province of error and the latter falls outside the scope of most accident scenarios, the violations of greatest interest are likely to be those occupying the middle ground, that is, violations having some degree of intentionality, but that do not involve the goal of system damage.

Within this broad hinterland of deliberate but nonmalevolent infringements, it is possible to make a further rough dichotomy between routine and exceptional violations. The former are largely habitual, forming an established part of an individual's behavioural repertoire; the latter are singular violations occurring in a particular set of circumstances. The road environment provides multiple examples of routine violations. The behaviour of the Chernobyl operators in the 20 or so minutes before the explosions offers a clear instance of an exceptional set of violations.

7.2. ROUTINE VIOLATIONS

Two factors, in particular, appear to be important in shaping habitual violations: (a) the natural human tendency to take the path of least effort; and (b) a relatively indifferent environment (i.e., one that rarely punishes violations or rewards observance). Everyday observation shows that if the quickest and most convenient path between two task-related points involves transgressing an apparently trivial and rarely sanctioned safety procedure, then it will be violated routinely by the operators of the system. Such a principle suggests that routine violations could be minimised by designing systems with human beings in mind at the outset. Landscape architects are forever making the mistake of laying out pathways to satisfy aesthetic criteria rather than human needs; as a consequence, their symmetry is soon marred by muddy diagonal tracks across protected grassland.

7.3. EXCEPTIONAL VIOLATIONS

But exceptional violations are not so clearly specified, being the product of a wide variety of local conditions. However, both the Chernobyl and the Zeebrugge disasters suggest the significance of what might loosely be called 'system double-binds'—particular tasks or operating circumstances that make violations inevitable, no matter how well-intentioned the operators might be.

8. PSYCHOLOGICAL GROUNDS FOR DISTINGUISHING ERRORS AND VIOLATIONS

One place where errors and violations are both abundant and relatively easy to observe is on the roads. In a recent study (Reason, Manstead, Stradling, Baxter, Campbell & Huyser, 1988), a Driver Behaviour Questionnaire (DBQ) was administered anonymously to 520 UK drivers of both sexes and covering a wide age range. The DBQ was made up of 50 items, each one describing either an error (a slip or a mistake) or a violation. The latter included both infringements of the Highway Code and deviations from accepted practice (e.g., driving too slowly on a two-lane rural highway). The respondents used a 5-point rating scale to indicate how frequently (over the past year) they had committed each type of 'bad behaviour.'

The data were analysed using a factor analytic technique involving varimax rotation. Three orthogonal factors accounted for nearly 40 per cent of the variance. Items loading highly on factor 1 were violations (e.g., drinking and driving, close following, racing with other drivers, disregarding speed limits, shooting stop lights, etc.). Factors 2 and 3, however, were clearly associated with erroneous behaviour. The items loading highly on factor 2 tended to be hazardous errors: slips and mistakes that could have adverse consequences for other road users (e.g., failing to see 'Give Way' signs, failing to check mirror before manoeuvres, misjudging the speed of oncoming vehicles when overtaking, etc.). Items associated with factor 3, on the other hand, tended to be inconsequential lapses (e.g., taking the wrong exit at a roundabout, forgetting where one's car is in a car park, driving to destination A when destination B was intended, etc.).

This analysis provided strong support for the belief that errors and violations are mediated by different cognitive mechanisms. This conclusion was further endorsed by the age and sex relationships. Violations declined with age, errors did not. Men at all ages reported more violations than women. Women were significantly more lapse-prone than men (or more honest!). These self-report data also correspond closely with what we know of the relative contributions of men and women at various ages to road accidents (Storie, 1977).

9. A RESIDENT PATHOGEN METAPHOR

The case studies considered earlier, along with numerous others (Turner, 1978; Perrow, 1984), indicate that major disasters in defended systems are rarely if ever caused by any one factor, either mechanical or human. Rather, they arise from the unforeseen and usually unforeseeable concatenation of several diverse events, each one necessary but singly insufficient.

These observations suggest an analogy between the breakdown of complex technological systems and the aetiology of multiple-cause illnesses such as cancer and cardiovascular disease. More specifically, there appear to be similarities between latent failures in complex technological systems and resident pathogens in the human body.

The resident pathogen metaphor emphasises the significance of causal factors present in the system before an accident sequence actually begins. All man-made systems contain potentially destructive agencies, like the pathogens within the human body. At any one time, each complex system will have within it a certain number of latent failures, whose effects are not immediately apparent but that can serve both to promote unsafe acts and to weaken its defence mechanisms. For the most part, they are tolerated, detected and corrected, or kept in check by protective measures (the auto-immune system). But every now and again, a set of external circumstances—called here local triggers—arises that combines with these resident pathogens in subtle and often unlikely ways to thwart the system's defences and to bring about its catastrophic breakdown.

In medicine, a good deal more is known about the nature of active failures (i.e., trauma, invasive agencies, acute diseases, etc.) than about the action of resident pathogens. The same is true in the systems reliability field; single component failures or simple human errors can be foreseen and contained by built-in safety devices, but these engineered defences offer little protection against certain combinations of system pathogens and local triggers. In addition, there are interesting parallels between the aetiologies of pathogen-related diseases and the catastrophic breakdown of complex, opaque technical installations. Both seem to require the breaching of defences by a concatenation of resident pathogens and external triggering events, though in both cases the precise nature of this interaction is hard to predict.

The resident pathogen notion directs attention to the indicators of 'system morbidity' that are present prior to a catastrophic breakdown. These, in principle, are more open to detection than the often bizarre and unforeseeable nature of the local triggering events. Implicit in the metaphor is the notion that the likelihood of an accident will be some function of the number of pathogens currently present within the sociotechnical system. The greater the number of pathogens residing in a system, the more likely it will encounter just that particular combination of triggering conditions sufficient to complete an accident sequence.

Other things being equal, the more complex, interactive, tightly-coupled and opaque the system, the greater the number of resident pathogens it is likely to contain. However, while simpler systems are usually less interactive, less centralised and more transparent, they tend to be considerably less evolved with regard to built-in defences. Thus, relatively few pathogens can often wreak greater havoc in simpler systems than in more advanced ones.

An important corollary of these arguments is that the risk of an accident will be diminished if these pathogens are detected and neutralized proactively. However, like cancer and heart disease, accidents have multiple causes. The occurrence of an accident is not simply determined by the sheer number of pathogens in the system; their adverse effects have to find windows of opportunity to pass through the various levels of the system and, most particularly, through the defences themselves. In short, there are a large number of stochastic factors involved.

The resident pathogen metaphor has a number of attractive features, but it is far from being a workable theory. Its terms are still unacceptably vague. Moreover, it shares a number of features with the now largely discredited accident proneness theory, though it operates at a systemic rather than at an individual level.

Accident proneness theory had two elements. First, the purely statistical observation that certain people have more than their chance share of accidents, as determined by the Poisson model. Second, and much more controversial, there was the assumption that this unequal liability originated in some relatively enduring feature of the individual (i.e., personality traits, information-processing deficiencies, physical characteristics and the like). In the pathogen metaphor, comparable assertions are being made about systems rather than individuals. Here it is argued that some systems have a greater accident liability due to their larger accumulation of resident pathogens. The major difference, of course, lies in their respective remedial implications. Accident proneness theory, predicated as it is upon stable dispositional factors, offers no alternative other than the screening out of high-liability individuals; pathogen theory leads to a search for preaccident morbidity indicators and assumes that these are remediable.

Accident proneness theory failed because it was found that unequal accident liability was, in reality, a 'club' with a rapidly changing membership. In addition, attempts to find a clearly definable accident-prone personality proved fruitless.

The pathogen metaphor would suffer a similar fate if it were found that pathogens could only be identified retrospectively in relation to a specific set of accident circumstances in a particular system. For the pathogen metaphor to have any value, it is necessary to establish an *a priori* set of indicators relating to system morbidity and then to demonstrate clear causal connections between these indicators and accident liability across a wide range of complex systems and in a variety of accident conditions.

10. A GENERAL VIEW OF ACCIDENT CAUSATION IN COMPLEX SYSTEMS

This section seeks to extend the pathogen metaphor in order to lay the foundations of a possible theoretical framework for considering the aetiology of accidents in complex technological systems. As indicated earlier, the challenge for such a framework is not just to provide an account of how latent and active failures combine to produce accidents, but also to indicate where and how more effective remedial measures might be applied. The framework has as its building blocks the basic elements of production common to any complex system (Wreathall, 1989).

10.1. THE BASIC ELEMENTS OF PRODUCTION

The notion of production offers a reasonably uncontroversial starting point. All complex technologies are involved in some form of production. The product can be energy, a chemical substance or the mass transportation of people by road, rail, sea or air.

Figure 5-4 identifies the basic elements common to all such productive systems. These elements are represented diagrammatically as planes, one behind the other. We can think of these planes as identifying the essential, benign components of effective production.

10.1.1. The decision makers

These include both the architects and the high-level managers of the system. Once in operation, they set the goals for the system as a whole in

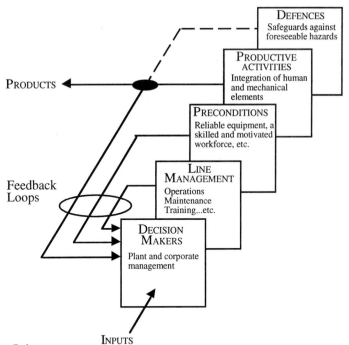

Figure 5-4
The basic elements of production. These constitute the necessary and benign components of any productive system.

response to inputs from the outside world. They also direct, at a strategic level, the means by which these goals should be met. A large part of their function is concerned with the allocation of finite resources. These comprise money, equipment, people (talent and expertise) and time. Their aim is to deploy these resources to maximise both productivity and safety.

10.1.2. Line management

These are the departmental specialists who implement the strategies of the decision makers within their particular spheres of operation. They go by various labels: operations, training, sales, maintenance, finance, procurement, safety, engineering support, personnel and so on.

10.1.3. Preconditions

Appropriate decisions and effective line management are clearly prerequisites for successful production. But they are not of themselves sufficient. We need something between the line managers and the productive activities. These are a set of qualities possessed by both machines and people: reliable equipment of the right kind; a skilled and knowledgeable workforce; an appropriate set of attitudes and motivators; work schedules, maintenance programmes, and environmental conditions that permit efficient and safe

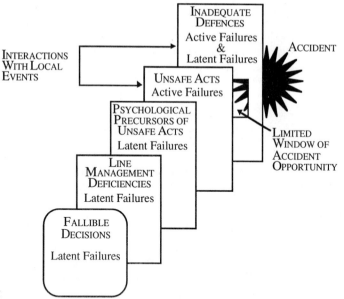

Figure 5-5
The various human contributions to the breakdown of complex systems are mapped onto the basic elements of production. It is assumed that the primary systemic origins of latent failures are the fallible decisions taken by top-level plant and corporate managers. These are then transmitted via the intervening elements to the point where system defences may be breached.

operations; and codes of practice that give clear guidance regarding desirable (safe and/or efficient) and undesirable (unsafe and/or inefficient) performance—to name but a few.

10.1.4. Productive activities

These are the actual performances of humans and machines: the precise synchronisation of mechanical and human activities in order to deliver the right product at the right time.

10.1.5. Defences

Where productive activities involve exposure to natural or intrinsic hazards, both individuals and machines should be supplied with safeguards sufficient to prevent foreseeable injury, damage or costly outages.

10.2. THE HUMAN ELEMENTS OF ACCIDENT CAUSATION

These are represented in Figure 5-5. It should be noted that a parallel diagram could equally well have been drawn for the purely mechanical or technical failures. However, our principal concern is with the human contribution to systems accidents, because accident analyses reveal that human factors dominate the risks to complex installations. Even what appear at first sight to be simple equipment breakdowns can usually be traced to some prior human failure. Nevertheless, it is important to acknowledge that any component or piece of equipment has a limited reliable life; all such items may fail for engineering rather than human reasons.

The essence of Figure 5-5 is that it portrays these human contributions as weaknesses or 'windows' in the basic productive 'planes' (shown in Figure 5-4). Here we show the dark side of the production picture. The causal sequence moves from fallible decisions, through the intervening planes to an accident, that is, the unplanned and uncontrolled release of some destructive force, usually in the presence of victims. In what follows, I will elaborate upon the nature of each of these 'malign planes,' beginning with fallible decisions.

10.2.1. Fallible decisions

A basic premise of this framework is that systems accidents have their primary origins in fallible decisions made by designers and high-level (corporate or plant) managerial decision makers.

This is not a question of allocating blame, but simply a recognition of the fact that even in the best-run organisations a significant number of influential decisions will subsequently prove to be mistaken. This is a fact of life. Fallible decisions are an inevitable part of the design and management process. The question is not so much how to prevent them from occurring, as how to ensure that their adverse consequences are speedily detected and recovered.

In considering fallible decisions, it is important to be aware of the context in which high-level decisions are taken. Figure 5-6 summarises some of the constraints facing corporate and senior plant managers. All organizations have to allocate resources to two distinct goals: production and safety. In the long term, these are clearly compatible goals. But, given that all resources are finite, there are likely to be many occasions on which there are short-term conflicts of interest. Resources allocated to the pursuit of production could diminish those available for safety; the converse is also true. These dilemmas are exacerbated by two factors:

(a) *Certainty of outcome.* Resources directed at improving productivity have relatively certain outcomes; those aimed at enhancing safety do not, at least in the short term. This is due in large part to the large contribution of stochastic elements in accident causation.

(b) *Nature of the feedback.* The feedback generated by the pursuit of production goals is generally unambiguous, rapid, compelling and (when the news is good) highly reinforcing. That associated with the pursuit of safety goals is largely negative, intermittent, often deceptive and perhaps only compelling after a major accident or a string of incidents. Production feedback will, except on these rare

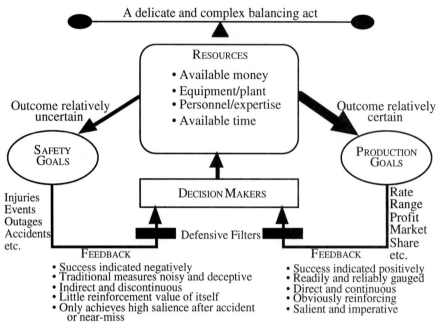

Figure 5-6
A summary of some of the factors that contribute to fallible, high-level decision making. Resources allocated to production and safety goals differ (a) in their certainty of outcome and (b) in the nature and impact of their respective feedback.

occasions, always speak louder than safety feedback. This makes the managerial control of safety extremely difficult.

Furthermore, decision makers do not always interpret feedback on either the production or the safety channels accurately. Defensive 'filters' may be interposed that both protect them from bad news and encourage extrapunitive reactions. Thus, poor achievement on the production front can be blamed upon an inadequate workforce, union interference, market forces, world recession, shortages of materials and the like. A bad safety record can be attributed to operator carelessness or incompetence. This position is sometimes consolidated by cataloguing the various safeguards, engineered safety devices and safe operating practices that have already been implemented. Indeed, given the almost diabolical nature of some accident sequences, these are perfectly understandable reactions. But they nevertheless block the discovery of effective remedies and contribute to further fallible decisions.

10.2.2. Line management deficiencies

On this 'plane', the consequences of fallible decisions manifest themselves differently in the various line management departments. Of course, it would be naive to assume that the pathology or otherwise of a given line department is purely a function of higher-level decision making. The native incompetence of any set of line managers could further exacerbate the adverse effects of high-level decisions or even cause good decisions to have bad effects. Conversely, competence at the line management level could do something to mitigate the unsafe effects of fallible decisions, make neutral decisions have safer consequences, and transform good decisions into even better ones. Nevertheless, the scope for line management intervention is, in very real terms, constrained by the size of their departmental budgets or the resources at their disposal. For theoretical purposes, we will assume that these allocations will have been decided at a higher level in the system. Indeed, such allocations constitute a major part of the output of higher-level decision making.

The interaction between line management deficiencies and the psychological precursors of unsafe acts is extremely complex. There is a many-to-many mapping between possible line management deficiencies and the various psychological precursors of unsafe acts. For example, deficiencies in the training department can manifest themselves as a variety of preconditions: high workload, undue time pressure, inappropriate perception of hazards, ignorance of the system and motivational difficulties. Likewise, any one precondition (e.g., undue time pressure) could be the product of many different line management deficiencies (e.g., poor scheduling, poor procedures, deficiencies in skills, rules, or knowledge and maintenance inadequacies).

A useful way of thinking about these transformations is as failure types converting into failure tokens (Hudson, 1988). Deficient training is a pathogen type that can reveal itself, on the precondition plane, as a variety of pathogenic tokens. Such a view has important remedial consequences. Rectifying a particular failure type could, in principle, remove a wide and varied class of tokens. The type-token distinction is intrinsically hierarchical. Condition tokens at this level of analysis become types for the creation of unsafe act tokens at our next stage of analysis.

10.2.3. Preconditions for unsafe acts

Preconditions or psychological precursors are latent states. They create the potential for a wide variety of unsafe acts. The precise nature of these acts will be a complex function of the task being performed, the environmental influences and the presence of hazards. Each precursor can contribute to a large number of unsafe acts, depending upon the prevailing conditions.

At this level, the type-token distinction becomes especially significant due to the some-to-many mapping between precursors and unsafe acts. A particular psychological precursor, either alone or in combination with other precursors, can play a significant part in both provoking and shaping an almost infinitely large set of unsafe acts. But the precise nature, time, place and perpetrator of any single act are almost impossible to anticipate, though we can apply some general predictive principles.

The stochastic character of this onward mapping reveals the futility of 'tokenism' —the focusing of remedial efforts upon preventing the recurrence of specific unsafe acts. Although certain of these acts may fall into an easily recognisable subclass (e.g., failing to wear personal safety equipment in the presence of hazards) and so be amenable to targeted safety programmes and training, most of them are unforeseeable, sometimes even quite bizarre. The only sensible way of dealing with them is, first, to eliminate their preconditions as far as possible and, second, to accept that whatever the measures taken, some unsafe acts will still occur, and so provide defences that will intervene between the act and its adverse consequences.

As in the case of line management deficiencies, not all unsafe act precursors result from fallible decisions. Many of the pathogens at this level are introduced directly by the human condition. The capacities for being stressed, failing to perceive hazards, being imperfectly aware of the system and having less than ideal motivation are brought by each person into the workplace. Thus, in causal terms, there is only a loose coupling between the line management and precursor 'planes'. The point to stress is that these predispositions can either be markedly exaggerated or considerably mitigated by the character of decisions made at the top levels of the system and communicated to the individual via line departments. Even the best-run organisations cannot eliminate the harmful psychological effects of negative life events (e.g., marriage breakdowns, sickness in the family, bereavements, etc.) occurring outside the workplace. But they can anticipate the possibility if not the particular form of occurrence of negative life events and provide adequate defences against their unsafe consequences.

10.2.4. Unsafe acts

Even more than their psychological precursors, the commission of unsafe acts is determined by a complex interaction between intrinsic system influences (of the kind described for the preceding three 'planes') and those arising from the outside world. This has to do both with protean environmental factors and with the particular form of the existing hazards. Thus, an unsafe act can only be defined in relation to the presence of a particular hazard. There is nothing inherently unsafe about not wearing a safety helmet or a life jacket. Such omissions only constitute unsafe acts when they occur in potentially hazardous situations (i.e., when heavy objects are likely to fall from above, or in close proximity to deep water). An unsafe act is more than just an error or a violation—it is an error or a violation committed in the presence of a potential hazard: some mass, energy or toxicity that, if not properly controlled, could cause injury or damage. A

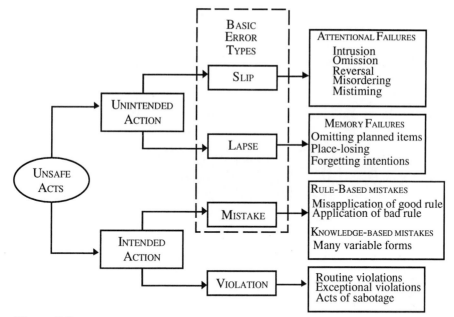

Figure 5-7
A summary of the psychological varieties of unsafe acts, classified initially
according to whether the act was intended or unintended and then distinguishing
errors from violations.

classification of unsafe acts based upon arguments presented earlier in this
book is shown in Figure 5-7.

10.2.5. Defences: The limited window of accident opportunity

A system's defences can be made up of many elements. At the lowest
level of sophistication, they may consist of little more than personal safety
equipment for the workforce and guards preventing direct contact with
dangerous materials or moving parts. At the other extreme, there are the
'defences in depth' of nuclear power plants. These comprise both people (the
control room operators) and many (both redundant and diverse) engineered
features such as automatic safety devices and levels of containment.

Very few unsafe acts result in actual damage or injury, even in relatively
unprotected systems. And in highly protected systems, the various layers of
defence can only be breached by the adverse conjunction of several different
causal factors. Some of these are likely to be latent failures of pathogenic
origin, others will be local triggering events such as the commission of a set
of unsafe acts in a highly specific set of circumstances—often associated
with some atypical system condition (i.e., the unusually low temperature
preceding the Challenger launch, the testing carried out prior to the annual
shut-down at Chernobyl A, and the nose-down trim of the Herald of Free

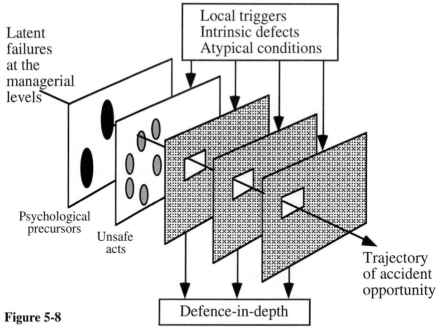

Figure 5-8

The dynamics of accident causation. The diagram shows a trajectory of accident opportunity penetrating several defensive systems. This results from a complex interaction between latent failures and a variety of local triggering events. It is clear from this figure, however, that the chances of such a trajectory of opportunity finding loopholes in all of the defences at any one time is very small indeed.

Enterprise due to a combination of high tide and unsuitable docking facilities).

Figure 5-8 tries to capture some of the stochastic features involved in the unlikely coincidence of an unsafe act and a breach in the system's defences. It shows a trajectory of opportunity originating in the higher levels of the system, passing via the precondition and unsafe act planes and then on through three successive layers of defence. Each of these planes has windows of opportunity, but they are in continual flux due to the largely unpredictable influences of both intrinsic and extrinsic factors. On each plane, the areas of permeability or windows vary over time in both their location and their size, and these changes have different time constants at different levels of the system. This picture emphasises the unlikelihood of any one set of causal factors finding an appropriate trajectory.

In a highly defended system, one of the most common accident scenarios involves the deliberate disabling of engineered safety features by operators in pursuit of what, at the time, seems a perfectly sensible goal (i.e., Chernobyl), but that fails to take account either of the side effects of these actions or of system characteristics. On other occasions, the defences are breached because the operators are unaware of concurrently created gaps in system security (i.e., at TMI-2, Bhopal, Herald) because they have an erroneous perception of the system state.

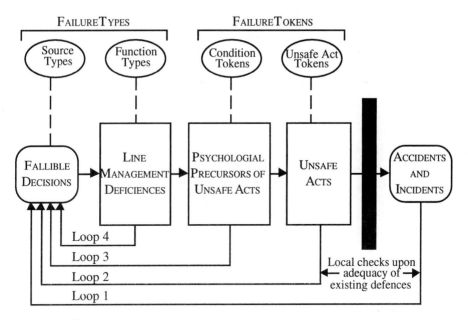

Figure 5-9
Feedback loops and indicators. The indicators are divided into two groups: *failure types* (relating to deficiencies in the managerial/organizational sectors) and *failure tokens* (relating to individual conditions and unsafe acts).

10.3. CONTROLLING SAFER OPERATIONS

The control of safe operations, like the control of production, is a continuous process. The prerequisites for adequate safety control are: (a) a sensitive multichannel feedback system, and (b) the ability to respond rapidly and effectively to actual or anticipated changes in the safety realm. These two aspects of control—feedback and response—are considered further below.

Figure 5-9 portrays the feedback loops and indicators potentially available to those responsible for the management of system safety. Together these various feedback loops and indicators constitute the safety information system (SIS).

It has been shown that an effective safety information system ranks second only to top management involvement in discriminating between safe and unsafe organisations matched on other variables (Kjellen, 1983).

Loop 1 (the reporting of accidents, lost time injuries, etc.) is the minimum requirement for an SIS. In most cases, however, the information supplied is too little and too late for effective anticipatory control. It is too little because such indices as fatalities and LTIs are simply the tip of the event iceberg. It is too late because they are retrospective; the events that safety management seeks to eliminate have already occurred.

Loop 2 is potentially—though rarely actually— available through such procedures as unsafe act auditing (Shell Safety Committee, 1987). Usually the information derived from such auditing is disseminated only at the lower levels of the organisation. However, since unsafe acts are the stuff from which accidents are made, a feedback loop that samples the incidence and nature of unsafe acts in various operational spheres would provide a greater opportunity for proactive safety control.

The main thrust of this view of accident causation is towards the establishment of loops 3 and 4: *pathogen auditing*. The theory dictates that the most effective way of managing safety is by acting upon types rather than tokens, that is, by influencing system states occurring early on in the accident sequence. To identify these failure types and to find ways of neutralizing the pathogens so revealed represent the major challenges facing human factors researchers concerned with preserving the safety of complex, high-risk systems.

10.4. GENERAL INDICATORS

The general indicators shown in Figure 5-9 cover two broad aspects of an organisation's safety functioning. The first relates to the variety and sensitivity of its feedback loops. The second deals with the decision makers' responsiveness to safety-related data. No amount of feedback will enhance an organisation's degree of safety if the information supplied is not acted upon in a timely and effective manner.

Westrum (1988) has provided a simple but meaningful classification of the ways in which organisations may differ in their reactions to safety data. His basic premise is that: "Organizations think. Like individuals, they exhibit a consciousness, a memory, and an ability to create and to solve problems. Their thinking strongly affects the generation and elimination of hazards." Organisational responses to hazards fall into three groups: denial, repair and reform actions.

Denial Actions

Suppression: Observers are punished or dismissed, and the observations expunged from the record.

Encapsulation: Observers are retained, but the validity of their observations is disputed or denied.

Repair Actions

Public Relations: Observations emerge publicly, but their significance is denied; they are sugar-coated.

Local Repairs: The problem is admitted and fixed at the local level, but its wider implications are denied.

Reform Actions

Dissemination: The problem is admitted to be global, and global action is taken upon it.

Reorganization: Action on the problem leads to reconsideration and reform of the operational system.

The more effective the organisation, the more likely it is to respond to safety data with actions from the bottom of this list (i.e., reform), while those less adequate will employ responses from the top (i.e., denial).

Westrum then uses these reactions to define organisations along a scale of what he calls 'cognitive adequacy', or the effectiveness of their ways of thinking about hazard. These are grouped under three headings: pathological, calculative and generative organisations.

(a) *Pathological organisations* are ones whose safety measures are inadequate even under normal conditions. These organisations sacrifice safety goals in the pursuit of production goals, often under severe economic pressures, and actively circumvent safety regulations. Information about hazardous conditions is suppressed at the source by suppressing or encapsulating the messenger (e.g., the Tennessee Valley Authority's nuclear power plant management).

(b) *Calculative organisations* try to do the best job they can using 'by-the-book' methods. These are usually adequate under normal operating conditions, but often fail when they encounter unforeseen circumstances. In short, they may implement many safety practices but have little in the way of effective disaster plans (e.g., the New Jersey chemical industry, the CEGB, the U.K Department of Energy).

(c) *Generative organisations* are characterised by a high degree of ostensibly irregular or unconventional activity in furthering their goals. They set targets for themselves beyond ordinary expectations and fulfill them because they are willing to do unexpected things in unexpected ways. They emphasise results rather than methods, and value substance more than form. Hazards tend to be quickly discovered and neutralised because lower-level personnel have both permission to see and permission to do (e.g., U.S. nuclear aircraft carrier flight deck operations—see Rochlin, LaPorte & Roberts, 1987).

11. LEARNING THE RIGHT LESSONS FROM PAST ACCIDENTS

It is not easy to learn the right lessons from past disasters, especially if these events are likely to further undermine public confidence in the safety of one's own similar technologies. Institutional reactions to other people's catastrophes reveal, among other things, two universal human failings: the fundamental attribution error and the fundamental surprise error.

The *fundamental attribution error* has been widely studied in social psychology (see Fiske & Taylor, 1984; see also Chapter 2, Section 3.5). This refers to a pervasive tendency to blame bad outcomes on an actor's personal inadequacies (i.e., dispositional factors) rather than attribute them to situational factors beyond his or her control. Such tendencies were evident in both the Russian and the British responses to the Chernobyl accident. Thus, the Russian report on Chernobyl (USSR State Committee on the Utilization of Atomic Energy, 1986) concluded that: "The prime cause of the accident was an extremely improbable combination of violations of instructions and operating rules." Lord Marshall, Chairman of the U.K Central Electricity Generating Board (CEGB), wrote a foreword to the U.K. Atomic Energy Authority's report upon the Chernobyl accident (UKAEA, 1987), in which he assigned blame in very definite terms: "To us in the West, the sequence of reactor operator errors is incomprehensible. Perhaps it came from supreme arrogance or complete ignorance. More plausibly, we can speculate that the operators as a matter of habit had broken rules many, many times and got away with it so the safety rules no longer seemed relevant." Could it happen in the U.K.? "My own judgement is that the overriding importance of ensuring safety is so deeply engrained in the culture of the nuclear industry that this will not happen in the U.K"

The term *fundamental surprise* was coined by an Israeli social scientist, Zvi Lanir (Lanir, 1986), in regard to the Yom Kippur War, but it is particularly apt for both the TMI-2 and Chernobyl accidents. A fundamental surprise reveals a profound discrepancy between one's perception of the world and the reality. A major reappraisal is demanded. Situational surprises, on the other hand, are localised events requiring the solution of specific problems.

Lanir likens the difference between situational and fundamental surprise to that between 'surprise' and 'astonishment' and illustrates it with an anecdote from Webster, the lexicographer. One day, Webster returned home to find his wife in the arms of his butler. "You surprised me," said his wife. "And you have astonished me," responded Webster. Mrs Webster experienced merely a situational surprise; Mr Webster suffered a fundamental one.

The natural human tendency is to respond to fundamental surprises as if they were only situational ones. Thus, the fundamental surprise error "is to avoid any fundamental meaning and to learn the situational lessons from the surface events" (Lanir, 1986).

At the Sizewell B public inquiry (Layfield, 1987), the CEGB witnesses sought to dissociate the future station from the troubles that beset the Metropolitan Edison pressurised water reactor (PWR) on Three Mile Island on 28 March 1979. They identified various salient features of the TMI-2 accident—the steam power plant, sticky relief valves, poor control room design, inadequate operator training, etc.—and asserted that these and more would be significantly improved in the Sizewell B PWR. In his assessment of this evidence, Sir Frank Layfield hinted at broader issues: "Some aspects of the TMI accident give warnings which are of general importance," but then concluded that they were not applicable in the U.K. due to organisational differences.

This natural urge to distance U.K. installations from foreign catastrophes was even more apparent in the UKAEA's (1987) analysis of the Chernobyl disaster that concluded: "the Chernobyl accident was unique to the [Russian] reactor design and there are few lessons for the United Kingdom to learn from it. Its main effect has been to reinforce and reiterate the importance and validity of existing UK standards."

So what are the right lessons to be learned from TMI and Chernobyl? These, I believe, have been well stated for TMI-2 by David Woods, previously of the Westinghouse Corporation (Woods, 1987). The same general conclusions apply equally to Chernobyl and to the Bhopal, Challenger, and Zeebrugge accidents (Woods, 1987):

> The TMI accident was more than an unexpected progression of faults; it was more than a situation planned for but handled inadequately; it was more than a situation whose plan had proved inadequate. The TMI accident constituted a fundamental surprise in that it revealed a basic incompatibility between the nuclear industry's view of itself and reality. Prior to TMI the industry could and did think of nuclear power as a purely technical system where all the problems were in the form of some technical area or areas and the solutions to these problems lay in those engineering disciplines. TMI graphically revealed the inadequacy of that view because the failures were in the socio-technical system and not due to pure technical nor pure human factors.

Regardless of the technology or the country that it serves, the message of this chapter is very clear: No one holds the monopoly on latent failures. And these resident pathogens constitute the primary residual risk to complex, highly-defended technological systems.

12. POSTSCRIPT: ON BEING WISE AFTER THE EVENT

This chapter has argued that most of the root causes of serious accidents in complex technologies are present within the system long before an obvious accident sequence can be identified. In theory, at least, some of these latent failures could have been spotted and corrected by those managing, maintaining and operating the system in question. In addition, there were also prior warnings of likely catastrophe for most of the accidents considered here. The Rogovin inquiry (Rogovin, 1979), for example, discovered that the TMI accident had 'almost happened' twice before, once in Switzerland in 1974 and once at the Davis-Besse plant in Ohio in 1977. Similarly, an Indian journalist wrote a prescient series of articles about the Bhopal plant and its potential dangers three years before the tragedy (see Marcus & Fox, 1988). Other unheeded warnings were also available prior to the Challenger, Zeebrugge and King's Cross accidents.

For those who pick over the bones of other people's disasters, it often seems incredible that these warnings and human failures, seemingly so obvious in retrospect, should have gone unnoticed at the time. Being blessed with both uninvolvement and hindsight, it is a great temptation for retrospective observers to slip into a censorious frame of mind and to wonder at how these people could have been so blind, stupid, arrogant, ignorant or reckless.

One purpose of this concluding section is to caution strongly against adopting such a judgemental stance. No less than the accident-producing errors themselves, the apparent clarity of retrospection springs in part from the shortcomings of human cognition. The perceptual biases and strong-but-wrong beliefs that make incipient disasters so hard to detect by those on the spot also make it difficult for accident analysts to be truly wise after the event. Unless we appreciate the potency of these retroactive distortions, we will never truly understand the realities of the past, nor learn the appropriate remedial lessons.

There is one obvious but psychologically significant difference between ourselves, the retrospective judges, and the people whose decisions, actions or inactions led to a disaster; we know how things were going to turn out, they did not. As Baruch Fischhoff and his colleagues have shown, possession of outcome knowledge profoundly influences the way we survey past events (Fischhoff, 1975; Slovic & Fischhoff, 1977; Fischhoff, 1989). This phenomenon is called *hindsight* bias, and has two aspects:

(a) The 'knew-it-all-along' effect (or 'creeping determinism'), where by observers of past events exaggerate what other people should have been able to anticipate in foresight. If they were involved in these events, they tend to exaggerate what they themselves actually knew in foresight.

(b) Historical judges are largely unaware of the degree to which outcome knowledge influences their perceptions of the past. As a result, they overestimate what they would have known had they not possessed this knowledge.

The historian George Florovsky described this phenomenon very precisely: "In retrospect, we seem to perceive the logic of the events which unfold themselves in a regular or linear fashion according to a recognizable pattern with an alleged inner necessity. So that we get the impression that it really could not have happened otherwise" (quoted by Fischhoff, 1975, p. 288).

Outcome knowledge dominates our perceptions of the past, yet we remain largely unaware of its influence. For those striving to make sense of complex historical events, familiarity with how things turned out imposes a definite but unconscious structure upon the antecedent actions and conditions. Prior facts are assimilated into this schema to make a coherent causal story, a process similar to that observed by Bartlett (1932) in his studies of remembering. But to those involved at the time of these same events would have had no such deterministic logic. Each participant's view of the future would have been bounded by local concerns. Instead of one grand convergent narrative, there would have been a multitude of individual stories running on in parallel towards the expected attainment of various distinct and personal goals.

Before judging too harshly the human failings that concatenate to cause a disaster, we need to make a clear distinction between the way the precursors appear now, given knowledge of the unhappy outcome, and the way they seemed at the time. Wagenaar and Groeneweg (1988) have coined the term impossible accident to convey the extreme difficulty of those involved to foresee any possible adverse conjunction between what seemed then to be unconnected and, in many instances, not especially unusual or dangerous happenings. They concluded their review of 100 shipping accidents with the following comment (Wagenaar & Groeneweg, 1988, p. 42):

> Accidents appear to be the result of highly complex coincidences which could rarely be foreseen by the people involved. The unpredictability is caused by the large number of causes and by the spread of the information over the participants. ... Accidents do not occur because people gamble and lose, they occur because people do not believe that the accident that is about to occur is at all possible.

The idea of personal responsibility is deeply rooted in Western cultures (Turner, 1978). The occurrence of a man-made disaster leads inevitably to a search for human culprits. Given the ease with which the contributing human failures can subsequently be identified, such scapegoats are not hard to find. But before we rush to judgement, there are some important points to be kept in mind. First, most of the people involved in serious accidents are neither stupid nor reckless, though they may well have been blind to the consequences of their actions. Second, we must beware of falling prey to the fundamental attribution error (i.e., blaming people and ignoring situational factors). As Perrow (1984) argued, it is in the nature of complex, tightly-coupled systems to suffer unforeseeable sociotechnical breakdowns. Third, before beholding the mote in his brother's eye, the retrospective observer should be aware of the beam of hindsight bias in his own.

APPENDIX: CASE STUDIES

THREE MILE ISLAND

Chain of events and active errors	Contributing conditions and latent failures
Maintenance crew introduces water into the instrument air system.	Although this error had occurred on two previous occasions, the operating company had not taken steps to prevent its recurrence. *(Management failure)*
Turbine tripped. Feedwater pumps shut down. Emergency feedwater pumps come on automatically, but flow blocked by two closed valves.	The two block valves had been erroneously left in the closed position during maintenance, probably carried out two days prior to the accident sequence. One of the warning lights showing that valves were closed was obscured by a maintenance tag. *(Maintenance failures)*
Rapid rise in core temperature and pressure, causing the reactor to trip. Relief valve (PORV) opens automatically, but then sticks in the open position. The scene is now set for a loss of coolant accident (LOCA) 13 seconds into the emergency.	During an incident at the Davis - Besse plant (another Babcock and Wilcox PWR) in September 1977, the PORV also stuck open. The incident was investigated by Babcock and Wilcox and the U.S. Nuclear Regulatory Commission. However, these analyses were not collated, and the information obtained regarding appropriate operator action was not communicated to the industry at large. *(Regulatory failure)*
Operators fail to recognise that the relief valve is stuck open. Primary cooling system now has hole in it through which radioactive water, under high pressure, pours into the containment area, and thence down into basement.	1. Operators were misled by control panel indications. Following an incident 1 year earlier, an indicator light had been installed. But this merely showed whether or not the valve had been commanded shut; it did not directly reveal valve status. *(Design and management failures)* 2. Operators wrongly assumed that high temperature at the PORV drain pipe was due to a chronically leaking valve. The pipe temperature normally registered high. *(Management/ procedural failure)*
Operators failed to diagnose stuck-open PORV for more than 2 hours. The resulting water loss caused significant damage to the reactor.	1. The control panel was poorly designed with hundreds of alarms that were not organized in a logical fashion. Many key indications were sited on the back wall of the control room. More than 100 alarms were activated with no means of suppressing unimportant ones. Several instruments went off-scale, and the computer printer ran more than 2 hours behind events. *(Design and management failures)* 2. Operator training, consisting largely of lectures and work in the reactor simulator, provided an inadequate basis for coping with real emergencies. Little feedback given to students, and training programme was insufficiently evaluated. *(Training and management failures)*
The crew cut back the high-pressure injection (HPI) of the water into the reactor coolant system, thus reducing the net flow rate from around 1000 gallons/min to about 25 gallons/min. This 'throttling' caused serious core damage.	1. Training emphasized the dangers of flooding the core. But this took no account of the possibility of a concurrent LOCA. *(Training and management failures)* 2. Following the 1977 Davis - Besse incident, the Nuclear Regulatory Commission issued a publication that made no mention of the fact that these operators had interrupted the HPI. The incident appeared under the heading of "valve malfunction" not "operator error". *(Regulatory failure)*

BHOPAL

Selected latent failures	Origins
1. System errors	
Locating a high risk plant close to a densely populated area.	Government/Management
Poor emphasis on system safety. No safety improvements after adverse audits.	Management
No improvement in safety measures, despite six prior accidents.	Government/Management
Storing 10 times more methyl isocyanate (MIC) than was needed daily. Poor evacuation measures.	Government/Management
Safety measures not upgraded when plant switched to large scale storage of MIC.	Management
Heavy reliance on inexperienced operators and supervisors.	Management
Factory inspector's warning on washing MIC lines neglected.	Management
Failure to release telex message on MIC treatment.	Management
2. Operator errors	
Reduction in operating and maintenance staff.	Management
Using a nontrained superintendent for the MIC plant.	Management
Repressurising the tank when it failed to get pressurised once.	Management/Operator
Issuing orders for washing when MIC tank failed to repressurise.	Management/Operator
Not operating warning siren until leak became severe.	Management
Switching off siren immediately after starting it.	Management
Failure to recognise that pressure rise was abnormal.	Management/Operator
Failure to use empty MIC tank to release pressure.	Management/Operator
3. Hardware errors	
Insufficient scrubber capacity.	Design
Refrigeration plant not operational.	Management/Maintenance
No automatic sensors to warn of temperature increase.	Design/Management
Pressure and temperature indicators did not work.	Management/Maintenance
Insufficient gas masks available.	Management
Flare tower was disconnected.	Management/Maintenance
Vent gas scrubber was in inactive mode.	Management
Iron pipelines were used for transporting MIC.	Management
A manual mechanism for switching off scrubber.	Design/Management
No regular cleaning of pipes and valves.	Maintenance/Management
No online monitor for MIC tanks	Design
No indicator for monitoring position of valves in control room.	Design
Pressure monitor underreading by 30 Psig.	Design

CHALLENGER

Date	Actions and latent failures
1977	During test firings of solid-rocket booster, Thiokol engineers discover that casing joints expanded (instead of tightening as designed). Thiokol persuades NASA that this is "not desirable but acceptable." It was discovered that one of the two O-ring joint seals frequently became unseated, thus failing to provide the back-up for which it was designed.
1981	NASA plans two lightweight versions of the boosters in order to increase payload. One is to be of steel, the other made of carbon filament. Hercules submits an improved design for the latter, incorporating a lip at the joint to prevent the O-ring from unseating (termed a "capture feature"). Thiokol continues to use unmodified joints for its steel boosters.
1981 November	Erosion (or "scorching") was noticed on one of the six primary O-rings. This was the same joint that was later involved in the Challenger disaster.
1982 December	As a result, NASA upgrades the criticality ratings on the joints to 1, meaning that the failure of this component could cause loss of both crew and spacecraft.
1983 April	Some NASA engineers seek to adapt the Hercules "capture feature" into the new thinner boosters. The proposal is shelved and the old joints continue to fly.
1984 February	Just prior to the 10th shuttle launch, high-pressure air tests are carried out on the booster joints. On return, an inch-long "scorch" is found in one of the primary O-rings. Despite the "critical-1" rating, Marshall Space Center reports that no remedial action is required. No connection noticed between high-pressure testing and "scorching," although pinholes in the insulating putty were observed.
1984 April	On 11th flight, one of the primary O-rings is found to be breached altogether. This was still regarded as acceptable. No connection made between high-pressure air testing and scorching, even though the latter was found on 10 of the subsequent 14 shuttle flights.
1985 January	Breaches ("blowbys") are found on four of the booster joints. Weather at launch coldest to date: 51 degr F with 53 degr F at the joints themselves. No connection noted.
1985 April	On the 17th shuttle mission, the primary O-ring in the nozzle joint fails to seal. Scorching found all the way round the joint.
1985 July	After another flight with three blowbys, NASA booster project manager places a launch constraint on the entire shuttle system. This means that no launch can take place if there are any worries about a Criticality-1 item. But waivers may be granted if it is thought that the problem will not occur in flight. Waivers are granted thereafter. Since top NASA management were unaware of the constraint, the waivers are not queried.
1985 July	Marshall and Thiokol engineers order 72 of the new steel casing segments with the capture features.
1985 July	Thiokol engineer writes memo warning of catastrophe if a blowout should occur in a field joint.
1985 August	Marshall and Thiokol engineers meet in Washington to discuss blowbys. Senior NASA manager misses meeting. Subsequently, 43 joint improvements ordered.
1985 December	Director of the solid rocket motor project at Thiokol urges "close out" on the O-ring problem (i.e., it should be ignored) on the grounds that new designs were on their way, and the difficulties were being worked on. But these solutions would not be ready for some time.
1986 January 23	Five days before the accident, the entry "Problem is considered closed" is placed in a NASA document called the Marshall Problem Reports.
1986 January 27	It is thought probable that, on the night before the launch, the temperature would fall into the twenties, some 15 degr F colder than the previous coldest launch a year earlier. (The actual launch temperature was 36 degr F, having risen from 24 degr F.) At this point, Allan McDonald, Thiokol's chief engineer at the Kennedy Space center (the "close out" man), experiences a change of heart and attempts to stop the launch.
1986 January 28	The Challenger shuttle is launched and explodes seconds after, killing all seven crew members. A blowout occurred on one of the primary booster O-rings.

CHERNOBYL

Chain of events and active failures	Contributing conditions and latent failures
At 1300 on 25 April 1986, power reduction starts with the intention of achieving test conditions. The tests are to be carried out at 25 per cent full power (in the 700MW range). They are to be conducted in Unit 4, sharing common facilities with Unit 3.	The test was to see whether the "coast-down" capacity of a turbine generator would be sufficient, given an appropriate voltage generator, to power the Emergency Core Cooling System(ECCS) for a few minutes. This would fill the time it took to get the diesel standby generators into operation. A voltage generator had been tested on two previous occasions, but had failed because of rapid voltage fall-off. The goal on this occasion was to carry out repeated testing just prior to the annual maintenance shut-down, scheduled to begin on the following Tuesday. According to Russian sources, the quality of the test plan was "poor and the section on safety measures had been drafted in a purely formal way." In addition, the test plan called for shutting off the ECCS for the entire test period (about 4 hours). Authority to proceed was given to station staff without the formal approval of the Safety Technical Group. In addition, there is some evidence that three other RBMK plants (at Leningrad, Kursk and Smolensk) had refused to carry out these tests on safety grounds. The principal testers were electrical engineers from Moscow. The man in charge, an electrical engineer, "was not a specialist in reactor plants" (Russian report). *(Institutional and managerial errors and violations)*
At 1400, the ECCS is disconnected from the primary circuit.	This was part of the test plan, but it stripped the plant of one of its main defences. *(Managerial failure)*
At 1405, Kiev controller asks Unit 4 to continue supplying grid. The ECCS is not reconnected.	Although this failure to reconnect the ECCS did not contribute directly to the subsequent disaster, it was indicative of a lax attitude on the part of the operators toward the observance of safety procedures. Subsequent 9 hours of operating at around 50 per cent full power increased xenon poisoning, making plant more difficult to control at low power. *(Managerial and design failures)*
At 0028, having been released from the grid at 2310, operators continue power reduction. But operator omits entry of "hold power" order; this leads to very low power.	The design of the RBMK reactor renders it liable to positive void coefficient at power settings below 20 per cent full power. After a long struggle, reactor power was stabilised at 7 per cent full power. At this point, the test should have been abandoned in view of the dangerously low power setting. Russian comment: "The staff was insufficiently familiar with the special features of the technological processes in a nuclear reactor." They had also "lost any feeling for the hazards involved." *(Managerial, design and operational failures)*
Operators and engineers continue to improvise in an unfamiliar and increasingly unstable regime to protect test plan. Plant goes super prompt critical. Explosions occur at 0124.	To ensure the continuance of the test, the operators and engineers gradually strip the reactor of its remaining defences. By 0122, the core had only 6 to 8 control rods inserted. An attempt to 'scram' the reactor at 0124 fails. Prompt criticality is now irreversible. *(Managerial, design and operational failures)*

HERALD OF FREE ENTERPRISE

Chain of events and active failures	Contributing conditions and latent failures
Herald is docked at No. 12 berth in Zeebrugge's inner harbour and is loading passengers and vehicles before making the crossing to Dover	This berth is not capable of loading both car decks (E and G) at the same time, having only a single ramp. Due to high water spring tides, the ramp could not be elevated sufficiently to reach E deck. To achieve this, it was necessary to trim the ship nosedown by filling trim ballast tanks Nos. 14 and 3. Normal practice was to start filling No. 14 tank 2 hours before arrival. *(System failure)*
At 1805 on 6 March 1987, the Herald goes astern from the berth, turns to starboard, and proceeds to sea with both her inner and outer bow doors fully open.	The most immediate cause is that the assistant bosun (whose job it was to close the doors) was asleep in his cabin, having just been relieved from maintenance and cleaning duties. *(Supervisory failure and unsuitable rostering)* The bosun, his immediate superior, was the last man to leave G deck. He noticed that the bow doors were still open, but did not close them since he did not see that as part of his duties. *(Maintenance failure)*
Chief officer checks that there are no passengers on G deck, and thinks he sees assistant bosun going to close doors (though testimony is confused on this point).	The chief officer, responsible for ensuring door closure, was also required (by company orders) to be on the bridge 15 minutes before sailing time. *(Management failure)* Because of delays at Dover, there was great pressure on crews to sail early. Memo from operations manager: "put pressure on your first officer if you don't think he's moving fast enough ...sailing late out of Zeebrugge isn't on. It's 15 minutes early for us." *(Management failure)* Company standing orders (ambiguously worded) appear to call for "negative reporting" only. If not told otherwise the master should assume that all is well. Chief officer did not make a report, nor did the master ask him for one. *(Management failure)*
On leaving harbour, master increases speed. Water enters open bow doors and floods into G Deck. At around 1827, Herald capsizes to port.	Despite repeated requests from the master to the management, no bow door indicators were available on the bridge, and the master was unaware that he had sailed with bow doors open. Estimated cost of indicators was £400-500. *(Management failure)* Ship had chronic list to port. *(Management and technical failure)* Scuppers inadequate to void water from flooded G deck. *(Design and maintenance failure)* Top-heavy design of the Herald and other "ro ro" ships in its class was inherently unsafe. *(Design failure)*

KING'S CROSS UNDERGROUND FIRE

Chain of events and active failures	Contributing conditions and latent failures
At 1925 on 18 November 1987, discarded smoker's material (probably) sets fire to grease and detritus in right hand running track of escalator 4 (up) Piccadilly Line.	Wooden escalator installed in 1939. Long recognized as being especially fire-prone. Water fog equipment installed in 1948. Could not be used nightly because of rust problems. Smoke detectors not installed: expense not justified. Forty-five per cent of the 400 fires recorded on London Underground over previous 20 years had occurred on MH escalator. Running tracks not regularly cleaned, partly due to organizational changes which blurred maintenance and cleaning responsibilities. Safety specialist scattered over three directorates focused on operational or occupational safety. Passenger safety neglected. Railway Inspectorate took a blinkered view of their role. They did not pursue issues of fire protection. Judged as having "too cosy" a relationship with London Underground. Smoking permitted on London Underground trains and premises. *(Hardware, organizational, and regulatory failures)*
At 1934, railway police evacuate passengers via Victoria Line escalator. They are unaware of the layout of the station.	Inadequate fire and emergency training given to staff. It was accepted by the LU that the quality of staff training at its White City training center had been inadequate. Only 4 of the 21 station staff on duty had had any training in evacuation or fire drills. *(Management failure)*
At 1930, passenger alerts booking clerk to small fire on escalator 4. Booking clerk rings Relief Station inspector (RSI), but does not specify precise location of fire.	Inadequate fire and emergency training given to staff. It was accepted by LU that the quality of staff training at its White City training center had been inadequate. Only 4 of the 21 station staff on duty had had any training in evacuation or fire drills. *(Management failure)*
Between 1935 and 1938, RSI enters lower machine room, but fails to detect fire. He enters upper machine room and sees smoke and flames. Fetches fire extinguisher, but cannot get close enough to use it. He is too preoccupied to activate water fog equipment.	Inadequate training. RSI was not regularly based at King's Cross, nor did he have any fire training. He had not so far informed either the station manager (located some distance away due to refurbishment of the station) or the line controller of the fire. Trains were still arriving. Location of water fog equipment not widely known *(Management, and communication failures)*
At 1939, police in ticket hall decided to evacuate the area. At 1940, police officer asks for Piccadilly and Victoria Line trains to be ordered not to stop at King's Cross. Trains continue to stop. At 1941, metal gates to ticket hall closed by police officers. At 1945, first fire engines arrive. Two firemen examine fire on escalator. At 1945, flashover occurs. Whole ticket hall engulfed in intense heat and flame. Thirty-one people are killed, many others are seriously injured.	No established evacuation plan. Locked doors and metal barriers blocked escape routes. LU control rooms last modernised in the 1960s. Outdated communications equipment. Headquarters controller had no access to station public address system, which was not used during the emergency. 5 of the 8 TV monitors were out of service. Trains do not have a public address system. No public telephones at King's Cross tube station. *(Management, hardware, maintenance, and communication failures)* Fires ("smoulderings") regarded as inevitable occurrence on LU. "They are part of the nature of the oldest, most extensive, most complex underground railway in the world. Anyone who believes that it is possible to act as though there are no fires ever is, I fear, misguided" (Dr Ridley, then Chairman of London Underground). *Management, system, and organizational failures*

REFERENCES

Bainbridge, L. The ironies of automation. In J. Rasmussen, K. Duncan & J. Leplat (Eds.), *New Technology and Human Error*. London: Wiley, 1987.

Baker, S., & Marshall, E. Chernobyl and the role of psychologists: An appeal to Reason. *The Psychologist: Bulletin of the British Psychological Society*, 1988, 3, 107-108.

Bartlett, F.C. *Remembering: A Study in Experimental and Social Psychology*. Cambrige: Cambridge University Press, 1932.

Bellamy, L.J. *The Safety Management Factor: An Analysis of the Human Error Aspects of the Bhopal Disaster*. London: Technica Ltd., 1985.

Collier, J.G., & Davies, L.M. *Chernobyl: The Accident at Chernoyl Unit 4 in the Ukraine, April 1986*. Barnwood, Gloucs.: Central Electricity Generating Board, 1986.

Cooper, H.S.F. Letter from the Space Center. *The New Yorker*, November 10, 1987.

De Keyser, V. Temporal decision making in complex environments. Paper presented at Workshop on New Technology, Distributed Decision Making and Responsibility. Bad Homburg, W. Germany, 5-7 May, 1988.

De Keyser, V., Decortis, F., Housiaux, A., & Van Daele, A. Les communications hommes-machines dans les systemes complexes. *Action Fast*. Bruxelles: Politique et Scientifique, 1987.

Duncan, K. Fault diagnosis for advanced continuous process installations. In J. Rasmussen, K. Duncan & J. Leplat (Eds.), *New Technology and Human Error*. London: Wiley, 1987.

Fennell, D. *Investigation into the King's Cross Underground Fire*. Department of Transport. London: HMSO, 1988.

Fischhoff, B. Hindsight does not equal foresight: The effect of outcome knowlege on judgement under uncertainty. *Journal of Experimental Psychology: Human Performance & Perception*, 1975, 1, 288-299.

Fischhoff, B. Simple behavioral principles in complex system design. Paper presented at the World Bank Workshop on Safety Control and Risk Management, Washington, D.C., October 18-20, 1989.

Fiske, S.T., & Taylor, S.E. *Social Cognition*. Reading, Mass.: Addison-Wesley, 1984.

Hudson, P.T.W. Personal communication, 1988.

INPO. *A Maintenance Analysis of Safety Significant Events*. Nuclear Utility Management and Human Resources Committee, Maintenance Working Group. Atlanta, Ga.: Institute of Nuclear Power Operations, 1985 (b).

INPO. *An Analysis of Root Causes in 1983 and 1984 Significant Event Reports*. INPO 85-027. Atlanta, Ga.: Institute of Nuclear Power Operations, 1985 (a).

INPO. *An Analysis of Root Causes in 1983 Significant Event Reports*. INPO 84-027. Atlanta, Ga.: Institute of Nuclear Power Operations, 1984.

Kemeny, J. *The Need for Change: The Legacy of TMI*. Report of the President's Commission on the Accident at Three Mile Island. New York: Pergamon, 1979.

Kerhli, R.R. The investigative techniques used by the *Challenger* Commission to address information system failures as they relate to the Space Shuttle accident. In J. Wise & A. Debons (Eds.), *Information Systems: Failure Analysis*. Berlin: Springer-Verlag, 1987.

Kjellen, U. An evaluation of safety information systems of six medium-sized and large firms. *Journal of Occupational Accidents,* 1983, 3, 273-288.

Lanir, Z. *Fundamental Surprise*. Eugene, Ore.: Decision Research, 1986.

Layfield, F. *Report on the Sizewell B Public Inquiry*. London: HMSO, 1987.

Lihou, D.A., & Lihou, S.J. *Bhopal: Some Human Factors Considerations.* Birmingham: Lihou Loss Prevention Services, 1985.

Marcus, A.A., & Fox, I. Lessons learned about communicating safety-related concerns to industry: The Nuclear Regulatory Commission after Three Mile Island. Presented at 1988 Symposium on Science Communication: Environmental and Health Research. Los Angeles, University of Southern California, 15-17 December, 1988.

Montmollin, M. *L'Intelligence de la Tache. Elements d'Ergonomie Cognitive.* Paris: Peter Lang, 1984.

Moray, N. Monitoring behavior and supervisory control. In K. Boff, L. Kaufman & J. Thomas (Eds.), *Handbook of Perception and Human Performance (vol. 2).* New York: Wiley, 1986.

Morehouse, W., & Subramaniam, M. A. *The Bhopal Tragedy.* New York: Council on International and Public Affairs, 1986.

Morris, P.A., & Engelken, R.H. Safety experiences in the operation of nuclear power plants. In *International Atomic Energy Agency Principles and Standards.* Vienna: International Atomic Energy Agency, 1973.

NUREG. *Loss of Main and Auxiliary Feedwater Event at the Davis-Besse Plant on June 9, 1985.* NUREG-1154. Washington, D.C.: U.S. Nuclear Regulatory Comission, 1985.

Perrow, C. *Normal Accidents: Living with High-Risk Technologies.* New York: Basic Books, 1984.

Presidential Commision on the Space Shuttle Accident (1986). *Report to the President.* Washington, DC.

Rasmussen, J. Interdisciplinary workshops to develop a multi-disciplinary research programme based on a holistic system approach to safety and management of risk in large-scale technological operations. Paper commissioned by the World Bank, Washington, D. C., 1988.

Rasmussen, J. What can be learned from human error reports? In K. Dunan, M. Gruneberg & D. Wallis (Eds.), *Changes in Working Life.* London: Wiley, 1980.

Rasmussen, J., & Pedersen, O.M. Human factors in probabilistic risk analysis and risk management. In *Operational Safety of Nuclear Power Plants (vol.1).* Vienna: International Atomic Energy Agency, 1984.

Reason, J. T. & Mycielska, K. *Absent-Minded? The Psychology of Mental Lapses and Everyday Errors.* Englewood Cliffs, N. J. : Prentice-Hall, 1982.

Reason, J. T. Chernobyl: A reply to Baker and Marshall. *The Psychologist: Bulletin of the British Psychological Society,* 1988, 7, 255-256.

Reason, J. T. Lapses of attention. In R. Parasuraman & R. Davies (Eds.), *Varieties of Attention.* New York: Academic Press, 1984(a).

Reason, J. T. The Chernobyl errors. *Bulletin of the British Psychological Society,* 1987, 40, 201-206.

Reason, J. T., Manstead, A.S.R., Stradling, S., Baxter, J., Campbell, K., & Huyser, J. *Interim Report on the Investigation of Driver Errors and Violations.* Univesity of Manchester: Department of Psychology, 1988.

Rochlin, G.I., La Porte, T.R., & Roberts, K.H. The self-designing high-reliability organization: Aircraft carrier flight operations at sea. *Naval War College Review,* Autumn 1987.

Rogovin, M. *Report of the Presidents's Commission on the Accident at Three Mile Island.* Washington, D.C.: Government Printing Office, 1979.

Sheen, Mr Justice. MV Herald of Free Enterprise. Report of Court No. 8074 Formal Investigation. London: Department of Transport, 1987.

Shell Safety Committee. *Unsafe Act Auditing.* The Hague: Shell Internatinale Petroleum Maatschappij B.V., 1987.

Sheridan, T.B., & Hennessy, R.T. (Eds.). *Research and Modeling of Supervisory Control Behavior*. Washington, D.C.: National Academy Press, 1984.

Slovic, P., & Fischhoff, B. On the psychology of experimental surprises. *Journal of Experimental Psychology*: *Human Perception and Performance*, 1977,3,544-511.

Turner, B.A. *Man-Made Disaster*. London: Wykeham, 1978.

UKAEA. *The Chernobyl Accident and its Consequences*. United Kingdom Atomic Energy Authority. London: H.M.S.O. 1987.

Union Carbide. Bhopal Methyl Isocyanate Incident Investigation Team Report. Danbury, Conn.: Union Carbide Corporation, March 1985.

USSR State Committee on the Utilization of Atomic Energy. *The Accident at the Chernobyl Nuclear Power Plant and Its Consequences*. Information compiled for the IAEA Experts' Meeting, 25-29 August, 1986. Vienna: IAEA, 1986.

Wagenaar, W.A., & Groeneweg, J. Accidents at sea: Multiple causes and impossible consequences. *International Journal of Man-Machine Studies*, 1987,27,587-598.

Westrum, R. Organizational and inter-organisational thought. World Bank Workshop on Safety Control and Risk Management, Washington, D.C., 16-18 October, 1988.

Woodham-Smith, C. *The Reason Why*. London: Constable, 1953.

Woods, D.D. Technology alone is not enough. In R. Anthony (Ed.), *Human Reliability in Nuclear Power*. London: IBC Technical Services, 1987.

Wreathall, J. Personal communication, 1989.

COMPUTERS IN WEAPONS: THE LIMITS OF CONFIDENCE[2]

David Lorge Parnas

The military assisted at the birth of the modern electronic computer because it was obvious that computers could be used to develop new defense technologies and to produce tables for use in artillery battles. Over the years, computers have made substantial contributions to the accuracy and effectiveness of the armed forces. Today, computers have been integrated into many weapon systems, and software errors have become a major concern for all the armed services. It is common for Department of Defense officials to speak of a software crisis because software has become a source of both long delays in development of weapons and unpredictable failures in the field. As a result, many experts are now concerned about the trustworthiness of the increasingly powerful weapons at our disposal. The Pentagon has funded a wide variety of research projects intended to ameliorate the situation by improving the quality of the software purchased as a part of weapon systems. This chapter explains the role of computer systems in modern warfare and discusses the limitations on our ability to develop trustworthy computer systems.

WHAT DO COMPUTERS DO IN WEAPON SYSTEMS?

To describe the role of computers in weapon systems we must introduce three terms. The "target" is the object we want to damage. "Weapon" refers to the destructive device—bomb, projectile, missile, energy beam—that will be directed to approach the target and damage or destroy it. "Platform" refers to an airplane, ship, satellite or surface vehicle that carries the weapon to the point where it can be aimed or directed at a target. Computers in weapon systems assist in the performance of functions in four categories, described below.

Communications

Modern warfare requires the exchange of large amounts of information. Computers are used to control the transmission of such information, to distribute it to its intended recipients, to perform consistency checks on the transmitted data, to control shared resources, and to transform the information into a form that humans or devices can use. Computers are particularly vital when communication is between rapidly moving platforms using highly directional transmissions. When the computer actually controls the communication between personnel and weapon system, it can also be used to enforce access restrictions, for example, to demand a password and identification from the operator. For example, computer programs control the locks that are intended to prevent unauthorized use of nuclear weapons.

Navigation

Often the platform from which a weapon can be fired is itself mobile. Accurate aiming at a target with known location requires accurate information about the location of the platform. Computers can be used to determine the present location of the platform. Computers can also be used to compute a path from the platform's current location to a position from which the weapon can be fired at the target. The information produced by the computer can be used to guide a human controlling the platform, or the platform may be directly controlled by the computer.

Weapon Path Prediction and Weapon Control

Computers can predict the path that would be followed by a weapon if released at a specified point in space, with a specified release velocity, wind velocity, air density, and so forth. These predictions are based on mathematical models whose complexity depends on the number of physical factors taken into account. Path predictions are used to determine when and how a weapon should be fired in order to hit a specific target. The computer can either inform someone of the projected impact point, letting that person decide when to fire, or the computer can control the firing or release of the weapon directly. For most weapons, there is no opportunity to control the weapon after release, but some newer weapons can be controlled from the platform after release. Some weapons contain their own computerized guidance system, which takes over after release.

Target Identification, Tracking, and Target Motion Prediction

Computers can be used to process data from a sensor such as a radar unit and determine whether or not a possible target is present. Once a potential target has been identified, either by the computer or by other means, the computer can process the sensor data to keep track of the location of that object relative to the platform while both platform and target move. Computers can control the sensors, aiming, tuning, or positioning them, to obtain the most useful data. The computer can also be used to make extrapolations from tracking data to predict where the target will be at the time that the weapon could reach it. In some sophisticated weapon systems, more than one computer may be used. For example, a computer in the platform may identify and track the object and control a device that "illuminates" the target so that another, smaller computer, in the weapon itself, may track it more easily. Computers allow adaptive behavior in which the weapon system bases its identification, tracking, and prediction on previous observations. In this way, the computer may compensate for evasive tactics used by an enemy if the enemy continues to behave in the same way.

HOW AUTOMATED ARE WEAPON SYSTEMS?

Each of the functions described may be performed by a combination of human and computer effort. It is useful to distinguish four different approaches to the use of computers in military applications:

Off-Line Preparation of Tables
for Use in Manually Controlled Systems

A weapon and platform may be controlled by one or more persons who use tables and charts that were produced with the help of a computer. The operator consults these references when aiming and firing a weapon. In such applications, the computer is used long before the battle; computing may be done in a secure position where power supplies and communications are reliable.

On-Line Calculations Providing
Data for a Human Controller

If the mathematical models used in the computation take many factors into account, the tables and charts may become so detailed and bulky that it is not practical to consult them in the field. Time restrictions may make it difficult for the operator to use manual charts. In such situations, it's useful to install computers near the equipment so that the information needed may be computed when needed and displayed to the operator in a convenient form. The operator can check the data, to make sure the values are reasonable, before using it to control the weapon or platform.

On-Line Calculations with Built-in
Computers and Human Supervision

It is often inefficient to compute data, display it to an operator who then enters that same data to control the weapon. Instead, one may feed the data directly from the computer to the weapon control equipment so that the equipment is under computer control. However, it is still useful to have the operator present to check the data for reasonableness and to be able to override the automatic control when it appears necessary. The operator often has additional data about the situation and can recognize a computer error. In such systems, the operator can choose to revert to a manual control mode in which he can control the weapon directly even when the computer fails. However, when the use of such systems is routine, the operator often allows the data to be used without checking it.

Full Automation

In some situations there is no time for human involvement, or it is impractical to have a human in a position to perform the necessary control functions. For example a pilot who has released an air-to-air missile may be too busy flying his airplane to be involved in controlling the missile. It would be inappropriate to place him on the missile and expensive to give him the information and control that he would have if he were located on or in the weapon. In these situations a computer could have full control of the missile, although sometimes the pilot would retain the ability to destroy the released weapon.

SOME EXAMPLES

We have classified computerized weapons by both the function that the computer performs and the degree of automation. The two classifications are independent and, together, characterize sixteen roles that computers can play in weapon systems. Below, we describe military computer applications in each of these categories. Each example is identified by its row and column in Table 5.5.

1-1 Bounce Tables

The characteristics of radio signals at various frequencies may be used to generate tables that guide a communications technician in selecting frequencies and orienting antennas. The operator is free to deviate from these guidelines if unusual operating conditions make it necessary.

1-2 Navigator Charts

Computers can produce a large variety of tables and charts that guide an aircraft navigator. For example, computer generated tables may help a navigator to determine his position when given the direction to two known transmitters.

The navigator can turn to other methods if spurious signals lead to unreasonable results.

1-3 Artillery Tables

Computers can be used to produce tables that give the distance to the impact point of a shell fired at a given angle. These are then used by the officer who directs the weapon. If field experience indicates that the tables are not accurate, the officer can adjust his aim based on information about the impact point of recent shots.

1-4 Target Locations

Computers may be used to produce tables describing the location of enemy installations that are potential targets. These can be used by pilots or artillery officers during a battle.

Table 5.5				
	Communications	**Navigation**	**Weapon Path Prediction**	**Target Identification Tracking**
Off Line	Bounce Tables	Navigator Charts	Artillery Tables	Target Locations
On Line Data Display	Antenna Aiming	Projected Map Display	Impact Point	Target Display
On Line Supervised Control	Antenna Control	Auto Pilot	Bomb Release	Target Selection
Full Automation	Satellite Communication	Drone Control	Missile Defense	Missile Defense

2-1 Antenna Aiming

Computers may compute antenna orientations given data about the location of the other station. They may also suggest frequencies. The radio operator can review the computer suggestions before adjusting his equipment and make a different selection under unusual conditions.

2-2 Projected Map Display

In many airplanes a computer controls the positioning of a projected map that shows a pilot the interesting features of the territory below. He can compare the map with what he sees and, if necessary, update the location information in the computer to make the actual location and the computed location the same.

2-3 Impact Point

The computer may indicate where a bomb would drop if released at the present moment. The pilot releases the bomb when the computer-indicated impact point coincides with the point that he wants to hit. He is free to compensate for factors, such as target motion, that are not known to the computer by selecting an impact point that he expects to be the location of the moving target at the time of impact.

2-4 Target Location Display

The pilot can identify the location of the target by positioning a marker on a display in the pilot's field of view. The computer keeps the marker positioned over the identified ground position even as the airplane moves. This information helps the pilot keep track of the target in periods of reduced visibility. He can designate a new target position, updating the information in the computer, whenever he finds that the computer-computed position is inaccurate.

3-1 Antenna Control

Antennae used in highly directional communications can be controlled by computers while the sender and receiver move. Operators can correct inaccuracies caused by unusual conditions or computer error. Computers can also set up routings for communications requiring several relays.

3-2 Automatic Pilot

Computers may serve as an automatic pilot controlling some of the flight surfaces while the pilot observes and relaxes, ready to take over when necessary.

3-3 Bomb Release

The pilot can designate a desired target and the computer can release the bomb when the impact point and the pilot-selected target coincide. The pilot can observe a display that shows both the location that the computer believes is the target and the computed impact point. He can override the computer if needed.

3-4 Target Selection

A computer can identify a target using, for example, the heat generated by an airplane or missile engine. It then displays the location of this target to the pilot and begins to track the target. The pilot can force a new target designation if he notes that the computer has focused on a friendly vehicle, the sun, or a flare designed to fool such heat-seeking systems.

4-1 Satellite Communication Control

Communication with satellites is routinely under computer control. Computers orient directional antennae, select network configuration, check for accuracy and confirmation of receipt. No human is involved in normal operation, but reprogramming is possible if bugs are noted. However, when reprogramming is needed, critical data may be lost.

4-2 Drone Control

Computers may control drone planes, satellite maneuvers and pilotless landers making course corrections when needed. Often there is no opportunity for intervention. Errors result in the loss of a vehicle and the program is corrected for use in future flights.

4-3 Missile Defense Weapon Control

The pace of a battle in missile defense is so rapid that computers are essential for weapon control. Humans cannot react fast enough to accurately aim and fire weapons. In a space-based ABM (antiballistic missile) system, the path of directed energy weapons, rail guns, or "smart rocks" would be computed and used to control firing. There would be no opportunity for human intervention and no opportunity to correct programming errors during the battle. Failure could allow the enemy missile to destroy its target.

4-4 Missile Defense Target Selection

In a missile defense system the pace of the attack would be so rapid that the computer would have to identify and select the targets. In a space-based ABM system, the computer would have to discriminate between decoys and real warheads as well as between five warheads and those that were damaged by a directed energy weapon. There would be little opportunity for human intervention in such decisions because of the large number of targets and short battle duration. There would be even less opportunity to correct discrimination algorithms during the battle. Failure could allow the enemy missile to destroy its target. In addition to the specific functions described above, computers in weapon systems play the same multitude of roles that they now play in commercial equipment such as automobiles. Computers can be involved in engine control, fly-by-wire control systems, and monitoring. Many small subsystems now include their own computers rather than the hard-wired logic used earlier. Unexpected interactions between these programs sometimes surprise everyone involved.

WHY IS THE USE OF DIGITAL COMPUTERS
AND SOFTWARE IN MILITARY SYSTEMS INCREASING?

There is a clear trend toward the use of programmable microprocessors to replace older technologies in many components of large systems. In part, this can be explained by the rapid decrease in prices for microprocessor hardware. However, there are at least three basic technological advantages to the use of this approach; these advantages are probably more significant than the price change.

1. When analog technology is used, increased accuracy can be obtained only by more accurate control of the manufacturing process for basic materials. With digital technology accuracy can be obtained by increasing the number of components rather than their quality. In analog technology, accuracy may require close control of environmental parameters such as temperature. Digital circuits, designed to have only two stable states, are less sensitive to variations in such parameters.

2. There are practical limits on the mathematical functions that can be implemented using analog technology. It is difficult to implement functions that are not continuous, functions where the value changes suddenly at some threshold. There are no such limitations on digital computers. Using them, we can implement programs that make sharp distinctions between cases that are almost the same. This allows digital computers to be used in highly

complex situations where small differences in input should result in a large change in the output.

3. With older technologies changes in the functions implemented usually require some changes to the hardware. One must physically move a wire, replace a part, and so on. Frequently the changes are so major that complete replacement is needed. The behavior of programmable digital machines can be changed by loading new data into the memory. When there are many installations, changes by this method are much easier to implement than actual revisions to the hardware.

WHAT ARE THE DRAWBACKS OF DIGITAL TECHNOLOGY?

The use of digital computer technology is not without its drawbacks. Serious design errors that are not discovered until the system is released and actually used are far more common than with other technologies. Software is known for being untrustworthy and hard to get right. Changes are sometimes unexpectedly costly. The three reasons for this correspond to the three advantages.

1. Although, theoretically, the accuracy of digital arithmetic is unlimited, the finite approximations to real numbers that are used in digital computers do not have all the properties that we intuitively expect of arithmetic. For example, in digital computers it may not be the case that $(x+2y+z)-y$ computes the same value as $x+y+z$. The results may not even be close! Hard-to-find errors are the result.

2. The technology that allows us to create arbitrary discrete functions allows us to create programs whose functions have no compact description. The result is that we produce programs whose behavior we do not understand. The objects are so complex that we cannot understand them completely and our own creations regularly surprise us with unexpected behavior. We cannot even find useful approximations! The nature of the technology is such that minor discrepancies can have spectacular results.

3. The ease of change of software seems to lead to sloppiness. Software is often built without careful analysis because we know we can change the programs when we find errors. Some computer scientists advocate building programs before we understand the problem. They argue that we will discover more about the problem as we try the program. They point out that, when we discover that we misunderstood the problem, we can correct the program. Unfortunately, this often results in a program that has lost its original structure, and is not adequately understood.

WHAT IS THE STATE OF THE ART IN THE DEVELOPMENT OF LARGE SOFTWARE SYSTEMS?

It is sad but true that software systems do not work adequately when first delivered to customers. The first time that they are put into actual use we discover errors of varying severity. Some of them are caused by our ignorance of the conditions that the program will encounter. Others are caused by our ignorance of the implications of the program that we have written. Substantial revisions are required after the first users report their problems. Software often delays the availability of products, both military and civilian. If we are able to persevere and use the software it usually, but not always, improves. The process is one of evolution. Serious problems cause the system to "die" or produce incorrect results, but each one can be corrected. The program is revised and the next version is better. If we can accept that the software will fail in its early use, we may be able to endure until the quality becomes acceptable. Often, the corrections introduce new errors. Some software projects have failed because, on the average, each correction introduced more errors than it removed. Eventually, the software was simply abandoned.

WHY CAN'T WE DISCOVER THE ERRORS BY TESTING BEFORE DELIVERY?

One of our most respected computer scientists, E.W. Dijkstra, said, "Testing can show the presence of bugs, never their absence." Practical software must deal with so many distinct situations (or states) that complete testing is impossible. Software can pass any practical test and still contain serious errors. All we can do is test a selected subset of the situations that the software could encounter. This can give us a statistical estimate of the number of errors that remain. Useful estimates require that we know the statistical distribution of states and inputs that will be encountered in actual use. If our only concern is reliability, that is, the frequency of failures, random testing can provide good estimates. However, if we are interested in showing that the probability of serious errors remaining is low, testing cannot help; the number of tests required is far too large. Even the positive results about reliability prediction through random testing are overly optimistic. They depend on our knowledge of the operating conditions. When we are not replacing an old system with one intended to perform the same functions, we do not know the operating conditions before installation. The true statistics and operating conditions are only discovered when the system is functioning reliably. While the system is considered unreliable, the usage may not be the same as it would be after the system has matured.

WHY CAN'T WE REPLACE TESTING WITH SIMULATION?

We are often told that, with computer systems, simulation can overcome our inability to test adequately. Simulation is a powerful tool, but it too has severe limitations. The most fundamental limitation is that simulation is just another form of testing. The statistical limitations that keep us from doing an adequate number of tests apply just as well to simulated tests as to real ones. However, there are further limitations. We do not usually anticipate all the conditions that will arise in actual use. Often, the simulation designers make the same false assumptions as the program designers. Equally important, in practice it has proved difficult to keep the simulation model consistent with the design. Frequently we find that the simulators are evaluating a design that is different from the actual design. It is difficult, sometimes impossible, to keep the two consistent as the system design evolves. The result is often simulation models that are detailed, well implemented, but useless; they are simulating a design substantially different from the one that is being considered.

WHAT IS THE EFFECT OF HARDWARE FAILURES ON OUR ABILITY TO PRODUCE TRUSTWORTHY SOFTWARE?

Hardware failures are a fact of life that must be dealt with in all computer systems. Systems that are expected to be reliable or trustworthy must have software that helps in the recovery from hardware failures. For example, the software should provide a reduced, but useful, level of service when a partial hardware failure occurs; it should not simply quit. We can design systems that can survive routine, limited hardware failures. Such systems can continue to operate without significant interruption when one device fails. Unfortunately, it is impossible to design software that can recover from all possible combinations of hardware failures. Hardware failures highlight the gap between theory and practice in computer science. For example, we can prove that a computer system will not get into a deadlock, waiting forever without making progress. Unfortunately, the proof must make simplifying assumptions about hardware failures. A proof that took all possible combinations of hardware failures into account would be impractical. Deadlock-free computer systems still experience deadlocks when hardware failures occur. Similarly, probability theory allows us to predict that certain computer systems will not fail more than a few hours in forty years. Unfortunately, such predictions are based on the assumption that failures in one part of the system are independent of failures in another part. In practice, such assumptions often prove false. Most treatments of the reliability of computer networks assume that when a component fails it will simply go "dead." The models that they use ignore the possibility of a component that continues to function but functions incorrectly, producing information that brings the rest of the network to a halt. Models that look at all the possibilities for partial malfunctioning are intractable. There are too many possibilities.

THE PROBLEM OF POLLUTED DATA

Another class of problems that exacerbates the gap between theory and practice in building trustworthy computer systems is the problem of incorrect data. Recall that some of the power of the digital computer comes from its ability to have a big change of output because of a small change in some input. This also means that if the change in the input is a small error, the error in the output can be catastrophic. All well-designed software systems include programs to test the input data to see if it is reasonable; they are designed to detect erroneous input and not respond to it. Unfortunately, it is not possible to detect all errors in input data because some errors result in valid, but incorrect, inputs. Certain systems are particularly vulnerable to data pollution. Systems dependent on large databases with data supplied by many sources are vulnerable because any of the sources may pollute the database. Computer systems that depend on communication channels that are subject to interruption or jamming are particularly vulnerable. Systems depending on very sensitive sensors are easily polluted. Human error is a frequent source of data pollution.

THE USE OF SAFETY-LIMITED COMPUTERS

Software has proved to be a technology in which major errors are common and the product is not error tolerant. Even minor errors can have major effects. High-quality software may have as many as 1 error per thousand lines. A large system might have 40,000 errors and be reliable, but it takes only one error to have a catastrophic effect. Because of this, it is common to use digital computers in systems designed in such a way that a computer software failure will not be a catastrophe. For example, an elevator may include mechanical interlocks so that it will not fail when the program controlling it fails. Airplanes can be built with an interlock that prevents dropping a bomb when the plane is on the ground. Airplanes do not crash if the air traffic control program fails because the pilots can continue to fly in safe patterns until it returns. A nuclear plant that is controlled by a computer can have a separate shutdown system that will prevent catastrophe if the computer program fails. In military software, the use of such techniques has been tried with mixed results. An airplane that depends on a digital computer for fine control of its flight surfaces may be able to outperform an airplane that is designed to be flyable even if the computer fails. Safety interlocks built into the hardware or software may prevent the use of unusual techniques when they are badly needed. In short, designers often feel that they must choose between limiting the damage that a software error can cause and getting the highest possible performance. In battle, performance means survival.

WHAT'S DIFFERENT ABOUT MILITARY COMPUTING?

Much of what we have said applies to all applications of digital computers. Software has been a problem for banks, airlines, and management information systems. However, there are certain aspects of military applications that make the situation worse:
1. Realistic testing of weapon systems is often dangerous and expensive and may in some cases violate treaties.
2. Actual use is essential in learning the real requirements; enemies often do not think the way the designers do. As one frustrated designer once put it, "You wouldn't believe the things those guys thought of, nobody would think of things like that."

3. In other applications, errors that evidence themselves only in unlikely situations may be assumed to cause problems infrequently. In military applications, one must assume an antagonistic and sophisticated user who will work to make these unlikely situations frequent. The worst case may become the normal case if an enemy becomes aware of an exploitable flaw in the software.
4. The limitations on our ability to handle hardware failures by software recovery techniques are particularly important in military computer systems. Such systems are often subject to coordinated violent attacks, which can cause failure in many components at once. Jamming and other sabotage can cause partial malfunctioning. These problems are far more severe with a determined and sophisticated adversary in a military situation than they are in relatively controlled commercial environments.
5. Errors in input data are also likely under battle conditions. The shock, noise, and dust created by battle can pollute the data. Human operators are more likely to make input errors under battle conditions.
6. Failures frequently result in a destruction of any evidence of the cause.
7. The correctness of many weapons, such as those that use computers to identify enemy targets, depends on assumptions about the enemy designs. This means that it is within the power of the enemy to invalidate the weapons if the weapon designers made any assumptions other than those whose validity is guaranteed by physical laws.
8. Those weapons that we hope never to use, or will be used only once, cannot benefit from the process of evolution. This is discussed more in the next section.

EVOLUTION: WHAT DOES IT MEAN?

Experienced designers know that trustworthy computer systems are not created in one step, they evolve. Projects that succeed are usually just one more step in a sequence of systems of a certain type. Each system in the sequence shares many characteristics with its predecessors. Even then, the individual systems are not satisfactory when first released to people other than software developers. They are used (and abused), and they fail. Each failure provides some information leading to correction. Sometimes, after a long sequence of such corrections, the system becomes useful. The computer-controlled systems that surround us have evolved through a sequence of changes so gradual that each new version was expected to do something close to what the old version was doing already. Each new system has required testing in actual use, and each has required revision after such use. Like natural systems, they have evolved so that they can handle conditions that resemble those encountered during the evolution, and, like natural systems, changes in the environment cause failures. As with natural evolution, the evolution of computer software succeeds only when we can afford to discard what is lost when failure occurs. Systems that are not used repeatedly and routinely as they will be used in battle are not likely to work in battle.

WHERE CAN WE TRUST COMPUTERS?

From Table 5.5 we can see that trustworthiness is far easier to obtain in the upper-left portion of the table than in the lower-right portion. Communications systems are inherently simpler than other types of systems because we control the requirements. Communications systems can be tested thoroughly and safely. Navigation systems are more easily tested than systems for weapon control or target identification. Navigation systems depend on physical laws, not the behavior of an opponent. Weapon control software is difficult to test under realistic conditions because such tests are dangerous and expensive. Target identification is the most difficult to test because it cannot be tested under battle conditions and because it is difficult to provide realistic targets. The characteristics of the targets are determined by the potential enemy, and only the enemy can know what those characteristics are. Systems with a lower degree of automation can be used and evolve because they can function in real battle conditions even when the computer fails. The completely automated systems at the lower end of the table will probably fail completely when first used in battle; for such systems, evolution will be expensive, perhaps prohibitively so. The lower-right end of the table represents weapons that seem to be attractive to the Pentagon. They promise revolutionary improvement in performance. They are attractive to weapons developers because they are expensive and fun to work on. However, they represent a much higher risk of failure and, in my opinion, are not likely to be useful when first needed. Some of the systems at the lower-right of the table are not testable; we will discover their flaws in the first real battle. If the past is a good predictor of the future, the flaws will result in system failure.

PRIDE GOETH BEFORE A FALL

Computer-controlled weapon systems from the lower-right end of the table are often declared, by their designers and promoters, to be a success. Significantly, none of the systems mentioned was ever used in battle. Four frequently mentioned examples include the SAFEGUARD ABM system, the HARDSITE ABM system, FAS, also an ABM system, and AEGIS, a shipboard missile defense system. Of these, only two have been deployed. One of the other two has been tested under completely unrealistic conditions, the other has not even been tested. One of the deployed systems, SAFEGUARD, an ABM system that could be considered the precursor to the Strategic Defense Initiative (SDI), was dismantled except for the surveillance portion. The warfighting component of the system was discarded after an independent analysis showed that it would not be effective. Note that surveillance systems fall in the second row of the table and can be tested in actual use. The portion of SAFEGUARD that was dismantled is in the bottom right of the table. The remaining system, AEGIS, a shipboard battle management system, is at sea but still under rapid development. It has never been tested with more than 25 percent of its rated load. It has never been tested with live attacking missiles exploding or with its missiles being used to destroy many incoming missiles. Safety and cost considerations prevent the testing of this system under conditions that would occur during a real battle. Retired Navy Rear Admiral Eugene Carroll, Jr., of the Center for Defense Information, remarks that when the AEGIS computer system fails, a ship has less defensive fire power than was available in World War II. If the computer system fails in its first real battle, it could be catastrophic for the fleet that the system is designed to protect. In each of these cases, those who called the system a success were asked why they thought it was a success. The immediate answer was that the Pentagon accepted, and paid for, the system. ("The Army was happy as a clam with what we did.") That may be the ultimate definition of success in the defense industry. When asked how they could be confident that the system would work in battle, the designer of one replied, "We thought of everything that could happen." All of this is a frightening reminder of the warning in Proverbs: "Pride goeth before destruction, and a haughty spirit before a fall." By basing our defense on systems that we cannot test, we are showing the kind of arrogance that is likely to lead to disaster. Computer technology faces weapon designers with a dilemma. It allows unprecedented flexibility, information processing capability, and decision-making ability. However, these capabilities are accompanied by an unprecedented complexity, which limits our ability to understand the system's behavior. Our own products regularly surprise us. As the capabilities of computer systems increase, the limitations on our own ability to design them become more apparent. It is in the self-interest of weapons manufacturers to pretend that there are no limits on our ability to develop highly sophisticated computer-based weapon systems. It is in their interest to promise that investment in such systems can increase our security. It is in the national interest to recognize that there are limits on our own ability to build such systems and limits on the ability of technologists to solve the political problems that make us insecure. We have been pursuing a technological solution to the problem of security throughout our history. It is time to recognize that this approach is both limited and, because of the power of modern weapons, unacceptably dangerous.

READING QUESTIONS

1) What is the difference between active and passive error?
2) Why will efforts to eliminate latent error have a better payoff than ones directed at active error?
3) What are the four levels of supervisory control, and how do they distance operators from the effects of their actions?

4) Why are complexity of interaction and tightness of coupling important?
5) What paradox does including automatic safety devices produce?
6) What is defense in depth?
7) Why attempt to decrease the *duration* of latent errors rather than attempt to decrease their frequency?
8) What are the "ironies of automation"? How are they associated with automatic safety devices?
9) Why might the most successful automated systems actually need the greatest investment in operator training?
10) What are the two parts of the "catch 22" of human supervisory control?
11) Why might the "active errors of stressed controllers" be the "delayed effects of system design failures"?
12) What is the difference in the level at which errors and violations are described?
13) What are the differences between routine and exceptional violations?
14) What are resident pathogens, and how are they related to the complexity of the system?
15) What is "accident proneness," and why is it an inadequate explanation for the occurrence of accidents?
16) How do certainty of outcome and nature of the feedback influence decision making?
17) Why is the distinction between a pathogen type and a pathogen token important?
18) What is pathogen auditing?
19) How do you tell if an organization is "cognitively adequate" with regard to its response to accidents?
20) What are the Fundamental Attribution Error and the Fundamental Surprise Error? How are they related to learning the right lessons from an accident?
21) Why is it important to recognize Hindsight bias in our analyses of an accident? How is this related to the Fundamental Attribution Error and the Fundamental Surprise Error?
22) How are each of the "drawbacks of digital technology" mentioned by Parnas related to the reasons that the military is increasingly using digital technology?
23) Why must we "accept that the software will fail in its early use"?
24) Why are automatic safety devices a problem in military computing?
25) How is military computing different from computing in other areas?
26) Why is "The Army was happy with it" an inadequate claim for success?

DISCUSSION QUESTIONS

1) Parnas provides many examples of military uses of technology in his table. Use the concepts of complexity, tightness of coupling, and resident pathogens to describe the risks associated with each type of system.
2) What is wrong with simulation as a means of testing systems? Are there any situations under which simulation might be useful? How could you avoid overconfidence based on simulation?
3) Take a few of the case studies that Reason provides and analyze them for resident pathogens.
4) To what extent is it the responsibility of a technology's designer to be concerned with the resident pathogens in any particular installation of the system (say, an electronic sensor for an ASD in a nuclear power plant)?

PRACTICING THE DESIGN ETHIC

1) Interview one of the project leaders in the computer department on your campus or business who led the development of an existing application. (You may also need to interview the computer operations manager to determine information about the site's Disaster Recovery Plan, if one exists.) During the interview determine the following information:

- How are test scenarios/plans developed for a new system?
- When are the scenarios/plans developed (during the analysis, design, programming, or test phase)?
- What would happen if there was a serious error or outage that prevented the application from running for more than one day? Would the outage endanger people's health? How much money would be lost if the system was out for a day? What other factors would be affected (i.e., customer satisfaction, scheduling, etc.)?
- What plans are in place to handle a situation where the system was out for more than a day? Was this plan tested to see if it would work? Why or why not?
- Were the users and managers of the application involved in planning and evaluating the application tests? Were they involved in planning and approving any backup plans?

2) Find a "critical system" on your campus and analyze it. It is best if it is a computing system, but telephone, power, or various safety systems are good candidates too. Look for resident pathogens in the system, and determine ways to eliminate or minimize them. Remember, the "system" includes the organization and the people in it, not just the technology.

CHAPTER 6

COMPUTERIZED CRIME

Spectacular crimes always make better press. Young crackers jumping from node to node on the internet and attempting defense system break-ins or high-stakes financial crimes are the mythology of computer crime. But they are not the mundane reality or even the most expensive kinds of computer crime. Most computer crime is done by regular folks who, because of a gap in an organization's security, can get access to restricted data. Another major category of computer crime is the standard habit of copying software without paying for it. These low-tech crimes make up the bulk of losses from computer crime.

Sacco and Zureik provide an analysis of the motivations behind these crimes for a set of technologically competent students of computing. Together with Hearnden's data from criminological reports, a profile of the real "computer criminal" hidden behind the rhetoric emerges: Most criminals are opportunists who take liberties only when it seems easy and when the chances they will get caught seem remote. In addition, an outline of the steps needed to prevent most damaging computer crime emerges. But the answers are nontechnical: education and basic organizational security. Again, what seems at first like a technical issue can only be understood in its social and organizational context.

CORRELATES OF COMPUTER MISUSE:
DATA FROM A SELF-REPORTING SAMPLE[1,2]

V. F. Sacco
E. Zureik
Queen's University

The increased economic and social dependence of advanced industrial societies on the computer has caused law enforcement agencies, the business community, computer specialists and social scientists to become concerned about the possible misuses of computer technology. Some claim that the computer has changed the form and the means by which traditional white-collar crime can be defined and perpetrated, thus creating the opportunity for a new array of abusive conduct previously not considered by criminal law (Fitzgerald 1986, Bequai 1987, Clemons 1987). While a commonly discussed feature of this new type of crime is the profile of the offender (Bequai 1987:33, Johnson 1984:64), there is little detailed knowledge about what propels individuals to engage in such activity. Similarly, there is little reliable data regarding the illegal use of computers by governments and organizations in the course of administering people (Burnham 1983).

This study examines attitudes toward and involvement in computer misuse among a sample of undergraduate students enrolled in computer science courses at Queen's University in Ontario, Canada. More specifically, the attempt is made to investigate empirically the relationship between students' self-reports of computer misuse and their perceptions of the ethics, prevalence and likelihood of detection of these behaviours. The investigation of perceptual predictors reflects a criminological tradition highlighting the role that definitions of the situation' play in crime causation (Henshel and Silverman 1975, Gottfredson and Gottfredson 1980). Techniques of multiple regression and path analysis are employed in the examination of social and demographic predictors, perceptual variables, and behavioural outcomes. Following a review of the relevant literature addressing the extent, definitions, social distribution of, and the motivations behind-computer crime, the methods will be described and the results presented.

[1] Sacco, V.F., & Zureik, E. (1990). Correlates of computer misuse: data from a self-reporting sample. *Behaviour & Information Technology, 9,* 353-369. Copyright © 1990 Taylor & Francis Ltd. Reprinted by permission.
[2] This research was made possible by a grant provided by the Unsolicited Grants Program of the Ministry of the Solicitor General of Canada. The authors would like to thank the anonymous reviewers for their very useful and constructive suggestions, the Department of Computing Science at Queen's University and the students who participated in the survey.

PREVIOUS RESEARCH

The extent of computer crime

In one of the early attempts to document the occurrence of computer crime. McKnight (1973) interviewed executives of computer firms, newspaper journalists and legal counsellors. He concluded that while theft and misappropriation of software may have been sufficiently rare to allow for concealment by corporations, such crimes could—unless checked—become familiar and accepted risks of computerized business life. Indeed, a decade or so later, experts began to provide widely divergent estimates of financial damage caused by computer crime, ranging from a low of 20 million to a high of 5 billion annually (Goldstein 1983:50, Bequai 1987:49), Bequai attributes the confusion in estimates surrounding computer crime to the peculiarity of the technology and the velocity with which this type of crime can be committed. Claims are made that crime costs Canadian businessmen millions of dollars every year although exact figures are not known and only crudely estimated.

Some Canadian authorities, such as the Royal Canadian Mounted Police estimate that only about 5% of computer crime is uncovered. In the USA the figure varies from a low of 5% (Hollinger and Lanza-Kaduce 1988:105) to a high of 15% (Pfuhl 1985:2), Fitzgerald (1986:79) notes that according to American commentators, the reported instances of computer abuse represent only the 'tip of the iceberg', with only one out of every 100 abuses ever being detected, and only 18% of those detected ever being reported (See also Bequai 1987:56).

Those subscribing to the theory that computer crime is proliferating attribute the low reported figures to: (1) the reluctance of companies to divulge information which may compromise their public reputations; (2) inadequate legislation to deal with computer crime; (3) judges who are too lenient with computer criminals (since computer crime tends to be considered a 'victimless' type of crime committed by violators who are educated and who in most cases lack criminal records); (4) difficulties in detecting computer abuse; (5) concern about possible liability for failing to prevent computer abuse; and (6) fear of stimulating the interest of would-be offenders by advertising the vulnerability of computing systems (Fitazgerald 1986, Parker 1976).

Yet some authors (Taber 1980, Watkins 1981) argue that these educated guesses tend to exaggerate the incidence of computer crime. Watkins (1981:45) labels these claims as 'myths' and Webber (1985:50) supports this line of argument, by contending that incidents involving computer crime are frequently sensationalized by media in order to enhance the newsworthiness of the issue. Webber also emphasizes the unreliability of selected research studies. In order to impress upon the general public the all-pervasive nature of computer crime, law enforcement agencies, politicians and the media have relied upon various (questionable) statistical studies of its incidence. As an example, he offers the Ontario Provincial Police's 'Computer Crime and Security Survey', which was based on an Ontario sample of 648 corporate offices and institutions. Of the 321 responding organizations, only 4.15% reported experiencing a loss through computer abuse even though the survey assured the participants of their anonymity. Nonetheless, the report's authors interpreted the low figure as an indication of reluctance by victims to disclose the true nature of computer crime for fear of losing public trust. Webber warns that similar aspersions may be cast upon the frequently cited statistical reports of the Stanford Research Institute, whose statistics are often collected from unverified newspaper clippings (Webber 1985:51).

The social distribution of computer abuse

The empirical literature abounds with attempts to map the social distribution of computer crime. These epidemiological accounts serve to reassure the casual observer that our current knowledge of the social and demographic correlates of computer offending is both significant and useful. Typical offenders are described as male, young, educated and of middle or upper socio-economic status (Bologna 1982, Archambeault and Archambeault 1984). Those who offend within the context of the work environment are said to be highly intelligent, aggressive, and verbal (Franklin 1976). According to Parker (1976:46) such 'perpetrators are usually bright, eager, highly motivated, courageous, adventuresome, and qualified people willing to accept a technical challenge. They have exactly the characteristics that make them desirable employees in data processing' (See also Clemons 1987:7). Bloom (1980:30) paints a sinister image of the prototype computer offender as 'a new type of criminal', who is 'a white-collar worker between the ages of 18 and 30, appears loyal to the company and is intelligent. He likes computer crime because it's intelligent'.

Bequai (1987) argues that the computer criminal, like the hacker, is an ordinary person. Very few computer thieves are electronic geniuses, and the majority have not previously broken the law. Although this may change as more professional criminals enter the area, the overwhelming number of thieves are trusted by honest insiders. There are no supercriminals; there is merely a technology that has given ordinary men and women the tools with which to steal a king's ransom with relative impunity.

For several reasons the findings of such studies must be read with caution. First, there does not exist any agreed-upon definition of computer crime. As a result, the term may be employed to reference activities as diverse as those of the adolescent 'hacker', the 'organized criminal' or the corporate embezzler, Obviously, such activities involve distinctive populations and consequently, any attempt to describe the 'typical computer criminal' must presuppose some understanding of the specific type of computer crime in question. Second, the correlates of computer crime are likely to be unstable with respect to temporal trends. Thus, as computer hardware becomes more accessible and as computer software becomes increasingly 'user friendly,' the social structure of offending may become more diffuse (Archambeault and Archambeault 1984). Finally, the inadequacies of the data sources that allow for the investigation of correlational questions must be recognized. The data made available by victims and official agencies have tended to underrepresent the 'true' population of cases. Similarly, studies of offender groups have tended to employ small and unrepresentative samples.

The causes of computer crime

These uncertainties regarding what constitutes computer crime and thus, who engages in such conduct, confound our efforts to comprehend the motivations which underlie offending. Nevertheless, the research literature identifies a variety of motivational factors. Some writers emphasize rational and instrumental, economic motives as causes of computer crime. In so doing, they suggest a parallel between such behaviour and other forms of theft (Bologna 1982). However, such economic calculations may be more relevant to some types of offending (such as industrial espionage or embezzlement) than others (Bequai 1987).

Other analysts emphasize an understanding of computer offending as a type of conduct that is more analogous to "electronic joyriding" than to serious crime (Franklin 1976, Nycum 1976, Myers 1980, Volgyles 1980). In particular, it is argued, much 'computer hacking' is understood by those who engage in this behaviour not as criminal or unethical but as exciting, instructive or intellectually challenging (Bequai 1987:38). Normative prohibitions against such conduct may be neutralized by definitions of the situation that minimize the harm that the behaviour produces,

It is also recognized that with respect to occupationally-related forms of computer crime, some type of environments may be particularly conducive to offending. Parker (1976:49) notes, for instance, that work situations that engender employee dissatisfaction with employers may increase the probability of computer misuse. In such environments, groups of employees working together may provide each other with reinforcement so that minor unethical acts eventually develop into more serious offences. In this way, each employee may support the rationalizations offered by others in the performance of such acts to the extent that computer misbehaviour comes to be defined as common and accepted practice.

Perhaps the most popular type of explanation of computer crime stresses the ineffectiveness of formal and informal sanctions in the deterrence of such behaviour (Johnson 1984, Best and Picquet 1985, Kurzban 1986, Bequai 1987). Such arguments suggest that in general, people may commit computer crimes because they do not experience the social or moral pressures that might encourage them to do otherwise. The ineffectiveness of legal deterrents is in part explained by the low visibility of many computer offences and by the reluctance on the part of corporate victims to prosecute (Gellman 1976,

Bequai 1987:37,113, Canada House of Commons 1983:13). Moreover, existing laws may be characterized as inadequate with respect to their associated sanctions, and those rare cases that do find their way to court often meet with prosecutors and judges ill-equipped to assess responsibility. Thus, successful prosecutions frequently result in legal penalties involving fines or probation rather than criminal sentence (Goldstein 1983, Kurzban 1986, Bequai 1987, Clemons 1987).

THE STUDY

An approach to the measurement of computer crime

Over the last several decades, considerable time and energy have been devoted to the problem of crime measurement. For researchers working within the mainstream empirical traditions, the ability to accurately map the social distribution of offenders is viewed as an essential preliminary step toward the development of both useful theoretical accounts of such behaviour and effective crime prevention policy. Customarily, criminological data have been derived from one of three major sources: social control agency records, victim surveys and self-report surveys.

The records of social control agencies are collated and aggregated by central state agencies such as Statistics Canada (or in the USA, the FBI), and are known as Uniform Crime Reports (UCR). They are probably the most venerable source of information about both temporal trends in offending and the social and demographic correlates of such behaviour.

Beginning in the 1960s and 1970s, however, an increasingly vocal group of empirical criminologists focused attention upon the measurement errors inherent in official data. Of central concern in this respect were the threats to validity characteristic of the procedures through which such data are generated. In particular, critics charged that since UCR data are based upon crimes known to the police, they may more appropriately be viewed as measures of the selective nature of police activity rather than as measures of crime *per se*.

An awareness of the apparent shortcomings of UCR data encouraged the development of the two, alternative, non-official data collection procedures. The victim survey is intended to circumvent the problems of agency data by asking samples of community residents to report directly about the victimization experiences in which they themselves have been involved during some specified period. In direct contrast, the self-report survey asks respondents to describe the forms of law-breaking behaviour in which they have engaged. However, critics have charged that victims surveys and self-report surveys, like the UCR, also tend to be plagued by sampling, measurement and other methodological problems (Nettler 1984, O'Brien 1983).

Thus all of these three data collection strategies have their own unique problems which compromise the validity and the reliability of the data which they generate. Yet, despite their limitations, a reasoned analysis of the accumulated evidence indicates quite clearly that these data do in fact converge with respect to key social and demographic correlates (O'Brien 1983). Thus, once the methodological limitations are taken into account, it is clear that all data sources suggest similar social distributional patterns. The use of multiple methods, therefore, permits a 'triangulation' of the data and, in so doing, increases our confidence in each of the data sources.

How adequate are the data of official agencies, or victim or self-report surveys, in revealing the correlates or determinants of computer crime? In theory, at least, each strategy should be as applicable to this particular form of offending as to more traditional forms of interpersonal predation. However, accumulated experience with these data sources is to date not yet so extensive as to allow definitive judgements to be made about the viability of data sources or about the potential of these research methods for triangulation.

Official data relating to computer crime seem to be characterized by many of the same problems as data relating to more traditional offences (Taber 1980). The more routine problems of victim non-reporting and selective enforcement, however, are exacerbated by definitional ambiguities regarding what computer crime is and how its various manifestations should be recognized (Wagner 1979, Bequai 1987). The available literature also indicates that victim surveys of computer crime face serious difficulties relating to sampling, measurement and data access (Bequai 1987, McKnight 1973),

To date, little attention has been paid to the possible utility of self-report methodologies in the study of computer crime. The study reported below was intended partially to fill this void through a preliminary application of the self-report technique to the investigation of computer abuse among the members of a university student sample.

Research design

The general research strategy involved the attempt to relate perceptions of various forms of computer misbehaviour to the self-reported frequencies of these behaviours. The findings reported below are derived from a survey of anonymous student respondents enrolled in computing courses at a medium-sized Canadian university, Respondents were asked to complete a 22 page questionnaire that dealt with a variety of computing behaviours, attitudes and perceptions. Only the data relating to questions about computer misuse are discussed here. A total of 202 questionnaires were distributed in class to students enrolled in courses required for a major in computing science and other applied science disciplines. The sample spanned the usual four years of instruction at the undergraduate level. Slightly more than 50% (105) of the participating students completed and returned the questionnaires.

Three types of perceptual measures are employed in this analysis: (1) judgements regarding the ethical nature of the behaviours in question; (2)

beliefs about the relative prevalence of these behaviours; and (3) beliefs regarding the probability that these behaviours are likely to be detected.

A relationship between each of the these perceptual measures and self-reported computer misuse is predicted by both the general literature on criminology and the more specific literature on computer crime. Judgements about the inherent ethical or unethical nature of a given form of behaviour can be seen respectively as allowing or prohibiting involvement in this behaviour. It has been argued that for a variety of reasons many forms of computer misbehaviour are defined as ethically ambiguous (Bequai 1987, Canada House of Commons 1983). Unlike more traditional crimes against persons or property, there does not exist widespread agreement that the misuse of computer technology is wrong, in and of itself. This would imply a lack of internalized prohibitions against involvement in such activity. It may therefore be suggested that those who define various forms of computer abuse as ethically inappropriate will be more likely to abstain from such behaviour.

Beliefs about the relative frequency of occurrence of offence types may affect involvement by facilitating the perception that the behaviour is widespread and therefore acceptable. The perception that 'everybody is doing it' may reinforce a belief that deterrents directed toward the behaviour are ineffective; or reaffirm a belief in group-supported definitions of the acceptability of such behaviour (Bologna 1982). Whatever the mechanism, it is expected that higher rates of misbehaviour should correlate with perceptions that computer abuse is more prevalent.

Perceptions that a behaviour is unlikely to be detected may allow individuals to feel free of the external social constraints which might prohibit such conduct. Thus, motivation in the absence of effective deterrence may produce deviant behaviour. It has been claimed that most forms of computer crime are characterized by low visibility. It has been suggested that those responsible for monitoring such behaviour learn about only a small proportion of the total universe of offences. It may also be suggested that the ineffectiveness of deterrents and the low degree of visibility associated with many such offences are accurately perceived by potential offenders. It is to be expected. therefore, that a tendency to perceive a low likelihood of detection with respect to such offences is associated with a greater self-reported frequency of such behaviour.

As stated, the research literature provides no consistent conceptual or operational definition of computer crime (Wagner 1979, Nycum 1984). Because our intentions were empirical rather than theoretical, we chose to escape the debate about the meaning of 'computer crime' by employing an operational rather than a conceptual definition. In other words, we focused upon several specific types of behaviour rather than upon some master concept or abstract typology. In some instances (the item relating to rummaging through discarded printout for 'interesting program listings'. for example), the term computer crime is quite inappropriate in that the

	Yes	No	No Answer
A: Used unauthorized password	15	85	—
B: Used program in a way that avoids charges	29	70	2
C: Rummaged through discarded printout for interesting program listings	15	85	2
D: Used program that was property of time-share	5	94	1
E: Made copy of disk for personal use	62	38	—

Table 6.1
Personal behavior items (n = 101).

behaviour is not illegal. Thus, the term is used in a generic rather than a formalistic sense and terms such as 'misuse', 'abuse', 'delinquency' or 'misbehaviour' might be more suitable and for present purposes may be used interchangeably.

MEASURES AND FINDINGS

Self-reported computer misuse

In one section of the questionnaire respondents were asked to indicate whether, during the previous year, they had engaged in any of five specific types of computer misbehaviour.[3] The univariate frequency distributions for these items are found in Table 6.1. It will be noted that there was considerable variability in the proportion of 'yes' responses. The most frequently reported behaviour was the unauthorized copying of copyrighted material for personal use (62%) and the least frequently reported was unauthorized use of a program that was the property of a time-sharing system (5%). Equal proportions (15%) reported that they had rummaged through discarded printout 'for interesting program listings' or used an unauthorized password. Twenty-nine per cent indicated that they used a program in ways that avoided being charged for its use.

For the sake of economy of presentation, the decision was made to construct a simple additive index of item responses. Thus, for each respondent, 'yes' responses were summed for items A through E. Possible scores on this index ranged from 0 to 5 but as might be expected, index scores were highly skewed (mean = 1.25; s.d. = 1.15). In essence, scores on the index distinguish between those who did and those who did not report an act. Two factors account for the highly skewed nature of these scores, First,

---

[3] These items are adapted from Carroll's investigation of student attitudes toward computer crime (Bologna 1982).

Variable	Description	Mean	s.d.	Range
X1	Use of unauthorized password	5.60	1.50	0-7
X2	Use of proprietary program	4.84	1.76	0-7
X3	Rummage unattended printouts	3.95	2.22	0-7
X4	Use of time sharing program	4.73	1.85	0-7
X5	Copy copyrighted software	4.42	2.10	0-7

Correlation matrix

	X1	X2	X3	X4	X5
X1	1.00				
X2	0.52***	1.00			
X3	0.34***	0.25**	1.00		
X4	0.47***	0.52***	0.35***	1.00	
X5	0.49***	0.64***	0.21**	0.51***	1.00

Principle components analysis

Variable	Factor Loading	Communality
X1	0.77	0.59
X2	0.82	0.67
X3	0.51	0.26
X4	0.78	0.60
X5	0.80	0.64
Eigenvalue	2.76	
reliability	0.77	

** $p < .01$; *** $p < .001$.

Table 6.2
Descriptive statistics—ethical judgements of behavior.

as the data in Table 6.1 make clear, the items from which the index is constructed are themselves highly skewed. Second, an analysis of relevant correlations suggests that the level of intercorrelation among these items is quite low (average intercorrelation = 0.21) implying that those who engaged in one of these behaviours did not necessarily engage in another; (it is also true, of course, that the skewed nature of these items attenuate the correlations).

The perceptual measures

Data relating to the perceptual measures are in Tables 6.2, 6.3 and 6.4. In each case the data are arranged so as to present three distinct types of information. The top panels provide univariate data for each of the items, the

Variable	Description	Mean	s.d.	Range
X1	Use of unauthorized password	2.78	1.08	1-5
X2	Use of proprietary program	3.58	1.14	1-5
X3	Rummage unattended printouts	2.40	1.07	1-5
X4	Use of time sharing program	2.78	1.20	1-5
X5	Copy copyrighted software	4.38	0.81	1-5

Correlation matrix					
	X1	X2	X3	X4	X5
X1	1.00				
X2	0.27*	1.00			
X3	0.37**	0.22	1.00		
X4	0.54***	0.33*	0.49***	1.00	
X5	0.38**	0.15	0.22	0.28*	1.00

Principle components analysis		
Variable	Factor Loading	Communality
X1	0.78	0.61
X2	0.53	0.28
X3	0.69	0.47
X4	0.81	0.66
X5	0.56	0.32
Eigenvalue	2.34	
reliability	0.71	

$* p < .05; ** p < .01; *** p < .001.$

Table 6.3
Descriptive statistics—occurrence of behavior.

middle panels provide the intercorrelations among the items and the third panels present the results of a principal components analysis.

Ethical judgements

The variables are scored so that higher scores reflect judgements that the behaviour in question is more unethical. The top panel of Table 6.2 indicates that sample respondents viewed the use of the unauthorized password as the most unethical and rummaging through discarded printout as least unethical. The remaining three items cluster about the midpoint of their respective scales.

The second panel indicates that the intercorrelations among the items were of moderate magnitude.

Variable	Description	Mean	s.d.	Range
X1	Use of unauthorized password	2.86	2.18	0-7
X2	Use of proprietary program	2.67	2.12	0-7
X3	Rummage unattended printouts	1.74	2.01	0-7
X4	Use of time sharing program	2.61	2.19	0-7
X5	Copy copyrighted software	0.95	1.60	0-7

			Correlation matrix		
	X1	X2	X3	X4	X5
X1	1.00				
X2	0.34**	1.00			
X3	0.25*	0.40***	1.00		
X4	0.36**	0.69***	0.50***	1.00	
X5	0.33**	0.53***	0.66***	0.55***	1.00

	Principle components analysis	
Variable	Factor Loading	Communality
X1	0.54	0.30
X2	0.80	0.64
X3	0.75	0.56
X4	0.84	0.70
X5	0.83	0.68
Eigenvalue	2.89	
reliability	0.80	

$* p < .05; ** p < .01; *** p < .001.$

Table 6.4
Descriptive statistics—detection of behavior.

The third panel suggests the presence of a clear single factor solution. In other words, judgements about the ethical quality of the behaviours tended to group together. With the exception of the question relating to discarded printout, the items shared at least 60% of the variance in common with the underlying factor. The Alpha value was 0.77.

Occurrence

The data in Table 6.3 relate to perceptions about the relative occurrence of each of the behaviours. The mean values suggest that, in general, respondents perceived relatively low rates of occurrence. The important exception in this regard was the item relating to the copying of copyrighted software which respondents estimated as occurring with greater frequency.

As suggested by the data in Table 6.1, this perception was supported by respondents' personal experiences.

The middle panel indicates that the intercorrelations were, on average, somewhat smaller in magnitude than those described in the previous table. Again, however, there was a strong single factor solution with an associated Alpha value of 0.71.

Detection

Table 6.4 presents data relating to the perceptions of the difficulty of avoiding detection for each of the behaviours. In general, as the top panel of this table indicates, respondents perceived that for all behaviours it was relatively easy to escape detection. For none of the items did the mean value even approach the mid-point on the scale. Particularly noteworthy, is the low mean (0.95) for the item relating to the copying of copyrighted software.

The correlations found in the middle panel are generally of moderate magnitude. The lower panel indicates a very strong single factor solution with all five variables sharing significant variation with the underlying factor. The reliability coefficient was also quite high (Alpha = 0.80).

The analysis of these items indicates that it is legitimate to speak of an ethical factor, an occurrence factor and a detection factor. Each of these sets of variables was thus transformed into a scale based upon their weightings as defined in the principal components analysis. The scales are scored in the same direction as the individual items.

Correlation analysis

Several other control variables were included in this analysis. For present purposes they are treated as exogenous variables, or as causally prior to the perceptual and behavioural measures described above.

Age was measured in reported number of years. Gender was dummy coded (0 = male; 1 = female). Prior access to computing was a variable derived from three other items that asked respondents about their experiences prior to coming to Queen's University, The variable access was dummy-coded (0 = access; 1 = no access). Programming proficiency was measured through the use of an ordinal item that asked respondents about their familiarity with computers prior to coming to Queen's. Programme major was dummy-coded (0 = not computing; 1 = computing). Finally, programme year was indicated by responses to an item that asked respondents about their current programme year.

Table 6.5 presents a zero-order correlation matrix for the variables included in this analysis. The bottom line of correlations suggests that there were negligible effects on self-reported misuse, of gender, prior access, self-reported programming proficiency and programme year. There were significant effects associated with being younger and not being a computing major. There were somewhat stronger effects associated with the perceptual variables and all of these effects were in the expected direction. The

	Gender	Age	Prior access to computer	Programming proficiency	Major	Program year	Detection	Ethics	Occurrence
Age	-.10								
Prior access to computer	.22	-.13							
Programming proficiency	.04	.35*	-.15						
Major	.09	.18	-.06	-.15					
Program year	-.02	.23	.18	.14	.33*				
Detection	.04	.37*	.03	-.10	.08	.18			
Ethics	.13	.28	.07	.13	.20	.17	.37*		
Occurrence	.16	-.14	.13	-.29*	-.15	.13	-.13	-.26*	
Personal behavior	.04	-.27*	.08	-.14	-.29*	-.05	.31*	-.53*	.50*

$* \ p < .05.$

Table 6.5
Correlation matrix.

behaviours in question were more likely to be reported by those who believed that it was easy to avoid detection, by those who defined them as less unethical and by those who defined them as occurring with greater frequency. A 'forced entry' multiple regression, including these variables and no others (not presented) revealed that they were able to explain 43% of the variation in the dependent variable. Further, the analysis indicated that the effects of these variables were additive; tests of increments in explained variation for all first order interaction terms yielded non-significant results.

An examination of the relationships involving the perceptual variables and those which were assumed to be causally prior indicated that being older is associated with the perception that it is difficult to avoid detection and that the behaviours are more unethical; and low programming proficiency is related to the perception that the behaviours occur more frequently.

With respect to the intercorrelations among the perceptual items, two of the three are statistically significant. Perceptions that it is difficult to avoid detection are associated with perceptions of the behaviours as unethical and perceptions that the behaviours are unethical are associated with the perception that the behaviours occur less frequently. The correlation between detection and occurrence while not statistically significant, was in the expected direction.

Multivariate analysis

As a final step in the data analysis, an attempt was made to estimate the coefficients of a causal model. The model was intended to bring together in a multivariate context certain of the empirical findings identified in the data and some of the assumptions about the causes of computer crime that are discussed in the literature. As is normally the case with the type of analysis described here, the goal was not to engage in formal model-testing but rather to pursue the implications of a particular set of causal assumptions.

The model which is pictured in Figure 6.1 is fully recursive. It pictures the personal behaviour measure as the dependent variable and describes four sets of causally prior variables. Reading from left to right, gender and age are

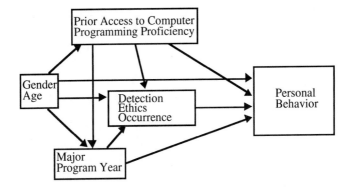

Figure 6-1
Model of path effects.

treated as exogenous variables, These demographic characteristics are conceptualized as affecting computing experience in the specific forms of prior access to computing facilities and computing proficiency, Both sets of variables are pictured as affecting the choice of a university major and program year. The proximate perceptual variables, detection, ethics, and occurrence form the final block of causal determinants. The results of this analysis are presented in Table 6.6. The effects were decomposed using the methods described by Alwin and Hauser (1975).

The data indicate that, consistent with the bivariate analysis, gender, prior access to computing, and self-reported programming proficiency were essentially negligible in their effects upon scores on the personal behaviour measure. There remains a moderate effect of age such that younger respondents are more likely to report computer misuse; and approximately

Dependent Variable	Predetermined Variable	Total effect	Indirect effect via			Direct effect
			X3-X4	X5-X6	X7-X9	
Personal Behavior	X1: Gender	.01	.01	-.04	.01	.04
	X2: Age	-.26	.02	-.02	-.15	-.07
	X3: Prior access to computer	.04		.04	-.03	.03
	X4: Programming proficiency	-.05		-.01	-.09	.05
	X5: Major	-.29			-.12	-.17
	X6: Program year	.11			.06	.05
	X7: Detection	-.09				-.09
	X8: Ethics	-.37				-.37
	X9: Occurrence	.36				.36

Table 6.6
Decomposition of path effects.

one-half of this effect is mediated by the perceptual measures, Higher scores on the dependent variable are also more likely among those who are not computing majors and slightly less than one-half of this effect is mediated by the proximate factors.

The strongest effects were associated with the perceptual variables. It will be noted that the total effect of 'detection' was much smaller than the zero-order correlation would have lead us to expect, although the effects of the ethics and occurrence measures remained strong. The effects of these latter variables were, however, reduced somewhat when the effects of prior variables were controlled. The reduction in the effect associated with detection was largely attributable to this variable's substantial correlation with the ethics measure ($r = 0.37$). As was true in the bivariate case, the effects were in the expected direction. Self-reported computer misuse was greatest among those who viewed such behaviour as least unethical and among those who perceived the behaviour as widespread. Taken together, the variables in the model explain about 47% of the variation in the dependent variable. The contribution of the proximate variables is sizeable and statistically significant and accounts for approximately 70% of the total explained variation.

SUMMARY AND DISCUSSION

This study examined self-reported computer misuse among a sample of university students enrolled in computing courses. Drawing upon the research into computer crime and the more general criminological literature, an attempt was made to investigate the relationship between such behaviour and some social and perceptual correlates with which it might be expected to be associated. The findings indicated that: (1) there exists considerable variation in the reported frequency of the various behaviours about which respondents were queried; (2) in general, the social characteristics of respondents are not useful predictors of misuse although such behaviour is more likely to be reported by those who are younger and who are not computing majors; (3) the likelihood of reporting misuse is greater among those who define such behaviour as less unethical, as widespread and difficult to detect although the effect of the latter variable is diminished when the effects of the remaining two are taken into account; (4) the effects of age and major programme of study upon self-reported misuse are largely mediated by the perceptual measures.

The empirical findings of this study are to some extent compromised by methodological limitations. Although a lack of resources made the self-completed questionnaire the only reasonable data collection procedure, it is not the most desirable one. Moreover, the exploratory nature of the research prohibited the use of well validated measures, specific to the substantive problems of computer misuse. In particular, we are aware that the dependent variable may lack validity as an indicator of computer misuse, The problem in this respect is not merely technical in nature but is one that more generally reflects the lack of conceptual development in the study of computer crime. Quite clearly, these measurement problems demand immediate attention if the empirical investigation of computer crime (self-reported or otherwise) is to become more sophisticated. All of these caveats require a tentative interpretation of our findings and extreme caution in any attempt to generalize beyond the sample surveyed.

Our data are consistent with the conclusion that much of what has been written about computer crime has been phrased in a 'rhetoric of crisis' which exaggerates the magnitude of the problem (Webber 1985). With one exception (copying copyrighted software) the majority of respondents reported that they did not engage in the behaviour in question. In some cases, the number of respondents reporting a given form of misbehaviour was smaller than we might have expected. It must be recalled, however, that our measure did not allow us to determine the number of times that respondents engaged in the behaviours to which they gave affirmative responses. It is also worth noting that the sample of respondents was skewed in directions that might have lead us to expect relatively high rates of misbehaviour. The members of the sample were, after all, generally knowledgeable regarding computing and had ready access to the technology and social opportunities that are likely to facilitate computer misuse.

The data also support the conclusion that the tendency to engage in computer misbehaviour is diffuse rather than highly concentrated in some neatly definable 'high risk' group (Bequai 1987). The basic social and demographic predictors used in this study explained little of the variation in the dependent variable.

The study suggests that potential benefits may be derived from a more detailed and more rigorous investigation of the perceptual determinants of computer misuse. There are two salient aspects to this observation. First, as we have seen, the perceptual variables included in the study proved to be the most effective predictors of computer misuse. Second, these perceptual variables suggest an apparent avenue for policy intervention.

The data imply that a firm grounding in 'computer ethics' may decrease the occurrence of computer misbehaviour (Bequai 1987). This is not to suggest however that increasing the ethical sensitivity of computer users is simply a technical matter that involves no more than the introduction of new or more extensive courses in the ethics of computing. The problem is more basic and relates to the pervasiveness of honest disagreements about the contents of such courses. The rapid development of computer technology has created a 'cultural lag' such that normative standards have not kept pace. To the extent that the law affects moral judgements, however, it may be that criminalization—despite its lack of short term utility with respect to deterrence or apprehension—may produce long-term benefits by shaping public opinion regarding the non-normative nature of particular forms of computer misuse. In any case, it is probably true that in the absence of firm standards which define computer abuse as unethical, those with even weak motivations may feel free to act upon alternative definitions of such behaviour as 'entertaining', 'exciting' or 'educational' (Franklin 1976, Bellin 1985).

The alteration of other types of perceptions may potentially pose even greater problems. To some extent, the belief that others commit such acts with impunity and that computer misuse may be effectively concealed are validated by personal experience. In the absence of effective formal controls that would decrease both the actual and the perceived risk of detection, the attempt to manage the perceptions themselves would probably prove futile.

REFERENCES

Alwin, D. F. and Hauser, R. M. 1975, 'The decomposition of effects in path analysis' *American Sociological Review*, 40, 37-47.

Archambeault, W.G. and Archambeault, B.J., 1984, *Computers in Criminal Justice Administration and Management.- Introduction to Emerging Issues and Applications*(Cincinnati: Pilgrimage).

Bellin, D. 1985, 'High school hackers: heroes or criminals?', *Computers and Society*, 14 and 15, 16-17.

Bequai, A. 1978, *Technocrimes* (Lexington, MA: D. C. Heath and Company).

Best, R. A. and Picquet, D. C. 1985, *Computer Crime, Abuse, Liability and Security,- A Comprehensive Bibliography*, 1970—1984, (Jefferson, NC: McFarland and Company, Inc.).

Bloom, R. P. 1980, 'Computer crime: a new white collar crook', *Infosystems*, 27, 30-35.

Bologna, J. 1982, *Computer Crime: Wave of the Future* (San Francisco: Assets Protection).

Burnham, D. 1983, *The Rise of the Computer State* (New York: Random House).

Canada House of Commons, 1983, Minutes of Proceedings and Evidence of the Sub-Committee on *Computer Crime* of the Standing Committee on Justice and Legal Affairs.

Clemons, K. 1987, 'Computer Security', *Computer Data*, 12, 7.

Fitzgerald, O. 1986, 'The criminalization of computer abuse in Canada', *Canadian Computer Law Reporter,* 3, 77—90,

Franklin, T. 1976, *Computer Abuse*, 1976, Litigation Course Handbook Series, No. 88 (New York: Practising Law Institute).

Gellman, H. S. 1976, *Electronic Banking Systems and Their Effects on Privacy*, A Study for the Privacy and Computers Task Force, Department of Communications (Department of Justice, Ottawa: Information Canada).

Goldstein, B. 1983, 'Electronic fraud: the crime of the future', *Police Chief* 50, 50-53.

Goottfredson, M. R. and Goottfredson, D.R. 1980, *Decisionmaking in Criminal Justice: Toward the Rational Exercise of Discretion* (Cambridge, MA: Ballinger Publishing Company).

Henshel, R. and Silverman, R. 1975, *Perception in Criminology* (New York: Columbia University Press).

Hollinger, R. and Lanza-Kaduce, L. 1988, 'The process of criminalization: the case of computer crime laws', *Criminology*, 26, 101—126.

Johnson, D. G. 1984, 'Mapping ordinary morals onto the computer society: a philosophicalperspective', *Journal of Social Issues*, 40, 63—76.

Kurzban, S. A. 1986, 'Careers in computer misuse— not so appealing after all', *Computers and Society*, 15, 7—9.

McKnight, G. 1973, *Computer Crime* (London: Michael Joseph).

Myers, E. 1980, 'Motives for Theft', *Datamation*, 26,82-88.

Nettler, G. 1984, *Explaining Crime*, 3rd edn (New York: McGraw-Hill).

Nycum, S. H. 1976, *The Criminal Law Aspects of Computer Abuse: Applicability of the Federal Criminal Code to Computer Abuse* (Menlo Park, CA: Stanford Research Institute).

Nycum, S. H. 1984, 'Some legal aspects of computer security', *Canadian Computer Law Review*, 1, 244.

O'Brien, R. 1983, *Crime and Victimization Data* (Beverly Hills: Sage).

Parker, D. 1976, *Crime by Computer* (New York: Charles Scribner's Sons).

Pfuhl, E. H. Jr. 1985, *Computer Abuse: Thoughts on the Social Construction of Crime*, Paper presented at the 1985 Annual Meetings of the American Society of Criminology, San Diego, CA [mimeo].

Taber, J. K. 1980, 'A survey of computer crime studies', *Computer/Law Journal*, 2, 275—328.

Vanderlee, D. P. 1980, 'Computer theft: plugging in to high tech', *Canadian Lawyer*, 4, 12-13.

Volgyles, M. R. 1980, 'The investigation, prosecution, and prevention of computer crime: a state-of-the-art review', *Computer Law Journal*, 2,385-402.

Wagner, C. R. 1979, *The CPA and Computer Fraud* (Lexington, MA: Lexington Books).

Watkins, P. 1981, 'Computer crime: separating the myth from the reality', *C.A. Magazine*, 114, 44-47.

Webber, C. 1985, 'Computer crime: what has not been considered?', *Canadian Law Reporter*, 2, 49-54.

COMPUTER CRIME:
MULTI-MILLION POUND PROBLEM[4]

Keith Hearnden
Loughborough University

For too long, the "experts" have overlooked the human dimension of computer crime. Much research, many learned publications and a wealth of sophisticated computer hardware and software are evidence of the direction the computer industry has taken in its attempt to contain computer crime. I would not deny that this "mechanistic" approach has provided many valuable aids to improved security, but I do feel sometimes that its proponents have lost sight of a fundamental truth—that it is people who commit computer crimes, and that attempting to deal with the problem in human terms often offers a cost-effective and more securely based solution.

One of the difficulties with this line of reasoning, however, is the absence of any great volume of data about computer-linked crime and the people who commit it, so that to some extent we are forced into making assumptions about important things like motivations, attitudes to crime, profiles of computer criminals and so on. However, it is perhaps also true that we have not made the best use of the information that is available, nor extracted from it those items that could be significant in our attempt to understand more about the people involved in computer-linked crime.

In this article I have looked again at those cases recorded in UK studies such as the Audit Inspectorate Report of 1981; the Audit Commission Report of l985; the BIS *Computer Related Fraud Casebook* (where this gives details of cases not covered by the 1981 Audit Inspectorate Survey); the 1984 EEC Report, *The Vulnerability of the Information Conscious Society*; a survey, *Computer Related Crime in Australia,* by the Computer Abuse Research Bureau in Victoria; some statistics produced by the American CPA about banking and insurance crime; and some crimes newly reported in press and journal articles.[5] I hope that what these reveal will give a clearer insight into how computer crime is committed and what kinds of people become involved in it; and that from this greater understanding we can deduce some lines of action designed to counter the problem and reduce our exposure to risk.

---

[4]Hearnden, Keith (1986, October). Computer crime: Multi-million pound problem. *Long Range Planning, 19(5)* 18-26. Copyright © 1986 Elsevier-Pergamon Press. Reprinted by permission.
[5]The full details of the reports referred to in this article are: Computer Fraud Survey, by the Local Government Audit Inspectorate (1981), now obtainable as Computer Fraud Survey, The Audit Commission for Local Authorities in England and Wales (HMSO, London, 1985). Computer Related Fraud Casebook, BIS Applied Systems LTD (Manchester, UK, 1983). The Vulnerability of the Information Conscious Society, Commission of the European Communities, Information Technologies and Telecommunications Task Force (Brussels, 1984). Computer Related Crime in Australia, Computer Abuse Research Bureau, Chisholm Institute of Technology (Victoria, 1984). Banking and Insurance EDP Fraud, Certified Public Accountants, EDP Fraud Review Task Force (USA, 1984).

Source of data	Types of crime included
1981 Audit Report	
1985 Audit Report	UK fraud (including misuse of computer resources)
BIS Fraud Survey	
EEC Report	EEC fraud; sabotage; deliberate attack
CARB Report	Fraud; sabotage; vandalism; misuse of resources
USA CPA Report	Banking and insurance fraud
press and journal reports	Fraud; extortion; industrial espionage

Table 6.7
What kind of crime?

WHAT KIND OF CRIME?

Let us first define what types of activity are included in this analysis (see Table 6.7). One omission from this survey is data on the theft of computer equipment. Whilst some information exists (in the EEC and Australian reports) it seems to me that this is a physical security problem, capable of being tackled by conventional crime prevention methods; which is why the subject is not dealt with here. I would just mention in passing, though, that theft of computers and associated equipment appears to be escalating, and there is some evidence to suggest that ready markets exist for high-technology second-hand products.

Our concern here, then, is primarily with fraud, embezzlement, misuse of computer resources and deliberately inflicted physical damage. In a computer context, fraud can be carried out in one of three ways. The first of these is by manipulating information fed into the system and falsifying data relating to accounts, stock records, funds transfer, etc.: this is commonly called "input" fraud. This is the type most commonly reported, and probably is genuinely the most widespread. Whether its ascendancy also in some way reflects the difficulty of ever discovering more sophisticated crimes that involve the alteration of computer programs, our second method, is an open question. Certainly, as we shall see, there is little evidence of fraud having been committed in this way.

The third technique involves the manipulation or misappropriation of computer output: theft of cheques, destruction of delivery notes, etc. This is also rarely in evidence and reflects the relatively limited opportunity up to now for fraud in this area. With the recent explosion in the use of micros at work, however, theft of output probably represents the area of most potential danger, due to the transportability of floppy disks and the poor performance of passwords and other control systems on such machines. "As microcomputer users convert their confidential information to disk files, that information which represents a competitive edge will become a target for industrial espionage."[6]

Misuse of resources covers a range of activities that in many ways are less serious than fraud, but which, nevertheless, represent an abuse of computer facilities. Unchecked and in excess they can seriously disrupt computer production schedules, by using resources required for legitimate work. A typical example is using an employer's computer to undertake private work—where effective controls are difficult to impose and will become an even greater problem as more employees have access to remote terminals and micros.

Sabotage, arson, and acts of vandalism directed against computers figure only in the EEC and Australian surveys, which makes widespread comparison impossible here. Nevertheless, even the limited information available provides some valuable insights into what are invariably high-cost incidents. Sometimes such acts appear to be politically motivated, whilst on other occasions they stem from employee frustration or aggression.

HOW MUCH CRIME IS THERE?

One aspect of computer-linked crime about which there seems to be general agreement is that "input" crimes dominate. This was not always the case. When business computing was in its infancy, it was conducted almost entirely by computer "experts," who operated on the fringes of mainstream company activity, secure both physically in their isolated computer suites and emotionally in the knowledge that they alone possessed the key that could unlock this new technological treasure-chest—and turn it into something at least partially useful to the businesses that employed them! What crimes there were that came to light back in the early 1960s always involved computer staff and were usually accomplished by amending the programs (software) in fraudulent ways.

Gradually, as computing technology has changed, so has the pattern of computer crime. The main thrust of recent years has been to progress from a batch production system, controlled by full-time computer operators, to widespread time-sharing systems that are capable of supporting simultaneously many separate terminals, usually remote from the actual computer.

Accompanying this fundamental change has been an improvement in the presentation of computer information and a facilitation of the way in which data can be entered into and processed by the computer. This is the so-called "user-friendly interface." The result is that computing has moved out of the era of black box mystique and is now just another business tool, available to a wide spectrum of staff from senior managers to first-line supervisors and

---

[6]Kevin Fitzgerald in CIT - CARB Report.

Source of data	Input	Output	Program	Misuse of resources	Sabotage/ vandalism
1981 Audit Report	42	2	1	22	n/a
1985 Audit Report	58	2	—	17	n/a
BIS Fraud Survey	46	1	5	2	n/a
EEC Report	25	8	4	2	21
CARB Report	39	13	19	29	9
USA CPA (Banks)	("Most" out of total of 120 crimes)				
1985 press reports	5	4	2	2	—
Totals	215	30	31	74	30
Percent	57	8	8	19	8

Table 6.8
How much computer crime?

clerical personnel. This has meant that the opportunity to misappropriate some of the wealth processed by the computer system is now available to many more people than used to be the case; for there is nothing like the daily use of a computer system for revealing any loopholes or imperfections that exist in its security.

Since manipulation of input data is perhaps the easiest avenue open to would-be computer criminals, this is where most evidence exists of attempts at fraudulent conversion. Table 6.8 shows the statistics culled from the various reports studied.[7]

From these figures, it appears that well over half of all known computer-linked crimes are perpetrated by falsifying in some way or another the information fed into the computer. Thus, typically, supernumeraries will be entered on the company payroll; fictitious invoices from non-existent suppliers will be passed for payment; genuine debts due to an organization will be written off the sales ledger balances; stock records will be falsified, in order to cover thefts; or, in a banking context, a cashier will manipulate say a spouse's checks so as to bypass the account debiting procedure.

From such examples, it can be appreciated that much of the computer crime that has been reported contains very little that is original or very sophisticated—perhaps that is why it was discovered in the first place! Most of it exploits weaknesses in the system controls, whilst it also reflects badly on the quality of management that often fails to implement such basic principles as the separation of duties between those responsible for handling goods or cash and those whose task it is to record all such transactions. In essence, much of what is now considered "computer crime" has existed since well before computers assumed their dominant role. Rather is it the case that,

---

[7] The CARB Report lists a total of 123 crimes. Those not included here are eight cases of theft of equipment and six cases where the technique used was not known.

Source of data	Managers/ supervisors	Clerks/ cashiers	Computer staff	Customers/ outsiders	Others/ unknown
1981 Audit Report	20	17	21	1	8
1985 Audit Report	29	27	8	6	7
BIS Fraud Survey	21	11	12	6	4
EEC Report	n/a	n/a	n/a	n/a	n/a
CARB Report	18	18	49	18	20
USA CPA (Banks)	26	68	13	0	13
1985 press reports	1	0	6	6	0
Totals	115	141	109	37	52
Percent	25	31	24	8	12

Table 6.9
Who commits computer crimes?

as the use of computers has mushroomed, so the means of committing fraud have adjusted to the new technology.

Less frequent, but of equal occurrence amongst themselves, are three other types of crime. These are those which involve the theft of computer output (checks, master programs), sabotage or vandalism, and those which involve the unauthorized adjustment of computer software. These all individually represent less than one in ten of recorded crimes but, as we shall see later, they have led to substantial financial losses where they have occurred.

You will notice an anomaly between the proportion of software-oriented crimes in Australia (17.5 percent) and that in our other surveys (3.5 percent). It is difficult to postulate reasons, unless it is that the Computer Abuse Research Bureau (CARB) there has more successfully teased out information than we have so far in Europe. Certainly, they are unequivocal in their concern.

> The categories that should perhaps cause us most concern are the ones that we do not know so much about; the processing oriented techniques and the output oriented techniques. These techniques probably represented the majority of the 'under-water iceberg'; the part we cannot see, because they are being executed either without detection or, if they have been detected, management has been too reticent to reveal the abuse.[8]

WHO COMMITS THE CRIMES?

Using the same source data, one conclusion is immediately clear: almost all the crimes involving computers are carried out by employees (see Table

---

[8] Computer Related Crime in Australia.

Type of Crime	Managers/ supervisors	Clerks/ cashiers	Computer staff	Customers/ outsiders	Others/ unknown
Input	64	51	9	11	16
Output	0	1	5	2	1
Program (Software)	0	0	8	0	0
Resources	4	3	28	3	5
Totals	68	55	50	16	22

Table 6.10
Crimes by type and occupation.

6.9).[9] From this broad analysis it is possible to refine the information, so as to link occupation with types of computer crime. By doing this, we can more accurately define the risks facing us and thereby concentrate on devising appropriate strategies to deal with them (see Table 6.10). (This further analysis is not possible from the data supplied in any of the foreign reports, and is therefore restricted to the UK information.)

Presented in this way, we can immediately see that clerical, supervisory, and managerial computer crime is almost exclusively undertaken by manipulating input data. This pattern of computer input crime (76 percent committed by end-users) is striking evidence of where the greatest risks now lie. As the authors of the 1985 Audit Commission Computer Fraud Survey have observed:

> The risk is not just that a greater number of staff in organizations are more computer literate; rather it is that while the generation of new entrants are familiar with computing, middle and senior management are invariably not so familiar. One generation is ready to grasp the potential, whereas another may well fail to grasp the implications. The risk is enhanced as computer facilities are provided on the office desk, rather than in a central processing area. As the number of users increases, so there is increased need for greater control, security and audibility.

Computer staff on the other hand, are much more prone to misuse the computer resource, have a not unexpected monopoly on program fraud, and are the major cause of output-oriented crime. The latter two techniques can be (and already have been) employed to defraud organizations of large sums of money, but abuse of resources in itself does not usually incur significant losses. Even including this last in our statistics, computer staff still account for only a quarter of all reported crimes.

---

[9] Available data only identify 36 cases in these two categories, without subdividing them between clerks and managers, etc. This division is therefore arbitrary.

MOTIVATIONS: THE IMAGE AND REALITY

There is a commonly held image of the computer criminal, widely promoted by the media, which depicts him as something of a "whiz kid." The respected American computer crime expert Donn Parker has described such people as, "Usually bright, eager, highly motivated, courageous, adventuresome and qualified people, willing to accept a technical challenge. They have exactly the characteristics that make them highly desirable employees in data processing." Match this personality profile with the assessment by F. W. Dennis in an article in Security World that "The common denominator in nearly all cases of computer fraud has been that the individual is very much like the mountain climber - he or she must beat the system because it is there," and you have all the ingredients for a successful Hollywood film.

However, when you are able to analyze how the (relatively few) reported computer crimes were committed, the substance for such an assessment is not really there. Not many of the crimes reported in the BIS Computer Related Fraud Casebook, for example, demonstrate high technical ingenuity on the part of the perpetrator. Most exhibit an opportunistic exploitation of an inherent weakness in the computer system being used.

On the question of the motivations behind computer-linked crimes, a US attorney, Jay BloomBecker, has produced a perceptive analogy which likens the criminal's attitude to the computer as either a "playpen" or a "cookie jar" (Computerworld, May, 1981). Some people, he says, view the computer as a playpen, where crime can result from an attempt to gain satisfaction from working with the computer that gets out of hand. He illustrates this by reference to attempts to gain use of computer time without paying for it: through, for instance, gaining unauthorized access to a time-sharing service; by illegally using a program, knowing that it was copyrighted and by running personal programs on your employer's computer. It is a theory that acknowledges the inherent satisfaction gained by many, adults and children alike, merely from manipulating a computer.

Others, perhaps the more dangerous category, view the computer world they live in as a cookie jar. In this case, personal problems like a gambling debt, drug-taking or investment losses may motivate an employee to view the funds available in the computer system as a solution to the problem. The criminal may try to take what he needs from the computer system; just like dipping into a "cookie jar." In such circumstances, the motivation is much more pressing than the observation of a loophole in the system security. In support of this view, an American study of white-collar crime has concluded that "situational pressures, such as a debt or loss" are a major factor in criminality.[10]

---

[10]Albrecht and Romney in Prosecutor's Brief, 1979.

One of the crimes reported in the BIS Casebook refers to a classic illustration of this. In 1981, a 23-year-old, rather naive bank clerk, earning only £200 a month, became infatuated with a 32-year-old, worldly wise woman. In order to meet what he perceived to be her expectations of him, he lavished money on expensive gifts, travel and general "good-living." He stole £23,000 from four bank accounts, covering the theft by transferring cash through a computer from seventeen other accounts. He then lost £10,000 in casinos, trying to repay the money. When he was finally caught, the woman deserted him!

ATTITUDES TO CRIME

Jack Bologna has spent longer than most examining the motivational aspects of computer crime and has published a collection of his own articles under the title Computer Crime Wave of the Future. In this, he reports the results of a fascinating questionnaire about attitudes to crime, which he put to two disparate groups in the United States - 100 accountants from public practice, industry and government and 90 data processing professionals of middle to higher rank, who were delegates to a Honeywell conference on computer security. The group were asked to express their agreement or disagreement with a series of statements seeking to rationalize why employees steal or embezzle from their employers. The statements were an attempt to synthesize the positions of the various schools of thought (from moral philosophers, through sociologists to economists and politicians) on crime motivations and causes.

There were both interesting similarities and differences in the responses he obtained. For both groups, the top four items were the same. They agreed that employees steal because:

1 "They feel they can get away with it and not be caught."
2 "They think stealing a little from a big company won't hurt it."
3 "Each theft has its own preceding conditions and each thief has his own motives, so there is no general rule."
4 "Most employee thieves are caught by accident, rather than by audit or design. Therefore, fear of being caught is not a deterrent to theft."

The fact that 70 percent of the accountants and 78 percent of the DP professionals believed that most thieves were caught by accident is a startling admission of the vulnerability of the accounting controls, audit trails, and programming documentation for which their professions are responsible.

However, the differences in the responses from the two groups provided equally interesting revelations. For the DP professionals gave significantly greater accord to the propositions that:

1 "They feel that 'beating the company' is a challenge and not a matter of economic gain alone." (DP = 70 percent v. Acc. 57 percent.)
2 "They feel frustrated or dissatisfied about some aspect of their personal life that is not job-related." (DP = 68 percent v. Acc. = 48 percent.)

Source of data	Input (£)	Output (£)	Program	Resource	Sabatoge
1981 Audit Report	858,170	3,600	26,000	17,379	n/a
1985 Audit Report	901,001	230,185	0	2301	n/a
BIS Fraud Survey	3,774,089	56	23,050	2000	n/a
EEC Report	6,112,800	n/a	11,880,000	n/a	1,674,000
CARB Report	1,580,925	106,845	152,038	34,323	461,550
1985 press reports	14,993,500	68,500	9,030,000	0	n/a
Totals	28,220,485	409,186	21,111,088	56,003	2,135,550
Percentage of total value	54	0.8	41	0.1	4
Number of cases with value assessed	193	13	21	27	8
Average value	146,220	31,476	1,005,290	2074	266,944

Table 6.11
The cost of computer crime.

3 "They feel frustrated or dissatisfied about some aspect of their job." (DP = 75 percent v. Acc. = 63 percent.)

In their identification of personal and job-related "frustration" as a contributory cause of criminality, it may be that the DP professionals were accurately reflecting the lack of autonomy, minimal job variety, and poor management communications often endemic in data processing work.

HOW MUCH DOES IT COST?

To ask this question is akin to the enquiry about the proverbial piece of string! The scale of losses ranges from that involving the simple misuse of a computer resource, with virtually no quantifiable costs, to a handful of sophisticated frauds perpetrated against banks and other financial institutions, where the costs have been measured in millions of pounds.

What I have undertaken here is a consolidation of the published information about computer crime costs right across the spectrum, followed by a detailed analysis of input crimes on their own. As we have already seen, input crimes are probably the major problem facing us and therefore represent the greatest potential return, if we tackle them successfully. No adjustment has been made for the effects of inflation on the values of crimes which, in a few cases, go back to the 1960s. Furthermore, these values seldom reflect the full costs of an incident, since the less easily quantifiable costs of disruption and subsequent recovery are missing from most calculations. To this extent, true costs are understated in the figures that follow.

Status	Source of data	No. of crimes	Total value (£)	Average value (£)
Managers/supvrs	1981	19	720,254	37,908
	1985	23	788,956	34,302
	BIS	20	678,081	33,904
		62	2,187,291	35,279
Clerks/cashiers	1981	14	77,619	5,554
	1985	24	100,920	4,205
	BIS	11	175,526	15,957
		49	354,065	7,226
Computer staff	1981	2	5,295	2,647
	1985	1	452	452
	BIS	4	201,405	50,351
		7	207,152	29,593
Outsiders/unknown	1981	5	54,802	10,960
Customers/others	1985	8	10,673	1,334
	BIS	9	2,719,077	302,120
		22	2,784,552	126,571

Table 6.12
Crimes by value and occupation

The overall costs, analyzed by type of crime in pounds sterling are shown in Table 6.11.[11],[12] One or two aspects of these figures call for comment. The two UK Audit Commission Surveys revealed a lower average cost per incident than any of the other reports; something they recognized, but for which they offered no explanation. The EEC Survey and the 1985 press reports include three major banking frauds achieved by program manipulation; together these account for about £20 million of the total £21 million in that category. The latest press reports also include nearly £ 15 million bank losses resulting from two cases of false input information, again greatly inflating the figures.

Obviously, cases of this magnitude tend to distort the "run-of-the-mill" crimes and inflate the "average" values given. However, we must also recognize that the computer systems of financial institutions do routinely process vast sums of money, and to that extent can expect to be the subject of regular fraudulent attacks. Banks themselves have been conspicuously reluctant to admit to losses through fraud — a fact strongly criticized by the authors of the Australian CARB report, whose data include no banking information at all. In some measure, then, the five high-value cases included here only help to balance earlier (suspected) omissions.

---

[11] European Currency Units (ecus) converted at 1 ecu 54p (UK).
[12] Australian dollars converted at $ 151p (UK).

Job roles	Average value (£)	Average duration (months)	Value per month (£)
Managers/supvrs	35,279	19	1,857
Clerks/cashiers	7,226	11	657

Table 6.13
Length and value of crimes.

Most of us, however, do not work in banks, and are therefore more likely to encounter the kind of input fraud covered so well by the two Audit Commission surveys and in the BIS Casebook. Between them, these three surveys examine 137 such cases,[13] enough to provide us with a number of useful insights.

First, let us look at how crimes relate to jobs (see Table 6.12). Whilst the number of cases involving computer staff is too small to provide a reliable result, there is an immediate comparison possible between the senior staff grades of manager and supervisor on the one hand and the more junior clerical and cash-handling roles on the other. Those in positions involving trust, responsibility and (presumably) greater technical know-how manage on average to extract five times greater value than their humbler counterparts. When you also take into account that there are fewer of them, the potential for causing harm where technical expertise co-exists with authority and opportunity can be readily appreciated. This message is reinforced by examination of the length of time such crimes go on before detection, and the rate at which value (normally money) is extracted (see Table 6.13).

Finally, the 1985 Audit Commission Survey has some additional information about the people who committed the crimes it reported. The information is interesting for the light it sheds on this particular manifestation of white-collar crime. For every grade of staff I have calculated the average time both in service to the one employer and also in the particular job occupied at the time the crime was committed. I have then compared them with the average duration of the frauds (see Figure 6-2). Remember, these are averages, which makes it a sobering thought indeed that staff with such long records of service can and do feature in the annals of computer crime.

All the information we have indicates that nearly all computer criminals are first-time offenders, motivated by greed, pressing financial problems or other personal difficulties. There seems to be no strong relation between the extent of the financial loss and length of service, for some trusted employees have been prepared to commit fraud for a relatively small reward. Like all fraud, it is the opportunity, rather than the actual sum involved, that determines behavior.

---

[13]In total, 144 cases, of which seven have no assessed value and have therefore been omitted here.

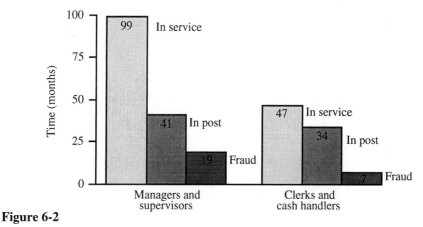

Figure 6-2
Average duration of fraudulent activity.

WHAT CAN BE DONE?

If we start from an acknowledgment that very few cases of computer fraud exhibit the ingenious application of technical skills (but that, on the contrary, most take advantage of inherent weaknesses in the basic system controls and procedures) then there is a range of counter-measures available for us to consider. The security manager should have a role to play in any such scheme, though it would be idle to pretend his is the only one.

The Audit Commission Survey makes the following observations:

If basic controls were introduced and enforced by management the risk of further frauds would be minimized. The ability to enforce such controls (particularly where there are increasingly complex terminal-based systems) will call for additional skills. A combination of accounting and computing knowledge will be essential for those responsible for verifying the adequacy of such controls—the auditor will need to be computer literate if he is to function effectively in the future.

The risks of fraud and abuse will be all the greater if internal controls and internal audit are inadequate. Poor supervision and ineffective audit will almost certainly encourage the opportunity for large-scale and long-running losses. Where the organization sustains such an environment and still encourages the widespread introduction of computing, the risks will be considerable.

I am a great believer in a four-pronged approach to computer security. For many reasons, I think it is completely impractical to rely on any single person or job role to carry out the security function effectively. I would not, therefore, rely on computer staff alone to develop system security; nor do I see it as just the auditors' responsibility to ensure effective controls. Both approaches would be rapidly undermined without the involvement of the managers using the computer and without the insights brought by them to the actual operation of the systems. Even an approach that combined these three elements would be missing the professional skills of the security expert in analyzing risks and probing for any weaknesses in the agreed security strategy.

To conclude, then, here are a few thoughts in the form of an aide-memoire about the contributions that could and should be made by those most closely involved.

Managers

- Define responsibilities of those involved: in systems design; in system use and in auditing.
- Develop for all users a "Code of Practice."
- Ensure adequate training is given at all levels.
- Become personally computer literate.
- Allow realistic time and budget schedules for developing security in computer systems.
- Counsel staff.

Auditors

- Liaise with computer staff in the development of systems.
- Ensure provision of adequate audit trails.
- Liaise with computer users.
- Become personally computer literate.

Computer Staff

- Be aware of the need for security.
- Ensure programmers and analysts possess general business skills, as well as technical expertise.
- Allow sufficient time to develop secure systems during program development.

Security Managers

- Become computer literate.
- Analyze the risks.
- Ask "awkward" questions: of computer staff, of auditors and of users.
- Apply security experience to the computer situation.
- Liaise with managers, auditors, and computer staff.

READING QUESTIONS

1) Why is most computer crime undetected and underreported?
2) Why might some educated guesses about the extent of computer crime exaggerate its frequency?

3) What is the disagreement about the "profile" of the typical computer criminal?
4) What is the problem with using the large category "computer crime" to describe all crime done with computers?
5) What are the four "causes" of computer crime and how do their arguments about computer crime conflict or converge?
6) What are the differences between uniform crime reports, victim surveys, and self-report surveys? How does each method bias its estimate?
7) How do the different "types" of crime in the survey differ in their frequency?
8) According to the self-report survey, are people who do one "type" of computer crime likely to engage in other "types"? Why does this say about the profile of the computer criminal?
9) What "social characteristics" were tested to see if they predicted computer crime? What is the reason they did not predict well?
10) What is the relationship between beliefs that computer crime is not wrong and the commission of computer crimes?
11) What is "input fraud"? What are the other two types of computer crime? Are there differences in the prevalence of these types?
12) How could "user friendly" computers contribute to computer crime?
13) Why should you separate the duties of those who handle goods and those who record these transactions?
14) What is the difference between "playpen" and "cookie jar" computer crime?
15) What is the difference in the size of the crimes committed by senior and junior personnel?

DISCUSSION QUESTIONS

1) There seems to be a clear association between the belief that computer crime is not wrong and the willingness to commit it. What does this say about the usefulness of courses that study "computer ethics"? What ways other than courses could we encourage a thoughtful approach to computer crime?
2) Why is there the widespread conception that computer criminals are "hackers"? Does this conception make common "input" computer crime easier to commit?
3) What is the profile of the "typical" computer criminal? What are the motive, means, and opportunity of the "typical" computer crime?

PRACTICING THE DESIGN ETHIC

1) Interview the security manager at a local computer department (or your university). It is possible there isn't a specific "security manager," in which case ask the computer operations manager who has responsibility for system and data security at that location. Arrange a brief interview to determine the following: (Note: ensure the confidentiality of the data you collect, and be sure to tell the person you are interviewing that confidentiality of names and business will be respected.)
   • Why does the installation have (not have) a "security administrator"?
   • What is considered a breach of security?
   • Have there been security violations in the past year? If so, how were they discovered?
   • What actions have been taken to prevent the breach of security from recurring?
   • Have the breaches of security been caused by employees, outsiders, or students?
   • What "damage" was caused by the breach of security?

Summarize your data and report your findings to the class. Include your perspectives on the information you collected. Also, describe any impacts you feel the security policies have on other social issues (i.e., privacy, freedom of expression, and property issues).

2) Interview, briefly, at least three people who are managers, security personnel, computer staff, end users, or students (be sure to cover at least three of these categories). Determine the following:

- Are they aware of a security policy on site? If so, can they explain to you what is covered in the policy?
- What issues do they feel ought to be covered in a security policy?
- What would they consider a breach of security of the computer system?
- What could happen to their data if security was breached?

Summarize your data and describe how your interviewees' perspectives differ.

CHAPTER

7

EXPERTS AND EXPERT SYSTEMS

In this chapter, we attempt to sidestep the usual heated rhetoric of the expert systems debate to look at two particular kinds of expert systems. One is XCON, the hardware configuration expert system that has been used with great effectiveness by Digital Equipment Corporation (DEC). The other is that group of expert systems which have attempted to solve the complex problem of medical diagnosis.

In the somewhat clean decision-making context of configuring computers, XCON seems a huge success. It made configuration a less expensive, more reliable, and more helpful process than it had been before at DEC. And its benefits extended beyond the narrow domain of configuration into sales and support. However, in the much noisier domain of medical diagnosis, expert systems seem not to do as well as expert humans, who in turn do not do as well as simple linear models.

But in both these contexts, we find that the models (either expert systems or linear models) do not remove the need for human oversight and intervention. In DEC, since the models are constantly changing, XCON must be updated to conform to the latest specifications. This requires maintaining a group of knowledgeable people who can monitor and update the system. It would quickly become obsolete without this maintenance. Thus, XCON does not remove the need for complex, human understanding but merely relocates it. The same is true for even the simple linear models in medical diagnosis. If they are adopted by practitioners, they will likely be used as advisors, removing some of the burden from diagnosticians by allowing them to concentrate on the hard cases—relocating their expertise to where it is most needed.

AN EXAMINATION OF THE IMPACT OF EXPERT SYSTEMS ON THE FIRM: THE CASE OF XCON[1]

J.J. Sviokla

Many consider XCON to be one of the most successful commercial expert systems in use. Its developers and users document $15 million plus in savings from 1980 to 1985. Yet few people understand how XCON created these benefits. There is even less understanding of the effects XCON use created for the underlying business task it supports. The purpose of this article is to provide an indepth analysis of the effects of XCON use on the process of computer configuration at Digital and the resulting managerial implications of these effects.

More generally there has been little or no attempt to relate ES to other issues that affect the information processing capacity of a firm. Moreover, there are omissions, particularly with regard to the organizational issues of ES building and long-term use. This lapse probably exists because ESs are so new to industry that, until recently, business academics and practitioners have had little chance to explore their complexities. Mumford (1987) suggests the need to study how expert systems are actually used as opposed to how designers expect them to be used.

This study uses pre/post field investigations to discover how use of XCON altered the execution of the task it was designed to support. It also examines the changes XCON engendered in the information processing capacity of the firm.

LITERATURE ON EXPERT SYSTEMS

Use of ES in commercial organizations is a relatively new phenomenon, and examination of their implications is just beginning to be explored. Currently, there are three categories of literature concerning ES. The first describes how to build expert systems. *Building Expert Systems* (Hayes-Roth, et al., 1983), a collection of articles designed to aid ES development and use, and *Expert Systems: A Practical Introduction* (Sell, 1985), which presents formulae for building ES based on the author's experience at Digital, are examples of a growing number of books written on the subject. Some publications focus on tools and applications (Harmon and King, 1985; Harmon and Rex Maus, 1988). Others focus on specific problem areas (e.g., Mockler, 1989).

---

[1] From Sviokla, J. J. (1990). An examination of the impact of expert systems on the firm: the case of XCON. *MIS Quarterly*, 14, 127-140. Reprinted by special permission from the *MIS Quarterly*, Volume 14, Number 2, June 1990. Copyright 1990 by the Society for Information Management and the Management Information Systems Research Center at the University of Minnesota.

The second category of literature, which chronicles the work of computer scientists, primarily describes theoretical issues, such as the methods of knowledge representation (Minsky, 1975), search strategies (Knuth and Moore, 1975), and so on. Often an ES has many developers, each of whom contributes to the lineage of writings that tracks the system over time. The series of articles from Shortliffe (1976) through van Melle, et al. (1981) for the MYCIN/EMYCIN project is one example of such a stream of research.

The third category of works focuses on commercial uses of ES. These "system biographies," written by practitioners, review the commercial ramifications of their handiwork. The *AI Business* (Winston and Prendergast, 1984), a collection of papers by managers and their academic allies, and the book *The Rise of the Expert Company* (Feigenbaum, et al., 1988) are two recent examples of this genre. The wealth of personal commentary and experience embodied in these works makes them valuable first-hand accounts of pioneering real-world efforts. Yet there are no unifying research themes in their observations because the authors are practitioners describing their experiences, not researchers seeking effects. Nor are any investigators looking at what effects these expert systems have on the user organization.

There are many possible ways to look at the impact of information systems on the organization, and there is a rich tradition of research in the more general area of information technology (IT) in organizations. In a classic review article, Kling (1980) highlights two schools of thought with fundamentally different assumptions about the organization: segmented institutionalist and systems rationalist. Kling points out that these assumptions drive very different analyses and interpretations of the phenomena observed. He notes that the technology is "malleable though not entirely plastic" (p. 100). Thus, to speak of the "social impact of computing" is as invalid as it is valid. The role of referent perspective shapes the investigation.

In an analysis of citations in the MIS field, Culnan (1987) notes a distinct sub-field concerning the impacts of computers on the organization. Citing Culnan and building on Kling (1980), Markus and Robey (1988) analyze the underlying causal agencies, beliefs about logical structure (static versus dynamic theory), and levels of analysis (micro, macro, or mixed). By going a level deeper in the review and analysis of existing impact literature, they observe that some of the differences result from the implicit themes and analyses of the different researchers. These observations are consonant with Fry (1982), who notes the wide variety of constructs for IT and organizations. Therefore, it is important to characterize the motivation for this study.

Expert systems explicitly set out to capture and assist or automate complex, non-algorithmic decisions. In an organizational context, the manager creating such a system is consciously designing a decision-making process for the firm. Simon (1945) and Huber (1984) both note the central importance of designing the decision processes to the effectiveness of modern firms. In a theoretical review and analysis of the strategic systems literature on MIS, Bakos and Treacy (1986) suggest that systems that help "skirt the limits of rationality" (p. 109) beyond the bounded rationality of humans (Simon, 1945; Cyert and March, 1963) are valuable opportunities for increasing the efficiency and effectiveness of the organization. Therefore, a large-scale, successful system, such as XCON, which explicitly attempts to re-design an existing decision process, should shift the information processing capabilities of the organization.

DESIGN OF CURRENT STUDY

Given the complexities described above, the first research design question was to choose the best method to gather an understanding of the impacts of ES use on the organization. Benbasat, et al. (1986), in a review of case research in information systems, note that one important motivation for case research occurs when "the research is interested in complex problems which cannot be removed from the setting without destroying the phenomenon" (p. 7). Bonoma (1985) advocates the use of case research in environments "where the existing body of knowledge is insufficient to permit the posing of causal questions, and when a phenomenon cannot be studied outside the context in which it naturally occurs" (p. 207).

The impact of expert system use on a firm's information processing capacity is intertwined with an understanding of the business process it is designed to support. Hence, a case study seemed appropriate.

The next research design question was to choose measures—within the case approach—to provide a useful organization for the data. After a review of the variety of measures from the literature, two measures of impact were chosen: *performance programs* (March and Simon, 1958) and *information processing capacity* (Galbraith 1973; 1977). Within the performance programs, two levels of analysis were chosen: individual and organizational. Rousseau (1985) defends this type of mixed-level analysis when the effects are not simply macro or micro. (See Markus and Robey, 1988.) In this exploratory case work on XCON, it was important to be open to potential changes at the micro and macro levels of the task.

March and Simon (1958) provide the most complete discussion of performance programs. They emphasize the limited nature of humans to process information and the various sources of uncertainty that an organization faces. One of the critical mechanisms that an organization uses to make decisions and carry out work is performance program, which March and Simon define as follows:

> We have seen that under certain circumstances the search and choice processes are very much abridged. At the limit, an environmental stimulus may evoke immediately from the organization a highly complex and organized set of responses. Such a set of responses we call a *performance program*, or simply a *program* (p. 141).

March and Simon (1958) have some helpful ideas on how to look for performance programs in organizations. Specifically, they suggest observing behavior, interviewing members of the organization, and examining documents. The data gathered for this study that identify performance programs closely parallel March and Simon's suggestions.

Thirty-three interviews were conducted during more than a dozen field visits over a period of five months. In addition to interviews, observational and archival data were collected. These three sources were analyzed by the author to create a before-and-after picture of the configuration process and XCON's role within Digital.[2] For data collection and analysis purposes, pre-XCON was defined as 1978—the period just before XCON was introduced. Post-XCON is defined as 1985—five years after the system was in active daily use.

The second measure used within the case research was information processing capacity. The information processing capacity of the firm was chosen as a means to capture the changes in input and output of the target task. As affirmed by Bakos and Treacy (1986), it was expected that the use of an expert system would expand the ability to the human problem solvers and increase the information processing capacity of the organization for the target task. In an extensive review of the information processing literature, Zack and McKenney (1989) note that there have been very few operationalizations of the information processing concept in field research. There is no completely satisfactory model for the information processing capacity of a firm (Galbraith 1973). It is not the focus of this research to find and prove such a model. Rather, the information processing capacity of the firm and performance programs are used as organizing concepts for data collection, analysis, and comparison to understand the impact of expert systems use on the firm.

For this study, the specific operationalization of this measure draws on the work of Galbraith (1973; 1977), who defines the information processing capacity of an organization to be the number of different input resources, the diversity of the outputs, and the level of task performances (Galbraith, 1977). These definitions are, for this study, pragmatic and simple: *inputs* are defined as the number of data sources used and people consulted in the delivery of the product or service; *outputs* are defined as the number of different versions of the product/service; the *level of task performance* is the management's assessment of performance and any available objective measures. In addition

---

[2] Historical information—especially interviews about past events—presents methodological challenges: people forget the correct facts; they remember the facts incorrectly; or, with time, they recollect the past in a manner inconsistent with the facts. Archival data and multiple interviews were used in this study to cross-check the recollections and verify important historical issues (Bonoma, 1985). Detailed process maps were drawn to create a flow of the decision process in the firm. Each iteration of these maps was reviewed for accuracy by three different experts within the firm. This article presents a verbal description of these maps and describes the significant differences from pre-XCON to post-XCON.

to the two measures (organizational programs and information processing capacity), an in depth study of the business situations was made in order to help the researchers interpret the data gathered.

THE COMPANY SETTING

With 1986 revenues of $7.6 billion, net income of $617 million, and more than 89,000 employees worldwide, Digital Equipment Corporation was the second-largest computer manufacturer in the United States. In an industry that experienced phenomenal growth during the past three decades, Digital had built a reputation for engineering excellence and an ability to deliver reliable computers with superior performance for the price. While most computer manufacturers restricted their offerings to a few standard systems with limited options, Digital designed its machines and marketing to give customers a broad and flexible set of basic systems with many add-on options. Using this strategy, Digital grew rapidly. In the 13 years from 1972 to 1985, its equipment revenues increased 29 percent per year compounded.

Because of the product line's flexibility, many Digital employees-especially those in manufacturing and sales-needed constant retraining and updating of their product knowledge. This almost continual learning process represented a significant price that the product strategy necessarily exacted.

THE ISSUE—CONFIGURATION

Configuration was one of the key controls Digital used to ensure that the products its salespeople sold were, in fact, buildable. The term "configuration" means translating a customer's needs into a complete computer system. In 1974, when a customer bought a Digital computer, the customer worked with a salesperson to identify needs and tailor a system and a list of options to match the customer's precise requirements. This process was the first step in configuration.

A typical configured order contained one or more main components, each with one to 100 (or more) options.

There were three basic tasks in configuration:
1. Translating customer needs into Digital products
2. Checking the completeness and accuracy of the sales order
3. Designing the specific placement and connection of all parts in the order

The configuration issue was important to Digital because sales orders—the raw material of configuration—constituted the most important customer information that flowed through the company. Configuration was the major means used to verify, process, and ensure the accuracy of sales orders.

As early as 1974-75, the complexity of the configuration process was substantial. There were approximately 50 types of central process with 400 core options, each of which had approximately 10 versions—that is, 4,000 options overall. No one knew for certain how many possible working configurations existed, but the number was estimated to be in the millions. Some customers needed minor variations, such as three tape drives instead of two. However, in the overall order population, many different types of configurations passed through the firm—hence the complexity.

Misconfiguration posed many possible problems. For example, large customers might place two identical orders but the delivered machines might have different assembly. This difference in assembly might be cosmetic, such as a different color cabinet, or functional, such as a different placement of a disk drive. This lack of standardization did not communicate the quality control Digital wanted to present to all its customers.

In creating an organizational program for configuration at Digital, it was discovered that, pre-XCON, every configuration was reviewed in at least three places in the order flow: initial technical edit, manufacturing technical edit, and final assembly and test. After a salesperson drafted a contract with a price, an initial technical editor—usually located in a field sales office scanned the order to ensure that all the necessary components were included. After this initial verification, the order was "accepted," which meant that Digital committed to deliver the stated gem on the specified dates and for the agreed-upon price.

Manufacturing management assigned primary technical editing responsibility to the second stopping point: the manufacturing technical edit group. Members of this group generated the configuration drawing and controlled the configuration through manufacture. The technical editors (TEs) within the manufacturing technical edit group usually began the configuration process by retrieving a sales order. The TE—equipped with a telephone, a bookshelf of technical manuals, and experience—was challenged with ensuring every order's technical completeness before creating a drawing showing the placement of all the system's modules. Because of the vast number of possible options and the exactness of assembly requirements, this task required intimate knowledge of an enormous amount of technical detail. The time spent on an order varied with its complexity, size, and frequency. On average, it took 15 minutes to configure an order by hand, but correctness was uneven. According to surveys conducted by the Intelligent Systems Technology Group (ISTG) within Digital, the human configurers were completely correct only 65 percent of the time. The ISTG criteria for correctness were relatively strict: a configuration could be scored "incorrect" if a cable was off by one foot.

The difficulty of configuring depended greatly on the newness, complexity, and frequency of the order. The actual time it took to edit an order varied from five to 10 minutes to an hour or more. The TEs and their management estimated that the cycle time to complete the technical editing process for an order—pre-XCON—was one to two days on a regular basis.

Task performance measures were largely subjective and locally determined by each technical editor. Given the immense number of possible configurations, each technical editor developed a repertoire that worked best for him or her. There were no optimal configurations; the evaluation of any particular configuration was simple: if it worked, it was right. Consequently, two people could configure the same systems differently, yet both could be correct according to the rating criteria.

A major method—perhaps the major step taken to ensure that systems were built correctly—was final assembly and test (FA&T), the third stopping point in the performance program for configuration. Before XCON, approximately 90 percent of Digital's system volume passed through FA&T, where all configuration changes and errors were settled by creating and testing the system. In a real sense, this was the final technical edit.

Because of a large backlog of orders for Digital products during this time as well as frequent changes to computer orders, it was not unheard of for the total order-processing time to extend four to six months—although such a situation was uncommon. Usually, the cycle time from when an order reached manufacturing technical edit until it was shipped to the customer was approximately 10 to 15 weeks. Of that time, once the parts were ordered and received, approximately four to six weeks were spent with the machine in FA&T.

SOLVING THE CONFIGURATION PROBLEM—XCON

By 1975, management recognized configuration as a serious issue with an overwhelming magnitude of potential problems. To support the massive FA&T effort necessitated by the growing volume of equipment sales, the company had created an FA&T facility in Westminster, Massachusetts. This facility covered more than 13 acres under one roof and cost between $15 and $20 million to build. Inventory to stock the plant cost approximately $20 million more. By 1975, Digital was grossing $433.2 million in equipment sales, and by the early 1980s that figure was projected to quadruple.[3] Such growth would necessitate four or five more FA&T plants. If the FA&T "solution" to the problem continued, tens of millions of dollars would be tied up in plant, equipment, and inventory simply to support the assembly operation.

Organizational dilemmas also confronted Digital managers. Estimates of the number of configuration experts at Digital ranged from 50 to 60 experienced individuals. The number of people projected to be required by the early 1980s ranged between 50 and 200. Furthermore, the underlying problem continued to become more and more difficult. It was clear that no human being could possibly remember and manage all the relevant technical data required to perform configurations while simultaneously tracking and learning about the onslaught of new product offerings and options.

The impetus to seek a solution began with the realization of the enormity of the FA&T cost. This search led to the development of XCON, which began with a collaboration between Digital and John McDermott, a professor of computer science at Carnegie Mellon University. During the period from

---

[3] In fact, Digital exceeded $4 billion in equipment revenue in 1981.

December 1978 to April 1979, McDermott—with the help of Digital personnel—created a prototype with 210 rules and 100 components. The system demonstrations were impressive enough to garner support to fund the XCON project, which was to provide the system with the basic knowledge of configuration. McDermott remained the principal designer/developer. Toward the end of 1979, the system was validated with 50 "representative orders" which were reviewed by six experts. The system made two "significant" and 10 "low-level" mistakes.

Conceptually, the system is very straightforward. There are three basic inputs to XCON:

• All VAX orders and selected PDP-11 orders
• Digital product information
• Engineering/marketing configuration guidelines

In processing an order, XCON performs the following activities, with the data provided from the three inputs above:

• Adds or deletes components necessary to make the order complete and correct (includes comments on the reason for each change)
• Assigns each component to its correct location
• Configures cable layout, lengths, and connections
• Calculates cable layout, lengths, and connections
• Calculates the address vectors (the logical addresses of the options in the computer)

The outputs from XCON are:

• Order line item summary
• Detailed configuration drawings at the cabinet, box, and backpanel levels
• Explanatory text regarding:
    — Parts not needed in configuration
    — Spare parts
    — Additional parts needed for completeness
    — Parts that, for technical reasons, were not configured
    — Address and vector settings
    — Unused controller capacities
    — Unused box power

The extent and precision of the output was much more complete than previous output by human configurers. By the end of 1979, Digital was using XCON in a pilot project at its Salem, New Hampshire, manufacturing plant. In 1980, the system was in active use at Salem. By early 1981, the system was in regular use throughout the company

PERFORMANCE PROGRAM: POST-XCON

There were two major changes to the performance program post-XCON. First, fewer areas in Digital continued doing technical editing. The coordination and control of configuration became standardized and centralized. Second, the roles and responsibilities of the technical editors

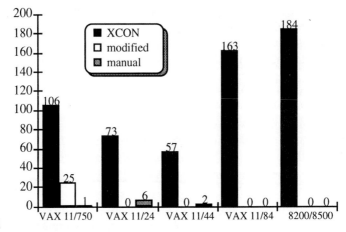

Figure 7-1
Configuration data—Digital Salem (4 months in 1986).

changed dramatically. With the use of XCON, 90 percent of all orders were put through the system. There was no need to have the sales office check a configuration. Nor was there a need to make substantial configuration adjustments at the FA&T operation. Manufacturing technical edit was the one and only major configuration generation point.

This centralization led to more control of the configuration process. It also standardized the execution of configuration policy on each and every XCONed order. Moreover, the best configuration expertise began to migrate to the ISTG organization—the software development team responsible for keeping XCON up to date.

The second major shift in performance programs came at the TE's desk. The homogenous task became differentiated, and three processes of configuration emerged: (1) XCON; (2) modified; and (3) manual.

In 1986, the vast majority of Digital orders went directly through the XCON system, as shown in the Salem plant's data (Figure 7-1).

"XCON" meant that the TE checked the XCON output. When the order—a list of line items— flashed on the screen, the editor would scan for part numbers, order completeness, and overall correctness. Often salespeople would include extra parts or parts for another system on the same order. When this occurred, these extra parts needed to be marked as "spares" so that XCON would not attempt to configure them and find them as mistakes. Consequently, a task for the technical editor was to ensure that all extra parts were correctly marked "spare." In cases where the spare components were similar to those requiring configurations, the TE might have to ask the salesperson for clarification.

At the other extreme, there were some configuration or planning tasks that could not be performed well on the machine. For XCON, this occurred relatively infrequently—only about four to six times per month per TE in the Salem sample. When it did happen, the Salem technical editors had to configure manually, as was done pre-XCON. There were also some special customer orders for which the technical editors decided not to use XCON at all, again configuring the entire order manually. For instance, military orders often specified the configuration in the purchase contract. In these cases, the TEs simply translated the contract specifications onto the configuration sheets because the military specifications might or might not agree with XCON's results.

The challenges arose in the second category of tasks, "modified" (for which XCON created less flexibility). Modifications to XCON content often occurred on brand new VAX models. Modifying an XCON configuration meant going back through the entire output—often 20 pages or more—to trace every reference to a particular line item or series of line items and their cable needs, address vectors, and other specifications. In the XCON case, this hybrid system of part ES, part manual seemed to be the most time-consuming and frustrating activity of all. As one TE noted:

> It is so boring! Often I have to take the output, lay it on a table, and get the white-out. I look through the entire thing, making all the necessary changes. People often expect to be able to see the XCON output on the computer, so I have to adjust it on the screen. To do this I call up the output file, put it in a word processor, and edit it line by line. It takes forever. We have been working with the people in Hudson [the XCON developers] to get an editor [software], which could do all that for us—especially tracking down all the dependent details (Source: author interview).

In general, TEs were guided by rules of thumb gained from experience to separate orders requiring careful review from those requiring less. For example, early versions of new products such as the 8600 series of VAX computers often contained mistakes. Therefore, technical editors, alert to the 8600 series, would carefully inspect orders containing one. Overall, the technical editor's job had changed significantly.

INFORMATION PROCESSING CAPACITY: POST-XCON

With the XCON system in place, the second measure—the information processing capacity of the firm—increased significantly. Table 7.1 shows the inputs, outputs, and task performance components for configuration—pre- and post-XCON—at Digital.

Inputs

Post-XCON, the inputs to the technical editing process were more numerous. It is important to remember that in the information processing assessment, an increase in inputs through specialization of tasks increases the information processing need of the task because each new input must be coordinated. With the XCON system, the information processing needs increased in this area because the XCON development group was another

Pre-XCON		Post-XCON
Inputs—Increased		
Sales order	=	Sales order
Memoranda/guides	=	Memoranda/guides
Training	=	Training
Experts consulted	+	Experts consulted
Technical Editors [a] (23 in 1981)	++	Technical Editors (17 in 1986) XCON Development Group [b] (30 in 1986)
Outputs—Significantly Increased		
Phone follow-up	-	Phone follow-up
8' x 10" hand drawing of configuration	++	Configuration including parts to be added exact layout assembly information, vectors cabling, etc. explanations
	++	Information for XSEL and other systems internal to Digital
Task Performance — Significantly increased		
In 1981 average review of 100-300 orders/editor/year	++	In 1986 average review of over 1000/editor/year
Correctness range 65% to 90%[c]	++	Correctness range 95% to 98%
Total volume — 4,000-5,000 VAX orders, -15,000 other orders	++	Order volume — 60,000 + orders
Even distribution of orders through TE	++	Short time windows; distribution uneven with high peaks
	++	Shorter cycle time (10-12 weeks in assembly to 2-3 weeks)

The indicators of effect and direction are shown for each item: + + is a large increase, + an increase, = stayed the same, - a decrease.

[a] This number excludes managers of technical editors

[b] There were approximately 40 people in the XCON/XSEL development group as of July 1986. Most of them worked on XCON.

[c] This estimate and the estimate of 95-98% correctness are based on tests conducted by the Intelligent Systems Technology Group at Digital.

Table 7.1

Digital's Pre- and Post-XCON task performance components for configuration.

input to the process. Of the 40 or more developers in the Intelligent Systems Technology Group (ISTG), approximately 30 were involved with the creation and maintenance of XCON—a net increase of 24 people with greater skill specialization. Simultaneously, the number of technical editors decreased from 23 to 17 in the period from 1981 to 1986. This decrease was more than offset by an increase in the number technical staff needed to create XCON. Within the working definition of information processing, this translates into an increase in inputs.

It should be noted that the focus of the information processing view of the firm is different from traditional views of input. In a traditional input/output analysis, an increase in inputs means more material, labor, or capital. In the information processing analysis, inputs and outputs are not productivity measures but rather are approximations of the complexity of the information processing task. Consequently, the framework is useful for describing information processing effects but is significantly different from traditional productivity approaches.

With XCON, manufacturing, engineering, and marketing were also involved in creating the rules for systems' configurations. As of early 1985, all products had to have established and complete configuration rules in the XCON system before release. Overall, there was an increase to the inputs for XCON.

Outputs

The outputs from the XCON-aided configuration process increased dramatically. Outputs are defined as the number of different versions of the product/service. XCON clearly increased outputs. Configuration done by the manufacturing technical editors was always intended to help assemblers and technicians build machines. However, XCON output was so superior to previous hand configurations in terms of its detail and scope that manufacturing managers attributed savings of at least two hours of assembly time, per system, to the XCON output. There were additional salary savings in terms of being able to use less-skilled individuals to assemble systems.

The pre-XCON configuration paperwork was a one-page hand-drawn document of the basic system layout. Post-XCON documents were 10 + pages of detailed specifications and drawings indicating where every module and component was to reside. A more consistent and complex set of documents reflects an increase in information processing capacity, as described by Galbraith (1973) and operationalized here.

Post-XCON output also had more audiences. Pre-XCON output was used primarily by manufacturing assembly people. Post-XCON output was used not only by manufacturing for assembly but also in the field engineering's assembly process. In addition, field service representatives used the customer's copy of the configuration as a trouble-shooting aid. It was assumed that there were many other users that ISTG simply did not know about. During the interviewing at the company, for example, it was discovered that the shipping department used XCON output as part of its training and packaging routine to assure that all the correct components were in the shipment going to the customer site.

Besides being more complete and precise, XCON output was also broader in scope. Before XCON, the manufacturing engineers or manufacturing technicians calculated address vectors and cable lengths. However, issues such as excess or unused capacities were not addressed. The XCON configuration document generated these numbers for every computer. This information could be communicated back to the salesperson to show the expandability of the system.

Another output of the technical editing process was a continual feedback of information to other areas in Digital. For example, XCON was used to support XSEL, the most important other use of XCON in Digital. XSEL is an expert system that helps a salesperson translate a customer's business needs into specific parts and computers. When a salesperson uses XSEL, the XSEL system accesses the configuration information and rules embedded in XCON. In this way, the XCON system helps support Digital's sales force in configuring the Digital product line.

There was one category of outputs—telephone follow-up—that decreased. The TEs at the Salem manufacturing plant stated that they were not called as frequently by marketing, sales, and manufacturing for advice on systems. However, this decrease did not change the assessment that outputs substantially increased overall.

Task Performance

The most striking effect of XCON was an increase in task performance. In 1981, 23 technical editors created approximately 4,000 VAX and an estimated 15,000 other system configurations by hand. With XCON, in 1986, 17 technical editors created over 60,000 system configurations with increased quality and detail. Quality estimates varied widely, but all pointed to improved performance. Technical editors estimated that pre-XCON, they were correct about 90 percent of the time, whereas the personnel at ISTG figured correctness at about 65 percent. The difference in estimates was largely a reflection of the increased expectations of the configuration output that XCON generated versus an unaided TE. For example, pre-XCON configurations did not contain address vectors for the components; post-XCON they did. Consequently, post-XCON the basic configuration was more thorough. In any event, the estimates for XCON's percentage of correct configurations were at approximately 95 percent to 98 percent in 1986 on all orders.

In addition, there had been a change in Digital's business environment that increased the information processing need of the task even more. During most of the 1970s, Digital had a large backlog of computer orders that allowed at least some pre-production planning time. In the computer market of the early 1980s, the firm had to be more nimble because the backlog had evaporated and customers were expecting—and getting—faster delivery. Not only were the lead times shorter, but customers were waiting until later in each quarter to book orders. In 1986, the majority of Digital orders were booked and filled in the last month of each fiscal quarter. The order capture rate, as it was called, was more compact with sharp peaks. This volatility meant that more orders were driven through the system within a shorter time frame. XCON was an essential component in allowing the organization to cope with these peaks, which had been generated by the changes in the business environment.

Another major improvement in task performance was a reduction in an order's cycle time. The estimated cycle time between configuration and actual order shipment decreased dramatically—from an average of three to four months during the late 1970s to a minimum of one to two days in 1986. Cycle time for a VAX computer varied, but the minimum time elapsed through the POM (point of manufacture) part of the manufacturing process—from technical edit to shipment—was estimated to be two to three days. The average time was approximately three to four weeks, reduced from 10 to 12 weeks using FA&T.

Many factors besides XCON have contributed to this dramatic decrease in cycle time of the order. Competitive pressures forced mini-computer makers to strive to be more responsive in their manufacturing. During the early 1980s, the market for computers began to soften; this rekindled Digital's efforts to improve the speed of the order-fulfillment cycle. Nevertheless, XCON was a significant enabling mechanism in the firm's improved cycle time.

In summary, looking across the three components of information processing, inputs increased while both outputs and task performance significantly increased.

ORGANIZATIONAL IMPLICATIONS OF XCON USE

The organizational adaptations fostered by the use of XCON had four revealing features.

Technical editing system replaced

First, the organization replaced a system of technical editing, which relied heavily on experts and apprentices to manage a complicated problem on a decentralized basis, with a centrally supported system of intelligent software plus human operators. The latter system was able to cope with a higher level of complexity than had ever been managed by the company's previous configuration support.

By creating the XCON software, Digital created an asset that had a different capacity from the previous method of configuration. Before XCON, configuration capacity was determined by the number of staff available to process configurations. Total configuration capacity was limited by the number of trained individuals. Furthermore, the total number of configurers would have to be sufficient to match peak demands; this might have necessitated inventorying talent to meet high volume. In contrast, XCON's capacity was limited only by the hardware and software constraints and could, in practice, cope with high peaks in configuration throughout the organization. Therefore, Digital did not need to inventory configuration talent to serve the new market demands. This allowed the firm to pursue a customization strategy that might not have been feasible if it had to build the organizational structure to support this strategy with human configurers.

Roles and responsibilities shifted

Second, roles and responsibilities shifted when XCON technology was introduced. In general, those associated with XCON's creation seemed to gain responsibility for development and maintenance. As the use of the system became an integral part of operating the business, responsibility for supporting the software became very real. As a software manager at Digital expressed it: "XCON is the only ES I know of today where the financial lights would dim if it were unplugged. That is a tremendous responsibility" (Source: author interview).

Transferring responsibility to users and developers, however, was not universal. In the case of XCON, the technical editors' job seems to have lost clout and become more clerical. As one of the TEs explained.

> It was more fun before XCON, when you had to figure out each system. You got to keep in touch with many parts of the company—engineering, sales, and marketing—to know what was happening. We still do that now, but not so much. Also, we have to do all that correcting (Source: author interview).

The most explicit recognition of the decreased responsibility was that, pre-XCON, technical editors could prevent an order from being built until all configuration issues were solved—post-XCON they could not. Also, the TEs used to be consulted more often. They did continue to get calls and electronic mail from different Digital people wanting information on how to configure a particular order, but this happened less frequently.

More subtly, XCON use enriched and reinforced the experts' assessment and role. This specific instance lends credence to Huber's (1984) general prediction that information technology would expand the reach of an expert's purview. It helps knowledgeable individuals communicate more effectively because it fosters a common language about computer configuration. Performance of a complex task improves when a common language is developed to state succinctly the relevant criteria and facts in the task domain (Macy, et al., 1953). Similarly, ESs themselves build a common language for a complex task. They codify opinions and integrate actions associated with the task, thus building a common set of recommendations, designs, and judgments in addition to the shared descriptive vocabulary.

Formal maintenance system developed

Third, the organization needed to formally cope with the maintenance of the configuration knowledge base. For both pre and post-XCON, there was no specific training for technical editors, nor was there a prescribed "inventory" of TE talent. An individual with experience in manufacturing or order processing often served a brief apprenticeship to become a TE. Post-XCON, a staff of approximately 40 programmers maintained the XCON knowledge base. Because of the changing nature of product knowledge, over one half of the XCON knowledge base was rewritten annually (Barker and O'Connor, 1989).

This centralization of the creation and maintenance of configuration knowledge raised some potential risks. For example, there was a risk that the reviewers of the system output would not understand the task well enough to modify XCON's results when modifications were needed. In 1985, the organization still had a mix of pre-XCON and post-XCON employees who could, together, bridge the operating procedures from one era to the next and make relevant adjustments to XCON output. The long-term effects of XCON use on the available pool of talent for configuration was an issue that had yet to be resolved in 1985.

Also, there was a risk that the expert system was a short-term solution for a long-term problem. Perhaps by 1985 it was time to revamp the entire XCON approach to order processing and product strategy; but because XCON could reasonably cope with the problem, the issue was never raised. This issue is always a problem when an expert system is used to augment a complex process. Designers and managers will always be confronted with the trade-off between managing the complex process with the aid of an expert system and simplifying the process itself.

"Progressive structuring" initiated

The fourth effect on the organization seen after XCON use is what I term *progressive structuring*. In the process of capturing and codifying the data, opinions, and suggested actions necessary to make XCON a useful tool, Digital personnel "progressively structured" the problem of configuration. The progressive structure of the problem articulates specific inputs, outputs, and increases in task performance. In short, progressive structuring increases the information processing capacity of the firm as defined by Galbraith (1973, 1977). The impact of progressive structuring on configuration was felt across the organization. The configuration acted as the focal point from which more and more structuring of the task emerged. Initial success with the system led to further development of new information processing tasks, thereby progressively structuring the total task of configuration.

With the task reasonably structured, new organizational options became available. ISTG managers felt that XCON was an integral part of Digital's move from an FA&T manufacturing strategy to a point-of-manufacture (POM) strategy. The FA&T strategy required that most systems (80 percent to 90 percent) be assembled before shipment, while the POM strategy shipped the same high percentage of the systems as separate components to be fully assembled for the first time at the customer site. XCON's robust, logical description of the configuration was an integral ingredient in coordinating and controlling the assembly necessary to execute a POM strategy successfully. ISTG attributed to XCON 20 percent of the savings (15 million-plus) made by changing from FA&T to POM. Information processing capacity, in a sense, substituted for physical capacity. Formalization of this complex decision task allowed the organization to pursue a strategy with high information processing needs.

CONCLUSION

The use of XCON at Digital changed the management and execution of the knowledge-intensive task of computer configuration. The pre-XCON management challenge was to keep a sufficient supply of technical editors available to configure and reconfigure Digital computers. Because the relevant base of configuration knowledge was constantly changing as the company introduced new products, the quality of the configuration decisions was spotty. Since many derivative decisions, such as sourcing and assembly, are built upon the configuration, not surprisingly, other departments responsible for derivative decisions undertook their own configuration efforts to double check the pre-XCON configuration.

Post-XCON, the control and application of the most up-to-date configuration knowledge was more consistent and correct, and the need for derivative examination of the configuration document dwindled. In fact, the robustness of the knowledge applied by XCON played a central role in the organization's removal of the last stage of the manufacturing process (e.g., final assembly and test). Meanwhile, the management challenge shifted from keeping staff up-to-date to keeping the software up-to-date.

From an organizational perspective, the information processing capacity of the firm increased. In particular, the combination of the knowledge based system and the individual decision makers allowed for quicker dispersion of expertise and faster, higher-quality decisions. The first leverage point created by the knowledge-based system seemed to be the leverage of scarce expertise, and the second leverage point seemed to be the elimination of the second-guessing that occurred when a critical decision was not robustly executed. Thus, the organizational implications showed up locally in changed roles and responsibilities of the individuals performing the task and globally in the tasks that depended on the decisions made by the local experts.

Many organizations are dependent on individuals (such as technical editors) who must make decisions in knowledge-intensive domains. Product configuration, product engineering, and product service are three areas in which organizations train and deploy scores of people to meet the decision needs of the organization. Often, the initial decisions of these individuals drive derivative activities; therefore, it is critical to get the decision correct the first time. In domains where knowledge is rapidly changing and where no algorithmic solution is available, organizations invest in both multiple checks and rechecks of the decision and in considerable training of key employees. This type of solution is not only costly, it creates ambiguity and uncertainty around a critical business process.

Knowledge-based systems maybe a powerful tool to aid organizations in addressing this problem. The creation of the system can help articulate a common solution to a complex problem. Use of the system can help standardize execution of corporate policy and directives. Overall, a combination of system knowledge and individual knowledge may lead to a more effective and efficient system for executing critical business decisions.

However, these systems create management challenges. To ensure ongoing viability of an organization's processes, the manager will need to consciously redesign the jobs of decision makers affected by the knowledge-based system. Moreover, use of these tools has the potential to severely de-skill talented individuals and create a knowledge-worker version of mindless work. At the extreme, the organization could become over-dependent on the knowledge embedded in the system and find it difficult to update the knowledge. However, the manager can act to consciously "grow" individuals who understand the task in enough depth so that they can monitor and update the system.

More generally, organizations are creating and implementing software tools that embed greater knowledge and skill. The ongoing management challenge is to understand the organizational implications of the use of these tools and redesign business processes and individual responsibilities in light of evolving technological capabilities.

REFERENCES

Bakos, J.Y. and Treacy, M.E. "Information Technology and Corporate Strategy: A Research Perspective," *MIS Quarterly* (10:2), June 1986, pp. 107-119.

Barker, V. and O'Connor, D. "Expert Systems for Configuration at Digital, XCON and Beyond," *Communications of the ACM* (32:3), March 1989, pp. 298-320.

Benbasat, I., Goldstein, D. and Mead, M. "The Case Research Strategy in Studies of Information Systems." unpublished paper, Harvard Business School, Boston, MA, May 1986.

Bonoma, T.V. "Case Research in Marketing Oportunities: Problems and a Process, *Journal of Marketing Research* (22). May 1985, pp.199-208.

Culnan, M.J. "Mapping the intellectual Structure of MIS, 1980-1985: A Co-Citation Analysis," *MIS Quarterly* (11:3), September 1987, pp. 341—353.

Cyert, R. and March, J. *Behavioral Theory of the Fjrm*, Prentice-Hall, Inc., Englewood Cliffs, NJ, 1963.

Feigenbaum, E., McCorduck, P. and Nii, H.P. *The Rise of the Expert Company*, Times Books, New York, NY, 1988.

Fry, L.W. "Technology-Structure Research: Three Critical Issues," *Academy of Management Journal* (25:3), 1982, pp. 532-552.

Galbraith, J. *Designing Complex Organizations*, Addison-Wesley, Reading, MA, 1973.

Galbraith, J. Organization Design, Addison Wesley, Reading, MA, 1977.

Harmon, P. and King, D. *Expert Systems: Intelligence in Business*, John Wiley and Sons, Inc., New York, NY, 1985.

Harmon, P. and Rex Maus, W.M. *Expert Systems Tools and Applications*. John Wiley and Sons, Inc., New York, NY, 1988.

Hayes-Roth. F., Waterman, D.A. and Lenat, D.B. *Building Expert Systems*, Addison-Wesley, Reading, MA, 1983.

Huber, G.P. "The Nature and Design of Post-Industrial Organizations." *Management Science* (30:8). August 1984, pp. 428-451.

Kling, R. "Social Analyses of Computing: Theoretical Perspectives in Recent Research," *Computing Surveys* (12:1), March 1980, pp. 61—110.

Knuth, D.E. and Moore, R.W. "An Analysis of Alpha-Beta Pruning," *Artificial Intelligence* (6:4), 1975, pp. 293-326.

Macy, J., Jr., Christie, L.S. and Luce, R.D. "Coding Noise in a Task-Oriented Group," *Journal of Abnormal and Social Psychology* (48), 1953, pp. 401-409.

March, J.G. and Simon, J.A. *Organizations*. Wiley, New York, NY, 1958.

Markus, M.L. and Robey, D. "InformationTechnology and Organization Change: Causal Structure in Theory and Research", *Management Science* (34:5), May 1988, pp. 583-598.

Minsky, M.L. "A Framework for Representing Knowledge," in *The Psychology of Computer Vision*, P. Winston (ed.), McGraw-Hill, New York, NY, 1975.

Mumford, E. "Managerial Expert Systems and Organizational Change: Some Critical Research Issues," in *Critical Issues in Informalion Systems Research*, R.J. Boland, Jr. and R.A. Hirschheim (eds.), John Wiley & Sons, New York, NY, 1987, pp. 135-155.

Rousseau, D.M. "Issues of Level in Organizational Research: Multi-level and Cross-level Perspectives," in *Research in Organizational Behavior* (7), L.L. Cummings and Barry M. Staw (eds.), JAI Press, Inc., Greenwich, CT, 1985, pp. 1-37.

Sell, P.S. *Expert Systems—A Practical Introduction*, Wiley, New York, NY, 1985.

Shortliffe, E.H. Computer-based Medical Consultations: MYCIN, American Elsevier, New York, NY, 1976.

Simon, H.A. *Administrative Behavior*, The Free Press, New York, NY, 1945.

van Melle, W., Shortliffe, E.H. and Buchanan, B.G. "Emycin: A Domain-independent System that Aids in Constructing Knowledge-based Consultation Programs," in *Machine Intelligence, Infotech State of the Art Report 9*, No. 3,1981.

Winston, P.H. and Prendergast, K.A. (eds). *The AI Business*, The MIT Press., Cambridge, MA, 1984.

Zack, M.H. and McKenney, J. "Organizational Information Processing and Work Group Effectiveness," working paper, #89-054, Harvard Business School, Boston, MA, 1989.

ARTIFICIAL INTELLIGENCE: EXPERT SYSTEMS FOR CLINICAL DIAGNOSIS: ARE THEY WORTH THE EFFORT?[4]

Barbara Carroll

Both psychologists and AI specialists have been interested in the ability of human experts to make good, accurate diagnostic decisions. Both have attempted to model the decision-making processes of experts in a number of fields. And both have used computers in the modeling process. However, despite similar aims, psychologists and those working in mainstream AI have approached the topic of human expertise very differently.

Within psychology, researchers have pursued three major themes. First, they have examined the accuracy of experts' diagnostic decisions. Second, they have focused on the judgment process itself and have been interested in the degree to which a particular regression equation can be used to predict an expert's decisions. And, third, they have considered the possibility of replacing experts by linear regression models and have investigated the decision-making contexts in which these models lead to an increase in predictive accuracy (c.f. Dawes & Corrigan, 1974; Hoffman, Slovic & Rorer, 1968).

In contrast to the approach taken by psychological researchers, those in AI who are interested in human expertise do not attempt to assess the accuracy of experts' diagnostic decisions. Instead they assume human experts are the ideal and that, on the basis of their knowledge, they are able to achieve an outstanding level of decision-making performance (Hayes-Roth, Waterman & Lenat, 1983). Thus, AI workers view human expertise as a highly valuable and scarce resource. This belief provides them with the rationale for expending the large amounts of time, effort, and money necessary to tap as much of the complexity of experts' knowledge and skill as possible, and to model it as an expert system.

When the products of the work on human expertise conducted in psychology and AI are compared an intriguing paradox emerges. While psychologists are content to model experts' decision-making processes by simple linear equations, those in AI favor the use of intricate and highly sophisticated expert systems. This paradox of simple versus complex decision-making models needs some form of resolution. Expert systems are extremely expensive. They require at least a five-year commitment to develop, and they represent an investment of several million dollars, even before they reach the stage of being tested prior to commercial release

---

[4]Carroll, Barbara (1987). Artificial intelligence: expert systems for clinical diagnosis: are they worth the effort? *Behavioral Science, 32,* 274-292. Reprinted by permission.

(Davis, 1982, 1984, Pople, 1984). Given this, expert system construction can be justified only if they do a significantly better diagnostic job than the simple non-interactive regression equations proposed by psychologists.

The critical question of how well expert systems do when pitted against the regression equations that model experts' decision-making processes has not as yet received research attention. In fact, at the moment a fair empirical comparison is hardly possible. In 1984 few of the major expert systems were in commercial use. Many were not even at the stage of extensive testing and most still required work on developing and debugging their knowledge bases (Davis, 1984). Two years later this situation was largely unchanged, at least for the medical expert systems discussed in this paper (Jackson, 1986). Although the simple versus complex paradox cannot be resolved empirically, at least not at the present time, it can be addressed conceptually and this is the task undertaken here. The cases for each side will be outlined in some detail and then integrated in an attempted resolution of the paradox.

THE PSYCHOLOGISTS' CASE FOR SIMPLE MODELS

In their research, psychologists have adopted a strategy reflective of the statistically based paradigm in the discipline. Thus, they analyze judgment tasks into a relatively small set of codable information sources, or cues, that are considered necessary to form an adequate judgment. These cues may be either objective as, for example, in the case of laboratory test results, academic examination grades, or scores on the scales of a personality inventory. Or they may be subjective, requiring interpretation by the expert, as in the reading of an X-ray film or the estimation of the severity of disease in a patient. In either case, psychologists have investigated the accuracy of diagnostic decisions based on integration of these cues.

The accuracy of clinical judgment

Although psychologists have investigated the diagnostic accuracy of a wide variety of experts, they have been particularly interested in expert clinicians, including both psychiatric and medical specialists. Perhaps the most striking finding of the studies that have examined the accuracy of clinicians' judgments is that, for a variety of judgment tasks clinicians do not seem to be highly accurate at all. While there is no doubt that some of them are excellent diagnosticians, Goldberg (1959) found that when diagnosing brain damage on the basis of Bender Gestalt test results, experienced clinicians made the correct diagnosis only about 65% of the time. The result is robust. It holds for judgments based on the Minnesota Multiphasic Personality Inventory (MMPI) where the input information consists of scores on 11 personality scales considered to be relevant for the diagnosis of psychiatric pathology (Meehl, 1954). It was replicated by Hoffman, Slovic and Rorer (1968) who argued that the judgment dimensions provided by assessment devices such as the MMPI may not, in fact, be those which clinicians naturally employ in the judgment task, and who had radiologists themselves generate the dimensions that they considered to be important in the diagnosis of malignant ulcers. And, finally, it holds when the information on which judgments are based is not quantified but, instead, presented in the form of a verbal description (Oskamp, 1965).

Given that clinicians' judgment and decision-making ability seems to leave a lot to be desired, psychologists have sought ways of improving their performance. Perhaps clinicians simply do not have enough information to do a good job. However, it seems, at least in the case of Hoffman, Slovic and Korer's (1968) radiologists, that even when there is sufficient information available, only a fraction of it is actually used in forming judgments (see also Slovic, 1969; Ebbeson & Konecni, 1976). Phelps and Shanteau (1978) have demonstrated that experts are capable of using a larger fraction but that, in reality, relationships between sources of information render a number of these sources redundant. Thus, attention to a greater information pool is not necessary to make better judgments. In addition Connolly (1980) has pointed out that cognitive limits will establish a firm upper bound on the number of information sources that can be attended to at once. However, overriding all this is the suggestion that increasing the amount of information on which judgments are based does not, in fact, translate into more accurate judgments. It merely implies greater confidence in mediocre judgments (Oskamp, 1965).

Related to this last point is the notion that clinicians are not more accurate in their judgments because they are not aware of their fallibility and therefore are not motivated to do anything about it. This question has been investigated by Goldberg (1959)and Lichtenstein and Fischoff (1976). Their results indicate that expert clinicians are overconfident in their assessment of their ability, but not to as great an extent as those with less experience and knowledge. Hence, they tend to be more aware of their limitations than their semi- or nonprofessional counterparts. They tend to underrate their ability in simple judgment tasks and overestimate their performance as the tasks become more difficult. In this latter situation, their unjustified faith in the accuracy of their judgments extends equally to both diagnosed and misdiagnosed cases.

Based on the premise that clinicians tend to place greater stock in their judgment ability than is warranted, Einhorn and Hogarth (1978) have investigated some of the reasons why this might be so. They argue that the fault lies in the nature of judgment tasks in the real world. In the real world, judgments are formed so that decisions can be made and then acted upon. Under these conditions individuals assess the quality of their judgments by observing the consequences of the actions resulting from those judgments. The more frequently these consequences are in accord with their judgments, the better they perceived the judgments to be. Yet there are biases in this type of feedback information. Specifically, it is easy to find confirming instances of a correct decision but typically much more difficult to find disconfirming evidence. A patient who is diagnosed as healthy when, in fact, he or she has some serious pathology, is not liable to return and so prove the physician wrong. Einhorn (1978) and Einhorn and Hogarth (1978) have stressed that this bias is exaggerated by such factors as a tendency to ignore base rate and selection rate information, to overlook the possibility that feedback is contaminated by treatment effects, and to be highly susceptible to partial positive reinforcement. In addition, Connolly (1980) has pointed out that people have a tendency to rationalize what are, at the time incorrect decisions, so that in retrospect they are perceived to be correct.

Together these factors effectively inflate individuals' perceptions of their judgmental accuracy; they become overconfident. This effect may be particularly pervasive for clinicians and similar groups whose judgment tasks are probabilistic in nature. When, for example, a patient has certain symptoms and blood test results he or she may have hepatitis with probability .7. In such situations, Einhorn (1980) has stressed that it is genuinely difficult to assess the accuracy of judgments precisely because clinicians expect to be wrong a portion of the time. Therefore for them to revise their evaluation of their ability, they must somehow be able to judge whether they have, in fact, been wrong too often. And this is difficult when they are not aware of how the probability estimates are derived, and when they make particular diagnoses infrequently and without immediate feedback.

The message in the above arguments is clear: provide clinicians with more accurate feedback about the quality of their diagnostic decisions. Then, on the basis of this information they can learn, from their mistakes, to form better clinical inferences. Of particular interest here is the suggestion by Fryback and Erdman (1979) and Kleinmuntz (1982), among others, that computers can be useful in this regard. They enable assessment and follow-up information on a large number of patients to be stored, and can therefore provide clinicians with accurate statistics, such as the relative frequencies of various diseases.

Computers do, however, have their limits. Most important, they can handle only certain types of information. Therefore, while they help to provide clinicians with accurate feedback, they do not solve the problem of judgment inaccuracy. For the fact remains that accurate feedback cannot always be obtained. For example, a doctor may diagnose a patient's illness and prescribe the appropriate medication. If the patient fails to improve, the clinician's diagnosis is not necessarily wrong: it may simply be that the patient is resistant to treatment and a different combination of medications is required. Similarly, if a university admissions' committee accepts a student who later withdraws, the selection decision is not automatically invalidated. Some personal tragedy may have played a major role in the student's decision and may even have lowered that student's grades prior to quitting. In summary, the psychological research on clinical judgment suggests that experts are not overwhelmingly accurate in their diagnostic judgments. There is no evidence that providing them with more information will rectify the situation. And furthermore, because accurate feedback on the effectiveness of experts' decisions is unavailable in many contexts, they are unlikely to learn to improve their diagnostic ability in those contexts. Faced with these results, many psychologists have tried to improve the decisions experts make by identifying and then attempting to eliminate sources of judgmental error. Thus, psychologists have focused on how experts integrate the sources of information available to them when they form the judgments that underlie their diagnostic decisions, and have sought mathematical models of this integration process which outperform the experts on whom they are based.

Appropriate models of experts' decision-making processes

According to Meehl (1954), in any decision-making context experts can integrate information in two possible ways. Judgments may be nonmechanical and reliant on experience, intuition, and hunches. Alternatively, cue combination may be mechanical. In this case, based on the model proposed by Brunswik (1952) and Hammond (1955) and his associates' (Hursch, Hammond & Hursch, 1964), psychologists have assumed clinical judgment can be represented by a regression equation.

Given that experts may integrate information clinically or statistically, psychologists have questioned whether one method is superior to the other in terms of its predictive accuracy. When clinical judgment is pitted against actuarial methods the results are unambiguous: statistical prediction is at least as good as clinical prediction (Dawes & Corrigan, 1974; Dawes, 1976; Meehl, 1965). Although the value of clinical intuition is recognized when, for example, input information involves feelings that are non-codable, the demonstrated superiority of actuarial methods of codable cues has meant that intuitive factors have received little attention from most psychologists working in the area of clinical judgment (c.f. Dawes & Corrigan, 1974; Meehl, 1973).

In 1960 Hoffman went beyond the idea that a regression equation could be used to predict clinical or selection outcomes. He suggested that a simple linear regression model could be used as a "paramorphic representation" or approximation of an expert's underlying decision making processes. Then, according to the assumptions of this model, the regression Beta-weights indicate the emphasis judges place on individual cues.

A number of psychologists have argued that this additive model is too simple and that clinicians process information configurally rather than independently, as assumed by the model. However, using ANOVA techniques, researchers concerned with this issue have generally failed to find evidence of significant configural processing, even when the judgment task has been specifically designed to promote it (Hoffman, Slovic & Rorer, 1968). Thus, it is generally agreed that a wide variety of judgment tasks can be adequately represented by a simple linear model (Hammond, Hursch & Todd, 1964; Slovic, Fischoff & Lichtenstein, 1977). Anderson (1972) goes as far as equating this linear model with clinicians' actual judgment processes. However, the majority opinion supports Hoffman's (1960) notion that a linear model is simply an approximation of those underlying psychological processes (see Goldberg, 1968; Meehl, 1954; Rorer & Slovic, 1966). Goldberg (1968), in particular, has argued that clinicians may, in fact, process information in a configural manner but seem not to only because a linear model is robust enough to reproduce most of the resultant judgments with very little error.

Given that experts' decision-making processes can be represented by a simple linear model, researchers have found that, in many contexts, these paramorphic models have greater predictive accuracy than the experts themselves (see Bowman, 1963; Goldberg, 1970; Yntema & Torgerson, 1961). This led Goldberg (1970) to propose a technique known as bootstrapping wherein clinicians are replaced by the regression equation that models what they do.

Dawes (1971,1976,1977,1979), based on his work on university graduate admissions selection procedures, has been particularly interested in why bootstrapping works and in what decision-making contexts it is liable to be of greatest utility. He, and others, argue that bootstrapping works simply because a regression equation is an abstraction of the process it models and therefore captures the principles experts use without their unreliability (Bowman, 1963; Dawes, 1971). Thus, it eliminates sources of judgment error that arise when experts are tired, bored, or preoccupied with personal problems (Goldberg, 1970).

Dawes (1971) also argues that bootstrapping is most valuable in decision-making contexts where there is an error of measurement in the predictors, where criteria are "noisy," or have a degree of error associated with them, and where deviations from optimal weighting do not make much of a practical difference. In these situations as long as there is a conditionally monotone relationship between each input variable and the criterion variable, experts' linear paramorphic models have substantially greater predictive accuracy than the experts themselves (Dawes & Corrigan, 1974).

The types of decision-making contexts just described are common in psychology. They occur in areas such as psychiatric and medical diagnosis and apply to problems such as selecting applicants to graduate school (Dawes, 1971). Furthermore, Dawes and Corrigan (1974) have demonstrated that in such contexts it is not necessary to approximate clinicians by their regression models. It is sufficient to replace them by any linear model. As long as the signs of the Beta-weights are correct, and the monotonicity between predictors and criterion preserved, their magnitude may be random. Or, more useful in a population that is changing over time, unit weights can be used without loss of accuracy (Dawes & Corrigan, 1974; Einhorn & Hogarth, 1975).

These types of bootstrapping models using non-optimal (in the least squares sense) methods of cue combination are not only valid for predicting numerical criteria. They are also valid, in contexts such as those just described, when there is no measurable outcome variable and the judgment task is one of establishing preferences (Dawes, 1977).

The Implications of Clinical Judgment Research

The results of the research on clinical judgment suggest that experts are not extremely accurate in their diagnostic decisions and that in many of the decision-making contexts studied by psychologists bootstrapping, using extremely simple linear models, can provide diagnoses that are both more reliable and more accurate. The major implication of these findings is that, at least in "noisy" decision-making contexts, clinicians can and should be replaced by these linear models so that diagnosis is strictly a mechanical matter (Dawes, 1976; Meehl, 1954). Given this, the value of computers in the diagnostic domain is obvious. They provide quick and reliable diagnoses. But, more important, when Beta rather than unit weights are used, sophisticated computer systems can derive them on the basis of large data bases of patient information. This procedure does not, of course, eliminate the fallibility of that subset of the data base of relying on clinicians' judgments (e.g., X-ray diagnoses). However, it does have two advantages. First, the data base can be easily updated to include case history and diagnostic information on new patients as they are treated. Therefore, the validity of the regression coefficients can he checked from time to time and adjusted to reflect changes when necessary (Kleinmuntz, 1982). Second, computers can be programmed to determine the relative frequency of various diseases. Thus, they can calculate the probability of each of a patient's potential diagnoses. Furthermore, they can perform this task accurately, thereby eliminating the biases to which clinicians are subject when they attempt the same calculations (see Lichtenstein & Fischoff, 1976; Fryback & Erdman, 1979; Einhorn, 1980).

From a psychological perspective, then, simple linear regression models and computer technology seem to hold the key to better diagnostic decisions. There is one problem, however. Psychological researchers and, in fact, people in general are simply not prepared to have clinicians' diagnostic role replaced by a machine (Kleinmuntz, 1982). Clinical intuition and experience seem to count for something. Consequently, psychologists have spent some time discussing and trying to redefine the clinicians' role.

Fryback and Erdman (1979) credit clinicians with the central role. They make the diagnostic decisions and computers simply provide realistic, unbiased feedback on those decisions. Kleinmuntz (1982) also sees clinicians in the primary role with computers, as described so far, serving strictly as diagnostic aids that calculate Beta-weights and probabilities and are essentially occupied with number crunching.

For Dawes (1976) the emphasis on experts' decision-making abilities is, in many situations, little more than cognitive conceit, coupled with our unwillingness to accept the fact that there are cognitive limits to our decision-making talents. In "noisy' decision-making contexts, such as the selection of graduate students, he argues that computerized models should make the decisions, with admissions' committees over riding these decisions only for social reasons such as ensuring adequate minority group representation.

Meehl (1954, 1973) is also comfortable with allowing the computer to diagnose when the data are objective and their combination is mechanical. He argues that in this realm diagnostic decisions are routine, clinical intuition does not have a role to play, and clinicians can be more effectively employed in those aspects of diagnosis that a computer cannot do. Thus, clinicians can observe and interview patients, be supportive and empathic, exercise their intuition and test out hunches, and make strategic decisions about the sequence of diagnostic tests and treatment steps.

Finally, several psychologists stress the need for a more integrated relationship between clinicians and computers. Einhorn(1972), for example, points out that computers can use objective, quantified input data, such as MMPI scores or blood test results. Alternatively, they can make use of qualitative information, provided a clinician subjectively interprets and codes that data to ensure monotonicity between predictors and criterion. When this type of clinical information is included as input to the computer, the resultant diagnosis can be said to capture, at least minimally, the clinician's knowledge and experience (see, also, Dawes, 1977). Hence, clinicians and computers become more interdependent.

Yntema and Torgerson (1961) carry this interdependence one step further when they claim "man and computers could cooperate more efficiently if a man could tell the computers how he wanted a decision made, and then let the machine make the decision for him" (p. 20). This idea is a critical one especially if, as Johnson, Hassebrock, Duran, and Moller (1982) have suggested, expert clinicians differ from novices in the reasoning strategies they employ to make their diagnostic decisions. This type of interdependence may be achieved, as Dawes (1979) has suggested, by allowing experts to establish the coefficients of the computerized regression model on the basis of intuition. Alternatively, the simple linear model may be abandoned as dehumanizing in favor of an approach which focuses more directly on experts' decision-making processes per se. Whether or not this is an example of cognitive conceit, it is precisely the approach taken by Kleinmuntz (1968,1975,1982) when he had both clinical psychologists and neurologists explain each step of their respective decision making processes. Moreover, it is this emphasis on how decisions are reached, together with the length of time involved in eliciting and editing 'talk aloud' protocols, that prompted Leal and Pearl (1977) to devise an interactive computer program capable of capturing the ways in which decision makers structure their knowledge in order to make their professional decisions. Finally, and most important, it is this kind of perspective that spawned expert systems.

EXPERT SYSTEMS: THE CASE FOR COMPLEX MODELS

Expert systems are sophisticated and highly specialized computer programmes that try to capture and reproduce experts' decision-making processes (Naylor, 1983). Their focus is on the knowledge experts possess and the ways in which they use it to solve problems within their specialties.

Thus, expert systems are, in technical terms, knowledge based. Furthermore, their power lies in this knowledge in the sense that the more accurately they reflect experts' knowledge, the better they are considered to be (Davis, 1984).

The way in which this knowledge is explicated and then programmed is quite specific. First of all, expert systems do not represent all types of knowledge and cannot model all decision-making tasks, or all experts. They do not deal with the type of firm, fixed, and formalized knowledge that can be handled within the scope of algorithmic programmes (Buchanan et al., 1983). Instead, they take a heuristic approach, based on the assumption that real-world decision problems are solved only semi-logically. Experts do not reason every decision from first principles; they take short cuts. Often they lack sufficient information to allow them to make purely logical decisions. However, over and above this, experts in a number of areas rely heavily on experience, professional judgment, and hunches in making decisions. It is just this type of subjective and rather elusive knowledge that expert systems attempt to capture (Buchanan et al, 1983; Duda & Gaschnig, 1981).

While the type of knowledge on which experts base their performance is one prerequisite for a knowledge-based expert system, there are others. The decision problem or task that is to be programmed as an expert system must be one that requires specialized knowledge or expertise. Hence, those who are recognized as experts in the area must outperform novices. Furthermore, within the set of experts it must be possible to identify at least one individual who is acknowledged to be particularly proficient in his or her decision-making capacity. In addition, the task domain must be such that experts can explain both the knowledge they require and the methods they use to apply it to particular decision problems in that domain. This will be the case, for instance, for tasks that are routinely taught to students or apprentices.

Other prerequisites for knowledge-based systems stem from consideration of machine limitations and the time and effort involved in constructing and implementing such systems. As yet expert systems can only deal with very narrow domains of expertise so that appropriate tasks are ones that have a specific, well-bounded domain of application. Furthermore, given the human and financial costs of expert systems mentioned earlier, the decision-making task to be modeled must be one that is commercially viable (Brachman et al, 1983; Davis, 1984; Duda & Gaschnig, 1981).

Although the list of prerequisites seems prohibitive, a fairly wide variety of expert systems has been developed so far. For instance, PROSPECTOR is a geological expert system that focuses on mineral exploration problems. It estimates the chances of finding certain minerals in a particular location and gives a rough guide to the quantity of each (Duda et al, 1978; see also Naylor, 1983). And DENDRAL infers chemical molecular structures on the basis of spectrographic information (Buchanan & Feigenbaum, 1978). However, perhaps the most popular area of expert system development is that of medical diagnosis. In addition to CADUCEUS (also known as

INTERNIST), medical expert systems include MYCIN, which diagnoses and suggests treatment for infectious diseases, and PUFF, which diagnoses pulmonary diseases (Shortliffe, 1976; Kunz et al, 1978 respectively; see also Johnson & Keravnou, 1985).

Expert system construction

The simplest way to understand expert systems, as complex models of experts' decision-making processes, is to observe how they are built. There are two aspects of this construction. The first involves the elicitation of an expert's specialized knowledge and decision heuristics. And the second concerns the computer representation and organization of that expertise.

The knowledge base.

The most popular way of representing knowledge in an expert system has been to use production, or situation-action rules consisting of IF THEN statements (Clancey, 1983; Duda & Gaschnig, 1981). There are alternatives. For example, Aikins (1983) has constructed CENTAUR, with a domain of pulmonary physiology, as an expert system whose knowledge base incorporates prototype representations (see also Jackson, 1986). However, alternatives such as this are very complicated technically and, on these grounds, expert system designers have generally been content to opt for a rule-based approach which assumes experts' rules of thumb are the most important component of their expertise.

The construction of an expert system normally requires an expert in the domain of interest and a knowledge engineer, or specialized programmer, to act as an intermediary between expert and computer. All of the systems built so far have relied on a single expert and, with one exception, there has been no discussion of how the expert involved was selected (Davis, 1984). The exception is the internist on whom CADUCEUS was modeled. He was concerned about capturing the type of generalized expertise traditionally used by internists and simply volunteered his services (Pople, 1184). While the expert's role in the construction team as well-defined, that of the knowledge engineer is more flexible. There are expert systems, such as TEIRESIAS, which focus on the domain of knowledge acquisition and lessen the dependence on knowledge engineers by allowing expertise to be transferred interactively from human expert to machine (Davis & Lenat, 1982; Politakis & Weiss, 1984). However, these presuppose that experts know something about the program's internal representational structures. And it has been suggested that usually they do not (Duda & Gaschnig, 1981). Thus, the expert-engineer partnership is, in practice, fairly well-established.

Within this partnership the expert identified his or her knowledge and the programmer transforms it into a machine-usable form. The stages of this process have been outlined by Hayes-Roth et al. (1983), Buchanan et al. (1983), and, more technically, by van Melle (1981). It sounds relatively straightforward. The boundaries of the problem domain are identified, the concepts relevant to that domain are elicited, the rules relating subsets of these concepts are specified and the hierarchical organization of the rules clarified. The rules are then formalized as IF ... THEN statements and organized hierarchically by a control structure. The resultant program as tested and, with the expert's help, the rules validated. The most reasonable strategy is to start small and construct a skeleton expert system. When this is working satisfactorily more knowledge (rules) can be added to flesh it out and, in the process, the control structure will usually be modified to reflect new and changed organizational links between rules.

The process is not as easy as it appears, however. The type of knowledge that expert systems try to capture and reproduce is generally not well structured, particularly at the level of detail required for the construction of such a system. Extracting the knowledge may not be too difficult. Typically arranging it in a systematic fashion proves more of a challenge (Buchanan et al, 1983). Together, these two tasks represent a considerable cognitive load and investment of time for the expert involved. For instance, Pople's (1984) internist contributed about three hours a week for six months to help build the skeleton of CADUCEUS.

The above prescription for expert system construction does more than oversimplify the mechanics of knowledge acquisition. In addition, it fails to do justice to the complexity of the program that models the expert's knowledge. To rectify this a more detailed account of the machine representation of this knowledge is required. The emphasis here will be more conceptual than technical. More complete general descriptions are available in van Melle (1981), Davis & Lenat (1982), or Clancey (1983). For a detailed description of the knowledge representation in MYCIN see Shortliffe (1976).

While an expert system may consist of up to seven components, only two of these are common to all existing systems (for descriptions of the remaining five specialty components see Hayes-Roth et al, 1983). All contain a knowledge base and a control structure which is alternately referred to as an inference engine or an interpreter. The knowledge base is usually composed entirely of rules: expert systems typically do not store raw data on individual cases. In many of the expert systems constructed so far these rules are exclusively production rules. MYCIN is the largest of these systems, with a total of about 450 rules (Shortliffe, 1976; van Melle, 1981). Each rule is a chunk of knowledge that is self-contained but which, by itself, cannot be used to form a diagnosis. Diagnoses are made on the basis of sets or chains of rules. Each rule is of the form IF antecedents A, B and C are satisfied THEN the conclusion D can be drawn. But it is more complicated than this even: conclusion D can rarely be drawn with certainty. Instead it holds with probability p (Davis, 1984).

As an example, consider the following MYCIN rule for identifying the organism responsible for a particular infectious disease:

If 1) the gram stain of the organism is gram negative, and

   2) the morphology is rod, and

3) the aerobicity of the organism is anaerobic

Then there is suggestive evidence (.7) that the identity of the organism is Bacteroides (Davis, 1984, p. 34)

Although the content may not mean much outside the field of bacteriology, there are several points that deserve mention. First, the probability (or, in technical terms, the certainty factor) of .7 is estimated by the expert clinician involved in the expert system construction. Moreover, the estimate is not mathematically but, rather, experientially determined. Second, while expert systems allow the rules to be expressed, as above, in English, this is not the language the computer uses. It works with highly esoteric languages such as LISP or INTER. LISP (Naylor, 1983; van Melle, 1981).

The third and final point deals with the ways in which the three antecedent conditions are fulfilled, and leads nicely into a discussion of the expert system's control structure. There are two means by which the premises of any production rules may be satisfied. The first, lower order method is simply to ask the user, in this case typically a physician, for the information directly. Thus, in a consultation interview MYCIN may ask, for instance: Is the organism a rod or coccus? The physician then types in the answer, say rod. Or he or she may type in "Unknown" in which case the rule above fails unless the conclusion can be reached with a lower probability on the basis of conditions (1) and (3) alone.

The second method of satisfying antecedent conditions is of a higher order. It involves employing the system's own knowledge base. Thus, in order to satisfy condition (1) the programmer effectively asks: What is the gram stain of the organism? However, instead of seeking the answer from the physician, as user, all the rules relating to the gram stain are called up and each is interpreted. In formal terms, the pursuit of the goal of diagnosing the organism is temporarily postponed while the subgoal of determining the gram stain is pursued (Davis, 1984; van Melle, 1981).

The two methods of satisfying the antecedent conditions of rules (rule interpretation) are employed together in an expert system. The system does what it can on the basis of its rule-based knowledge and, when it gets stuck, it asks the user to provide the necessary information. Obviously some overall organization is required. For example, there must be a way of knowing which rules are related to the gramstain property of an organism so that they can be called up without simply churning through the entire set of rules. And there must be a way of knowing when there are no pertinent rules and the user must provide the information. Finally, there must be a way of keeping track of where one is in the diagnostic process, and how the various strands are related to each other. These organizational tasks are the province of the second major component common to all expert systems: the control structure, rule interpreter, or inference engine (Davis, 1984).

The control structure

The control structure consists of metarules (van Melle, 1981; Clancey, 1983). As an illustration, consider the following metarule from MYCIN:

If 1) the infection is a pelvic abscess, and
   2) there are rules which mention in their premise enterobacteriaceae, and
   3) there are rules which mention in their premise gramposrods,
Then there is suggestive evidence (.4) that the former should be done before
   the latter (Clancey, p. 238).

The function of the control structure, then, is to manipulate the rules that comprise the knowledge base. The implication is that control structure and knowledge base are separate components. While such independence is not essential, it is, from a programming perspective, by far the easiest approach (Davis, 1984). In fact, it is just this distinction between knowledge base and control structure that differentiates expert systems from other types of computing programs (Duda & Gaschnig, 1981; Hapgood, 1985).

All expert system control structures manipulate knowledge-base rules according to one of two strategies. Either they employ what is known as forward-chaining or, alternatively, they use backward-chaining. Of the two, backward-chaining, or consequent reasoning, is by far the most popular [for descriptions of forward-chaining procedures see Duda & Gaschnig, 1981; van Melle, 1981). It is the strategy employed by MYCIN and, hence, by most of its derivatives (e.g., PUFF).

Backward-chaining is goal-directed. It assumes that diagnostic problems can be represented by a tree diagram (a goal tree); with a diagnosis (goal) at the apex, and branching out into increasingly specific configurations of signs and symptoms necessary for the diagnosis. The procedure begins with a diagnosis. This is the physician's best guess (c.f., condition one of the metarule above). It is entered into the computer and the expert system then tries to confirm it. To do so the control structure calls up all rules relating directly to the diagnosis of, say, pelvic abscesses. These will be fairly general rules. Next, the control structure tries to satisfy each of these rules. When it runs across a rule that cannot be satisfied, that rule is considered to be a subgoal and the control structure calls up all the more specific rules that must be fulfilled in order to achieve that subgoal, and so on. Obviously backward-chaining is a "depth-first" technique. It is methodical and in that sense it is an efficient way of arriving at a diagnosis. However, it is costly an terms of the amount of information it requires from the user. If the same knowledge-base rule occurs in two different contexts and if that rule needs a piece of information, then the user will have to provide that piece of information twice (Davis & Lenat, 1982; Duda & Gaschnig, 1981; van Melle, 1981).

To illustrate, consider an example from MYCIN's repertoire. A particular infectious disease may be caused by one of four organisms. MYCIN considers each possibility in turn. In trying to identify organism 1 it will, among other things, ask for the aerobicity of the organism. The physician will type it in. If, in the end, there is insufficient evidence to conclude that the diagnosis is attributable to organism 1, then organism 2 will be considered. Again the aerobicity will be requested and again it must be supplied.

The above discussion of expert systems, how they are constructed and how they work, has been a fairly general one. Nevertheless, even at this level it is apparent that expert systems are highly sophisticated (and becoming even more so) and represent complex models of experts' decision-making processes in a number of rather narrowly defined specialty areas. Furthermore, the way in which this specialty knowledge is represented in the computer is not primarily dictated by the nature of the expertise. Instead, it seems to be largely a function of constraints imposed by existing computer technology and programming techniques. It is still the case that in most expert systems knowledge is represented by production rules, with a separation of the knowledge base and control structure. This is not necessarily the most appropriate or the most flexible knowledge representation. It is simply the one that is most tractable from a programming perspective.

The evaluation of expert systems

The preceding discussion provides some understanding of the type of decision-making model captured in an expert system. Now the question is: How good are expert systems? There are at least two ways of interpreting this question. A good expert system may be one in which there is a close match between the system and the expert on whom it is modeled. Alternatively, a good expert system may be one that out-performs those professionals who would make use of such a system.

Experts and expert system: How close is the match?

Within the field of AI, a number of researchers have recognized that the degree of concordance between the expert and the model of the expert may be modest. In many of the existing expert systems the knowledge base contains only production rules and Aiken (1983) and Davis (1982), among others, claim that this type of knowledge representation is too limited for many diagnostic problems. When this is the case, an expert system relying on production rules will not model its expert closely and, given that the human expert is assumed to be the ideal, it will therefore not be judged to be as good. Consistent with this there is a recent trend in AI toward expert systems that combine production rules with more general rule-based knowledge representations (see, e.g., Hayes-Roth et al., 1983). However, even with these modifications, the match between experts and expert systems may not be good. Although experts do use rules to solve their diagnostic problems, Dreyfus (1972) has suggested that they do not use only rules. Thus, expert systems, as they exist now, will inevitably miss some—perhaps important—aspects of clinicians' decision-making processes. The nature of these limitations is acknowledged by some expert system proponents (see, e.g., Winston & Prendergast, 1984). But there seems to be no discussion of the seriousness of those limitations. There is only an underlying optimism that future technological advances will make it possible to approximate the activities of experts more closely.

Assuming, for the moment, that clinicians' diagnostic decisions are rule-based, the question of how adequately these rules can, in fact, be captured in an expert systems arises because of the nature of the decision problems faced by clinicians. In very many instances these tasks are ill-structured. Clinicians are often required to make decisions on the basis of incomplete information. And their job is further complicated by the fact that the set of information they do have is not standard; data are collected in a different order for different patients so that, given limited time, the set of missing data will vary across patients.

If the set of information clinicians use to form diagnoses varies from patient to patient, even when those patients actually have the same disease, then their resultant decision rules would be expected to be extremely complex. Hapgood (1985) has suggested that they fall into two categories. The first contains more general rules that work for routine cases. And the second contains those rules which govern the exceptions and qualifications to the normal rules of the first type. It is these rules that it seems most difficult to elicit. And it is precisely these rules that are critically important, for they provide clinicians with diagnostic flexibility.

The difficulty of elucidating this second category of rules is acknowledged by those who build expert systems. Even though one of the prerequisites for an expert system is that the expert be able to explain his or her specialized knowledge and experience, a large proportion of the knowledge engineer's task is still devoted to helping the expert structure that expertise into an interlocking network of rules (Buchanan et al., 1983; Duda & Gashnig, 1981). Part of the problem seems to be that clinicians use rules, particularly those in the second category, without being fully aware of what those rules are. The assumption that knowledge engineers operate under is that it is possible, through discussion, to make clinicians conscious of these rules. They can then be captured in an expert system. Some psychologists would challenge this assumption. For instance, Nisbet and Wilson (1977) would argue that clinicians do not necessarily become aware of the rules they use. Instead, they may simply invent rules which seem plausible within the decision-making context. These "invented" rules may, in fact, work. However, at the time of expert system construction their validity has not been established by prior experience as is the case for the other "noninvented" rules. Instead, it must be assessed in terms of future diagnostic applications.

Dreyfus (1972) has stressed the importance of the decision-making context. He argues that regardless of whether the rules elicited from clinicians are actual or invented, they are embedded in a certain context. In the interaction between expert and knowledge engineer, the decision rules are removed from this context and reinserted into a context which is dictated by the knowledge representation of the expert system. Dreyfus warns that the two contexts are not synonymous and, to the extent that they differ, distortions would be expected to occur in the translation of rules from expert to machine.

In summary, then, it appears that expert systems may be limited in their ability to capture experts decision-making processes. At present most of them are capable of capturing only rules, and these comprise only a portion of clinicians activities. Furthermore, they may have to be content with accepting the fact that the rules they do capture may well be distortions of those clinicians actually use. Thus, expert systems are generally not superb models of human expertise. This does not, however, automatically imply that they are inaccurate in their diagnostic decisions.

The accuracy of expert system diagnosis

Published empirical evidence on the level of performance attained by expert systems is relatively hard to come by. Much more common are statements, presumably based on experience, attesting to the systems capabilities. Thus, Brachman et al. (1983) claim that no existing expert system comes close to the ideal, exceptionally high level of performance supposedly achieved by human experts. However, it seems that the medical expert systems do a reasonably good diagnostic job within their domains. Members of the medical profession consider MYCIN's diagnostic and treatment judgments to be as good as their own (Davis, 1984; Naylor, 1983). And PUFF is able to produce diagnoses that are accepted by clinicians between 90% and 95% of the time although it is unclear whether the clinicians would actually have made the identical diagnosis themselves (Davis, 1984; van Melle, 1981). Finally, Pople (L984) claims that CADUCEUS does a fairly good diagnostic job in internal medicine.

This somewhat informal evaluation of medical expert systems indicates that, at least in some medical specialties, expert systems can approach but not exceed the diagnostic ability of clinicians. However, Yu et al.'s (1979) results would dispute this. In their study independent evaluators compared MYCIN's performance in the treatment of meningitis to that of clinicians with varying degrees of expertise. The results favoured MYCIN: its prescriptions were more often rated as acceptable by the evaluators than were those of the clinicians. They were even rated as slightly better than the prescriptions of the best clinician. However, lest the picture look too rosy, it should be emphasized that only 65% of MYCIN's diagnoses were acceptable (versus an average of 55.5% for the clinicians).

Overall, the discussion of expert systems presented here demonstrates that they are extremely complex models of experts decision-making processes but that the degree of congruence between expert and model is often limited. And, furthermore, while MYCIN may outperform clinicians, it is more often the case that the accuracy of expert systems is bounded by the performance levels attained by the experts on whom they are modelled.

A RESOLUTION OF THE SIMPLE VS. COMPLEX PARADOX

The paradox of simple versus complex models of experts' decision-making processes arose as a result of applying two different research traditions to the same underlying problem. Psychologists base their linear models on sources of information that are codable. Hence, they capture experts' experience only minimally, in the coding of subjective input variables, and they exclude the role of clinical intuition. Those in AI, on the other hand, credit experience and intuition with a central role and they go to considerable lengths to capture these qualities in the form of decision heuristics. The question is: Are expert systems worth all this effort? Do they do a better job of making expert decisions than the models proposed by psychologists?

Yu et al.'s (1979) results suggest that while MYCIN's performance is not outstanding, it is comparable with the level of judgment accuracy achieved by clinicians in psychological research. However, while expert systems can perform as well as human experts, they typically do so only in an ideal research environment where they are required to make decisions on the basis of refined "textbook" cases that are well within their problem domains. In real world settings where they must deal with, for example, actual patients who provide case histories in which symptoms are misrepresented and relevant information forgotten, expert systems attain only very modest accuracy levels (c.f. Davis, 1984; Meehl, 1954; Pople, 1984). Similarly, at the boundary of their specified problem domains, the quality of expert systems' diagnostic decisions declines much faster and to a much lower level than it does for human experts (Davis, 1984). This is to be expected. Whereas experts have some background knowledge outside their specialty, expert systems do not.

The conclusion to be drawn from this is that when any decision problem is attempted under realistic conditions containing noise or error, expert systems will fare significantly worse than experts. Within a medical context, for instance, when patients misrepresent their symptoms, clinicians provide the expert system with faulty information. And when decision problems test the limits of an expert system's problem domain, some of the rules needed in the diagnostic process will simply be absent from the system's knowledge-base and the system will therefore be unable to request the information required to make an adequate diagnosis. The result of these two sources of error will be that the expert system can confirm a number of diagnoses, each with low probability. This leaves clinicians in a quandary over the most appropriate course of treatment and, in choosing between alternatives, error is introduced into the criterion.

If expert systems can do as well as experts under ideal conditions, but are less accurate in those real-world settings that introduce error into the diagnostic process, then the question is: How does the performance of these same expert systems compare with that of the linear decision models proposed by psychologists? And the answer seems to depend upon the nature of the decision problem.

Psychologists such as Dawes (1971) and Goldberg (1970) claim that the predictive accuracy of linear models is greater than or equal to that of expert judgment because such models eliminate important sources of error in the decision-making process. If this claim is valid, experts can be expected to be about as accurate as their paramorphic models when the decision problem is inherently noise-free.

In a medical context, for instance, it is often the case that there is very nearly a one-to-one relationship between diagnosis and treatment outcome. Therefore, it follows that when patients present their symptoms accurately, when physicians have important test results available, and when the diagnostic problem is well within an expert system's domain, expert systems can be as accurate as their experts who, in turn, can be as accurate as their linear models. Thus, expert systems can do as well as the linear models favored by psychologists for noise-free decision problems under ideal conditions. In real-world settings that are noisy, however, linear models have the edge over expert systems, even when the decision problem is error-free in nature.

The situation is considerably different in decision-making contexts that are inherently noisy. In selecting graduate students, for example, there is only a fuzzy relationship between present academic qualifications and future academic success (Dawes, 1971, 1976). Similarly, when there as no measurable criterion and the decision problem is to establish preferences, the analogous relationship is complex and weak (Dawes, 1979). In cases such as these, experts are not and cannot be expected to be very accurate. However, it is in these contexts that bootstrapping works and even linear models with unit weights outperform experts (Dawes, 1977, 1979; Dawes & Corrigan, 1974). Given that expert systems typically are no more accurate than experts, the conclusion that, for noisy decision problems, the performance of expert system's is inferior to that of very simple linear models is justified.

If the conceptual conclusions drawn here are substantiated empirically, expert systems are likely to perform as well as linear decision models only for problems and in contexts that are noise-free. This assertion, if correct, seriously undermines the rationale for expert system construction. It does not, however, automatically follow that expert systems should be abandoned in favor of linear models. If there is some way of modifying expert systems to improve their accuracy, they may still be competitive with psychology's simple alternative. From the reviews of the literature in psychology and AI just presented there are a number of possibilities for such improvement.

As already mentioned, expert systems perform very badly when the limits of their knowledge bases are tested. Thus, their accuracy may be improved by adding production rules to expand the scope of their knowledge base. This is the approach taken by knowledge engineers in AI. Rules are modular so their addition should be a simple matter. In practice it is not. There is no problem with the knowledge base. It is for the control structure that the difficulty arises. The major function of the control structure is to determine the order in which the branches of the decision tree are to be searched and to guide the decision-making process within each of these branches. When new rules are added both the order in which the branches are to be searched and the decision-making strategy within one or more branches are changed. Thus, a great number of the control structure links between production rules must be changed. This process is eased to a degree by systems such as TIERIASIS. Nevertheless, these systems offer somewhat limited explanations of control structure functioning, and altering the control structure of an expert system is still an exceedingly complicated process (Buchanan, 1983; Davis, 1984).

Expanding the knowledge base, however, is not the only possible strategy for improving the decision-making ability of expert systems. At least two others are suggested by the psychological literature. First, the level of performance of an expert system is bounded by the talents of the expert on whom it is modeled. If that expert clinician misapplies rules or uses rules that are wrong, then the expert system will do likewise. While those in AI assume all experts are highly accurate, psychologists caution that only some experts are actually excellent diagnosticians (see, e.g., Goldberg, 1959). Obviously, then, it is crucial to develop means of identifying one of these outstanding clinicians and having him or her serve as the source of the expert system knowledge base (see Kleinmuntz, 1968, for recognition of this point).

The suggestion is promising and perhaps suffers from only one major drawback. As already mentioned, the construction of an expert system requires a considerable commitment on the part of the expert clinician (Pople, 1984). Good diagnosticians are usually also extremely busy consultants and may well be unwilling to invest the time and effort required. To the extent that this is so, knowledge engineers will have to sacrifice and model their expert systems on those with less diagnostic skills.

The second way in which psychologists can contribute to the improvement of expert systems has to do with the certainty factor associated with each production rule in the knowledge base. These are judgments of the plausibility of a particular rule (Hayes-Roth et al, 1983). They are not, strictly speaking, probabilities but they are linear transformations of them (Davis & Lenat, 1982). Furthermore, they are provided by the specialist or clinician on whom the expert system is based and reflect his or her experience. Therefore, the psychological results which suggest that clinicians are not well calibrated, or not very good at estimating probabilities, are pertinent. In fact, these findings may have particular relevance because it seems likely that knowledge engineers would not automatically be alerted to this tendency: clinicians generally announce their probability judgments with a larger dose of confidence that is warranted (Fryback & Erdman, 1979; Lichtenstein & Fischoff, 1976).

The fact that medical specialists are not well calibrated may not be too serious for expert systems. It may be more crucial for the patients awaiting diagnosis if, as Fryback and Erdman (1979) have suggested, this lack of calibration is manifested as a tendency to play it safe and overestimate the probability of disease. In order to offset this tendency psychologists have argued for a computing system that stores patient information and calculates empirically based probabilities. If there is some way of transforming these probabilities into production rule certainty factors, then expert systems should be less reflective of experts' biases and, on these grounds, they may become more accurate decision makers.

Knowledge engineers are sensitive to this idea. From their perspective they, too, understand the utility of storing patient data so that the expert system can learn from examples and so can modify its own rules, refine its certainty factors, and so on (Duda & Gaschnig, 1981). The problem they face is that it is simply not feasible, as yet, to build an expert system that incorporates such a data base. First it is, in itself, an extremely challenging task. And second, the vast majority of expert systems are neither complete nor in commercial use. Consequently, all available time and effort is channeled into improving expert systems in their existing form, leaving very little of either commodity for the expansion of the concept of an expert system (Davis, 1982; 1984).

The foregoing arguments suggest that while there are ways of improving the performance of expert systems in principle, in practice these strategies are either technologically infeasible or place unrealistic demands on busy professionals. Therefore, at least within the forseeable future, expert systems are unlikely to match the performance of simple linear models for some decision problems and under most conditions. Is there, then, any case to be made for the construction of expert systems?

Although linear models are often superior to expert systems, there are some specialized contexts in which expert system can hold their own. For example, in those medical subspecialties where decisions are typically made on the basis of objective (laboratory tests, unambiguous clinical signs) rather than subjective patient reports, expert systems can perform as well as highly trained specialists. In the absence of such specialists, however, expert systems are likely to have the advantage over the attending physician or family practitioner. Hence, they may be useful in smaller medical institutions which do not have consultants in the more esoteric subspecialties at staff.

Of course, even in these situations, linear models will probably do as well as expert systems. However, the latter may be preferred over the former because, being based on particular individuals' experience, the diagnostic decisions seem more "human' Such a preference, if it actually exists, is understandable. It is also potentially dangerous. To the extent that an expert systems decisions are "humanized" the distance between the computer model and physician user is minimized. Thus, when physicians rely on expert system diagnosis there is the concern that they will effectively learn to think like the expert system. In this case, they may not be overly sensitive to evidence that questions the provided diagnosis and, if so, they are unlikely to override the expert system's diagnosis treatment recommendations. And, in that case, diagnostic errors will most probably be machine errors.

When regression equation diagnosis is preferred over the expert system option, intuition suggests that it will be easier to override suspect diagnoses. Clinicians will often possess, or interpret, details of a patient's history that are not available to the computer but which render the computer's diagnosis highly suspect (see, also, Dawes & Corrigan, 1974; Kleinmuntz, 1982). In addition, a patient's overall history and pattern symptoms may be strongly reminiscent of a past case. When this happens, Gilovich (1981) has suggested that clinicians will be inclined to base their diagnosis on whatever pathology was diagnosed in that past case. If the computer diagnosis is at odds with this, then it may be overridden. To the extent that clinicians actually do override the mechanical diagnoses of a regression equation, the use of linear models will lead to an increase in diagnostic errors that are errors in human judgment. Perhaps in the end, the choice between complex expert systems and simple linear models, in contexts where they do equally well, is really a choice between living with the consequences of machine versus human error. And this choice is a matter of both taste and ethical and moral debate.

The preceding discussion of the simple versus complex paradox suggests a resolution in favor of psychologists' simple linear models. They can outperform expert systems in all but nearly perfect decision-making contexts, and there seems little hope that technological advances in the near future will alter this ranking. Furthermore, even in those situations where expert systems and linear equations are closely matched, it is not at all certain that the machine errors of expert systems will be more acceptable than the human errors that are likely to accompany linear equations.

There is, however, one argument that could be used to challenge this resolution. When experts make decisions their task is essentially one of pattern recognition. For example, a patient presents a certain pattern of symptoms and a physician must decide whether or not that patient belongs to the class of people with stomach cancer. The problem of pattern recognition has received a great deal of attention in AI over the past 20 years or so and there is a substantial body of literature in this area which deals with pattern recognition algorithms (perceptrons) that are based on linear regression equations (see, e.g., Nilsson, 1965; Sebestyen, 1962; Watanabe, 1985). In these algorithms Beta-weights are assigned to local features of patterns and can be modified in light of cases of misclassification. Thus, by considering dimensions of the decision-making problem to be local features and misclassification to be synonymous with a wrong decision, perceptions are very close to the kinds of decision-making algorithms proposed by psychologists such as Dawes (1979).

Given this similarity, it can be argued that Minsky and Papert's (1969) critique of perceptrons also applies to psychologists' simple decision-making models. In their book Minsky and Papert identify some limitations of perceptron algorithms. A detailed analysis of these limitations is beyond the scope of this paper. However, in brief, they argue that perceptrons cannot recognize patterns when classification is based on global properties such as connectedness or openness. In these cases perceptrons fail because there is no finite set of local properties such that a linear combination of those properties defines membership in the class of, for example, objects that are connected. And, in these cases, pattern recognition, at least in part, depends on configural processing.

The types of expert decisions studied by psychologists are typically of this "global" type. For example, consider the class of people with stomach ulcers or the class of students who will be successful in graduate school. In both these cases the classification criterion is a global one. Hence, it could be argued that the linear models used by psychologists to approximate experts' decision-making processes in such situations are not valid and that, by default, the construction of expert systems is justified.

There are at least two arguments against this conclusion. First, Minsky and Papert's (1969) critique has not stopped work on perceptrons in AI. Although some, for example, Nilsson (1971), seem to have taken the criticism seriously, others, such as Watanabe (1985), have been content to make minor modifications so that perceptron algorithms are "good enough" and perceptrons are still popular pattern recognition algorithms.

The second argument against the conclusion that the regression decision-making algorithms proposed by psychologists are invalid is that while Minsky and Papert's (1969) conclusion is warranted, its applicability to the area of expert decision making may be limited. Minsky and Papert's argument is a mathematical one and so tacitly assumes ideal conditions. Therefore the conclusion that linear models are not appropriate decision-making algorithms seems justified for decision problems that are virtually noise free. However, very often the decision problems studied by psychologists are not of this type. In the case of graduate student selection and in many types of medical diagnosis, input information is noisy and/or has a stochastic relationship to a valid decision. In these cases to adopt Minsky and Papert's conclusions is to adopt configural decision-making methods. However, it is in just these cases that bootstrapping is most effective and linear regression algorithms are particularly robust with respect to configural strategies (see, e.g., Dawes, 1976, 1979; Dawes & Corrigan, 1974). Thus, in noisy decision-making contexts the empirical evidence suggests that Minsky and Papert's critique is not applicable. The use of regression equations as a model of experts' decision-making processes as therefore not invalidated in such contexts and a resolution of the simple versus complex paradox which advocates the use of expert systems by default is not justified.

The resolution of the complex versus simple paradox is not an acclamation of the merits of psychologists over knowledge engineers. Nor does it imply that linear models are a closer representation of experts' underlying decision-making processes than expert systems. It simply means that linear models are extremely robust. Given the degree of error that exists in the real world, in both the nature of decision problem and the measurement of predictor and criterion variables, linear models simply do a better predictive job than other algorithms.

REFERENCES

Aikins, ,J. S, Prototypical Knowledge for Expert Systems. *Artificial Intelligence*, 1983, 20, 163-210.

Anderson, N. H. Looking for Configurality in clinical judgment. *Psychological Bulletin*, 1972, 78, 93-102.

Bowman, E. H. Consistency and optimality in management decision making. *Management Science*, 1983, 9, 310-321.

Brachman, R. J., et al. What are expert systems? In F. Hayes-Roth, D. A. Waterman & D. B. Lenat (Eds.) *Building Expert Systems. Vol. 1.* Reading MA: Addison-Wesley Publishing Co., 1983, 127-167.

.Brunswik, E. *The conceptual framework of psychology.* Chicago: University of Chicago Press, 1952.

Buchanan, B. G., et al. Constructing expert systems. In F. Hayes-Roth, D. A. Waterman, & D. B. Lenat (Eds.) *Building expert systems. Vol. 1.* Reading, MA: Addison-Wesley Publishing Co., 1983, 127—167.

Buchanan, B. G. & Feigenbaum, E. A. DENDRAL and meta-DENDRAL: Their applications dimension. *Artificial Intelligence,* 1978, 11(1), 5-24.

Clancey, W. I.. The epistemology of a rule-based expert system: A framework for explanation. *Artificial Intelligence*, 1983,20,215—251.

Connally, T. Uncertainty, action and competence: Some alternatives to omniscience in complex problem-solving. In S. Fiddle (Ed.) *Uncertainty: Social and behavioural dimensions.* New York Praeger, 1980,69-91.

Davis, R. Expert systems: Where are we? And where do we go from here? *The AI Magazine*, 1982, Spring, 3—22.

Davis, R. Amplifying expertise with expert systems. In P. H. Winston, & K. A. Prendergast (Eds.), *The AI business: The commercial uses of artficial intelligence.* Cambridge, MA: The MIT Press, 1984,17-40.

Davis, R. & Lenat, D. B. *Knowledge-based systems in artificial intelligence.* New York: McGraw-Hill, 1982.

Dawes, R. M. A case study of graduate admissions: Applications of three principles of human decision making. *American Psychologist*, 1971,26, 180-188.

Dawes. R. M. Shallow psychology. In J. S. Carroll & J. W. Payne (Eds.) *Cognition and social behavior.* Hillsdale, N: Lawrence Erlbaum Associates, 1974, 3—11.

Dawes, R. M. Predictive models as a guide to preference. *IEEE Transactions on Systems, Man, and Cybernetics,* 1977,7(5), 355-357.

Dawes, R. M. The robust beauty of improper linear models in decision making. *American Psychologist*, 1979,34(7), 571-582.

Dawes, R. M. & Corrigan, B. Linear models in decision-making. *Psychological Bulletin,* 1974, 81(2), 95-106.

Dreyfus, H. L. *What computers can't do.* New York: Harper & Row, 1972.

Duda, R. O., et al. Semantic network representations in rule-based inference systems. In D. A. Waterman, & F. Hayes-Roth (Eds.) *Pattern-directed inference systems.* New York: Academic Press, 1978, 203-221.

Duda, R. C. & Gaschnig, J. G. Knowledge-based expert systems come of age. *Byte*, September, 1981, 238-281.

Ebbeson, E., & Konecni, V. Decision-making and information integration in the courts: The setting of bail. *Journal of Personality and Social Psychology*, 1975, 32, 805-821.

Einhorn, H J. Decision errors and fallible judgment: implications for social policy. In K. R. Hammond (Ed.) *Judgment and decision in public policy formation.* Denver, Colorado: Westview Press, 1978, 142-169.

Einhorn, H. J. Overconfidence in judgment. *New Directions for Methodology of Social and Behavioral Science*, 1980, 4,1-16.

Einhorn, H. J. & Hogarth, R. M. Unit weighting schemes for decision making. *Organizational Behavior and Human Performance*, 1975, 13, 171—193.

Einhorn, H. J. & Hogarth, R. M. Confidence in judgment: Persistence of the illusion of validity. *Psychological Review*, 1978, 85(5), 374-416.

Fryback, D. G. & Erdman, H. Prospects for calibrating physicians' probabilistic judgments: Design of a feedback system. *IEEE*, 1979, 1, 340-345.

Gilovich, T. Seeing the past in the present: The effect of associations to familiar events on judgment and decisions. *Journal of Personality and Social Psychology*, 1981, 40, 797-808.

Goldberg, L. R. The effectiveness of clinicians' judgments: The diagnosis of organic brain damage from Bender-Gestalt test. *Journal of Consulting Psychology*, 1959, 23(1), 25-33.

Goldberg, L. R. Simple models or simple processes? Some research on clinical judgments. *American Psychologist*, 1968, 23(7), 483-496.

Goldberg, L. R. Man versus model of man: A rationale, plus some evidence, for a method of improving clinical inference. *Psychological Bulletin*, 1970, 73(6), 422-432.

Hammond, K. R. Probabilistic functioning and the clinical method. *Psychological Review*, 1955, 62, 255—262.

Hammond, K. R., Hursch, C. I. & Todd, F. I. Analyzing the components of clinical inference. *Psychological Review* 1964, 71, 438-456.

Hangood, F. Computers: Experts to a point. *Atlantic Monthly*, February, 1985, 90-92.

Hayes-Roth, F., Waterman, D. A. & Lenat, D. B. An overview of expert systems. In F. Hayes-Roth, D. A. Waterman, & D. B. Lenat (Eds.) *Building expert systems. Vol. l.* Reading, MA: Addison Wesley Publishing Co., 1983, 3-29.

Hoffman, P. J. The paramorphic representation of clinical judgment. *Psychological Bulletin*, 1960, 57(2), 116-131.

Hoffman, P. J., Slovic, P. & Rarer, L. G. An ANOVA model for the assessment of configural cue utilization in clinical judgment. *Psychological Bulletin*, 1968, 69, 338-349.

Hursch, C. J., Hammond, K. R. & Hursch, J. Some methodological issues in multiple-cue probability studies. *Psychological Review.* 1964, 71, 42— 60.

Jackson, P. *Introduction to expert systems.* Workingham. England: Addison-Wesley, 1986.

Johnson, L. & Keravnou, I. E. *Expert system technology.* New Hampshire, Abacus Press, 1985.

Johnson, P. E., Hassebrock, F., Duran, A. S. & Moller, J. H. Multi-method study of clinical judgment. *Organizational Behavior and Human Performance*, 1982, 30, 201-230.

Kleinmuntz, B. The processing of clinical information by man and machine. In B. Kleinmuntz (Ed.) *Formal representation of human judgment.* New York: John Wiley, 1968, 149-186.

Kleinmuntz, B. The computer as clinician. *American Psychologist*, 1975, 30, 379-386.

Kleinmuntz, B. Computational and non-computational clinical information processing by computer. *Behavioral Science*, 1982, 27, 164-175.

Kunz, J. C., et al. *A physiological rule-based system for interpreting pulmonary function test results.* Heuristic programming Project, Computer Science Dept., Stanford University, HPP-78-19 (Working paper), 1978.

Leal, A. & Pearl, J. An interactive programme for conversational elicitation of decision structures. *IEEE Transactions on Systems, Man and Cybernetics*, 1977, 7(5), 368-376.

Lichtenstein, S. C. & Fischoff, B. Do those who know more also know more about what they don't know? *ORI Bulletin*, 1976, 16(1).

Meehl, P. E. *Clinical vs. statistical prediction.* Minneapolis: University of Minnesota Press, 1954.

Meehl, P. E. Seer over sign: The first good example. *Journal of Experimental Research in Personality*, 1965, 1, 27-32.

Meehl, P. E. *Psychodiagnosis: Selected papers.* New York: W. W. Norton & Co., 1973.

Minsky, M. & Papert, S. *Perceptrons: An introduction to computational geometry.* Cambridge, MA: MIT Press, 1969.

Naylar, C. M. *Build your own expert system.* Cheshire, U. K.: Sigma Technical Press, 1983.

Nilsson, N. J. *Learning machines: Foundations of trainable pattern-classifying systems.* New York: McGraw-Hill, 1965.

Nilsson, N. J. *Problem solving methods in artificial intelligence.* New York: McGraw-Hill, 1971.

Nisbet, R. H. & Wilson, T. D. Telling more than we can know: Verbal reports on mental processes. *Psychological Review*, 1977, 84(3), 114—124.

Oskamp, S. Overconfidence in case-study judgments. *Journal of Consulting Psychology*, 1965, 29(3), 261-265.

Phelps, R. H. & Shanteau, J. Livestock judges: How much information can an expert use? *Organizational Behavior and Human Performance*, 1978, 21, 209-219.

Palitakis, P. & Weiss, S. M. Using empirical analysis to refine expert system knowledge-bases. *Artificial Intelligence*, 1984, 22, 23-48.

Pople H. E. CADUCEUS: An experimental expert system for medical diagnosis. In P. H. Winston, & K. A. Prendergast (Eds.) *The AI business: The commercial uses of artificial intelligence.* Cambridge, MA: The MIT Press, 1984, 67-80.

Rorer, L. G. & Slovic, P. The measurement of changes in judgmental strategy. *American Psychologist*, 1966, 21, 641-642.

Sebestyen, G. S. *Decision making processes in pattern recognition.* New York: The Macmillan Co., 1962.

Shortliffe, E. H. *Computer-based medical consultations: MYCIN.* New York: Elsevier, 1976.

Slovic, P. Analyzing the expert judge: A descriptive study of a stockbroker's decision processes. *Journal of Applied Psychology*, 1969, 53(4), 255- 263.

Slovic, P., Fischoff, B. & Lichtenstein, S. Behavioral decision theory. *Annual Review of Psychology*, 1977, 28, 1-39.

van Melle, W. J. *System aids in constructing consultation programs.* Ann Arbor, MI: UMI Research Press, 1981.

Waranabe, S. *Pattern recognition: Human and mechanical.* New York: John Wiley & Sons, 1985.

Winston, P. H. & Prendergast, K. A. (Eds.) *The AI business: The commercial uses of artificial intelligence.* Cambridge, MA: MIT Press, 1984.

Yntema, D. B. & Torgerson, W. S. Man-computer cooperation in decisions requiring common sense. *IRE Transactions of the Professional Group on Human Factors in Electronics,* 1961, 2(1).

Yu, V. L. et al. Antimicrobial selection by a computer. A blinded evaluation by infectious disease experts. *Journal of the American Medical Association*, 1979, 242(12), 1279-1282.

READING QUESTIONS

1) Why is it "just as invalid as it is valid" to speak of the social *impact* of computing?
2) Why should a large-scale, successful experts system be expected to shift the information processing capacities of an organization?
3) What is a *performance program,* and how is it related to what an expert system does?
4) How did Sviokla collect the pre- and post-XCON data for the study? What are the disadvantages of this method?
5) What is information processing capacity, and how is it related to activity in an organization?
6) Why was configuration a central problem for DEC?
7) Why was final assembly and testing not a good solution to ensuring quality?
8) What were the two major changes to the performance program post-XCON?
9) How did the technical editor's task become split post-XCON?
10) What effect did XCON have on employment at DEC?
11) What increases in complexity (measured by input and output)were produced by XCON?
12) In what specific ways did task performance improve post-XCON?
13) How was responsibility and power shifted in DEC as a result of XCON's success?
14) Why was a formal program for maintenance of the "knowledge base" necessary?
15) What is progressive structuring? How did the implementation of XCON produce it?
16) What is the difference between the psychologists' and the AI researchers' approach to understanding how experts make accurate diagnostic decisions?
17) What is the case against medical experts' diagnosis skills? Does increasing the information available to them help?
18) What is the problem with how experts determine if they have made an incorrect diagnosis?
19) How is a linear equation like an expert's judgments?
20) In what kinds of situations do linear equations do better diagnosis than experts?
21) What are the advantages and disadvantages of having a linear equation substitute for clinical judgment? Is there a compromise position?
22) What are the prerequisites for building an expert system?
23) Explain the procedure for constructing an expert system. Why does the procedure sound easier than it actually is?
24) What are the two major parts of all expert systems?
25) How close is the match between the judgments of expert systems and the judgments of experts?
26) What is the difficulty with eliciting the rules that experts have for exceptions?
27) Why might the rules that expert systems use be distortions of those that experts use?

28) "Experts have some background knowledge outside their specialty; expert systems do not." Why is this important?
29) How does the relative performance of linear equations and expert systems depend on the nature of the decision problem?
30) What are some ways that our psychological knowledge about experts could help us make better expert systems?

DISCUSSION QUESTIONS

1) Was XCON a benefit to the employees of DEC? To answer this you will need to take into consideration changes in job quality, in employment, and in productivity.
2) What risks were created by the adoption of XCON? Use some of the ideas from the chapter on risk in this analysis.
3) How does the decision problem for XCON differ from the decision problem for medical experts? What might this indicate about the effectiveness of expert systems in each area?
4) You have a choice of three diagnosis systems: a doctor with a 65 percent reliability, an expert system with a 70 percent reliability and a linear equation with a 75 percent reliability. Which would you prefer? Why? Who would you sue if the diagnosis was wrong?

PRACTICING THE DESIGN ETHIC

1) Investigate an introductory course on expert systems or AI offered on your campus. Determine whether the course covers the following issues. (You should check the syllabus and reading material for the course, as well as the instructor, or a student who took the course.)
   • How does an AI system change the decision-making responsibilities in the organization?
   • What do you do if an expert is unwilling to provide his knowledge to you?
   • How do you answer the question from an employee, "If I provide my expert knowledge to you, will the computer eventually take over my job?
   • How will an expert system benefit the employees, customers, managers, and owners of a business?
   Summarize the information and report to the class. How would you change, if at all, the issues covered in the class?
2) Imagine your school has designed an expert system to advise you which classes to take, based on its knowledge of your test scores, your current GPA, your current transcript, and your career goals. Assume that it is at least as accurate in its advice about courses as the typical student advisor. Interview several students and student advisors to determine how they would use such a system. What part of their decision making would it replace? What would it leave undone? How might it change advising and course taking?

CHAPTER
8

TECHNOLOGY AND EMPLOYMENT

There are two competing mythologies of computing and employment: the utopic and the dystopic. The utopic vision claims that computing will make work easier, will make workers happier by upgrading their jobs, will make the workplace a more democratic place, and will create employment by increasing productivity. The dystopic vision claims that computing will deskill workers, create electronic sweatshops, replace workers with machines, and create intrusive and controlling electronic monitoring of work.

By now you will not be surprised to learn that the real picture is more complicated than either story. Attewell and Rule investigate some of these claims in their classic "what we know and what we don't know" paper. They find that the data are inconclusive for either mythology. Either it is too difficult to collect the data needed to make large claims, or the actual data support a conclusion somewhere in the middle. The "middle of the road" conclusion that squares best with the data is that the effects of computing on work are not uniform but depend on the organizational culture that implements the technology. Though this paper is a little dated, the empirical picture has not changed in the interim, and more recent work confirms the authors' earlier conclusions.

The report by the National Academy of Science Panel on Technology and Employment is also complex in its findings. Though the conclusion is that technological advancement in the long run produces more jobs, it also produces what economists call "displacement." Displacement is the need for workers to move from one job to another, and from the worker's perspective looks suspiciously like unemployment. Thus the panel calls for support for displaced workers while warning that a failure to support technological innovation will result in permanent employment losses.

Both papers, then, make the point that the utopic and dystopic mythologies are misguided. The real work resides in dealing with the social and organizational problems in the "middle of the road."

COMPUTING AND ORGANIZATIONS: WHAT WE KNOW AND WHAT WE DON'T KNOW[1]

Paul Attewell
James Rule
SUNY, Stony Brook

A few issues in the evolution of computing draw equal attention from specialists and from the public at large. Nearly everyone, for example, wants to know what kind of social world is emerging from the continuing permeation of organizational life by computing. The most urgent of these questions are socioeconomic—for instance, whether new technologies will reduce employment, enhance organizational efficiency, or strengthen managers' decision-making power. However, hardly of less interest are issues relating to the changing nature of social *experience* in the face of technological change: Is work becoming more or less fulfilling, thanks to the computer? Are computerized organizations more or less humane than their conventional counterparts?

We like to think of these questions as topical, yet they echo themes that have long played a part in the history of social and economic thought. They were by no means new, for example, when Marx entertained them. He and other nineteenth-century commentators devoted much attention to what we would now call automation and technologically induced unemployment. No less was Marx attentive to what he saw as degradation in the *content* of work through technologically induced deskilling. The widespread use of computing by government and private organizations is obviously a phenomenon of the last two or three decades. Yet the same questions we are now asking about computing, others have long asked about other technologies.

What puzzles us is that people remain so willing to speak and write as though the overall effects of computing technologies were a foregone conclusion, as though they could be determined a priori. People still make broad claims that computerized work is manifestly more fulfilling than conventional work or that computerization obviously and evidently robs work of its inherent rewards. Similar a priori claims are made on the effects of computing on employment or on its role in organizational decision making. Often buttressed by studies of small sets of cases, such works give people the impression that we understand more about the repercussions of

[1] Attewell, P., & Rule, J. (1984). Computing and organizations: What we know and what we don't know. *Communications of the ACM, 27,* 1184-1192. Copyright © 1984, Association for Computing Machinery Inc. Reprinted by permission.

computing in organizations than we really do and that research will only confirm what we already know.

We argue the opposite; that evidence on these subjects is actually fragmentary and very mixed, and that a priori arguments are particularly inappropriate in light of the range and variety of variables at work in these situations. In this article we examine the literature on the effects of computing on the numbers and quality of jobs, on management decision making, and on organizational dealings with clients and customers. We also consider various perspectives on the causes of organizational decisions to adopt computing in the first place. We pay much more attention to the first questions, where the existing literature is larger. However our conclusions are similar for all of these areas: Virtually none of the studies mounted so far have been capable of yielding a persuasive and comprehensive view of computer-induced social change.

QUALITY OF WORK

The research literature on the impact of new information technologies on job content and job satisfaction provides a mass of contradictory findings. The wide range of informed opinion can best be defined by describing the two extreme positions: *deskilling* and *upgrading.*

The deskilling perspective suggests that automation is used to strip relatively skilled jobs of their conceptual content [13]. Those conceptual tasks previously integrated into work are either built into computer algorithms or transferred to a numerically smaller number of high-level specialists.

Deskilling manifests itself in two ways: *intra*occupational changes, where the skill content of a particular job decreases over time, and *inter*occupational changes, where the number of people in skilled jobs shrinks and the number in less skilled jobs increases. In the second of these cases, one empirical indicator of deskilling is a shift in the occupational distribution of the white-collar work force. Thus, the deskilling position implies that new information technologies produce a more polarized pyramidal distribution of skill: a mass of unskilled clerical workers at the bottom, and a small number of "conceptual workers" at the top, alongside management. James Driscoll of MIT [25] has put this rhetorically: "The office of the future would. . . leave people in only two roles: bosses and garbage collectors. "

In contrast, several researchers have argued that computerization and other new information technologies upgrade rather than deskill white-collar workers [8, 35, 81]. They maintain that automation primarily occurs in already-routinized work situations; the new technology takes the drudge work out of information processing by automating filing and information retrieval, preparing repetitive paperwork (e. g., form letters), doing simple computational tasks, moving messages, and so on. As automation absorbs many of the *manual aspects* of information processing, humans have more time to concentrate on conceptual and decision-making tasks.

The potential victims in this net upgrading of white-collar work are the lowest level clerical workers whose work consists almost entirely of manual manipulation of data (e.g., file clerks, correspondence typists, mailroom workers). These jobs can be largely replaced by the new technologies. However, proponents of the upgrading thesis argue that negative impacts need not occur even for this lowest stratum of workers. The process manifests itself in the relative growth of higher level white-collar jobs and the relative shrinkage of low-level jobs; the absolute number of low-level clerical workers need not decline in the short run. In addition. retraining schemes can modestly upgrade even lowest level clerical workers: File clerks become dataprocessing and entry clerks, bank tellers become officers or collections agents, typists retrain on text editors, and other workers join the computer operations staff (cf. [76. (p. 63)]).

With upgrading, then, the impact of computer technology is a net increase in skill and job satisfaction [35]. The occupational distribution of white-collar jobshifts from a pyramid shape (few skilled, many semiskilled or unskilled) toward a diamond shape (few top managers, many professionals and middle managers, few low-skilled clericals) [124].

At the case-study level, many observers have described a loss of conceptual content, fragmentation, and deskilling of various clerical and professional white-collar jobs after computers were introduced [7, 20, 36-38, 46, 76, 116]. Groups representing clerical workers have also complained about computer-generated degradation of their work [41, 92]. On the other hand, several observers (Sometimes the same observers!) give examples of the reversal of the division of labor with the introduction of new information technologies. Tasks are consolidated rather than further fragmented [20, 72, 76 (p. 62), 102].

The most plausible explanation for these opposed viewpoints is not that either group of observers is wrong but that both processes (deskilling and upgrading) are occurring within white-collar occupations. The riddle, then, is to determine which tendency predominates. For this purpose, single-case studies are not useful.

These difficulties are partially overcome in Attewell's [5] study of the insurance industry, utilizing Bureau of Labor Statistics (BLS) surveys on a large sample of insurance firms. Using detailed job descriptions, the BLS divides each occupation into several skill levels: file clerk A, file clerk B, file clerk C, etc., Since the surveys provide the numbers of persons in each skill category and since surveys have been carried out at five-year intervals during a period of rapid computer automation, one can analyze the data to determine intraoccupational skill changes over time. Consistent with the case studies above, Attewell reported a mixed picture. Four occupations showed modest but statistically significant downgrading over the last 15 years, six showed similarly significant upgrading, and three showed no trends. Thus both upgrading and deskilling are occurring within occupations as automation affects information-processing jobs. The unanswered question is, What is the overall effect of intraoccupational shifts in skills economy wide? Are the findings for the insurance industry generalizable to other sectors?

Horowitz and Herrenstadt [47] examined intraoccupational skill changes in five industries between 1949 and 1965, using occupational skill data as determined by successive editions of the Department of Labor's *Dictionary of Occupational Titles* (*DOT*) and found little overall change in skills. Spenner [107] examined change within 545 occupations using the 1965 and 1977 *DOT* skill measures and found "very little change—if any, a slight upgrading in the actual skill content of work over the last quarter century" [107, (p. 973)]. Rumberger [101] examined the *DOT* measure of educational requirements of jobs (as a proxy for skill) for the period 1960-1976. He found that intraoccupational change had led to a narrowing of skill differences: upgrading in lower occupations, downgrading in higher ones.

Although these *DOT* studies have a great advantage over the case studies in terms of correctly representing a large range of occupations and industries, they are unfortunately flawed. In an exhaustive study of the *DOT* skill-measurement system, carried out under the auspices of the National Academy of Science, Cain and Treiman [14] found that successive editions of the *DOT* do not accurately assess changes in skill content. They also echoed Howe's [48] criticism of the *DOT* as systematically biased because it undervalues the skill levels of many jobs predominantly held by women. Taken together, these objections vitiate the *DOT* as a tool for studying skill changes.

This leaves us with an unsatisfactory situation. We have a variety of case-study evidence indicating both upgrading and downgrading but no way to map this onto the economy as a whole or onto a representative sample of firms.

The evidence on interoccupational change (i. e., the relative growth of high-skill versus low-skill occupations) has similar difficulties. A series of early case studies reported that lower level clerical positions were eliminated by automation and that the proportion of higher level clerical jobs increased [18, 21, 43, 68, 94, 112, 120]. More recently, Menzies [76 (p. 63)] documented the retraining of displaced low-level clerical workers associated with "a radical upgrading of information work in Canadian industry, characterized by a diminishing demand for low-level clerical workers [and] increasing demand for technical and professional workers." Attewell [5], using BLS data on interoccupational shifts in the insurance industry from 1966 to 1980 (a period of intense automation), documents a marked growth in the proportion of insurance workers in higher level white-collar occupations (38 to 60 percent) and a corresponding decrease in the proportion of the work force in lower level jobs. These findings support the upgrading thesis.

Unfortunately, in attempting to generalize beyond these case-specific or industry-specific studies to the economy as a whole, we confront some of the problems encountered with the *DOT* data discussed above. Jaffe and Froomkin [51 (pp. 73-82)] suggested a modest aggregate upgrading of skills, most especially due to the changing industrial composition of the economy, rather than to an occupational mix within industries. Dubnoff [26] looked at the interoccupational distribution of jobs between 1900 and 1970, again using the *DOT* to measure skill levels. He found no aggregate deskilling in the nonfarm sector since 1900. Rumberger [101 (p. 578)] used *DOT* educational requirements as a proxy for skill and found that "between 1960 and 1976 changes in the distribution of employment have favored more-skilled jobs. " But each of these studies stands or falls on the accuracy of *DOT* determinations of skill levels of jobs,

The third source of data for examining changes in the quality of worklife due to technological change comes from surveys of workers' own opinions. Muller [79] surveyed a representative sample of the U. S. work force (blue and white collar) about their experience of many kinds of technological change between 1962 and 1967. She found that reports of job enlargement and increased job satisfaction greatly exceeded reports of downgrading [79 (p. 14)]. More recently, Kling [59] surveyed 1200 managers, clerks, and data analysts in municipal government jobs about the impact of new information technologies on their work. He concluded that "computer use did not profoundly alter the character of their jobs. " However, the new technology did have an effect on the quality of worklife. Kling found a modest upgrading of skill and job satisfaction across the occupational hierarchy from clericals to middle-level professionals to managers.

Kraemer and Danziger [62] also analyzed opinion survey data from a large sample of municipal government employees, examining several dimensions of job satisfaction and four levels of information workers (managers, staff professionals, bureaucrats who work with the public, and "desk-top bureaucrats"). Consonant with Kling's observations, they found that about half of the workers experienced an increased sense of accomplishment in computerized work, whereas only 4 percent reported a lowered sense. Most respondents did not experience computer-generated changes in supervision, nor did respondents report that computers diminished their control over others. Time pressure was experienced differentially; Forty-eight percent of the sample was unaffected, 29 percent reported decreased pressure, and 22 percent reported increased pressure. Overall, then, the effects of new technology were not dramatic, but where change was reported, computers were most often said to be enhancing job satisfaction.

Kraemer and Danziger's analysis did not support Kling's finding that the job-enhancing benefits of computerization increase as one climbs the organizational hierarchy. They found no significant differences between the occupational levels in terms of an increased sense of accomplishment. Surprisingly, they found that managers and bureaucrats directly serving the public reported higher increases in supervision than more routinized desk-top bureaucrats. Perceived changes in time pressure were also distributed across occupational strata in unexpected ways; Street-level bureaucrats experienced the highest incidence of decreased work pressure, followed by managers, desk-top bureaucrats, and professionals. The one finding that did support Kling's view of the hierarchical impact of the new technology concerned control over others. Computers allowed for an increased control over others toward the top of the occupational hierarchy.

Surveys of worker satisfaction in the private sector do not match in quality, detail, or representativeness the above research on the public sector [93, 114], Shepard's [102] study remains the most ambitious. He compared various groups of blue- and white-collar workers on several dimensions of alienation. He found that automated workers were less alienated than both mechanized and nonmechanized groups. Unlike the surveys discussed earlier, Shepard's study did not ask workers within an occupation to compare their pre- and post-automation work, but instead contrasted quite different occupations cross-sectionally. Since pay, promotion prospects, prestige, and other factors differentiated these occupations, in addition to level of technology, Shepard's observed difference in alienation/dissatisfaction between occupational groups may have little to do with technology.

To summarize: Surveys of workers' perceptions of the new technology generally contradict the deskilling/job degradation thesis. Most workers surveyed regard the new technologies in a positive light. There are, however, three caveats concerning these findings: First, existing opinion-survey data depend mainly on studies of public bureaucracies. The application of computer technology in the public sector may be more "humane" than in private-sector profit-oriented businesses that are pressured by competition-hence, the need to study a representative sample of businesses. Second, existing studies do not distinguish among levels of information technology. Thus we do not know whether the reports of job enhancement come from those individuals who work eight hours a day on state-of-the-art computer work stations or from individuals who only indirectly or intermittently use computer data. (Kraemer and Danziger [62] suggest this as a possible after-the-fact explanation for some of their findings.) The issue needs to be tested more rigorously. Finally, there is a possibility that increased satisfaction reflects a "novelty effect," a temporary increase in interest that will fade as the technology becomes more familiar. Surveys therefore should take account of the length of time for which respondents have used the technology they are assessing.

EFFECTS ON UNEMPLOYMENT

Fears of automation-generated unemployment swept the United States and Europe in the late 1950s and early 1960s, resulting in several volumes of research and commentary [1, 42, 50, 64, 82, 89, 109]. At that time, the main focus was on blue-collar unemployment and the automation of manual tasks, although computer impacts on white-collar workers were considered. These early concerns faded as the 1960s brought both increases in productivity and a rapid expansion of the American work force, thus apparently proving that automation need not generate unemployment.

However, by the early 1970s concerns over technologically generated unemployment surfaced again. By the late 1960s the manufacturing sector of the U. S. economy was exhibiting "jobless growth"—expansion in output with no corresponding increase in employment. In the industrialized nations of Europe and Japan there were absolute declines in manufacturing employment alongside increases in output [97 (pp. 3-4, 38-39)]. The rapid growth of the service sector (18. 5 million new jobs in the United States between 1970 and 1981) seemed to offset stagnation and contraction in manufacturing employment during the 1970s, although some argued that this trend was heavily dependent on the expansion of government and would not continue into the 1980s, even in private-sector services (e. g., [34]).

A spate of studies then appeared, many sponsored by European governments, assessing the unemployment consequences of new microelectronic technology [2, 6, 15, 16, 29, 31, 53, 84-86, 104, 111]. These studies were generally pessimistic, predicting substantial levels of technologically induced unemployment (10 percent and greater). However, each national study concludes that the unemployment consequences for that nation of not adopting the new technology would be more severe than the consequences of adopting it, since nonadoption would result in loss of international competitive standing and hence loss of export markets. The pessimistic position is well expressed by the titles of books: *The Collapse of Work* [52] and *Automatic Unemployment* [45].

Pessimists point out that microelectronics technology is simultaneously affecting all parts of industry and commerce, from product and process design to welding, forging, molding, diecasting, and painting [55] to assembly [45 (pp. 21-24), 55] and office work [30, 35, 54]. Empirically, the pessimists' case rests on a series of daunting but quite unsystematic case studies, which show employment shrinkages of 50 percent in metal-working, 25 percent in telecommunications [97 (U. K. data)], 30 percent in banking [86 (French data)], 16-35 percent in female clerical work (76 (pp. 71-73, Canadian data)], and so on.

There are two major problems with the empirical bases of the pessimists' position. First, most of the national studies utilizing sophisticated input/output analyses [e. g., (69, 85)] are grounded in percentage estimates of the degree of increased productivity due to microelectronic technology for each industrial/commercial sector. These estimates are at best informed guesses and at worst complete speculation. There have been no systematic industrywide measurements of productivity increases resulting from the new technology because of the near impossibility of the task, from a methodological standpoint. Different firms take incompatible approaches to productivity measurement; many do not measure it at all. Attempts to compare productivity before and after automation in a few exemplary automated corporations are frustrated by the fact that such businesses often abandon or change their productivity measurement systems when production is reorganized around new technology, thus vitiating such comparisons. Separating the effects of the new technology from other factors affecting productivity (economic contractions, good or bad management, etc.) is also quite complex.

A second and easier approach has been to directly measure changes in employment in automating firms and to extrapolate these findings to the economy at large (e. g., [97]). This approach has similar pitfalls, If, as is often the case, one looks at firms in the avant-garde of computer automation, one risks choosing totally atypical businesses, Also, automating enterprises may be more competitive, stealing market shares from less advanced firms— the employment impact may be felt not in the automating firm itself but in backward non-competitive firms in the same business. Observed employment decreases may also be due to nationwide contraction rather than new technology, and so on.

A better way to assess employment changes due to the new technology would be to draw a systematic representative sample of businesses, study each firm's level of automation, and analyze changes in employment for each firm, controlling for (1) degree of automation and (2) changes in total constant dollar sales. Such a sample would have to include the full spectrum of automated and nonautomated businesses.

Optimists argue that studies of the apparent negative employment effects of the new technology are overstated, since they ignore several countertendencies. They maintain that by cutting the costs of goods and services, new technology stimulates increased demand. The work force need not shrink if increases in production balance increases in productivity, These "economic multiplier" effects might help to create a new technological "long wave" that could revive the international economy. Other such waves were triggered by the introduction of the railroads, electric power, etc. (17, 33) Optimists also point out that automation frequently occurs in industries experiencing a labor *shortage* and increased consumer demand. Automation in such industries only slows down the growth rate of labor; it does not shrink the labor force [30]. Again, these claims, although plausible, cannot be measured without a representative sampling of businesses and an examination of their occupational and output growth rates.

MANAGEMENT EFFECTS

Students of organizations have frequently observed their control of information as a source of power [19, 75, 91]. New technologies that alter the quality and availability of information are likely to shift balances of power between various groups of organizational actors—workers, supervisors, middle managers, executives, etc. [88] The rerouting of information may also create new dependencies between parts of organizations and dissolve old ones, paving the way for structural changes.

One group of researchers finds evidence that such processes lead to increased centralization of power and decision making in computer-automated organizations [65]. Leavitt and Whisler [66] predicted in 1958 that the new information technologies would eliminate whole levels of middle management as improved information led to centralized decision making at the higher levels of the corporate hierarchy. Those middle-level managers who remained would have less discretion than before, since they would be supervising according to standardized procedures and decisions set from above, and since their clerical subordinates would face more routinized work [119]. Centralization would also lead to the merging of departments and a general simplification of organizational structure.

Early case-study research confirmed this prediction, especially as regards the decline of middle management [3, 49, 80, 81, 119]. Subsequent studies of computer-mail systems have reinforced this view by showing the predominance of "top-down" communication [67, 70].

A further indication of centralization is the development of executive information systems that allow top executives to bypass line administrators and to monitor activity on the "factory floor" via computer tallies [12].

There is some evidence for an opposite view, however: The increase in communication resulting from new computer technologies may be *decentralizing* managerial decision making. Withington [122] reported case-study observations that management-information-system (MIS) data enhanced decision making by middle managers and strengthened their authority (cf. [58]). Pfeffer [90, 91] has argued that computerization allows for delegation of decision-making authority to lower level managers because such decisions can be easily monitored by higher level managers via MIS data, Blau et al. [10], in a comparative study of manufacturing companies, found that on-site computers do foster decentralized operational decisions, at least down to the level of plant manager. Also contra Whisler, Blau et al. and Blau and Schoenherr [11] found that, far from eliminating levels of middle management, computers are associated with an increase in the number of levels of line management and that differentiation into multiple departments increases with computerization. They contend computers lead to a more differentiated, more complex organizational structure.

Between the extremes of centralization and decentralization, we find a number of studies that suggest that power shifts resulting from computerization are complex and cannot be understood in terms of the single dimension of centralization/decentralization. Kling [60 (p. 24)] has argued that even where new information technologies provide the potential for increased managerial surveillance, this potential has often not been used by managers. He also cites instances where subordinates put false information into MIS systems in order to evade managerial control [60 (p. 84)].

Nor is it clear that upper management is always the group that benefits from improved access to information. Markus [74, (p. 55)] discusses a situation where junior officers in a U. S. military logistics group gained status vis-à-vis senior officers because of their access to on-line data, Bjorn-Anderson and Peterson [9] found that planners gained power at the expense of plant and production managers in several computerized Danish factories. Kraemer and Danziger [62] found in a sample of municipal governments that managers and staff did experience an increase in control over subordinates but that they themselves also experienced a relative increase in supervision. Meanwhile, a substantial proportion of their subordinates—"desk-top bureaucrats"—reported a lessening of supervision following computerization (see also [59, (p. 21)]). Such examples indicate that control is not a simple zero-sum relationship and that various groups may experience enhanced power and decision-making opportunities after computerization. Kling, Kraemer, and Dutton (summarized in [60 (p. 92)]) found that the pattern of power shifts following office automation in large municipalities differed from that found in smaller cities. Contextual variables thus play important mediating roles in influencing the outcome of the introduction of the new technology.

Robey [95, 96], in reviewing this literature and in presenting his own international case-study data, provided the following conclusion: "Computers do not necessarily affect the distribution of authority and control. " In most cases either there is no change following the introduction of a MIS or an existing organizational structure is simply reinforced. Where changes are observed, centralization is a more common outcome than decentralization. Computerized information systems are clearly compatible with a wide variety of lateral and vertical power relationships in organizations [96].

Contradictory conclusions can be drawn from these case studies, if we assume that there must be a single accurate characterization of these effects. If we instead assume that a range of management effects is possible following the introduction of new information technology and that a variety of factors influences a particular outcome, our task becomes clear. We must identify those variables that can account for differential outcomes and examine them in a comparative study of a stratified sample of organizations. Variables include organizational size, industry type, degree of prior routinization or variability of work, degree of dependence upon a professional or high-skilled work force, and the patterns of information usage and information flow associated with the technologies in use.

ORGANIZATIONS AND THE PUBLIC

Social relationships within organizations are not the only ones to change in response to new bureaucratic uses of information. Relationships between organizations and their environments—particularly the general public—are also affected. It is easier to collect, disseminate, store, analyze, and use information with modern information technologies, and this is bound to make a difference in how organizations interact with the public.

This category of relationships has been the focus of much less theoretical attention and empirical investigation than those discussed earlier. To be sure, students of formal organization have long acknowledged that the flow of information between organizations and the public represents an important constraint on these relationships (see Deutsch [22] and Stinchcombe [108]). However, this recognition has not been attended by systematic attention to these issues in specific organizations. A few authors (e. g., Shils [103], Rule [98], and Rule et al. [99, 100]) have focused on the growing appetite of centralized organizations, especially governments, for information on the people with whom they deal. Other authors (e. g., Mowshowitz [77], Hiltz and Turoff [44], and Smith [106]) have speculated about new kinds of informational services that computerized organizations could provide and the concomitant changes that could be expected in modern ideas of what organizations are and do. However, none of these writings take us close to a comprehensive assessment of how informational relations between organizations and the public are changing through the rise of computing.

Any perceptive casual observer could cite additional evidence that such relationships are indeed changing. All of us find ourselves interacting more with machines, and less with live human beings, as we deal with organizations. Bank accounts, bills, responses to complaints, correspondence, and other transactions are now routinely computerized. A few authors (e. g., Turkle [110] and Weizenbaum [117]) have begun to study the effects of these interactions, but we still know little about the prevailing forms and extent of computerized processes that organizations may substitute for direct dealings with people.

We suspect that profound economic forces will lead to further automation. It is widely acknowledged that human beings are becoming more and more expensive, relative to computer time. Hiring people to deal with the general public may thus become a luxury that organizations feel they cannot afford. A major New York bank recently tried to institute rules permitting only account holders with substantial deposits the privilege of doing business with a human teller. The effort was abandoned in the face of public protest and editorial reproach, but one can hardly doubt that similar moves will be attempted elsewhere.

Still, it would be wrong to conclude that the growing reliance on computing for mediation between organizations and the public must necessarily restrict and impoverish these relations. As with job content and worker satisfaction, a variety of tendencies and possibilities seems to be present. Computerization, after all, affords the capability of providing more information to more customers or account holders in less time, The only reliable grounds for judging which tendencies will prevail would be a study of a representative sample from a large and significant population of organizations.

THE IMPETUS TO INNOVATION

For most observers, the reasons for adopting computing in organizations are moot. It is taken as self-evident that organizations computerize in order to pursue long-standing goals of efficiency and cost-effectiveness. Rationalization, or the relentless effort to adopt the most efficient means to established ends, is seen as the hallmark of modern organizations. Computerization is considered the most eminently rational of present-day technological trends.

Against this view there is a long-standing alternative, originally and most persuasively articulated by Jacques Ellul [28]. In this view, new technologies do not arise simply as superior responses to preexisting problems, Rather, the "need" for innovation is the product of a mind-set that demands that every available technological possibility be developed as a matter of course. The evolution of technology is thus self-sustaining and autonomous—a catalyst for change in other sectors of society, rather than a response to interests generated elsewhere. Though planners may believe they are acting rationally in adopting new technologies, their decisions actually reflect a pervasive mystique that what can be developed, must be developed. This idea continues to have influence among modern critics of technology (e. g., Winner [121]).

In fact, this critical view is by no means unsupported in the empirical literature. True, the earliest writers on subjects like office automation considered the cost-benefit justifications of new technologies as too obvious to question [66]. However, other early studies that actually examined the effects of computer innovations in detail reported a more mixed picture [65, 118]. More recently, the URBIS study by the Irvine group has again shown how strong the tendency is, among managers in municipal governments, to perceive that the use of computers is the most rational choice (e. g., [27]). However, the participating authors themselves by no means take these perceptions at face value; indeed, they find savings through computing quite uneven among local governments and among departments within governments. They are confident that a savings is possible in the most favorable circumstances but unconvinced that any savings will necessarily be realized [57].

Downs [23] has pointed to some possible explanations. He shows, much as Laudon [65] has done, that changes in information organization may also be changes in power relations. Such findings suggest that efficiency claims for computing innovations may actually mask the political motives of the parties making the claims.

In the most penetrating empirically oriented study of these issues, King and Kraemer [57] examine why innovations in computing often seem to fail to yield expected benefits. They identify a number of hidden costs attached to new computing systems that are often ignored by planners-the interruptions of established organizational routines brought about by computing use, for instance. Even more important, they offer what strikes us as a very telling observation: New computing systems are often applied not only to existing organizational problems but to qualitatively new organizational activities. Thus, a new computing system for an accounting and finance department may be used to undertake much more thorough and far-reaching audits of the activities of other departments than anyone had previously considered necessary. In such cases it may be more reasonable to conclude that the availability of the technology incited the organizational "needs" to which it was applied, rather than the other way around.

These and other findings by members of the Irvine group provide tentative and tantalizing support for some of Ellul's seemingly incredible ideas. To be sure, their observations at this stage must be considered straws in the wind. Dutton and Kraemer base their observation on their sample of 572 larger municipal and county governments, for example. Are profit-making organizations more rigorous in their cost-benefit rationality? Can managers in most organizations even cite evidence for the cost-effectiveness of their systems? Does adoption of such systems correspond to shifts in organizational agenda?

CONCLUSIONS

The sheer variety of disparate and seemingly conflicting conclusions that can be derived from the studies noted may seem to warrant despair, Why do all these works add up to so few conclusive results? Is there really so little to show, by way of direct answers to the questions with which this review began?

For our part, we are obviously skeptical but by no means discouraged. The literature reviewed offers important lessons for future inquiry, especially by way of cautionary conclusions on relations between theories and empirical investigation on these issues. In particular, we believe that a priori reasoning proceeding from assumptions about principles that logically must describe the social impacts of computing in organizations is unproductive. On the contrary, we suspect that the transformations in organizational life through computing are so multifarious as to encompass the most disparate cause-effect relations in different contexts. There is no reason why computing should not result in deskilling in some settings and the enhancement of job content elsewhere, or in greater responsiveness to public needs in some organizations and diminished responsiveness in others. Indeed, one might well expect quite different effects to ensue from what appear to be the "same" causes in similar or even identical organizations, according to contextual changes in such things as the environments in which organizations act. In short, we see no reason to believe that any simple set of theoretical relationships can account for all the data that one might expect empirical inquiry to bring to light on these subjects.

The problem for research, as we see it, is twofold. First, one must determine, as far as possible, what particular cause-effect relations prevail in specific contexts. Where, for example, is computerization an authentic response to needs that are demonstrably fulfilled by the new technologies; and where, by contrast, might computerization actually create the needs that it is supposed to be fulfilling? Second, one must locate such cases as closely as possible within larger ranges of cases in which similar cause-effect relations can be expected to prevail. Clearly these requirements point to an ambitious program of inquiry. They suggest that large samples and extensive replication will be necessary—not so much to isolate the effects of computing in organizations, but to characterize such effects in their full variety.

We do not expect any of the problems considered above to be "solved" definitively, no matter how widely they are investigated. This does not dismay us. We believe that the social impacts of computing are infinitely variable but that the sources of these variations are eminently accessible to study. As long as investigators continue to study new organizations in new settings, new effects can be expected to emerge. The essential thing is that we continue confronting our theories with new data and that we not be afraid to modify theories in light of such confrontations.

REFERENCES

1. American Assembly. *Automation and Technological Change*. Prentice. Hall, Englewood Cliffs, N. J., 1982.
2. ANZAAS (Australian and New Zealand Association for the Advancement of Science). *Automation and Unemployment*. The Law Book Company, Sydney, Australia, 1979.
3. Argyris, C. Management information systems: The challenge to rationality and emotionality. *Manage. Sci.* 17, 6 (Feb. 1971), 275-292,
4. Attewell, P. The de-skilling controversy. Mimeo manuscr., Dept. of Sociology, State Univ. of New York, Stony Brook, 1982.
5. Attewell, P. Microelectronics and employment. Paper presented at the Conference on Microelectronics in Transition. Univ. of California, Santa Cruz, 1983.
6. Austrian Academy of Sciences. *Mikroelectronick: Anwendungen, Ver breitung und Auswirkungen: Am Beispiel Osterreichisches*. Springer-Verlag, Berlin, West Germany, 1981,
7. Barker, J., and Downing, H., Word processing and the transformation of the patriarchal relations of control in the office, *Cap. Cl,* 3 (1978), 64-99.
8. Bell, D. *The Coming of Post-Industrial Society*. Basic Books, New York, 1903.
9. Bjorn-Anderson, N., and Pederson, P., Computer facilitated changes in management power structures, *Account. Organ. Soc.* 5, 2(1977), 203-216.
10. Blau, P. M., McHugh Falbe, C., McKinley, W., and Tracy, P, Technology and organization in manufacturing. *Adm. Sci. Q,* 21, 1 (Mar. 1976), 20-40.
11. Blau, P. M., and Schoenherr, R, *The Structure of Organizations*. Basic Books, New York, 1971.
12. Bralove, M. Direct data: Some chief executives bypass and irk staffs in getting information. *Wall St. J.* (Jan. 12, 1983). 1.
13. Braverman, H. Labor and Monopoly Capital: The Degradation of Work in the Twentieth Century. *Monthly Review,* New York, 1974.
14. Cain, P., and Treiman, D. The D. O. T. as a source of occupational data, *Am. Sociol. Rev.* 46, 3(1981), 235-278.
15. Central Policy Review Staff. *Social and Employment Implications of Microelectronics*. H. M. Government, London, 1970.
16. Chern, A. B. Speculations on the social effects of new microelectronics technology. *Int. Labor Rev.* 119, 6 (Nov. -Dec, 1980), 705-721.

17. Cooper, C. M., and Clarke, J. A. *Employment, Economics and Technology: The Impact of Technological Change in the Labour Market.* St. Martin's Press, New York, 1982.
18. Craig, H. *Administering a Conversion to Electronic Accounting.* Division of Research, Graduate School of Business Administration, Harvard Univ., Boston, Mass., 1955.
19. Crozier, M. *The Bureaucratic Phenomenon.* Univ. of Chicago Press. Chicago, Ill., 1964.
20. DeKadt, M. Insurance: A clerical work factory. In *Case Studies in the Labor Process*, A. Zimbalist, Ed. Monthly Review, New York, 1979.
21. Delehanty, G. Office automation and occupation structure: A case study of five insurance companies. *Ind. Manage. Rev*, 7 (Spring. 1966), 99-108.
22. Deutsch, K. *The Nerves of Government.* The Free Press, New York, 1966.
23. Downs, A. A realistic look at the final payoffs from urban data systems. *Public Adm. Rev.* 27, 3 (Sept, 1967), 204-209.
24. Driscoll, J, How to humanize office automation. *Off. Technol. People* 1, 2-3 (Sept. 1982), 167-176.
25. Driscoll, J, Office automation: The dynamics of a technological boondoggle. In *Emerging Office Systems*, R. M. Landau and J. H. Blair, Eds. Norwood, N. J., 1982.
26. Dubnoff, S. Inter-occupational shifts and changes in the quality of work in the American economy, 1900-1970. Paper presented at the annual meetings of the Society for the Study of Social Problems, San Francisco, Calif., 1978.
27. Dutton, W., and Kraemer, K. Determinants of support for computerized information systems: The attitudes of local government chief executives. *Midwest Rev. Public Adm*, 12, 1 (Mar. 1970), 19-40.
28. Ellul, J, *The Technological Society.* Knopf, New York, 1964.
29. Equal Opportunities Commission. *New Technology and Women's Employment: Case Studies from West Yorkshire.* Equal Opportunities Commission, Manchester, England, 1982.
30. Ernst, M. The mechanization of commerce. *Scientific American* 247. 3 (Sept. 1982), 132-147.
31. ETUI (European Trade Union Institute). *The Impact of Microelectronics on Employment in Western Europe in the 1980s.* European Trade Union Institute, Brussels, Belgium, 1979.
32. Faunce, W. A, Automation and the division of labor. *Soc. Problems* 13 (Fall 1985), 149-160.
33. Freeman, C., Clark, J., and Soete, L. *Unemployment and Technical Innovation: A Study of Long Waves and Economic Development*, Francis Pinter, London, 1982.
34. Gershuny, J. I. *After Industrial Society?* Humanities Press, Atlantic Highlands, N, J., 1978.
35. Giuliano, V, The mechanization of office work, *Scientific American* 217, 3 (Sept. 1982), 140-165.
36. Glenn, E., and Feldberg, R, Degraded and deskilled: The proletarianization of clerical work. *Soc. Probl.* 25, 1 (Oct. 1977), 52-64.
37. Glenn, E., and Feldberg, R. Proletarianization of clerical work: Technology and organizational control in the office. In *Case Studies on the Labor Process.* A. Zimbalist, Ed. Monthly Review, New York. 1979.
38. Glenn, E., and Feldberg, R. Technology and work degradation: Re-examining the Impacts of office automation. Mimeo manuscr. . Dept. of Sociology, Boston Univ., Boston, 1980.
39. Granovetter, M. Small is bountiful: Labor markets and establishment size. *Am. Sociol. Rev.* To be published.

40. Greenbaum, J. *In the Name of Efficiency: A Study of Change in Data Processing Work.* Temple Univ. Press, Philadelphia, Pa., 1979.
41. Gregory, J., and Nussbaum, K. Race against time: Automation in the office. *Off. Technol. People* 1, 2-3(1982), 197-236.
42. Haber, W., Ferman, L., and Hudson, J. *The Impact of Technological Change: The American Experience.* W. E, Upjohn Institute for Employment Research, Kalamazoo, Mich., 1983.
43. Helfgott, R, B. EDP and the office workforce. *Ind. Labor Relat. Rev.* 19 (July 1966), 503-517.
44. Hiltz, S, R., and Turoff, M. *The Network Nation.* Addison-Wesley. Reading, Mass., 1978.
45. Hines, C., and Searle, G. *Automatic Unemployment.* Earth Resources Research, London, 1979.
46. Hoos, I, *Automation in the Office.* Public Affairs Press, Washington. D. C., 1960.
47. Horrowitz, M., and Herrenstadt, I. Changes in skill requirements of occupations in selected industries, In *The Employment Impact of Technological Change, vol, 2.* National commission on Technology, Automation. and Economic Progress, U. S. Government Printing Office, Washington, D. C., 1966.
48. Howe, L. *Pink Collar Workers,* G. P. Putnam, New York, 1977.
49. Huse, E. The impact of computers on managers and organizations: A case study in an integrated manufacturing company, In The *Impact of Computers on Management,* C. A. Myers, Ed, MIT Press. Cambridge, Mass., 1967.
50. International Conference on Automation, Full Employment. and a Balanced Economy. In *Proceedings.* American Foundation on Automation and Employment, 1967.
51. Jaffe, A. J., and Froomkin, J. *Technology and Jobs: Automation in Perspective.* Praeger, New York, 1966.
52. Jenkins, C., and Sherman, B. *The Collapse of Work,* Eyre Methuen. London, 1979.
53. JIPDEC (Japan Information Processing Development Center). The impact of microelectronics on employment. *JIPDEC Rep.* (Spring, 1980), 1-19.
54. JIPDEC (Japan Information Processing Development Center), The office of today and tomorrow. *JIPDEC Rep.* 47(1981).
55. JIPDEC (Japan Information Processing Development Center), The robots are coming. *JIPDEC Rep.* 50(1982).
56. Kahn, H. The future of the corporation. In *The Future of the Corporation,* H. Kahn, Ed. Mason and Lipscomb, New York, 1974.
57. King, J. L., and Kraemer, K. Cost as a social impact of telecommunications and other information technologies. Public Policy Research Organization, Irvine, Calif:, 1980.
58. Klatzky, S. R. Automation, size, and locus of decision-making, *J. Bus,* 43, 2 (Apr. 1970), 141-151.
59. Kling, R. The Impacts of computing on the work of managers, data analysts and clerks, Mimeo manuscr., Dept. of Information and Computing Science, Univ., of California, Irvine, Calif., 1978.
60. Kling, R. Social analyses of computing: Theoretical perspectives in recent empirical research, *ACM Comput. Surv.* 12, 1 (Mar. 1980), 61-110.
61. Kling, R., and Scacchi, W. The web of computing: Computer technology as social organization, *Adv. Comput.* 21(1982), 1-90.
62. Kraemer, K., and Danziger, J, Computers and control in the work environment, Mimeo manuscr., Public Policy Research Organization, Irvine, Calif., 1982.

63. Krail, P, Programmers and Managers: *The Routinization of Computer Programming in the United States*, Springer-Verlag, New York, 1977.
64. Kreps, J. M. *Automation and Employment*. Holt, Rinehart and Winston, New York, 1964.
65. Lane, R. The decline of politics and ideology in a knowledgeable society. *Am. Sociol. Rev.* 31, 5 (Oct, 1966), 649-662.
66. Laudon, K, *Computers and Bureaucratic Reform.* Wiley, New York. 1964.
67. Leavitt, M., and Whisler, T. Management in the 1980s, *Harvard Bus. Rev.* 36, 6 (Nov. -Dec. 1958), 41-48.
68. Leduc, N. Communicating through computers. *Telecommun. Policy* (Sept. 1979). 235-244.
69. Lee, H. C. Electronic data processing and skill requirements. *Pers. Adm,* 29 (May-June 1966), 50-53.
70. Leontief, W. The distribution of work and income, *Scientific American* 247, 3(1982), 188-204.
71. Lippitt, M., Miller, J. P., and Lalamaj, J. Patterns of use and correlates of adoption of an electronic mail system, *Proceedings of the American Institute of Decision Sciences*, Las Vegas, Nev., 1980.
72. Lowi, T. The Information revolution, politics, and the prospects for an open society, In *Government Secrecy in Democracies, I* Galnoor, Ed. Harper and Row, New York, 1977.
73. Mann, F., and Williams, L. Organizational impact of white collar automation, In *Annual Proceedings.* Industrial Relations Research Association, Madison, Wis., 1958, pp. 59-69.
74. Mann, F., and William, L. Some effects of the changing work environment in the office, 18(1962), 90 -101.
75. Markus, M. L. *Systems in Organizations.* Pitman Publishing Marshfield, Mass., 1984.
76. Mechanic, D. Sources of power and lower participants in complex organizations. *Adm. Sci. Q.* 7(1982), 349-364.
77. Menzies, H. *Women and the Chip: Case Studies of the Effects of Informatics on Employment in Canada.* Institute for Public Policy, Montreal, Canada, 1981.
78. Mowshowitz, A, *The Conquest of Will: Information Processing in Human Affairs,* Addison-Wesley, Reading, Mass., 1976.
79. Moynihan, D. P. The professionalization of reform. *Public Interest 1.* 1 (Fall 1985), 6-16.
80. Mueller, E. *Technological Advance in an Expanding Economy: Its Impact on a Cross-Section of the Labor Force*, Institute for Social Research, Ann Arbor, Mich., 1969.
81. Mumford, E., and Banks, O. *The Computer and the Clerk* Routledge, Kegan Paul, London, 1967.
82. Myers, C. *The Impact of Computers on Management.* MIT Press, Cam bridge, Mass., 1967.
83. National Commission on Technology, Automation and Economic Progress. *Technology and the American Economy*, vol. 1. U. S. Government Printing Office, Washington, D. C., 1966.
84. National Commission on Technology, Automation and Economic Progress. The employment impact of technological change. In *Technology and the American Economy*, vol. 2. U. S. Government Printing Office, Washington, D. C., 1966.
85. Netherlands Government, *The Impact of Chip Technology on Employment and the Labour Market,* Ministerie Van Sociale Zaken, The Hague, The Netherlands, 1979.

86. Netherlands Government, *The Social Impact of Micro-Electronics.* Netherlands Government Publishing Office, The Hague, The Netherlands, 1980.

87. Nora, S, . and Minc, A. *The Computerization of Society: A Report to the President of France.* MIT Press, Cambridge, Mass., 1980.

88. Olson, M. H, New information technology and organizational culture, *Manage. Inf Syst. Q.* (1982).

89. Olson, M. H., and Lucas, H. C. The impact of office automation on the organization: Some implications for research and practice. *Commun. ACM* 25, 11 (Nov. 1982), 838-847.

90. Organization for Economic Cooperation and Development. *The Requirements of Automated Jobs.* OECD, Paris, France, 1965.

91. Pfeffer, J. *Organizational Design.* AHM Publishing, Arlington Heights, Ill., 1978.

92. Pfeffer, J. *Power in Organizations,* Pitman Publishing, Marshfield. Mass., 1981.

93. *Processed World 1.* 1 (Spring 1981).

94. Response Analysis Corporation, *Office Automation and the Work place.* Honeywell, Minneapolis, Minn., 1983.

95. Rico, L. The staffing process and the computer. *Manage. Pers. Q. 1.* 4 (Autumn-Winter 1962), 32-38.

96. Robey, D. Computers and management structure: Some empirical findings re-examined. *Hum. Relat.* 30, 11(1977), 963-976.

97. Robey, D, Computer information systems and organizational structure. *Commun. ACM* 24, 10 (Oct. 1981), 679-687.

98. Rothwell, R., and Zegveld, W. *Technical Change and Employment.* Frances Pinier, London, 1979.

99. Rule, J. *Private Lives and Public Surveillance,* Schocken, New York. 1974.

100. Rule, J., McAdam, D., Stearns, L, and Uglow, D. *The Politics of Privacy.* Elsevier, New York, 1980.

101. Rule, J., McAdam, D., Stearns, L., and Uglow, D. Documentary identity and bureaucratic surveillance in America. *Soc. Probl.* To be published.

102. Rumberger, R. The changing skill requirements of jobs in the U. S. economy. *Ind. Labor Relat. Rev.* 34(1981), 578-590.

103. Shepard, J. *Automation and Alienation: A Study of Office and Factory Workers,* MIT Press, Cambridge, Mass., 1971.

104. Shils, E. *Center and Periphery: Essays in Macrosociology,* Univ. of Chicago Press, Chicago, Ill., 1975.

105. Sleigh, J., Boatwright, B., Irwin, P., and Stanyan, R. *The Manpower Implications of Micro-Electronic Technology.* H. M. Stationery Office. London, 1979.

106. Smith, A. *The Geopolitics of Information.* Oxford Univ., New York. 1980.

107. Smith, A. *Goodbye Gutenberg.* Oxford Univ., New York, 1980.

108. Spenner, K. Temporal changes in work content. *Am. Sociol. Rev.* 44. (1979), 985-975.

109. Stinchcombe, A. Institutions of privacy in the determination of police administrative practice. *Am. J. Sociol.* 69, 2 (Sept. 1981), 1-10.

110. Terborgh, G. *The Automation Hysteria,* W. W. Norton, New York. 1965.

111. Turkle, S. Study of human interactions with computers. *The Second Self* Simon and Schuster, New York, 1984.

112. United Kingdom Government. *Technological Change: Threats and Opportunities for the United Kingdom,* H. M, Stationery Office, London, 1979.

113. U. S. Bureau of Labor Statistics. The introduction of an electronic computer In a large insurance company. In *Studies on Automation Technology 2*, U. S. Government Printing Office, Washington, D. C., 1955.

114. U. S. Dept. of Health, Education and Welfare, *Work in America*, MIT Press, Cambridge, Mess., 1973.

115. Verbatim Corporation. *The Verbatim Survey: Office Worker Views and Perceptions of New Technology in the Workplace*. The Verbatim Corporation, Sunnyvale, Calif., 1982.

116. Wallace, M., and Kalleberg, A, Industrial transformation and the decline of craft: The decomposition of skill in the printing industry, 1931-1978, *Am. Sociol, Rev.* 47, 3(1982), 307-324.

117. Weber, C. E. Impact of electronic data processing on clerical skills. *Pers. Adm.* 22-33, 1 (Jan. -Feb. 1959), 20-26.

118. Weizenbaum, J. *Computer Power and Human Reason*. W. H. Freeman, San Francisco, Calif., 1976.

119. Westin, A., and Baker, M. *Databanks in a Free Society*. Quadrangle Times Books, New York, 1972.

120. Whisler, T. *The Impact of Computers on Organizations*. Praeger, New York, 1970.

121. Whisler, T., and Meyer, H. The impact of EDP on life company organization. Pers. Adm. Rep. 34, Life Office Management Association, 1987.

122. Winner, L. *Autonomous Technology*. MIT Press, Cambridge, Mass. . 1977.

123. Withington, F. *The Real Computer: Its Influences, Uses and Effects*. Addison-Wesley, Reading, Mass., 1969.

124. Zimbelist, A., Ed, *Case Studies on the Labor Process*, Monthly Review, New York, 1979.

TECHNOLOGY AND EMPLOYMENT:
INNOVATION AND GROWTH IN THE U.S. ECONOMY[2]

Panel on Technology and Employment
National Academy of Sciences
National Academy of Engineering
Institute of Medicine

TECHNOLOGY AND AMERICAN ECONOMIC WELFARE

Technological change transforms the production of goods and services and improves the efficiency of production processes. It also allows the production of entirely new goods and services. Since the beginnings of American industrialization, such change has been a central component of U.S. economic growth, growth that has been characterized by the creation of new industries and the transformation of older ones as a result of innovations in products and processes. Technological advance has also played an increasingly important role in the growth of income per person during the past 100 years; its contribution to that area and to economic growth is likely to increase still further as the United States becomes more closely linked to the global economy.

The use of new technologies in production processes frequently reduces the labor and other resources needed to produce a unit of output; these reductions in turn lower the costs of production and the employment requirements for a fixed output level. If reductions in the demand for labor were the only effect of technological change on employment, policymakers addressing the problem of maintaining U.S. economic welfare would only have to balance the contributions of technological change against the costs of higher unemployment.

However, technological change has other important effects that historically have enabled society to achieve greater prosperity without sacrificing employment. By reducing the costs of production and thereby lowering the price of a particular good in a competitive market, technological change frequently leads to increases in output demand; greater output demand results in increased production, which requires more labor, offsetting the employment impacts of reductions in labor requirements per unit of output stemming from technological change. Even if the demand for a good whose production process has been transformed does not increase significantly when its price is lowered, benefits still accrue because consumers can use the savings from these price reductions to purchase other goods and services. In the aggregate, therefore, employment often expands. Moreover, when technological change results in the development and production of entirely new products, employment grows in the industries producing these new goods. Historically and, we believe, for the foreseeable future, reductions in labor requirements per unit of output resulting from new process technologies have been and will continue to be outweighed by the beneficial employment effects of the expansion in total output that generally occurs. Indeed, the new realities of the U.S. economy of the 1980s and 1990s will make rapid development and adoption of new technologies imperative to achieving growth in U.S. employment and wages.

One crucial new reality of the U.S. economy of the 1980s is that it is more "open" to international trade than was the American economy of the 1950s and 1960s. The increased importance of trade means that higher productivity growth, which is supported by technological change, is essential to the maintenance of higher real earnings and the preservation of U.S. jobs. Moreover, the more rapid rates of international technology transfer characteristic of the modern economic environment mean that the knowledge forming the basis for commercial innovations need not be domestic in origin, just as U.S. basic research has underpinned the technological advances of firms in other nations.

The relative rates of development and adoption by U.S. and foreign industries of new process technologies affect the rates of growth in labor productivity (output per worker) in those industries and therefore can produce differences in labor costs among U.S. and foreign firms. To the extent that foreign firms develop and adopt new technologies faster than U.S. firms, the production costs of foreign producers will fall more rapidly. Barring shifts in U.S. and foreign currency exchange rates, declines in the wages of U.S. workers, or comparable technological advances by U.S. firms, these reductions in foreign producers' costs will decrease markets for U.S. firms and ultimately reduce jobs for American workers within the affected industries. To remain competitive in the absence of technological change and labor productivity growth in these industries, U.S. labor costs, relative to those of foreign producers, must be lowered, either by direct reductions in wages or through government policies that support devaluation of the dollar. Either of these methods decreases U.S. workers' incomes relative to those of foreign workers. Thus, if U.S. firms fall behind foreign firms in developing and adopting new technologies, the alternatives are not attractive—U.S. workers must accept fewer jobs or lower earnings.

Yet, if U.S. firms consistently develop and adopt new technologies more rapidly than foreign producers, the picture is quite different. The resultant higher productivity growth in U.S. industries will support reductions in production costs, which will enable U.S. workers to retain higher-wage jobs. Because new knowledge and technologies developed in the United States now are transferred to foreign competitors more rapidly than they were in the past, however, any technology-based advantages held by U.S. firms and workers over foreign firms and workers are likely to be more fleeting in the future. A key factor in sustaining American living standards and employment thus is continued public and private investment in the generation of new knowledge. Of equal importance, however, is the need for U.S. firms to advance from fundamental knowledge to commercial innovations more rapidly than in the past.

We have defined our task in this study as that of analyzing the contribution of technological change to employment and unemployment. Because technological change plays a limited role in determining total employment, its impacts in this area are primarily sectoral in nature, and those impacts are affected only indirectly by aggregate economic conditions. We therefore regard the design of macroeconomic policies aimed at achieving high levels of aggregate demand and employment as outside this panel's charge. Despite the increased importance of international trade for this economy and the role of technological change within it, a discussion of trade policies also would have taken this panel far beyond its charge; trade policy therefore was not considered in detail by the panel.

Our principal finding may be succinctly stated:

> Technological change is an essential component of a dynamic, expanding economy. Recent and prospective levels of technological change will not produce significant increases in total unemployment, although individuals will face painful and costly adjustments. The modern U.S. economy, in which international trade plays an increasingly important role, must generate and adopt advanced technologies rapidly in both the manufacturing and nonmanufacturing sectors if growth in U.S. employment and wages is to be maintained. Rather than producing mass unemployment, technological change will make its maximum contribution to higher living standards, wages, and employment levels if appropriate public and private policies are adopted to support the adjustment to new technologies.

Technological change often involves difficult adjustments for firms and individuals. Workers must develop new skills and may be required to seek employment in different industries or locations. In many cases, workers suffer severe financial losses as a result of permanent layoffs or plant closings. Managers also face serious challenges in evaluating and adopting new manufacturing and office technologies in an increasingly competitive global economy.

Given these realities, we recommend policies to help workers adjust to technological change. Our recommendations propose initiatives to aid displaced workers through job search assistance, basic skills training, training in new job-related skills, and advance notice of plant shutdowns and large-scale permanent layoffs. Through these initiatives we focus on the need to assist individuals who experience hardship as a result of technological change and to aid them in securing new employment. We also offer recommendations that call on U.S. firms to develop and adopt new technologies more rapidly and suggest policies—both public and private—that might encourage them to do so.

The technological revitalization of American industry that is the goal of these recommendations is essential to the national welfare. The alternative to rapid rates of technological change is stagnation in U.S. wages and employment. In the end, no trade-off need be made between the goals of high levels of employment and rapid technological change. Policies that help workers and managers adjust to technological change can aid and encourage the adoption of productivity-enhancing technologies.

Technological change poses significant challenges to government policymakers, business, and labor, as well as to individual workers. Although the United States remains a technological and economic leader, the performance of this economy in adopting new technologies, achieving higher levels of productivity, and dealing with the adjustment of workers to new technologies leaves a great deal to be desired. If business, labor, and government fail to develop appropriate adjustment policies, the eventual price may be reduced technological dynamism and a decline in the international competitiveness of the U.S. economic system.

CENTRAL FINDINGS

In addition to the principal finding already stated, the central findings of this panel cover a number of dimensions of the employment impacts of technological change and form the basis for our policy recommendations, summarized below and discussed in greater detail in Chapter 10 of our full report. The complete set of findings for this study is compiled in Chapter 9.

EMPLOYMENT AND WAGE IMPACTS
OF TECHNOLOGICAL CHANGE IN AN OPEN ECONOMY

• *Historically, technological change and productivity growth have been associated with expanding rather than contracting total employment and rising earnings.* The future will see little change in this pattern. As in the past, however, there will be declines in specific industries and growth in others, and some individuals will be displaced. Technological change in the U.S. economy is not the sole or even the most important cause of these dislocations (see Chapters 2 and 3).

• *The adoption of new technologies generally is gradual rather than sudden.* The employment impacts of new technologies are realized through the diffusion and adoption of technology, which typically take a considerable amount of time. The employment impacts of new technologies therefore are likely to be felt more gradually than the employment impacts of other factors, such as changes in exchange rates. The gradual pace of technological change should simplify somewhat the development and implementation of adjustment policies to help affected workers (see Chapter 2).

• *Within today's international economic environment, slow adoption by U.S. firms (relative to other industrial nations) of productivity increasing technologies is likely to cause more job displacement than the rapid adoption of such technologies.* Much of the job displacement of the past 7 years does not reflect a sudden increase in the adoption of laborsaving innovations but instead is due in part to increased U.S. imports and sluggish exports, which in turn reflect macroeconomic forces (the large U.S. budget deficit and the high foreign exchange value of the dollar during 1980—1985), slow adoption of some technologies in U.S. manufacturing, and other factors (see Chapters 2 and 3).

• *The rate of technology transfer across national boundaries has grown; for the United States, this transfer increasingly incorporates significant inflows of technology from foreign sources, as well as outflows of U.S. research findings and innovations.* In many technologies, the United States no longer commands a significant lead over industrial competitor nations. Moreover, technology "gaps" (the time it takes another country to become competitive with U.S. industry or for U.S. firms to absorb foreign technologies) are likely to be shorter in the future (see Chapter 3).

TECHNOLOGY AND THE CHARACTERISTICS OF TOMORROW'S JOBS

• *New technologies by themselves are not likely to change the level of job-related skills required for the labor force as a whole.* We do not project a uniform upgrading or downgrading of job skill requirements in the U.S. economy as a result of technological change. This does not deny the need, however, for continued investment and improvement in the job-related skills of the U.S. work force to support the rapid adoption of new technologies that will contribute to U.S. competitiveness (see Chapter 4).

• *Technological change will not limit employment opportunities for individuals entering the labor force with strong basic skills.* The most reliable projections of future job growth suggest that the number of jobs in the broad occupational categories accounting for the majority of entrant employment will continue to expand. Combined with a projected lower rate of growth in the entrant pool, this conclusion suggests that labor force entrants with strong basic skills (numerical reasoning, problem solving, literacy, and written communication) will fare well in the job markets of the future (see Chapter 5).

TECHNOLOGY AND WORK FORCE ADJUSTMENT

• *A substantial portion—from 20 to 30 percent—of displaced workers lack basic skills.* These workers often remain unemployed longer and have difficulty finding new jobs without incurring significant wage reductions. In view of the fact that technological and structural change in this economy will place increasing demands on the ability of workers to adjust, experienced workers who lack basic skills will face even greater difficulties in future job markets (see Chapter 3).

• *The evidence suggests that displaced workers who receive substantial advance notice of permanent job loss experience shorter periods of unemployment than workers who do not receive such notice.* Substantial advance notice (several months) of permanent layoffs or plant shutdowns appears to reduce the severity of worker displacement. Moreover, such a policy can improve the effectiveness of job search assistance, counseling, and retraining programs, thereby reducing the public costs of unemployment (see Chapter 7).

• *The primary federal program for displaced workers, Title III of the Job Training Partnership Act (JTPA), emphasizes the rapid placement of workers in new jobs. It does not appear to serve the needs of many displaced workers.* JTPA provides little training for the substantial number of displaced workers who need better basic skills; it also provides little extended training in job-related skills for other workers (see Chapter 7).

• *Displaced worker adjustment assistance programs reduce the duration of unemployment after displacement and result in higher wages in new jobs obtained immediately after participation in such programs.* There is limited evidence on the specific contribution of retraining in basic and job-related skills (a component of many such programs) to the employment and earnings prospects of displaced workers. Nevertheless, it would be wrong to conclude from this that retraining is ineffective or that it has a negative impact on earnings or reemployment prospects. Too little is known about the components of effective adjustment programs for displaced worker populations with different characteristics because of the paucity of rigorous evaluations of such programs. Additional policy experiments and evaluations are badly needed to improve these programs (see Chapters 7 and 8).

POLICY OPTIONS AND RECOMMENDATIONS

Our policy options and recommendations are based on the conclusion that, with an appropriate policy structure, technological change can support growth in U.S. employment and living standards. Toward that end, we have developed options and recommendations for the public and private sectors that emphasize three broad initiatives in public and private sector policies: (1) public policies to aid worker adjustment to technological change; (2) public policies to support the development and application of advanced technologies; and (3) improvements in labor-management cooperation in the adoption of new technologies, as well as improvements in private managers expertise in evaluating and implementing new technologies.

Although the overall U.S. standard of living and average real (inflation-adjusted) wages generally increase as a result of technological change, individuals suffer losses. Many of our public policy recommendations stem from the belief that a portion of the affluence created by technological change should be used to assist those suffering losses as a result of it. In addition, public policies that deal with the equitable distribution of gains and losses from technological change can facilitate such change by reducing the resistance of potential losers to new technologies in the workplace. Just as management policies to support adoption of new technologies within the firm must address worker concerns about adjustment and employment security (see Chapter 7 of our full report), public policies that aid adjustment can reduce potential resistance to new technologies and support their more rapid adoption. On balance, if policies are developed that will ease the burden of adjustment for those individuals faced with job loss and thereby facilitate the adoption of new technologies, all members of our society can benefit.

RECOMMENDATIONS FOR THE PUBLIC SECTOR

Policies For Worker Adjustment

Our options and recommendations for assisting worker adjustment to technological change focus on the two groups that may be affected adversely by such change: experienced workers who may lose their jobs as a result of the adoption of technology, and labor force entrants, whose employment prospects may be reduced by technological change. Our options and recommendations to assist experienced displaced workers focus primarily on modifications in the primary federal program for which technologically displaced workers, as well as workers displaced by other causes, are eligible, Title III of JTPA. We also suggest other policies (advance notification of plant shutdowns and large-scale layoffs) to enhance the effectiveness of Title III. Our recommendations to aid labor force entrants focus on the need for additional research and actions based on the reports of other expert groups, a decision that reflects the fact that a complete evaluation of policies affecting the educational attainment and basic skills preparation of entrants is beyond the scope of this report. Our public policy recommendations also address the impacts of technological change on the employment prospects for minority and female members of the labor force.

Options for Adjustment Assistance for Displaced Workers

We recommend that action be taken to improve existing JTPA Title III programs of job search and placement assistance and training in both basic and job-related skills for displaced workers. We recommend that some or all of the following options be implemented:
- broadening the range of employment services provided to displaced workers and those facing imminent displacement, including job counseling, skills diagnosis, job search assistance, and placement services;
- increasing the share of Title III funds devoted to training in basic and job-related skills;
- broadening income support for displaced workers engaged in training;

• instituting a program of federally provided direct loans or loan guarantees, administered by state or local authorities, to workers displaced by technological change, plant shutdowns, or large-scale layoffs (these loans could be used by displaced workers to finance retraining or relocation or to establish new businesses); and

• establishing a program for demonstrations and experiments with rigorous evaluation requirements to test and compare specific program designs.

In addition to these modifications to JTPA, we recommend revising state unemployment compensation laws to guarantee explicitly that displaced workers who are eligible for unemployment compensation can continue to receive benefits while undertaking retraining.

We have concluded that the federal government should be the primary source of funding for the abovementioned policy options. Federal financing is preferable to state funding because of the inequities created by differences in the level of state resources for such programs. Indeed, states that are experiencing severe economic dislocations are likely to face serious problems in funding significant displaced worker programs. In view of the fact that one of the central motives for worker adjustment programs is the equitable distribution of the costs and benefits of new technology adoption among the U.S. population, the avoidance of regional inequities is an important consideration. One option for financing the economic adjustment loans, like the arrangements for other federal loan programs, would employ the Federal Financing Bank and therefore would not require federal funds from general revenues.

Estimates of the costs of these adjustment assistance options for displaced workers depend on estimates of the population of displaced workers. In Chapter 3, we note that estimates of the number of workers displaced annually range from 1 million, if displaced workers are defined as individuals with 3 years' employment in their jobs prior to layoff, to 2.3 million. Cost estimates also depend on assumptions about the rates of worker participation in such programs, an area in which reliable data are scarce. Existing programs that combine income support with retraining for displaced workers, such as the UAW-Ford program, have enrolled 10—15 percent of the eligible population (see Chapter 7). Although we lack conclusive evidence on this point, it may be that participation rates would be higher in programs involving displaced workers from industries that pay lower wages than the automotive industry.[3]

We have compiled estimates of the costs to the federal government of job search assistance, training, and extended unemployment compensation for two values of the annual flow of displaced workers (the two values are drawn

---

[3]Participation rates also will be affected by the policies and guidelines adopted by states in administering any system of training, job search assistance, and income support.

from the 1984 survey of displaced workers conducted by the U.S. Bureau of Labor Statistics): 1 million workers, which is the estimated number of displaced workers who had been employed for 3 or more years in the job from which they were displaced; and 2.3 million, which is the estimated total number of workers suffering permanent job loss. As estimated rates of participation in these programs range from 5 to 30 percent of the displaced worker population, the estimated costs of these policy options range from $131 million (5 percent participation rate) to $786 million (30 percent) for an annual flow of 1 million displaced workers. It is important to note that the highest estimated participation rate exceeds any observed thus far in a displaced worker training program in the United States. If we assume that the flow of eligible displaced workers is 2.3 million annually, the estimated costs of the program range from $301 million (5 percent participation rate) to about $1.8 billion (30 percent).[4] JTPA Title III outlays for fiscal year 1987 are roughly $200 million, although a significant expansion has been proposed in the President's budget for fiscal year 1988.

How could these policy options be financed? The panel discussed revenue alternatives and found no single method that was preferable to all others on equity and other grounds. In the absence of evidence suggesting that one alternative is superior to all others, the decision on funding sources and budgetary reallocations is properly political, involving considerations that extend well beyond this panel's charge.

Advance Notice of Plant Closures and Large Permanent Layoffs[5]

We have concluded that substantial (a minimum of 2–3 months) advance notice of permanent plant shutdowns and large permanent layoffs offers significant benefits to the workers who are displaced and to the nation by reducing the average duration of the workers' unemployment and lessening the public costs of such unemployment. The current system of voluntary advance notice, however, fails to provide sufficient advance notice to many U.S. workers. We therefore recommend that federal action be taken to ensure that substantial advance notice is provided to all workers. Although the panel agreed on the need for federal action to broaden the coverage of advance notice within the U.S. work force, panel members were not unanimous in their support of a specific legislative or administrative mechanism to achieve this goal. The panel believes that the following alternatives are viable options to achieve broader advance notice, with appropriate provisions to reduce the burden on small business and provide for unforeseen circumstances:

---

[4]If the annual flow of displaced workers is estimated to amount to 1.2 million workers (the estimate used by the Secretary of Labor's Task Force on Economic Change and Dislocation, 1986), the estimated costs of these options range from $157 million to $943 million.

[5]Panel member Anne O. Krueger dissents from this recommendation. Her statement appears at the end of the Executive Summary and in Appendix D of the full report.

• federal action to require employers to provide substantial advance notice of permanent plant shutdowns and large permanent layoffs; or

• federal action to provide tax incentives for employers to give such notice.

The current system of voluntary advance notice does not provide workers with the "best-practice" amount of advance notice (a minimum of 2–3 months)—as Chapter 7 notes, too few workers are notified in advance of permanent plant closures or large permanent layoffs, thus hampering their adjustment. When workers receive sufficient advance notice, the evidence suggests that they adjust more rapidly and more successfully to job loss, which reduces the costs of displacement to them and to the public sector. We believe that the benefits of advance notice more than outweigh the costs of such a policy—costs that exist, but that are distributed differently, when no advance notice is provided. When advance notice is given, the costs of worker displacement are shared by taxpayers, by the displaced workers, and by the firms closing plants or permanently discharging workers, rather than being borne primarily by taxpayers and the workers being laid off.

Through its public policies, this society has made a judgment that the costs of many regulations (e.g., those covering health and safety, consumer protection, or securities markets) that enhance the flow of information to workers and consumers and distribute costs more equitably among workers, consumers, and firms are more than offset by the benefits of such policies. We believe that advance notice falls into the same category of public policy and that steps to mandate this practice should be taken by the federal government.

Training for Labor Market Entrants

We share the concerns of other studies, set forth in the reports of the COSEPUP Panel on Secondary School Education for the Changing Workplace ("High Schools and the Changing Workplace: The Employers' View," 1984), the Task Force on Teaching as a Profession, of the Carnegie Forum on Education and the Economy ("A Nation Prepared: Teachers for the 21st Century," 1986), and the U.S. Department of Education ("A Nation at Risk: The Imperative for Educational Reform," 1983), regarding the amount and quality of basic skills preparation provided to laborforce entrants by U.S. public schools. Improvement in the basic literacy, problem-solving, numerical reasoning, and written communication skills of labor force entrants is essential. We endorse additional public support for research on strategies to achieve this goal, as well as financial support for the implementation of programs that improve the basic skills of laborforce entrants and of those already in the labor force who lack these skills.

Equal Employment Opportunity

We recommend more vigorous enforcement of policies to combat racial and sexual discrimination in the labor market as a means of improving the ability of minority and female workers, as well as minority and female labor force entrants, to adjust to the demands of technological change.

Science And Technology Policy To
Support The Adoption Of New Technologies

We support continued high levels of investment by industry and the federal government in basic and applied research—this is the essential "seed corn" of innovation, and such investments play a significant role in the education of scientists and engineers. Federal support for nondefense R&D is particularly important, in view of the limited commercial payoffs from the high historical levels of defense R&D in this country (there are important but limited exceptions to this generalization, as noted in Chapter 2). The foreseeable contribution of defense R&D to the civilian U.S. technology base appears to be limited at best.

In addition to a strong research base, however, public policies to support more rapid adoption of new technologies within this economy deserve consideration. The historic focus of post-World War II science and technology policy on the generation rather than the adoption of new civilian technologies (once again, a generalization with several important exceptions) contrasts with the orientation of public science and technology policy in several other industrial nations (e.g., Japan, Sweden, and West Germany) and may have contributed to more rapid adoption of manufacturing process innovations and more rapid commercialization of new product technologies in those nations. We therefore support the development and evaluation of additional public policies to encourage the more rapid adoption of new technologies within the United States.

We recommend increased federal support for activities and research to encourage more rapid adoption of new technologies. Although the achievement of this goal requires actions in a number of areas not considered by this panel, our review of policies leads us to recommend the following options for consideration:

• Strengthen research on technical standards by public agencies (primarily the National Bureau of Standards) to support, where appropriate, private standard-setting efforts.

• Strengthen research programs supporting cooperative research between industry and the federal government in the development and application of technologies.

• Increase support for federal programs to improve U.S. firms' access to foreign science and engineering developments and innovations.

The Adequacy Of The Data

In the course of this study, the panel has found that the data available from public sources are barely sufficient to analyze the impacts of technology on employment. In some cases this data problem reflects the rapid expansion of new sectors of the economy, such as services, for which federal agencies have been hard-pressed to monitor and collect data comparable in quality and quantity to those available for manufacturing. In other cases these data have declined in quality during the past decade as a result of reductions in data collection budgets. The amount and quality of data on evaluations of worker adjustment assistance programs also must be improved.

• We recommend that post-fiscal year 1980 reductions in key federal data collection and analysis budgets be reversed and that (at a minimum) these budgets be stabilized in real terms for the next decade in recognition of the important "infrastructural" role data bases play within research and policymaking. We urge that a portion of these budgets be devoted to improvements in the collection and analysis of employment, productivity, and output data on the nonmanufacturing sector of this economy.

• We recommend that a new panel study or a supplement and follow-up to the Current Population Survey be undertaken by the Bureau of Labor Statistics to examine the effects of technological change on the skill requirements, employment, and working conditions of individuals of working age. We also support the development by the Census Bureau of better data on technology adoption by firms.

• We recommend that the Bureau of Labor Statistics expand its survey of displaced workers (the special supplement to the Current Population Survey) to allow annual data collection and that this survey improve its question on the nature and effect of advance notice of layoffs.

• We recommend that any expansion of adjustment assistance services for displaced workers be accompanied by rigorous evaluations of these programs to provide information on the long-term effectiveness of different program designs and strategies.

To reduce the potential for conflicts of interest that may arise when an organization charged with operating adjustment assistance programs has sole responsibility for the design and administration of evaluations of these programs, we recommend that federal or state agencies responsible for the operation of such programs share with other agencies the responsibility for evaluating them, or conduct such evaluations with the advice of independent expert panels.

• We recommend that evaluations be undertaken of the implementation of the provisions of the Perkins Vocational Education Act of 1984 that allow federal and state funds to be used for improving the skills of the employed work force. In addition, a federally sponsored evaluation of a sample of state-level programs in upgrade training should be undertaken to determine the overall effectiveness of such programs and the specific design features that contribute to success.

Health And Safety Impacts Of Technological Change

We recommend a major interdisciplinary study of the consequences of technological change for workplace health and safety and the regulatory structure designed to ensure that worker health and safety are protected. These areas also should be monitored carefully by federal and state agencies.

RECOMMENDATIONS FOR THE PRIVATE SECTOR

Labor-Management Collaboration In Technology Adoption

Rates of adoption of new technologies, as well as the exploitation of computer-based manufacturing and office automation technologies to increase worker productivity, satisfaction, and safety, are affected significantly by the management of the adoption process. If the process proceeds smoothly, both workers and management can benefit from these technologies, which have the potential to enrich work as well as to enhance its efficiency. The potential payoffs from cooperation between labor and management in technology adoption are high, but such cooperation has been lacking in some U.S. industries. Our recommendations in this area highlight some key components of successful adoption strategies.

Elements of "Best-Practice" Strategies for Technology Adoption

• We recommend that management give advance notice of and consult with workers about job redesign and technological change.

• We recommend that the adoption of new workplace technologies be accompanied by employment policies that strengthen employment security; such policies include retraining of affected workers for other jobs and a reliance on attrition rather than on permanent layoffs wherever possible. At the same time, workers and unions must recognize their stake in a more productive workplace and consider modifications of work rules and job classifications in exchange for such employment security policies.

Protection from the Costs of Displacement

We recommend that management and labor explore the use of severance paymentsfor permanent layoffs of experienced workers. To preserve such benefits in the event of a firm's bankruptcy, we also recommend that employers and workers consider establishing a joint insurance fund.

Education For Managers

We recommend that the current efforts to strengthen the quality of managerial education in the management, adoption, and evaluation of advanced manufacturing and service production processes be continued, both within business schools and through other institutions. Additional research on this topic is needed and could be funded through university—industry research collaboration, among other possibilities. Education for those currently employed as managers also must be strengthened to incorporate instruction in the adoption of new technologies and in strategies for helping the work force adjust to technological change.

STATEMENT OF ANNE O. KRUEGER

Advance notification of layoffs is undoubtedly beneficial to those workers who will lose their jobs. If there were no negative side effects associated with advance notification, it would clearly be beneficial to all.

There will be several side effects, however, if notification is mandatory. First, the necessary enforcement apparatus would increase the cost of doing business. Second, for all firms, but especially for risky ones, knowledge that layoffs could not be made on short notice would increase incentives to use capital and hire fewer workers. To the extent that fewer jobs would be created, the proposed requirement would hurt the employment prospects of those the proposal is designed to assist. That mandatory periods prior to layoffs can result in smaller levels of employment has been well documented in a number of developing countries. Third, requirements of advance notification reduce the flexibility of firms already in difficulty. The requirement is, in effect, the same as a tax for these firms.

I conclude that advance notification is desirable, and efforts to educate employers of its value to employees should be encouraged. With respect to mandatory notification, however, I believe that the evidence is far from sufficient to warrant such a step.

REFERENCES

Carnegie Forum on Education and the Economy, Task Force on Teaching as a Profession. (1986). *A nation prepared: Teachers for the 21st century.* New York: Carnegie Corporation.
COSEPUP (Committee on Science, Engineering, and Public Policy) Panel on Secondary School Education for the Changing Workplace. (1984). *High Schools and the changing workplace: The Employers' view.* Washington, DC: National Academy Press.
Secretary of Labor's Task Force on Economic Adjustment and Worker Dislocation. (1986). *Economic adjustment and worker dislocation in a competitive society.* Washington, DC: US Government Printing Office.
U.S. Department of Education. (1983). *A nation at risk: The imperative for educational reform.* Washington DC.

READING QUESTIONS

1) How were Marx's concerns about technology similar to those we express today?
2) What is wrong with the broad *a priori* claims that are usually made about technology and employment?
3) What is the deskilling argument? According to this argument, what are the social and technological causes and their effects on job skills?
4) What is the upgrading argument? According to this argument, what are the social and technological causes and their effects on job skills?
5) How can we best explain the contradictory finding in the deskilling/upgrading literature?

6) What are the DOT studies, and are they better than single-case studies? What are their shortcomings?

7) What are the advantages of the survey techniques reported here, and what do these studies say about the deskilling/upgrading argument?

8) Why might the private sector differ from the public sector in it mix of deskilling and upgrading?

9) What is the "novelty effect"? How can it explain perceived upgrading?

10) What is "jobless growth," and why might technology be implicated in it?

11) What are the pessimistic and optimistic explanations for the connection between employment and technology?

12) What are the difficulties of using case study data to answer questions about the effects of technology on employment?

13) What are the arguments of those who think technology will centralize or decentralize power and authority relations in organizations? What data argue for each position?

14) What conclusion does Robey draw about these studies?

15) Why would it be wrong to conclude that technology will inevitably restrict the communication between organizations and the public?

16) How can efficiency claims for a new technology mask the political motives of those parties making the claims?

17) What would be the problem if reductions in the demand for labor were the only effect of technological change on employment?

18) How can increases in demand come from technological change?

19) What is the panel's conclusion about the effects of technology on unemployment?

20) Why is high productivity growth essential to continued employment?

21) Why might foreign firms' adoption of technology decrease markets for U.S. firms and reduce jobs for American workers?

22) What are the alternatives if U.S. firms fall behind foreign firms in adopting new technology?

23) Why is it important for U.S. firms to advance from fundamental knowledge to commercial innovation more rapidly than in the past?

24) What difficult individual and organizational adjustments result from the necessary increase in adoption of technology by U.S. firms?

25) Why is there a gradual pace of technological change, and how does this effect the displacement of workers?

26) Why are strong basic skills (rather than technical skills) emphasized by the panel?

27) Why is substantial advance notice helpful for those who are laid off because of technological advances?

28) Why are "policy experiments" needed with advance notice of layoffs"

29) What three broad initiatives does the panel recommend?

30) What basic belief underlies the panel's recommendations?

31) How does the equitable distribution of costs reduce the resistance to new technologies in the workplace?

32) What is the purpose of the several adjustment assistance options that the panel recommends?

33) What factors influenced the panel's cost estimates for the implementation of these programs?

34) What was the disagreement about with regard to advance notice of plant closings?

35) Why is it important to change government funding of defense projects into government funding of other basic and applied research?

36) Why is data collection important to planning for federal assistance to displaced workers?
37) What recommendations does the panel make to the private sector? What is the panel's reasoning for these recommendations?

DISCUSSION QUESTIONS

1) Attewell & Rule present a number of simple claims about the effects of technology on the workplace. What is similar about all these claims? What is similar about all the "It's more complicated than that" answers?
2) If there is no requirement for advance notice of plant closings, do the costs associated with unexpected layoffs go away? If not, who has to bear them? How does this square with the panel's assumptions about equitable distribution of cost?

PRACTICING THE DESIGN ETHIC

1) Test some of the findings mentioned in the executive summary on Technology and Employment. The class should form five groups; each group should be assigned to interview one of the following categories of people: managers of computer departments, officials from a local union, managers from local business sites using computers, end users from local businesses that use computers, and computer science professors. Each group should interview at least four people in their assigned category. For each interview, test the Central Findings mentioned in the executive summary. State the findings and ask for the interviewee's opinion about the statement. Ask all the interviewees to describe their experiences that lead them to their conclusions, and their views on how to address the issue:
   - Technological change and productivity growth have been associated with expanding rather than contracting total employment and rising earnings.
   - The adoption of new technologies generally is gradual rather than sudden.
   - Within today's international economic environment, slow adoption of productivity increasing technologies is likely to cause more job displacement than rapid adoption of such technologies.
   - New technologies by themselves are not likely to change the level of job-related skills required for the labor force as a whole.
   - Technological change will not limit employment opportunities for individuals entering the labor force with strong basic skills (numerical reasoning, problem solving, literacy, and written communications).
   - A substantial portion - from 20 to 30 percent - of displaced workers lack basic skills.

   Summarize your findings and report to the class. Then, compare and contrast the opinions of the different groups. Are there different perspectives and opinions among the various groups. Compare the solutions described by the interviewees to the policy recommendations mentioned in the executive summary.
2) Draw a flow chart of the effects of technological change on employment. Be sure to include all the feedback loops. Use the flow chart to describe the effects of some of the policy recommendations the panel made.

CHAPTER
9
WORK IN ONLINE COMMUNITIES

Technological determinism is the idea that if a technology is appropriate to a task, it will be applied in the way the designers intend and will have the effects that the designers envision. When applied to technology and office work, this view suggests that there are simple communication problems organizations face that technology can address. Furthermore, these problems are isolated and solving them will not change the way the organization basically functions, except to streamline it. Finally, the view suggests that managers and executives will adopt the technology and use it in the ways the designers envision.

Both articles in this chapter take issue with this model. Kraut argues that the telework revolution has not occurred—and may never occur—because the traditional office supports "a large number of activities crucial to the functioning of any work organization." Thus, radical changes will be resisted, since they may not support these activities. For this reason, the conservative world of business has attempted to appropriate the gains from technology without radically changing the traditional office. This means that most "telework" is done by professional (rather than clerical) office workers, and that it is primarily a supplement to regular office work. The technology also allows organizations to move office work to areas that have lower wages, while still replicating the traditional office environment.

Although it may not eliminate the traditional office, technology can change it. Sproull and Kiesler investigate the ways that incorporating electronic communication into the traditional organization will change the ways people in those organizations interact. Electronic interaction reduces time and space restrictions on communication and reduces cues that indicate status in the organization. This has the potential to change the ways that workers in an organization interact with each other. Though not as revolutionary as the (sputtering) "telework revolution," this change is significant, and is likely to be long-lasting.

PREDICTING THE USE OF TECHNOLOGY:
THE CASE OF TELEWORK[1]

Robert E. Kraut
Bell Communications Research

Recently a number of scholarly articles and articles in the popular press have argued that new computer and telecommunication technology is enabling flexibility in work arrangements that was previously unavailable (e.g., Becker & McClintock, 1981; Giuliano, 1981a & 198 lb; If home is where the worker is, 1982; McClintock, 1981; Nilles, Carlson, Gray, & Hanneman, 1976; Olson, 1982, 1983; Schiff, 1983; Toffler, 1979). In the extreme, Toffler argues that new technology enables an "electronic cottage" and the radical transformation of work in America. In a more cautious and scholarly tone, Olson (1983) argues that the technology enables "space and time independence" of work. Commentators predict by the 1990s that between 10% (e.g., Kelly cited in Chabrow, 1985) and 40% (J. Carpenter, cited in Bell Communications Research News, 1985) of work will be performed from home using computers and telecommunications equipment. These predictions are based on changes in the occupational structure of the United States economy and changes in the technology with which people do work. But they also are based on a technologically deterministic view of the world that assumes if technology is appropriate it will be applied. By 1980, about 40% of the United States work force were office workers (Panko, 1984). Commentators make the claim that office automation technology—the electronic storage, retrieval, manipulation, and communication of records, messages, documents and other information—frees office workers from the confines of a standard 9-to-5 business day in a conventional office. Because white-collar workers can remotely receive, send, and act on the information they need to do their jobs, they can now work whenever and wherever their circumstances and their bosses allow them.

The intention of this chapter is to examine two components of these claims, that remote work is a transformation of the way work currently is done in America and that new technology is a cause or at least an enabler of that transformation. I treat telework as a workplace innovation and examine it in the context of what we already know about the spread of innovations across people and across organizations. My conclusion is that the new technology, indeed, has the potential for transforming work, but that it does not now serve that function and it may never do so. The independence of space enabled by the telephone in the early part of this century did not lead to

---

[1]From Kraut, R. E.. (1987). Predicting the use of technology: the case of telework. In R. Kraut (Ed.). *Technology and the transformation of white collar work* (pp. 113-133) Hillsdale, NJ: Lawrence Erlbaum. Copyright © 1987 by Lawrence Erlbaum Associates, Inc. Reprinted by permission.

the dissolution of the conventional office (Pool, 1977). So too the current technology, per se, is unlikely to lead to a dispersed work force.

At the present time, much white-collar work is done outside of the confines of the standard workplace and standard worktime (Giuliano, 1981a), much of it without the help of computers or new telecommunications technology. In addition, the new technology that has been introduced into the workplace is being used to maintain current work styles rather than transform them. I conclude from these observations that the use of new computer and communication technology is neither a necessary nor a sufficient condition for the work style flexibility implied in the remote work or electronic cottage concepts.

WHAT IS TELEWORK?

Telework, remote work, or telecommuting[2] is the use of computers and telecommunications equipment to do office work away from a central, conventional office. Work can be performed at the alternate site full time or for several days a week. The alternate work site can be the employee's home, a satellite work center close to the worker's residence, or transient locations such as hotels or public transportation. Although working in homes, hotels, and planes frees workers from the constraints of a conventional office, work in a satellite work center simply moves a conventional office closer to home without changing the work style likely to be performed at that site. In this chapter I concentrate on telework at home.

Large numbers of workers are potentially able to work at home, although as Kraemer (1982) points out, reliable estimates of the numbers of jobs that are appropriate for telework or the numbers of workers who might ultimately adopt teleworking are not available. Some work requires that the worker be at a particular location (e.g., assembly-line work or work requiring face-to-face contact with others). Other work doesn't require a worker in a fixed location. This is especially true for "information workers," whose task is the production, collection, transformation, and distribution of information (Kraemer, 1982).

The United States economy consists of large numbers of information workers. Porat (1977), using detailed input/output analyses of the United States market, estimated that by 1975 information workers had accounted for over 50% of the United States labor force. Unfortunately, even among information workers, we have no precise definition of the type of work that could be done remotely and no good mappings of our vague definitions to the U.S. Census Bureau's or Labor Department's occupational classifications.

---

[2]*Telecommuting* (Nilles et a.. 1976) is a frequently used term for this phenomenon, but the word is an awkward back formation from such terms as *telecommunication* and *television. Tele* means at a distance or from afar and thus telecommuting would be redundant, meaning commuting from afar (i.e., standard commuting), just as telecommunication is communication from afar. *Telework* (Giuliano, 1981a, 198lb), working from afar or at a distance, is the better term and will be used here.

Some white-collar information workers may be able to perform much but not necessarily all of their work remotely. This would include such job categories as accountants, computer specialists, librarians, writers, editors, purchasing agents, sales managers, stock and bond sales agents, billing clerks, and stenographers. Other white-collar information workers, such as therapists, teachers, photographers, curators, insurance adjusters, office managers, bank tellers, cashiers, and mail carriers, could perform little if any of their work remotely as it is now constituted with current technology. A rough estimate of the maximum number of workers who could work remotely at least part time is 50% of white-collar workers (Harkness, 1977) or roughly 26 million workers.[3]

TELEWORK NOW

Energy conservation was the initial justification for research on telework (Harkness, 1977; Nilles et al., 1976). As a result, the primary focus of research on this topic has been on workplace substitution, that is, working at home or other remote sites in lieu of work at the central office. The thesis of this section is that remote work occurs to a large degree now, but in ways that do little to shake the dominance of work at a conventional office. Instead, individuals and corporations use computers and telecommunications equipment for workplace augmentation, in which work at home or another remote site is added to work done in a convention office. In addition, corporations have suburbanized work, moving components of their conventional offices away from central cities to the suburbs, and have exported office jobs as well.

NATIONAL SAMPLES

Despite optimistic predictions, workers who work at home represent only a small proportion of the nation's workforce. According to Census Bureau figures, the proportion of people who work at home has been decreasing. The decennial census asks respondents about their means of transportation to work during the week preceding the census survey. Respondents could indicate that they worked at home. This census question is certainly not an ideal measure of the prevalence of home work in general and of telework (i.e., electronic home work) in particular. For example, respondents were asked only about their primary work site. Multiple job holders were asked only about the job at which they spent most hours. The census provides no information about the technology used on jobs. The target week may not

---

[3] Many professional occupations that are candidates for teleworking are growing quickly in percentage terms (e.g., para-legal personnel, computer systems analysts, computer programmers, and aero-astronautic engineers all have estimated growth rates over 70% from 1978 to 1990; Carey. 1982). The candidate occupations with the greatest growth in terms of numbers, however, tend to be clerical. For example, general office clerks, secretaries, typists, accountants and auditors, and hand bookkeepers all have projected employment growth of over 200,000 from 1978 to 1990 (Carey, 1981).

Occupational grouping	N (thousands)	% home work
All nonfarm workers	82,235	1.6%
Executive, administrative, and managerial	10,079	2.1
Professional	12,409	1.9
Technicians and related support	3,002	.6
Sales Occupation	9,478	1.8
Administrative support, including clerical	16,441	1.1
Private household service	480	11.7
Protectice service	1,276	.4
Service, except private and protective	10,089	2.3
Farming, forestry, and fishing	1,552	8.8
Precision production, craft, and repair	12,396	1.1
Machine operators	6,156	.6
Fabricators, assemblers, & hand work	3,073	.6
Transportation, & material moving	3,336	.5
Handlers, cleaners, helpers, laborers	5,385	.5

Note: Computed from U.S. Bureau of The Census (1980).

Table 9.1
Percentage of home work by occupation.

have been a typical work week. And yet the census is the only source of data on a large, representative sample of the United States labor force and is therefore the source of the best available data in the United States on the prevalence and distribution of home work.

In 1960, only 3.6% of the nonfarm labor force worked at home as their primary place of employment. In 1970 the figure was 2.0%, and in 1980 it was 1.6% (unpublished data computed from the U.S. Census public use micro sample). These figures are, of course, old and do not encompass the 1980s when personal computers were spreading rapidly through corporations and homes. They do, however, encompass the last major wave of office automation, in banking and insurance during the 1970s.

Table 9.1 shows the distribution of home work among occupations. We see a small amount of home work among white-collar workers: executives, professionals, technicians, sales, and administrative support. In 1980, if we look only among white-collar workers, home workers were disproportionately managers and executives, writers, editors, and entertainers, sales people, information clerks, social workers and social scientists. On the other hand, white-collar workers who disproportionately work in conventional locations include communications equipment operators, college teachers, scientists and engineers, mathematics professionals, health professionals, and administrative support personnel.

These data, of course, estimate the amount of work done from home regardless of technology. Thus, daycare providers, who run a daycare business in their basements are counted as well as authors who write on a personal computer or computer programmers who communicate with a mainframe computer in another state. If we restrict our search to telework the use of computers and telecommunications to substitute for travel to a conventional work site—the data are virtually nonexistent and the estimates, unreliable as they are, are much lower. For example, Electronic Services Unlimited (1984), a consulting firm specializing in telework, after reviewing the literature and analyzing a number of company pilot projects, estimated that there were about 10,000 teleworkers in the United States.

Although few people work at home as their major place of employment, many people work at home as an adjunct to their conventional office jobs. An AT&T (1982) national probability sample of households found that a large proportion of American households had members who worked at home on at least a part-time basis. Of the households in the AT&T sample, 54% contained individuals who were employed outside the home; more than 30% of those employed brought work home with them. That is, about 16% of the households in their sample had workers who brought work home from outside employment. Those who brought work home were primarily employed in white-collar, information sector, office jobs. Thus, 88% of those who brought work home were in managerial, professional, technical, sales, or administrative support occupations compared to only 52% of those who brought no work home. Similarly 60% of those who brought work home had an office or school as the location of their outside employment versus only 36% of those who brought no work home. These home workers tended to work in the evenings and on weekends.

In addition, 22% of households had some income-producing business conducted from home, generally small (grossing less than $5,000), young businesses (less than 2 years old) employing only the proprietor. These tended to be service or product sales businesses.

The tasks that both groups—those who brought work home and those who operated a business from home—performed at home did not require sophisticated computer or telecommunications equipment. They used the telephone frequently. Over half also read and did clerical and financial work, although financial work was not done frequently. Besides the telephone, paper, pencil and calculators were the only frequently employed tools.

In summary, these national samples show only a small proportion of workers whose home is their major place of employment. Furthermore, this proportion is decreasing. On the other hand, the data show large numbers of information workers who occasionally bring work home, using the telephone, but no sophisticated computer equipment. In addition, a surprisingly large number of small sales and service businesses are run from home.

HIGH TECHNOLOGY CASE STUDIES

We can get another perspective on the numbers of information workers who use telecommunications technology to work at home by looking at the behavior of workers in high technology companies. (See also Olson, 1987). These workers have relatively sophisticated computer and telecommunication technology available to them in their conventional office work, may have similar, company-provided facilities available at home, and are likely to be among the American households who currently have personal computers at home. They are therefore likely to use or want to use the technology available in the conventional workplace when they work at home. As such, they act as innovation leaders (Hippel, 1983), previewing the behavioral adaptations that the general public is likely to make as new technology becomes more widely distributed.

IBM

As an example, consider IBM's telecommuting experiment (Miller, 1983). In 1981, because the management at IBM feared future shortages of computer scientists and electrical engineers, they conducted a large scale experiment in which 300 volunteer programmers worked at home. The management believed that teleworking would allow them to attract and retain qualified workers. IBM implemented teleworking on a larger scale for programmers and marketing representatives after establishing through their trial that employee productivity had increased and that the company could manage logistics and security. In 1983, IBM paid for telephone line, modem, and terminal costs for over 8,000 professionals who worked at home. Company guidelines stated, however, that the home work was not in lieu of work during regular hours at a company location. According to official company policy, these employees could work as much as they wanted at home as long as they put in a standard work week in the office. (Informal arrangements, of course, may have been different.)

Other Teleworking Experiments

The National Academy of Sciences (1985) recently held a symposium on telework, at which a number of organizations described their experiences with this form of work reorganization. Five large employers described pilot projects they had initiated with teleworking. These projects typically allowed a small number of highly motivated, volunteer employees to perform most or all of their normal work from home. I briefly describe the organizations' evaluations in the following section on benefits. For the present purposes, I should just note that most organizations were satisfied with their ability to manage employees who worked from home and with these employees' productivity. However, perhaps the most surprising finding reported at the National Academy of Sciences' conference was that despite the testimonials these organizations bestowed upon their telework experiments, none was dramatically increasing the numbers of its teleworking employees to even 1% of its work force. For none of these organizations was telework to be routine.

Variable	Office workers	Home workers	t (Office > Home)
	(n = 169)	(n = 153)	
Age in years	31.7	33.7	-1.98
% female	30.3	24.3	1.19
Years of education	16.2	17.3	-5.44
% living with spouse	58.6	69.9	-2.13
Number of children	.49	.54	-.55
Minutes commuting	29.3	28.4	.52
Salary level			
(1 = low, 7 = high)	4.3	4.9	-4.4
% with clerical job	10	2	2.8
% with administrative job	6	6	.01
% with technical job	81	90	-2.17
Job autonomy			
(1 = low, 5 = high)	3.5	3.7	-1.6
Job satisfaction			
(1 = low, 5 = high)	3.0	3.1	-1.1
Work group satisfaction			
(1 = low, 5 = high)	3.7	3.5	-1.9
Hours worked at office	33.5	36.5	-3.4
Hours worked at home	0	7.5	-17.0
Hours not worked	.55	1.4	-3.4
Hours interested in			
home work	13.6	17.7	-3.4
Hours job would allow			
home work	16.6	19.6	-2.4

Table 9.2
A comparison of office workers versus home workers

Informal Work at Home

In 1983 and 1984 I conducted a study of over 300 computer users at AT&T Bell Laboratories and AT&T Information Systems to examine informal home work arrangements in a high technology company. (Additional details of the research are available in Kraut, in press.) Respondents were employed by research and development companies that had, to a large extent, automated clerical work and provided managers and professionals with relatively mature computer-based tools to perform work. For example, virtually all document preparation in these companies was done using computer terminals attached to mini-computer-based text-processing systems. Much of the clerical work was done personally by professionals and managers, rather than through a clerical support staff. Virtually no professional or managerial workers had typewriters and almost all had terminals at their desks, ranging from stand-alone graphics workstations to personal computers, to dumb terminals connected to mini-computer hosts. Most technical employees were on corporate electronic mail networks that allowed them to communicate with and send documents to co-workers in their own departments or across the country; in addition, electronic mail gateways allowed them to communicate with researchers in universities and private research organizations. Electronic bulletin-boards and news programs brought in information from around the country. With the pervasive use of office automation technology in this setting, we would expect that workplace effects that might follow the widespread diffusion of office automation more generally would already have occurred here.

I sent an electronic survey to 727 computer users, selected at random from among the recent users of 14 company-owned computers in New Jersey, Illinois, and Colorado. Four hundred and fourteen users answered the questionnaire, of whom 327 gave relatively complete and usable answers.

Table 9.2 shows some characteristics of the sample. The sample was 68% male, 64% were married or living with a person of the opposite sex, had an average age of 32 years, and had an average of 17 years of education (i.e., some graduate training). Most were technical professionals divided among researchers in mathematics, computer science, and the behavioral sciences, software developers, hardware developers, and systems engineers; the proportion of clerical workers and administrative workers underestimated the proportions working in the company as a whole.

The central concern of this research was identifying the amount of time workers actually worked at home and the factors that allowed them and impelled them to work there. It is important to note that according to company policy, a standard work week was 37.5 hours long and was performed on site. These was no company-wide provision for home work and no company-sponsored experiments on this work arrangement, but individual workers could work out informal arrangements.

The first major point to be noted from this research is that although many people worked at home on an informal basis, they tended to augment work at their conventional offices, not substitute for it. Although on average, workers worked a full work week in the office, about 50% of them also worked at home. Although some employees substituted work at home for work in the office on an hour by hour basis, others added time in the office whenever they worked at home. Overall, the more time people spend working at home the more time they also spend working in the office (or vice versa). Of the 322 respondents who answered the appropriate question, 153 had worked at home in the week preceding the survey, an average of 7.5 hours, (i.e., a full working day). But they also worked 36.5 hours at a company location, significantly more than the 33.5 hours put in by those people who did no work at home.

Second, employees would like to work at home much more than they did. Figure 9-1 shows this dramatically. The employees who worked at home an

Category		Office	Home	t (Office > Home)
Cognitive	Read	1.02	1.50	-5.0
	Write	0.78	1.16	-4.6
	Program	0.28	0.86	-22.1
Social	Talk about work (face-toface)	1.30	0.16	1.5
	Talk about nonwork (face-to-face)	0.18	0.08	7.3
	Attend meetings	0.28	0.0	3.9
	Telephone	0.72	0.39	3.9
	Electronic mail	0.34	0.67	-4.3

Note: Entries have been standardized within location, so that a 0 indicates activity was never performed at a given location and a 1 indicates that an activity was performed a standard deviation more frequently than other activities at that location.

Table 9.3
Tasks in office and at home.

average of 7.5 hours per week were interested in working at home almost 18 hours per week. Those who at the time of the survey did no work at home were interested in working there almost 14 hours per week. Respondents to this survey also believed that their jobs would allow them to work 18 hours per week at home on average. Figure 9-1 compares the distribution of actual hours worked at home with the distribution of the number of hours employees wanted to work at home and thought that their jobs would allow them to do so. The discrepancy between these two distributions suggests that organizational constraints rather than personal or job-related ones had limited the amount that employees worked at home.

Third, employees who worked at home showed a division of labor across space. A comparison of the work they did at home with the work they did in their offices is presented in Table 9.3. Respondents estimated the frequency in the previous week with which they engaged in each of a number of work tasks, separately for tasks performed at home and in a company work location. One can summarize the findings by noting that employees use their conventional office for social tasks and their home for cognitive tasks. Thus, as Table 9.3 shows, compared to their work in an office, when these employees worked at home they were more likely to read, write, and program, and less likely to talk to colleagues face-to-face or on the phone. Among the social activities, only the use of electronic mail was performed from home more than from the office. Presumably, this results from the asynchronous nature of electronic mail communication. Although telephone communication can overcome the spatial isolation of working at home, it cannot overcome the temporal isolation.

Finally, the variables predicting the amount people actually worked at home were not the same ones that predicted the amount they wanted to work

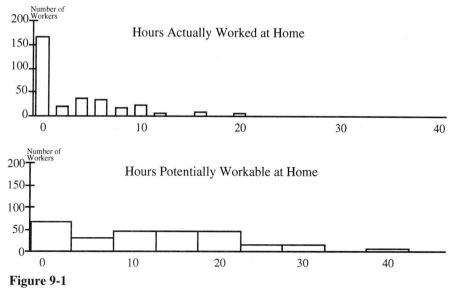

Figure 9-1
Comparison of actual versus potential home-based work.

at home or the degree to which their jobs allowed them to work successfully at home. The effects of family life on working at home were complex. Interestingly, in this sample of salaried employees who performed supplementary home work, having a spouse led them to work at home, but having children made them less likely to want to work at home and to believe that they could do it successfully.

BENEFITS OF REMOTE WORK

Given that large numbers of people could potentially work at home, how many will ultimately do so and who will they be? It's hard to predict the future and harder yet when the past is so poorly understood. Our abilities to predict the extent to which telework will transform the nature of work in America must of course be based on our knowledge of current trends in the workplace, such as I've presented here. But, in addition, we can draw inferences from parallel processes, the spread of other technological and behavioral innovations.

The literature on the spread of innovations is a rich one, dating from anthropological and sociological work in the early part of this century (see Katz, Levin, & Hamilton, 1963; Rogers, 1983 for reviews). By 1983, the literature contained over 2,200 empirical books and articles as well as many more essayistic discussions. Despite the limitations of the work to date (see Brewer, 1980 for a good review), work on diffusion of innovation generally can raise our sensitivity to factors that may be important in predicting the spread of telework, as well as other workstyle innovations (cf. Walton 1975,

1977). A fundamental dictum in this literature is that characteristics of an innovation are only some of the many factors that influence its spread.

To understand the diffusion process, we need to know much about the potential adopters, especially their values and pre-existing behavior patterns, and the benefits they may derive from the innovation, because these are the attributes that have the strongest associations with the adoption of innovation across studies (Tornatzky & Klein, 1982). The following sections below consider in detail two of these characteristics: the potential benefits that adopters of telework are likely to derive and the behavioral and value shifts they are likely to endure.

TELEWORK: WHO BENEFITS?

Of what value is teleworking to its adopters? For telework to succeed both organizations as employers and the people they employ need to accept it. The benefits of telework, therefore, depend on whether we are considering employers or employees. In addition, we must distinguish between professional/managerial and clerical/support workers.

The Professional-Clerical Distinction

Differences in the nature of the work of professional and managerial workers and clerical and support workers, differences in their labor supply, differences in their labor market characteristics, differences in their working conditions, and differences in their power all have implications for the suitability of telework for these workers and the benefits that they and their employers could derive from it.

First, consider the major difference in their sex composition and associated characteristics. As Figure 9-2 shows, compared to managerial or professional work, clerical work is women's work. Overall, in 1982 the United States labor force was 43.5% female. Among professional and technical workers, 45.1 % of the workers were female and among managers and administrators it was 28.0% female. On the other hand, clerical work is 80.7% female.[4]

Women are an increasing proportion of the labor force (up from 33% in 1960, to over 43% in 1983). In 1960 35% of women were in the labor force; by 1980 this had risen to 52%. Much of this rise came from married women,

---

[4]These summary statistics misrepresent the degree of occupational segregation by sex by aggregating heterogeneous collections of occupations. Occupational segregation by sex within particular occupations is much higher (Reskin, 985) and within jobs in particular firms is almost total (Bielby & Baron, 1985). For example, although professional and technical workers are 43.5% female, some occupations suitable for telework within this class are heavily male (e.g., engineers are 94.3% male and lawyers and judges are 84.6% male) whereas others are heavily female (eg., librarians, archivists. and curators are 80.7% female). Even among heavily female clerical workers, some occupations are heavily male (eg. shipping and receiving clerks are 75.2% male) whereas others are almost exclusively female (eg., secretaries are 99.2% female, typists 96.6%, receptionists 97.5%).

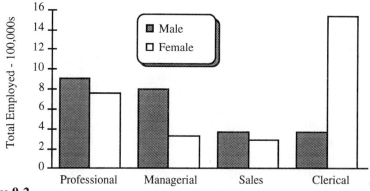

Figure 9-2
Occupation and gender of white collar workers, 1982.

especially those with children. In 1960 18.6% of married women with children under 6 in intact families were in the labor force; by 1981 this had risen to 48.7%. Most separated and divorced women with children have always had to work to support their children. As a result, their labor force participation isn't increasing as dramatically, because it started at a high level.

Given that clerical work is primarily women's work, that in our society women are primarily responsible for childcare, and that large numbers of women with young children work, a major difference between clerical workers and others is the extent to which they must integrate their work lives with their child-care responsibilities.

The second major difference between clerical workers and professional or managerial workers inheres in the work itself. Professional or managerial work is more autonomous than is clerical work (Hackman & Oldham, 1980). The greater freedom for professional employees to decide what tasks to perform and when to perform them, their greater freedom from supervision, their vaguer performance standards, and the longer deadlines associated with their tasks may make their jobs more appropriate than clerical ones for telework. Certainly, these factors change the style of remote supervision that would be appropriate for remote professional as opposed to remote clerical workers.

The third major difference between clerical work and professional or managerial work is in its legal definition. Clerical work is generally covered under the Fair Labor Standards Act. This act, as amended, covers such conditions of work as minimum wages and overtime pay. Professions and managers are generally exempt from these standards.

Finally, as Iacono and Kling (1987) point out, clerical workers are generally at the bottom of an office power hierarchy and have little power to shape their conditions of work.

BENEFITS TO EMPLOYERS

Availability

The major benefits of telework to employers are personnel-related. Employers who allow or encourage their professional or managerial employees to telework generally expect two gains: a larger pool of scarce, skilled labor and increased productivity from that labor (National Academy of Sciences, 1985). Professional workers who might be more available as a result of telework are those who need to mesh family and work obligations (e.g., female heads of households or members of dual career families).

Employers of clerical workers often are interested in cheaper, more docile labor, although more abundant supplies of more productive labor also would be appreciated. In part, they achieve this cost reduction by coupling home work with an arms-length employment relationship to their employees, for example, by hiring them as independent contractors rather than as regular employees. Thus, employers of teleworking clerical workers typically pay piece-rate wages to temporary workers who receive no fringe benefits (e.g., Geisler, 1985; Olson, 1987).

Productivity

The data on the effects of teleworking on workers' productivity are sparse; they suggest that people who work at home are more productive than office-based workers. McClintock (1981), for example, interviewed 20 university professionals. He noted that increased time spent teleworking was associated with greater efficiency on routine work tasks, greater effectiveness on complex and nonroutine work tasks, and resultant gains in productivity.

Supplementing formal research by academics, corporations have evaluated their own pilot projects less formally. Teleworking has been tried in a small number of well-publicized pilot projects. Electronic Services Unlimited (1984), a private consulting firm, had identified 24 teleworking experiments or pilot projects with evaluation. The pilot projects typically had 6 to 25 highly motivated, volunteer participants performing most or all of their normal work at home. The pilot projects reported at a recent National Academy of Sciences (1985) conference on teleworking were unanimous in concluding that teleworking increased productivity. Productivity among both clerical and managerial teleworkers typically increased about 15% to 25%, using a variety of productivity measures, both subjective and objective. For example, Blue Cross/Blue Shield of South Carolina reported more claims processed with fewer errors for clerical workers keying in transactions (Geisler, 1985); the U.S. Army reported programmers writing more lines of code (McDavid, 1985); Mountain Bell reported course writers writing more courses that helped students learn better (Phelps, 1985).

These same studies suggest that employees were generally happy working at home. (The unhappy workers in these pilot projects were able to return to conventional employment.) To the extent that teleworking increased workers' job satisfaction, it should also increase their time at work and their commitment to the job (i.e., decrease absences, tardiness, and turnover), for both professional and clerical workers. Job satisfaction, itself, however, has no effect on productivity, the quality or quantity of output per unit time worked (Locke, 1976).

One must hesitate about accepting these findings, however, given the generally poor research methodologies, non-comparable control groups, and selective samples used in these evaluations. A careful reading of the literature suggests that to the extent that productivity gains are associated with telework, they are probably the result of highly motivated, volunteer workers putting in more time on their jobs when they were working at home than when they were working in a conventional office, (i.e., a self-selection effect). The gains may not be sustained with more general use of teleworking by less motivated workers who have no choice but to work at home.

Overhead

Finally, most employers can reduce their overhead costs by encouraging teleworking, either by moving some employees to cheaper locations (e.g., satellite locations away from expensive, central cities) or by shifting the cost of office space, equipment, or utilities to the employee (e.g., through unreimbursed home offices). Whether employers actually reduce costs, of course, depends on the trade-off between reduced overhead, increased productivity, and increased communications costs.

Miscellaneous benefits to employers include decreases in relocation costs and decreases in disability payments when disabled workers can maintain employment at home. When the teleworkers use central computing resources, doing so from home tends to distribute the computer use throughout the day and night and effectively decreases the organization's needed computer capacity.

BENEFITS TO EMPLOYEES

Some benefits to employees accrue regardless of the type of employee. Thus, teleworkers reduce their commuting time (which in the United States averages about 1 hour per day round trip), reduce their incidental costs (e.g., transportation,[5] clothes, or restaurant costs), and increase their flexibility to coordinate their work with their personal schedules and responsibilities.

---

[5]Reduction in transportation costs is in the national interest as well as in the interest of particular employees. The original research on teleworking (Nilles, et at 1976) was interested in the cost trade-offs between travel and communication, especially as this trade-off affected energy needs. Nilles et al. predicted substantial declines in energy consumption with increases in the numbers of people working at or near their homes. Harkness (1977) estimated that 25% of all United States motor fuel consumption and 11% of the nation's petroleum consumption were due to commuting or the journey to work. For example, in 1980 the 38 standard metropolitan statistical areas with populations of 1 million or more represented

	Work-site last week			
	On-site		Home	
Variable	Male	Female	Male	Female
N (thousands)	23,638	26,936	371.2	456.0
White	91.1%	87.9	95.6	96.1
Age	38.8	36.1	46.8	43.3
Years of education	14.8	13.5	14.6	13.5
Married couple household	57.1%	31.9	44.9	54.0
Own children at home	92.2%	85.0	66.5	95.2
Preschool children at home	17.9%	13.2	10.8	19.7
Work-limiting disability	4.9%	3.2	10.6	7.1
Part-year or parttime	25.8%	51.8	40.6	74.0
Self-employed or employee of own corporation	14.0%	3.7	65.0	50.8
Wages & self-employment income (all white collar workers)	$18.0K	8.0	12.0	3.0
Wages & self-employment income (full-time white collar workers)	$20.0K	10.8	17.0	8.1
Below poverty cutoff	2.6%	4.1	8.3	6.7

Note: Computed from U.S. Bureau of The Census

Table 9.4
Descriptive statistics for home workers versus conventional workers (white collar workers only).

Other benefits depend on whether the worker is professional or clerical and male or female. For workers who also are responsible for child care—especially female clerical workers, whose wages are too low to afford fulltime, paid child care—teleworking provides an opportunity to combine at least part-time work with childcare. Table 9.4 shows a demographic profile of men and women who were identified as working at home on the 1980 U.S. Census. It shows that compared to those who work in conventional places, a home worker is likely to be a married women in an intact family with a young child, who is self-employed, and works part-time. This constellation suggests that home work is indeed being used to combine paid employment and childcare (see Kraut & Grambsch, 1985). Similarly, tele-working provides the handicapped, the elderly, or otherwise homebound workers with new employment opportunities.

Professional workers, with others to care for children (e.g., paid child-care or compliant spouses), gain a more distraction-free work environment

---

about 49% of the employed civilian labor force. Approximately 79% of these workers commuted to work in private automobiles, 61.2% alone and 17.7% in car-pools (U.S. Bureau of the Census, 1983).

that meshes better with their lifestyles. On the other hand, because women with young children and other homebound workers have few other options in the labor market, their situation leaves them vulnerable to exploitation by employers.

Organized labor is very sensitive to the exploitation that teleworking may invite. Labor unionists point to the abuses of the past in the garment, glove, and jewelry trades that led to the Federal Government's banning of some home-production work (Chamot, 1987; Chamot & Zalusky, 1985). These abuses included low wages, poor benefits, long hours without overtime pay, hazardous working conditions, and the use of child labor. These are the issues about home work that have concerned social reformers since at least the turn of the century (e.g., Cadbury, Matheson, & Shann, 1906). Similar abuses are starting to reappear in home production work (Johnson, 1982). In addition, the effects of merging home and work domains on the family, especially on children, are not understood. Organized labor argues that protective labor laws such as the Fair Labor Standards Act, which were instituted to curb child labor and other sweat-shop abuses, are unenforceable when employees work at home. As a result, the AFL-CIO and the National Association of Working Women (9 to 5) has called on the U.S. Labor Department to institute a ban on home clerical work (National Academy of Sciences, 1985, Appendix C).

DISCUSSION

The major question that remains from this review of the motivations for working at home and evidence on its current status is why there is so little true workplace substitution. We have seen that large numbers of people could potentially work at home; the nature of the occupations, of the work tasks, and of the technology all allow this. The analysis of the relative advantages of telework suggests that it would be useful to corporations and to managerial and professional workers. It may provide a work option for homebound workers and those with child-care responsibilities, although it may be susceptible to abuse. Yet, corporations who test teleworking on a trial basis rarely implement it on a large scale, even when they have deemed the trial a success. Workers in a high technology company who currently work the equivalent of 1 day a week at home do so relatively independently of their full-time work in a conventional office. For these workers there is a large discrepancy between the amount of time they actually work at home and the amount of time they would like to work at home and think that they could. Even people who do no work at home would like to work at home almost two days a week and believe that the nature of their jobs would allow them to do so.

It is of course possible that we currently see such little workplace substitution because we are only at the beginning of a social phenomenon that is accelerating. The diffusion of innovation literature shows that the interval from the introduction of an innovation to its ultimate acceptance by most of the relevant consumers can vary widely, from less than 10 years, in the case of some consumer products like the television, to almost a century, in the case of other products, like the telephone. More importantly, from the shape of the S-shaped curve showing the degree of acceptance of an innovation over time, one cannot tell during the beginning of the diffusion process what the ultimate acceptance of the innovation will be. In the beginning, innovation failures and innovation successes look much the same.

In the beginning of the innovation cycle, temporary circumstances may hinder the spread of the innovation. These include phenomena common to most innovations, such as size limitations on the formal and informal communication networks through which knowledge of the innovation spreads or high price, which decreases with increased production. The hindering phenomena also may be specific to the innovation. In the case of telework, for example, acceptance may be retarded until the majority of the information that workers use is available on-line or until the majority of co-workers are accessible through electronic mail. Similarly it is possible that computer and communication services need to be easier to use or that communications costs must fall or that communications speed and quality must increase before telework will become a wide-scale social phenomenon. We could expect, however, that these inhibitors will weaken over time, as the community of teleworkers increases and as proponents, change agents, and entrepreneurs work to solve technical problems.

THE STABILITY OF THE CONVENTIONAL OFFICE

But we should not expect a widespread adoption of telework simply because the technology allows it to happen. A more resistant barrier to the spread of telework is its incompatibility with the current work ethos. Although the adoption of any innovation requires some change on the part of the adopters, the adoption of telework requires unusually large changes in an especially central and stable component of the contemporary work culture. The conventional office structure, in which office workers congregate in a central office, is an indirect outgrowth of industrial automation. By the early part of the 20th century, manufacturing had primarily changed from an home-based, artisan production process to a factory system, in which masses of workers were brought together to accomplish related tasks. This industrial model eventually permeated education and office institutions as well (Zuboff, 1982).

Office structure has remained virtually unchanged since the late 19th century, despite both major changes in office technology (e.g., account books, shorthand transcription, telephones, dictation equipment, adding machines, letter presses, mimeo-machines, typewriters, and electronic copiers). The office also has remained stable in the face of explicit attempts to reorganize it (e .g., job redesign, flextime, and participatory management). Even the major change in the composition of the office—the feminization of office work—did little to change the structure of the office (cf. Baker, 1973; Davies, 1983; Scott, 1982).

The introduction of the telephone to the office is an especially apt comparison to the current introduction of computer and high-speed telecommunications technology. The telephone in the early part of this century could have allowed the dispersion of the white-collar work force, but the evidence is that it had the opposite effect (Pool, 1977). Physicians were able to move their surgeries away from their homes, and the management of industries moved from factories to conventional offices in central cities, not to their homes.

What causes this stability in office structure? My conclusion is that conventional, 9-to-5 office arrangements support a large number of activities crucial to the functioning of any work organization. Radical changes in the conventional office have the potential to disrupt these other activities and may be resisted.

The defining component of the conventional office is the co-presence of other workers for substantial parts of the work day. The presence of coworkers is the basis for a major satisfaction that workers derive from work: socializing and friendly social interaction (Locke, 1976). It also is a source of the social support that, among other factors, makes employment a contributor to the mental health of workers (Thoite, 1983). Social interaction as a source of satisfaction and support is even more important for office work than for factory work, because much of the work itself involves face-to-face dealings with others (e.g., Bair, 1987; Teger, 1983).

The presence of co-workers also facilitates the socialization of new workers to the workplace. The literature on socialization among both children and adults shows that modeling and observational learning are major ways for people to learn particular skills and general attitudes and values. In a modern office, the skills may be very specific ones, such as how to operate the copying machine or the text editor or how to complete an expense voucher, or they might be general ones, such as how to write well, to be a "good worker," or to get ahead.

In a related vein, the presence of co-workers aids the informal communication networks through which much information in an office flows. Informal communication networks generally follow proximity (e.g., Festinger, Schachter, & Back, 1950). People communicate most with, and are most influenced by those with whom it is easiest to communicate, those literally next door. The informal communication networks aid in the flow of both organizational norms and organizational information. Organizational norms include, among others, standards for dress, punctuality, and productivity. Organizational information includes gossip about individuals through which some organizational norms are enforced, information about organizational goals, and information about organizational structure (e.g., transfers and job openings). In addition, the informal communication networks aid organizational creativity, by fostering communication and collaboration among individuals who happen to be near each other.

The conventional office aids in at least one style of supervision or staff management. Managers can use the informal communication network to communicate tasks and goals and can get feedback about a subordinate's performance both from the informal communication network and from direct observation.

Finally, the conventional office structure helps workers structure their time. A basic social arrangement in modern society is that the individual tends to sleep, play, and work in different places, with different coparticipants, under different authorities, and without an overall rational plan (Goffman, 1961). One of the ways individuals have adapted to the consuming and often incompatible demands of work and family life is to spatially and temporally segregate them. Telework by definition breaches this segregation and exposes workers to potential role conflict.

This discussion described several organizational and personal arrangements that are likely to be disrupted by telework. One might be able to devise technological and organizational solutions for some of the disruptions. The far-reaching nature of these disruptions, however, is an important reason why telework may not spread as a workplace innovation.

ALTERNATE ROUTES TO ORGANIZATIONAL GOALS

The second major reason why telework as a workplace innovation may not spread is that employers have alternative means through which they can reap the benefits of introducing new technology into office work. They can use the new computer and communications technology to automate office work and to spread conventional offices to areas of more abundant or cheaper labor. These alternate routes do not disrupt conventional office structure and the activities it supports.

First, employers can partially solve the problem of insufficient labor supply by using the new technology to replace workers, rather than using telework to attract them. Two technological trends are leading to increased replacement of human labor and mental activity with computers; both indirectly stem from continual decreases in computer costs and increases in computing and telecomunications capabilities. The first trend is the increasing availability of information in computer readable form. The information may have originated in this form, as when a customer orders from a mail order catalog by punching the buttons on a touch-tone telephone, replacing data entry clerks, or when an author writes a manuscript on a personal computer, replacing typesetters. In addition, the increased pattern recognition abilities of computers means that other information can be made computer readable without labor intensive transcribing of information by human operators. Thus, optical character recognition and voice recognition can be used, for example, to replace data-entry clerks in the insurance industry, one of the clerical jobs for which telework is currently being used.

The second technological trend is the increased abilities of computer software to incorporate human knowledge and intelligence. The intelligence of computers includes the ability to encode unambiguous knowledge and decision rules, as, for example, in accounting or statistical analysis programs or programs to compute a loan client's credit risk. It also includes the ability to encode ambiguous knowledge and heuristic reasoning processes, in, for example, medical diagnostic programs, equipment configuration programs, or computer program writing programs. This capturing of human intelligence decreases the demand for some skilled professionals, either by automating their functions, allowing less skilled para-professionals to perform some of the professional's tasks, or by making the remaining professionals more productive.

The second way in which employers can use new technology is to relocate conventional offices from areas with high costs and poor labor supplies to more favorable sites. The trends have been to relocate those parts of an office that require no face-to-face contact with the public (i.e., back office work) from northern central cities to southern and southwestern locations, to suburban locations, and to foreign locations. These sites have in common large numbers of potential clerical workers, generally nonunionized, who will work for below the prevailing wage rates in United States northern cities (Noyelle, 1984; Working Women, 1985). The important point to note for the present purposes is that the conventional office structure is being reproduced in these alternative locations.

We have seen that employers have alternate ways to meet their goals that do not entail the organizational and personal disruptions associated with telework. Given this state of affairs, if telework spreads as a workplace innovation, it is likely to happen because workers themselves find it in their interest to work at home. We have seen that managers and professionals seem to benefit most from telework. In addition, their jobs are likely to be most autonomous and therefore most suitable for telework. Finally, because their skills are in high demand, they are likely to be able to arrange the personal accommodations with their supervision to enable them to telework without wholesale changes in company policy. Thus, as a result of these considerations, if telework spreads, it is likely to do so as a bottom-up social movement spreading on an individual basis among managerial and professional workers through normal, individual diffusion processes.

SUMMARY

In summary, we have seen that telework is feasible and has benefits for employers and at least management and professional employees. It may not, however, spread as a workplace innovation because it threatens to disrupt too many basic facets of organizational and personal life and because employers have alternate ways to reap technological benefits without such widespread disruption.

REFERENCES

American Telephone & Telegraph. (1982). *The structure of the work-at-home market: Job/volunteer/school.* (Unpublished manuscript). Basking Ridge, NJ: Author.

Bair, J. H. (1987). User needs for office system solutions. In R. Kraut (Ed.). *Technology and the transformation of white collar work* (pp. 177-194) Hillsdale, NJ: Lawrence Erlbaum.

Baker, E. (1973). *Technology and women's work.* New York: Columbia University Press.

Becker, F., & McClintock, C. (1981, March). *Mixed blessings: The office at home.* Paper presented at the National Telecommunications Conference, Houston.

Bell Communications Research News. (1985, March 8). *Integrated services digital network.* Livingston, NJ: Bell Communications Research.

Bielby, W., & Baron, J. (1985). A women's place is with other women: Sex segregation in the workplace. In B. Reskin (Ed.), Sex segregation in the workplace. (pp. 27-55). Washington, DC: National Academy Press.

Brewer, G. D. (1980). On the theory and practice of innovation. *Technology in Society, 2,* 337- 363.

Cadbury, E., Matheson, M., & Shann, G. (1906). *Women's work and wages.* London: T. Fisher Unwin.

Carey, M. (1981). Occupational employment growth through 1990. *Monthly Labor Review,* 104,42-55

Carey, M. (1982). Occupational employment growth through 1990. In U.S. Department of Labor, Bureau of Labor Statistics, *Economic Projections to 1990.* Washington DC: U.S. Government Printing Office.

Chabrow, E. (1985, April). Telecommuting: Managing the remote workplace. *Information Week,* 27-35.

Chamot, D. (1987). Electronic work and the white collar employee. In R. Kraut (Ed.). *Technology and the transformation of white collar work* (pp. 23-34) Hillsdale, NJ: Lawrence Erlbaum.

Chamot, D., & Zalusky, J. (1985). Use and misuse of workstations at home. In *Office workstations in the home* (pp. 76-84). Washington, DC: National Academy Press.

Davies, M. (1983). *Woman's place is at the typewriter: Office work and office workers 1870-1930.* Philadelphia: Temple University Press.

Electronic Services Unlimited. (1984). *Telework: A multi-client study.* New York: Author.

Festinger, L., Schachter, S., & Back, K. (1950). *Social pressures in informal groups: A study of human factors in housing.* New York: Harper & Row.

Geisler, G. (1985). Blue Cross/Blue Shield of South Carolina: Program for clerical workers. In *Office workstations in the home* (pp. 16-23). Washington, DC: National Academy Press.

Giuliano, V. (1981a). Teleworking: A prospectus. *Telephony, 200,* 65-75.

Giuliano, V. (1982b). Teleworking: Future shock. *Telephony, 200,* 56-62.

Goffman, E. (1961). *Asylums.* Garden City, NY: Anchor.

Hackman, J. R., & Oldham, G. R. (1980). *Work Redesign.* Reading, MA: Addison-Wesley.

Harkness, R. C. (1977). Technology assessment of telecommunications-transportation interactions. Menlo Park, CA: Stanford Research Institute.

Hippel, E. von. (1983). *Novel product concepts from lead users: Segmenting users by experience.* (Working paper no. 1476-83). Cambridge, MA: Massachusetts Institute of Technology, Sloan School of Management.

Iacono, S., & Kling, R. (1987). Changing office technologies and transformations of clerical jobs: A historical perspective. In R. Kraut (Ed.). *Technology and the transformation of white collar work* (pp. 53-76) Hillsdale, NJ: Lawrence Erlbaum.

If home is where the worker is. (1982, May). *Business Week*, 66.

Johnson, L. (1982). *The seam allowance: Industrial homework in Canada.* Toronto: The Women's Press.

Katz, E., Levin, M. L., & Hamilton, H. (1963). Traditions of research on the diffusion of innovation. *American Sociological Review, 28,*237-252.

Kraemer, K. (1982). Telecommunications-transportation substitution and energy productivity: A re-examination. *Telecommunications Policy, 6,*39-59.

Kraut, R. E. (in press). Telework as a work-style innovation. *Information and Behavior,* 2.

Kraut, R. E., & Grambsch, P. (1985, June). *Prophecy by analogy: Potential motivations for and consequences of electronic homework.* Paper presented at the Computer and Society Conference, University of Rochester, Rochester, NY.

Locke, E. (1976). The nature and causes of job satisfaction. In M. Dunnette (Ed.), *Handbook of industrial and organizational psychology* (pp. 1297-1349). Chicago: Rand McNally College Publishing.

McClintock, C. (1981, March). *Working alone together: Managing telecommuting.* Paper presented at National Telecommunications Conference, Houston.

McDavid, M. (1985). U.S. Army: Prototype program for professionals. In *Office Workstations in the Home* (pp. 24-32). Washington, DC: National Academy Press.

Miller, D. (1983, October). *The IBM teleworking experiment.* Paper presented at the National Executive Forum: Office Workstations in the Home. National Academy of Sciences, Board on Telecommunications and Computer Applications, Washington, DC.

National Academy of Sciences. (1985). *Office workstations in the home.* Washington, DC: National Academy Press.

Nilles, J. M., Carlson, F. R., Gray, P., & Hanneman, G. (1976). *The telecommunications-transportation tradeoffs: Options for tomorrow.* New York: Wiley.

Noyelle, T. (1984, October). *Employment discrimination in the service economy.* Paper presented at the Conference on Women, Clerical Work, and Office Automation: Issues for Research, Organized by the Women's Bureau, U.S. Department of Labor and the Panel of Technology and Women's Employment, National Research Council, Washington, DC.

Olson, M. H. (1982). New information technology and organizational culture. *MIS Quarterly, 6,* 71-92.

Olson, M. H. (1983). Remote office work: Changing work patterns in space and time. *Communications of the ACM, 26,* 182-187.

Olson, M. H. (1987). Telework: Practical experience and future prospects. In R. Kraut (Ed.). *Technology and the transformation of white collar work* (pp. 135-152) Hillsdale, NJ: Lawrence Erlbaum.

Panko, R. (1984). Office work. *Office: Technology and People, 2,*205-238.

Phelps, N. (1985). Mountain Bell: Program for managers. In *Office workstations in the home.* Washington, DC: National Academy Press.

Pool, I. (Ed.). (1977). *The social impact of the telephone.* Cambridge, MA: MIT Press.

Porat, M. (1977). *The information economy: Definition and measurement.* (U.S. Department of Commerce, Office of Telecommunications, U.S. Government Printing Office Stock No. 003-000-00512-7). Washington, DC: U.S. Government Printing Office.

Reskin, B. (1985). *Women's work, men's work: Sex segregation on the job.* Washington, DC: National Academy Press.

Rogers, E. M. (1983). *The diffusion of innovations.* New York: Free Press.

Schiff, F. W. (1983). Flexiplace: An idea whose time has come. *IEEE Transactions on Engineering Management, EM-30,* 2630.

Scott, J. (1982). The mechanization of women's work. *Scientific American, 247,* 166-187.

Teger, S. L. (1983). Factors impacting the evolution of office automation. *Proceedings of the IEEE, 71,*503-511.

Thoite, P. (1983). Multiple identities and psychological well-being: A reformulation and test of the social isolation hypothesis. *American Sociological Review, 48,* 174-187.

Toffler, A. (1979). *The third wave.* New York: Morrow.

Tornatzky, L. G., & Klein, K. (1982). Innovation characteristics and innovation adoption-implementation: A meta-analysis of findings. *IEEE Transactions on Engineering Management, EM-29,* 28-45.

U.S. Bureau of the Census. (1980). *Census of population and housing, 1980: Public-use micro- data sample A.* [MRDF] Washington, DC: Author.

U.S. Bureau of the Census. (1983). *Statistical abstract of the United States: 1984* (104th ed.). Washington, DC: U.S. Government Printing Office.

Walton, R. E. (1975). The diffusion of new work structures: Explaining why success didn't take. *Organizational Dynamics, 3,*2-22.

Walton, R. E. (1977). Successful strategies for diffusing work innovations. *Journal of Contemporary Busines*s, 1-21.

Zuboff, S. (1983, Winter). Problems of symbolic toil. *Dissent, 29,* 51-61.

COMPUTERS, NETWORKS, AND WORK[6]

Lee Sproull
Sara Kiesler
Carnegie Mellon University

Although the world may be evolving into a global village, most people still lead local lives at work. They spend the majority of their time in one physical location and talk predominantly to their immediate co-workers, clients and customers. They participate in only a few workplace groups: their primary work group, perhaps a committee or task force and possibly an informal social group.

Some people, however, already experience a far more cosmopolitan future because they work in organizations that have extensive computer networks. Such individuals can communicate with people around the world as easily as they talk with someone in the next office. They can hold involved group discussions about company policy, new product design, hiring plans or last night's ball game without ever meeting other group members.

The networked organization differs from the conventional workplace with respect to both time and space. Computer-based communication is extremely fast in comparison with telephone or postal services, denigrated as "snail mail" by electronic mail converts. People can send a message to the other side of the globe in minutes; each message can be directed to one person or to many people. Networks can also essentially make time stand still. Electronic messages can be held indefinitely in computer memory. People can read or reread their messages at any time, copy them, change them or forward them.

Managers are often attracted to networks by the promise of faster communication and greater efficiency. In our view, the real potential of network communication has less to do with such matters than with influencing the overall work environment and the capabilities of employees. Managers can use networks to foster new kinds of task structures and reporting relationships. They can use networks to change the conventional patterns of who talks to whom and who knows what.

The capabilities that accompany networks raise significant questions for managers and for social scientists studying work organizations. Can people really work closely with one another when their only contact is through a computer? If employees interact through telecommuting, teleconferencing and electronic group discussions, what holds the organization together? Networking permits almost unlimited access to data and to other people.

[6]Sproull, L.S., & Kiesler, S.B. (1991). Computers, networks, and work. *Scientific American, 265 (3).* 116-23. Reprinted with permission. Copyright © 1991 by Scientific American Inc. All rights reserved.

Where will management draw the line on freedom of access? What will the organization of the future look like?

We and various colleagues are working to understand how computer networks can affect the nature of work and relationships between managers and employees. What we are learning may help people to exploit better the opportunities that networks offer and to avoid or mitigate the potential pitfalls of networked organizations.

Our research relies on two approaches. Some questions can be studied through laboratory experiments. For instance, how do small groups respond emotionally to different forms of communication? Other questions, particularly those concerning organizational change, require field studies in actual organizations that have been routinely using computer networks. Data describing how hundreds of thousands of people currently use network communications can help predict how other people will work in the future as computer-based communications become more prevalent. Drawing on field studies and experiments, researchers gradually construct a body of evidence on how work and organizations are changing as network technology becomes more widely used. The process may sound straightforward, but in reality it is often full of exciting twists. People use technology in surprising ways, and effects often show up that contradict both theoretical predictions and managerial expectations.

One major surprise emerged as soon as the first large-scale computer network, known as the ARPANET, was begun in the late 1960s. The ARPANET was developed for the Advanced Research Projects Agency (ARPA), a part of the U.S. Department of Defense. ARPANET was intended to link computer scientists at universities and other research institutions to distant computers, thereby permitting efficient access to machines unavailable at the home institutions. A facility called electronic mail, which enabled researchers to communicate with one another, was considered a minor additional feature of the network.

Yet electronic mail rapidly became one of the most popular features of the ARPANET. Computer scientists around the country used ARPANET to exchange ideas spontaneously and casually. Graduate students discussed problems and shared skills with professors and other students without regard to their physical location. Heads of research projects used electronic mail to coordinate activities with project members and to stay in touch with other research teams and funding agencies. A network community quickly formed, filled with friends and collaborators who rarely, if ever, met in person. Although some administrators objected to electronic mail because they did not consider it a legitimate use of computer time, demand grew sharply for more and better network connections.

Since then, many organizations have adopted internal networks that link anywhere from a few to a few thousand employees. Some of these organizational networks have also been connected to the Internet, the successor to ARPANET. Electronic mail has continued to be one of the most popular features of these computer networks.

Anyone who has a computer account on a networked system can use electronic mail software to communicate with other users on the network. Electronic mail transmits messages to a recipient's electronic "mailbox." The sender can send a message simultaneously to several mailboxes by sending the message to a group name or to a distribution list. Electronic bulletin boards and electronic conferences are common variants of group electronic mail; they too have names to identify their topic or audience. Bulletin boards post messages in chronological order as they are received. Computer conferences arrange messages by topic and display grouped messages together.

The computer communications technology in most networked organizations today is fairly similar, but there exist large differences in people's actual communication behavior that stem from policy choices made by management. In some networked organizations, electronic mail access is easy and open. Most employees have networked terminals or computers on their desks, and anyone can send mail to anyone else. Electronic mail costs are considered part of general overhead expenses and are not charged to employees or to their departments. In the open-network organizations we have studied, people typically send and receive between 25 and 100 messages a day and belong to between 10 and 50 electronic groups. These figures hold across job categories, hierarchical position, age and even amount of computer experience.

In other networked organizations, managers have chosen to limit access or charge costs directly to users, leading to much lower usage rates. Paul Schreiber, a *Newsday* columnist, describes how his own organization changed from an open-access network to a limited-access one. Management apparently believed that reporters were spending too much time sending electronic mail; management therefore had the newspaper's electronic mail software modified so that reporters could still receive mail but could no longer send it. Editors, on the other hand, could still send electronic mail to everyone. Clearly, technology by itself does not impel change. Management choices and policies are equally influential.

But even in organizations that have open access, anticipating the effects of networks on communication has proved no easy task. Some of the first researchers to study computer network communications thought the technology would improve group decision making over face-to-face discussion because computer messages were plain text. They reasoned that electronic discussions would be more purely intellectual, and so decision making would be less affected by people's social skills and personal idiosyncrasies.

Research has revealed a more complicated picture. In an electronic exchange, the social and contextual cues that usually regulate and influence group dynamics are missing or attenuated. Electronic messages lack

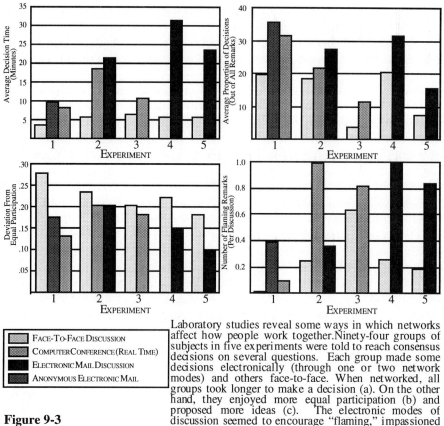

Figure 9-3

Legend:
- FACE-TO-FACE DISCUSSION
- COMPUTER CONFERENCE (REAL TIME)
- ELECTRONIC MAIL DISCUSSION
- ANONYMOUS ELECTRONIC MAIL

Laboratory studies reveal some ways in which networks affect how people work together. Ninety-four groups of subjects in five experiments were told to reach consensus decisions on several questions. Each group made some decisions electronically (through one or two network modes) and others face-to-face. When networked, all groups took longer to make a decision (a). On the other hand, they enjoyed more equal participation (b) and proposed more ideas (c). The electronic modes of discussion seemed to encourage "flaming," impassioned self-expression (d).

information regarding job titles, social importance, hierarchical position, race, age and appearance. The context also is poorly defined because formal and casual exchanges look essentially the same. People may have outside information about senders, receivers and situations, but few cues exist in the computer interaction itself to remind people of that knowledge.

In a series of experiments at Carnegie Mellon University, we compared how small groups make decisions using computer conferences, electronic mail and face-to-face discussion (see Figure 9-3). Using a network induced the participants to talk more frankly and more equally. Instead of one or two people doing most of the talking, as happens in many face-to-face groups, everyone had a more equal say. Furthermore, networked groups generated more proposals for action than did traditional ones.

Open, free-ranging discourse has a dark side. The increased democracy associated with electronic interactions in our experiments interfered with decision making. We observed that three-person groups took approximately four times as long to reach a decision electronically as they did face-to-face. In one case, a group never succeeded in reaching consensus, and we were ultimately forced to terminate the experiment. Making it impossible for people to interrupt one another slowed decision making and increased conflict as a few members tried to dominate control of the network. We also found that people tended to express extreme opinions and vented anger more openly in an electronic face-off than when they sat together and talked. Computer scientists using the ARPANET have called this phenomenon "flaming."

We discovered that electronic communication can influence the effects of people's status. Social or job position normally is a powerful regulator of group interaction. Group members typically defer to those who have higher status and tend to follow their direction. Members' speech and demeanor become more formal in the presence of people who have high status. Higher status people, in turn, talk more and influence group discussion more than do lower-status people.

Given that electronic conversations attenuate contextual cues, we expected that the effect of status differences within a group should also be reduced. In an experiment conducted with Vitaly Dubrovsky of Clarkson University and Beheruz Sethna of Lamar University, we asked groups containing high- and low-status members to make decisions both by electronic mail and face-to-face. The results confirmed that the proportion of talk and influence of higher-status people decreased when group members communicated by electronic mail.

Is this a good state of affairs? When higher-status members have less expertise, more democracy could improve decision making. If higher-status members truly are better qualified to make decisions, however, the results of consensus decisions may be less good.

Shoshanah Zuboff of Harvard Business School documented reduced effects of status on a computer conference system in one firm. People who regarded themselves as physically unattractive reported feeling more lively and confident when they expressed themselves over the network. Others who had soft voices or small stature reported that they no longer had to struggle to be taken seriously in a meeting.

Researchers have advanced alternative explanations for the openness and democracy of electronic talk. One hypothesis is that people who like to use computers are childish or unruly, but this hypothesis does not explain experimental results showing that the same people talk more openly on a computer than when they are face-to-face. Another hypothesis holds that text messages require strong language to get a point across; this hypothesis explains flaming but not the reduction of social and status differences. The most promising explanation of the behavior of networked individuals is that when cues about social context are absent or weak, people ignore their social situation and cease to worry about how others evaluate them. Hence, they devote less time and effort to posturing and social niceties, and they may be more honest.

Researchers have demonstrated decreased social posturing in studies that ask people to describe their own behavior. In one of our experiments, people were asked to complete a self-evaluation questionnaire either by pencil and paper or via electronic mail. Those randomly assigned to reply electronically reported significantly more undesirable social behaviors, such as illegal drug use or petty crimes. John Greist and his colleagues at the University of Wisconsin found similar decreases in posturing when taking medical histories from clinical patients. People who responded to a computerized patient history interview revealed more socially and physically undesirable behavior than did those who answered the same questions asked by a physician.

These studies show that people are willing to reveal more about undesirable symptoms and behavior to a computer, but are these reports more truthful? An investigation of alcohol consumption conducted by Jennifer J. Waterton and John C. Duffy of the University of Edinburgh suggests an affirmative answer. In traditional surveys, people report drinking only about one half as much alcohol as alcohol sales figures would suggest. Waterton and Duffy compared computer interviews with personal interviews in a survey of alcohol consumption. People who were randomly assigned to answer the computer survey reported higher alcohol consumption than those who talked to the human interviewer. The computer-derived reports of consumption extrapolated more accurately to actual alcohol sales than did the face-to-face reports.

These and other controlled studies of electronic talk suggest that such communication is relatively impersonal, yet paradoxically, it can make people feel more comfortable about talking. People are less shy and more playful in electronic discussions; they also express more opinions and ideas and vent more emotion.

Because of these behavioral effects, organizations are discovering applications for electronic group activities that nobody had anticipated. Computers can be valuable for counseling and conducting surveys about sensitive topics, situations in which many people are anxious and cover their true feelings and opinions. Networks are now being used for applications ranging from electronic Alcoholics Anonymous support group to electronic quality circles.

Just as the dynamics of electronic communications differ from those conducted orally or by letters, so electronic groups are not just traditional groups whose members use computers. People in a networked organization are likely to belong to a number of electronic groups that span time zones and job categories. Some of these groups serve as extensions of existing work groups, providing a convenient way for members to communicate between face-to-face meetings. Other electronic groups gather together people who do not know one another personally and who may in fact have never had the opportunity to meet in person.

For example, Hewlett-Packard employs human-factors engineers who work in widely scattered locations around the world. These engineers may meet one another in person only once a year. An electronic conference creates ongoing meetings in which they can frequently and routinely discuss professional and company issues.

In some ways, electronic groups resemble nonelectronic social groups. They support sustained interactions, develop their own norms of behavior and generate peer pressure. Electronic groups often have more than 100 members, however, and involve relationships among people who do not know one another personally.

Employees whose organization is connected to the Internet or to a commercial network can belong to electronic groups whose members come from many different organizations. For example, Brian K. Reid of Digital Equipment Corporation reports that some 37,000 organizations are connected to USENET, a loosely organized network that exchanges more than 1,500 electronic discussion groups, called newsgroups. Reid estimates that 1.4 million people worldwide read at least one newsgroup.

Networked communication is only beginning to affect the structure of the workplace. The form of most current organizations has been dictated by the constraints of the nonelectronic world. Interdependent jobs must be situated in physical proximity. Formal command structures specify who reports to whom, who assigns tasks to whom and who has access to what information. These constraints reinforce the centralization of authority and shape the degree of information sharing, the number of organizational levels, the amount of interconnectivity and the structure of social relationships.

Organizations that incorporate computer networks could become more flexible and less hierarchical in structure. A field experiment conducted by Tora K. Bikson of Rand Corporation and John D. Eveland of Claremont Colleges supports the point. They formed two task forces in a large utility firm, each assigned to analyze employee retirement issues. Both groups contained 40 members, half of whom had recently retired from the company and half of whom were still employed but eligible for retirement. The only difference between the two groups was that one worked on networked computer facilities, whereas the other did not.

Both task forces created subcommittees, but the networked group created more of them and assigned people to more than one subcommittee. The networked group also organized its subcommittees in a complex, overlapping matrix structure. It added new subcommittees during the course of its work, and it decided to continue meeting even after its official one-year life span had ended. The networked task force also permitted greater input from the retirees, who were no longer located at the company. Although not every electronic group will be so flexible, eliminating the constraints of face-to-face meetings evidently facilitates trying out different forms of group organization (see Figure 9-4).

○ EMPLOYEE △ RETIREE

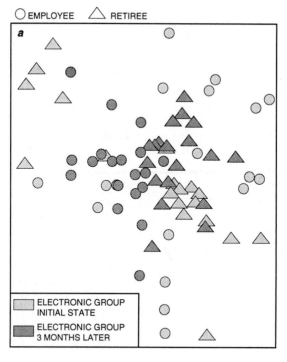

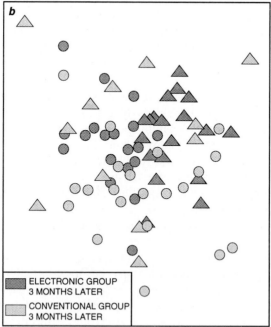

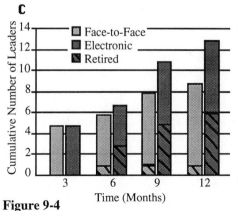

c

Cumulative Number of Leaders

(Chart legend: Face-to-Face, Electronic, Retired)

Time (Months): 3, 6, 9, 12

DYNAMIC GROUP STRUCTURES emerge when people converse electronically. These charts depict the behavior of two study groups, each containing a mix of employees and retired workers. One group worked in person, the other over a network. Members having the most information and social contacts appear near the center of the charts. Over time, the electronic group becomes more socially cohesive (*a*). Chart *b* compares the electronic group with the conventional three months into the project and shows that retirees in particular become better integrated in the electronic group. Networks also encourage more people to take on leadership roles (*c*).

Figure 9-4
Dynamic group structures in electronic communication.

Another effect of networking may be changed patterns of information sharing in organizations. Conventional organizations have formal systems of record keeping and of responsibilities for distributing information. Much of the information within an organization consists of personal experience that never appears in the formally authorized distribution system: the war stories told by service representatives (which do not appear in service manuals), the folklore about how the experimental apparatus really works (which does not appear in the journal articles) or the gossip about how workers should behave (which is not described in any personnel policy).

In the past, the spread of such personal information has been strongly determined by physical proximity and social acquaintance. As a result, distant or poorly connected employees have lacked access to local expertise; this untapped knowledge could represent an important informational resource in large organizations. Electronic groups provide a forum for sharing such expertise independent of spatial and social constraints.

One significant kind of information flow begins with the "Does anybody know...?" message that appears frequently on computer networks. A sender might broadcast an electronic request for information to an entire organization, to a particular distribution list or to a bulletin board. Anyone who sees the message can reply. We studied information inquiries on the network at Tandem Computers, Inc., in Cupertino, Calif., a computer company that employs 10,500 workers around the world. In a study we conducted with David Constant, we found an average of about six does-anybody-know messages broadcast every day to one company-wide distribution list.

Information requests typically come from field engineers or sales representatives who are soliciting personal experience or technical knowledge that they cannot find in formal documents or in their own workplace. At Tandem, about eight employees send electronic mail replies to the average question. Fewer than 15 percent of the people who answer a question are personally acquainted with the questioner or are even located in the same city.

Question askers can electronically redistribute the answers they receive by putting them in a public computer file on the network. About half of the Tandem questioners make their reply files publicly available over the company network to other employees. Tandem takes this sharing process one step further by maintaining an electronic archive of question-and-reply files that is also accessible over the company network. The firm has thereby created a repository of information and working expertise that is endlessly accessible through space and time (for example, the expertise remains available when an employee is out of the office or he or she leaves the organization). A study by Thomas Finholt in our research program found that this archive is accessed more than 1,000 times a month by employees, especially those located in field offices away from the geographic center of the company (see Figure 9-5).

The discretionary information sharing we discovered at Tandem and at other networked organizations seems to run contrary to nonelectronic behavior in organizations. The askers openly admit their ignorance to perhaps hundreds or even thousands of people. The repliers respond to requests for help from people they do not know with no expectation of any direct benefit to themselves.

One might wonder why people respond so readily to information requests made by strangers. Part of the explanation is that networks make the cost of responding extremely low in time and effort expended. Also, open-access networks favor the free flow of information. Respondents seem to believe that sharing information enhances the overall electronic community and leads to a richer information environment. The result is a kind of electronic altruism quite different from the fears that networks would weaken the social fabric of organizations.

The changes in communication made possible by networks may substantially alter the relationship between an employee and his or her organization, the structure of organizations and the nature of management. Senior managers and key professionals usually have strong social and informational connections within their organizations and within their broader professional communities. Conversely, employees who reside on the organizational periphery by virtue of geographic location, job requirements or personal attributes have relatively few opportunities to make contact with other employees and colleagues.

Reducing the impediments to communication across both physical and social distance is likely to affect peripheral employees more than central ones. We, along with Charles Huff of St. Olaf College, studied this possibility for city employees in Fort Collins, Colo. Employees who used electronic mail extensively reported more commitment to their jobs and to their co-workers than did those who rarely used the network. This correlation was particularly strong for shift workers, who, because of the nature of their

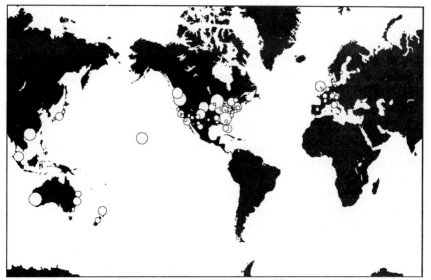

Figure 9-5 Electronic links have the greatest effect on workers located at outlying sites. Workers in field offices of Tandem Computers, Inc., whose headquarters are in Cupurtino, Calif., have access to data files via a network. Circles indicate how many times each office tapped into one file (consisting of employee-initiated questions and answers about company products and services) over a one-year period; the greater the usage, the larger the circle. Workers in distant or isolated offices, where local expertise is relatively limited, made the most use of the information provided through the network.

work, had fewer opportunities to see their colleagues than did regular day workers. As one policewoman told us, "Working the night shift, it used to be that I would hear about promotions after they happened, though I had a right to be included in the discussion. Now I have a say in the decision making."

Organizations are traditionally built around two key concepts: hierarchical decomposition of goals and tasks and the stability of employee relationships over time. In the fully networked organization that may become increasingly common in the future, task structures may be much more flexible and dynamic. Hierarchy will not vanish, but it will be augmented by distributed lattices of interconnections.

In today's organizations, executives generally know whom they manage and manage whom they know. In the future, however, managers of some electronic project groups will face the challenge of working with people they have never met. Allocating resources to projects and assigning credit and blame for performance will become more complex. People will often belong to many different groups and will be able to reach out across the network to acquire resources without management intervention or perhaps even without management knowledge.

A recent case in mathematics research hints at the nature of what may lie ahead. Mathematicians at Bell Communications Research (Bellcore) and at Digital Equipment sought to factor a large, theoretically interesting number known as the 9th Fermat number. They broadcast a message on the Internet to recruit researchers from universities, government laboratories and corporations to assist them in their project. The several hundred researchers who volunteered to help received-via electronic mail software and a piece of the problem to solve; they also returned their solutions through electronic mail.

After results from all the volunteers were combined, the message announcing the final results of the project contained a charming admission:

> We'd like to thank everyone who contributed computing cycles to this project, but I can't: we only have records of the person at each site who installed and managed the code. If you helped us, we'd be delighted to hear from you; please send us your name as you would like it to appear in the final version of the paper. (Broadcast message from Mark S. Manasse, June 15, 1990.)

Networking in most organizations today is limited to data communications, often for economic or financial applications such as electronic data interchange, electronic funds transfer or remote transaction processing. Most organizations have not yet begun to confront the opportunities and challenges afforded by connecting their employees through networks.

Among those that have, managers have responded in a variety of ways to changes that affect their authority and control. Some managers have installed networks for efficiency reasons but ignored their potential for more profound changes. Some have restricted who can send mail or have shut down electronic discussion groups. Others have encouraged using the network for broadening participation and involving more people in the decision-making process. The last actions push responsibility down and through the organization and also produce their own managerial issues.

A democratic organization requires competent, committed, responsible employees. It requires new ways of allocating credit. It increases unpredictability, both for creative ideas and for inappropriate behavior. Managers will have to come up with new kinds of worker incentives and organizational structures to handle these changes.

The technology of networks is changing rapidly. Electronic mail that includes graphics, pictures, sound and video will eventually become widely available. These advances will make it possible to reintroduce some of the social context cues absent in current electronic communications. Even so, electronic interactions will never duplicate those conducted face-to-face

As more people have ready access to network communications, the number and size of electronic groups will expand dramatically. It is up to management to make and shape connections. The organization of the future will depend significantly not just on how the technology of networking evolves but also on how managers seize the opportunity it presents for transforming the structure of work.

READING QUESTIONS

1) What is technological determinism? How has the belief in it shaped the predictions about telework?
2) Explain some of the models of telework (e.g. satellite work centers).
3) Could all "information workers" completely switch to telework?
4) How is augmentation different from replacement in telework?
5) Has work at home been increasing or decreasing ?
6) What percentage of people bring work home? What are these people, and their work, like? What tools are they most likely to use?
7) Kraut's survey suggests that people would like to work more at home, and that the technology allows this to happen. Why, then, don't they?
8) For Kraut's respondents, how was telework different work from office work?
9) What are several differences between clerical and professional/managerial workers?
10) What gains do employers expect from clerical and professional/managerial workers?
11) Are teleworkers more productive? What alternative explanation can explain this result from company studies?
12) Does the job satisfaction (some) teleworkers experience increase their productivity? What other effects does it have?
13) How does telework reduce overhead costs?
14) What are the general benefits of telework to employees?
15) What is the likely profile of a homeworker?
16) What are the concerns of organized labor about telework?
17) "In the beginning, innovation failures and innovation successes look much the same." Explain.
18) What temporary factors could be restraining the development of telework?
19) What changes in office technology have occurred since the late nineteenth century? Have they changed the basic structure of office work?
20) Why is social interaction important to office work?
21) What benefits does the physical presence of coworkers provide to workers? To managers?
22) Why is role conflict a problem for teleworkers?
23) How does the replacement or relocation of work avoid the need for telework and preserve the traditional office?
24) If teleworking does catch on, what group is most likely to adopt it?
25) What are the time and space differences that electronic communication can produce?
26) Why was it a surprise that electronic mail was popular on ARPANET?
27) What kind of choices can management make that will affect the way electronic communication is used in an organization?
28) Why might we expect that plain text communication would lead to a more intellectual and rational discussion? Why does this not seem to happen?
29) How does electronic communication change the effects of status in a discussion? Does this guarantee good decision making?
30) What are the various explanations for the openness and democracy of electronic talk?
31) Why are people more comfortable and honest in electronic interaction?
32) How are "electronic groups" different from face-to-face groups?
33) How might electronic communication change the patterns of information sharing in an organization?
34) What is electronic altruism?

35) Why is electronic communication more likely to help those who are peripheral in an organization?

DISCUSSION QUESTIONS

1) Even if we can replace the functions of the traditional office, what will be the problems encountered during a transition?
2) Use the most conservative picture from Kraut's article and the examples and research from Sproull and Kiesler to produce a description of the "office of the future." How is it different from the "standard" picture? How does it differ from the "traditional office"?
3) Explain the paradoxical effects of electronic communication on human interaction. Make sure you explain: flaming, honesty in survey taking, more equitable participation, electronic altruism, and increased decision times for discussions.

PRACTICING THE DESIGN ETHIC

1) If you are a member of online forums or conferences, or you can temporarily sign on to one or more of them, analyze the content of the forums in light of some of Sproull and Keisler's findings. Browse the forums for examples of: flaming (i.e., does it appear that some of the entries are very emotional and angry), electronic altruism (i.e., when a request for help or information is entered, how quickly and how many responses do you see in response to the request), level of participation of people in the forum (i.e., in a given period of time - one day - how many people participated in the forum and how often), and openness (i.e., does it appear that the participants in the forum are especially open about personal matters). Summarize your findings and provide examples in a report.
2) Get in touch with a local business or university that provides some form of telework for its employees. Interview at least one manager (preferably one manager who works, at least in part, at home and one who doesn't work at home), one worker who doesn't participate in the telework program, and one worker who does participate in the program. Determine each person's job description and what portion of the job they do at home versus in the workplace. During the interview, determine the following information:
    • What is their view of telework? Do they think it increases productivity?
    • Do they think working at home affects a person's chances for raises or promotions?
    • Do they use electronic mail to communicate with each other? Is that sufficient to allow those who work at home and those at work to do their jobs.
    • For those working at home: Do they like working at home? Why or why not? How do they schedule their time? Do they miss seeing their co-workers? Why or why not? If yes, how do they solve that problem?
    • For those who don't work at home: What are their feelings about those people who work at home? Would they like to work at home in the future? Why or why not? Do they miss seeing those who work at home? Why or why not?
    • For managers: What issues does telework raise in managing an employee who works at home? How does it affect those who work in the workplace?

Analyze the information that has been gathered, and summarize the class findings. Do you notice any differences in perspective among the groups that were interviewed? Are there any apparent differences based on type of work performed? Any differences based on gender?

CHAPTER

10

EQUITABLE ACCESS TO COMPUTING

Lost in the hyperbole of the advancing technology are issues of access to that technology by the broad array of people that make up our society. The goal of providing equal access to technology can be based in several values that computer scientists share. First, because of our egalitarian heritage, we desire to eliminate barriers that keep some segments of our population from enjoying the economic benefits of participating in technology. Second, regardless of our intentions, when we exclude certain segments of our population from access, we deny ourselves the contributions those people could have made to our profession and our society. Finally, and recently in the area of handicapped access, the design of curricula, of buildings, and of technology in a way that excludes certain groups is illegal.

The three articles included in this chapter are a guide to these issues. Anderson, Lundmark, Harris, and Magnan review the extensive research on access differences based on gender, ethnicity, and social stratification. Their review suggests that though technology may be more widely available today, the gaps in access based on these three dimensions are not diminishing, and in some instances may even be growing larger.

Cisler's article addresses the technical, organizational, economic, social, and user interface issues involved in the debate over "ubiquitous access" to the emerging national network. This issue is currently being considered at national, state, and local levels and may become one of the central debates as this network emerges.

Finally, the paper by EASI (EDUCOM's Equal Access to Software for Instruction project) address the issue of access for the handicapped. The review of this issue is timely, given recent passage of federal legislation mandating equal access. Potential designers will find the appendix of specifications for accessibility useful as a guide and as a reference.

EQUITY IN COMPUTING[1]

Ronald E. Anderson
Vicki Lundmark,
Linda Harris,
Shon Magnan
University of Minnesota

While the research on the impacts of computing tends to view social processes as "computer-mediated," some effects of computers are more appropriately viewed as socially mediated technology processes. Technology transfer or diffusion is a case in point. To best understand and predict how evenly or equitably computing technology spreads throughout a society, one should start with a conceptual model of a technology transfer process shaped largely by social factors. In this investigation we look at three important sociological concepts and ask to what extent these factors yield inequity or an uneven distribution of computing experiences. In brief, we will ask to what extent participation in computing is mediated by gender roles, social stratification, and ethnicity. After defining inequity, we will review each of these three concepts and consider some sociological issues. Following the conceptual discussion will be a review of the trends from research studies on equity and inequity in computing.

WHAT IS INEQUITY?

Synonyms of inequity are injustice and unfairness; not only does it refer to a lack of equality but it implies an ethical or moral problem as well. In a society where equality of educational opportunity is highly valued, evidence of significant obstacles to such opportunity produces moral, political, and policy issues. Those carrying the banner of computer inequity believe that computing is essential for learning and a prerequisite for employment. They argue for actions to remove the obstacles that block women, minorities, the poor, and other classes of people from computer resources. Since much computer learning occurs outside of school and is therefore income-dependent, it is argued that educational systems have a special obligation to compensate for this disparity.

Within computing and computer education, the main equity concerns have not been fair salaries but issues of access, activity, participation, and performance. Access refers to availability of resources (software as well as hardware); activity refers to the amount and quality of time that people use computing systems; participation consists of enrollment in computer courses and other learning opportunities; and performance has to do with measures of

---

[1] This article was written expressly for inclusion in this text.

computer literacy and other computer-related capabilities. In our review, higher education and career differences will also be considered under the heading of performance issues.

THE SIGNIFICANCE OF COMPUTER EQUITY

One argument challenging the usefulness of research on computer inequity is that differences among racial and other social groups should be minimized because reporting these differences perpetuates negative stereotypes of less powerful groups. The flaw in this argument is that without solid data allowing their problems to be systematically monitored and the situation addressed., disadvantaged groups may rapidly become even more disadvantaged. Furthermore, without such data it is impossible to evaluate the effectiveness of educational programs designed to rectify the problems.

Another argument against the study of computer inequity is that computers are irrelevant or at least insignificant for addressing the requirements of education and problems of the society. Here are the main arguments offered to refute this contention:

Improved quality of education

Undoubtedly some of the ways that computers have been applied to learning have yielded ineffective or even negative consequences. However, the overall impact appears to have been beneficial to education. The general consensus in the educational computing community is that computing improves educational quality when it is used to facilitate creativity and problem solving (Scott, Cole, & Engel, 1992). For computer-assisted instruction (CAI) and integrated learning systems (ILS), the conventional wisdom is quite divided. Nonetheless, the research for even these computer methods shows impressive gains in achievement (Kulick & Kulick, 1987).

In addition to the evidence from studies on effectiveness of alternative learning methods, an economic analysis shows affirmation of the contribution of computers to educational quality (Krueger, 1991). Using data from the High School and Beyond Survey, Krueger estimated that at least one-third of the observed increase in education's rate of return to graduates during the 1980s was due to their computer training and use. In other words, during the 1980s, school experience with computers led to greater wage advantage.

Employment

Folk wisdom has perpetuated the belief that computer experience in school leads directly to success in entering the job market, and recently an economic analysis found statistical data to support this claim. On the basis of their analysis of data from the U.S. Bureau of the Census, Boozer, Krueger, & Wolkon (1992) concluded that "school-related computer training is linked to obtaining a job that utilizes computer technology" (p. 308).

Economic productivity

Nearly every study commissioned on national or international productivity has concluded that a labor force with computing skills is essential to long-term productivity and global competitiveness (e.g., National Governors Association, 1991; U.S. Congress, 1988). This does not mean that computer education should be reduced to vocational training, but there are learning areas such as keyboarding where the training needs of industry intersect with the educational needs of students. In a society filled with computerized information systems, this is especially true for the general area of decision making.

Computer efficacy

All the benefits of school computing listed so far derive in part from their contribution to students' confidence in dealing with a complex and empowering technology. Computer utilization often requires accomplishing new, unspecified tasks that require more than routine training. Critical to effectiveness in this type of environment is a strong attitude of self-confidence in dealing with the computer technology. While such an attitude must be grounded in some basic knowledge, effective performance depends heavily upon one's sense of efficacy regarding one's creative application of computer techniques.

Computer perspective

Closely related to computer efficacy is an awareness of the general capabilities of computers, especially their limitations. Without an understanding of the role of computers and how they are used, it is more difficult to function effectively in a society where large computer systems are commonly used for managing information about the public.

Given all these outcomes from the use of the computer in education, any effective, though unintended, segregation of specific groups from computer education poses a threat to our human values of equality and educational opportunity, to say nothing of our values concerning economic productivity. Before looking at the evidence on computer inequity, there is some conceptual groundwork to review.

SOCIOLOGICAL CONSIDERATIONS

Gender roles

Every society differentiates its expectations for females and males, and this is why women and men tend to have different hairstyles, lifestyles, interests, and preferences. These different sets of expectations are called gender roles, and particular individuals conform more or less to these roles. Life course socialization, a major school of sociological thought regarding gender roles, emphasizes all the different sources and influences of expectations throughout one's lifetime. Especially effective in socialization are the family and peers, but social institutions such as church, state, business, and school also shape and enforce gender roles. Socialization theorists concentrate on how expectations work and therefore tend to be more conservative and pessimistic about changing gender roles. Feminist theorists, on the other hand, focus on differences in gender roles, and share a more liberal perspective on change. The overarching goals for feminists are to explain and prevent social inequities in gender roles. As we shall see, the story for females in computing begins with disenchantment sometime in the adolescent years, evolves into avoidance of computing courses and specialized careers, and culminates in the ghettoization of huge numbers of women in low-paying, low-level, computer-based clerical jobs.

When a teenage girl hears a comment such as "computers are nerdy" or "software engineering is not for girls," she is receiving socialization messages and may as a consequence be less likely to work on computers or take a computer course. Social psychological research has found more subtle socialization outcomes. Anderson et al. (1982) and Huff, Fleming, & Cooper (1992) found women more susceptible to negative self-attributions in response to computer malfunctions. Huff & Cooper (1987) discovered that when software designers were asked to write programs for female users, they produced programs that were more polite, considerate, and practical than those they wrote for male users. The major feminist critique of educational computing is that not only is it largely dominated by males but the symbolism of computers and computer applications is largely male-oriented (Griffiths, 1988). It is argued that the only solution to the inequity problem is to replace the maleness of the computer with either a neutered computer or one equally allied with femaleness and maleness (Bryson & Castell, 1992).

Social stratification

Economic dualism presumes an economic system separated into two main parts: the core (or center) and peripheral economies. The core consists chiefly of large, well-capitalized organizations, whereas the periphery tends to be small companies with less technological sophistication (Hodson & Kaufman, 1982). One labor market serves the core with highly trained workers that receive high economic rewards, possibilities for promotions, and on-the-job training. In sharp contrast, the secondary labor market serves the peripheral economic sector with workers who tend to lack specialized skills and remain vulnerable to economic instability and job insecurity. Serious barriers between the two labor markets prevent most workers in the peripheral market from ever moving out and achieving the benefits available to those in the primary labor market. Technology, and computerization in particular, make these barriers to mobility more formidable because of extensive requirements for specialized education and training (Bluestone, 1970). In addition, computer jobs in the core sector tend to be arranged in sequences where entry job skills serve as prerequisites for more advanced jobs. Another more recent barrier to a great many higher-paying, core-sector jobs is the expectation for computer literacy and other computer-related skills.

The advent of computer technology in schools may have put students of poor families, including many ethnic minorities, at a further disadvantage. If students in these categories emerge from school with lower levels of computer experience, this creates one more handicap in the filtering process of recruitment into the primary labor pools. Furthermore, technology may perpetuate an existing stratification system in other ways, especially by giving those at higher levels greater ability to control the structuring of lower-level processes.

New technology often gives those with power and wealth additional advantage over the weak or poor. In very primitive societies, weapons and agricultural inventions made possible the subjugation of slaves and serfs. In modern times, the "haves" often get access to new technology long before the "have nots," and this has been true with computer technology because of its expense and the learning required.

Ethnicity

The term "ethnicity" refers to one's identification with a particular race or ethnic group, a people of the same race or nationality who share a common and distinctive culture. The cultural values of ethnic groups differ, which to some extent accounts for differential participation in computing. However, the relative lack of computer experience in minority communities is more a matter of scarce income, educational, and occupational benefits. Sociologists often characterize such situations as indirect discrimination, the perpetuation of unfair decisions that produce intergroup inequities (Pettigrew & Taylor, 1992). Direct discrimination occurs when hiring and other important decisions are made, either intentionally or unintentionally, on the basis of irrelevant characteristics such as race. A large flow of recent immigrant ethnic minorities into European and North American countries may create additional problems of direct and indirect discrimination over and above those of the indigenous ethnic communities.

As income-related disadvantages persist in ethnically defined communities, the schools also tend to struggle with limited resources. While there have been programs in the United States for buying computers and training teachers in schools with a high proportion of minority students, there is striking evidence of computer discrimination in urban schools (Piller, 1992). It would appear that the only way to ensure that computers do not become a discriminatory technology further disenfranchising minorities and the poor is to establish institutional programs such as free computing in libraries or community centers, installing a computer in every school desk, and other interventions to compensate for the unaffordability of new computing resources by the poor. Also critical to creating and maintaining computer equity are special interventions to ensure quality instruction in the schools (Smith & O'Day, 1990) as well as support for national educational technology initiatives (Branscum, 1992).

SCOPE AND METHOD

In this investigation, we have narrowed our scope primarily to the United States and to social groups defined by three characteristics: gender, income, and ethnicity. This limitation can be justified by the literature on computer equity; most of the published research was done in the United States and almost all of it deals with these three types of social groups.

Data on computer equity from several other countries have appeared in the literature. These include Canada (Collis, 1985; Collis & Williams, 1987), Australia (Chambers & Clarke, 1987), and New Zealand (McKinnon & Nolan, 1990). Published discussions of equity issues, particularly in the context of developing countries, are becoming more common (Hawkridge, Jaworski, & McMahon, 1990). Nonetheless, very few of these investigations contain large, representative samples of schools or students. During the next decade, we anticipate more and more data forthcoming from other countries.

Gender, income, and ethnicity are only a few of the bases of inequality and discrimination in modem societies. Persons with physical disabilities, students with low school-related abilities, and children whose families speak another language are all susceptible to receiving fewer opportunities for school computing experience. These groups of students have not been compared in this study because relatively little data are available to make any generalizations. By neglecting them in our review we do not intend, by any means, to suggest that their problems are less serious or that they can be neglected within educational programs. In the future, these and other bases for social groupings will be the subject of scrutiny in evaluating ongoing computer equity.

The method of our study is that of secondary analysis. First we reviewed and carefully evaluated the rapidly growing body of literature on computer inequity. Then we did additional analysis of equity data from the United States portion of the IEA (International Association for the Evaluation of Educational Achievement) Computers in Education Study (Pelgrum & Plomp, 1991). Data were obtained from the first stage of the IEA study, a survey of over 1,200 representative schools in the United States, that was directed by Henry Jay Becker of The Johns Hopkins University. We gave special attention to the IEA Study because it is the most recent large-scale survey of computing in U.S.A. schools.

In the next three sections we review the evidence for computer equity and inequity. First, we discuss gender as a basis for inequity (an area where considerable research has been conducted), then social stratification, and finally ethnicity. Following that, we discuss the overall implications of the state of computer inequity and alternative interventions.

GENDER

Access

School access

As Sutton (1991) notes in her overview of the research on equity and computers in the schools, the literature implicitly defines access in two major ways. The first approach computes the "students per computer" ratio in a school. The second estimates the percentage of students who have used a computer in school. Because differences in access defined the latter way are strongly intertwined with activity or type of use, we have included such reports under the topic of activity in the next section. While differential in-school access for racial, ethnic, and socioeconomic groups is a major concern, for gender groups it virtually becomes a nonissue because boys and girls in the U.S.A. are so seldom segregated into different schools.

Home access

Surprisingly, however, it appears that gender matters to the prospect of having access to computers in the home. The 1985 National Assessment of Educational Progress (NAEP) study (Martinez & Mead, 1988) randomly sampled nearly 40,000 United States students at three grade levels (3, 7, and 11). It asked all students if their families "owned a home computer." In the third grade, 31 percent of the boys compared with 26 percent of the girls had home computers; in the seventh grade, it was 37 percent for boys, but 28 percent for girls; and by the eleventh grade, it was 35 percent compared with 25 percent, a 10 percent gender gap. Similarly, in a Canadian study of 3,000 representative urban eleventh graders, 50 percent of the boys reported having a computer at home while only 35 percent of the girls reported home access (Collis, Kieren, & Kass, 1988). Localized studies in California and Montreal showing the same kind of gender differential in home access to computers add even more evidence to these findings (Braun, Goupil, Giroux, & Chagnon, 1986; Chen, 1986).

Access to computing at home for school-age children may have a strong bearing on women's ensuing success with computers. Martinez and Mead (1988) concluded that home usage was as important as instruction, and perhaps more important, to improving computer competence scores, and a number of studies have found that home computer use improved confidence with computers (Campbell, 1989; Johanson, 1985). Furthermore, early home access may increase the odds of recruitment to computer fields in college. A West Coast study of 312 students enrolled in two semesters of "Introduction to Computer Science," the gateway course for the computer science major, found the enrolled men were twice as likely as the women to have had a personal computer during high school (Kersteen, Linn, Clancy, & Hardyck, 1988).

	1984			1989		
	Male	Female	Difference	Male	Female	Difference
Children (3-17 years old)						
Have computer at home	17	14	3	25	23	2
Use computer at home	14	9	5	21	17	4
Use computer at school	29	27	2	46	46	0
Adults (18 years and older)						
Have computer at home	10	8	2	19	16	3
Use computer at home	6	4	2	12	8	4
Use computer with a job	21	29	-8	32	43	-9

Source: U.S. Bureau of the Census, 1988, 1991, Tables 2 and 4.

Table 10.1
Percentage of Computer Access and Activity for Children and Adults by Sex in 1984 and 1989.

Activity

School activity

The U.S. Census data in Table 10.1 concur with two other national reports (Martinez & Mead, 1988; Platter, 1988) that males and females about equally claim to have used computers in school. But the concept of having ever used a computer in school takes into account neither the extent nor the type of computer use, both areas where large gender differences occur.

Becker and Sterling's (1987) national study of 2,331 U.S. schools in 1985 was based upon teacher estimates rather than student responses. However, it adds more detail to the picture by first dividing schools into three groups based upon whether they rated high, medium, or low in their overall gender equity efforts. Boys dominated game playing at every school regardless of the overall equity level, and boys dominated after-hours use of computers in all schools except the high-equity schools. The only category displaying greater female than male activity was word processing at the high school level.

Home activity

Table 10.1 suggests that home ownership and home use as well as school use all rose considerably in the years between 1984 and 1989 while the gender differences in those categories remained small and similar. However, it is possible that some real differences are masked by methodological limitations and the lack of additional detail on type of use. The studies mentioned earlier indicated that differences in home ownership do indeed exist between men and women. In addition, evidence suggests that men use home computers more frequently than women, at least in the high school and college years (National Center for Education Statistics, 1991b, Table 395). In the 1982-1983 California study (Fetler, 1985), boys were more likely to report learning about computers away from school, at home, from friends, and with video games. Of the eleventh graders who had home computers in the 1987 national Canadian study (Collis, Kieran, & Kass, 1988), significantly more males than females labeled themselves persistent home users while more females disclosed that they never used their home computers.

The strongest gender contrasts in nonschool computing include work as well as play. A striking difference in Table 10.1 is the extent to which female adults surpass males in reporting use of computers with their jobs. Data from the High School and Beyond study (Platter, 1988) support this conclusion. Questioning more than 15,000 randomly sampled young adults four years after they were high school sophomores in 1980 on the contexts of their experience with computers revealed that 26 percent of the women compared with 15 percent of the men had used computers at work while 31 percent of the men compared with 22 percent of the women had used computers for personal or recreational reasons.

Participation

There are no detailed data on the distribution of boys and girls in precollege computer classes, and available reports are somewhat contradictory. The NAEP study (Martinez & Mead, 1988) found boys were only slightly more likely than girls to be "studying computers" at the time of the assessment. In high school, the difference was barely 1 percent. Likewise, our analysis of the 1989 IEA survey found that girls, if anything, outnumbered boys in middle school computer courses and constituted 46 percent of the enrolled students in typical high school computer courses.

In his study of five Bay Area high schools, Chen (1986) found little enrollment difference by gender in nonprogramming computer courses, while Linn's study (1985) of California high school students found 86 percent of the word processing enrollees but only 37 percent of those in programming were female. Becker and Sterling's (1987) national analysis with a 1985 survey of schools agrees with this insofar as it reported widespread female dominance of word processing and male dominance of elective programming in middle schools and high schools. Only at high-gender-equity schools did females participate equally in elective programming; only at low-gender-equity schools did males dominate word processing.

Performance

The topic of computer performance also sustained dual definitions in the equity research literature of the 1980s with a focus placed either upon computer literacy (general understanding of computing) or computer programming (Sutton, 1991). For computer literacy (and competence), small gender differences have been reported. Those found by the NAEP study (Martinez & Mead, 1988) favored boys and were significant--that is, they were not likely to have occurred by chance but small enough to cause question of their practical importance. Those found by Fetler (1985) among California twelfth graders likewise favored boys significantly, but again the differences were small and achievement levels for both girls and boys were quite low. For computer programming, several small-scale studies found no gender difference in skill with either BASIC or LOGO. By the end of the decade, however, schools had shifted their emphasis from programming to applications and using the computer as a tool (Becker, 1990). In one of the earliest representative studies of computer performance, Anderson (1987) found Minnesota eighth and eleventh grade girls and boys to perform equally in programming tests as well as overall computer literacy. His results may be unusual, however, in that when the assessment was taken in 1979—before the deluge of microcomputers—Minnesota already had pioneered special programs to incorporate computers into the classroom. Nevertheless, the evidence all together implies that minimal gender differences exist in precollege computer performance.

It could be said that a third realm of performance related to computer use in the schools consists of the efforts to enhance learning in other subject areas such as reading and writing and math with computer-aided instruction. In general, CAI became a popular mode of school computer activity in the second half of the 1980s (Becker, 1990). Studies on its effectiveness suggest that CAI accrues greater benefits to males than to females (Niemiec & Walberg, 1985). But the findings in this area must be met with considerable caution because the research approaches used may have confounded the medium with the design of instruction (Sutton, 1991).

Higher education

As with enrollment status by gender at the high school level, no comprehensive data exist to settle the question of how much men and women might differ in the particular kinds of computer courses taken in college. Yet we do know that many women fall away from computing fields at this point, i.e., they show low persistence rates, continuing the trend apparently begun in high school to opt out of the full range of computer related courses. In a study of 368 representative undergraduates at an urban California university, only 23 percent of the women compared with 53 percent of the men stated they had taken or planned to take a course in computer science. But these results are undoubtedly somewhat shaped by how relevant the students believed computer science would be to their chosen majors (Miura, 1987). In another study of 305 students in introductory psychology and sociology courses at the University of Winnipeg, fewer women than men claimed intentions to major in computer science. Although the women had studied computing as much as men had in non-computer science courses, they displayed significantly lower levels of prior coursework in computer science itself (Temple & Lips, 1989).

Source: National Center for Education Statistics, 1991a, Table 2:10-3.

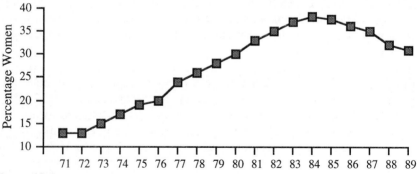

Figure 10-1

Percentage of B.A. Degrees in Computer and Information Sciences Earned by Women 1971 - 1989.

Even when women enroll in college computer programs, they show lower persistence rates than men (Jagacinski, LeBold, & Salvendy, 1988). Whereas women accounted for less than 20 percent of the undergraduate degrees in computer and information sciences before 1977, their share had climbed to 37 percent by 1984. Since then, as Figure 10-1 demonstrates, the rate has been steadily falling. North American enrollments in college computer science have been dropping for both men and women since 1984, but the decline is considerably steeper for women (National Center for Education Statistics, 1991a, Table 2:10-2). This puzzling decline in female representation in college computer science programs has given the computer science community cause for serious concern.

Careers

If, for the moment, we look only at the distance from college to employment, low persistence rates in higher education training programs can be cited as a major factor in the occupational segregation women experience in computing and computer-related jobs. The difference in the computing positions men and women hold are pronounced. Department of Labor annual statistics for 1988 show that men are overrepresented in the three highest-paying computing fields, as analysts, programmers, and repairers, while women disproportionately occupy the computing jobs of operators and keyers.[2] Weekly median salaries for the former group range between $513 and $674; for the latter, between $303 and $342 (Banks & Ackerman, 1990).

---

[2]Computer scientists are omitted from this discussion because they are grouped with math scientists into a single category.

In noncomputing fields as well, women as a whole relate to computers in ways that are distinctive from men. For example, the major occupational grouping of "technical, sales, and administrative support" workers accounts for 44 percent of all working women and only 20 percent of all working men. In every subcategory of this grouping, which includes secretaries and sales clerks, women claim higher rates of computer usage (except for computer equipment operators, whose computer usage rates show no gender difference). Moreover, women use the computers in these jobs differently. Female administrative support workers report word processing, bookkeeping, and invoices among their most common uses considerably more often than the males in administrative support, whose computer work emphasizes inventory and analysis instead (U.S. Bureau of Census, 1991, Tables D, 6, & 7).

This interesting contrast in computer activity by gender is likewise played out among managerial and professional workers, the occupational group that reports the highest rates of specific computer uses. Accounting for about one fourth of each sex in the workforce, women and men have a roughly equal hold on this occupational territory. But if we separate professionals from managers, we first find that women have higher rates of computer use in managerial work than men and a greater emphasis on word processing, bookkeeping,, and communications whereas male managers (like the male administrative support workers) are more likely to emphasize inventory and analysis in their computer activities. Second, we find that female professionals, a category that includes schoolteachers and other professionals, use their computers less than professional men and are more likely to cite instruction as one of their most common computer uses while male professionals cite programming instead (U.S. Bureau of Census, 1991, Tables D, 6, & 7). In short, even when women share occupational categories of equal prestige with men, they tend to use their computers for less prestigious activities in those jobs. It appears that women's computer activities tend to maintain information while men's are more likely to manage and control property.

Summary

Boys have been and continue to be more likely than girls to have and to use computers at home. Also, while the evidence indicates that little to no gender difference exists in computing skills and that equal numbers of boys and girls participate in computing courses well into the middle school years, the kinds and amount of computer activities they pursue at school have already begun to divide along gender lines by that time.

Existing data cannot provide a clear picture of how much these gender divisions intensify in high school, but Figure 10-2 suggests that the gap widens significantly. In 1989, women who had entered the college pipeline to computer science occupations accounted for less than one-third of the bachelor's and master's degrees awarded in the field and approximately one-

Source: National Center for Education Statistics, 1991b, Table 233.

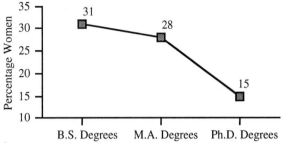

Figure 10-2
Percentage of Women in the Computer Science Pipeline 1988-1989.

seventh of the doctoral degrees. Aside from the moral and political implications of this pipeline shrinkage, it poses serious economic consequences for women and to the future of the workforce (Pearl, Pollack, Riskin, Thomas, Wolf, & Wu, 1990).

SOCIAL STRATIFICATION

The main bases of social stratification are occupation, education, wealth, and power. Researchers operationalize these concepts in a variety of ways, but household income, educational attainment, and occupational prestige, either separately or in some combination, serve as measures of socioeconomic status (SES). Here we concentrate upon income measures because the available computer-related data contain little with regard to education or occupation.

Access

School access

Do low-SES schools offer students the same access to computers as other schools? The annual survey by Quality Education Data, a Denver, Colorado research company, in 1983 reported that the 12,000 wealthiest schools were four times as likely to have computers as were the 12,000 poorest schools. The next question is whether or not such a wide disparity existed at the end of the decade after over two million computers had gone into the schools.

Data from the 1989 IEA Computers in Education Study confirmed that a significant relationship remained between the concentration of computers and wealth of the school district in all but senior high schools. Figure 10-3 gives the number of students per computer by district poverty for each school level. The poverty grouping in this study was based upon the percentage of each school district's children whose family income fell below the federal government poverty guideline. The three groups, low-, medium-, and high-poverty, were created by ranking all schools by the percentage of district families below the poverty line, and then dividing them into the three groups.

Source: IEA Computers in Education 1989 (The Johns Hopkins University, Henry Jay Becker, Study Director).

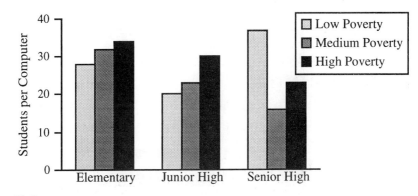

Figure 10-3
Students per Computer by Poverty Level within School Level, 1989.

In both elementary and junior high schools, wealthier (lower-poverty) groups have fewer students per computer than schools with higher poverty. The data on senior high schools, however, show that wealthier schools have a lower students-to-computer ratio than the poorer schools. This reversal can be attributed to special financial assistance for computer equipment to poorer high schools.

This trend in high schools where poorer schools have a greater concentration of computers than wealthier schools should be interpreted in the context of findings from qualitative studies. Piller (1992) found that even though some poor high schools had obtained large numbers of computers, the equipment was often unused because of maintenance problems and lack of human resources. He found one computer lab serving primarily as a detention center. Another lab filled with new, multimedia Macintoshes was used only for teaching typing. Clearly the statistics on access do not serve as adequate indicators of the quality of instruction. Nor should these access statistics be used as a basis for concluding that there is greater equity now in senior high schools.

Home access

Another aspect of access is the availability of computers in the home. In the early years of the microcomputer, the high cost inhibited most persons of modest income from purchasing them (Gaziano, 1983). Now that the costs of home computing have dropped, one would imagine the relationship between income and home computing may have diminished. The data in Figure 10-4 from the 1984 and 1989 Current Population Survey conducted by the U.S. Bureau of the Census reveal that the household computer gap had widened. In 1984, only 2 percent of the households with a family income under $10,000 had a computer, and this rose to 5 percent in 1989. But in 1984, for

Source: U.S. Bureau of the Census, 1988 and 1991, Table 1.

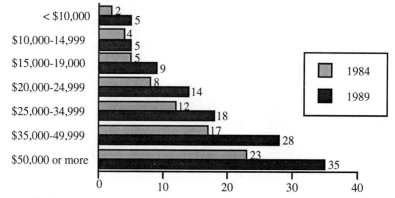

Figure 10-4
Percentage of Households with Computers by Family Income in 1984 and 1989.

those families with incomes over $50,000, 23 percent had a computer in the home; and this increased to 35 percent in 1989. This means the gap widened from 21 percent to 30 percent.

Data from many smaller-scale studies support this trend. For instance, Miura (1987) found when comparing two randomly selected subsets of seventh graders from two California schools that 46 percent of the high socioeconomic status students compared with only 12 percent of the low socioeconomic status students reported access to computers at home.

Activity

School activity

Socioeconomic status also can affect the amount of time that students use computers in school and at home. As Figure 10-5 indicates, the use of computers in school is clearly related to income. For example, in 1984, only 18 percent of those students whose family income was less than $10,000 used a computer in school, and this increased to 37 percent in 1989. Those whose household incomes were more than $50,000, however, used computers in schools at rates of 38 percent in 1984 and 51 percent in 1989. The trend lines show that while the income gap for in-school computer use diminished slightly, it remains quite large.

Platter (1988) analyzed data from the High School and Beyond Study, which asked about the computer activity of a stratified probability sample of the 1980 sophomore cohort three times over a four-year period. Respondents within the lowest SES quartile consistently reported the lowest percentage of computer use. The highest SES quartile reported twice as much educational use and 2 1/2 times more personal use than did the lowest SES quartile

Source: Bureau of the Census, 1988 and 1991, Table 2.

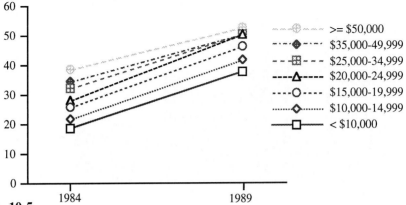

Figure 10-5
Percentage of Children (Ages 3 to 17 Years) Who Used Computers in School, by
Family Income in 1984 and 1989.

(Platter, 1988). Similar relationships of computer experience with family
income and father's education were reported by Platter.

Home activity

Although the difference between the rich and the poor in school
computer use is pronounced, the difference in home computer use by
household income is even more so, as shown in Figure 10-6. The Current
Population Survey found only 3 percent of those students whose household
income was less than $10,000 used computers at home in 1984. This
increased by 5 percent to 8 percent in 1989. Those students whose household
incomes were above $50,000 used computers at home at rates of 22 percent

Source: Bureau of Census, 1988 and 1991, Table 2.

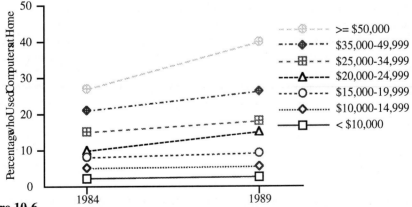

Figure 10-6
Percentage of Children (Ages 3 to 17 Years) Who Used Computers at Home, by
Family Income in 1984 and 1989.

Source: National Assessment of Educational Progress (Martinez & Mead, 1988).

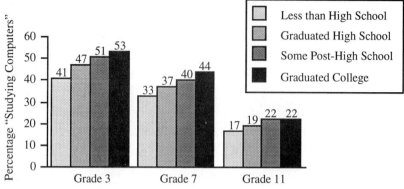

Figure 10-7
Percentage of Students Who Were "Studying Computers," by Parent's Education.

and 44 percent in 1984 and 1989, respectively—a 22 percent jump. In both 1984 and 1989, the percentage of students whose household income was less than $15,000 and used computers at home never exceeded 10 percent. The same statistic for those students whose household income exceeds $40,000 never fell below 20 percent.

Participation

Differences are also evident in the types of classes that students enroll in. Figure 10-7 shows data from the 1985 NAEP study. These percentages show that for all three grade levels tested, 3, 7, and 11, the more education one's parents had, the more likely one was to be "studying computers" in school. This difference was strongest for grades 3 and 7. Numerous studies have noted that minority and poor students spend more time on computer-assisted-instruction (CAI) and less time on programming than do other students. Anderson, Welch, and Harris (1984) analyzed data from the 1978 and 1982 National Science Assessments and stated that not only were more non-Title 1 (higher-income) students studying programming, but that this gap had increased between 1978 and 1982. Campbell (1989) found that affluent suburban schools taught more programming and computer literacy than poorer areas. West, Miller, and Diodato (1985) found that high-SES students were twice as likely as low-SES students to have earned computer science credit.

Summary

Our review of the relationship between socioeconomic status and computer exposure revealed that low-SES students are often disadvantaged when compared with high-SES students both in school and at home. In some cases, however, this disadvantage is changing; while we found a greater concentration of computers in wealthier elementary and middle schools,

Percentage Nonwhite	Elementary	Lower Secondary	Upper Secondary	Total
0 - 25%	28.58	20.63	25.60	24.76
	(237)	(268)	(246)	(751)
26 - 56%	33.62	25.48	18.82	26.01
	(61)	(45)	(61)	(168)
57 - 100%	39.40	41.78	29.73	37.74
	(54)	(51)	(37)	(143)
Total	31.13	24.20	24.83	26.71
	(352)	(365)	(344)	(1062)

Source: IEA Computers in Education Study, 1989 (The Johns Hopkins University, Henry Jay Becker, Director).

Table 10.2
Ratio of Students per Computer by Percentage Nonwhite in School and School Level, 1989.

senior high schools in 1989 no longer followed that statistical pattern. Even though the cost of microcomputers has dropped, students with higher family incomes still have greater access to computers at home. This gap has widened since the early 1980s.

Low-SES students are less likely to be enrolled in computer science classes, and when they do use computers, they are more likely to use them for computer assisted instruction instead of programming or computer literacy. There is evidence that the mere presence of microcomputers may not be enough to reduce this difference in type of use. The evidence on home computer activity is comparable. Those students with lower family incomes are least likely to use a computer at home, and this gap has widened since 1984.

ETHNICITY

Access

School access

The concentration or density of computers, as measured by the ratio of number of students to the number of computers has been the most common measure of computer equity among schools. However, breakdowns of this ratio have rarely been available by the concentration of minority students within schools. The first major exception to this data vacuum was Becker's 1983 school survey (Becker, 1985a). Among elementary schools, he found that the median ratio of students per computer was 182 to 1 for all schools, but 215 to 1 for predominantly minority schools. This pattern was replicated at both the elementary and secondary school levels in his 1985 survey (Becker & Sterling, 1987).

Source: U.S. Bureau of the Census, 1991, Table 2.

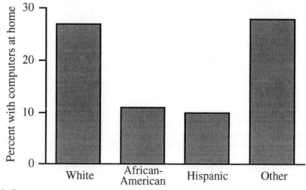

Figure 10-8

Percentage of children (ages 3-17 years) with computers at home, by ethinicity, 1989.

This pattern has continued through the 1980s, as our analysis of data from the 1989 IEA survey demonstrates. In the 1989 data, inequities were greatest at the elementary and lower secondary school level (see Table 10.2). For instance, at the lower secondary level in predominantly white schools the student-to-computer ratio was 21 to 1 compared with 42 to 1 in predominantly nonwhite schools. During the 1980s both lower secondary and elementary schools which were populated primarily by minority students provided less access to computers than predominantly white schools.

Home access

The earliest report which described home computing access by ethnicity was from the 1985 National Assessment of Education Progress (NAEP). It found fewer minority students reporting that their "families own a computer." For instance, among seventh graders, 36 percent of the white students said their families owned a computer, but only 26 percent of African-American and 21 percent of Hispanic students reported that their families owned one (Martinez & Mead, 1988).

The most recent data available on ethnicity and home computing is found in the 1989 Current Population Survey, summarized in Figure 10-8. These data are based upon the counts of children in the 3-to-17-year-old range who reside in homes with a computer (U.S. Bureau of the Census, 1991). The results show that while 26 percent of the white children in this age range lived in homes with a computer, only 14 percent of Hispanic children and 11 percent of African-American children did. However, 28 percent of those whose race was classified as "other" reported a computer at home. Presumably, most Asian students fell into this group, which most likely accounts for the higher concentration of home computers. These data show

Source: U.S. Bureau of the Census, 1991, Table 2.

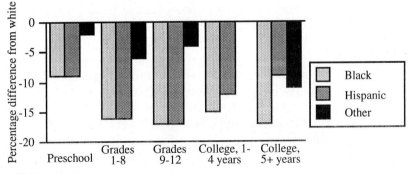

Figure 10-9
Minority Student Gap: Percentage Difference in Home Computer Use with White
Students as Baseline, 1989.

that the ethnic disadvantage in access to school computers in general is not
counterbalanced by access to home computers. Given the persistent income-
based computing gap, it is not surprising that ethnic minorities, who on
average have lower incomes, might be less likely to have home computers.
This technological disadvantage for minority students begins in the home,
and is perpetuated in elementary school and beyond.

Activity

School activity

The 1989 Current Population Survey also found that white students were
much more likely to use computers in school than African-American,
Hispanic, or those describing their race as "other." This gap again was
considerably larger in the elementary grades than at the secondary school
level. In grades 1 to 8, the reported current computer use in school was 36
percent of African-Americans, 40 percent of Hispanics, 58 percent of whites,
and 49 percent of other ethnic groups (National Center for Education
Statistics, 1991b, Table 395).

Home activity

The disparities between ethnic groups loom even larger when comparing
them on the percentage actually using computers in the home. The 1989
Current Population Survey found that not only were African-American and
Hispanic students much less likely to have a computer at home, but if they
did have one, they were much less likely to use it. Figure 10-9 shows this gap
by using the white students as a baseline. At nearly every level in the
educational system, minority students who had computers at home were less
likely to be using them from preschool through college. This difference is

magnified in high school: African-American and Hispanic high school students were 17 percent less likely than white students to use their home computers. Even at the college and postgraduate levels, minority students were less likely to use home computers.

Participation

Access to computers at school is least for minority students in the early grade levels. Inequity in use at school parallels this finding. When asked whether school-age children in the home were "studying computers," the differences between minority and ethnic groups across the third and seventh grades were small but significant. The differences narrowed to a percentage point or two by the eleventh grade (Martinez & Mead, 1988). It appears that students of minority racial and ethnic backgrounds may be studying computers as frequently as whites, but whites are more likely to be taking higher-level computer classes such as programming. School-level findings suggest that the programming course participation rate among students in predominantly minority schools was half that of students in predominantly white schools, which was 21 percent (Becker & Sterling, 1987).

Performance

Inequities in home computer use were substantial across high school years and college years. This pattern in inequities led to significant aggregate differences in computer capabilities, and these differences were particularly in evidence among high school students. African-American and Hispanic students scored approximately 5 to 8 percent lower on a test of computer competence than white students (Martinez & Mead, 1988).

Higher education

The decades of the '70s and '80s witnessed increased rates of high school graduation for racial and ethnic minorities and women. More than ever, minorities and women were working on college degrees, but the field of study was not likely to be computer science. The proportion of African-American and Hispanic college students who received undergraduate degrees in computer and information sciences was very low. Of all undergraduate degrees given for computer and information sciences in 1988-1989, African-Americans received only 8 percent and Hispanics received only 3 percent. Less than 4 percent of master's degrees and doctorates in computer and information sciences were awarded to African-Americans or Hispanics that year (National Center for Education Statistics, 1991b, Tables 246, 248, and 250).

Careers

Data from the 1988 annual Department of Labor Statistics (Banks & Ackerman, 1990) demonstrate that there have been clear discrepancies in computer occupations across racial and ethnic groups. By comparing a racial or ethnic group's proportion in the population with its proportion in each computer job category, it is possible to determine that group's relative overrepresentation or underrepresentation in the job category. The higher-paying careers, which include analyst positions and programmers, were disproportionately occupied by white males. Nonwhite males were underrepresented in all computer occupations except repairers.

Women of all ethnic and racial backgrounds, including whites, were underrepresented in all relatively higher-level computer occupations (analysts, programmers, and repairers). Nonwhite females were underrepresented by at least 50 percent in each of the higher-level computer-using occupations. White females were also underrepresented in these higher-level occupations, but not to the degree of nonwhite females. All females were dramatically overrepresented among computer operators and keyers. In the key-entry occupational category, African-American women were overrepresented by a factor of 2 (Banks & Ackerman, 1990).

Summary

Racial inequities are found at nearly each possible juncture in computing, starting with fewer computers available for minority students to use—at school as well as at home. Predominantly minority schools have tended to have more students competing for computers, thus reducing access. The disparities in home computer use were particularly significant, and became greater for minority students in secondary and postsecondary school.

Ethnicity-based gaps in frequency of computer use exacerbate the gaps in computer access. Even though most high schools had computers, minority students were using them less. This may be a latent effect of underexposure to computers in early years; yet even when computers were available to minority students in later years, they did not get used. High school is often the first chance many students have to choose certain courses. Computer courses often fall into this optional category, attracting students who have both prerequisite skills and an interest in the subject. A higher proportion of white students were enrolled in computer courses and, in particular, computer programming courses. This difference in enrollments is noteworthy because it impacts postgraduation job skills.

Disproportionately fewer minority students obtained undergraduate or graduate degrees in computer and information science, and after graduation a substantial gap opened in computer employment. Nonwhite males were disproportionately underrepresented in all computer occupations while white males were overrepresented in higher-level computer jobs. Females of all ethnic backgrounds were underrepresented in all higher-level computer jobs, and overrepresented in lower-level computer jobs, including operators and keyers.

GLOBAL ISSUES

Our analysis thus far has focused primarily upon the educational context of one country, the United States. Computer equity, especially gender equality, is of interest in a number of countries, and data are just beginning to become available for making international comparisons (Pelgrum & Plomp, 1991). Because of the controversial nature of ethnicity and social stratification, as well as differing definitions and procedures, it will be difficult if not impossible to investigate questions of computer equity across countries. One type of international comparison that is possible to examine is the extent to which student access to computers depends upon the relative wealth of nations. The data from the IEA Computers in Education Study provide such an opportunity. Figure 10-10 shows that student access to computers as measured by the average number of computers per thousand students is correlated with the country's per capita gross national product (GNP). Countries with higher average income, such as Japan, Switzerland, and the U.S.A., tend to have a greater computer density in their schools, whereas countries with lower average income levels, such as India and Portugal, tend to have very few school computers available. A country's per capita GNP is not the only determinant of the number of computers in its schools, but these data from only a few countries show that it can have a major influence on student access. The implications of this relationship for third world countries are serious and suggest how difficult it will be to achieve global computer equity (Hawkridge, Jaworski, and McMahon, 1990).

AGENDAS FOR CHANGE

Attempts to reform or otherwise improve education are called interventions by program evaluators, who try to measure program impacts. To determine the effectiveness of interventions it is necessary to identify both desired and undesired outcomes and to attempt to measure them. There have been very few computer equity interventions that have been accompanied by this type of evaluation research. Consequently the state of knowledge on how to implement computer education programs is quite primitive. In this section we first review the equity interventions that have been reported in the research literature and then outline some of the key factors that account for more or less success in the implementation of equity programs.

Interventions

Teacher training

In one of the first tests of an intervention for gender inequities (Fish, Gross, & Sanders, 1986), staff at three experimental middle schools attended equity workshops and implemented strategies for involving girls with computers that had been suggested in *The Neuter Computer* by Sanders and Stone (1986). Three findings emerged. Mandating the implementations

Source: IEA Computers in Education Study, 1989 (The Johns Hopkins University, Henry J. Becker, Study Director).

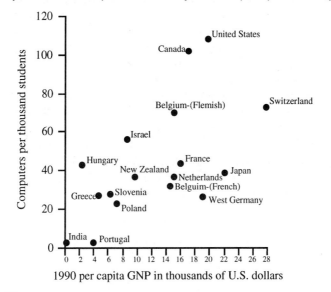

Figure 10-10
International comparisons of upper secondary systems: Computers per 1,000 students by per capita GNP, 1989.

mattered; in one control school, staff had been sensitized to the same information, but no behavior change occurred without a requirement to make change. Offering girls exclusive time and activities mattered; students and teachers in common reported that the most effective strategies had been those that allowed girls to work in same-sex contexts, and half of the girls said contexts where no other girls were present discouraged them from participation. Finally, girls' computer use did increase in the experimental schools while it did not in control schools. A similar effort in Kansas produced reports of increased computer use and enjoyment among upper elementary and middle school girls (Thurston, 1990).

Computer experience

The effects of school computer experience varies greatly from study to study depending presumably upon the instructional and technological context. For college women, experience apparently improves computer comfort and sense of competence (Arch & Cummins, 1989; Miura, 1987; Wilder, Mackie, & Cooper, 1985). Likewise for younger students, some research has linked experience to improved attitudes and higher competence (Levin & Gordon, 1989; Martinez & Mead, 1988). In other research, however, increased familiarity seemed to produce decreases in girls' liking, enjoyment, and self-confidence with computers (Collis, 1985; Krendl & Broihier, 1991; Wilder , Mackie, & Cooper, 1985).

Chambers and Clarke (1987) studied the infusion of new computer technology in seven schools in Australia during the 1985 school year. They conducted student surveys and tests before the computers were introduced at these schools and repeated these measures at the end of the school year. Four "disadvantaged" student groups were tracked: girls, low-SES students, those with low "school ability," and students with parents born outside of Australia. Students belonging to these groups were less likely to benefit from the computer initiative. (The researchers' criteria for benefit were greater computer use both inside and outside school, greater knowledge about computers, and more positive attitudes toward computers.) Ironically, the introduction of new computer technology in these Australian schools resulted generally in greater inequities. Until more details are known about the school context and the quality of student computer experiences, these research findings and other inconsistencies will remain unexplained. In any event, the existing research does suggest that the mere introduction of new technology into a school does not guarantee greater computer equity, much less improved computer instruction.

School policy initiatives

Without knowing the details or the results of their efforts, we do know that a share of American schools are involved in implementing equity actions. In the IEA 1989 Computers in Education Study directed by Henry Becker at The Johns Hopkins University, some school principals reported efforts to provide special computing opportunities for girls, to educate parents and staff on gender equity issues, or to recruit female role models to positions as computer teachers and aides. Our analysis of these data found that high schools showed higher rates of such action than middle or elementary schools. Interestingly, high rates of equity action were associated with the "gender isolation" of the principal; that is, in elementary schools where school principals are predominantly female, male principals were more likely to implement equity actions; and in high schools where principals are predominantly male, female principals engaged in the most gender equity intervention.

Computer networks

We highlight one type of technological intervention, computer networks, because of its potential for education in cultural diversity. Evaluation research on the impact of educational networking projects is only beginning but suggests bases for optimism.

Cummins and Sayers (1990) reviewed cross-cultural telecommunications projects which bring together students of different geographical and cultural backgrounds on a common theme. Such projects did not focus on the computer but rather used the computer as a tool for empowering students who come from diverse disadvantaged backgrounds. Project Orillas is one example where teachers from North America were paired with teachers from

South America, and these "sister" classes shared perspectives on social issues related to societal power relations. Cummins and Sayers concluded that this method of empowerment goes beyond providing equitable computer experience and encourages students to critically examine the larger societal issues of equity.

DeVillar and Faltis (1991) cite educational computer technology as key to facilitating the reduction of educational inequities in multicultural settings. Their "socio-academic achievement model" promotes a combination of social learning and independence. They note, however, that barriers to effectively implementing such technology are "formidable," in large part because the policies of implementation tend to be "divisive rather than integrative." For, as Diem (1986) has noted, the socially mediated processes of computer use in the classroom tend to favor those most facile with the technology.

Key Factors

Even though the amount of intervention research has been slim, discussions in the literature point to key factors that clarify the underlying processes. In planning and studying change it is essential to take the following factors into account.

Social support

Socialization theories emphasize psychology and individual processes as the mediums for change. What this overlooks is the social side of the picture: how family, school, work, government, and the media all structure people's opportunities. Redressing inequities in computing is a lot bigger task than simply enticing girls and minority students to take part.

Considerable research has documented how the lack of social support discourages girls and young women from computing. Two studies suggest how much the computer industry shortchanges girls by stereotyping software and by portraying women in subordinate images remote from the computer in mass market magazines (Huff & Cooper, 1987; Ware & Stuck, 1985). At the school level, role models are often available; however, concern exists over the extent to which parents, teachers, and school counselors depend upon traditional stereotypes in their interactions with students and pay less attention to girls (Fox & Hesse-Biber, 1984). A startling finding in the research is how consistently boys more than girls will say that girls are unsuitable for computing in some ways (Collis & Williams, 1987; Johnson, Johnson, & Stanne, 1986; Levin & Gordon, 1989; Smith, 1987; Temple & Lips, 1989; Wilder, Mackie, & Cooper, 1985). Boys and girls alike view a girl computer enthusiast as attractive in primary school. By junior high, she is likely to be seen as a lonely girl who has problems with her femininity (Lage, 1991).

From his observational research, Diem (1986) found that students when given a choice tended to do computer work in small groups. In these groups, students were likely to assume one of three roles, the "expert,"the "experimenter," or the "observer." The expert and the experimenter were quasi-leaders of the groups and tended to be those with more experience or knowledge of computers, as well as more confidence. Observers made up the bulk of the groups and were essentially peripheral to the hands-on action.

Diem (1986) suggests that problems in inequitable learning are sometimes compounded by teacher behavior. Teachers tend to reward those students who are the most technologically literate by giving them additional or alternative tasks. Those who already have more knowledge and experience are given opportunities to further learn while students of lesser ability are given fewer options and very likely more lower-level opportunities. This effectively stratifies the classroom, essentially "tracking" students from different ability levels into different computer learning activities. Thus, students of different backgrounds tend to get involved in different types of computer activity that serve to differentially equip them in computer skills and experience.

While there has been relatively little research on social support systems in computing, a growing consensus among specialists and researchers claims the most effective action that can be taken to reduce the low persistence of females in computing is the establishment of mentoring programs (Martin & Murchie-Beyma, 1992). A critical element of effective mentoring is the availability of role models and social support.

Efficacy

Self-confidence with regard to computer-related tasks appears to be a major determinant of performance and desire to participate in computer activities. While this affects all disadvantaged student groups, most of the efficacy research has concentrated on gender. Adolescent girls, more than boys and more than younger girls, exhibit lower confidence and self-esteem, higher rates of depression, and tendencies to blame failure on themselves rather than circumstances (American Association of University Women, 1992; Fox & Hesse-Biber, 1984). In math and science, such lowered self-confidence, along with perceptions of the irrelevance of math and science to girls, is linked to lowered motivation and accounts for much of the gender differences achievement (Marini & Brinton, 1984). Similarly (as the discussion of performance indicated), it is not girls' abilities that seem to be the hindrance in computing. Girls themselves will assert that boys and girls are equal in ability with computers (Collis & Williams, 1987; Martinez & Mead, 1988). But when girls are asked to rate themselves individually, they indicate a sense of efficacy significantly lower than boys do. The label Collis (1985) created for these findings also summarizes this research theme fairly well. She calls it the "We Can, But I Can't" paradox. It is easy to blame the victim for this state of affairs by concluding that the solution to inequities is to raise efficacy levels. But structural deterrents such as stereotyped segregation by gender must also be altered.

Cultural software bias

As Scott, Cole, and Engel (1992) point out, student interactions with computers are a form of communication, dependent upon shared culture. Until recently, software was written primarily for English language users; keyboards and screen drivers did not facilitate other languages. This effectively may restrict computing experiences to students comfortable with North American or European middle-class language and culture. Students whose first language is not English, particularly Southeast Asians and Hispanics, suffer a disadvantage. It is quite possible that other ethnic minorities, such as African-American students, also may be hampered by the lack of cultural diversity in educational software. Elementary-level students who come from home environments in which a different language is spoken may be disadvantaged most.

Gender bias

Feminists have become particularly interested in examining how computing is constructed as a male domain (Griffiths, 1988; Perry & Greber, 1990; Turkle & Papert, 1990). Computer user seems to be one of those social roles that masquerades as sex-neutral when in fact it is defined largely by male opinion leaders. For example, either males or females can ostensibly fill the role of worker, but females appear less successful in that role because its ideal definition has been constructed as male (Acker, 1990). Huff and Cooper's (1987) findings demonstrate a similar gendering of the supposedly neutral within computing. When software designers were asked to develop programs for students in general, they created programs almost identical to the ones they had specifically produced for boys and distinctly different from the ones they had produced for girls.

Females are demonstrably sensitive to the masculine connotations of computing's image. They are more likely than males to see computers as impersonal, dehumanizing, and rigid (Badagliacco, 1990) and computer users as sedentary, asocial eggheads (Collis, 1985). The question is how far female-associated values and skills have been rendered invisible by the social construction of computing when in fact they might be integral or advantageous pieces. Anderson (1987) argues that the substance of computing is grounded as much in words as in numbers, and Kramer and Lehman (1990) suggest that the old number crunching images of computing are giving way to new metaphors about interaction, communication, and cooperation. Image alterations such as these might work toward balancing the current one-sidedness of computing's gender associations.

Quality of computing

Computer activity has a qualitative dimension: All uses of the computer are not equal. Playing games on the computer uses and develops different skills than using word processing software or writing programs. Intensive concentration in certain areas will lead to a deficit in other areas. The implicit premium is put on experience in higher-order activities such as programming skills over lower-order activities such as computer-assisted drills and practice. Therefore, inequities in type of computer activity are as important as overall usage. In his 1983 national survey of schools, Becker (1985a) found that the focus in predominantly minority schools was more likely to be on drill and practice sessions on the computer. Schools which were predominantly white, on the other hand, had a stronger emphasis on use of the computer for programming-related activities.

Sutton illustrates the rationalization for this differential pattern of use:

> The low-SES children who are disproportionately African-American were gaining most of their experience with a computer when it was in control, informing the student when he or she was correct. In contrast, the high-SES students, who were disproportionately white were gaining considerable experience when they were in control, giving the computer a series of instructions, and observing the consequences of these instructions. This differential is consistent with the long standing beliefs that children must first master the basics before moving to higher order thinking and that poor and minority children lack the basics. (Sutton, 1991, p. 482)

This difference in the quality of interaction with computers serves to differentially equip students for computer problem solving. As a result, many lower-SES and minority students gain experience with computers which does not equitably prepare them for higher-level computer activities, such as programming.

Educational system policies

Problems of computer inequity must be addressed both qualitatively by improving computer instruction and quantitatively by installing computer resources on a large scale. All levels of an educational system from the classroom up to the national government must take action. A few model schools cannot solve the problem; actions must be taken at the national level as well. Current national policy on educational computing is characterized by Borrell (1992) as embarrassing and ineffective. Not only does "America lack direction" on educational technology, he argues, but "America will march into the future without adequate planning, effective implementation, or a national agenda, while other countries such as Japan and France implement well-coordinated policies" on computer education (p. 30). Those few who continue to champion major reform in educational computing seek large-scale funding of innovative educational software, teacher training and support systems, as well as additional technology (Branscum, 1992). However, Kondracke (1992) predicts that in the current political climate another decade may pass before the problems are addressed on a large scale.

CONCLUSIONS

Our systematic review of the data from large, representative studies has found strong evidence of persistent patterns of computer inequity among gender, income, and racial groups. The complex patterns of ongoing computer inequity confirm the usefulness of the sociological concepts of gender roles, social stratification, and ethnicity in understanding the implications of computer technology.

While the quantitative evidence for widespread computer inequity is substantial, the qualitative studies reveal that the actual inequities probably are vastly greater than the statistics indicate. Underutilization of computing resources has not been measured effectively in statistical studies, and disadvantaged students are much more likely to go to schools that waste computing resources becasue of lack of teacher training and other constraints. In fact, the condition of educational computing in urban ghettos is so impoverished that the cover of the September 1992 issue of *Macworld* magazine called it "America's Shame."

Not everyone shares concern over evidence of gross computer inequity. Some argue that in the future computer inequity will dissipate because computer applications will be so user-friendly. Another claim is that computers will be ubiquitous—that is, embedded everywhere in both our work and personal spaces (Weiser, 1991), and that everyone will be exposed to them outside of school. The problem with these arguments is that new ways to use computers will continue to expand in number and complexity. These new applications will continue to challenge designers of human interfaces and expand the need for training and specialized expertise rather than diminish it. While the cost of computers will continue to drop, the cost of new applications and the associated training will be sufficiently high that not everyone will be able to afford it. In fact it is quite likely that large, lower-income sectors of the society will not have opportunities to experience cutting-edge computing technology unless they find it at school.

A recent economic analysis of U.S. Census data found that after eliminating the effects of SES, education, and type of job, workers who used computers in their jobs during the 1980s earned an average of 15 percent higher wages (Krueger, 1991). It is unlikely for the reasons just given that the value of computer skills will decline during the 1990s and beyond. Consequently, inequities will not only continue but will reinforce the dual economy and reduce the relative economic well-being of large segments of the society.

What can be done to remedy these computer inequities in the educational system? Regrettably, there has been so little research on this question that we only can speculate about what consequences might result from alternative reforms to produce greater computer equity. Therefore, the first agenda for change should be to initiate and fund research on the outcomes of various strategies to reduce inequity and improve the quality of computer utilization in education.

In this review of research on computer equity we have attempted to avoid making value judgments about computer equity, its priority, and what should be done about it. Nonetheless it is the personal opinion of the authors that computer equity is a serious social problem and that major steps should be taken to ameliorate existing conditions. We urge that these steps be accompanied by extensive research on the outcomes of such programs.

REFERENCES

Acker, J. (1990). Hierarchies, jobs, bodies: a theory of gendered organizations. *Gender and Society, 4(2)*, 139-158.

American Association of University Women (1992). How schools shortchange girls. Washington, DC: AAUW Educational Foundation.

Anderson, R. E. (1987). Females surpass males in computer problem solving: findings from the Minnesota computer literacy assessment. *Journal of Educational Computing Research, 3(1)*, 39-51.

Anderson, R. E., Klassen, D. L., Krohn, K. R., & Smith-Cunnien, P. (1982). Assessing computer literacy. St. Paul, MN: Minnesota Educational Computing Consortium.

Anderson, R. E., Welch, W. W., & Harris, L. J. (1984, April). Inequities in opportunities for computer literacy. *The Computing Teacher*, 10-12.

Arch, E. C., & Cummins, D. E. (1989). Structured and unstructured exposure to computers: sex differences in attitude and use among college students. *Sex Roles, 20(5-6)*, 245-254.

Badagliacco, J. M. (1990). Gender and race differences in computing attitudes and experience. *Social Science Computer Review, 8(l)*, 42-63.

Banks, M. E., & Ackerman, R. J. (1990). Ethnic and gender computer employment status. *Social Science Computer Review, 8(1)*, 75-82.

Becker, H. J. (1985a). How schools use microcomputers: summary of the 1983 National Survey. Second National Survey of Instructional Uses of School Computers. Baltimore, MD: The Johns Hopkins University.

Becker, H. J. (1985b). Men and women as computer using teachers. *Sex Roles, 13(3-4)*, 137-148.

Becker, H.J. (1990, April). Computer use in United States schools: 1989. An initial report of U.S. participation in the I.E.A. computers in education survey. Paper presented at the Annual meeting of the American Educational Research Association, Boston.

Becker, H. J., & Sterling, C. W. (1987). Equity in school computer use: national data and neglected considerations. *Journal of Educational Computing Research, 3(3)*, 289-311.

Bluestone, B. (1970). The tripartite economy: labor markets and the working poor. *Poverty and Human Resources, 5*, 15-35.

Boozer, M. A., Krueger, A. B., & Wolkon, S. (1992). Race and school quality since Brown v. Board of Education (pp. 269-338). In M.N. Bailey and C. Winston (eds.), *Brookings Papers on Economic Activity: Microeconomics*. Washington, D.C.: The Brookings Institution.

Brookings Papers on Economic Activity: Microeconomics 1992. Washington, DC: The Brookings Institution.

Borrell, J. (1992). Personal computers in education. *Macworld, 9(9)*, 25-30.

Branscum, D. (1992). Conspicuous consumer. *Macworld, 9(9)*, 83-88.

Braun, C. M., Goupil, G., Giroux, J., & Chagnon, Y. (1986). Adolescents and microcomputers: Sex differences, proxemics, task and stimulus variables. *Journal of Psychology, 120(6)*, 529-542.

Bryson, M., & Castell, S. (1992). So we've got a chip on our shoulder!: sexing the texts of educational technologies. In J. Willingskey & J. Gaskell (eds.), *Gender Enriches Curriculum.* New York: Teachers College Press.

Campbell, N. J. (1989). Computer anxiety of rural middle and secondary school students. *Journal of Educational Computing Research. 5(2)*, 213-220.

Chambers, S. M., & Clarke, V. A. (1987). Is inequity cumulative? The relationship between disadvantaged group membership and students' computing experience, knowledge, attitudes and intentions. *Journal of Educational Computing Research, 3(4)*, 495-518.

Chen, M. (1986). Gender and computers: the beneficial effects of experience on attitudes. *Journal of Educational Computing Research, 2(3)*, 265-282.

Collis, B. (1985). Psychosocial implications of sex differences in attitudes toward computers: results of a survey. *International Journal of Women's Studies, 8(3)*, 207-213.

Collis, B., Kieren, T. E., & Kass, H. (1988, April). A multidimensional study of adolescent gender differences in computer use and impact. Paper presented at the annual meeting of the American Educational Research Association (AERA), New Orleans, LA.

Collis, B. A., & Williams, R. L. (1987). Cross cultural comparison of gender differences in adolescents' attitudes toward computers and selected school subjects. *Journal of Educational Research, 81(1)*, 17-27.

Cummins, J., & Sayers, D. (1990). Education 2001: learning networks and educational reform. *Computers in Schools, 1(1-2)*, 1-29.

DeVillar, R.A., & Faltis, C.J. (1991). Computers and cultural diversity: restructuring for school success. New York: State University of New York.

Diem, R. A. (1986). Computers in a school environment: preliminary report of the social consequences. *Theory and Research in Social Education, 14(2)*, 163-170.

Fetler, M. (1985). Sex differences on the California statewide assessment of computer literacy. *Sex Roles, 13(3-4)*, 181-191.

Fish, M. C., Gross, A. L., & Sanders, J. S. (1986). The effect of equity strategies on girls' computer usage in school. *Computers in Human Behavior, 2(2)*, 127-134.

Fox, M. F., & Hesse-Biber, S. (1984). *Women at Work.* Palo Alto, CA: Mayfield Publishing Co.

Gaziano, C. (1983, November). "Megatrends" and knowledge gaps: future predictions. Paper presented at the meeting of the Midwest Association for Public Opinion Research, Chicago, IL.

Griffiths, M. (1988). Strong feelings about computers. *Women's Studies International Forum, 11(2)*, 145-154.

Hawkridge, D., Jaworski, J., & McMahon, H. (1990). *Computers in Third-World Schools.* New York: St. Martin's Press.

Hodson, R., & Kaufman, R. (1982). Economic dualism: a critical review. *American Sociological Review, 47(6)*, 727-739.

Huff, C., & Cooper, J. (1987). Sex bias in educational software: the effect of designers' stereotypes on the software they design. *Journal of Applied Social Psychology, 17(6)*, 519-532.

Huff, C., Fleming, J. H., & Cooper, J. (1992). Gender differences in human-computer interaction. In C. D. Martin & E. Murchie-Beyma (eds.), *In Search of Gender-Free Paradigms for Computer Science Education* (pp. 19-32). Eugene, OR: International Society for Technology in Education (ISTE).

Jagacinski, C. M., LeBold, W. K., & Salvendy, G. (1988). Gender differences in persistence in computer related fields. *Journal of Educational Computing Research, 4(2)*, 185-202.

Johanson, R. P. (1985, March). School computing: some factors affecting student performance. Paper presented at the annual meeting of the American Educational Research Association (AERA), Chicago, IL.

Johnson, R. T., Johnson, D. W., & Stanne, M. B. (1986). Comparison of computer assisted cooperative, competitive, and individualistic learning. *American Educational Research Journal, 23(3)*, 382-392.

Kersteen, Z. A., Linn, M. C., Clancy, M., & Hardyck, C. (1988). Previous experience and the learning of computer programming: the computer helps those who help themselves. *Journal of Educational Computing Research, 4(3)*, 321-333.

Kondracke, M. (1992). The official word. *Macworld, 9(9)*, 232-236.

Kramer, P. E., & Lehman, S. (1990). Mismeasuring women: a critique of research on computer ability and avoidance. *Signs, 16(l)*, 158-172.

Krendl, K. A., & Broihier, M. (1991). Student responses to computers: a longitudinal study. Paper presented at the annual meeting of the International Communication Association, Chicago, IL.

Krueger, A. B. (1991). How computers have changed the wage structure: evidence from microdata 1984-89 (Working Paper #291). Princeton, NJ: Princeton University, Industrial Relations Section.

Kulick, J. A., & Kulick, C. C. (1987). Review of recent literature on computer-based instruction. *Contemporary Educational Psychology, 12*, 222-230.

Lage, E. (1991). Boys, girls, and microcomputing. *European Journal of Psychology of Education, 6(l)*, 29-44.

Levin, T., & Gordon, C. (1989). Effect of gender and computer experience on attitudes toward computers. *Journal of Educational Computing Research, 5(1)*, 69-88.

Linn, M. C. (1985). Fostering equitable consequences from computer learning environments. *Sex Roles, 13(3-4)*, 229-240.

Marini, M. M., & Brinton, M. C. (1984). Sex typing in occupational socialization. In Barbara Reskin (ed.) Sex segregation in the workplace: trends, explanations, remedies (pp. 192-232). Washington, DC: National Academy Press.

Martin, C.D., & Murchie-Beyma, E. (eds.) (1992). *In Search of Gender Free Paradigms for Computer Science Education*. Eugene, OR: International Society for Technology in Education (ISTE).

Martinez, M. E., & Mead, N. A. (1988). Computer competence: the first national assessment (Tech. Rep. No. 17-CC-0l). Princeton, NJ: National Assessment of Educational Progress & Educational Testing Service.

McKinnon, D. H., & Nolan, P. C. J. (1990). Curriculum innovation with computers: redressing inequities of access and use in the Freyberg Integrated Studies Project. In A. McDougal & C. Dowling (eds.). *Computers in Education: Proceedings from the Fifth World Conference on Computers in Education* (pp. 145-153). Amsterdam, The Netherlands: North-Holland.

Miura, I. T. (1987). The relationship of self-efficacy expectations to computer interest and course enrollment in college. *Sex Roles, 16(5-6)*, 303-311.

National Center for Education Statistics (1991a). *The Condition of Education: Volume 2: Postsecondary Education*. Washington, DC: U.S. Department of Education.

National Center for Education Statistics. (1991b). *Digest of Current Education Statistics 1991*. Washington, DC: U.S. Government Printing Office.

National Governors Association (1991). *Time for Results: The Governors' 1991 Report on Education*. Washington, DC: National Governors Association.

Niemiec, R. P., & Walberg, H. J. (1985). Computers and achievement in the elementary schools. *Journal of Educational Computing Research, 1(4)*, 435-440.

Pearl, A., Pollack, M., Riskin, E., Thomas, B., Wolf, E., & Wu, A. (1990). Becoming a computer scientist: a report by the ACM Committee on the Status of Women in Computing Science. *Communications of the ACM, 33(11)*, 47-57.

Pelgrum, W. J., & Plomp, T. (1991). *The Use of Computers in Education Worldwide*. Elmsford, NY: Pergamon Press.

Perry, R., & Greber, L. (1990). Women and computers: an introduction. *Signs, 16(l)*, 74-101.

Pettigrew, T. F., & Taylor, M. C. (1992). Discrimination. In E. F. Borgatta & M. L. Borgatta (eds.). *Encyclopedia of Sociology* (pp. 498-503). New York: Macmillan Publishing Co.

Piller, C. (1992). Separate realities. *Macworld, 9(9)*, 218-230.

Platter, A. E. (1988). Computing experiences of young adults: An empirical analysis. *Social Indicators Research, 20*, 291-302.

Sanders, J. S., & Stone, A. (1986). *The Neuter Computer: Computers for Girls and Boys*. New York: Neal-Schuman.

Scott, T., Cole, M., & Engel, M. (1992). Computers and education: a cultural constructivist perspective. *Review of Research in Education, 18*, 191-251.

Smith, M. S., & O'Day, J. (1990). Systemic school reform. *Politics of Education Yearbook 1990* (pp. 233-267).

Smith, S. D. (1987). Computer attitudes of teachers and students in relationship to gender and grade level. *Journal of Educational Computing Research, 3(4)*, 479-494.

Sutton, R. E. (1991). Equity and computers in the schools: a decade of research. *Review of Educational Research, 61(4)*, 475-503.

Temple, L., & Lips, H. M. (1989). Gender differences and similarities in attitudes toward computers. *Computers in Human Behavior, 1(4)*, 215-226.

Thurston, L. P. (1990, June). Girls, computers, and amber waves of grain: computer equity programming for rural teachers. Paper presented at the annual conference of the National Women's Studies Association, Towson, MD.

Turkle, S., & Papert, S. (1990). Epistemological pluralism: styles and voices within the computer culture. *Signs, 16(l)*, 128- 157.

U.S. Bureau of the Census (1988). Computer use in the United States: 1984 (Current Population Reports, Special Studies Series P-23, No. 155). Washington, DC: U.S. Government Printing Office.

U.S. Bureau of the Census (1991). Computer use in the United States: 1989 (Current Population Reports, Special Studies Series P-23, No. 173). Washington, DC: U.S. Government Printing Office.

U.S. Congress (1988). Power on! new tools for teaching and learning (OTA-SET-379 Office of Technology Assessment). Washington, DC: U.S. Government Printing Office.

Ware, M. C., & Stuck, M. F. (1985). Sex role messages vis a vis microcomputer use: a look at the pictures. *Sex Roles, 13(3-4)*, 205-214.

Weiser, M. (1991, September). The computer for the 21st century. *Scientific American*, pp. 94-104.

West, J., Miller, W., & Diodato, L. (1985). *An Analysis of Course-Taking Patterns in Secondary Schools as Related to Student Characteristics*. Washington, D. C.: U.S. Government Printing Office.

Wilder, G., Mackie, D., & Cooper, J. (1985). Gender and computers: two surveys of computer related attitudes. *Sex Roles, 13(3-4)*, 215-228.

ACCESS ISSUES FOR THE NATIONAL RESEARCH AND EDUCATION NETWORK (NREN)[3]

Steve Cisler
Apple Computer

UNIVERSAL SERVICE

Only connect!
–E. M. Forster. Howards End

In 1908, the manager of the Bell telephone system, Theodore Vail, announced the policy that has affected the development of both voice and data services up to the present day:

> ...one system with a common policy, common purpose and common action: comprehensive, universal, interdependent, intercommunicating like the highway system of the country, extending from every door to every other door, affording electrical communication of every kind, from every one at every place to every one at every other place.[4]

Some years later, during the New Deal, the Communications Act of 1934 charged the Federal Communications Commission with "the enhancement of commerce in communication by wire and radio so as to make available, so far as possible, to all the people of the United States a rapid, efficient, nation-wide and world-wide wire and radio communication service."

These goals of universal service, of ubiquitous access to various technologies have been quite successful. In 1990 the percentage of American households with different technologies were: electricity 99.8 percent; telephone 93 percent; radio 99 percent; television 99 percent; VCR 64.6 percent.[5]

With the growth of the Internet and the enactment of the High Performance Computing and Communications Act of 1991, many groups and individuals have been pressing for access not to consumer products but to a network originally intended for researchers in companies, national laboratories, and universities. Some people have briefly surveyed the electronic landscape of the Internet and want to settle there for a variety of

---

[3]This article was written expressly for inclusion in this text, by Steve Cisler, Apple Computer Library, Apple Computer, Inc., Cupertino, California. Internet: sac@apple.com.
[4] de Sola Pool, Ithiel. (1983). *Technologies of Freedom*. Belknap. Pool's works have stood the test of time, and I recommend this title as well as *Technologies without Boundaries* (Harvard University Press, 1990) and *Forecasting the Telephone* (Ablex, 1983). Unless you have extremely good network access, you will not be able to reach Professor Pool. He died in 1984.
[5] Hadden, Susan G. (1991.) Technologies of Universal Service. *Universal Telephone Service*. Institute for Information Studies..

reasons: the culture of sharing, the lack of rules, the seemingly free access to hundreds of sources of information and millions of files, the ability to reach colleagues in another state or another country with a single click of the mouse. Just as explorers and guides in the American West returned to civilization to lecture and write, writers on the network return to their analog lives and spin tales of digital riches, wide-open cyberscapes, and the opportunities for the not-yet-enfranchised to get online and drive a stake in the ground and extend their intellectual lives.

In the extreme this becomes a binary way of dividing people. Either they are on the Net,[6] or they are not. There is a big division between those with access to the Internet and those with none. Much of that gap is in the heads of the many network users who tend to believe that somehow cyberspace is a more valid place to exist than a world devoid of connectivity. Another view is that a transaction or piece of information is more worthwhile because it is digital as opposed to verbal or print or some other analog storage or transmission medium. This attitude comes partly from the long hours that Internauts, net.citizens, info-surfers, and cybertrash spend online. It is an exciting place, and it is hard to explain what it is and why it is important and will change people's lives, even if they can't afford the technology.

METAPHORS FOR THE NETWORK

When people try to explain electronic networks such as the Internet or the National Research and Education Network to people who are not "on the Net," they frequently make use of metaphors: subdivisions on the edge of a metropolis, highways, rivers, mines, fields, information silos, and even Zen-like electronic Koans. Former Senator Al Gore spoke of information silos and the electronic data highway—the most popular metaphor; the California Educational Computing Consortium used the term "mining the Internet" for finding useful resources and individuals on the network; and Merit, the Michigan organization that has been so central to the development of the National Science Foundation Network (NSFNET) chose the metaphor of an ocean cruise as the best way to introduce the Net to new initiates.

The Merit Internet Cruise software was distributed free-of-charge beginning early in 1992. It allowed people with access to a Macintosh to take a tour of the various services and functions of the Internet. Upon reflection I realized that gaining access to the Internet is similar to booking passage on a cruise ship that calls in many ports with many attractions, and the other passengers are interesting but nowhere as diverse as the population at large. This is usually borne out in the many conferences or sessions where parts of NREN or telecommunications policy are hammered out. Most of us are forty-

---

[6]   The Net: This is a loose, ill-defined term meaning the Network, which can be the Internet, the future NREN or, as John Quarterman calls the conglomerate of all global, interconnected networks, the Matrix.

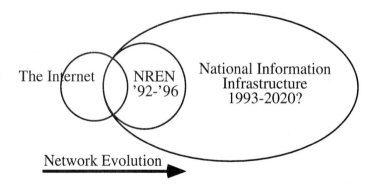

Figure 10-11

something white men trying to do what is best for our constituents, our university, our company, and even the country at large.

The restaurant on board the S.S. NREN has hundreds of different menus but only a relatively small amount of food to actually sample, and other passengers as well as some of the crew are furiously crafting the right tools for people who want to get something from the restaurant, fish from the side, or learn to cook themselves. Although most everyone's passage is prepaid, there is not much to buy once you are on board. Everyone shares what they have to some extent, but with each additional port, new markets open up and more goods appear for sale.

As part of a research department in a computer company, I travel first class on this cruise ship. Many of my fellow passengers share my good fortune mainly because they are affiliated with the right organization (a computer company, research university, national laboratory), but some are in the tourist class and some are stuck in steerage. By this I mean that their network connections are slow, intermittent, or quite costly to them personally. Some other first-class travelers are concerned about the people below decks, about those scaling the hull of the good ship Internet, and they worry that their own progress will be slowed by the increasing number of life rafts, freighters, barges, and yachts heading for our vessel. They are concerned that many of those trying to get aboard will not want to pay full fare or any fare at all, nor will they contribute enough of their resources to be shared with others on the voyage. In the engine room the technicians are devoting their energies to increasing the range, speed, and carrying capacity of the ship, but that may not change quickly enough for the boat people who are hoping to be picked up. Some of us on board are signaling those adrift and are sending semaphore to land-bound travelers, telling them of the pleasures and benefits of the voyage.

But let's drop the metaphor and ask ourselves: Should we be raising expectations of high school students, public library patrons, hospital patients, independent learners, businesspeople, freelance writers, and unaffiliated researchers by singing the praises of a network that they may not be able to

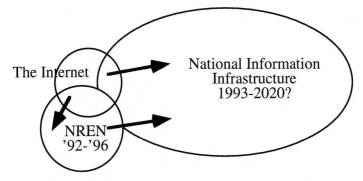

Figure 10-12

access? In past years the research community felt that the ARPAnet would suffer if the university users were allowed on. Now, the Internet constituents and the interest groups pushing for the development of the NREN are not at all united on the many issues, including the subject of this article: access– who should be able to use the NREN and under what guidelines and at what cost.

WHO IS THE NETWORK FOR?

> Panhandler to man having lunch: Got any spare change, man?
> Diner: Say, are you on the Net? What's your address?
> –Overheard in an outdoor restaurant in California

In Figure 10-11 we see a crude diagram to show the difference (not to scale) between the Internet, the NREN, and the future National Information Infrastructure–NII (a.k.a. National Public Network by the Electronic Frontier Foundation).[7] The Internet is international in scope and encompasses many networks connected mainly by the TCP/IP protocols. Other networks connect with it to exchange mail. The NREN will be built on the American part of the Internet. That is part of the overlap. A little later, perhaps as early as 1993,[8] the NII will begin to emerge. Some people see the NII built on top of the NREN, as shown in the diagram; others see NREN as a network reserved for researchers and academicians that will serve as a testbed and may be connected in some ways to the NII (Figure 10-12).

Here is the statement of Michael Roberts of EDUCOM and currently the director of the Internet Society: "...Planning the NII is like designing a large, urban city. The NREN is a big new subdivision on the edge of the

---

[7] I have chosen to avoid the term "Interagency Interim NREN," a Washington beltway term for the transition network between the Internet and the full-blown gigabit NREN.

[8] This was originally written in 1993. We are now a few days into 1994, and the parameters of the NII are still being discussed by Congress and the Clinton Administration. By the time you hold this book, the outlines of the NII will (perhaps) be more clear [Chuck Huff, editor].

metropolis, reserved for researchers and educators. It is going to be built first and is going to look lonely out there in the middle of the pasture for a while."[9] Let's hope the inner city of the NII does not languish while the suburbs flourish.

Whether or not the NII grows from NREN or uses it as a model for the larger, more public infrastructure, the populist politics of some Internet evangelists have shaped the perception that the NREN will develop in one of two ways: kilobits for the masses or gigabits for the elite. While that fits nicely on a bumper sticker, the situation is far more complex. Many of the so-called elite are pushing for ubiquitous access, or at least access for K-12 students and teachers and administrators. Mitchell Kapor of the Electronic Frontier Foundation states, "These high-end low-end visions of the NREN are strikingly different. There is no assurance that one size network fits all. In principle, it might be possible to satisfy everyone with one technical scheme; in practice, this is unlikely."[10] Having a single network structure that can handle short ascii messages, interlibrary loan transactions, fax images over TCP/IP, full-motion digital video, sound, high-resolution digital photographs from museums,[11] and large data sets for weather modeling research presents an enormous architectural challenge.

Dave Hughes, a telecommunications activist and electronic grass roots organizer who has worked with rural schools and Indian reservations. as well as electronic bulletin board system operators, fears that the NREN will only benefit the relatively prosperous research universities and not the thousands of school districts around the country. Instead of "highways for the mind" NREN could mean "super toll roads between castles."[12]

The 1991 White House Conference on Library and Information Services passed a resolution stating that "the network should be available in *all* libraries and other information repositories at every level. The governance structure for NREN should include representation from all interested constituencies. . . ."[13]

The Coalition for Networked Information,[14] which is composed primarily of universities, some computer firms, and American and foreign publishers, takes the stance that the evolving NREN should be for the research and education communities. However, CNI's definition of education

---

[9]   Roberts, Michael (1991). Positioning the National Research and Education Network. *EDUCOM Magazine*. Summer issue. <roberts@educom.edu>
[10]   Karraker, Roger (1991). Highways of the Mind. *Whole Earth Review*, Spring issue. (anonymous ftp from ftp.apple.com in the alug directory)
[11]   Cisler, Steve (July 1992). "Project Chapman" *Apple Library Users Group Newsletter*. Details on the plans to mount free JPEG-compressed images from the Smithsonian Institution on the Internet.
[12]   Ibid.
[13]   *Information 2000: Library and Information Services for the 21st Century*. U.S. GPO 1991 (ISBN 0-16-035978-3).
[14]   See the anonymous ftp archives on a.cni.org.

is not spelled out but is quite broad, and extends beyond postsecondary education.

Dr. Tom Grundner of the National Public Telecomputing Network and originator of the Free Net concept, wrote to suggest that a nationwide system of public access computer systems be established. "These systems would be free to the user in the same sense that the public library is free to its patrons. Of equal importance, each of these systems would have a place on them for the library community, the K-12 community, the medical community, government officials, and anyone else who wanted to use it. In addition, each system would be linked by, and would provide its users with controlled access to the Internet/NREN."[15]

I would add that it is necessary to open the network up to commercial firms, from small entrepreneurs, mom-and-pop software firms, chambers of commerce, large chains, multi-national firms, and phone companies. This is often overlooked when we speak of access issues, but without a thriving commercial substratum, it will be impossible to finance the growth of the networks. Ensuring that present network users are not subjected to bombardment by sophisticated electronic mail marketing campaigns, but still allowing the firms to conduct business will have to evolve as the Acceptable User Policy (ies) of the Internet/NREN change.

LOWERING THE BARRIERS THAT PREVENT ACCESS

Today a child can go to a library and use a computer to get the title of a book. a faster network would bring the book to the child at home, pictures and all. But how do we get there? [16]

–Al Gore

While many individuals and some groups are calling for open access for all, many barriers prevent a new user or prospective information provider from gaining access to and using the network. What follows is a list of the problems and the solutions that are working for some areas and some users.

Technical expertise

Setting up and maintaining a network node is based partly on the knowledge of the TCP/IP protocol suite. As Ken Klingenstein, director of computing services at University of Colorado–Boulder, points out, "this knowledge base unfortunately is more folklore than codified rules; there is no shrink-wrapped alternative."[17] Even in companies with a sizable MIS department to handle internal network issues, knowledge of these protocols is lacking. Many of the networks are proprietary, and linking the internal and

---

[15] Grundner, Tom (July 1992). Whose Internet is it anyway?—A Challenge *ONLINE.*
[16] Gore, Al (September 1991). Infrastructure For the Global Village *Scientific American.*
[17] Klingenstein, Ken (1992). A Coming of Age: The Design of the Low-End Internet. In Brian Kahin (ed.). *Building Information Infrastructure.* McGraw-Hill.

Internet mail services takes significant time and expense. As an example, my own company, Apple Computer, Inc., has internal local area network mail systems that span thousands of employees. In addition, there is AppleLink, which runs on a General Electric network, and finally there is an IP network connected to the Internet. Building gateways by writing software and getting agreements between the various centers of power and software firms has been a time-consuming but enormous achievement for Erik Fair and others on the engineering network services staff. This sort of talent is not widely available, even to many firms larger than ours.

Education

In a recent survey Syracuse University's Charles McClure and his staff found that 92 percent of the public librarians questioned were very concerned about the limited knowledge that they had about networks and their content. Academic librarians shared this concern (75 percent), but not to the same extent.[18] Judging by the number of times I and others have been asked to speak or write about issues related to Internet resources, connectivity, and policy, education of potential network participants and users is a top priority. In most conferences and workshops these classes and talks attract overflow audiences. By the end of 1992 there will be at least nine new titles in print from various publishers and individuals covering the Internet. Most of them will be for novices.[19]

Costs

Expenses associated with education and technical expertise are just part of the total cost. The Internet is often perceived as being free to the user. As Bruce Sterling states in his science column in *Fantasy and Science Fiction:* "The Internet is also a bargain. The Internet as a whole, unlike the phone system, doesn't charge for long-distance service. And unlike most commercial computer networks, it doesn't charge for access time, either. In fact the 'Internet' itself, which doesn't even officially exist as an entity, never 'charges' for anything." The charges have typically been made to the institution. The institution has absorbed these costs, charged back to the department or in some cases to the individual user. One of the reasons for the rapid growth of the Internet has been the end users' lack of concern for any

---

[18]   McClure, Charles et al. (1992). Public libraries and the Internet/NREN: new challenges, new opportunities. School of Information Studies. Syracuse University.
[19] This prediction has been accurate. There are many more than 9 books on the Internet now and several of them are written for novices. Here are some of them: Tennant, Roy, Ober, John, & Lipow, Anne G. (1993). *Crossing the Internet threshold: an instructional handbook*. Berkley, CA: Library Solutions Press; Marine, April (1993). *Internet: getting started*. Englewood Cliffs, NJ: Prentice Hall; Krol, Ed. (1992). *The whole Internet: user's guide & catalog*. Sebastopol, CA: O'Reilly & Associates; Kehoe, Brendan P. (1993). *Zen and the art of the internet: a beginner's guide, 2nd ed.* Englewood Cliffs, NJ: Prentice Hall. [Chuck Huff, editor].

ticking meter that measures packets of data transmitted or received or elapsed connect time. Would Internet usage grow as fast with meters running? Probably not.

The meter does run for the class of user who has connected through a network service provider such as The WELL or Netcom in California, World in Massachusetts, or Colorado SuperNet where there is usually a monthly fee as well as an hourly fee. All these regional services offer very attractive rates for the unaffiliated user, but they are not free. In a region such as the San Francisco Bay area where competition has attracted at least eight Internet service providers (PSI, ANS, AlterNet, BARRNet, The WELL, Netcom, a2i, CERFnet, and Holonet), sophisticated users will shop around. Those who need more handholding (technical support) may choose one company or another. Those who need more bandwidth will have fewer choices.

One network service provider went from a flat rate per month to a flat rate for a certain number of hours and an hourly charge after the maximum was exceeded. Why? Many subscribers were tying up the dialup lines using IRC. Internet Relay Chat, a sort of digital citizens' band service that has thousands of devotees, is banned in some colleges, and even has a recovery discussion group for IRC junkies on Usenet, the distributed bulletin board that itself is quite addictive. I suppose it is sort of a methadone treatment to have IRC addicts on Usenet, but the whole phenomenon is serious enough to have generated at least one thesis.

In 1993 a group of amateur radio operators set up, with the approval of the FCC, a TCP/IP backbone network in the San Francisco Bay Area to provide license-free, wireless access to the Internet for public libraries (and their patrons) as well as accounts for business and professional people.[20]

A valuable service for all users would be nationwide 800 numbers, both data and voice, whereby a prospective Internet user could answer basic questions about her address (the heart of Silicon Valley or a wheat farm in America's heartland), level of service needed (2400 baud dialup to 45 megabits per second clear channel), intended use (selling images, playing games, collaborating with a teacher or a research lab), and affiliation (lifelong learner, farmer, entrepreneur, government official, librarian) and receive a list of service providers, if there were any at all, that would fit the new user's needs. This sort of referral service should be provided by a national network information center, and the queries could be used to improve coverage and service. If the center received numerous inquiries from a certain job category or region, service providers could respond more quickly.

---

[20] As reported by Dewayne Hendricks of Tetherless Access. Ltd. <dewayne@netcom.com>

Variable regional network policies

The regional TCP/IP networks have been coordinating their roles more in the past few years, but as new players enter the field, the rules change and for competitive reasons prices and practices do too. In some areas there is strict compliance with the NSF Acceptable Use Policy. In others, the signing of such an agreement by a new user, if it is done at all, is not enforced or taken seriously.

In this era of network cultural diversity and the flowering of hundreds of virtual communities, one cannot expect identical network policies. An anarchist art collective in San Francisco will have different rules from the MIS department of a large pharmaceutical firm, but they both may use the same network. However, we are likely to see a common denominator of rules, perhaps expressed as network etiquette, more than we will see the growth of network protocol police. If the network culture begins to mirror the outside world beyond research laboratories and computing centers, there may be more demand for net.cops, fines, and expulsion from the community. "Yes, Professor Harkin, you were clocked at 1.5 megabits per second in a 56-kilobit zone. I'll have to see your E-mail address and password. Please step away from the workstation. . . ."

User interfaces to network services

If a user is able to log in to the Internet/NREN and only sees a prompt such as this

>

he may sign off and never return. Many Internet host systems have no greeting or assistance that is much friendlier than that lonely prompt sign. Most network administrators and designers realize this shortcoming. A few believe the austere interface is a good filter to keep the riffraff off "their" network, but most can provide pointers to software that makes it much easier to navigate the network. For a new user with a free account, help should be available in the form of on-screen assistance, a phone number to converse with a more experienced user, and manuals for basic navigation of the network. Fortunately, a cluster of electronic and print titles began appearing in 1992. The network community has already provided graphic interfaces for many Internet tasks, and most of the software is in the public domain or is free for educational purposes. The popularity of mail readers such as Eudora,[21] the Gopher client-server software with interfaces for most popular computers,[22] and NCSA Telnet[23] are strong evidence that some of the best things in Internet life *are* free.

---

[21] Available via anonymous ftp from ux1.cso.uiuc.edu
[22] Available via anonymous ftp from boombox.micro.umn.edu
[23] Available via anonymous ftp from sumex-aim.stanford.edu in the info-mac directory.

The Electronic Frontier Foundation[24] has signed a contract for the production of integrated software for Internet users of MS-DOS, Macintosh, and Unix computers. The software and source code will be distributed free of charge. This too will simplify access for many users. Similar projects are being undertaken by the Texas Education Agency and by the Technical Education Research Center (TERC) in Cambridge, Massachusetts.

Addressing the needs of the disabled user of telecommunications services merits a chapter by itself. People with disabilities are as diverse as all of humanity. The term is not limited to someone in a wheelchair or a blind or deaf person. What is recognized is that as a group these people face the risk of social and physical isolation. Therefore, telecommunications access can be more important to them than it is to people without disabilities. The World Institute on Disability has issued a report explaining the problems, the issues, and how to work toward solutions. It makes the important point that "services designed with maximum accessibility for consumers with functional limitations will attract most consumers, including those without obvious limitations. . . . If it's easier to use, it's easier to market."[25] By providing electronic curb cuts for NREN access, disabled people as well as the nondisabled will have an easier time crossing the data highways we are building.

Governance and security issues

It is important to remember that individual-access issues are not the only ones network designers are concerned about. Whole organizations will not participate in the Internet until they are satisfied that the structure of the network is more defined. Until a system administrator can get a correct answer from a single phone call when a problem arises with a network connection, many firms will not treat the Internet with the respect that many of us already have for it. These same firms also see the Internet as a haven for intruders, many of them youthful, talented, and persistent. They must be assured that security measures will allow easy access from the organization to the network but not the other way around.

Copyright

Earlier in this essay I mentioned that the Internet cruise ship had hundreds of menus but very little food to sample. By this I meant that there are many bibliographic databases from libraries all over the world but no way to actually obtain most of the books, journal articles, or technical reports. Creators of knowledge, the agents, and the publishers need to have some mechanisms to reward them for their work. These distribution mechanisms

---

[24] Background electronic information available from ftp.eff.org
[25] Kaplan, Deborah et al. (1991). *Telecommunications and Persons with Disabilities: Laying the Foundation.* World institute on Disability. 510 16th St., Suite 100, Oakland, California 94612.

and royalty agreements are well established in the world of print. Although some publishers are reluctant to venture outside their known world of ink and paper, others are experimenting with new forms of information delivery, new types of contracts between buyer and seller, and are even looking closely at the basic assumptions about copyright and intellectual property. The Copyright Clearance Center and the Corporation for National Research Initiatives have issued a paper discussing copyright in the electronic environment.[26] It is highly recommended for those willing to plunge into these swirling waters where the only creatures able to stay afloat are lawyers. Unfortunately, the Copyright Clearance Center was afraid of making this white paper available in electronic format. This would indicate that the organization setting itself up to deal with technological change and copyright has many reservations about the use of networks to disseminate ideas as opposed to products.

CONCLUSION

In tackling the problems of access this paper has not addressed some of the larger issues. If you advocate ubiquitous access for extending the benefits of high speed telecommunications to those other than academic researchers, national laboratories, and large businesses, you must ask yourself (or others surely will):   What is the public good, and who will pay for this? Congress?[27] Consumers? Taxpayers? Rather than try to provide an answer, let me point the reader to several important works.

Henry Geller, former general counsel of the FCC and an assistant secretary in the NTIA, advocates the construction of the broadband network by the phone companies, but it should not "supplant all other delivery systems: it should be envisioned as a bedrock assurance that First Amendment and other vital interests will be well served in the next century through universal, high-speed data access."[28]

The Electronic Frontier Foundation takes a more gradual approach, advocating an open system with low-cost basic ISDN services available on a wide basis to encourage the explosion of development and entrepreneurship that accompanied the growth of the personal computer hardware and software industries.[29]

---

[26] Garrett, John R., and Joseph S. Allen. (March 1992). *Toward a Copyright Management System for Digital Libraries.* Coalition for Networked Information..

[27] *New York Times.* (1992, August 31). Editorial page. In taking a cautious stance against the telephone companies providing video dialtone services in order to build the broadband network, the paper suggests in passing that perhaps Congress will fund the construction of the Net!

[28] Geller, Henry. (1992). *Fiber Optics: An Opportunity For A New Policy?* Annenberg Washington Program. Washington, DC. (202) 393-7100.

[29] Kapor, Mitchell (1991). *Building the Open Road.* Electronic Frontier Foundation. Available via anonymous ftp from ftp.eff.org. RFC 1259.

A collection of essays by policy and telecommunications experts focuses on universal telephone service in the 21st century.[30] Barbara O'Connor writes about NREN and universal service. Daniel Brenner discusses privacy issues. Eli Noam writes about the growth of private networks and how this may restrict the exercise of free speech. Susan Hadden's chapter on "Technologies of Universal Service" matches many of my concerns and was instrumental in helping me sort out various issues, some of which are not covered in this chapter. Specifically, what sort of information should be free to all users who access the Internet or NREN? Many people confuse access to the Net with access to the resources that are on the Net. It is one thing to have a password on a 45-megabit-per-second backbone host computer, but if you can only use a few of the thousands of other hosts, how valuable will it be?

In the past, cross-subsidies in the regulated monopoly have permitted those companies to provide consumers with various free services, subsidized or lifeline rates, directories delivered at no charge, and, for many years, unbilled directory assistance. The new competitive marketplace makes this sort of service impossible to continue. Yet we must consider the continued need for what Hadden calls "essential information"[31] and I call "core information."[32] In an electronic environment, any host machine would have a public directory of information available at no charge. In an electronic public library, it would be the bulk of that institution's offerings; in a consulting firm hanging out its electronic shingle, it might be limited to résumés of the principals and some electronic infomercials to convince a buyer that buying their expertise is a good idea. In a government agency, it might be abstracts of full reports or a directory of forms, services, and personnel. In short, this core information would provide access to the thousands of services that will undoubtedly emerge, just as they have in the French Minitel industry. The equivalents in the Internet world are the anonymous ftp sites, some of which have been listed in the footnotes, and the so-called gopher holes which number in the hundreds in Australia, Europe, Israel, and North America.

Another book that shaped my thinking was W. Russell Neuman's study of the shifts in postindustrial society caused by new technologies. "The hero of the piece is communications technology, or at least its increasing capacity to enhance communications and empower the individual to control the communications process. There is no villain per se. There are, however, social, economic, and political forces that threaten to constrain, to limit, and perhaps to pervert the new technology's potential for intellectual diversity and openness."[33]

---

[30] Institute for Information Studies (1991). *Universal Telephone Service: Ready for the 21st Century?* The Aspen Institute, Wye Center, Box 222, Queenstown, MD 21658.

[31] Ibid., p. 80.

[32] Cisler, Steve. Electronic public spaces. *The Matrix News*, Austin, TX.

[33] Neuman, W. Russell (1991). *The Future of the Mass Audience*. Cambridge University Press.

My own belief is that the technology is moving forward, not of its own accord but because that is the nature of the technologists and the enterprises that develop new systems and hardware. This does not mean that the public policy or the laws or the users will change as rapidly. As Neuman points out, the communications revolution "encourages both a diverse pluralism and increased participation in public life," but the social psychology of the mass audience (the extreme example being the generic couch potato) operates in opposition to this liberating technological trend. Buttressing that opposition is the regulatory climate and traditions of the mass media.[34]

The Internet and National Research and Education Network offer opportunities for many individuals and for many organizations, as users of the services, as service providers, or as suppliers of intellectual content and tools for users. Understanding the complex issues and the dynamic political and technological environment will help the reader make more informed decisions about the direction in which they would like to see the network evolve.

---

[34] Ibid., pp. 42-43.

COMPUTERS AND STUDENTS WITH DISABILITIES: NEW CHALLENGES FOR HIGHER EDUCATION[35]

Project EASI
(Equal Access to Software for Instruction)
A Project of the EDUCOM Educational Uses of
Information Technology (EUIT) Program

COMPUTING AND DISABILITY

Disability is the direct result of the relationship between people, their goals, their environment, and the resources available to them within that environment. (Richard Read, Center for Computing and Disability SUNY-Albany)

Accessibility is the degree to which resources are used to bridge the gap between a person's goals and the requirements of his or her environment. New technologies continue to provide new resources to people with disabilities for bridging educational and employment gaps. Such an application of computer technology is referred to as adaptive computer technology.

Computer technology redefines and expands every aspect of the postsecondary environment. Computer use has expanded from a few technical disciplines to nearly every aspect of academic and administrative activities. Academic courses now include computer-based assignments in writing, architectural design, business management, and library research, in addition to the traditional areas of computer programming, statistical analysis, and engineering design. Increasing numbers of campuses now use computers for administrative tasks such as student admissions, registration, financial operations, and library services.

This widespread integration of computing technology into postsecondary education accentuates the need to provide adaptive computing support and services to faculty, staff, and students with disabilities. Adaptive computer technology can create environments where people with disabilities have an equal opportunity to develop and apply their abilities.

Although technology can create opportunities in higher education for people with disabilities, it can also erect barriers that lead to decreased participation. Problems can result from the often inaccessible nature of the

---

[35]This chapter was adapted for this text from the EDUCOM publication of the same title. Project EASI is an international volunteer organization dedicated to assisting higher education in the development of computer support services for students with disabilities. EASI provides information and guidance on campus applications of adaptive computer technology for access to information resources, instruction, research, and employment. For more information on Project EASI, its publications and other resources contact: EUIT Program, EDUCOM, 1112 16th Street NW, Suite 600, Washington, DC 20036. Tel: 202-872-4200. Bitnet: EASI@EDUCOM Internet: EASI@EDUCOM.EDU.

standard computer interface. With appropriate institutional planning, adaptive computing support and services can join forces to create accessible environments and to provide equitable educational and employment opportunities.

ACCESS TO INFORMATION TECHNOLOGY

Computer access technology has allowed students with disabilities to compete and succeed in secondary education. As these computer-liberated students mature, they will expect similar access in postsecondary education and the workplace. (Jay Brill, Maryland Technology Assistance Program)

Institutions of postsecondary education are increasingly challenged to provide equal access to computing technology for all users—both disabled and nondisabled. The range of necessary adaptive computing services is in proportion to the magnitude of established computing activities. Whether provided to the general campus population or required for coursework, degree completion, or campus employment, computing services must accommodate people with disabilities.

A number of issues should be considered when implementing adaptive computing support and services, such as site renovation, workstation acquisition, software and hardware evaluation, access to instructional software, support needs, and user and staff training. People with disabilities require training and ongoing support to use adaptive equipment and to develop basic computing skills. Thus, it is important to determine the extent of adaptive computing services needed and to identify and train personnel who will provide these services.

In addition, the implementation of adaptive computing requires research. This research should be twofold: (1) identifying adaptive systems that are compatible with the current and future computing environments, and (2) identifying and implementing computing systems that compensate for specific disabilities. Research should identify new barriers and prevent them from developing as the technology evolves.

The academic environment

As institutions provide adaptive computing access, they must consider three areas of the academic environment: general facilities and support, discipline-specific computing, and academic support.

In the first of these areas—general facilities and support—people with disabilities require access to the same hardware, software, and services that are provided to the general campus population. This may include general computing sites, computing resale programs, technical support and repair services, and consultation and support services, as well as library catalog, database searches, and course registration. When campus personnel establish adaptive computing access in general facilities, their primary concern should be the flexibility of the adaptive computer systems. As the ideal, adaptive systems should accommodate the wide range of abilities and preferences of all users.

The second area is discipline-specific computing. This area includes computing activities as general as freshman composition and as specialized as computer-aided design. Faculty, staff, and students will require increasing levels of support as adaptive computing is integrated into discipline-specific computing. Solutions may prescribe adapting course-specific hardware and software, training faculty and staff in the use of adaptive technology, and identifying and/or developing accessible courseware.

The third area is individualized academic support, which refers to use of the computer as a compensatory tool for educational tasks not normally accomplished with a computer. Examples include reading, note taking, and the writing of exams. As research and technology evolve, this area promises people with disabilities new degrees of independence and participation in every aspect of life.

> For most people, advances in technology are a luxury; for persons with disabilities, the area of adaptive technology is a key to independence. (Darren Gabbert, Coordinator, Adaptive Computing Technology Center, University of Missouri-Columbia)

Students may require access to a wide variety of computer hardware and software throughout their academic careers. Obstacles to accessibility often occur when classes are held across campus from adaptive computing services. Different courses may require different computer systems, each of which presents unique access/interface challenges. Access to library catalogs and databases is limited when specially adapted terminals are installed only at central locations.

Providing adaptive computing services to meet student requirements may be costly. However, training and support costs can be reduced by using consistent adaptive strategies that are best achieved by careful needs analysis. By examining the demographics of the disabled population, as well as the extent to which computing exists in the academic environment, computing personnel can determine the extent of training and support required. An effectively designed computing infrastructure can effectively meet the needs of current and future users, and at the same time amortize the cost of services over a longer time period.

Administrative environment

In addition to instructional uses, campuses are using computers more often for tasks that range from admissions and registration to business operations. Access to administrative computing for employees with disabilities is required to meet affirmative action employment mandates.

Administrative computing typically is not as diverse as academic computing. Employees with disabilities in business or departmental offices, libraries, and labs may require customized computer resources. Once these resources are tailored, they remain relatively constant. Thus, the training and support needs of employees with disabilities should be fewer than those of students.

Access to administrative computing for students with disabilities should also be considered. For example, telephone registration might be supplemented with a TDD (telecommunication device for the deaf).

Campus networks

With the widespread availability of computer networks comes the need for students with disabilities to have network access through adaptive computer technology. Networks may cut down certain access problems, such as those encountered when students access programs and files from residence halls and other remote locations. Network access also reduces the need to manipulate floppy disks and decreases travel across campus. From adapted workstations, networks can allow access to many campus resources such as library catalogs, databases, and electronic mail.

USER CONSIDERATIONS

While the computer is advancing handicapped individuals two steps through the use of special programs designed for handicapped individuals, the computer is advancing everyone else in society five steps. Moreover, the five steps are being designed in such a way that the handicapped individual cannot take advantage of them, thus leaving them actually three steps behind in the net result. (Gregg Vanderheiden, 1983, Trace Research and Development Center)

Demographics

There are approximately 43 million Americans with disabilities (U.S. Census, 1990). Of the 4.3 million youth in special education, an estimated 150,000 enter postsecondary training each year (National Norms for Freshmen, 1988). In addition, many adults enter postsecondary institutions for retraining after acquiring disabilities.

According to Profiles of Handicapped Students in Postsecondary Education (Greene & Zimbler, 1989), approximately 10.5 percent of college students report having some type of disability. Of those, 39 percent report having a visual handicap, 24 percent report health impairments, 20 percent report being hard of hearing, 17 percent report orthopedic impairments, 12 percent report specific learning disabilities, 6 percent report deafness, and 4 percent report speech impairments.

Considerations for effective access

Listed below are examples of adaptive technology in the four areas which affect computer use: computer input, computer output, documentation, and environment. In addition, the best sources of information on any of these topics are likely to be experienced users on campus who may have already found products and strategies which improve their ease of computer use.

Computer input

Individuals with limited use of their hands may have difficulty operating standard input devices (such as a keyboard or mouse) or handling storage media such as floppy disks. Adaptive technology for people with mobility impairments includes alternatives to keyboards and mice, software and hardware that enable the standard keyboard to be modified, keyguards that reduce the likelihood of mistyped keystrokes, mouthsticks and headwands used to strike keys, and floppy disk guides that make it easier to handle disks.

Hard disk drives reduce the need for manual manipulation of stored data. Voice input is increasingly becoming an option for some applications. Power strips can facilitate access to computers that have switches located in inaccessible areas. Transparent labels with raised dots are available to mark keys, such as the Return Key. They help users with visual impairments to locate the keys. Braille can also be used to mark floppy disks, drives, and other components.

Computer output

For computer users with visual impairments, access to computer output is a major problem. Solutions involve alternate displays, which include screen-reading programs, speech synthesizers, modified word processors and other software, Braille-conversion programs, and Braille or large-print output devices. If the user has some vision, technology is available to magnify screen output. Much of this technology also is useful to individuals with learning disabilities.

Computer users with hearing impairments need an alternative to standard auditory output. For example, the primary alternative at present is visual redundancy, in which a part of the screen flashes on and off when a sound is emitted by the computer.

Documentation

Most standard computer documentation is in print form. Access to documentation for people with disabilities is often overlooked. At the user's request, some software and hardware vendors now provide ASCII, Braille, large-print, videotape, or audiotape versions of their documentation.

Optical character recognition (OCR) can convert print into a computer file, which can then be accessed through speech or printed in large print or Braille. Although only about 10 percent of blind people use Braille effectively, in some instances—particularly for users who are deaf-blind—it may be the necessary format.

Many users on campuses prefer to obtain help from a computer consultant rather than a manual. Technology, such as a TDD at the consulting center, may increase accessibility. Moreover, consultants should be sensitized to the needs of users with various disabilities. In addition, they should learn to use specialized equipment and should, whenever possible, be available to assist users who may require help.

Environment

There are two types of environmental adaptations. The first provides physical access to the computing facility. It may include appropriate signage to indicate that a computer lab has adaptive equipment; wheelchair access with unlocked, accessible doors between the building entrance and the lab; the provision of accessible restrooms; and housing adaptive equipment in labs that are open a maximum number of hours. Within the computing lab, accessibility factors include computer tables that are wheelchair-accessible, well-lit monitors, keyboards positioned within reach of the user (at eye level for someone using a headwand), and conveniently placed printers.

The second type of adaptation temporarily modifies the environment for an individual. For example, many people with learning disabilities have a great deal of difficulty working in a noisy environment. Ear protectors, such as those worn by construction workers, may enable the computer user to block out enough background conversation and computer noise to be able to work productively. The use of earphones instead of speakers can assure privacy for blind individuals using speech output and can reduce environmental noise. Antiglare screens are another example of this type of temporary modification.

FEDERAL INFORMATION RESOURCE MANAGEMENT REGULATIONS

The Federal Information Resource Management Regulations (FIRMR) became effective for all federal procurement beginning in October 1988. The FIRMR guidelines address the needs of people with disabilities, outlined in the previous section, by defining functional specifications in three areas: input, output, and documentation. One effect of the guidelines will be to encourage industry to integrate the needs of the disabled community into standard products. The functional performance specifications that define an initial and basic level of electronic equipment accessibility are listed in the appendix.

SUMMARY

Rapidly changing technology promises solutions not previously envisioned—solutions to the problem of providing equal access to learning resources for all students. This promise presents the challenge to build a sound but flexible computing infrastructure capable of incorporating and exploiting new technologies. Lack of technology and lack of awareness, coupled with the fear of obsolescence or the belief that a panacea is just around the corner, are forces that have previously forestalled the establishment of adaptive computing on campuses.

The technology and information resources for implementing adaptive computing currently exist. Immediate planning to provide technological access for people with disabilities—while campuses are developing computerization plans—could reduce the financial impact of future technology accessibility legislation and would meet current legal requirements. The adaptive technology field is dynamic. Its evolution promises to benefit people with disabilities, many service providers, and, ultimately, society as a whole.

APPENDIX: FUNCTIONAL PERFORMANCE SPECIFICATIONS FOR TECHNOLOGY ACCESSABILITY[36]

These specifications are organized by functional requirement into three categories: input, output, and documentation. This organization reflects the major areas that need to be addressed during agency acquisition planning and procurement. All the capabilities set forth in these specifications are currently available from industry in various degrees of functional adequacy except for access to screen memory for translating bit-mapped graphic images.

A. *Input.* Access problems concerning the input interface to a microcomputer differ by the type and severity of the functional limitation of the employee. Some users with disabilities are capable of using a keyboard if it can be modified slightly. Other users with disabilities require an alternate input strategy. The following is an overview of common input alternatives, and other input functional requirements which should be considered:

(1) *Multiple Simultaneous Operation Alternative.* Microcomputers have numerous commonly used functions that require multiple, simultaneous striking of keys and/or buttons. Sequential activation control provides an alternative method of operation by enabling the user to depress keys or buttons sequentially.

(2) *Input Redundancy.* Some programs require a mouse or some other fine motor control device for input. However, some users with motor disabilities cannot operate these devices. An input redundancy feature provides the functionality of these devices through the keyboard and/or other suitable alternative input devices (e.g., voice input).

(3) *Alternative Input Devices.* The capability to connect an alternative input device can be made available to a user who is unable to use a modified standard keyboard. This feature supplements the keyboard and any other standard input system used. The alternative input capability consists of a physical port (serial, parallel, etc.) or

---

[36]From FIRMR Bulletin 56, Managing end user computing for users with disabilities, Appendix J (GSA 1989).

connection capability that allows an accommodation aid to be connected to the system to augment or replace the keyboard. For example, an alternative input device can be customized as the most effective method of input (e.g., switches, eye scan, headtracking) for the user while supporting transparent hardware emulation for standard input devices (i.e., keyboard and the mouse).

(4) *Key Repeat.* A typical microcomputer generates repetitions of a character if that key remains depressed. This is a problem for users without sufficient motor control. A key repeat feature gives a user control over the repeat start time and rate by allowing either the timing parameters to be extended or the repeat function to be turned off.

(5) *Toggle Key Status Control.* Microcomputer toggle keys provide visual feedback indicating whether a key is on or off. A toggle key status feature provides an alternative mode to visual feedback to show the on or off status of a toggle key.

(6) *Keyboard Orientation Aids.* To orient a visually impaired user to a particular keyboard, a set of tactile overlays should be available to identify the most important keys. The tactile overlays can be in the form of keycap replacements or transparent sticky tape with unique symbols to identify the various keys.

(7) *Keyguards.* To assist a motor-disabled user, a keyguard should be available to stabilize movements and ensure that the correct keys are located and depressed. A keyguard is a keyboard template with holes corresponding to the location of the keys.

B. *Output.* Auditory output capability, information redundancy, and monitor display should be considered as functional requirements.

(1) *Auditory Output Capability.* The auditory output capability on current microcomputers is sufficient to beep and play music. However, some users with disabilities may require a speech capability. A speech synthesizer is required to generate speech on today's computers. The capability to support a speech synthesizer should continue to be available in future generations of computers or this capability may be internalized through an upgrade of the computer's internal speaker. The speech capability should include user adjustable volume control and a headset jack.

(2) *Information Redundancy.* Currently, several programs activate a speaker on the microcomputer to provide information to the user. However, some programs do not have the capability to present this information visually to the hearing-impaired user. This feature provides information redundancy by presenting a visual equivalent of the auditory information presented.

(3) *Monitor Display.* The requirement to enhance text size, reproduce text verbally, or modify display characteristics is crucial for some users with visual disabilities. To ensure that this access continues, the following capabilities are required:

(a) *Large Print Display.* There should be a means for enlarging a portion of the screen for the low-vision user. The process uses a window or similar mechanism that allows magnification to be controlled by the user. A user can invoke the large-print display capability from the keyboard or control pad for use in conjunction with any work-related application software. If applications software includes graphics, then enlargement of graphic displays should also be available.

(b) *Access to Visually Displayed Information.* The capability to access the screen is necessary to support the speech and/or Braille output requirement of many blind users. Currently, blind users are able to select and review the spoken or Braille equivalent of text from any portion of the screen while using standard applications software. Third-party vendors should continue to have access to the screen contents in a manner that can be translated and directed to any internal speech chip, a speech synthesizer on a serial or parallel port, or a Braille display device. Information that is presented pictorially also needs to be available in a manner that, as software sophistication improves, it may be eventually translated using alternate display systems.

(c) *Color Presentation.* When colors must be distinguished in order to understand information on the display, color–blind end users should be provided with a means of selecting the colors to be displayed.

C. *Documentation.* The vendor should be responsive in supplying copies of the documentation in a usable electronic format to disabled federal employees.

SELECTED RESOURCES

Organizations and Programs

American Association for the Advancement of Science (AAAS), Project on the Handicapped in Science, 1333 H Street NW, 10th Floor, Washington, DC 20005; (202) 326-6671. The project is a national center for addressing the concerns of handicapped people in science and engineering and for improving the science career information available to youths with disabilities.

Association on Handicapped Student Service Programs in Postsecondary Education (AHSSPPE), P.O. Box 21192, Columbus, OH 43221; (614) 488-4972. AHSSPPE is an umbrella group for disabled-student service organizations around the country. The goal is equal access for disabled students in higher education. AHSSPPE offers resources, contacts, and several publications.

Center for Special Education Technology, 1920 Association Drive, Reston, VA 22091; (703) 620-3660, 1-800-873-8255. The Center's Resource Inventory series provides listings of information and service resources in special education technology. The inventories are organized by state and topic. This information is intended to help technology users locate needed services.

Closing the Gap, P.O. Box 68, Henderson, MN 56044; (612) 248-3294. CTG (SpecialNet); X0060 (AppleLink); X0060@AppleLink.Apple.com (Internet). Closing the Gap publishes a bimonthly newspaper on microcomputer applications for people with disabilities; the paper emphasizes special education and rehabilitation uses. The organization also provides hands-on training, an annual conference, and a database of resources.

Committee on Personal Computers and the Handicapped (COPH-2), 2030 Irving Park Road, Chicago, IL 60618; (312) 477-1813. COPH-2 is a consumer organization that searches out, evaluates, and shares information about personal computers relevant to people with disabilities.

Computer Center for the Visually Impaired, 17 Lexington Avenue, Box 515, Baruch College, New York, NY 10010; (212) 725-7644. Baruch College of CUNY is a leader in the field of teaching blind and visually impaired people to use computers for personal, educational, and occupational purposes, and has published a guide to computer equipment for the blind and visually impaired.

HEATH Resource Center, One Dupont Circle, Suite 800, Washington, DC 20036-1193; (800) 544-3284 or (202) 939-9320 (both available for TDD). The HEATH Resource Center is a clearinghouse that operates under a Congressional legislative mandate to collect and disseminate information about disability issues in postsecondary education. Funding from the United States Department of Education enables the Center to increase the flow of information about educational support services, policies, and procedures related to educating or training people with disabilities after they have left high school.

IBM National Support Center for Persons with Disabilities, P.O. Box 2150, Atlanta, GA 30301-2150; (800) 426-2133 (Continental US Voice); (800) 284-9482 (Continental US TDD); and (404) 238-4761 (Atlanta-local). The Center was created in 1985 to help professionals learn how computers can enhance the education, work, and life-styles of people with disabilities. The Center provides information on what technology is available and where it can be obtained, but does not recommend solutions. A Disability Resource Center is maintained and equipment is available to demonstrate this new technology. Provides information on computerized systems and technology for disabled people in the workplace, home, and school environments.

Job Accommodation Network, 809 Allen Hall, P.O. Box 6122, West Virginia University, Morgantown, WV 26506-6122; (800) 526-7234 (voice/TDD, outside WV), (800) 526-4698 (voice/TDD, inside WV). The Job Accommodation Network (JAN) is a national information and consulting service providing free accommodation information to businesses wanting to hire or retain people with disabilities.

Radio Shack Technical Support, Radio Shack Customer Service, 400 Atrium, Fort Worth, TX 76102; (800) 433–5682. Radio Shack's Technical Support Office provides technical support to Radio Shack/Tandy users and publishes Selected Products for People with Special Needs, a catalog of special-needs products available through any local Radio Shack store.

RESNA--Association for the Advancement of Rehabilitation Technology (formerly the Rehabilitation Engineering Society of North America), Suite 700, 1101 Connecticut Avenue NW, Washington, DC 20036; (202) 587-1199. RESNA is an interdisciplinary society for the advancement of rehabilitation through technology. RESNA members use leading-edge technology to resolve problems in rehabilitation.

Trace Research and Development Center for Communication, Control, and Computer Access for Handicapped Individuals, S-151 Waisman Center, 1500 Highland Avenue, Madison, WI 53705; (608) 262-6966, TDD (608) 263-5408. X0059 (AppleLink); X0059@AppleLink.Apple.com (Internet). The Trace Center has a wealth of information on using current technology to meet the communication and environmental control needs of severely disabled people, as well as information on hardware, firmware, and software that may be used to make standard computer equipment accessible.

Worldwide Disability Solutions Group, Apple Computer, Inc., MS 36SE, 20525 Mariani Avenue, Cupertino, CA 95014; 408-974-7910. APPLE.OSEP (SpecialNet); SPECIAL.ED (AppleLink). This office is responsible for special education and rehabilitation technologies used on the Apple II and Macintosh families of computers to meet the needs of people with disabilities.

Publications

Adaptive Technology Lab Kit. Southern Connecticut State University, 501 Crescent Sreet, New Haven, Conn. 06515.

AHSSPPE Network (Newsletter for the Computer Special Interest Group of the Association on Handicapped Student Service Programs in Postsecondary Education). P.O. Box 21192, Columbus, OH 43221.

AHSSPPE Publications and Products Catalog. P.O. Box 21192, Columbus, OH 43221; (614) 488-4972.

Apple Computer Worldwide Disability Solutions Group. *Toward Independence: A Guide to the Accessible Macintosh.* Cupertino, CA: Apple Computer Worldwide Disability Solutions Group.

Apple Computer Worldwide Disability Solutions Group (1990). *Apple Computer Resources in Special Education and Rehabilitation.* Allen, TX: DLM Teaching Resources ([800] 527-4747, [800] 442-4711 [TX]).

Berliss, J. (1990). *Checklists for Implementing Accessibility in Computer Laboratories at Colleges and Universities.* Madison, WI: Trace Research and Development Center.

Berliss, J., and Vanderheiden, G. (1988). It's academic: Computer accessibility issues in higher education. In *Proceedings of RESNA 12th Annual Conference.*

Berliss, J., Borden, P., & Vanderheiden, G. (eds.) (1989). *Trace Resource Book.* Madison, WI: Trace Research and Development Center.

Bowe, Frank (1984). *Personal Computers and Special Needs.* Berkeley, CA: Sybex (2344 Sixth Street, 94710).

Brown, C., et al. (1987). *Computer Access in Higher Education for Students with Disabilities.* Sacramento, CA: High Tech Centers for the Disabled.

Closing the Gap. Bimonthly newspaper that includes software and equipment reviews, annual resource guide, and glossary of accessible computing terminology, published by Closing the Gap, Henderson, MN.

Computer-Disability News. Periodical newsletter published by the National Easter Seal Society, 2023 Ogden Avenue, Chicago, IL. 60612; (312) 243-8400.

Computer Equipment and Aids for the Blind and Visually Impaired: A Resource Guide (1985). New York: Computer Center for the Visually Impaired, Baruch College.

Connections: A Guide to Computer Resources for Disabled Children and Adults. Cupertino, CA: Apple Office of Special Education Programs, Apple Computer, Inc.

General Services Administration (1987). *Access to Information Technology by Users with Disabilities, Initial Guidelines.* Washington, DC: Clearinghouse on Computer Accommodations, General Services Administration (Room 2022, KGDO, 18th and F Streets NW 20405; (202) 523-1906 [voice/TDD]).

General Services Administration (1989). *Managing End User Computing for Users With Disabilities.* Washington, DC: Clearinghouse on Computer Accommodations, General Services Administration.

Greene, B., & Zimbler, L. (1989). *Profile of Handicapped Students in Postsecondary Education*, 1987, Doc. # CS 89-337. Washington, DC: U.S. Department of Education, Office of Educational Research and Improvement, National Center for Education Statistics. (202) 357-6366 or 357- 6834.

Hagen, D. (1984). *Microcomputer Resource Book for Special Education.* Reston, VA: Reston Publishing Company.

HEATH, Information from HEATH newsletter. Numerous reprints of articles on technology and disability in higher education. One Dupont Circle, Suite 800, Washington, DC 20036; (800) 5544-3284; (202) 939-9320 (both lines available for voice or TDD).

HEATH Resource Center, Resource Directory. Selection of resources in the field of postsecondary education and disability. One Dupont Circle, Suite 800, Washington, DC 20036, (800) 544-3284, (202) 939-9320 (both lines available for voice or TDD).

Horn, C., Shell, D., and Benkofske, M. T. H. (1989). What we have learned about technology usage for disabled students in postsecondary education: Results of a three-year demonstration project. *Closing the Gap, 8(3),* pp. 26-29.

IBM National Support Center for Persons with Disabilities. (1991). *Technology for Persons with Disabilities: An Introduction.* Atlanta, GA: IBM National Support Center.

IBM National Support Center for Persons with Disabilities. (1991). *Hearing Impairments, Learning Impairments, Mobility Impairments, Speech or Language Impairments, and Vision Impairments*. Atlanta, GA: IBM National Support Center.

Information Available from the Trace Center Reprint Service (1988-1989). A complete listing of the books, papers, and software available through the Trace Center. A list of reference sheets on specific access issues is also available. Madison, WI: Trace Research and Development Center.

Iowa Program for Assistive Technology. *Assistive Technology Information Network* (quarterly periodical). University Hospital School, University of Iowa, Iowa City, IA 52242.

Jamison, S. L. (1983). *Signs for Computing Terminology: A Sign Reference Book for People in the Computing Field*. Silver Spring, MD: National Association of the Deaf.

Kramer, K. (1988). Computer accessibility for students with disabilities. *Academic Computing, 3(2)*, 26-27, 38-39.

Margolis, V. (1986). The role of college disabled student service programs in providing access to the microcomputer. *AHSSPPE Bulletin, 4(2)*, 66-75.

Mendelsohn, S. B. *Financing Adaptive Technology: A Guide to Sources and Strategies for Blind and Visually Impaired Users*. New York: Smiling Interface (2792 Church Street Station, 10008-2792; (212) 222-0312, also available in large print, Braille, audiotape, or ASCII).

National Braille Press. *Add-On's: The Ultimate Guide to Peripherals for the Blind Computer User*. Boston, MA: National Braille Press (88 St. Stephens Street, 02115, also available in Braille and audiotape; (617) 266-6160).

Parette, Howard P., Jr., Ed.D., & Van Biervliet, Alan, Ph.D. (1990). *Assistive Technology Curriculum: A Module of Instruction for Students in Arkansas Colleges and Universities*. University of Arkansas at Little Rock, Arkansas Technology Information System (ARTIS), 2201 Brookwood, Suite 117, Little Rock, AR 72202; (800) 828-2799 or (501) 371-3566.

Read, R. (1988). Our basic beliefs. *CCD Newsletter, 1(2)*, 1-4, 13. Center for Computing and Disability, Milne 303, SUNY-Albany, 135 Western Avenue, Albany, NY 12222.

Shell, D., Horn, C., & Severs, M. (1988). Effects of a computer-based educational center on disabled students' academic performance. *Journal of College Student Development, 29*, 432-440.

Vanderheiden, G. C. (1984). Curbcuts and computers: providing access to computers and information systems for disabled individuals. *Discovery 83: Computers for the Disabled Conference Papers*. University of Wisconsin-Stout.

Vanderheiden, G. C., & Lee, C. C. (1988). *Considerations 4.2: Results of the Industry/Government Cooperative Effort on Computer Accessibility for Disabled Persons.* Madison, WI: Trace Research and Development Center.

Wheels for the Mind. Periodical published by Wheels for the Mind, 23L, P.O. Box 810, Cupertino, CA 95015.

READING QUESTIONS

1) How do gender role socialization, economic dualism, and indirect discrimination contribute to computing inequity?
2) Where did the data that Anderson et al. cite come from?
3) Why is differential in-school access a nonissue in terms of gender?
4) What gender-based differences in home access are there, and why do they matter?
5) Why is it important to look at the extent and type of computer use when analyzing gender inequity in schools?
6) Are there differences in general enrollment in computing classes in elementary and high school? What about differences in skill?
7) What differences in enrollment and persistence emerge in college?
8) How are the jobs women hold in computing different? Make sure to include employment rates, salary, occupation, and type of work within occupation.
9) What economically based differences are there in terms of access to computers in school? Are these the same for all levels of school?
10) Why do the statistics on access "not serve as adequate indicators of the quality of instruction"?
11) Low-SES homes with computers jumped from 2 percent to 5 percent from 1984 to 1989. Compared with high-SES homes, is this a significant improvement?
12) Does computing access at school offset the large, ethnically based differences at home?
13) For minority students, there seems to be equal participation in computing at school. Why, then, is there not equal performance?
14) In what way does being female *and* minority influence participation in careers involving computing?
15) Why does mandating computing equity programs matter in schools?
16) "…the mere introduction of new technology into a school does not guarantee greater computer equity…" Why?
17) How could computing networks be important in overcoming computer inequity?
18) Why is social support for computing important in achieving computing equity?
19) How does "tracking" influence the access of students to computers?
20) What is the "We can, but I can't" paradox?
21) How might the new image of "interactive" computing change its perceived "gender"?
22) "…inequities in type of computer activity are as important as overall usage." Why?
23) What is "the Net"?

24) Why is there a "big division" between those with access to the Internet and those with none?

25) What is the difference among first-class passengers, steerage passengers, boat people, and land-bound travelers?

26) Some have argued that the NREN will develop in one of two ways: "kilobits for the masses or gigabits for the elite." Why is it more complicated than this?

27) What is an "acceptable use policy"? How do they vary now? What pressures are there for change?

28) In what way are technical expertise, education, cost, network policies, user interfaces, security, and copyright issues that might be addressed to resolve equity in access to the Net?

29) How do fees structure use patterns?

30) What are net.cops? Why might we need them?

31) What issues are involved in deciding how to pay for equitable net access?

32) What is "essential" or "core" information? Why is it core? How does this relate to cost & equity issues?

33) How has past experience with TV, radio, etc., left people unprepared for net access?

34) How are general facilities and support, discipline-specific computing, and academic support crucial for access for the disabled?

35) How might network access help those with disabilities?

36) What percentages of people with various disabilities are there? Use a calculator and the figure for your campus to determine the numbers at your campus.

37) What four areas are important to consider when attempting to make computing more accessible to the disabled?

38) What is FIRMR, and how will it affect standards for computing in the future?

39) What have been some of the obstacles to the adoption of procedures and technologies that make computing more accessible to the disabled?

DISCUSSION QUESTIONS

1) Anderson et al. claim that computer skills are crucial in gaining well-paid employment. Contrast this with the claim of the NAS panel that "basic skills" are the important ones.

2) There are few gender-based differences in computing equity in students' early years, but these differences get quite large after high school. For SES and ethnicity, the differences start out large and get slightly larger or remain relatively constant. Why these differences in pattern?

3) Role-play the parts of various constituencies in a discussion on how to provide Net access to all the schools, libraries, and businesses in your county. Make sure to include low-SES groups, those with needs for high security, school officials, elected officials, and large and small business representatives—the more the merrier (up to a point). Make sure to include discussion of technical expertise, education, cost, network policies, user interfaces, security, and copyright issues. For a shorter discussion, try just one of the issues.

PRACTICING THE DESIGN ETHIC

1) Develop a survey to determine the level of access to computers in your local area. Form several teams, with each team focused on one of the following categories: gender, SES, disabilities, ethnicity. Each team should develop a survey/questionnaire that will be used in a local elementary school, high school, university, or business. Each team should ensure that it gets at least 10 responses from each site it chose. Also ensure that there are no more than 6 questions on each questionnaire so that the questionnaire can be filled out quickly by the respondents. Each questionnaire should request the appropriate information for its specific inquiry (i.e., gender, family income, ethnic background, or disability). In addition, each questionnaire should request the following information:
   - Do you have access to a computer? If so, where is it located? Circle all that apply: work, school, home.
   - What activities do you do on the computer?
   - On average, how much time do you spend on the computer each week?
   - Have you ever had formal training on the use of computers?

   Evaluate the data you gathered and determine if there are any patterns to the data. Does the data confirm or contradict the findings described in the paper "Equity In Computing?" Why do you think that is the case?

2) Use the appendix's FIRMR guidelines to evaluate the hardware and software on your campus available to those with disabilities. What changes could be made? Rank-order these changes in terms of both their urgency and their cost. Have a discussion with one of your institution's officials about these alternatives and the school's plan.

Chapter 11

NATIONAL DATABASES AND PRIVACY

Organizations face two "identification" questions when dealing with an individual. Is that individual entitled to the services he or she requests? And is that individual a threat to the organization's concern? These are not merely questions of whether "big brother" can achieve control over individuals. Many individuals request, even demand, that organizations take these actions to protect citizens or shareholders from danger or loss. The two articles in this chapter provide an overview of the issues and problems with surveillance in modern society.

Clarke's classic review presents a categorization of types of "dataveillance" that are currently being used or proposed. Just his listing of the broad array of techniques for surveillance is intimidating and worrisome. But the list provides two additional benefits. It makes us aware of the broad scope of surveillance in modern society, and it provides a balanced approach to issues in this area. For instance, the current (well-deserved) concern over the clipper chip has tended to displace all other coverage of surveillance issues. The chip is designed to allow U.S. authorities to decrypt any message over public lines, and is thus primarily a "personal dataveillance" technique. In light of Clarke's claim that mass dataveillance is by far the most widespread technique in use, and the one most likely to cause harm to individuals, the computer science community may be in danger of straining out the gnat but swallowing the camel in the area of privacy invasion and surveillance.

Rule, McAdam, Stearns, and Uglow's systematic investigation of personal documents in the United States suggests just how big the camel may be. They present a study of the historical development, current practice, and certainty of identification associated with six of the most widely held personal documents in the United States: birth certificates, driver's licenses, social security cards, passports, bank books, and bank-issued credit cards. Their conclusions that "mass surveillance through personal documentation feeds on itself" suggests that if we want the convenience and safety associated with personal identification, we may be in for a rough ride in terms of our privacy.

INFORMATION TECHNOLOGY AND DATAVEILLANCE[1]

Roger A. Clarke
Australian National University

Concern about freedom from tyranny is a trademark of democracy. Between 1920 and 1950, the anti-utopian novels of Zamyatin [78], Kafka, Huxley [21], and Orwell [45] unleashed a visionary, yet paranoiac "literature of alarm" (see, e.g., [5], [12], [15], [19], [32], [36], [49], [53], and [62]).

Surveillance is one of the elements of tyranny. The word conjures up unpleasant visions of spies, repression of individuals, and suppression of ideas. Nevertheless, some classes of people, at least when they undertake some classes of activity, are deemed by society to warrant surveillance. Few would contest that people reasonably suspected of terrorism and organized, violent crime are candidates for surveillance. Meanwhile, the growth in crimes against property has resulted in the widely acclaimed "neighborhood watch" movement.

The computer has been accused of harboring a potential for increased surveillance of the citizen by the state, and the consumer by the corporation. Most accusations have been vague, asserting that harm will result, rather than showing the mechanisms by which it will come about. Some have even claimed that the potential is already realized: "It is possible ...to imagine what one might call a 'central clearing house' for mass surveillance and control, without straining the limits of present-day [i.e., 1974] technology and organisational skills... [A]ll major agencies would render unlimited assistance to one another. Information generated in the relationship between a client and any one system would automatically be available to any other system...[T]he client's contact with one would have the effect of contact with all ...[N]o favorable decision from any agency would be implemented while there remained a dispute between the client and another agency" [55, p. 319].

Apart from research by Kling [23, 24] and Laudon [27—31], there has been little discussion in the computing literature. Most of the important contributions have been by observers rather than practitioners of computing, particularly Rule [55—59], Marx [33, 34]. and Reichman and Marx [35, 50]. See also [2, 11, 52].

The purpose of this article is to make the work of such authors more readily accessible to computing practitioners and academics, to extend it somewhat, and to propose a framework for policy. It commences by

---

[1]Clarke, R. A. (1989). Information Technology and Dataveillance. *Communications of the ACM*, 31-35. 498-512. Copyright © 1989, Association for Computing Machinery Inc. Reprinted by permission.

clarifying the concept of *dataveillance*, and then describes the manner in which information technology (IT) is stimulating its development. Popular publications have tended to deal with the topic in colorful, at times even hysterical, fashion (see, e.g., [1], [4], [6], [7], [12], [13], [37], [64], [70], and [73]). To enable the problems to be appreciated and responded to rationally, I will attempt to deal with the topic in a more neutral and dispassionate manner. In particular, I explicitly reject the notion that surveillance is, of itself, evil or undesirable; its nature must be understood, and society must decide the circumstances in which it should he used, and the safeguards that should be applied to it.

SURVEILLANCE

The *Oxford Dictionary* explained surveillance as "watch or guard kept over a person, etc., esp. over a suspected person, a prisoner, or the like; often spying, supervision; less commonly, supervision for the purpose of direction or control, superintendence" [46]. The oldest usage noted was in the "Committee of Surveillance" immediately after the French Revolution. *Webster's 3rd Edition* defines it as "1. close watch kept over one or more persons: continuous observation of a person or area (as to detect developments, movements or activities); 2. close and continuous observation for the purpose of direction, supervision or control" [71].

Rule uses the term for "any form of systematic attention to whether rules are obeyed, to who obeys and who does not, and how those who deviate can be located and sanctioned" [55, p. 40]. and later as "the systematic collection and monitoring of personal data for the purpose of social control" [59, p. 47] (see also [20, p.90]. In this article the following definition is used:

Surveillance is the systematic investigation or monitoring of the actions or communications of one or more persons. Its primary purpose is generally to collect information about them, their activities, or their associates. There may be a secondary intention to deter a whole population from undertaking some kinds of activity.

The basic form, physical surveillance, comprises watching and listening (visual and aural surveillance). Monitoring may be undertaken remotely in space, with the aid of image-amplification devices like field glasses. Infrared binoculars, light amplifiers, and satellite cameras, and sound-amplification devices like directional microphones: and remotely in time, with the aid of image and sound-recording devices. Several kinds of communications surveillance are practiced, including mail covers and telephone interception. The popular term *electronic surveillance* refers to both augmentations to physical surveillance (such as directional microphones and audio bugs) and to communications surveillance, particularly telephone taps.

These forms of direct surveillance are commonly augmented by the collection of data from interviews with informants (such as neighbors, employers, workmates, and bank managers). As the volume of information collected and maintained has increased, the record collections (or personal data systems) of organizations have become an increasingly important source.

Dataveillance is the systematic use of personal data systems in the investigation or monitoring of the actions or communications of one or more persons.

The terms *personal surveillance* and *mass surveillance* are commonly used, but seldom defined. In this article the following definitions are used:

Personal surveillance is the surveillance of an identified person. In general, a specific reason exists for the investigation or monitoring.

Mass surveillance is the surveillance of groups of people, usually large groups. In general, the reason for investigation or monitoring is to identify individuals who belong to some particular class of interest to the surveillance organization.

Personal surveillance is an important weapon in the fight against such social evils as terrorism and organized crime. It is used to collect evidence in civil cases. It is also a means of learning sufficiently embarrassing facts about a person to assist in discrediting him or her in the eyes of some other person or group, or buying his or her silence or agreement. At its most secret, it can deny the subject natural justice, and at its most open, it can be tantamount to coercion or blackmail.

Personal surveillance activities are undertaken by "private investigators" for corporate and personal clients. The majority of these activities, however. are undertaken by staff employed by government agencies, including police, national security, customs, and telecommunications officials.

Mass surveillance is difficult to discuss dispassionately because of the impact on our culture of the anti-utopian novels, particularly *1984* [45]. Its primitive forms include guards on raised walkways and observation turrets. More recently, closed-circuit television has offered a characteristic that significantly enhances the effectiveness of surveillance: The subjects, even if they know they are subject to monitoring, cannot know precisely when the observer is actually watching.

"Modern techniques have made possible a new intensity of governmental control, and this possibility has been exploited very fully in totalitarian states .… [E]mphasis upon the value of the individual is even more necessary now than at any former time" [60, p. 35]. Such a sentiment could be expected from the contemporary civil libertarian lobby. In fact, the words predate the use of computers even in information management, let alone personal data management, having been written in 1949 by Bertrand Russell. Ubiquitous two-way television *a la* 1984 has not arrived, even though it is readily deliverable. It is unnecessary because dataveillance is technically and economically superior.

RELEVANT IT TRENDS

Computers were originally developed for their high-speed computational capabilities. They subsequently spawned or stimulated a wide variety of

• Magnetic data-storage capabilities have improved immensely between 1965 and 1985, and optical storage is expected to have a significant impact in at least some application areas.	• Inroads have been made into natural language understanding, at least in respect of the more formal usages of language by humans.
• A rich assortment of input and output technologies has been developed to support the capture and dissemination of data.	• The hitherto numerical bias of computing technology is being augmented by symbolic manipulative capabilities. Many kinds of complex deterministic problems can now be tackled, and progress is being made in modeling probabilistic, "fuzzy," and stochastic processes.
• Textual and conventional "structurable" data have been dealt with successfully for some years by DBMS technology. The management of image and voice data is improving, and integrated data management, and conversion between the various forms are now being addressed.	• Significant improvements in telecommunications continue, particularly in speed, cost, reliability, robustness, security, and standardization.

Figure 11-1
Relevant components of IT development.

related technologies and have been married with telecommunications. Data can now be captured, stored, processed, and accessed readily and economically, even when the facilities and their users are physically dispersed. Figure 11-1 identifies some particularly pertinent aspects of current developments in IT.

Apparently distinct technologies have drawn together very quickly, as in electronic funds transfer systems (EFTS) and their nephew EFT/POS (point of sale). Change is being wrought less by computers themselves than by amalgams of many interacting and mutually supporting technologies. Optical-storage technology may portend a new surge in such compound high-technology ventures.

IT crystal-ball gazing is fraught with danger. Nevertheless, discernible trends include the integration with EFTS of air-travel systems and telephone charging; road-traffic monitoring, including vehicle identification, closely integrated with ownership and driver's-license records; computerization and integration of court records, criminal records, fingerprint records, and criminal-investigation systems; integration of structured and textual data to support criminal investigation and national-security applications; computerization and integration of birth, death, and marriage records; and homes wired for reasons of employment, security, entertainment, and consumerism.

As a consequence of the centralizing tendency of early IT, a "data imperative" arose, with government agencies and private companies alike collecting ever more data. Rule interpreted this as commitment to the "efficiency criterion," whereby privacy concerns should be recognized, but not at the cost of administrative efficiency. IT led to increasingly information-intensive practices and increasingly fine-grained decision making [55, 59].

With the repeal of Grosch's law during the 1970s, economies of scale no longer apply to processing power. Other factors that are militating against the old centralist notions are the systems software overheads of large-scale centralized processing; risks associated with single-site activities; standardization of local and site networking standards; fast-growing capabilities of network workstations and servers; decreasing cost and increasing portability and robustness of dense storage, as in the so-called "smart card"; established techniques of distributed DBMS; and emerging techniques of distributed operating systems. The once-obvious tendency of computers to centralize information, and hence power, is quickly giving way to the looser concepts of networking and dispersion.

The National Data Center Issue

In the mid-1960s the U.S. government considered creating a national data center. The prime motivation was slated to be the need for more coherent data management to support economic and sociological research. Such a data collection, however, had clear potential for supporting administrative decision making. A few people recognized the vital role of data dispersion: "One of the most practical of our present safeguards of privacy is the fragmented nature of present information. It is scattered in little bits and pieces across the geography and years of our life. Retrieval is impractical and often impossible. A central data bank removes completely this safeguard" (Representative Frank Horton, 1966-67 hearings on a proposed national data center, quoted in [59, p. 56]). Concerns such as these resulted in the proposal not proceeding.

Centralized storage, however, is no longer a precondition of the dossier society that Horton feared. For dataveillance purposes a single centralized data bank is unnecessary, provided that three conditions are fulfilled:
(1) A range of personal data systems must exist, each processing data for specific purposes.
(2) Some, preferably all, personal data systems must be connected via one or more telecommunications networks.
(3) The data must be identified consistently.

A recent report of the Office of Technology Assessment (O.T.A.) of the U.S. Congress discussed the manner in which use of IT is quickly leading to a de facto national identification system [43, pp. 3, 68-74]. There are also reports suggesting that both the NCIC (National Crime Information Center) and NSA (National Security Agency) are providing foci for such a system (e.g., [54, pp. 185-186]).

Beyond assisting in the investigation of people's pasts, IT is also dramatically improving the monitoring of people's ongoing activities and present location. A person's "most recent financial (or indeed any other kind of) transaction indicates where the person can currently be found. If that location is communicated to surveillance staff immediately, they can literally be on their way to the scene before the person leaves the checkout counter. A recent Australian report commenced with the sentence "EFTPOS is not a Greek island" [3]. The comment had a poignancy that its authors may not have appreciated. People go to Greek islands to escape from it all. EFT/POS constitutes a real-time locator service: You cannot escape from it at all. This was recognized at least as long ago as 1971, when, it was suggested as an appropriate surveillance tool for the KGB (Armer, quoted in [59, p. 115]).

Physical and even communications surveillance are labor-intensive activities, which have so far proved difficult to automate. Dataveillance is essentially computer-based, with the "watch and report" responsibility delegated to a reliable, ever-wakeful servant. It is increasingly cost-effective for organizations to place people under surveillance via their records and transactions, and traditional methods are being relegated to the role of complementary techniques. Furthermore, because dataveillance is cheaper than traditional methods, there is a tendency for more organizations to monitor more people: Both personal and mass surveillance are becoming routinized [35, 51].

The Central Role of Identification Schemes

Of the three requirements for a dispersed national data center identified earlier, the first two are already fulfilled. The third has not as yet been achieved, because of the difficulties of reliably identifying surveillance subjects, in associating stored data with individuals, and in associating new data with old.

The vast majority of personal data systems use schemes based on documentary evidence, possession of tokens, and personal knowledge. None of these can provide a satisfactory basis for a high-integrity system [9]. Many organizations that need to recognize identities in successive transactions assign their data subjects a more-or-less arbitrary unique identifying code. Some organizations prefer to (or have to) identify individuals by their names, usually supplemented by additional data such as date of birth. This approach involves a great deal of ambiguity, and name-matching routines have been developed to apply algorithms to such data in order to display synonyms "most-likely-first."

These various schemes may be of a reasonable level of integrity where data subjects have an interest in their accuracy, but are otherwise of, at best, only moderate integrity. Organized crime finds such low-integrity schemes as a social-security number a positive boon in its aims to legitimize false identities.

A high-integrity identification scheme is only possible if some physiological attribute is used that the person cannot alienate, and that the organization can capture, recognize, and store with its records. During 1987 the New South Wales (N.S.W.) Police Department implemented a fingerprint-record system based on Japanese technology. Although some U.S.

state and local government law-enforcement agencies have installed such systems, the N.S.W. initiative is quite significant, since its bureau operates on behalf of all police departments throughout Australia, and it appears to have been the first national system to enter operation anywhere in the world. Apart from criminal records, and limited applications in building security arrangements, fingerprint identification has not been socially acceptable. It can confidently be expected that there will be considerable efforts to make it so.

Historically, organizations have developed their identification schemes independently of one another, and large, multifunction organizations have run multiple schemes. However, organizations are increasingly using a single code for multiple purposes. For example, since at least the early 1970s, financial institutions have been moving toward "client-oriented" data management, whereby all of a client's data carry the same identifying code. The Australian Department of Social Security has committed itself to a common identification scheme for recipients of all classes of benefits by 1990.

Some identifiers were designed to be used for multiple purposes, whether by a single organization or by several. For example, in European countries it is normal for the same number to be used for the national superannuation fund as for taxation. Despite successive reports recommending the contrary (e.g.. [48. 68]), the United Slates is continuing its trend toward using the (originally single-purpose) social security number as a de facto national identification code. For example, in 1985 a database called ESVARS was established, explicitly to enable any organization (federal, state, or private sector) to verify social-security numbers (43, p. 73].

General-purpose schemes, for use by all organizations for all purposes, have been attempted in a number of countries during wartime, including the United Kingdom and Australia, when the "inducement of rationing has made them workable" [55, p. 314]. The few countries that have considered such a scheme in peacetime have rejected the idea. The United States did so in the mid-1970s [68]. The Australian government proposed such a scheme in 1985, although the proposal was subsequently amended to a multipurpose scheme for three main agencies. and finally withdrawn in the third quarter of 1987 when serious public concern arose about its implications [9]. As the scope of use of an identification scheme moves from single-use via multiple-use toward general-purpose use, the ease with which dataveillance can be undertaken increases significantly.

TECHNIQUES OF DATAVEILLANCE

This section discusses the techniques used in personal dataveillance, mass dataveillance, and facilitative mechanisms. Figure 11-2 provides a summary.

Personal dataveillance of identified individuals who have attracted attention	*Mass dataveillance* of groups of people, with the intention of finding individuals in need of attention.
• *Integration of data* hitherto stored in various locations within the organization • *Screening or authentication of transactions*, against internal norms • *Front-end verification of transactions* that appear to be exceptional, against data relevant to the matter at hand and sought from other internal databases or from third parties. • *Front-end audit of individuals* who appear to be exceptional, against data related to *other* matters and sought from other internal databases or from third parties. • *Cross-system enforcement against individuals,* where a third party reports that the individual has committed a transgression in his or her relationship with the third party.	• *Screening or authentication of all transactions*, irrespective of whether or not they appear to be exceptional, against internal norms. • *Front-end verification of all transactions*, irrespective of whether or not they appear to be exceptional, against data related to other matters and sought from other internal databases or from third parties. • *Front-end audit of individuals,* irrespective of whether or not they appear to be exceptional, against data related to *other* matters and sought from other internal databases or from third parties. • *Single-factor file analysis of all data held or able to be acquired*, irrespective of whether or not they appear to be exceptional—variously involving transaction data compared against a norm, and against a norm inferred from a population a posteriori; transaction data compared against permanent data; and transaction data compared against other transaction data. • *Profiling, or multifactor file analysis, of all data held or able to be acquired*, irrespective of whether or not they appear to be exceptional—variously involving singular profiling of data held at a point in time, and aggregative profiling of transaction trails over time.
Facilitative mechanisms:	
• *Matching*—expropriation and merger of data held in separate data systems, whether operated by the same organization or by third parties.	° *Data concentration*—by organizational merger or by the operation of data-interchange networks and hub systems.

Figure 11-2
Techniques of Dataveillance.

Personal Dataveillance Techniques

Organizations maintain records about individuals they are concerned with (their *data subjects*). In most cases data subjects are clients of the organization, because they have a known and fairly explicit relationship with them. This relationship may be direct (as with financial institutions and the Internal Revenue Service (IRS) or indirect (as is sometimes the case with superannuation funds). With some record-keeping organizations, there may be no overt relationship (e.g., counterintelligence agencies, private investigators, and credit bureaus).

Subjects of personal dataveillance have attracted attention for some reason. The reason may be benign, for example, because they have applied for employment or a service. An investigation will usually have the intention of disqualifying the person from the employment or service they seek, but sometimes the organization may be considering whether the person may qualify for extra assistance, say, because of aboriginal ancestry. Another class of reasons for investigation is suspicion that the person has committed a crime or misdemeanor. A transaction may have taken place that appears inconsistent with existing records, or potentially incriminating information may have been received from outside the organization.

Dataveillance depends on data that identify people. Despite the increase in information intensity in recent years, there remain many economic relationships in which the parties do not necessarily identify themselves. These include barter and cash transactions ranging from hunting and fishing licenses, through gambling, and bus, train, and ferry tickets to quite large consumer items, including expensive cars and boats. Authorities throughout the world, concerned about the base with which organized crime "washes" its illegally gained cash, have set, or are considering setting, maximum limits on unidentified cash transactions.

Given that identified records exist, a variety of dataveillance techniques are available. The most primitive technique, record integration, brings together all of the data an organization holds about each person. For many organizations this is not the trivial exercise it appears. Data may be dispersed in many ways, such as geographically across different offices and files, or under different codes or names (e.g., where the person has changed name; operates under multiple identities, including married and maiden names, and business and company names; operates joint accounts, sometimes with another party's name first; uses various combinations of given names; or has a name that is subject to spelling variants). In addition, during the early years of administrative and commercial applications of computing, it has been cost-effective and even necessary to store transaction data separately from permanent data, and transaction data for each period of time in distinct files. Financial institutions have undergone the transition to client-oriented data storage, the insurance industry is going through it, and airlines have commenced the changeover.

An approach adopted by most organizations is to monitor new transactions. Each transaction an organization receives (e.g., an application for employment, a loan, or a government benefit) is processed according to standard rules to determine whether the transaction is valid and acceptable. Additional rules may be applied, expressly designed to detect both inaccuracies and attempts to cheat the decision criteria. Exceptional cases generally are submitted to a more senior authority for more careful nonroutine consideration.

Where the processing rules depend only on data already available to the organization, these practices are generally referred to as screening or authentication. Some commercial and administrative activity is impractical without such basic data processing, and in many cases the law requires it, as, for example, in the processing of applications for government benefits. Moreover, the stewardship responsibilities to which any organization is subject generally require that controls be built into transaction processing, subject to cost-effectiveness constraints.

Front-end verification of transactions represents a future development beyond screening (25; 43, pp. 67-83). It involves the collection of data from other personal-data systems in order to facilitate the processing of a transaction. The source of the data may be elsewhere the same organization, for example, a driver's-licensing authority might consult its traffic-offenses database when renewing licenses. More commonly, however, front-end verification involves communication between two or more distinct organizations, either on an ad hoc basis or under a standing data-interchange arrangement.

Front-end verification is a personal dataveillance, technique when the transaction has been identified as exceptional, and the purpose of collecting the additional data is to establish whether there is any inconsistency between the various sources of data. An inconsistency may disqualify the transaction or be evidence of some wrongdoing such as providing misleading information. The data-interchange arrangements necessary to support front-end verification are not well documented in the literature. Rule provides one good reason: "No topic evoked less candour . .. or gave rise to more vivid displeasure when I insisted on pursuing it" [55, p. 308].

Front-end verification tests transactions. A broader form of personal dataveillance is what might be termed *front-end audit*. This uses the occasion of the detection of an exceptional transaction as an opportunity to further investigate other matters relating to the individual. For example, when a driver is stopped for a traffic offense, it is becoming standard practice for the police officer to initiate on-line inquiries. Those typically concern the vehicle (whether it is currently registered and whether it has been reported stolen), the vehicle's registered owner, and the driver (whether the driver is being sought for questioning or has an outstanding arrest warrant). The first transaction generally arises because there are reasonable grounds for believing that an offense has been committed. The justification for the subsequent transactions is less clear.

Intersystem and interorganizational arrangements can be pursued a step further by means of cross-system enforcement. This technique makes an individual's relationship with one organization dependent on his or her performance in relation to another. For example, there have been proposals in some U.S. states whereby renewal of a driver's license or entry to a turnpike would be precluded until the person has paid all outstanding parking fines. Steps have been taken in this direction (e.g., to preclude the sale of books of turnpike tickets), but to date their effectiveness appears to be doubtful.

In those cases the systems to be used for cross-enforcement are different, but to some extent related. There have been suggestions in New York City that even the issuing of a marriage license might be made dependent on payment of outstanding parking fines. In this case the link between the two systems is rather tenuous—it is merely that the same organization has responsibility for both functions. Such a mechanism was included in the Australian government's proposed national identification scheme: The individual's right under Medicare to free treatment or a refund of medical expenses would have been suspended until that person's obligation to have a national identity card was fulfilled [9].

Mass Dataveillance Techniques

Personal dataveillance is concerned with identified individuals about whom some kind of concern or suspicion has arisen. On the other hand, mass dataveillance is concerned with groups of people and involves a generalized suspicion that some (as yet unidentified) members of the group may be of interest. Its purposes are to identify individuals who may be worth subjecting to personal surveillance. and to constrain the group's behavior.

Screening or authentication of transactions. discussed earlier, is arguably a form of mass surveillance to the extent that it is routinely or automatically applied to every transaction, whether or not it appears to be exceptional. Similarly, when data are routinely sought from other internal databases or third parties in order to undertake front-end verification of all transactions. mass dataveillance is being undertaken. This is a recent development in which IT's role has been criticized: "In the past, such verification was done manually on a random basis or when the accuracy of information provided was suspect. Today, ...computerized databases and on-line networking make it possible to carry out such verification routinely" [43, p. 67]. Similarly, front-end audit is a mass-surveillance technique if the investigation of multiple aspects of a person's performance arises without any explicit cause, rather than as a result of some exceptional transaction.

The application of such techniques to existing records, rather than to new transactions, is referred to here as *file analysis*: "The files are most useful where they enable the system quickly and unerringly to single out the minority of their clients who warrant some measure of social control" (Rule, quoted in [67]). File analysis can be effective in searching out what Marx and Reichman refer to as "low-visibility offenses" [35]. In a recent instance in the United Kingdom, government investigators applied file-analysis techniques to detect and prosecute multiple applications for shares to "privatized" government enterprises such as Telecom and British Petroleum.

Screening, front-end verification, front-end audit, and file analysis may all be undertaken with varying degrees of sophistication. Transaction data may be compared against a formal standard or other norm, for example, highlighting those lax returns that include deductions above a certain value or show more than, say, eight dependents. The norms against which the data are compared may be either legal or other a priori norms that have been set down in advance by some authority, possibly for good reasons, possibly quite arbitrarily. Alternatively, they may be a posteriori norms that were inferred from analysis of the collection of records.

Alternatively, transaction data may be compared against permanent data, for example, highlighting tax returns where the spouse's name does not match that on file. Or transaction data may be compared against other transaction data, for example, highlighting people whose successive tax returns show varying numbers of dependents.

The previous examples are each based on a single factor. Judgments of any complexity must be based on multiple factors, rather than just one. Profiling, as it is commonly known, may he done on the basis of either a priori arbitrary or pragmatic norms, or on a posteriori norms based on empirical evidence. Rule noted in 1974 that the IRS used an a posteriori technique for predicting the "audit potential" of different returns. It did this by inferring unknown characteristics from known characteristics by applying discriminant analysis to a small random sample of returns [55, p. 282]. Marx and Reichman's description of this technique is "correlating a number of distinct data items to order to assess how close a person comes to a predetermined characterization or model of infraction" (35, p. 429). These authors further distinguish "singular profiling" from "aggregative profiling," which involves analyzing transaction trails over a period of time.

Sophisticated profiling techniques are claimed to hold great promise because they can detect hidden cases amid large populations. Benefits could be readily foreseen from profiles of young people with proclivities toward particular artistic and sporting skills; propensity for diseases, disorders, delinquency, or drug addiction or suicidal or homicidal tendencies. A recent O.T.A. report noted that most U.S. federal agencies have applied the technique to develop a wide variety of profiles including drug dealers, taxpayers who underreport their income, likely violent offenders, arsonists, rapists, child molesters, and sexually exploited children [43, pp. 87-95].

Facilitative Mechanisms

Mass-dataveillance techniques may be successfully applied within a single personal-data system, but their power can be enhanced if they are applied to data from several. These systems might all be operated by the organization concerned or by a number of distinct organizations. In such cases a preliminary step may be undertaken:

Computer matching is the expropriation of data maintained by two or more personal-data systems. in order to merge previously separate data about large numbers of individuals.

Matching has become technically and economically feasible only during the last decade, as a result of developments in IT. The first large program was Project Match, undertaken by the U.S. Department of Health, Education and Welfare (HEW), now known as Health and Human Services (HHS). By 1982 it was estimated that about 500 programs were carried out routinely in U.S. state and federal agencies [69], and O.T.A. estimated a tripling in use between 1980 and 1984 [43, p. 37]. Moreover, a succession of federal laws, culminating in the 1984 Budget Deficit Reduction Act, imposed matching on state administrations as a condition of receiving federal social-welfare funding. (For references descriptive of and supportive of matching, see [25], [39]-[41], [65]. and [66]. Cautionary and crucial comments are to be found in [22], [23], [26], [35], [43], [50], and [61]).

Matching makes more data available about each person and also enables comparison between apparently similar data items as they are known to different organizations. Rather than relating to a single specified person for a specific reason, matching achieves indiscriminate data cross-referencing about a large number of people for no better reason than a generalized suspicion: "Computer matches are inherently mass or class investigations, as they are conducted on a category of people rather than on specific individuals …in practice, welfare recipients and Federal employees are most often the targets" [43, p. 40].

Matching may be based on some common identifier that occurs in both files, in which case the error rate (measured by the proportion of undetected matches and spurious matches) will tend to be fairly low. There are few opportunities for such matching, however, and instead it is usually necessary to correlate several items of information. Intuitively, name, birth date, and sex seem appropriate, but it appears that greater success has been achieved by using some component of address as a primary matching criterion.

Individuals may be judged to be interesting because of:
• the existence of a match where none should exist,
• the failure to find a match where one was expected,
• inequality between apparently common data items (e.g., different numbers of dependents), or
• logical inconsistency among the data on the two files (e.g., the drawing of social-welfare benefits during a period of employment).

Curiously, the current U.S. government matching guidelines [40] define matching only in terms of the first of these criteria.

An additional facilitative mechanism for both personal and mass dataveillance is referred to here as *data concentration.* The conventional approach is to merge existing organizations in search of economies of scale in administration. If the capabilities of large-scale data-processing equipment were to continue to increase, the merger of social-welfare and internal-revenue agencies could be anticipated enabling welfare to be administered as "reverse taxation."

Organizational merger is an old-fashioned "centralized" solution. The modern, dispersed approach to data concentration is to establish systems that can function as the hub of a data-interchange network. For example, the U.S. government has developed new systems to facilitate routine front-end verification. These initiatives, in the name of waste reduction, involve both

Dangers of personal dataveillance
• Wrong identification • Low data quality • Acontextual use of data • Low-quality decisions • Lack of subject knowledge of data flows • Lack of subject consent to data flows • Blacklisting • Denial of redemption

Dangers of mass dataveillance	
To the individual	To society
• Arbitrariness • Acontextual data merger • Complexity and incomprehensibility of data • Witch hunts • Ex ante discrimination and guilt prediction • Selective advertising • Inversion of the onus of proof • Covert operations • Unknown accusations and accusers • Denial of due process	• Prevailing climate of suspicion • Adversarial relationships • Focus of law enforcement on easily detectable and provable offenses • Inequitable application of the law • Decreased respect for the law • Reduction in the meaningfulness of individual actions • Reduction in self reliance and self determination • Stultification of originality • Increased tendency to opt out of the official level of society • Weakening of society's moral fiber and cohesion • Destabilization of the strategic balance of power • Repressive potential for a totalitarian government

Figure 11-3
Real and potential dangers of dataveillance.

federal government sources (including IRS and criminal records) and private-sector credit bureaus, and their use not only extends across many federal government agencies, but is also imposed on state welfare administration agencies (14; 42, pp. 68-74]. The Australian government's proposal for a national identification scheme involved just such a coordinating database [9].

DATAVEILANCE'S BENEFITS AND DANGERS

In this section the advantages dataveillance techniques offer are briefly discussed. Greater space is then devoted to the threats dataveillance represents. Figure 11-3 summarizes these dangers.

Benefits

Significant benefits can result from dataveillance. The physical security of people and property may be protected, and financial benefits may accrue from the detection and prevention of various forms of error, abuse, and fraud. Benefits can be foreseen both in government activity (e.g., tax and social welfare) and in the private sector (e.g., finance and insurance). (For the limited literature on the benefits of matching, see [16], [25], [43. pp. 50-52], [65], and [66]. Literature on the benefits of other dataveillance techniques is very difficult to find).

Some proponents claim that the deterrent effect of public knowledge that such techniques are applied is significant, perhaps even more significant than direct gains from their actual use. There may be symbolic or moral value in dataveillance, irrespective of its technical effectiveness.

Few people would question the morality of an organization applying the more basic techniques, for example, record integration and screening. Some would go so far as to regard organizations that did not apply modern IT in such ways as failing to fulfill their responsibilities to taxpayers and shareholders. Nevertheless, dataveillance is, by its very nature, intrusive and threatening. It therefore seems reasonable that organizations should have to justify its use, rather than merely assuming its appropriateness.

Dangers of Personal Dataveillance

Because so few contemporary identification schemes use a physiological identifier, they are, at best, of moderate integrity. Rather than individuals themselves, what is monitored is data that purport to relate to them. As a result there is a significant likelihood of wrong identification.

The vast majority of data systems operators are quite casual about the quality of most of their data; for example, the O.T.A. reported that few federal government agencies have conducted audits of data quality [43, p. 26]. For many organizations it is cost-effective to ensure high levels of accuracy only of particular items (such as invoice amounts), with broad internal controls designed to ensure a reasonable chance of detecting errors in less vital data. Some errors are intentional on the part of the data subject, but many are accidental, and some are a result of design deficiencies such as inadequate coding schemes. Similar problems arise with other elements of data quality such as the timeliness and completeness of data. Even in systems where a high level of integrity is important, empirical studies have raised serious doubts [30; 43, pp. 52-53]. Data quality is generally not high, and while externally imposed controls remain very limited, it seems likely that the low standards will persist.

People and matters relating to them are complicated, and organizations generally have difficulty dealing with atypical, idiosyncratic cases or extenuating circumstances [35, p. 436]. A full understanding of the circumstances generally requires additional data that would have seemed too trivial and/or expensive to collect, but also depends on common sense, and abstract ideas like received wisdom, public opinion, and morality [54]. When the data are used in their original context, data quality may be sufficient to support effective and fair decision making, but when data are used outside their original context, the probability of misinterpreting them increases greatly. This is the reason why information privacy principles place such importance on relating data to the purpose for which they are collected or used [44], and why sociologists express concern about the "acontextual" nature of many administrative decision processes [35].

Much front-end verification is undertaken without the subject's knowledge. Even where an organization publicizes that it seeks data from third parties, the implications of the notice are often unclear to the data subject. International conventions stipulate that data should not be used for purposes other than the original purpose of collection, except with the authority of law or the consent of the data subject (e.g., [44]). Where consent is sought, the wording is often such that the person has no appreciation of the import of the consent that is being given, or the bargaining position is so disproportionately weighted in favor of the organization that the data subject has no real option but to comply. Effective subject knowledge and consent mechanisms are necessary, both as a means of improving data quality, and to avoid unnecessary distrust between individuals and organizations.

Front-end audit and cross-system enforcement give rise to additional concerns. Their moral justification is not obvious, and they create the danger of individuals being effectively blacklisted across a variety of organizations. Credit-bureau operations are extending in some countries into insurance, employment, and tenancy. Acute unfairness can arise, for example, when organizations blacklist a person over a matter that is still in dispute. It is particularly problematic where the person is unaware that the (possibly erroneous, incomplete, or out-of-date) data have been disseminated. Finally, even where individuals have brought the problems upon themselves, blacklisting tends to deny them the ability to redeem themselves for past misdemeanors.

Dangers of Mass Dataveillance to the Individual

Mass dataveillance embodies far greater threats. In respect of each individual, mass surveillance is clearly an arbitrary action, because no prior suspicion existed. The analogy may be drawn with the powers of police officers to interfere with the individual's quiet enjoyment. If a police officer has grounds for suspecting that a person has committed, or even is likely to commit, an offense, then the police officer generally has the power to intercept and perhaps detain that person. Otherwise with rare and, in a democratic state, well justified exceptions, such as national security emergencies and, in many jurisdictions, random breath testing, even a police officer does not have the power to arbitrarily interfere with a person.

With mass dataveillance, the fundamental problem of wrong identification, unclear, inconsistent, and context-dependent meaning of data, and low data quality are more intense than with personal dataveillance. Data arising from computer matching are especially problematic. Where there is no common identifier, the proportion of spurious matches (type (1) errors) and undetected matches (type (2) errors) can be very high. The causes include low quality of the data upon which computer matching depends (variants, misspellings, other inaccuracies, and incompleteness), inappropriate matching criteria, widely different (or subtly but significantly different) meanings of apparently equivalent data items, or records with differing dates of applicability. Marx and Reichman report a New York State program in which half of the matches were spurious due to timing problems alone [35, p. 435]. In addition. the meaning of the record as a whole must be properly understood. Although it might seem improper for a person to be both in employment and in receipt of a social welfare benefit, many pensions and allowances are, in law, either independent of, or only partially dependent on, income from other sources.

Data on the error rates of matching programs are difficult to find: They are mostly conducted away from the glare of public, or indeed any other kind of supervision. In an incident in Australia in 1986, the federal agency responsible for the Medicare scheme calmly, and without apparent legal authority, expropriated and merged data from several federal government agencies, relating to all inhabitants of the small island state of Tasmania. The agency reported the 70 percent hit rate across the databases as a good result, confirming its belief that a national identification scheme could be based on such a procedure. They ignored the implication that across the national population the records of nearly five million persons would remain unmatched, and failed to apply any tests to establish what proportion of the 70 percent were spurious matches and what portion of the 30 percent nonmatches were failures of the algorithm used. Australians embrace a popular mythology that everyone in Tasmania is related to everyone else. For this reason alone, the agency might have been expected to recognize the need for such testing.

The complexities of each system (particularly a country's major data systems such as taxation and social welfare) are such that few specialists are able to comprehend any one of them fully. It is arguably beyond the bounds of human capability to appreciate the incompatibilities between data from different systems and to deal with the merged data with appropriate care. Computer matching, therefore, should never be undertaken without the greatest caution and skepticism.

Profiling makes a judgment "about a particular individual based on the past behavior of other individuals who appear statistically similar" [43, p. 88]. Statistical techniques such as multivariate correlation and discriminant analysis have limited domains of applicability that are often poorly understood or ignored. Even if the statistical procedures are properly applied, a profile needs to be justified by systemic reasoning. In the hands of the inadequately trained, insufficiently professional, or excessively enthusiastic or pressured, profiling has all the hallmarks of a modern witch-hunting tool.

Profiling is not restricted to retrospective investigation. It purports to offer the possibility of detecting undesirable classes of people before they commit an offense. O.T.A. documents a "predelinquency" profile developed for the U.S. Law Enforcement Assistance Administration [43, p. 90]. Even if the technique is perceived to be successful, its use seems to run counter to some fundamental tenets of contemporary society. It is unclear on what moral and, indeed, legal grounds profiling may be used to reach administrative determinations about individuals or discriminate between individuals. Such vague constraints may not be sufficient to stultify an attractive growth industry. With computer displays and printouts lending their (largely spurious) authority to such accusations, how will the tolerance needed in complex social environments be maintained?

Not only in government, but also in the private sector, dangers arise from both the effectiveness and ineffectiveness of profiling. The combination of consumer profiles with cheap desktop publishing is dramatically altering the cost-effectiveness of customized "mail shots." Applied to cable television, the technique will enable the operator to selectively transmit "commercials" to those subscribers who seem most likely to be susceptible to the client's product (or perhaps just the advertisement). Whereas Vance Packard could only prophesy the development of such technology [41], the components can now be identified, and the economics described.

Conventional justice is expensive and slow. Some procedures are now being structured, particularly in such areas as taxation, such that a government agency makes a determination, and individuals who disagree must contest the decision [61]. This inversion of the onus of proof exacerbates the problems of misinterpretation resulting from data merger, and uncertainly arising from correlative profiling. It is further compounded by the imbalance of power between organization and individual. Marx and Reichman provide an example in which individuals were confronted by a complex of difficulties: A remote examination authority statistically analyzed answer sheets, and threatened students who had sat in the same room and given similar (incorrect) answers with cancellation of their results unless they provided additional information to prove they did not cheat [35, p. 432].

Some dataveillance is undertaken with dubious legal authority or in the absence of either authority or prohibition. To avoid being subjected to public abuse and perhaps being denied the right to undertake the activity, it is natural for organizations to prefer to undertake some operations covertly. There are also cases where the benefits of surveillance may be lost if it is not undertaken surreptitiously (e.g., because of the likelihood of the person temporarily suspending, rather than stopping, undesirable activities; or of "skips" on consumer credit transactions).

To protect the mechanism or the source, an individual may not be told that dataveillance has been undertaken, the source of the accusation, the information which the accusation is based or even what the accusation is. Such situations are repugnant to the concept of due process long embodied in British law and in legal systems derived from it. Dataveillance tends to compromise the individual's capacity to defend him or herself or to prosecute his or her innocence. In its most extreme form, one Kafka could not anticipate, the accuser could be a poorly understood computer program or a profile embodied in one.

Social Dangers of Mass Dataveillance

At the social level, additional problems arise. With personal dataveillance, investigation and monitoring normally take place after reasonable grounds for suspicion have arisen. Mass surveillance dispenses with that constraint because the investigation is routinely performed and the suspicion arises from it. The organization therefore commences with a presumption of guilt on the part of at least some of the data subjects, although at the beginning of the exercise it is unknown which ones. The result is a prevailing climate of suspicion.

The organizational functionary who communicates with the data subject often only partially understands the rationale underlying the decision, prefers not to admit that lack of understanding, and is often more concerned with case resolution than with public relations. Hence, there is an increased tendency for organizations and data subjects to develop adversarial relationships. Moreover, since organizations generally have the information, the size and the longevity, the bargaining positions are usually unequal.

Some of the "atypical, idiosyncratic, and extenuating cases" that are uncovered by mass dataveillance are precisely the deviants who are being sought. But others are just genuinely different, and such people tend to have difficulties convincing bureaucrats that their idiosyncrasies should be tolerated. Dataveillance encourages investigators to focus on minor offenses that can be dealt with efficiently, rather than more important crimes that are more difficult to solve. Law enforcers risk gaining a reputation for placing higher priority on pursuing amateur and occasional violators (particularly those whose records are readily accessible, like government employees and welfare recipients), rather than systematic, repetitive, and skilled professional criminals. The less equitably the law is perceived to be enforced, the greater the threat to the rule of law.

An administrative apparatus that has data available to it from a wide variety of sources tends to make decisions on the person's behalf. Hence, a further, more abstract, yet scarcely less real impact of dataveillance is reduction in the meaningfulness of individual actions, and hence in self-reliance and self-responsibility. Although this may be efficient and even fair, it involves a change in mankind's image of itself, and risks sullen acceptance by the masses and stultification of the independent spirit needed to meet the challenges of the future.

Some people already opt out of official society, preferring bureaucratic anonymity even at the costs of foregoing monetary and other benefits, and, consequently, attracting harassment by officialdom. There may already be a tendency toward two-tiered societies, in which the official documentary level of government facts and statistics bears only an approximate relationship to the real world of economic and social activity. If uncontrolled dataveillance were to cause the citizens of advanced Western nations to lose confidence in the fairness with which their societies are governed, it would be likely to exacerbate that trend.

An increase in the proportion of economic activity outside mainstream society would prompt, and be used to justify, a further increase in the use of mass surveillance. Assuming that world politics continues to be polarized into an East-West confrontation, it would be very easy to justify tighter social controls since any serious weakening in the moral fiber and integrity of the West would be destabilizing. Since "mastery of both communications and mass surveillance is necessary for an elite to maintain control" [57, p. 176], IT will be a major weapon whereby ruling groups seek to exercise control over the population.

Finally, it is necessary to mention (but not over-dramatize) the risk of dataveillance tools supporting repressive actions by a future invader, or by the "dirty-tricks department" of some democratically elected government gone, as Hitler's did, somewhat off the rails: "Orwell foresaw—and made unforgettable—a world in which ruthless political interests mobilized intrusive technologies for totalitarian ends. What he did not consider was the possibility that the development of the intrusive technologies would occur *on its own without the spur of totalitarian intent.* This, in fact, is what is now happening" [57, p. 179].

In general, mass dataveillance tends to subvert individualism and the meaningfulness of human decisions and actions, and asserts the primacy of the state.

SAFEGUARDS

Intrinsic Controls over Dataveillance

Some natural controls exist that tend to limit amount of dataveillance undertaken. The most apparent of these is its expense. There have been claims of dramatic success for matching schemes, but these have generally been made by the agencies that conducted them, and independent audits are hard to come by. The U.S. government's original (1979) guidelines on matching required that cost/benefit analyses be undertaken prior to the program being commenced [39]. However, there are many difficulties in undertaking a cost/benefit analysis of such a program. Many benefits are vague and unquantifiable, and many expenses are hidden or already "sunk." As a result, the requirement was rescinded in 1982 and has not been reimposed [40]. Moreover, there is seldom any other legal or even professional requirement that a cost/benefit analysis be performed [61, p. 540]. In 1986 O.T.A. concluded that few U.S. government programs are subjected to prior cost/benefit assessment [43, pp. 50-52].

Although reliable audits are difficult to find, anecdotal evidence throws doubt on the efficacy of matching. In the original Project Match, HEW ran its welfare files against its own payroll files. The 33,000 raw hits that were revealed required a year's investigation before they could be narrowed to 638 cases, but only 55 of these were ever prosecuted. Of a sample of 15 cases investigated by the National Council for Civil Liberties after HEW released the names of the people involved, 5 were dismissed, 4 pleaded guilty to misdemeanors (theft under $50), and only 6 were convicted of felonies. No prison sentences resulted, and the fines totaled under $2,000 [14, 49]. A 1983 match between Massachusetts welfare and bank files found 6,500 hits in five million records, resulting in 420 terminations of benefits, but also much confusion and recrimination [50]. Recent U.S. government reports have also raised doubts about the economic worth of many matching programs. A more positive report on several local government systems is to be found in [16].

There is very little evidence concerning the economics of other dataveillance techniques. Effective cost/benefit assessment, however, appears to be very rare (e.g., [43, pp. 80-81]). Unless credible cost/benefit analyses are undertaken, at least retrospectively, and preferably in advance, the potential economic safeguard against excessive use of dataveillance cannot be realized.

Economic controls, even if they were effective, may be sufficient to protect individual freedoms. In the early years of personal-data systems, the dominant school of thought, associated with Westin, was that business and government economics would ensure that IT did not result in excessive privacy invasion [74-76]. This view has been seriously undermined by Rule's work, which has demonstrated that, rather than supporting individual freedoms, administrative efficiency conflicts with it. Organizations have perceived their interests to dictate the collection, maintenance, and dissemination of ever more data, ever more finely grained. This is in direct contradiction to the interests of individuals in protecting personal data [55-59]. Meanwhile, onward march of IT continues to decrease the costs of dataveillance.

Another natural control is that surveillance activities can incur the active displeasure of the data subject or the general public. Given the imbalance of power between organizations and individuals, it is unrealistic to expect this factor to have any relevance outside occasional matters that attract media attention. Another, probably more significant control is that an organization's activities may incur the displeasure of some other organization, perhaps a watchdog agency, consumer group, or competitor.

In any case, these natural controls cannot be effective where the surveillance activities are undertaken in a covert manner. Intelligence agencies in particular are subject to few and generally ineffective controls.

Also, many controls, such as the power to authorize telephone interception, may not be subject to superordinate control. Intrinsic controls over dataveillance are insufficient to ensure that the desirable balance is found.

Extrinsic Controls over Dataveillance

The establishment of extrinsic controls over dataveillance cannot even be embarked upon until comprehensive information privacy laws are in place. Proper protection of privacy-invasive data handling was stillborn in the United States in the early 1970s by the limited official response associated with Westin [74—76], the Privacy Act of 1974, and the PPSC report [48]. Westin found no problems with extensive surveillance systems as such, only with the procedures involved, and the PPSC's aim was to make surveillance as publicly acceptable as possible, consistent with its expansion and efficiency [59, pp. 75, 110].

The U.S. Privacy Act was very easily subverted. Publication of uses in the Federal Register has proved to be an exercise in bureaucracy rather than control. The "routine use" loophole in the act was used to legitimize virtually any use within each agency (by declaring the efficient operation of the agency to be a routine use) and then virtually any dissemination to any other federal agency (by declaring as a routine use the efficient operation of the federal government) (see [35, p. 449; 43, pp. 16-21; 48]).

Rule's thesis [55-59]—that privacy legislation arose out of a concern to ensure that the efficiency of business and government was not hindered—has been confirmed by developments in international organizations and on both sides of the Atlantic. The OECD's 1980 Guidelines for the Protection of Privacy were quite explicitly motivated by the economic need for freedom of transborder data flows [44]. In the United States, the President's Council for Integrity and Efficiency (PCIE) and Office of Management and Budget (OMB) have worked not to limit matching, but to legitimize it [25]. In the United Kingdom, the Data Protection Act of 1984 was enacted explicitly to ensure that U.K. companies were not disadvantaged with respect to their European competitors.

There have been almost no personal-data systems, or even uses of systems, that have been banned outright. Shattuck [61, p. 540] reported that, during the first five years, the OMB's cavalier interpretation of the Privacy Act had resulted in not a single matching program being disapproved. Few sets of Information Privacy Principles appear to even contemplate such an extreme action as disallowing some applications of IT because of their excessively privacy-invasive nature. Exceptions include those of the New South Wales Privacy Committee [38], which are not legally enforceable, and, with qualifications, Sweden. This contrasts starkly with the conclusions of observers: "At some point ...the repressive *potential* of even the most humane systems must make them unacceptable" [59, p. 120]; and "We need to recognize that the potential for harm from certain surveillance systems may be so great that the risks outweigh their benefits" [33, p. 48].

Some countries, such as Australia, have no information privacy legislation, and only incidental protections exist, such as breach of confidence, telephonic interception, trespass, and official secrecy [18]. In jurisdictions where information privacy safeguards do exist, they are piecemeal, restricted in scope, and difficult to enforce. In particular, many countries restrict the protections to government data or computer-based systems, or make no provision for such conventional safeguards as detailed codes of practice, oversight by an adequately resourced and legally competent authority, or the right to sue for damages.

Moreover, technological developments have rendered some information privacy protections ineffective. For example, the O.T.A. concluded that "the Privacy Act ...offers little protection to individuals who are subjects of computer matching" [43, p. 38] (see also [17] and [63]).

Avenues of Change

Only once the principles of fair information practices have been engrained into our institutions and our ways of thought will it be possible to address the more complex, subtle, and pervasive threats inherent in contemporary IT.

In some countries the courts have absolved themselves of responsibility to change the law for policy reasons, unequivocally asserting not just Parliment's primacy in, but its exclusive responsibility for, law reform. In the United States, although the Bill of Rights does not mention a right to privacy, the courts have progressively established such a right based on elements of several of the amendments. The likely present view of the U.S Supreme Court, however, might be indicated by this quotation: "I think it quite likely that self-discipline on the part of the executive branch will provide an answer to virtually all of the legitimate complaints against excesses of information-gathering" (Rehnquist, 1971, then a spokesperson for the Justice Department, now Chief Justice, quoted in [59, p. 147]). Moreover, courts throughout the world have difficulty with cases involving recent developments in technology [10, 72]. Accordingly, they prefer to await statutory guidance from parliaments, with their generally better- financed and less-fettered access to technological know-how.

However, parliaments also tend toward inaction on difficult technological matters, particularly when they are proclaimed to be the salvation of the domestic economy or are tangled up with moral issues, such as "dole cheating" and "welfare fraud." Consumer protection laws in many countries still have yet to be adapted to cater for the now well-developed EFTS. Although the early literature on EFTS omits mention of its social impact, testimony was given before U.S. Senate subcommittees at least as early as 1975 on the repressive potentials of computerized payment systems [59, p. 151] (see also (24) and [55]). The call for protection was still necessary in 1984 in the United States [77] and in 1986 in Australia [3]. Parliaments in some countries such as Australia look less like sober lawmaking institutions than gladiatorial arenas. There are serious difficulties in convincing such legislatures to constrain the development of new "wonder technologies."

The conclusion is inescapable that the populations of at least some at the advanced Western nations are severely threatened by unbridled. IT-driven dataveillance.

POLICY PROPOSALS

New and Improved Safeguards

Since its brief period in the sun it the early 1970s, privacy has became unfashionable among lawmakers, and the momentum that the fair information practices/data protection/information privacy movement once had, has been lost. The PPSC concluded that "the real danger is the gradual erosion of individual liberties through the automation, integration and interconnection of many small, separate record-keeping systems, each of which alone may seen innocuous, even benevolent, and wholly justifiable" [48, p. 533]. Its recommendations were ignored and are now in serious need of resuscitation, not just in the United States, but also in other countries whose information privacy protection regime has not kept pace with developments in IT.

In some countries an effective foundation for dealing with information privacy problems was established during the 1970s. In others, such as the United States, the first attempt failed to establish an adequate basis. Still others have not taken the first step. That necessary foundation can be roughly equated with the OECD's 1980 guidelines [44].

Additional steps must now be taken. It is clear today that the dictates of administrative efficiency are at odds with individual freedoms, and the power of dataveillance techniques is far greater than a decade and more ago. It is now essential that governments consider each dataveillance technique and decide whether it should be permitted under any circumstances at all; if so, what those circumstances are and how each proposal should be assessed in order to judge its compliance with those criteria; what code of practice should apply to its use; and what control mechanisms will ensure that each of these safeguards operates effectively and efficiently.

Further, it must be recognized that IT continues to develop, and mechanisms are needed to ensure that legislators in particular, and the public in general, are kept up-to-date with the salient features of new applications.

The Responsibilities of IT Professionals

It would be inappropriate for the purveyors of any technology to be responsible for decisions regarding its application. The technologist has an unavoidable interest in the outcome, and cannot appreciate and take into consideration the interests of the many different social groups who may be affected.

• Society demands many different services, and many different organizations exist to provide them. Each of these organizations designs its information systems to support the functions it performs

• For each system, the data definitions, the level of integrity of identification, and the degree of data quality are chosen to ensure cost effectiveness. The definitions, identification mechanism, and data quality features of each system are therefore qualitatively different from those of every other system.

• Hence, a singe information system cannot economically serve the interest of all organizations. Clusters of organizations may be supported by a single information system, but only at the risk of compromising the effectiveness of each of them. Economies of scale will only be achieved when the functions and priorities of the organizations are closely aligned.

Figure 11-4
The law of requisite variety in information systems.

However, this necessary neutrality must not be interpreted as an excuse for inaction. IT professionals and academics alike have a moral responsibility to appreciate the power of the technology in which they play a part. Academe should commit some amount of research effort to the testing of the contentions in this paper as well as originate and evaluate proposals for technical safeguards. Both groups must publicize the nature and implications of their work, both for classes of affected individuals and for society as a whole. This applies as much to the negative consequences as it does to the potential benefits.

Finally, where there are acknowledged shortfalls in the regulatory environment in which IT is being applied, the IT practitioner has a responsibility to lobby for effective and efficient safeguards. This article has argued that existing safeguards are entirely inadequate. This implies a responsibility to approach lawmakers about the urgent need for developments in information privacy law. Although the actions of individual practitioners can be significant, coordinated policy efforts by professional bodies, such as the British and Australian Computer Societies, and by common-interest groups, such as ACM and the IEEE Computer Society, are likely to have greater effect.

IT as an Antidote to Information Concentration

If society is to control its fate, it must recognize a new Law of Requisite Variety in Information Systems (see Figure 11-4). Dispersion of authority and power, and, hence, of information, has long been regarded as vital to the survival of individualism and democracy. This law goes further, by recognizing that dispersion of data is also economic. Contrary to conventional wisdom, it is not administratively wasteful to treat the organs of executive government as distinct agencies, but rather administratively sensible.

Society may be better served by an alternative to centralization and its concomitant notions of rigidity and risklessness. If looseness. diversity, tolerance, initiative, enterprise, experimentation, and risk management were adopted as the bases for social and economic organization, then society could develop the adaptiveness needed to cope with technology-induced change. In the words of one philosopher, "The problem is...to combine that degree of security which is essential to the species, with forms of adventure and danger and contest which are compatible with the civilised way of life" [60, p. 21].

Some elements will be critical to a human-oriented IT. For example, the alternative approach to identification proposed by Chaum [8] proposes that the capabilities of "smart cards" be used not only for the benefit of organizations, but also of individuals. Each organization would know each individual by a different "digital pseudonym," which would be the joint property of both parties. Each individual could deny organizations the ability to link their data about him or her without consent. Both parties would have their interests protected. By such approaches, contemporary, decentralizing IT can support the evolution of human-oriented society, rather than hasten the demise of the age of individualism.

CONCLUSION

Dataveillance applications of IT have serious implications for individualism and society. The limited improvements in information practices that were achieved during the last decade have been outpaced by technological developments. Yet until and unless comprehensive information privacy protection is in place, effective controls over the new and emerging techniques of dataveillance will not be possible.

This article does not argue that personal and mass dataveillance are intrinsically evil and should be proscribed. However, their serious implications must be traded off against their benefits in each and every instance. Moreover, those benefits must not be assumed, but carefully assessed. We must appreciate the implications of the new technological capabilities, and create safeguards such that some applications are proscribed and the remainder controlled. We need to harness the new decentralizing potential of IT as a means of achieving a looser, more tolerant, diverse, robust, and adaptive society.

REFERENCES

1. Ackroyd, C., Margolis. K., Rosenhead, J., and Shallice, T., *The Technology of Political Control*. Penguin Books, New York, 1977.
2. Askin, F. Surveillance: The social science perspective. *Columbia Hum. Rights Law Rev. 4*, 1 (Winter 1972). (see also the remainder of the issue).
3. Australian Science and Technology Council. *Towards a Cashless Society*. ASTEC. Canberra Australia. May 1986.
4. Bramford, J. *The Puzzle Palace*. Penguin Books, New York, 1983.
5. Brenton, M. *The Privacy Invaders*. Coward-McCann. 1964.

6. Burnham, D. *The Rise of the Computer State*. Random House/Weidenfeld and Nicolson, 1983.
7. Campbell, D., and Connor, S. *On the Record*. Michael Joseph, 1986.
8. Chaum, D. Security without identification: Transaction systems to make Big Brother obsolete. *Commun. ACM 28*, 10 (Oct. 1985), 1030-1044.
9. Clarke, R. A. Just another piece of plastic for your wallet: The Australia card scheme. *Prometheus 5*, 1 (June 1987), 29-45.
10. Clarke, R. A. Judicial understanding of information technology. *Comput. J. 31*, 1 (Feb. 1988).
11. Cowen, Z. *The Private Man*. Australian Broadcasting Commission. 1969.
12. Crispin, A. *Who's Watching You*. Penguin Books, New York, 1981.
13. Donner, F. J. *The Age of Surveillance*. Knopf, New York, 1980.
14. Early, P. Big Brother makes a date. *San Francisco Exam*. (Oct. 12, 1986).
15. Ellul, J. *The Technological Society*. Knopf, New York, 1964.
16. Greenberg, D.H.. and Wolf, D.A. Is wage matching worth all the trouble? Public Welfare (Winter 1985), 13-20.
17. Greenleaf. G.W., and Clarke. R. A. Database retrieval technology and subject access principles. *Aust. Comput. J. 16*, 1 (Feb. 1984), 27-32.
18. Greenleaf. G.W., and Clarke. R. A. Aspects of the Australian Law Reform Commission's information privacy proposals. *J. Law and Inf. Sci. 2*. 1 (Aug. 1986), 83-110.
19. Cross, M. L. *The Brain Watchers*. *Signet*, 1963.
20. Hoffman, L. J., *Ed. Computers and Privacy in the Next Decade*. Academic Press, New York, 1980.
21. Huxley, A. *Brave New World*. Penguin Books, New York, 1975 (originally published in 1932).
22. Kircher, J. A history of computer matching in federal government programs. *Computerworld* (Dec. 14, 1981).
23. Kling, R. Automated welfare client-racking and service integration: The political economy of computing. *Commun. ACM 21*, 6 (June 1978), 484-493.
24. Kling, R. Value conflicts and social choice in electronic funds transfer system developments. *Commun. ACM 21*, 8 (Aug. 1978), 642-657.
25. Kusserow, R. P. The government needs computer matching to root out waste and fraud. *Commun. ACM 27*, 6 (June 1984), 542-545.
28. Langan, K. J. Computer matching programs: A threat to privacy? *Columbia J. Law Soc. Probl. 15*, 2 (1979).
27. Laudon, K. C. *Computers and Bureaucratic Reform*. Wiley, New York, 1974.
28. Laudon, K. C. Complexity in large federal databanks. *Soc./Trans.* (May 1979).
29. Laudon, K. C. Problems of accountability in federal databanks. In *Proceedings of the American Association for the Advancement of Science* (May). American Association for the Advancement of Science, 1979.
30. Laudon. K. C. Data quality and due process in large interorganizational record systems. *Commun. ACM 29*, 1 (Jan. 1986), 4-11.
31. Laudon. K. C. Dossier Society. *Value Choices in the Design of National Information Systems*. Columbia University Press, New York, 1986.
32. Long. E. V. *The Intruders*. Praeger, New York, 1967.
33. Marx. G. T. The new surveillance. *Technol. Rev.* (May-June 1985).
34. Marx. G. T. I'll be watching you: Reflections on the new surveillance. *Dissent* (Winter 1985).
35. Marx. G. T., and Reichman. N. Routinising the discovery of secrets. *Am. Behav. Sci. 27*, 4 (Mar.-Apr. 1984), 423—452.
36. Miller. A. R. *The Assault on Privacy*. Mentor, 1972.
37. Neier. A. *Dossier*. Stein and Day, 1974.

38. New South Wales Privacy Committee. *Guidelines for the Operation of Personal Data Systems*. NSWPC. Sydney, Australia, 1977.
39. Office of Management and Budget. *Guidelines to Agencies on Conducting Automated Matching Programs*. OMB, Mar. 1979.
40. Office of Management and Budget. *Computer Matching Guidelines*. OMB, May 1982.
41. Office of Management and Budget President's Commission for Integrity and Efficiency. *Model Control System for Conducting Computer Matching Projects Involving Individual Privacy Data*. OMB/PCIE. 1983.
42. Office of Technology Assessment. Federal government information technology: Electronic surveillance and civil liberties. OTA-CIT-293. U.S. Congress. Washington, D.C., Oct. 1985.
43. Office of Technology Assessment. Federal government information technology: Electronic record systems and individual privacy. OTA-CIT-296. U.S. Congress, Washington, D.C.. June 1986.
44. Organisation for Economic Cooperation and Development. *Guidelines for the Protection of Privacy and Transborder Flows of Personal Data*. OECD. Paris, France, 1980.
45. Orwell, G. *1984*. Penguin Books., New York, 1972 (originally published in 1948).
46. *Oxford Dictionary*. Vol. X 1933, p. 248.
47. Packard, V. *The Naked Society*. McKay, New York, 1964.
48. Privacy Protection Study Commission. *Personal Privacy in an Information Society*. U.S. Government Printing Office. Washingtion, D.C., July 1977.
49. Raines, J. C. Attack on Privacy. Judson Press, 1974.
50. Reichman, N., and Marx, G. T. Generating organisational disputes: The impact of computerization. In *Proceedings of the Law and Society Association Conference* (San Diego, Calif., June 6-9). Law and Society Association, 1985.
51. Rodota, S. Privacy and data surveillance: Growing public concern. Inf. Stud. 10, OECD., Paris, France, 1976.
52. Rosenberg J. M. *The Death of Privacy*. Random House, 1969.
53. Rosenberg, R. S. *Computers and the Information Society*. Wiley, New York, 1986.
54. Roszak, T. The Cult of Information. Pantheon, 1986.
55. Rule, J. B. *Private Lives and Public Surveillance: Social Control in the Computer Age*. Schocken Books, 1974.
56. Rule, J. B. *Value Choices in E.F.T.S*. Office of Telecommunications Policy, Washington, D.C., 1975.
57. Rule, J. B. 1984-The ingredients of totalitarianism. In *1984 Revisited-Totalitarianism in Our Century*. Harper and Row, New York, 1983, pp. 166-179.
58. Rule, J. B. Documentary identification and mass surveillance in the United States. *Soc. Probl. 31*, 222 (1983).
59. Rule, J. B., McAdam, D., Sterns, L. and Uglow D. *The Politics of Privacy*. New American Library, 1980.
60. Russell, B. *Authority and the Individual*. George Allen and Unwin, 1949.
61. Shattuck, J. computer matching is a serious threat to individual rights. *Commun. ACM 27*, 6 (June 1984), 538-541.
62. Stone, M. G. Computer Privacy. Anbar, 1968.
63. Thom, J., and Thorne, P. Privacy legislaton and the right of access *Aust. Comput. J. 15*, 4 (Nov. 1983).
64. Thompson, A. A. *A Big Brother in Britain Today*. Michael Joseph, 1970.

65. U.S. Dept. of Health and Human Services. *Computer Matching in State Administered Benefit Programs*: *A Manager's Guide to Decision-Making.* HEW, Washington, D.C., 1983.

66. U.S. Dept. of Health and Human Services. *Computer Matching in State Administered Benefit Programs.* HEW, Washington, D.C., June 1984.

67. U.S. Dept. Of Health, Education and Welfare, Secretary's Advisory Committee on Automated Personal Data Systems. *Records, Computers and the Rights of Citizens*, MIT Press, Cambridge, Mass., 1973.

68. U.S. Federal Advisory Committee on False Identification. *The Criminal Use of False Identification*, FACFI, Washington, D.C., 1976.

69. U.S. Senate. *Oversight of Computer Matching to Detect Fraud and Mismanagement in Government Programs.* U.S. Senate, Washington, D.C., 1982.

70. Warner, M., and Stone, M. *The Data Bank Society: Organisations, Computers and Social Freedom.* George Allen and Unwin, 1970.

71. *Webster's 3rd Edition.* 1976, p. 2302.

72. Weeramantry, C. G. *The Slumbering Sentinels: Law and Human Rights in the Wake of Technology.* Penguin Books, New York, 1983.

73. Wessell, M. R. *Freedom's Edge: The Computer Threat to Society.* Addison-Wesley, Reading, Mass., 1974.

74. Westin, A. F. *Privacy and Freedom.* Atheneum., New York, 1967.

75. Westin, A. F., Ed. *Information Technology in a Democracy.* Harvard University Press, Cambridge, Mass., 1971.

76. Westin, A. F., and Baker, M. *Databanks in a Free Society.* Quadrangle New York, 1974.

77. Yestingsmeier, J. Electronic Funds transfer systems: The continuing need for privacy legislation. *Comput. Soc. 13*, 4 (Winter 1984), 5-9.

78. Zamyatin, Y. *We.* Penguin Books, New York, 1983 (originally published in Russian, 1920).

Acknowledgments. This article arises from collaborative research undertaken with Graham Greenleaf, of the Faculty of Law at the University of New South Wales. Assistance is also gratefully acknowledged from research assistants Louise Macauley and Chris Keoth, and Jim Nolan, executive member of the New South Wales Privacy Committee. The constructive criticism of referees and the area editor was also very helpful.

DOCUMENTARY IDENTIFICATION AND MASS SURVEILLANCE IN THE UNITED STATES.[2]

James B. Rule   *Douglas McAdam*
SUNY Stony Brook   *University of Arizona*

Linda Stearns   *David Uglow*
Louisiana State University *DCI Research Associates*

A distinctive feature of advanced industrial societies is the importance of personal documentation in relations between individuals and organizations. By personal documentation we mean two things: (1) the identification cards, certifications, licenses, and other organizationally generated tokens of identity held by private individuals; and (2) the data on persons developed by organizations and stored in computers or files for use in dealing with these people. These two forms of personal documentation usually work together: issuance or use of the first requires creation of, or recourse to, the second. Together, the two structure ongoing exchanges of information between persons and organizations which, we argue, bear importantly on the interests of both parties. Many social scientists have studied these exchanges and expressed concern about their effects upon individual privacy and autonomy (Rule, 1974; Rule *et al.*, 1980; Shils, 1975; Westin, 1967; Westin and Baker, 1972; Wheeler, 1969).

Social scientists are not the only ones to note the growing impact of personal documentation. It is practically impossible for an adult to live in the United States without frequent recourse to such things. One finding of our research underscores this fact: in 1976 and 1977 we surveyed 192 randomly selected households in Brookhaven Town, New York, and found an average of 28.8 different *kinds* of personal documents per household. The documents most often reported were Social Security cards, insurance policies, driver's licenses, birth certificates, personal checks, insurance payment records, marriage licenses, insurance identification cards, bank statements, tax returns, and savings passbooks. Social Security cards, the most widely held of these, were reported in 98 percent of the households; savings passbooks, the least widely held, were reported in 87 percent. When documents such as these are lost or accidentally destroyed, the resulting inconvenience dramatizes the importance of the documentary link between the individual and the relevant organizations.

This paper presents a study of six of the most widely held personal documents in the United States: birth certificates, driver's licenses, Social

---

[2]From Rule, J. B., McAdam, D., Stearns, L., Uglow, D. (1983). Documentary identification and mass surveillance in the United States. *Social Problems*, 31(2), 222-234. Copyright © 1983 by the Society for the Study of Social Problems. Reprinted by permission.

Security cards, passports, bank books, and bank-issued credit cards. Each of these documents marks some kind of ongoing relationship between the individual holding them and the organization relying on them. Normally these relations entail complex claims and responsibilities between the two parties—claims and responsibilities specified and governed at least partly by information from the written or computerized records. Many aspects of these relations involve what we call *mass surveillance* and *social control* (Rule *et al.*, 1980).

By surveillance we mean any systematic attention to a person's life aimed at exerting influence over it. By social control we mean efforts to define and bring about "correct" actions or statuses. Surveillance and social control are ubiquitous social processes, but our concern here lies with *mass* forms—that is, surveillance and control by organizations over large, otherwise anonymous publics. Such relations need not be malevolent or disadvantageous to the latter. A preventive health care system entails surveillance and control just as much as a system of political repression. Mass surveillance and social control, moreover, are often just two aspects of much more multifarious relationships between individuals and organizations—as indeed is the case in the six personal documents we studied.

There are two kinds of social control processes involved in these six personal documents. First, they enable organizations to exclude "inappropriate" individuals from roles or privileges to which they are not considered entitled. Second, they enable organizations to take coercive action against those whose behavior they consider threatening. Examples range from simply depriving minor violators of their documentation—as in revocation of driver's licenses—to arrest or imprisonment for tax fraud or other illegalities brought to light through bank records.

Personal documentation thus serves organizations by providing grounds for certainty in dealing with large numbers of otherwise anonymous individuals. It enables organizations to know what resources and actions they should apply to which individuals. Which motorists are entitled to renewed licenses, and which are wanted for serious motoring offenses by the police? Which credit card holders are entitled to the most generous credit privileges, and which are liable to arrest for fraudulent credit card use? Which passport applicants are entitled to the document as native-born citizens, and which applicants are illegal aliens seeking to travel back and forth to their country of origin? Recourse to personal documentation represents an effort to generate certainty about people in settings like these, where such certainty would otherwise be a problem for organizations.

Generating certainty about people is a problem for organizations where the interests of individuals and organizations are apt to conflict. Passports help representatives of the state distinguish between those entitled to enter their country without hindrance and others. Credit cards facilitate purchases by authorized consumers only, and control the amount of credit available to them. Whatever their other purposes, most forms of personal documentation exist at least partly to help organizations discriminate in their treatments of individuals. Most people, most of the time, may not he tempted to circumvent such discriminations—but those who are must be dealt with.

This study explores the origins, workings, and future of mass surveillance through personal documentation. How have these six documentary systems and others like them evolved? What are their strengths and weaknesses as sources of certainty for organizations dealing with the public? And what are the prospects for further growth and development in these respects?

We spent several years trying to find answers to these questions. From 1977 to 1980 we conducted interviews and observed encounters between the public and those who issue documents at more than 34 different bureaucratic sites in the United States. These included such diverse settings as a small bank in New York State; a large bank headquarters in San Francisco; offices engaged in passport issuance in the Washington, D.C. vicinity; offices of the Department of Health, Education and Welfare in Maryland; and local, county, and state birth certification offices in New York. In many cases, these interviews and observations entailed repeated visits to the same site; a minority of the interviews were by telephone. Most interviews were with middle-level officials responsible for managing the issuance or use of personal documentation in one specific location; some were with higher-level officials more concerned with broad policy than with day-to-day operations. In addition, we analyzed a variety of published and unpublished reports on the organizations depicted in this paper.

First we chart the origins of these documentary systems and the broad patterns of their historical development. Then we look at the strengths and weaknesses of these systems as instruments of surveillance and social control. Finally, we show how the continuing perfection of technology and organization promise growing efficiency for organizational interests over the years to come.

HISTORICAL DEVELOPMENT AND SPONSORSHIP

Mass use of personal documentation is a relatively recent historical development in the United States. Of the six documents we studied, three— Social Security cards, driver's licenses, and credit cards—did not exist at the beginning of the 20th century. The other three—birth certificates, passports, and bank books—were restricted to much smaller subsets of the population than they are today. The growth in coverage and importance of these personal documents mirrors the growing role of direct relations between centralized organizations and private individuals.

Birth Certificates

Birth registration and certification have been carried out by government agencies in North America since well before the American Revolution. One of the earliest laws requiring registration of births with government agencies (as distinct from recording in parish registers) dates from Virginia in 1632 (U.S. Department of Health, Education and Welfare, 1954:3). But we estimate that the majority of births in the United States remained unrecorded with any government agency until at least the end of the 19th century. In 1903, the U.S. Congress passed a joint resolution requesting states to develop a uniform system of registering births (1954:8). Since then, federal authorities have been urging the states to increase the coverage and rigor of their registration and certification procedures. Individual states were declared part of a birth "registration area" when they had registered an estimated 90 percent of births within their boundaries (1954:8). The first states to meet this criterion—generally older, more urban ones such as Massachusetts and New York—did so in 1915; the last—Nevada, New Mexico, South Dakota, and Texas—did so between 1928 and 1933 (1954:13).

By 1950, census officials estimated that 97.9 percent of all births in the United States were being registered (U.S. Department of Health, Education and Welfare, 1954:12). Today, documentary requirements make it difficult for anyone born in the United States to do without a birth certificate; it is often essential for access to schooling, insurance, and pension coverage—as well as applying for a variety of other personal documents. Issuing birth certificates remains a state responsibility; in 1976, there were at least 7,000 offices across the United States authorized to issue certificates or copies (U.S. Department of Justice, 1976:17). States vary enormously in the degree of centralization and rigor they apply in issuing birth certificates, according to state and federal officials we interviewed. Some states issue only through a single central office, while New York State, at the other extreme, maintains some 1,500 issuing locations. According to a knowledgeable federal official,[3] the federal government continues to promote greater centralization, and co-ordination within and among the states in birth certification—particularly in matters relating to the use of the documents for surveillance and social control. This source estimated that federal requirements, such as those for documentary substantiation of applications for Social Security cards, account directly or indirectly for about half the demand for birth certificates in the United States. By 1976, there were at least 10 million such requests per year (U.S. apartment of Justice, 1976:17).

Driver's Licenses

Licensing drivers has always been a state responsibility, and as with birth certificates there has been considerable variety in practices from state to state. According to an official of the American Association of Motor Vehicle

---

[3] Loren Chancellor, Registration Methods Branch Chief, Department of Health, Education and Welfare, Rockville, Maryland, May 11, 1977: personal interview.

Administrators,[4] Massachusetts was the first state to license drivers, in 1907, and South Dakota the last, in 1957. Initially, licenses seem to have been strictly a way of generating revenue, but gradually they became a means of surveillance and control.

In 1950, there were an estimated 62 million driver's licenses in force throughout the United states. By 1978, that figure had risen to 140.8 million, and some 50.6 million new and renewed licenses were issued that year (American Association of Motor Vehicle Administrators, 1979:D-L-1). Quite beyond its role in surveillance over driving, the driver's license has become essential identification in a variety of other settings, such as check cashing and car rentals. So pervasive is the need for driver's licenses that by 1977 at least 40 states issued "non-driver's licenses" for those who did not drive, but who needed the documentation for other purposes (Tritsch and Kumbar, I977:H-19).

Passports

Passports were first issued in North America before the Revolutionary War. It was not until 1856 that the U.S. federal government claimed exclusive rights to issue passports; until then these documents could also be issued by state and even local officials (U.S. Department of State Passport Office, 1976:31). From 1801 to 1809, the State Department issued 587 passports, while from 1898 to 1905 they issued 108,404 (1976:220). At the end of 1978 there were some 13.9 million valid, domestically issued U.S. passports (as distinct from those issued by U.S. officials abroad) and some 3.2 million new passports were issued that year.[5]

The growth in passport use is attributable both to the rise in international travel and to the development of the modern state. During the 19th century, few countries required the use of passports except in wartime. The United States did not require U.S. nationals to use passports for travel in peacetime until 1952, and it is estimated that most U.S. travelers did not carry passports in peacetime until the late l940s (1976:4).

Social Security Cards

Social Security was founded through legislation passed in 1935 (Booth, 1973:7), and 45 million accounts were opened by the end of the first year the system was in operation (Westin and Baker, 1972:33). Because of the advantages associated with participation in Social Security, the number of accounts rose quickly to approximate the number of employed persons. By mid-1983, according to a Social Security official, there were 205 million

---

[4] Arthur Tritsch, Director, Driver Services, American Association of Motor Vehicle Administrators, Washington, D.C., May 23, 1983: telephone interview.
[5] Norbert J. Krieg, Deputy Assistant Secretary for Passport Services, November 14, 1979: personal communication.

active accounts, each with a Social Security number and card corresponding to it. Some 5.5 million new accounts are being added each year.[6] Because nearly every economically active adult in the United States has a Social Security number, the number is ideal for other surveillance and management purposes. Since 1961, the Internal Revenue Service (IRS) has adopted the use of Social Security numbers for ordering income tax records and for identifying taxpayers.[7]

Credit Cards

The earliest credit cards in the United States, available for relatively narrow ranges of products and services, appear to have been issued in the early decades of the 20th century (Rule, 1974:225). Some general-purpose cards catering to affluent users (e.g., Diner's Club, Carte Blanche) were issued in the decade or so after the Second World War. But it was not until banks began issuing credit cards to middle and even lower-middle income groups that the majority of the adult population gained access to this form of documentary relationship. Today VISA and MasterCard account for virtually all of the bank-issued credit cards in use in the United States. In 1978, there were some 52 million MasterCards and 54 million VISA cards in use, and these two systems issued some eight and 10 million new cards respectively that year (American Bankers Association, 1979).

In 1979, responsibility for issuing and managing VISA and MasterCard accounts was dispersed among 10,000 and 11,000 banks respectively throughout the United States (American Bankers Association, 1979). These thousands of companies observe a variety of policies, but all maintain careful surveillance and control over issuance and use of their cards. All exchange information and other services with other surveillance and control organizations, as we discuss below. Partly because of the sophistication of surveillance and control achieved by the managers of VISA and MasterCard, the cards have become required for use in other transactions such as cashing checks and renting cars.

Bank Books

According to officials of the American Bankers Association, only a small minority of U.S families had bank accounts at the beginning of the 20th century. By 1977, however, 77 percent of U.S. families had checking accounts, and 81 percent had savings accounts—including accounts both in banks and savings and loan institutions (Curtin and Neubig, 1979:22).

---

[6] Nicky Bonacci, Press Office, Social Security Administration, Woodlawn, Maryland, July 8, 1983: phone interviews.
[7] Income tax was first collected in peacetime in 1913. By the eve of the Second World War, according to an IRS official, only about 8 million U.S. citizens paid federal income tax, a small minority of the adult population.

THE PURSUIT OF CERTAINTY: SELF-IDENTIFICATION

Organizations use systems of personal documentation to cope with people who attempt to circumvent organizational purposes by concealing or distorting information about themselves. The importance of this task warrants the considerable expense and effort of building and maintaining the bureaucratic systems which stand behind these personal documents. But how well do these bureaucratic activities serve the surveillance goals for which they are intended? One of the things to strike us as we began this study was the wealth of apparent opportunities for circumventing the surveillance purposes of the six systems we looked at: in fact, it is easy to obtain six personal documents under false pretenses. We make this observation not to appeal for tighter controls, but to note a sociological puzzle: personal documents which are widely regarded as authoritative, and which figure in important bureaucratic surveillance processes, often do not seem to warrant the credence placed in them.

These weaknesses seem particularly marked where organizations must rely on applicants' own accounts, and upon documents presented by applicants, in deciding whether to issue documentary identification. For example, birth certificates are widely perceived as a basic and trustworthy form of identification and are used to generate other personal documents. Yet officials in organizations relying on birth certificates for surveillance acknowledge that these documents can be easily obtained fraudently. People who wish to conceal their true identities may check obituaries or other death records of persons about their own age, then request a birth certificate in the name of the deceased person (U.S. Department of Justice, 1976:1). The widely varying rigor among offices issuing birth certificates makes this practice quite easy. A few states seek to restrict distribution of certificates by requiring a signed statement establishing a "legitimate need" for the document. But others officially grant anyone the right to obtain a certified copy of any birth certificate which can be identified (1976:18). Since certificates and official copies of certificates issued in the United States provide no way of identifying the person presenting the document with the person whose birth is recorded there, consumers of birth certificates normally have only the individual's own account to establish this link.

Nevertheless, self-identification *via* the birth certificate plays a key role in generating other personal documents. Issuance of driver's licenses, for example, depends overwhelmingly on self-identification by the applicant. Indeed, as recently as 1977 several states required no personal document to substantiate information on driver's license applications. Where supporting documentation is required, the birth certificate is by far the document most often used (Tritsch and Kumbar, 1977:D-1). Other documents acceptable in applying for a driver's license, such as baptismal certificates or the Social Security card, are also readily available under false pretenses. For female applicants, the family name given on the birth certificate or other documents dating from before marriage need not agree with the name in which the license is sought. Our observations of driver's license issuance in New York State convinced us that the face-to-face transactions between applicants and staff were much too superficial to enable the latter to verify the authenticity of substantiating documents. We doubt that greater scrutiny is the rule elsewhere (U.S. Department of Justice, 1976:F-15).

Social Security cards are also issued almost entirely on the basis of self-identification. Prior to 1974, applicants were not required to produce supporting documentation (U.S. Department of Justice, 1976:24). Among documents currently used for this purpose are birth certificates, library cards, and voter registration cards, all readily obtainable under false pretenses (U.S. Department of Health and Human Services, 1982). One official whose work involved issuing Social Security cards reported that she was instructed to issue cards on presentation of the officially required documentation, even if applicants' accounts of their background and circumstances were blatantly implausible.[8]

Passports are issued with only slightly more rigor than Social Security cards. Passport applications must be submitted in person, and passport officials are supposed to question applicants about details put forward there. This first stage of the application process is aimed at establishing the applicant's identity; one of the documents most widely used for this purpose is the driver's license (U.S. Department of Justice, 1976:21). Passport officials are supposed to question applicants about statements on their applications and about the accompanying identification; the exchanges we observed appeared more perfunctory than probing, lasting about 10 to 15 minutes. The application is then forwarded to a central location, where officials scrutinize further supporting documents to determine the applicant's citizenship. The document most often used for this purpose, according to passport officials, is the birth certificate.

Reliance on self-identification in the issuing of personal documentation leads to a kind of chain-reaction process, in which acquisition of a birth certificate affords access to a succession of further documents. Each item of documentary identification strengthens the case for access to further items. Not only the birth certificate, but also other documents even more easily available under false pretenses—such as voter's registration cards—serve as "breeder documents," each etching the holder's documentary identity more deeply in a document-oriented world.

A SUPERIOR SOURCE OF CERTAINTY: DIRECT CHECKING

The dilemma facing organizations is clear. Surveillance systems are developed to enable organizations to distinguish between those worthy of friendly treatment and others. Yet self-identification leaves the responsibility

---

[8] Social Security official, San Francisco, August 10, 1979.

of transmitting vital data in the hands of the very people who may be tempted to seek a "better deal" of some kind by circumventing the purpose of the system.

But superior techniques of surveillance are increasingly available. Organizations can use direct channels to move personal data from points of origin to where they are needed for decision-making without requiring the interested individuals to act as intermediaries. Reliance on such direct checking both helps reduce the costs of dealing with individual documents on a one-by-one basis and, more importantly, obviates the weaknesses inherent in direct checking.

Direct checking is essential in screening VISA and MasterCard applications. Supporting documents are rarely required here, and crucial information provided on application forms is nearly always checked against data from independent, outside sources—usually credit bureaus. These are profit-making firms which specialize in compiling and selling data on consumers credit-worthiness. They either confirm or supply information on applicants' current indebtedness, past payment of credit accounts, and history of litigation, liens, bankruptcies, and the like. Where data from credit bureaus are lacking, credit card firms may rely on other forms of direct checking, such as telephone contacts with applicants' employers or banks to determine their salary and financial status. Exchange of such information among these organizations is a routine part of their clerical practice.

Direct checking also plays a key role in surveillance over the ongoing use of credit cards. VISA and MasterCard maintain elaborate systems to monitor use of their cards, both by intended users and by criminals. One way they do this is by continually analyzing records of purchases made with cards, to detect overspending and fraud. Another is by requiring that certain large charges be first cleared by telephone with the bank which issues the card (Rule, 1974:240). The latter form of direct checking sometimes leads to the arrest of fraudulent users before they leave the store. BankAmericard (predecessor of VISA) reported making 450 such arrests in California alone in 1970 (Rule, 1974:246).

Direct checking is also used in processing driver's license applications. Many states rely on their own data files compiled by state police and courts. Other states check license applications against the National Driver Register. a computerized central listing of persons whose licenses have been revoked or suspended throughout the United States. The latter practice was used in 26 states in 1977 (Tritsch and Kumbar. 1977:B- l). During 1978, the National Driver Register reported 180,000 "hits," or probable identifications of ineligible persons seeking new licenses; most of these no doubt resulted in denials of new licenses. In addition to the National Driver Register, the National Law Enforcement Telecommunications Network (NLETS) acts as a central switchboard for direct checking on drivers by law enforcement agencies throughout the United States; for example, it can determine whether an out-of-state driver's license is valid where issued (U.S. Congress, Office of Technology Assessment, 1982:p 40). In March 1983 alone, according to an NLETS official[9], this system handled about half a million such interstate inquiries.

Direct checking is an option in issuing other forms of documentary identification as well. Requests for *duplicate* Social Security cards are checked with data on the card-holder held in central files before the duplicate is issued. Similarly, passport authorities can sometimes directly check documents submitted with passport applications. But such checks are unlikely unless the documents appear inauthentic; applicants bent on fraud may simply submit authentic documents referring to someone else.

Direct checking in surveillance over the use of passports, however, is well developed. The Treasury Department has developed a comprehensive computerized data base against which it checks the names of many incoming travelers as they cross the U.S. border. The goal is to extend these checks, which apply both to U.S. nationals and foreigners, to all such travelers, though present rates of coverage are uneven among the many border points. The data base includes the names of persons whose movements are of interest to a wide variety of local, state, and federal officials. Part of the data base consists of the FBI's computerized listing of wanted and missing persons from throughout the United States. During 1978, some 49.7 million persons and vehicles were checked against this listing as they entered the United States; 21,760 "hits" were made in this way, and 2,070 persons were arrested as a result.[10] In some instances government agencies are unable or unwilling to authorize arrest, but nevertheless have the system retain a record of the person's movements.

Finally, direct checking is sometimes involved in issuing savings passbooks and check books. Banks try to confirm the identities of those seeking to open accounts when they doubt the applicant's background. If they suspect an account is being sought for fraudulent purposes such as writing bad checks, bank officials may contact the applicant's employer or personal and business references. Banks appear responsive, in these matters, both to their own interests in avoiding fraud and those of local businesses and law-enforcement agencies.

Symbiosis in surveillance: the elaboration of direct checking

The six personal documentation systems also act as sources of personal data for direct checking by other organizations. These flows of data across organizational lines are taking on increasing importance in the national organization of mass surveillance in the United States. The fact that more and

---

[9] Tim Sweeney National Law Enforcement Telecommunications Network, Phoenix, Arizona, May 11, 1983: telephone interview.

[10] Jay Corcoran, Director, Information Services Staff, Department of the Treasury U.S. Customs Service, March 3, 1981: personal communication.

more routine bureaucratic paper work is being done electronically means that organizations have more personal data to offer one another. Such symbiotic relations among organizations warrant close attention.

Ironically, birth certification is perhaps the least developed of these six systems in this respect. Certificates and certified copies are readily available, but the means of disseminating them are relatively primitive. Organizations seeking birth certificate information must normally depend on the person whose birth is certified, because of the difficulty of identifying the source of the certificate and obtaining it independently. New social structures and technologies which would transmit birth certificate data directly from its source to organizational consumers as readily, say, as credit reports would surely be a boon to the organizations concerned.

By contrast, data from driver's license files are provided freely to outside interests. Police forces and other law enforcement agencies share data via the NLETS. The next most frequent users of driver's license data are undoubtedly insurance companies, who seek the data for screening and processing insurance applications. In 1976, all but two states made at least some data from a driver's record available to insurance companies. Nineteen states routinely granted access to the entire record, and many states realized significant revenues ranging from eight cents to four dollars per inquiry (Tritsch and Kumbar, 1977:H-ll). The volume of data so provided can be great. The state of Illinois in 1982 answered some 2.5 million requests for data from driver's license files. About 179,000 of these were from law-enforcement officials; the overwhelming balance no doubt came from insurance companies (State of Illinois, 1983).

Information from Social Security files, including both income data and the account-holder's whereabouts, is intensely attractive to many outside interests. When the Social Security system was founded in 1935, elaborate assurances were offered that data would remain confidential (Rubinstein, 1975). But confidentiality has been eroded over the years, especially since the 1970s. Social Security files are now open to state welfare departments and food stamp programs (to control access to benefits), the FBI and the Secret Service, the Immigration and Naturalization Service (to control employment of undocumented aliens), and others (U.S. Department of Health, Education and Welfare, 1977:52239). One of the more controversial users of Social Security information is the Parent Locator Service. This agency, established by Congress in 1975, uses such data for action against parents who desert spouses with dependent children (U.S. Privacy Protection Study Commission, 1977b:16). In creating the service, Congress also granted it access to personal data held by other federal agencies, including the Internal Revenue Service

Data generated by credit card companies are provided routinely to a variety of organizations. Probably the biggest data consumers are credit bureaus, who normally demand an exchange of data: organizations which purchase the credit bureaus' reports must then provide data from their own files. Such data are increasingly provided in large quantity by direct computer links. In addition, many credit card issuers provide the addresses of card holders to merchants who have accepted the card as identification for a check which subsequently bounced. This is apparently why credit cards are so often preferred as identification in check cashing: the merchant may have no other way of contacting the writer of the check. Credit card issuers help merchants in this way because of their shared desire to control bad checks written by card-holders. Credit card firms, like most other large-scale creditors, also provide information from their files to law-enforcement agencies, including the Internal Revenue Service, the FBI, and other local, state, and federal bodies. Data of interest here include the amounts of the card-holder's indebtedness and the nature of expenditures, as well as the individual's whereabouts at particular times (U.S. Privacy Protection Study Commission, 1977a:53).

Finally, data generated through use of checking and savings accounts are regularly provided to credit bureaus, prospective creditors, and a variety of law enforcement agencies. The effects of such provision, in terms of social control, range from extension or withdrawal of credit to prosecution for tax evasion and other felonies. A few banks and savings institutions resist such disclosure, but these seem to be a distinct minority (Linowes, 1979:11). Demands from law enforcement agencies for data are often backed by subpoena, leaving court action the only available avenue for resistance.

Besides responding to inquiries from such outside bodies, savings institutions are required to report yearly to the federal government all interest paid to depositors. Such institutions also must report foreign currency transactions in excess of $10,000 (U.S. Privacy Protection Study Commission, 1977a:104). And, in compliance with still other federal regulations, virtually *all* personal checks paid by United States banks are microfilmed; the records are retained for five years to be available for scrutiny by federal officials (U.S. Privacy Protection Study Commission, 1977a:105)

THE FUTURE OF MASS SURVEILLANCE

The dramatic proliferation of personal documentation since the beginning of the 20th century means much more than growing possession of certificates, cards, and computer records. It reflects the growth of an important new category of *relationships* between ordinary people and large, centralized organizations. These new relationships entail increasing demands on personal privacy as organizations consume more and more personal data and use these data to shape their treatment of persons with whom they deal. As we have shown, these demands are growing apace with the further refinement of technological and organizational resources. Where, we must ask, are these trends leading? What sort of social world is emerging from the changes detailed here?

To answer such questions, one must consider the limitations of organizational mass surveillance as much as its strengths. These limitations are by no means trivial. Organizations cannot achieve mass surveillance goals without data, and such data are by no means available simply for the asking. Indeed, we have shown how even the most seemingly powerful organizations often must accept significant limitations on their ability to master important data on the people with whom they deal.

A key example is the widespread reliance on self-identification, including personal documentation presented by those being identified. It is widely acknowledged by officials of surveillance organizations that such practices as permitting people to provide their own birth certificates lead to significant evasion of social control. Yet the organization of information flow in the United States does not yet offer an alternative to this practice at acceptable cost.

Similarly, some organizations do not even exploit relevant data already contained in files accessible to them. This is true of some state driver's licensing systems, which issue licenses on the strength of data provided by the applicants, without checking their own records of the applicants' driving histories (Tritsch and Kumbar, 1977:2-1). Here, we conclude, organizations are responding both to the costs of clerical time in searching for potentially relevant data, and to costs in terms of public complaints over delays in issuing documents. A number of officials reported that the latter were an especially important consideration for their organizations. This appears particularly true for the four government documents: birth certificates, passports, driver's licenses, and Social Security cards. The public are apt to insist on quick access to these as a matter of right (U.S. Department of Justice, 1976:F-15).

Still, the effect of such weaknesses in surveillance may be a good deal less than it would appear. Organizations do not advertise the laxity of their surveillance procedures. They are much more likely to require applicants to read and sign statements such as the following, from the application for Social Security cards:

> WARNING. Deliberately furnishing (or causing to be furnished) false information on this application is a crime punishable by fine or imprisonment, or both (U.S. Department of Health and Human Services, Social Security Administration, 198).

In fact, fraudulent applications for Social Security cards are rarely prosecuted unless they are compounded with other, more serious infractions. There were 117 prosecutions and 62 convictions in the years 1980 to 1982 inclusive, according to a Social Security official.[11]

---

[11] Robert Sedlak, Inspector General's Office, Department of Health and Human Services, Baltimore, May 13, 1983: telephone interview.

The effectiveness of mass surveillance and social control depends most directly on the public's *perceptions* of what systems can and cannot know about them. Most U.S. citizens are apparently aware that large organizations are capable of sophisticated data linkages. They realize that income not listed on tax returns is likely to be reported directly to the Internal Revenue Service by the paying organization, or that creditors have ways of finding out about debts not acknowledged on credit applications. But relatively few people, we suspect, can distinguish between the risk that a credit applicant's recent bankruptcy will be reported to a prospective creditor and the risk that the Passport Office will spot an application for a passport in the name of someone who already has one. The first risk is relatively great, since credit bureaus systematically collect and report such data, while the second is relatively low, since the Passport Office ordinarily does not check new applications against records of outstanding passports.

The overall picture that emerges from these observations is one of dialectical tension between the efforts of organizations to maximize the scope and effectiveness of mass surveillance, and the efforts of certain subsets of the public to evade organizational intent in these respects. Organizational reliance on bluff and intimidation is part of one side of this dialectic; yet such feints would mean little without the other weighty organizational efforts considered here—particularly the development and exploitation of new sources of data. Countervailing against such forces are individuals' efforts to escape the effects of had credit records, poor driving histories, ineligibility to enter the United States, and the like.

We do not portray this opposition in simplistic terms, as nothing other than efforts by oppressive institutional interests to manipulate innocent individuals In fact, there is considerable grass-roots support and even demand for increased mass surveillance—for example, to keep undocumented aliens out of the labor force, to keep dangerous drivers off the roads, or to keep poor credit risks from spoiling the credit markets enjoyed by others. But whatever the mixture of elite initiatives and popular demand fueling the growth of mass surveillance, there can be no doubt that organizational powers in this respect are in the ascent, and opportunities for individual evasion of mass surveillance increasingly restricted.

The key consideration mediating the interests of mass surveillance and those of evasion are the significant *costs* of the former. While the per-case costs of operating large data systems is ordinarily small, the starting-up costs of creating such systems is great. Thus, even relatively powerful and well-financed organizations such as those considered in this paper cannot extend their sway as rapidly as they might. Paying the armies of clerical staff who must assemble and process personal data is one significant source of these costs; procuring and operating computing systems and other data-management technologies are another. Yet the conspicuous trend in mass surveillance is toward a cumulative decline in such costs.

Consider the growing reliance of organizations on direct checking, as distinct from self-identification. At the beginning of the 20th century there were few organizations which could be counted on to generate authoritative personal information on a mass basis. Even birth certification probably covered no more than half of those being born. And without sources of "breeder documents," the bases for generating further documents were weak.

As sources of authoritative personal data available for direct checking grow, however, the costs of mass surveillance drop. Indeed, viewing the broad sweep of historical change, we conclude that *mass surveillance through personal documentation feeds on itself.* The more important events in life entail production or consumption of personal documentation, the more feasible it is to institute effective surveillance through direct checking based on such data. Imaginative administrators of surveillance organizations are constantly seeking new uses for personal data in these ways.

This, then, is the special appeal of direct checking, from the standpoint of surveillance interests. When accomplished through computer links, it is relatively inexpensive on a per-case basis, extremely quick, and unobtrusive from the standpoint of the individuals involved. These same qualities both excite the enthusiasm of bureaucratic planners and politicians and spur the anxiety of privacy advocates and civil libertarians. In the last few years, the former have been putting their concerns aggressively into practice, while the latter have mostly been on the defensive. One of the best publicized instances of new forms of mass surveillance through low-cost direct checking have been the programs of "computer matching" sponsored by federal agencies. Here computerized lists of, say, welfare recipients are checked against other computerized data such as payrolls in order to detect fraud. Originally sponsored by Joseph Califano during his tenure as President Jimmy Carter's Secretary of Health, Education and Welfare, these efforts have been pursued with increased vigor under the administration of President Ronald Reagan. Proponents of these techniques have lauded them as essential to government efficiency and costcutting; opponents have characterized them as violations of due process, privacy, and civil liberties. Both positions were voiced in the 1982 hearings of the Subcommittee on Oversight of Government Management of the Senate Government Affairs Committee (U.S. Congress: Senate, 1983).

The perfection of direct checking within and among organizations is the wave of the future in mass surveillance. By substituting direct checking for self-identification, organizations can transcend the limitations which have beset mass surveillance in the past, and which continue to limit the effectiveness of a number of the processes described above. Instead of relying on individuals to provide information and documents themselves, organizations will increasingly seek personal data directly from other organizations. Such exchanges will increasingly take the form of computers talking to computers. And as data management in all kinds of organizations becomes computerized, the machines will have more and more to talk about.

Such exchanges will transcend limitations on mass surveillance and control in the interests of enhanced efficiency.

But inefficiency may protect important values. Whatever one thinks of the goals of specific surveillance procedures, few really want to see the ability of organizations to keep track of people grow without limit. At best, such developments would foster a more intrusive, less private world. At worst, they would lower institutional defenses against threats of totalitarianism. Thus, we favor limitations on direct checking in many settings, especially where personal data provided for one purpose are reused for another purpose unfriendly to the individual (Rule *et al.*, 1980:153). We hope this study helps to show what is at stake in these developments, and what price is paid for making personal documntation and mass surveillance more efficient.

REFERENCES

American Association of Motor Vehicle Administrators
1979 Driver's License, 1978. Statistical Report. Washington, D.C.: American Association of Motor Vehicle Administrators.
American Bankers Association
1979 ABA Bank Card Letter, March 1979. Periodical. New York: American Bankers Association.
Booth, Philip
1973 *Social Security in America*. Ann Arbor, Michigan: Institute of Industrial and Labor Relations, University of Michigan and Wayne State University.
Curtin, Richard T., and Thomas S. Neubig
1979 *Survey of Consumer Finances 1977-78*. Ann Arbor, Michigan: Survey Research Center, University of Michigan.
Linowes, David
1979 *"Privacy in banking."* Mimeograph. University of Illinois, 308 Lincoln Hall, Urbana, Illinois.
Rubinstein, Walter D.
1975 *Confidentiality Under the Social Security Act*. Pamphlet. Woodlawn, Maryland: Social Security Administration.
Rule, James B.
1974 *Private Lives and Public Surveillance*. New York: Schocken.
Rule, James, Douglas McAdam, Linda Stearns, and David Uglow
1980 *The Politics of Privacy*. New York: Elsevier.
Shils, Edward
1975 *Center and Periphery: Essays in Macrosociology*. Chicago: University of Chicago Press.
State of Illinois
1983 *Report of State Advisory Committee on Distribution of Government Information*. Springfield: Office of the Secretary of State.
Tritsch, Arthur, and Albert Kumbar
1977 *Comparative Data Analysis of State Motor Vehicle Administration*. Washington, D.C.: National Highway Traffic Safety Administration.
U.S. Congress: Office of Technology Assessment
1982 *An Assessment of Alternatives for a National computerized Criminal History System*. Washington, D.C.: Office of Technology assessment.
U.S. Congress: Senate

1983 *Oversight of Computer Matching to Detect Fraud and Mismanagement in Government Porgrams.* Committee on Governmental Affairs, Subcommittee on Oversight of Government Management 97th congress, 2nd Session. Washington, D.C.: U.S. Government Printing Office.

READING QUESTIONS

1) What is dataveillance?
2) What is the "efficiency criterion"?
3) Under what conditions is a single, centralized data bank unnecessary for dataveillance?
4) What is the difference between high- and low-integrity identification schemes? Give some examples in each category.
5) Why is it easier to do dataveillance when a single identifier has multiple uses?
6) Why is record integration not the trivial exercise it appears to be?
7) What is authentication, and how does it differ from front-end verification and front-end audit?
8) In what ways does personal dataveillance become mass dataveillance?
9) What is file analysis?
10) What is profiling? Why are statistical methods central to profiling?
11) What is computer matching? In what way is it "indiscriminate"?
12) What are the benefits of dataveillance? Why might the deterrent effect be more important than the direct gains?
13) "Rather than individuals themselves, what is monitored is data that purport to relate to them." Explain.
14) "When data are used outside their original context, the probability of misinterpreting them increases greatly." Why? Give some examples.
15) What role does consent play in the use of data for dataveillance?
16) What is blacklisting? Why is it a problem when many organizations use the same data?
17) What are the practical and ethical problems with a "predelinquency profile"?
18) Why is inverting the "onus of proof" pose a problem?
19) What are some of the intrinsic controls over dataveillance?
20) Why is it important to do a cost/benefit analysis before implementing a system?
21) What are some of the shortcomings in the implementation of the Federal Privacy Law?
22) What responsibilities does Clarke say information technology professionals have with regard to the uses to which their technology is put?
23) What is the "Law of Requisite Variety"? How does it act as a safeguard against undue dataveillance?
24) What are the two major forms of personal documentation, and how are they related?
25) What two kinds of social control do personal documents make possible? What are the advantages of each?
26) When did birth registration start? How long did it take until reasonably good coverage was achieved across the U.S?
27) What has the federal government been pressuring states to do with regard to birth registration?
28) How did the purpose of driver's licenses change over time?

29) Why have VISA and Mastercard become required documents for check cashing and car rental?
30) What is the sociological puzzle of widespread personal documentation?
31) Why is the birth certificate a weak foundation for personal documentation?
32) Why is direct checking a way of resolving the documentation dilemma that faces organizations?
33) How well developed are cross-checking schemes between organizations for each form of documentation?
34) What are the limitations of mass surveillance?
35) *"Mass surveillance through personal documentation feeds on itself."* Explain.

DISCUSSION QUESTIONS

1) Would profiling to identify suspects in a criminal case be acceptable if it relied on a pattern of past offenses (e.g., past serial rapists)? What if this behavior included living in a certain area (e.g., a zip code)? What if it included skin color? What are the differences in these cases? Would your judgments change with the severity of the crime? How about with the source of the data? What other characteristics would influence your judgments?
2) Take three databases, each with a reliability of .8. Their joint reliability becomes about .5 (making very large assumptions). What characteristics of these databases would reduce the joint reliability? What would increase it?
3) Make a plot of how prevalent each form of personal identification has become in the U.S. over the past two centuries? What does the pattern of data suggest?
4) Both articles talk about the dangers that mass surveillance would pose if it were to be used by a totalitarian state. As a counterexample, consider the control the Chinese state exerts over its citizens. This is actually done with a form of "local control"—block leaders, work group leaders, party members. It is done *without* a large national database. Would control for the Chinese state dramatically increase with one?

PRACTICING THE DESIGN ETHIC

1) Interview at least five friends or family members about their experiences with data accuracy. During the interviews, determine the following information:
   • Have they ever discovered inaccuracies in the data that have been collected about them? If so, have they ever tried to correct those inaccuracies? How?
   • Have they ever been refused credit, loans, etc., because of inaccurate information?
   • What public and private organizations do they think have information about them? What types of information are these groups likely to have?
   • What are their feelings about these organizations having information about them?
   • Are they aware of their legal rights concerning information collected about them? (For example, are they aware of the legal restrictions concerning the use of a social security number as a means of identification?)
   • If they refused to supply certain information about themselves, what do they think the reaction would be from the requesting organization?

Summarize and report your findings. Did you discover any patterns to the responses you received? Why do you think your respondents said the things they did?

2) How many different forms of personal identification do you have? What is the average for the class? For each one in turn, list the things you would not be able to do if they were lost. Determine what information might be used across the various IDs to match record information about you across databases.

Chapter 12

PRIVACY IN THE WORKPLACE

This chapter deals with privacy issues in the workplace. We present two articles that look at practical, legal, and social aspects of this issue.

Adler, Parsons, and Zolke provide a valuable service in summarizing both the legal and the social science data on privacy. They suggest that the issue is framed by three questions: (1) What personal data is actually required? (2) How will such data be obtained? (3) Under what circumstances will these data be released? They conclude that all employers should adopt an "information practices plan" that will guide the collection and distribution of employee information.

Adler et al. suggest that employees are reasonably comfortable that their organization keeps performance-related data about them. However, the second article we reprint (by Grant, Higgins, and Irving) makes clear that what is thought by many to be merely a privacy issue is connected in a direct way to the morale and performance of the employees. Perversely, the close monitoring of employees' performance may actually produce decreases in the quality of the work. Grant et al. show that when explicit production data are monitored, "what isn't counted doesn't count." Both supervisors and employees shape their perceptions about the job on the basis of the dimensions that are explicitly monitored—to the detriment of those aspects not monitored. Customer service, a key aspect of this organization's business, is lost in the rush to production. Thus, even if monitoring is perceived as reasonable, and is legal, it may have adverse effects if not well designed.

EMPLOYEE PRIVACY: LEGAL AND RESEARCH DEVELOPMENTS AND IMPLICATIONS FOR PERSONNEL ADMINISTRATION[1]

P. A. Adler
C. K. Parsons
S. B. Zolke
Georgia Institute of Technology

Picture the following scenario. A supervisor's relationship with a subordinate has deteriorated to an antagonistic stage. The supervisor learns that the employee has been diagnosed by a physician as being paranoid. Seeking to strengthen his position and credibility in the matter, the supervisor circulates an interoffice memorandum indicating the physician's assessment of the employee's mental state. The employee challenges this action in court as libelous and an unnecessary invasion of privacy.

Can the previous situation occur? In fact, it has occurred and a state supreme court ruled in the employee's favor by stating that the employee's privacy had been violated by the interoffice memorandum.[2] This recent case, though another appeal is still possible, indicates the difficulty in maintaining the delicate balance between employer managerial interest and employee personal privacy. It also establishes another benchmark in the growing relationship between law and employee privacy which is now an integral area of concern within the field of personnel administration.

The issue of employee privacy has experienced a dramatic increase in attention from human resource administrators during the past few years. After a relatively slow start, perhaps triggered by an Orwellian philosophy revolving around fear of "Big Brother," concern for personal privacy has rapidly moved from the realm of science fiction to the reality of governmental law and corporate ethics, becoming, in the process, a central issue of employee relations.

A right to privacy is routinely associated with citizenship in the United States. However, there is a growing debate concerning the extent to which the government should become involved as an explicit protector of this right. This debate is carried on in books, articles, technical reports, and other documents. Stone, Gardner, Gueutal, and McClure have reported that over

---

[1] From Adler, P. A., Parsons, C. K., & Zolke, S. B. (Winter, 1985). Employee Privacy: Legal and research developments and implications for personell administration. *Sloan Management Review*, 13-21, by permission of the publisher. Copyright 1985 by the Sloan Management Review Association. All right reserved.

[2] See "SJC Outlines Rules on Employer Role in Workers'Privacy," *Boston Globe*, 7 July 1984. Decision upheld August 6,19 84 in U.S. Court of Appeals, First Circuit.

2,100 written documents have been recently published on the privacy issue.[3] In addition, both state and federal governments have become involved to some extent, continuing to gather information and to consider advocacy positions in the privacy area.

The fact that personal information is required in order to conduct business effectively in an increasingly complex society must be considered a principal contributor to the privacy issue. The question of what personal data is required to effectively conduct business affairs can be considered from a triangular perspective:

1. What personal data is actually required?
2. How will such data be obtained?
3. Under what circumstances will this data be released?

The utilization of this data usually falls into two categories. The first category involves the use of personal information about the employees as an input to managerial decisions regarding hiring, employee work assignment, compensation and benefits, promotions, terminations, etc.. The second category concerns the release of employee personal data to external individuals and organizations for such purposes as job references, credit checks, etc.

There appear to be two major sources of ambiguity when formulating and interpreting management policy in the area of employee rights to privacy. The first is "What are the specific statutes and legal framework under which employees have a formal right to privacy?" The second is "What information handling practices and managerial actions are likely to be perceived as privacy violations by employees?" We will address these two topics and discuss their implications for management policy making.

LEGAL BACKGROUND OF THE GENERAL PRIVACY ISSUE

"There can be no public opinion without full publicity in respect to all consequences which concern it. Whatever obstructs and restricts publicity, limits and distorts public opinion and checks and distorts thinking on social affairs."[4] Nevertheless, many societal functions would be ineffective were they not exercised in confidence.

The First Amendment serves to ensure the free flow of information and ultimately protects the idea of an informed public. This concept finds its origin as far back as the Magna Carta. However, the First Amendment freedoms are not absolute, and are tempered by three important restrictions: (1) the privilege to withhold records in safeguarding the national security;

---

[3] See E. F. Stone, D.C. Gardner, H. G. Gueutal, and S. McClure, "A Field Experiment Comparing Information Privacy Values, Beliefs , and Attitudes across Several Types of Organizations," *Journal of Applied Psychology* 68 (1983):459-468.
[4] See J. Dewey, "The Public and Its Problems," in Civil *Liberties in American History*, ed. L. W. Levy (New York: Da Capo Press, 1941).

(2) compliance with statutory law; and (3) the prevention of unwarranted invasions of privacy.

Though commonly assumed to be a right of citizenship, the U.S. Constitution does not make specific mention of the right to privacy. However, as Duffy notes, Amendments 1, 2, 3, 4, 5, 9, and 14 have been interpreted as collectively providing some privacy protection. In addition, several states (Alaska, Arizona, California, and Washington) have enacted some degree of constitutional protection.[5] Rather than review these protections state by state, we suggest that interested readers further consult their particular state codes.

Although there is no general explicit constitutional right to privacy, many state and federal courts have recognized certain protected "zones" of privacy. The most widely recognized "zones" have centered on sex and marriage.

This growing concern for privacy has been the subject of many disputes, especially given the limited applicability of the Privacy Act of 1974. In resolving the tensions between the opposing needs of disclosure and confidentiality, the courts have been without any uniform rules.

The Privacy Act requires that: (1) federal agencies inform individuals (including federal employees) that there are personal data record-keeping systems containing information about them; (2) agencies permit individuals to copy, correct, and amend the recorded personal information; and (3) the type of data agencies may collect about an individual be limited. With certain exceptions, the agency must obtain written consent from the individual before making disclosures of personal information to outsiders.

The 1974 Privacy Act created the Privacy Protection Study Commission, which was to recommend to Congress principles and practices that should be required of private businesses. These recommendations, reported in 1977, include that the 1974 Privacy Act not be extended to the private sector, that employees be given some new privacy protection, and that private sector organizations adopt some privacy policy protection on a voluntary basis.

As of 1981, nine states (Arkansas, California, Connecticut, Indiana, Massachusetts, Minnesota, Ohio, Utah, and Virginia) had passed privacy acts similar to the federal Privacy Act of 1974. Two other states (New York and Colorado) have passed less comprehensive laws. These laws, like their federal counterpart, apply to government agencies only. Eight states (California, Connecticut, Maine, Michigan, North Carolina, Oregon, Pennsylvania, and Wisconsin) now have legislation giving employees the right to inspect their own personnel file. Michigan's statute is the most detailed and provides safeguards as summarized by Duffy:

---

[5] See D. J. Duffy, "Privacy vs. Disclosure: Balancing Employee and Employer Rights," *Employee Relations Law Journal* 7(1982):594-609.

[E]mployees may, upon written request, examine and copy personnel records at a reasonable time and place. (The term personnel records appears to be broadly defined although the Act specifically excludes certain reference letters, comparative evaluations, medical reports. and investigative or grievance files maintained separately.) Employees may request that information in their personnel files may be amended or corrected. If the request is denied, they may file dissenting statements that are to be kept in a file with the disputed information. If the employer maintains investigative files, employees must be notified of their existence at the end of the investigation or after two years. Investigative files must be destroyed if no action is taken

Duffy goes on to note that other states have not been as comprehensive, but specific information items have drawn attention. Polygraphs and other so-called truth verification devices have at least some limitations in twenty-one states with Massachusetts, New York, and Rhode Island absolutely prohibiting their use in the employment context. Other statutes limit the use of arrest records and restrict access to medical records and financial data by outside parties .[6]

In addition to the federal and state statutes, many courts now recognize an independent tort for invasion of privacy. The legal concept is founded upon that body of unwritten principles originally based on the usages and customs of the community, recognized and enforced by the courts. However, invasion of privacy is a separate and distinct entity from defamation.

Invasion of privacy occurs where information not reasonably related to a legitimate interest is disclosed. Defamation applies to those instances where false or misleading information is disclosed. In the context of employee-employer relationships, most courts will recognize the furtherance of the employer's business or the public good as constituting a legitimate interest.

Cases do exist where the disclosure of defamatory information, if reasonably believed to be true and necessitated by a need to protect a business interest, will not be actionable. On the other hand, disclosure of true, embarrassing, private facts to people who do not possess a legitimate interest in the subject matter, will constitute an invasion of privacy.[7]

One federal court has already recognized that an employer can be liable for negligence in the maintenance of a personnel file.[8] Along the same line of reasoning, Representatives Barry Goldwater, Jr., and Edward Koch introduced legislation in 1975 which would have set privacy guidelines applicable in the private sector. The "Comprehensive Right to Privacy Act"

---

[6] Ibid.
[7] See: *Quinones v. United States*, 492 F. 2d 1269 (3r d cir., 1974); W. Prosser and W. P. Keeton. *On Torts.* 5th ed. (St . Paul. MN: West Publishing, 1984). pp. 856— 857.
[8] See *Bulkin v. Western Kraft East, Inc.*, 422 F. Supp. 437 (E.D. Pa. 1976).

(H.R.. 1984) was never voted upon; however, the findings of the seven member Privacy Protection Study Commission are worthy of mention. The Commission recommended that legislation:

1. Require businesses to publish notice of their file and information systems;
2. Require businesses to collect, directly from the individual, only personal information necessary to accomplish proper business purposes;
3. Restrict the transfer of information between businesses;
4. Require businesses to ensure that personnel files are kept accurate and timely;
5. Allow individuals to inspect files;
6. Require businesses to provide written notice to any person concerning whom it has information;
7. Provide strong penalties for violations; and
8 . Establish a board to oversee compliance.

It is suggested that regardless of which of these recommendations (if any) are codified by law, some type of uniform code is needed to clarify for the courts and personnel administrators those actions which are permissible. Consistent with the Commission's findings, most states' privacy statutes provide the employee with three procedural safeguards:

1. The right to be informed of the existence of the personnel file;
2. The right to inspect the personnel file; and
3. The right to correct inaccuracies in the personnel file.

Position of the Courts

In the decisions regarding privacy, most courts have concerned themselves with the preservation of two competing interests: the interest in avoiding disclosure of personal matters and the interest in providing for the free flow of information in making important business decisions. William Prosser, an authority on tort law in American jurisdictions, wrote that privacy could be categorized into four areas, two of which directly apply to the employment relationship: intrusion into private affairs and public disclosure of embarrassing private facts.[9]

Accordingly, when controversies arise regarding personnel files, employers will first have to be able to establish that they only retain information reasonably related to their business and that they have taken reasonable steps to preserve the privacy of their employees. For example, an employers obligation to protect the privacy interests of its employees often conflicts with the needs of a labor union, which seeks to review personnel

---

[9] See W. Prosser, "Privacy," *California Law Review* 48 (1960):383.

files in order to protect its members from discriminatory hiring and firing practices. These conflicting interests require a careful balancing of the respective harms should such information be disclosed or withheld.

The privacy question has further been clouded by administrative investigations. When an employer receives a request to produce the personnel records of its employees, the employee has no standing from which to attack the request. It becomes incumbent upon the employer either to comply with the request, thereby breaching the employee's privacy, or to assert the employee's privacy rights and run the risk of being held in contempt for refusal to comply. These are the types of problems, absent any uniform legislation, with which today's personnel administrators are faced.

Landmark Court Decisions

Several noteworthy decisions indicate the direction that the United States Supreme Court is taking with respect to the privacy question. The most significant privacy case of the 1970's was *Whalen v. Roe*.[10] There, a state health agency required employers to disclose employee medical records in order to document the outbreak of contagious diseases. Roe contested this practice and argued that such disclosure was an unwarranted invasion of privacy. The United States Supreme Court rejected Roe's argument and held that the public interest in health was more important than the individual interest in keeping medical records private. Further, there was no showing of any immediate, physical, tangible injury, and hence the disclosure was upheld.

Privacy is often measured in terms of the expectations of the individual versus the public's interest in gaining access to the information. A recent decision by the United States Court of Appeals for the Sixth Circuit, permitted a similar disclosure as in *Whalen v. Roe*, but required the National Institute for Occupational Safety and Health to provide adequate security measures to protect the privacy of those employees whose medical records were reviewed.[11]

It would appear that where a federal agency, which is governed by strict procedures for the safekeeping of records, seeks access to confidential employee records, the courts will permit disclosure as long as there exists a reasonable relation to a job-related health hazard, and adequate safeguards are employed. However, one federal court has held that the interests in protecting employee health are superior to the privacy interests of the individual. As justification for such a position, the federal court held that the fact that the employees were willing to divulge sensitive information to their employer constituted a dilution of their privacy interests.[12]

---

[10]See *Whalen v. Roe,* 429 U.S. 589 (1977).
[11]See *General Motors Corp. v. Director of NIOSH*, 636 F. 2d. 164 (6th Cir., 1980).
[12]See *United States v. Allis-Chalmers Corp.* 498 F. Supp. 1027 (E.D. Wis. 1980).

Many times, before an agency can obtain employee records, the employee is asked to consent to disclosure. This is especially true in cases dealing with psychological testing data. The United States Supreme Court has ruled that where there exists substantial evidence of actual adverse effects to the employee from disclosure, a governmental agency cannot compel the employer to release sensitive information.[13] Hence, although the employee may have diluted his privacy interest by permitting his employer to accumulate sensitive information, any showing of actual harm will prevent forced disclosure.

As seen from these cases, the risk to the affected employee is a key component in determining whether information can be disclosed. Most government agencies have policies and procedures which minimize the risk that confidential information will be disclosed to noninterested parties. Should the disclosure pose such an adverse effect on the employee that to do so would offend reasonable sensibilities, most courts will refuse to compel an employer to comply with a request. On the other hand, as long as the agency has adequate safeguards and the need for the information is related to health and safety, disclosure will be mandated.

Most courts have held that there is no infringement of privacy when ordinary sensibilities are not offended. So long as there is not a flagrant breach of decency and propriety, the courts will recognize that no individual can expect complete noninterference from the society in which he or she lives. Accordingly, information regarding salary, business connections, age, experience, education, and criminal convictions will not constitute an unwarranted intrusion into an individual's right to privacy.

Major Privacy Ambiguities

There continues to be confusion in the minds of many individuals, including personnel administrators, as to the legal status of employee privacy. The dividing line between legal and ethical controls affecting the privacy of employees is not as vague, however, as is frequently believed. In fact, there are actually few direct legal constraints pertaining to protecting employee privacy. At present, there are no broad federal regulations protecting the privacy of private sector employees. As noted earlier, the privacy of federal employees is protected by the Privacy Act of 1974. This federal law has been held by the courts to cover, in certain in stances, state, county, and municipal employees.

Employees in the private sector must still depend primarily upon the traditional legal implications of slander and libel, as well as ethical considerations, for the protection of personal data accumulated by their employers. However, due to the uncertainty of some personnel administrators

---

[13]See *Detroit Edison Co. v. National Labor Relations Board,* 440 U.S. 301 (1979).

about the existence and coverage of "privacy laws," private sector employee privacy is often artificially protected by "government regulations" which in reality, have no direct legal impact upon privacy matters. Some personnel administrators appear unaware that their "legal" concern for protecting employee privacy is actually based on governmental nondiscrimination laws, rather than on laws directly concerned with the employee privacy issue.

Accordingly, private sector employee may gain a certain subtle degree of privacy protection from their employers simply because of confusion about nondiscrimination laws with which managers desire to comply These personnel administrators believe they are complying with "nonexistent" privacy laws, when they actually are basing the actions on familiarity with provisions of governmental nondiscrimination statutes.

In fact, a recent federal court decision has stated that an employer's invasion of employee privacy may constitute a civil rights violation.[14] However, this issue arose because of the existence of pertinent civil rights legislation, rather than as a result of privacy laws per se. Thus, even if compliance occurs for the wrong legal reason personnel administrators "properly" protecting employee privacy will find themselves legally correct.

For another example, consider a recent case before the District Court of Appeals in Ohio. There, a jury verdict of $10,000 was sustained in an invasion of privacy case brought by an employee against his privately held corporate employer. The controversy centered on the employee's answer to a question regarding whether he had ever been convicted of a criminal offense. He answered in the negative and failed to note that he had previously been convicted of armed robbery in a juvenile delinquency proceeding. Several months after he was hired, the personnel director learned of the juvenile proceedings from the local police. His employment was terminated as a result of the alleged false statement.

At the grievance hearing, wherein the nature of the juvenile conviction was disclosed, the personnel director, a union representative, and other employees were present. The employee's lawsuit sought damages for the invasion of his privacy, alleging that his employer should not have disclosed anything more than the existence of a juvenile delinquency conviction.

In affirming the verdict, the appellate court noted that the right of privacy is concerned with a person's peace of mind that his private affairs will not be made public. Although an employer does have a qualified privilege to make limited communication to parties who possess a legitimate interest in the information, the publication of the nature of the juvenile offense, that is, the armed robbery, went beyond that privilege. This decision is especially significant inasmuch as the appellate court held that there exists no

---

[14]See *Phillips v. Smalley Maintenance Services*, 711 F. 2d 1524(11th Cit., 1983), 436 So. 2d 705 (Ala. 1983).

requirement that a plaintiff prove malice to sustain an invasion of privacy action.[15]

Currently, because of various court interpretations of the privacy issue, there is considerable question as to what is proper employee privacy protection under civil rights and nondiscrimination laws. The federal courts are clearly increasing their attention to the employee privacy issue, even if under the guise of civil rights laws, and consequently, personnel administrators should be aware of a rapidly increasing number of pending cases and plaintiffs' awards in this regard. Accordingly, what may be "traditionally" accepted as proper protection of employee privacy is subject to sudden legal change.

Although the courts seem to recognize that employers must have a reasonable opportunity, relevant to possessing employee personal data, to conduct their business affairs, personnel administrators should not take this to mean they have a broad license regarding the collection and protection of such data. Even if employee personal data is kept secret upon acquisition by employer, the mere obtaining of some of that information may be a civil rights violation. Thus, employers should be most cautious of asking the "wrong" questions (per court decisions) of employees regardless of their reasons why such information is necessary to the conduct of "normal" business activity.

Summary of Legal Background

There are multiple indicators that protection of employee privacy will receive even more emphasis in the near future. First, as noted above, the right to privacy is commonly assumed to be a basic right of U.S. citizens. However, there are several trends in our society indicating that the protection of these rights is becoming more problematic. Many people have heard of the Privacy Act of 1974 , but it is a common misconception that the Act applies to a wide range of employment situations. In fact, the Act only covers employees of federal agencies. It does prohibit certain information dissemination practices without employee approval, and requires that employees be permitted to review their personal employment information files upon request; however, these protections have not yet been extended to the private sector.

Second, several states have passed some form of law to protect privacy rights, but these vary in comprehensiveness. Although most of the state laws are relatively new, it is probable that both interpretation and enforcement of the laws will be inconsistent across these states.

Third, there are commercial and governmental interests in information about people, and employers provide a potentially rich source for this

---

[15]See *Chambers v. Terex Corp. Cuyahoga County, Ohio*, 8th District Court of Appeals, March 31, 1984.

information. For instance, the concept of credit rating is based on the idea that credit bureaus should gather individual financial data, including present salary and salary history.

Fourth, there is also a growing capacity within organizations to gather, save, and rapidly transmit employee information through computers and telecommunications devices. The improvement in technological capacity has been accompanied by the creation of centralized databases within organizations that link together many pieces of information about an employee which, in the past, had been scattered throughout the organization. All of these above conditions are viewed by some as threats to the basic right of privacy, leading to the continuing debate on workplace privacy.

On a national level, the debate will be fueled by incidents of employee privacy violation that gain national attention. For a given organization, the amount of conflict surrounding issues of employee privacy will be determined by the accumulation of privacy violations. Therefore, it becomes very important to understand what factors and information handling practices affect employee perceptions of privacy violations. We will now review the recent research on perceptions of privacy violation.

RESEARCH ON PERCEPTIONS OF PRIVACY VIOLATION

Research on employee perceptions of privacy is only beginning to accumulate. However, the studies that do exist suggest that there are a number of factors that affect perceptions of privacy violation. The first point of interest is whether or not employees know how their employers handle employee personal information . In a survey of 2,047 employees from five companies, Woodman, Ganster, Adams, McCuddy, Tolchinsky, and Fromkin found that across sixty information items (e.g., demographics such as age and sex, financial situation, medical information), employee beliefs about whether or not the company retained information were accurate an average of 68 percent of the time.[16] Management in each of the five companies had reported actual practices.

Employees tended to overestimate the maintenance of affiliation information (union, religious, political) and underestimate the maintenance of medical information. These inaccuracies are understandable because 65 percent of the employees reported that they had never inspected their personnel file. When asked whether or not they had experienced an upsetting incident in their company's handling of their personal information, 7 percent said yes to a disclosure within the firm and 3 percent said yes to some disclosure outside the firm. As a general reaction to the company's

---

[16] See R. W. Woodman, D. C. Ganster, J. Adams, M. K. McCuddy, P. D. Tolchinsky, and H. L. Fromkin, "A Survey of Employee Perceptions on Information Privacy in Organizations," *Academy of Management Journal,* 25 (1982): 647—63.

information handling practices, 44 percent were satisfied, 22 percent were dissatisfied, and 34 percent reported uncertain.

One of the most disturbing findings from this study is the general lack of knowledge about what is maintained and what is not. A lack of knowledge sets a fertile ground for rumors based on isolated incidents of privacy violations.

As part of the same survey, Tolchinsky, McCuddy, Adams, Ganster, Woodman, and Fromkin reported which information handling practices employees felt were most disturbing.[17] Each respondent in the survey responded to one of sixteen hypothetical job situations that reflected different practices. The four factors studied were: (1) type of information (personality or performance); (2) permission for disclosure (yes or no); (3) consequences of disclosure (positive or negative outcome for employee) ; and (4) location of disclosure (released to sources within the organization (internal) or sources outside the organization (external)).

All factors were found to be statistically significant, with greater perceived privacy invasion occurring: (1) for release of personality rather than performance information, (2) for permission not obtained prior to release, (3) for a negative rather than a positive consequence, and (4) for information released to an external rather than an internal party. Probably more interesting was the finding that permission was the most important factor. In fact, when previous permission is obtained, there is no difference between releasing information to internal or external parties. Also of interest was the finding that the outcome of the information release (positive or negative) was a relatively minor factor compared to whether or not permission was obtained prior to disclosure. Clearly, an individual's perceived control over personal information (permission obtained before release) is more important than the eventual outcome as far as perceptions of privacy are concerned.

This latter conclusion was also supported in a study by Fusilier and Hoyer who used a hypothetical personnel selection situation. Respondents felt a greater degree of privacy invasion when personal information from their current employer was released without their consent than when permission was obtained.[18] In addition, if the respondent received a job offer, perceived privacy violation was lower than if he or she did not get the offer. In this study, the location of the disclosure (within the university or outside the university) and type of information (personality or performance) did not make a difference.

---

[17]See P. D. Tolchinsky, M. K. McCuddy, J. Adams, D. C. Ganster, R. W. Woodman, and H.L. Fromkin, "Employee Perceptions of Invasion of Privacy: A Field Simulation Experiment," *Journal of Applied Psychology* 66(1981): 308—13.

[18]See M. R. Fusilier and W. D. Hoyer, "Variables Affecting Perceptions of Invasion of Privacy in a Personnel Selection Situation," *Journal of Applied Psychology* 65(1980): 623—26.

Though the current article has focused on the employer-employee relationship, there are many other institutions that gather, retain, and disseminate personal information (e.g., insurance companies, the Internal Revenue Service, lending and other credit granting institutions, law enforcement agencies). The question about public perceptions of the relative likelihood of privacy violations in different institutions was the topic of a study. In interviews with 193 subjects, Stone et al. asked about individuals' values, beliefs, attitudes, experiences, and future intentions concerning information handling practices in one of six different types of institutions, one of which was an employer. The researchers found that individuals felt more confident about their ability to control personal information maintained by their employer than their ability to control that maintained by any other type of institution. However, this difference in confidence did not produce significant differences in willingness to support legislation that would control information handling practices in these different institutions. The researchers also noted that the average scores for the legislation support scale were relatively high across all institutions.[19]

MANAGERIAL IMPLICATIONS AND CONCLUSIONS

From our review of both the legal and psychological literature on workplace privacy, it is clear that the handling of employee information in organizations has important implications for personnel administrators. Present case law leaves many questions unanswered and the private sector is not covered by legislation in most states. Therefore, the enactment of uniform guidelines incorporating the recommendations of the Privacy Commission would be helpful to personnel administrators.

Regardless of further governmental standards, personnel administrators essentially have two broad internal roles to perform regarding the protection of employee privacy. The first role relates to privacy considerations involved in carrying out their standard staff unit activities such as hiring, training, compensating, and grievance administration. The second role relates to providing staff technical guidance in the privacy arena for managers throughout their organization. Clearly, the performance of the first role establishes the basic pattern for handling employee privacy within that organization, since managers will likely follow the tone of the "examples" on this issue set by their personnel administrators.

Personnel administrators also have an external role to perform for their organizations relevant to protecting privacy of employees. This role involves the furnishing of employee personal information to third parties regarding job references, credit checks, legal investigations, insurance risks, etc. Ironically,

---

[19] See E. F. Stone, D. G. Gardner, H. G. Gueutal, and S. McClure, "A Field Experiment Comparing Information Privacy Values, Beliefs, and Attitudes Across Several Types of Organizations," *Journal of Applied Psychology* 68(1983): 459—68.

this external role, with its lesser direct bearing on internal organizational operations, may create the most difficult and potentially dangerous employee privacy challenges for management. We offer some of the more obvious implications and suggest that concerned readers follow up with more detailed suggestions provided by Duffy or Noel.[20]

1. Develop a formal information practices plan. To avoid sensitizing people, do not use the phrase "privacy plan." The plan should be written and circulated to all employees. Supervisors and managers must be made especially aware of their responsibilities concerning their own behavior and that of their subordinates.

2. Get employees involved and have them review their personnel file on a scheduled basis. Have employees formally acknowledge this review.

3. Be careful about personal data not directly related to job performance. Eliminate outdated information. Identify the purpose of each piece of data and who can have access to it.

4. Be careful about outside release. Have employees formally acknowledge what data can and cannot be released to which type of institution. It is the party that releases the information that is at risk, not the party that seeks the information.

Finally, the current dynamics of the employee privacy issue preclude the statement of exacting positions that will eliminate risk in this sensitive area. However, this fluidity does not prevent personnel administrators from understanding general positions and trends in the area.

---

[20]See Duffy (1982), pp. 594—609; A. Noel, "Privacy: A Sign of Our Times," *Personnel Administrator* 26(1981): 59—62.

COMPUTERIZED PERFORMANCE MONITORS: ARE THEY COSTING YOU CUSTOMERS?[21,22]

Rebecca A. Grant & Christopher A. Higgins
University of Western Ontario

Richard H. Irving
York University

Why is my work important? Because good customer service improves the company's image. You're building up clientele.

Most processors will cut a customer off the phone if the call gets long or starts undermining their production.

A listener might conclude that the employees who made the statements above worked in companies with different products or philosophies. In fact, both speakers are claims processors, doing identical jobs in the same division of a major insurance company. The difference between them is that one processor's work is monitored by a computer, and the other's is not.

Computerized performance monitoring and control systems (CPMCS), which record and report computer-driven activity, are now common in the insurance, banking, and airline industries.[23] A report from the Office of Technology Assessment indicates that anywhere from 25 percent to 35 percent of all U.S. clerical employees are now monitored electronically.

Reaction to computer monitoring has been intense and varied. Critics describe CPMCS as impersonal mechanisms that undermine trust, reduce autonomy, and fail to measure the most important parts of a service job. They predict that monitors will trigger a return to Taylorism and turn offices into information sweatshops.[24] Heather Menzies, an authority on workplace

---

[21] From Grant, Rebecca and Higgins, Christopher and Irving, Richard (1988). Computerized performance monitors: Are they costing you customers? *Sloan Management Review, 29,* pp. 39 - 45, by permission of the publisher. Copyright 1988 by the Sloan Management Review Association. All right reserved.

[22] The authors wish to acknowledge the support this research received from the Plan for Excellence (University of Western Ontario School of Business Administration), the Social Sciences and Humanities Research Council, and the Labour Canada Technology Impact Research Fund.

[23] The simplest monitors (such as word-processing logs) count lines or keystrokes and accumulate them into periodic summares. The most sophisticated designs record private conversations between employees, or alert supervisors when a worker is not connected to the system. They may also compare actual performance to productivity standards on a minute-by-minute basis. Some, such as Citibank's customer-sensor and AT&T's switching system, pace the work by directing inquiries to unoccupied employes.

[24] C. Oreskovich, "Computer Monitoring Debate Rages," Financial Post. 7 September 1985; J. Gregory and K. Nussbaum, "Race against time: Automation in the office," Office: Technology and People 1(1982): 197-236.

automation, argues that "the computer's silent monitoring of every action and its implicit pressure for greater output depersonalizes the workplace."[25]

Supporters of computerized monitoring contend that these systems substitute clear, accurate performance measures for stressful, subjective assessments. Furthermore, they contend, computer monitoring enhances the ability of managers to motivate and measure employee performance. These factors make it an attractive tool for increasing productivity.[26]

Our initial research in this area showed that most material on CPMCS impact was based on a few well-worn anecdotes about employee protests of pervasive systems. There was little empirical evidence to suggest that problems were widespread. There was, however, a consensus that monitoring encouraged employees to focus on the quantity of work produced.

This focus is effective if the job is essentially production. Typically, however, monitored employees are doing work that has a strong customer service element. Does the focus on productivity block out attention to customer service? This question has not been adequately addressed.

This article describes a study that we conducted in a multibranch division of a service-sector firm. We compared the attitudes and behavior of monitored workers to those of unmonitored workers doing identical jobs. In particular, we focused on two broad questions:
• Does use of CPMCS increase the worker's perception that production is more important than customer service and teamwork?
• If so, what are the effects of this perception?
    The answer to the first was a resounding "yes."
    The answer to the second was less clear—but was disturbing nonetheless.

RESEARCH FRAMEWORK

Jobs in the service sector typically involve both production and customer service. A travel agent may spend time doing simple ticketing for experienced business travelers, which is essentially production work. During holidays she may also have to handle frequent inquiries from callers wanting to compare seat prices or alternate routes; this work is customer service. When time constraints bring service and production into conflict, workers must decide whether to direct their attention to the production or the service aspect of the job. Conflicts between the two are a normal occurrence.

Our study examines how computer monitoring influences the decisions a service worker makes when resolving conflicts between service and

---

[25]H. Menzies, Women and the Chip: Case Studies of the Effects of Informatics on Employment in Canada (Montreal: Institute for Research on Public Policy, 1981).
[26]See, for example, C. J. Ferderber, "Measuring Quality and Productivity in a Service Environment," Industrial Engineering, July, 1981, pp. 38-47; and M.H. Olsen and H.C. Lucas, Jr. "The Impact of Office Automation on the Organization: Some Implications for Research and Practice," Communications of the ACM 25(1982): 838-847.

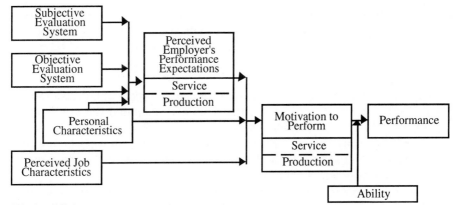

Figure 12-1
Role of performance evaluation systems in motivating performance.

production. Figure 12-1 shows a general model of the process.[27] Working backward, an employee's job performance develops from her intentions to perform in a certain way. We have called these intentions "motivation to perform." Performance is also affected by ability.

Motivation is formed around the answers to the following questions:
• What does my employer seem to want me to do? ("perceived employer's performance expectations")
• Who am I and what do I know about doing this job? ("personal characteristics")
• What does the job seem to demand? ("perceived job characteristics")

Employees tend to direct efforts at the tasks stressed or rewarded by the employer, so the "perceived employer's performance expectations" are important. But the employer's message is not necessarily always clear. CPMCS are objective evaluation systems that provide feedback primarily about the quantitative aspects of the work. Supervisors, co-workers, and customers all contribute to the subjective evaluation system. They may give feedback about work quality as well as about quantity, and add their own interpretations to the message while doing so. The employee's interpretation of both types of feedback will be influenced by her personality and perceptions of the job.

The model in Figure 12-1 represents a complex process. There are numerous dimensions to each of the concepts and complicated relationships

---

[27]This model is derived from the work of Ilgen, Fisher, and Taylor on feedback, and that of Fishbein in the area of motivation. It also incorporates, at a less abstract level, Lawler's concepts of thermostat models of control. See D. Ilgen, C. Fisher, and M Taylor, "Consequences of Individual Feedback on Behavior in Organizations" Journal of Applied Psychology 64 (August 1979): 349—371; M. Fishbein. "A Theory of Reasoned Action: Some Applications and Implications," Nebraska Symposium on Motivation, 1979, pp. 65—116: and E.E. Lawler III, "Control Systems in Organizations" in Handbook of Industrial and Organizational Psychology, ed. M.D. Dunnette (New York: Rand McNally, 1976).

among them. We will concentrate on the paths that go from "subjective evaluation system" and "objective evaluation system" through to "performance."

RESEARCH DESIGN

We conducted our research in the group-claims-processing division of a major North American insurance firm. The sites included the company's head office as well as its two largest branch offices. The sample consisted of seventy-nine nonsupervisory employees, fifty-five of whom were monitored by computer. We also included ten unit supervisors, one department supervisor, and two department managers.

Claims processors in this company perform two primary tasks: entering and paying claims using the automated claims-processing system and dealing directly with plan subscribers to resolve disputes and answer inquiries. In eight of the units studied, a computer program (the "monitor") counts the number of checks produced on a daily basis. The fifty five monitored employees receive a report of their average daily production at the end of each month. Daily production averages are also calculated over each quarter and annually. Head office processors also keep their manual log of the number of checks produced, predeterminations (coverage estimates) and letters handled, and phone calls answered. These logs go to the unit heads each Friday.

One head office unit (Life Claims) consists of unmonitored processors. These processors perform tasks identical to those of other units, but have not been incorporated into the control system. Instead. they submit weekly manual counts of checks produced, which are verified by the unit head. These counts are used to assess the productivity of life claims processors. (just as the monitor data is used in other units).

We also collected data for a tenth unit, the clerical support group for the head office department. These fifteen employees handle incoming and outgoing mail, register claims on the automated system, pull and replace manual files for processors, and provide other clerical assistance. The only counts kept for these employees are manual tallies of the total volume of work processed by the group. There are no productivity figures kept for individual employees.

Claims processors have a quota of sixty-five checks per day, set by senior management. According to interviews with processors, this target is easy to reach. Individual supervisors are free to increase this quota as they see fit.

Supervisors sample each processor's claims to arrive at quantitative measures of work accuracy on a monthly, quarterly, and annual basis. Two types of accuracy are measured: "statistical accuracy" and "payment accuracy." The first refers to the number of typographic errors made, such as wrong addresses, misspelled names. or missing postal codes. "Payment accuracy" refers to errors in the amount paid to the customer as a result of

	Monitored workers	Unmonitored workers
Production Quantity	44 (80%)	3 (14.3%)
Work Quality: Service, Accuracy, Teamwork, etc.	11 (20%)	18 (85.7%)

Table 12.1
"What is the most important factor in how your work is evaluated?"

approving claims for treatments not covered, paying claims against canceled policies, or using the wrong treatment code when determining payable benefits. These statistics are collected for all processors.

The data we collected included the following:

- All employees and supervisors completed a ninety-four-question survey that measured attitudes and perceptions about the work, the environment, the evaluation process, and motivation.
- We conducted semistructured interviews with each full-time employee and supervisor, elaborating on the qualitative aspects of the topics measured in the survey and the factors underlying survey responses. Each interview lasted one-half to three-quarters of an hour and consisted of fifteen open-ended questions.
- We collected actual performance data for each nonsupervisory monitored employee. This data included production counts and error statistics for the previous quarter overall and for the two months immediately prior to the survey, days absent in the previous year, and the overall performance rating. We took this data directly from the CPMCS and the performance appraisals for each person.
- We collected the data two weeks after the annual performance review. Employees were thus aware of their most recent evaluation when completing the survey and when being interviewed. The timing enabled us to test the validity of employees perceptions. For example, was the rating actually highly correlated to the production count, or was this a misconception?

PERCEIVED IMPORTANCE OF PRODUCTION QUANTITY

The interview responses provide important insights into the relative importance of production quantity. As Table 12.1 shows, 80 percent of monitored employees said that production quantity was the most important factor in their performance ratings. Accuracy (a measure of quality) was cited second most often by monitored employees. More than 85 percent of unmonitored employees, on the other hand, called work quality (customer service and teamwork) most important.

The company describes claims processing as customer service work, and we did observe extensive customer contact. Thus, while we expected monitored employees to place more emphasis on productivity, we did not expect them to reject "customer service" as a formal job description. But from comments made during the interviews, it is clear that workers do not agree with management's formal description of their jobs.

The majority of monitored employees who volunteered a description called their work a "production" or "assembly line" job. One monitored employee who had worked previously in the unmonitored processing unit said, "This is just a production job—not like processing in Life [the unmonitored unit] where you were doing customer service." Another said that customer service was not an important aspect of the job and was of interest to management only if it was "really bad."

The tendency of monitoring to focus employee attention on output is evident in other ways, as well. We asked what role the monitor played in evaluating performance. Monitored respondents emphasized the importance of the count; one said, "People are aways comparing themselves to each other on production." Another said, "It's always push, push, push to make your quota every day."

These comments were in direct contrast to those of unmonitored employees, who, without exception, described their jobs as "customer service." They believed the manual counts were used primarily to "make sure everyone's doing her fair share of the group work" and "ensure that no one processor is overloaded."

Clearly, monitored employees perceive pressure about productivity levels from management. The next question becomes whether this perception results in boosted productivity. One might expect that employees whose supervisors relied heavily on productivity measures would produce more to ensure good ratings. To examine this issue we asked employees to indicate the degree to which they believed their supervisor relied on productivity and accuracy statistics in evaluating performance. There was no significant correlation between this perception and the employee's actual productivity.

In fact, only one variable was significantly correlated with productivity: the importance the individual gives it. Individual productivity seems to be higher among those who consider it important regardless of its importance to the employer. Further research may demonstrate conclusively that monitoring designs are effective in improving productivity only if they reinforce personal motivation to achieve greater output.

Finally, it may be interesting to look at the actual importance of productivity in performance ratings. The monitored employees all agreed that productivity was an extremely important factor in performance appraisal.

Unit	Statistical accuracy	Payment accuracy	Average daily production	Attendance
A	X		S	
B	X		X	S
C	S		X	
D	S		S	
E		X		
F	no significant correlation			
X = measure most significantly correlated to overall performance rating S = measure significantly correlated, but less so than primary measure				

Table 12.2
Relationship between overall performance rating and performance on specific quantitative measures of job (monitored units only).

While supervisors differed in their approaches to motivating employees to be productive, they also agreed quantity was important. Thus we expected to see a strong correlation between a claims processor's productivity and her overall performance rating, but this did not turn out to be the case. When we tested the relationship between overall performance ratings and the measures of individual elements of performance, the importance of criteria other than average daily production was clear. Those criteria (presented in Table 12.2) included attendance and accuracy.

These results suggest that other factors strongly influence individual supervisors and that productivity may be a "hygiene" factor. That is, if it is too low, it will hurt the overall rating. But beyond the point at which it becomes good enough, higher productivity per se does not improve a rating.

The results suggest that monitored workers *believe* quantity is a critical factor in performance evaluation, regardless of the actual relationship between the monitored dimensions and overall ratings. At the same time, results do not suggest that supervisors with access to electronically monitored performance data rely primarily on that data during performance evaluation.

IMPACT ON CUSTOMER SERVICE

We used three items to measure the perceived importance of customer service. Ratings were high, with mean scores of 6.5, 6.2, and 5.8 on a seven-point Likert-type scale for each of the three measures. However. the fact that customer service was considered important did not necessarily guarantee that it would be given priority.

Customer service in this company has two components: fast and accurate claims payment and courteous and effective contacts with customers who phone for assistance. There is little problem with the first component; the company has a long-standing reputation in the industry for rapid turnaround of claims. Interviews suggested that processors thought primarily of that component when completing customer service items on the survey.

In the interviews, we asked how the company evaluated workers on the quality of customer service. The most common responses were, "By checking the accuracy of the claims we pay'" and "I don't know." Those who said they did not know suggested that, if no customer complaints were lodged, then management assumed the service was acceptable. Only eight of the processors (13.3 percent) mentioned that supervisors had discussed field service evaluations (prepared by sales representatives) or commented on processors' phone behavior.

Management's lack of concern about the quality of personal service, combined with its attention to production counts, does affect employees. Other research has noted an attitude of "when in doubt, pay out" among claims processors evaluated with quantitative measures.[28] We observed another pattern: if it isn't counted, it doesn't count. As one employee remarked, "People don't want to handle problems because it slows them down." Another monitored processor explained this attitude:

> I like the challenge of solving customer problems, but they get in the way of hitting my quota. I'd like to get rid of the telephone work. If [the company] thought dealing with customers was important, I'd keep it, but if it's just going to be production that matters, I'd gladly give all the calls to somebody else.

Monitored processors also believed that management's emphasis on production lowered the quality of processing that difficult or special claims received. Referring to such claims as "scrapwork," they told us how nonstandard claims or those requiring processor evaluation were regularly set aside. They were not handled until "I hit a day when I'm ahead of my quota."

This same aversion to difficult claims surfaced in complaints about eroded teamwork and cooperation. Those who complete their own work are expected to help others in the unit. However, processors indicated that the "helper" frequently sifts through the available work and takes the most straightforward claims. This practice reached the point where two supervisors established and enforced a rule that helpers must take claims from the top of a stack and complete every claim taken. Processors continued to suspect the help did more harm than good: "She's still going to try to work fast ... I'm the one who has to correct the mistakes in the end, so she doesn't really care."

Customer service also involves the preparation of coverage estimates and letters. This process is lengthy and requires close attention to complex coverage information; it is not monitored by computer. Employees submit

---

[28] Kerr, "On the Folly of Rewarding A, While Hoping for B," *Academy of Management Journal* 18(1975): 769—783.

counts of these activities, and management tries to assign contracts to ensure even distribution of the work. However, monitored employees complained that these activities are not considered when productivity is evaluated. Twenty of the monitored processors (36.3 percent) did not believe the manual counts of nonstandard work are used by management in any way. Another seven (12.7 percent) thought the manual tallies are reviewed only for individuals whose productivity is down during a particular period.

Members of one unit even described how they routinely bypass standard procedures to produce null checks for estimates and thus "fool" the CPMCS into counting them.

DISCUSSION

Because research in this area is virtually nonexistent, our findings must be considered preliminary.[29] Nonetheless, managers should be aware of the following patterns:

- Performance monitoring measures that cannot appropriately measure an important aspect of performance seem to promote bureaucratic behavior. The effects of inappropriate measurement appeared in three forms in this study: Interaction with customers was subordinated to production quantity; tasks requiring special attention became "scrapwork." despite assertions by processors that these were the tasks they found most challenging and satisfying; and processors became suspicious of coworkers trying to relieve a heavy workload. These effects degrade the quality of the product offered to the customer and the work environment within the processing division.

- If it isn't counted, it doesn't count. Companies that market CPMCS suggest that it reduces costs by reducing the need for supervision. However, systems that cannot completely monitor a job should be supplemented by active supervision. Employees must receive frequent feedback about their performance on unmonitored dimensions if they are to believe those dimensions are being evaluated.

- "Objective" measurement of performance is not necessarily perceived as fair measurement. Monitored employees were very aware that the performance data did not measure many parts of their job, and they perceived this as unfair. (Supervisors acknowledged that the criticism was justified.) While we cannot quantify what effect this perception of unfairness has, it is clearly not positive. Managers and CPMCS designers need to create control systems that can accommodate the host of contingencies that arise in service work.

---

[29] An extensive rewiew of research in this area by the U.S. government's Office of Technology Assessment concluded, "There is still little research separating the effects of monitoring from job design, equipment design, lighting, machine pacing, and other potentially stressful aspects of computer-based office work." See U.S. Congress, Office of Technology Assessment, The Electronic Supervisor: New Technology, New Tensions OTA-CIT-333 (Washington DC: U.S. Government Printing Office, September 1987).

- Monitored workers who internalize the CPMCS standards and gain intrinsic motivation from the system feedback may function more comfortably and productively in the monitored environment than those who do not. Workers who felt that the quotas eliminated the intrinsic satisfaction of providing good service commented more often on the stress of being "watched" constantly by an inanimate boss. Processors who considered the standards attainable or saw quantity as an important objective in itself reported little concern about being monitored.

The relationship between the processor's assessment of how important quantity is and his or her productivity is not conclusive. Our results do suggest that it is not the implementation of CPMCS per se that improves productivity. But the monitor may play a role in increasing motivation to be productive. The most effective use of monitoring may be to give employees direct, regular feedback and to give appraisers feedback less frequently. Supervisors can nurture employees' motivation to produce, and they can also help employees resolve conflicts between personal standards and perceived expectations.

READING QUESTIONS

1) How do you decide what personal data are required to effectively conduct business affairs?
2) What are the three requirements for federal agencies under the Privacy Act?
3) What civil (e.g., tort) protection do employees have for invasion of privacy?
4) What three procedural safeguards for privacy do most states recognize?
5) How have "administrative investigations" further clouded the privacy question?
6) How do the cases regarding public health show the courts' reasoning on the balance between public interest and privacy?
7) Though no federal "privacy laws" have been passed that apply to private organizations, how does the misperception that they have change organizational privacy procedures?
8) What information do employees *think* their employers keep on them?
9) What four dimensions of private information matter to employees. Which is most important?
10) What is an "information practices plan"? Why have one?
11) How widespread is electronic monitoring?
12) What are the various sources of information that a worker has for evaluating his or her performance in a job?
13) Explain the process of monitoring in the insurance firm studied by Grant et al. Include both human and computer-based monitoring.
14) Why did they collect the data within two weeks after the annual performance reviews had been held?
15) What was perceived to be the most important criterion of performance for monitored and unmonitored workers?
16) How did the workers perceive the purpose of making "counts" of work in the two departments?

17) Why was there no correlation between the perception that productivity was used to evaluate performance and employee's actual productivity?
18) How were supervisors actually using productivity in their ratings of employees? How were they perceived to be using it?
19) Which of the two components of customers service was thought of as the more important?
20) "If it isn't counted, it doesn't count." Explain.
21) What is "scrapwork," and how did monitoring affect its perception?
22) Why do performance monitoring measures that do not measure important aspects of performance promote bureaucratic behavior?
23) Why is an "objective" measure not always perceived as a "fair" one?
24) Why is intrinsic motivation important to employee productivity?

DISCUSSION QUESTIONS

1) What information about you does your organization keep? Under what circumstances will it be released to others? Does your organization have a formal "information practices plan"?
2) Use Figure 12-1 from Grant et al. to explain your approach to the work in this class. How does the particular sort of evaluation used in this class affect your approach to the class? Does the evaluation in another class also affect your approach to this one? If class discussions were held online (so contributions could be easily counted), how would that affect your approach?

PRACTICING THE DESIGN ETHIC

1) Work in groups of 3 or 4. Design a new computer system for an insurance company (like that in the Grant et al. paper) that would improve both quantitative (productivity) and qualitative (customer service) measures over the current system. How will you measure both the quantitative and qualitative aspects? Consider one or more of the following design approaches and discuss why you chose the approach you did.
    • No system monitoring
    • Monitor each individual's output, report to manager
    • Monitor each individual's output, report back to individual only
    • Monitor each individual's output, consolidate and report department's composite numbers
    • Monitor group-level output, using one of the above reporting schemes
2) Design an "information practices plan" for the performance information kept by the insurance company in the Grant et al. paper. What information would be kept? Who would review it for accuracy? Under what circumstances would performance information be made public?

Chapter 13

SOFTWARE OWNERSHIP: WHO OWNS WHAT AND WHY?

Surely, property rights in computing is an issue that deserves a book all to itself. And it would need to be revised monthly as court cases were decided in various countries. In presenting these three articles on property issues we hope to provide you with an introduction to the practical, social, and organizational dimensions that will always be present in this area. Future copyright and patent discussions will still have to deal with these issues when the current court cases have become history.

Levin reminds us that patent law is not the only mode of protection that is available to manufacturers of a product. Other forms include secrecy, lead time, moving quickly down the learning curve, and sales and service efforts. In fact, with the exception of the chemical industry, most industries view patent protection as no more effective than these other methods of protection of their economic interests. Levin explores the implications this has for patent policy.

Swinyard, Rinne, and Kau investigate the different perceptions of copying software that are held in the United States and in Singapore. They note that Singaporeans are more likely to make their moral decisions on the basis of the good that copying will do for themselves or others they know. This utilitarian (rather than rule-based) attitude is reinforced by cultural differences in the idea of ownership. Swinyard et al. conclude that resolving this international issue will take more than merely punishing offenders.

Samuelson and Glushko report the results of a survey done at the 1989 Computer-Human Interaction conference. After providing a 90-minute presentation of the legal issues involved, they asked the assembled researchers, designers, and developers what their opinions were about patent and copyright protection in software. They then compared these results with the opinions of legal scholars in the field of intellectual property. Their conclusion suggests that these designers may have more in common with Asian attitudes about sharing property than we might first think.

A NEW LOOK AT THE PATENT SYSTEM[1]

R. C. Levin
Yale University

In theory, a patent confers perfect appropriability by granting legal monopoly of an invention for a limited period of time in return for a public disclosure that assures, again in theory, widespread diffusion of social benefits after the patent's expiration. The rationale for this social contract rests on the recognition that technological knowledge has certain attributes of a public good. From this perspective, knowledge, once created, is believed to be freely appropriable by others, and the "free-rider" problem thus limits the incentive to create new knowledge. By conferring property rights that restrict temporarily the wide use of new knowledge, the patent system is supposed to create the incentive to engage in inventive activity and to undertake the costly investment typically required to reduce an invention to practice.

PATENTS IN THEORY VS. PATENTS IN PRACTICE

This idealized representation characterizes almost all theoretical work concerning the economics of patents. In the recent literature on "patent races" and R&D competition, patents are typically represented as providing perfect appropriability, although at least two papers are notable exceptions (Jennifer Reinganum, 1982, and Ignatius Horstmann et al., 1985). Recent attempts to model licensing behavior, surveyed by Carl Shapiro (1985), similarly treat patents as perfect property rights. On the other hand, theoretical work that takes account of unintended spillovers of knowledge from innovators to rivals (see, for example, Michael Spence, 1984, and my paper with Peter Reiss, 1984) typically pays no explicit attention to the role of patents.

In fact, empirical research, especially that of F. M. Scherer et al. (1959) and C. T. Taylor and Z. A. Silberston (1973), has made it clear that patents rarely confer perfect appropriability. Many patents can be "invented around." Others provide little protection because they would fail to survive a legal challenge to their validity. Still others are unenforceable because it is difficult to prove infringement.

Equally at variance with the theory, unprotected knowledge does not flow freely. Indeed, substantial real resources are often required to imitate an innovation, even one entirely lacking legal protection (Edwin Mansfield et al., 1981). As a consequence, public disclosure of a patent claim does not assure eventual diffusion of the knowledge required to make economic use of an innovation.

---

[1]Levin, R. C. (1986). A new look at the patent system. American Economic Review, 199-202.

The failure of actual patents to conform to the theoretical ideal does not necessarily signal the existence of a policy problem. There is no theoretical presumption that improving appropriability is desirable. Strengthening the patent system may simply reinforce the tendency for patenting to represent a "capture" of property rights, with the associated potential for the dissipation of social benefits through excessive effort to achieve an invention first. Moreover, as a practical matter, powerful incentives to innovate may exist despite the absence of strong patent protection. In the aircraft industry, for example, new products are protected by the inherent difficulty and high cost of reverse engineering complex, multicomponent systems. In the semiconductor industry, where imitation costs are relatively low, returns to new technology are garnered through quick market penetration supported by a steep learning curve. It is by no means obvious that patent protection needs to be strengthened in these two well-studied industries.

NEW EVIDENCE

Until recently, detailed investigation of the effects of the patent system has been confined to a handful of industries. In an effort to develop more comprehensive evidence, my colleagues and I have obtained information from 650 R&D executives in 130 different industries. Our survey contained numerous questions concerning the appropriability of returns from R&D, as well as questions about the nature of technological opportunity, and the results are described elsewhere (see my 1984 report with others). Here I simply note some conclusions concerning the effectiveness of patents and proceed to discuss some of their implications for public policy.

I focus on one particular set of questions. We asked respondents to rate (on a 7-point Likert scale) the effectiveness of six different means of "capturing and protecting the competitive advantages of new and improved production processes." We repeated the set of questions for new and improved products. The listed means of appropriation were patents to prevent duplication, patents to secure royalty income, secrecy, lead time, moving quickly down the learning curve, and sales and service efforts.

We learned that the effectiveness of patents is highly nonuniform across the industries we surveyed. In general, patents were viewed by R&D executives as an effective instrument for protecting the competitive advantages of new technology in most chemical industries, including the drug industry, but patents were judged to be relatively ineffective in most other industries.

Consider the 18 industries in which we had 10 or more respondents: pulp and paper, inorganic chemicals, organic chemicals, plastic materials, drugs, cosmetics, petroleum refining, plastic products, steel mill products, pumping equipment, computers, motors and generators, communications equipment, semiconductors, motor vehicle parts, aircraft and parts, measuring devices, and medical instruments. These industries are among the most R&D-intensive of the 130 on which we have information, and the average effectiveness of all six means of appropriation was higher in this set of 18 industries than in the full sample. Yet in none of these industries did a majority of respondents rate one of the two patent-related mechanisms as more effective than the most highly rated of the other four means of appropriating returns from new *processes*, although in drugs and petroleum refining a majority regarded process patents as at least the equal of the most effective of the other mechanisms of appropriation. In 5 other industries, one-third to one-half of the respondents thought process patents were no less effective than the most highly rated alternative. Three of these are chemical industries: inorganic chemicals, organic chemicals, and plastic materials.

Patents on new products were seen as more effective than process patents in most industries, but only in the drug industry were product patents regarded as strictly more effective than other means of appropriation by a majority of respondents. In 3 other industries—organic chemicals, plastic materials, and steel mill products—a majority of respondents rated patents as no less effective than the best alternative. In several industries producing equipment—pumps, motor vehicle parts, measuring devices, and medical instruments—a significant minority of respondents thought product patents to be at least as effective as other means of appropriation.

In our 1984 study, we analyzed these data in a variety of other ways (Levin et al.), and the conclusions reported here are very robust. Patents were regarded as most effective, absolutely and relatively, in industries with chemical-based technologies. Product patents were seen as moderately effective in a few industries producing relatively uncomplicated mechanical equipment and devices. In most other industries, patents were not viewed as a particularly effective means of appropriation. In addition, we found that patents tend to raise substantially the cost of imitation only in those industries that reported patents to be an effective means of appropriation.

SOME PRELIMINARY REFLECTIONS ON PUBLIC POLICY

These findings raise as many new questions as they settle. For example, if patents are an ineffective means of appropriation in many industries, why do firms use them? Further study is needed, but one possible answer is that patents are useful for purposes other than establishing property rights. patents may be used to measure the performance of R&D employees, to gain strategic advantage in interfirm negotiations or litigation, or to obtain access to foreign markets where licensing to a host-country firm is a condition of entry.

Suppose it is true that the appropriability of investment in technology is greatly enhanced by patents in chemicals, drugs, and several mechanical engineering industries, but not elsewhere. Some implications for public policy follow directly. In the majority of nonchemical industries, for example, there would be little to gain from lengthening the patent life, since the effect on R&D incentives would be negligible. Indeed, even where patents are effective, discounting implies that lengthening the patent life beyond 17 years would not have much impact on incentives unless there is a substantial lag between the grant of a patent and the peak years of its commercial impact (as there is in the drug industry, where the patent life has been lengthened).

Other public policy implications are more subtle and require further study. Consider the treatment of patent exploitation under the antitrust laws. Current law is a woeful tangle of apparently arbitrary and sometimes conflicting doctrines concerning the restrictions that patent holders may impose on licensees. Some practices that are unlikely to have adverse economic impact are illegal per se, although others, potentially more harmful, are subject to a rule of reason. Careful analysis of the efficiency considerations in this area is clearly warranted, and our survey results can inform such an analysis.

To illustrate, note that patent holders seek restraints on licensees to extract more profit from an innovation than could be obtained in the absence of such restraints. In the assessment of any such restraint under the rule of reason, we would wish to discern whether the favorable incentive effect from enhancing the value of patent rights outweighs the anticompetitive effect of the restraint. In such an assessment, general appropriability conditions in the relevant market are an important consideration. If patent protection were inherently strong and imitation costs were high, then restraints on licensees with substantial anticompetitive consequences might be viewed with great disfavor. On the other hand, in markets where patent protection is relatively weak and no other mechanism of appropriation is particularly effective, we might be inclined to take a more permissive posture toward a firm's attempt to extract all it can from a patent.

One more area of public policy deserves mention. During the past year, the Congress and trade policy officials have become increasingly concerned about the possible adverse impact of the intellectual property laws and enforcement policies of some of our trading partners. Considerable attention focuses on infringement by foreign producers of U.S.-owned copyrights on software, books, and audio and video recordings. But there is also substantial support for a policy that would pressure foreign governments to adopt stronger patent laws and to enforce existing laws. Given the absolute and relative inefficacy of patents in many industries, pursuit of these objectives might involve great political cost but generate little benefit to U.S. producers or consumers.

Scrutiny of the specific complaints of U.S. firms, however, reveals that the perceived problems are almost exclusively confined to the treatment of chemical and pharmaceutical patents by foreign governments. Many countries do not permit the patenting of chemical products, although in some of these it is possible to protect a product by patenting the process. Other countries, notably Canada, impose severe restrictions on the exploitation of pharmaceutical patents. Since patents appear to be very important in precisely the industries in which complaints have arisen, efforts to reach some international agreement on appropriate levels of statutory protection and enforcement may be well worth the cost.

REFERENCES

Horstmann, Ignatius, MacDonald, Glenn M. and Slivinski, Alan, "Patents as Information Transfer Mechanisms: To Patent or (Maybe) Not to Patent," *Journal of Politlcal Economy*, October 1985, 93, 837-58.

Levin, Richard C., Klevorick, Alvin K., Nelson, Richard R., and Winter, Sidney G., "Survey Research on R and D Appropriability Technological Opportunity: Part I," Working Paper, Yale University, July 1984.

_____ and Reiss, Peter C., "Tests of a Schumpeterian Model of R & D and Market Structure," in Zvi Griliches, ed., *R&D, Patents, and Productivity*, Chicago: University of Chicago Press, 1984, 175—204.

Mansfield, E., Schwartz, M. and Wagner, S., "Imitation Costs and Patents: An Empirical Study," *Economic Journal*, December 1981, 91,907—18.

Reinganum, Jennifer F., "A Dynamic Game of *R&D*: Patent Protection and Competitive Behavior," *Econometrica*, May 1982, 50, 671—88.

Scherer, F.M. et al., *Patents and the Corporation*, 2nd ed., Boston: privately published, 1959.

Shapiro, Carl, "Patent Licensing and R&D Rivalry," *American Economic Review Proceedings*, May 1985, 75,25—30.

Spence, Michael, "Cost Reduction, Competition, and Industry Performance," *Econometrica*, January 1984, 52, 101—21.

Taylor, C. T. and Silberston, Z A., *The Economic Impact of the Patent System: A Study of the British Experience*, Cambridge: Cambridge University Press, 1973.

U.S. Deparment of Health and Human Services, Social Security Admtistration 1982 Application for a Social Security Number. Flyer. Washington, D.C.: U.S. Government Printing Office.

U.S. Department of Health, Education and Welfare 1954 Vital Statistics of the United States, 1950, Volume l. Washington, D.C.: U.S. Government Printing Office.

_____ 1977 Privacy Act lssuances. Annual Publication, Federal Register. Washington, D.C.: U.S. Government Printing Office

U.S. Department of Justice 1976 The Criminal Use of False Identification. Washington, D.C.: U.S. Government Printing Office.

U.S. Department of State, Passport Office 1976 The United States Passport: Past, Present, Future Washington, D.C.: U.S. Government Printing Office.

U.S. Privacy Protection Study Commission 1977a Personal Privacy in an Information Society. Washington, D.C.: U.S. Government Printing Office.

1977b Citizen as Taxpayer. Washington, D.C.: U.S. Government Printing Office

Westin, Alan 1967 Privacy and Freedom. New York: Atheneum.

Westin, Alan, and Michael Baker 1972 Data Banks in a Free Society. New York: Quadrangle Books.

Wheeler, Stanton (ed.) 1969 On Record: Files and Dossiers in American Life. New York: Russell Sage Foundation.

THE MORALITY OF SOFTWARE PIRACY: A CROSS-CULTURAL ANALYSIS[2]

W. R. Swinyard
H. Rinne
Brigham Young University

A. Keng Kau
National University of Singapore

As long as the personal computer has existed, software piracy has been an important issue. Software producers have tried just about everything to protect themselves from losses due to unauthorized copying. They have made the copying difficult, using unformatted or oddly formatted disk sectors, laser holes and burns, and special error codes. They have created software which works only with key disks or plug-in port keys. They use license-agreements or lease-contracts with probably unenforceable break-seal acceptance provisions. And through it all, ADAPSO (an anti-piracy trade association representing 750 computer and software companies) promotes an understanding of copyright law and the moral notion, "Thou Shalt Not Dupe" (ADAPSO. 1984).

Despite these efforts, as the personal computer industry has grown, so has software piracy. The International Trade Commission, for example, estimates that theft of "intellectual property" costs the U.S. more than US$40 billion annually in lost sales and royalties. For software, it is estimated that one illegal copy is made for every software program sold (Bailey, 1984).

Though software piracy is a troublesome issue in every corner of the globe, the popular press has singled out Asia for particular condemnation. Articles in the U.S. computer press often comment with disdain about Hong Kong's "Golden Arcade", Singapore's "Funan Center" and "People's park," or Taipei's "Computer Alley"—retail outlets where the computer shopper can buy pirated copies of virtually any copyrighted software for little more than costs of a blank disk (see Hebditch, 1986, for example). The illegal sales from these outlets are impossible to measure. Lotus Development Corporation believes that software piracy from Taiwan alone cost them lost sales of US$200 million annually (Wall Street Journal, 1989). In a single 1986 raid on one Hong Kong shopping arcade US$130,000 worth of pirated software was confiscated (Warner, 1986). The shops stop making and selling pirate copies for only a few hours after such raids.

---

[2]Swinyard, W.R., H. Rinne and A. Keng Kau (August, 1990) The morality of software piracy: a cross-cultural analysis. *Journal of Business Ethics, 9* (8), 655-664. Copyright © 1990 Kluwer academic publishers. Reprinted by permission of Kluwer academic publishers.

A casual reader of these articles could logically conclude that the people of these Asian nations are behaving immorally about software copyright law. Possibly even that they are immoral people. If we hold a belief—say, that Asians pirate software—we may form a belief structure that leads to broader conclusions about them (Bem, 1970).[3] Are these conclusions warranted? By copying software are Asians behaving immorally? What *drives* their morality on this? How do they justify it? Is their moral development here different than that of Westerners? Or do they have similar moral development but different moral behaviors?

This paper investigates such issues. In particular, it contrasts the historical cultural development of proprietary intellectual property in Asia with that of the U.S. The piracy issue is specifically addressed using data collected in the United States and Singapore.

CULTURAL FOUNDATIONS

Protection legislation originated in the Western World. This legislation, which deals with patents, copyrights, trademarks, trade secrets, etc., reflects the traditional value of the West on the preservation and protection of individual creative efforts. Software can be protected through a variety of legal means. Program code has received both patent and copyright protection, but its most popular protection is under international copyright law (Harris, 1985). Copyright law originated centuries ago with British common law. In the U.S. its origins are found in the first draft of the Constitution. Article 1, Section 8 of that document contain these clauses:

> The Congress shall have power to promote the progress of science and useful arts, by securing for limited times to authors and inventors the exclusive right to their respective writings and discoveries . . .

and

> To make all laws which shall be necessary and proper for carrying into execution the foregoing powers, and all the powers vested by this constitution in the government of the United States, or in any department or officer thereof.

However, more thorough protection provided by statutory copyright law became available in 1909. These laws were strengthened with the 1976 Copyright Act (Davis, 1985) and the 1980 Software Amendments to that act (Benheshtian, 1986), which specifically included the visual representation of program code as appropriate to copyright.

---

[3] In this case, the belief structure would be "vertical" and resemble a syllogism:
1. The Asians pirate software.
2. Software piracy is both illegal and immoral, and so
3. The Asians must be immoral law-breakers.

Copyright laws and the West

Copyright and patent protection reflect a characteristic value of the Western World in general and the U.S. in particular. In the United States, individual freedom and benefits are emphasized over societal benefits. Many other western nations generally hold that individual creative developments have individual ownership. This view is reflected widely; artists' signatures on their creative work, journalists' bylines in newspaper articles, authors' names on their work, individual claims to design or copyright ownership, individual patent ownership.

Not only have artists and authors have historically taken full credit for and signed their work, but also glass-blowers, ceramicists, silversmiths, photographers, clock-makers, leatherworkers, woodworkers and furniture-makers, welders, inventors of all kinds, and even sometime masons, cement-layers, clothing inspectors, and automobile workers.

The West's preoccupation with protecting original creative work led it to originate copyright, patent, and trade-secret legislation.

Copyright laws and the East

Asia presents quite a contrast. Asian cultures (and particularly the Chinese culture, which has dramatically influenced the culture of most Asian nations), has traditionally emphasized that individual developers or creators are obliged to share their developments with society. A Chinese proverb heralds this view: "He that shares is to be rewarded; he that does not, condemned." Indeed, third-world and Asian nations traditionally believe that copyright is a Western concept created to maintain a monopoly over the distribution and production of knowledge and knowledge-based products (Altback, 1988).

Barnes (1989) suggests that, the inclination to create identical clones of a single product can be explained by [Asian] calligraphy. Becoming a master calligrapher in Japan takes countless hours of copying the works of a master until the student's work is indistinguishable from the original (Sanson, 1943). Barnes (1989) points out that moveable type—not accidentally a Chinese invention—allowed exact copies of the master's original calligraphy. A likely motivation for the Chinese to invent moveable type was that it permitted them to precisely reproduce classically elegant calligraphy time after time, thus reflecting their cultural value of sharing creative work

It is also noteworthy that in Asia books often feature both the name of the translator and the author with equal standing on the title page. Asian paintings often are signed with the name of the school that produced the work, rather than the name of the artist. Indeed, these schools typically have numerous artists, all precisely duplicating the same creative work.

We can see the legislative reflections of such values. Software was slow to achieve copyright protection in Japan and the Philippines, and it still does not exist in Indonesia, Malaysia, and Thailand (Greguras and Langenberg, 1985). And while mainland China is an attractive market for U.S. software firms, their major concern for that country is its lack of legal protection for software (Blois, 1988; Greguras and Foster-Simons, 1985).

And so we see that the cultural history of Asia does not generally support the notion of protecting proprietary creative work. In many Asian nations the highest compliment one can be paid is to be copied. Emulation is not only admired, it is encouraged. It is no surprise then that protection concepts would be adopted slowly.

Moral decision-making

Asians also have a different perspective on moral decision-making than people of many western nations. Americans, in particular, tend to be more rule-oriented in their decisions than Asians, who tend to be circumstance-oriented. Swinyard, Delong, and Cheng (1989) reported that Americans tend to make moral decisions based on fundamental value rules of right and wrong. That study found that Americans see little relativity in their moral choices; what is moral in one situation is also moral in another. The research concluded that they are relatively rule-oriented or deontological in their moral decisions.

By contrast, the study found that Asians (at least, Singaporeans) seem to make moral decisions less on rules and more on the basis of the consequences of their moral behavior. Thus, it concluded that Asians seem to follow a more utilitarian ethic. This tencency, too, suggests that Americans would be more likely be obedient to copyright laws than Asians, who would more carefully examine the situation, outcomes, or benefits which would result from a copyright violation.

HYPOTHESES

As a result of the above discussion we are led to expect that,

1. Americans will have both attitudes and intentions which are more congruent with copyright laws than Asians, and
2. Asians will tend to base their moral decisions on the outcomes of the behavior, while Americans will tend to base their moral decisions on the nature of the decision itself

METHODOLOGY

Sample

Our study uses a pilot sample of 371 student subjects: 221 attending a major western U.S. universiry and 150 attending the National University of Singapore.

Extensively pretested versions of a questionnaire were administered in classroom settings to students all across both campuses. The questionnaires were completed in private and subjects were assured of complete anonymity in their responses. The courses chosen typically contained students of all major fields of study in the respective schools of management for the two universities. While the sample does not represent "Americans" and "Singaporeans" it does reasonably represent the business management students of two Universities within those countries.

Measures of cognition, attitudes, and intentions

The questionnaire measured cognition of or knowledge toward pirating copyrighted software using three summed statements. Using five-point scales (anchored with 1—"strongly disagree" and 5—"strongly agree"), subjects were asked to indicate their view toward these statements:
- Making a copy of copyrighted software and giving it to a friend is illegal,
- When you buy a copyrighted software program, you usually are only buying the right to use the software. The program itself remains the property of the publisher, and
- It is illegal to copy "public domain" software (reverse scored).

Three measures were also summed to obtain subjects' attitudes toward software copyright laws:
- I would feel guilty about even having unauthorized copies of copyrighted software,
- I would not feel badly about making unauthorized copies of software (reverse scored), and
- I would feel badly about giving even my close friends copies of copyrighted software.

And, similarly, three measures were summed to obtain their behavioral intentions toward these laws:
- I wouldn't hesitate to make a copy of a copyrighted software program for my own personal use (reverse scored),
- I wouldn't hesitate to accept a copy of copyrighted software if someone offered (reverse scored), and
- I would never offer a friend a copy of a copyrighted software program.

For these three measures, then, higher scale values correspond with greater knowledge of copyright law, and attitudes and behavior more consistent with software copyright law.

Measures of personal utility

Tradeoff analysis was used to measure personal utility. The first moral reasoning study to use tradeoff analysis was that by Swinyard *et al.* (1989). Tradeoff analysis is a powerful method of analysis most often used to measure the relative importance of one product attribute (say, the quality or durability of a product) compared with another (for example, price). Tradeoff analysis requires that people ask themselves, "Are some attributes so important to me that I should sacrifice others to get them?" It takes into consideration context and situational contingencies.

- Do not copy the software and do not use it.
- Copy the program and destroy the copy after using it for the assignment
- Copy the program and keep a copy for use on other projects
- Copy the program and sell copies to other people that ask for it.

Table 13.1
Decision alternatives.

It also fits comfortably with the requirements of a circumstantial study of moral decision-making. For example, suppose a manager of research is faced with both a depleted budget and a need for a second copy of a new but costly business software package to complete a project. She has some choices. Among them: she can make the sacrifice and buy the package, perhaps by using budget allocated to another necessary area, but escape any threat of prosecution, or spasm of conscience. Or she can make an illegal duplicate copy of the software package and risk an entanglement with the law or even her own boss, but preserve her meager budget. If the project had important outcomes for her, she would undoubtedly be more inclined to somehow obtain the software. What should she do? Tradeoff analysis permits the computation of her utility or preference level for her alternative actions, given the results or outcomes that face her.

Similar to this example, our questionnaire asked the subjects to role-play each of three different scenarios. Each scenario placed the subjects in charge of an important business project which could be successfully completed with some new software, but there was no money available for its purchase. The scenarios explained, however, that a friend who owns this software has offered to let it be illegally copied. Subjects were given several alternatives in dealing with this software dilemma, shown in Table 13.1.

But each alternative carried with it some consequences or outcomes or benefits for the completion of a project in whIch the copied software will be used. The three scenarios differed, in fact, only in these outcomes (shown in Table 13.2), which were those having personal benefits, family benefits, or community benefits. For each of these sets of benefits, some outcomes may be viewed as a more attractive incentive to pirate the software, while others are not. One scenario shown to subjects is found in Appendix 1.

Moral acceptability and tradeoff measures

In each scenario subjects completed a measure of "moral acceptability" for each of the four alternative decisions shown in Table 13.1 (scaled on a 7-point "acceptable" to "unacceptable" scale (with "7" as "acceptable"). This is illustrated in Appendix 1. After reading the scenario, subjects were then asked to complete a 16-cell "tradeoff" table having the moral choices in the columns, and the outcomes (Table 13.2) in the rows. One tradeoff table, using "personal benefits" as the outcomes, is shown in Appendix 2.

Personal Benefits
  1. Provide you with a significant promotion and raise—a much better position and a 50 percent salary increase
  2. Provide you with a modest promotion and a raise—a somewhat better position and a 10 percent salary increase
  3. Not affect your job, position, or salary with the company

Family Benefits
  1. A large financial reward—one which will totally pay all family bills, and completely relieve your family from its critical financial condition
  2. A modest financial reward—one which will pay some of the financial bills, and provide temporary relief from your family's critical condition
  3. Non financial reward—thus providing no relief for your family's critical financial condition.

Community Benefits
  1. Significantly benefit thousands of people in your community
  2. Significantly benefit hundreds of people in your community
  3. Provide no benefits to people in your community

Table 13.2
Possible outcomes from successful completion of the project.

RESULTS

Cognition, attitude, and intentions measures

As shown in Figure 13-1, compared with the U.S. group, the Singaporean subjects were more *knowledgeable* about software copyright law ($t = 4.70$, p < 0.001). Despite this however, their attitudes were less supportive of those laws ($t = 7.78$, p < 0.001). And their behavioral intentions were consistent with their attitudes—the Singaporeans were significantly more inclined to

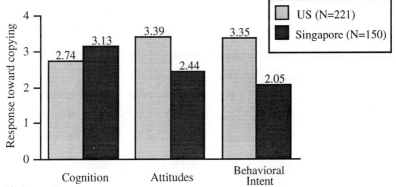

Figure 13-1
Response toward software copying: cognition, attitudes, and behavioral intent.

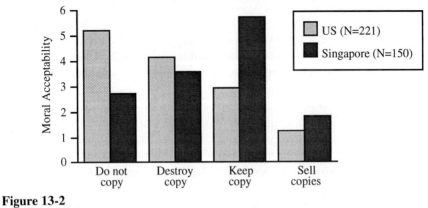

Figure 13-2
Moral acceptability.

make pirated copies of software than the Americans ($t = 10.59$, p < 0.001). These data support our first hypothesis—that Americans will have attitudes and intentions more congruent with copyright laws than Asians.

Moral acceptability

Figure 13-2 provides further support for the first hypothesis. This Figure shows that the U.S. subjects differed from the Singaporeans on measures of moral acceptability. Of the four decision measures shown in Table 13.l, the two groups were similar in their evaluations of the "destroy copy" and "sell copies" decisions ("copy the program and destroy the copy after [use]": $t = 1.85$. n.s. and "copy the program and sell copies": t 0.056, n.s.). But "do not copy" and "keep copy" were rated very differently. The Singaporeans found "copy the program and keep a copy . . ." significandy more acceptable ($t = 3.53$, p < 0.001), and "do not copy the software" significantly less acceptable than the Americans (t = 3.58, p < 0.001).

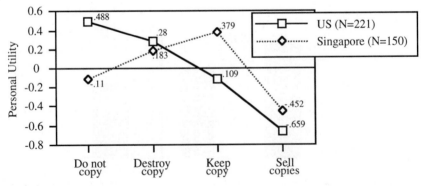

Figure 13-3
Utility of copying decision.

Outcome for you:	Do not copy or use	Copy but destroy after use	Copy & keep a copy	Copy and sell copies	
Benefit thousands of people in your community	1	2	5	10	US
	5	2	1	6	Asian
Benefit hundreds of people in your community	3	4	7	11	US
	7	4	3	8	Asian
Provide no benefit to people in your community	6	8	10	12	US
	11	10	9	12	Asian

Table 13.3
Tradeoff table results.

Tradeoff utilities

The tradeoff results reflect the above tendencies. For example, a typical tradeoff table is shown in Table 13.3 for the U.S. and the Asian groups.

As Table 13.3 shows, in completing the tradeoff table the U.S. group tended to favor the columns. In particular, their low numbers in the first column show that they preferred the "do not copy" alternative over all others, followed next by the "copy and destroy" column. Indeed, five of their first six preferences are in these first two columns. Thus, the U.S. students showed preference for their "decisions" over the "outcomes." That is, in making a moral decision, the U.S. group was more influenced by the legality of the copying than its impact on people.

The Singaporean subjects, on the other hand, specifically favored the "copy and keep a copy" over the other alternatives. They also tended to favor the rows—their lower numbers in Table 13.3 show concern toward the row variables of having a desirable outcome, rather than showing compliance with copyright laws. Thus, the Singaporean students showed preference for the "outcomes" over the "decisions."

The calculated tradeoff utilities from these data (and the two other tradeoff tables which were completed similarly) confirm this. The utilities are shown in Figure 13-3.[4] These utilities are simply calculated representations of what we have already observed in Table 13.3. For example, because the U.S. subjects tended to favor the "do not copy" column more than the Singaporeans, it is no surprise to us that Figure 13-3 shows that the

---

[4]While tradeoff analysis provides no difference tests of significance, it does provide a "badness of fit measure." Measures above 0.2 are to be considered unreliable. Our measures were all at 0.03 or lower, and no more than 6.5 inconsistencies out of a possible 198 comparisons, which suggests a very good fit with the original data.

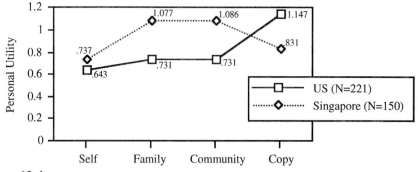

Figure 13-4
Importance of decision vs outcome.

calculated utilities for "do not copy" are substantially greater for the U.S. subjects than for the Singaporeans. And for "copy and keep a copy". the utility is somewhat greater for the Singaporeans than for the Americans.

The calculated tradeoff utilities representing the importance of the copying decision versus the outcome are shown in Figure 13-4. Figure 13-4 plots four points along the horizontal axis. The first three of these—"self," "family," and "community"—represent utilities or importance for the outcomes to come from copying the software:
• personal benefits, or benefits to self
• family benefits, and
• community benefits.

The fourth point on the horizontal axis of Figure 13-4—"copy"— represents the utility or importance of the copying *decision*. Thus, Figure 13-4's utility shown for "copy" represents the value or importance subjects are placing on the legality of the copying decision over the outcomes. On the other hand, the utilities shown for "self", "family", and "community" represent the value or importance subjects are placing on the actual outcomes of the project.

And so we see that, for the Singaporean subjects, the higher utilities in Figure 13-4 show their greater interest in the outcomes or benefits of the copying decision than in the legality of the copying. That is, in making a moral decision, the Singaporean group was more influenced by the benefits of their actions on self, family, or community than by the legality of copying the software. By contrast, the U.S. group was more influenced by the legality of the decision than by the benefits of the decision.

We view these results in support of our second hypothesis—that Asians will base their moral decisions more on the outcomes of the behavior, while Americans will base their moral decisions more on the nature of the decision itself.

DISCUSSION AND CONCLUSIONS

While Asians seem to have a more casual attitude than Americans toward software piracy, those in the West must understand that it is not simple lawbreaking we are dealing with. Copyright and other protection legislation goes firmly against the grain of Asian culture, which supports the concept of sharing, not protecting, individual creative work. One should not expect Asians to quickly support copyright legislation nor to immediately embrace it in their attitudes or behavior.

Meanwhile, police-action enforcements of copyright laws are being used in Asia. Despite the fact that many Asians are behaving illegally, to conclude that they are behaving immorally is inappropriate. More accurately, it appears that their moral values respecting this matter are simply very different from Westerners. Software copyright runs afoul of deeply rooted and somewhat fundamental Asian-cultural beliefs. Not only does their culture provide less support for copyright legislation, it provides more support for the human benefits which might come from the piracy.

We should expect relatively little voluntary compliance, until the Asian cultural norms change. Culture changes slowly, and people in the U.S. and other Western nations must have patience with Asia as it changes. Achieving Asian congruence of thought on it will likely take years; perhaps even generations.

APPENDIX 1

The Scenario

Suppose you are working for a private company on a government consulting project. The timing and the completion of the project is critical, and you are committed to the project.

You have just found out that there is *a computer software program which is essential to finish the project correctly and on time.* The software is copyrighted and costs $800. However, the company has not budgeted for the software and is not willing to purchase it.

You have a friend who has purchased this software program. Your friend has offered to let you copy the programs and use the copy however you wish.

Alternatives

You have the four alternatives listed below available for you. Please check the space which best reflects your personal view how acceptable or unacceptable each alternative is for you.

Acceptable Unacceptable

---A. Do not copy the software and do not use it.

---B. Copy the program and destroy the copy after using it for the assignment.

---C. Copy the program and keep a copy for use on other projects.

---D. Copy the program and sell copies to other people that ask for it.

Outcomes for your decision

Suppose that if you get the project finished correctly and on time the following three alternatives exist for you. The successful completion of the project could:

1. Provide you with a significant promotion and raise - a much better position and a 50 percent salary increase, or it could
2. Provide you with a modest promotion and raise—a somewhat better position and a 10 percent salary increase, or it could
3. Not affect your job, position, or salary with the company.

APPENDIX 2

Tradeoff Table for the Scenario

Now please consider both the four alternatives (A, B, C, and D) available to you with regards to the software, and the three personal outcomes (1, 2, and 3) and indicate the order of your preference for each combination, by numbering each box from 1 to 12:

Alternatives

	Do not Copy or use	Copy, but destroy after use	Copy and keep a copy	Copy and sell copies
Outcome for you: provide you with a significant promotion & raise				
provide you with a modest promotion & raise				
Not affect your position with the company				

REFERENCES

_____ 1984: *Thou Shalt Not Dupe*, ADAPSO, (Arlington, VA).

_____ 1989: 'Trade Thievery: U.S. Companies Curb Pirating of Some Items But by No means All', *Wall Street Journal* March 16.

Altbach, Philip G.: 1988, 'Economic Progress Brings Copyright to Asia', *Far Eastern Economic Review* **139** (9), 62—3.

Bailey, Douglas M.: 1984, 'A War of Attrition: Software Companies vs Crafty Pirates', New England Busines **6** (6), 22—23.

Barnes, Howared W.: 1989, 'Cost Leadership and Differentiation: Contrasting Strategies of Japan and the Federal Republic of Germany', working paper (Brigham Young University).

Bem, Daryl: 1970, *Beliefs, Attitutes and Human Affairs* (Brooks/Cole: Belmont, CA).
Benheshrian, Mehdi: 1986, 'Computer Copyright Law', *Journal of Systems Management* **37** (9), 6—11.
Blois, Keith: 1988, 'Supermarkets in China', *Retail & Distribution Management* **16** (1), 40—2.
Davis, G. Gervaise: 1985, Software Protection (Van Nostrand Reinhold, New York).
Greguras, Fred, and Frances Foster-Simons: 1985, 'Software Protection in the People's Republic of China', *Information Age* **7** (4), 220—8.
Greguras, Fred, and Peter M. Langenberg: 1985, 'Trends in Proprietary Protection in Asia and the Pacific Region', *Information Age* **7** (1), 3—9.
Harris, Thorne D.: 1985, *The Legal Guide to Computer Software Protection* (Prentice-Hall, Inc. New Jersey).
Hebditch, David: 1986, 'Pirate's Paradise', *Datamation* 32 (17), 71—2.
Sanson, G.B.: 1943, *Japan: A Short Cultural History* (Appleton Century-Crofts, New York).
Swinyard, William R., Thomas L. DeLong, and Peng Sim Cheng: 1989, 'The Relationship Between Moral Decisions and their Consequences: A Tradeoff Analysis Approach', *Journal of Business Ethics* **8**, 289—97.
Warner, Edward: 1986, 'U.S. Attempts to Take Wind from Asian Software Pirates' Sails', *Computerworld* **70** (18), 123.

SURVEY ON THE LOOK AND FEEL LAWSUITS[5]

Pamela Samuelson
Emory University School of Law

Robert J. Glushko
Search Technology

The software copyright look and feel lawsuits have created a climate of uncertainty in the user interface design field [3, 4]. Although individuals may have opinions about how these lawsuits should be decided, it is difficult for them to know how representative their views are. This column will report on a survey on the user interface field's perspective on these lawsuits which was conducted at the sixth ACM Conference on Computer-Human Interaction (CHI '89) on May 2, 1989. This forum was chosen because the annual CHI meeting is the largest gathering of user interface researchers, designers, and developers—the people who have the most to gain or lose by the outcome of the look and feel controversy. (An in-depth report on the survey findings, which includes detailed statistical analysis, is available [4].) This column will compare the results of this survey with a report jointly written by 10 intellectual property scholars [1] concerning copyright protection for look and feel and other aspects of user interfaces. The CHI survey results are, in general, consistent with the scholars' conclusions based on copyright principles [4]. The legal experts see a basis in copyright law for denying copyright protection to look and feel, which is what the user interface field thinks would be in the field's best interest.

The results of the CHI survey can be summarized briefly. More than 80 percent of the 667 respondents to the survey opposed copyright protection for the look and feel of user interfaces, although they strongly supported copyright protection for source and object code. They regard the kind of strong copyright protection being sought in the current look and feel lawsuits as likely to have a negative effect on their own work and on the user interface design community and industry. They oppose strong copyright protection for user interfaces because they think such protection would adversely affect the climate of open exchange and discussion of research and design innovations that has brought progress to the field.

[5] Samuelson, P., & Glusko, R. J. (1990). Survey on the look and feel lawsuits. *Communications of the ACM, 33(5)*, 483-487. Copyright © 1990, Association for Computing Machinery Inc. Reprinted by permission.

BACKGROUND ON THE CHI SURVEY

To assist the user interface design community in becoming more aware of the legal issues involved In the current round of look and feel lawsuits, Pamela Samuelson organized and moderated a 90-minute legal debate on copyright protection for user interfaces as a plenary session at CHI '89 [2]. The debate featured Jack Brown, the chief lawyer for Apple Computer in the Apple-Microsoft litigation, and Thomas Hemnes, a former defense lawyer in the Lotus case. They debated the legal perspectives on the pros and cons of protecting the look and feel of software user interfaces through copyright law. Michael Lesk of Bell Communications Research was an industry discussant.

Brown's argument emphasized the significant amount of creative work that went into the design of a user interface and the role of copyright in protecting those whose intellectual labor had produced a valuable product from those who found it easier to imitate a creative work than to do something creative themselves. Hemnes pointed out that not every valuable intellectual product was protectable by copyright law. Moreover, copyright law should and would respect nonprotection of certain aspects of intellectual works would further progress in a field.

We realized the CHI legal debate would provide a unique and efficient opportunity to survey a large sample of the user interface field about the legal issues. Such a survey should not be distributed until after the lawyers had their say, so the audience would have been educated about the terms of the legal controversy and each side had presented Its view. As the debate drew to a close, Samuelson informed the audience about the survey being distributed to them, and said although judges would make the final rulings on the look and feel lawsuits, this was a chance for representatives of the user interface design community to vote on the legal issues, and urged them to do so. Before filing out of the auditorium, 667 members of the audience filled out the survey.

A PROFILE OF SURVEY RESPONDENTS

The survey asked a number of questions about the respondents and their firms so it would be possible to analyze whether characteristics of the respondents or their firms might predict their views on the look and feel lawsuits and related issues. For example, respondents were asked to select from a list of job functions the one or two descriptions that best fit (1.68 was the average rate of response by job function). Table 13.4 shows the respondents' profile by job

User interface designer	44%
Researcher	32%
Software engineer	29%
Human factors engineer	15%
Manager	15%
Faculty	8%
Consultant	6%
Student	6%

Table 13.4
Respondent population by job function.

Computer manufacturer	26%
R and D organization	23%
University	20%
Software vendor	14%
Other	17%

Table 13.5
Respondent population by
employer.

function for the most frequently indicated categories.

Respondents were also asked to identify the one best description of the organization or company for which they work. Table 13.5 reflects the results of this question. The survey did not ask respondents to identify the organization or firm for which they worked, but since the respondents made up 42 percent of the total conference registration, this information provides a reasonable substitute without compromising the identity of particular respondents. The 10 organizations with the highest number of attendees at CHI '89 were, in decreasing rank order; IBM, Hewlett-Packard, Apple, MCC (the host organization in Austin), AT&T, Texas Instruments, Xerox, Bell Communications Research, the University of Michigan, and Carnegie-Mellon University. In addition to look and feel litigants Hewlett-Packard, Apple, and Xerox in positions two, three, and five, there were several representatives each from Ashton-Tate, Lotus, and Microsoft in attendance.

None of the factors characterizing the survey respondents were found to predict statistically significant differences in their answers to the questions concerning the role of copyright and patent in the protection of various aspects of software or concerning predicted effects of strong copyright protection. In view of the support the survey gives to the minimalist interpretation of the appropriate reach of copyright law as applied to software [2], it is worth pointing out that the respondents were among the leading designers and researchers in their field, responsible for creating many of the most commercially valuable user interfaces in the software industry. They typically worked for commercial firms that rely on copyright law to protect their software products [4].

SURVEY FINDINGS ON PROTECTION OF LOOK AND FEEL

One of the principal findings of the survey was that the user interface field thinks the look and feel of user interfaces should not be given protection by copyright or patent law. Some 77 percent of the respondents with an opinion felt that look and feel should not be given protection by either copyright or patent law, while 82 percent opposed copyright protection for look and feel.

Quite a few of the survey respondents explained their reasons for opposing legal protection for look and feel of user interfaces. Some said they were not sure what look and feel meant. Some were unsure how similar interfaces could be in look and feel before infringement might be found. Others thought look and feel related largely to functionalities of the interface which copyright should not protect. Still others expressed concern for the

Aspect	copyright	patent	both	neither
Source code	71%	10%	12%	7%
Object code	65%	10%	11%	15%
Pseudo code	39%	7%	6%	48%
Module design	18%	16%	6%	60%
Algorithms	8%	32%	7%	53%
Commands	6%	4%	2%	88%
Icons	37%	3%	3%	57%
Screen layout	25%	4%	2%	69%
Screen sequence	13%	6%	2%	79%
Look and feel	15%	5%	3%	77%
UI functionality	4%	12%	2%	83%

Table 13.6
Support for copyright and/or patent for software aspects.

effect on the users, as well as the industry, if the pending look and feel lawsuits established strong copyright protection for user interfaces [4].

In addition to asking about look and feel, the survey asked for views about legal protection of five other aspects of user interfaces, all of which (either explicitly or implicitly) are at issue in the current round of look and feel cases. The survey revealed even stronger opposition to copyright protection for commands, user interface functionalities, and screen sequence than to look and feel protection, as well as strong (but somewhat less opposition) to such protection for screen layouts. (See Table 13.6) Icons were the aspect of user interfaces for which there was strongest sympathy for protection, but not even this feature enjoyed majority support among respondents. Strongest opposition was registered as to protection of commands and user interface functionalities, with more than 8 of every 10 respondents objecting to their protection by copyright.

Because many of those features overlap significantly with the kind of look and feel being sought to be protected in the lawsuits, it is not surprising the respondents would view protection of these aspects of interfaces in much the same way they viewed protection of look and feel.

However, opposition to protection of look and feel was not part of wholesale rejection of intellectual property protection for software, as shown in Table 13.6. The respondents overwhelmingly supported intellectual property (and mainly for copyright) protection for source and object code. Fully 93 percent of those with an opinion supported intellectual property protection, either through copyright or patent, for source code. The 85 percent support for object code protection was nearly as strong.

As a group, the respondents strongly supported copyright protection for source and object code, but did not support copyright protection for pseudocode or modular design. Least of all did they support copyright protection for algorithms, although nearly 40 percent of the respondents supported patent protection for algorithms.

PREDICTED NEGATIVE EFFECT FROM COPYRIGHT PROTECTION FOR LOOK AND FEEL

Another major finding of the CHI survey was that respondents regarded the kind of strong copyright protection being sought in the look and feel lawsuits as likely to have a clear negative effect both on the industry/community and on their own work.

In response to a survey question about the effect such protection would have "on your own work," the average rating (on a five-point scale ranging from "1" for "significant negative effect" to "5" for "significant positive effect") was 2.049, a clear overall expectation of a negative effect. But it was not just a minority of respondents with "significant negative" votes who swayed the average; 72 percent expected a negative impact on their own work (ratings of "1" or "2") if the current lawsuits established strong copyright protection, while only nine percent expected the effect on their work to be positive (ratings of "4" or "5").

The predicted effect "on the user interface design industry/community" was even more strongly negative, with an average rating of 1.646 on the same five-point scale. Indeed, 86 percent of the respondents expected the kind of strong copyright protection for user interfaces being sought in the look and feel lawsuits to have a negative impact on the industry, while only 10 percent viewed the prospect as positive. Table 13.7 gives the results of the respondents' predictions about the likely effect of strong protection on their own work and on the industry.

Lest the reader interpret these results as only reflecting the opinion of worker bees or ivory-tower types. we hasten to point out that 15 percent of the respondent population identified themselves as managers, and their responses to the prediction questions and the protectability of individual features question did not differ in a statistically significant way from the responses of the respondent group as a whole. The average predicted industry effect among the managers, for example, was 1.74. The average responses by job function closest to the manager predictions were those of faculty (1.76), students (1.73) and user interface designers (1.72). All were still well under a 2.0 rating, which itself was a negative rating. Not a single category of respondents measured by job function predicted even a neutral, let alone a positive, effect on the industry if the look and feel lawsuits established the kind of copyright protection being sought.

When we compared the answers respondents gave concerning their predictions of effect on their own work with their predictions about the industry effect, we noted that while there was some shifting in both

Effect	- 1	2	3	4	+ 5
Own work	35%	36%	19%	7%	2%
Industry & Community	57%	29%	4%	7%	3%

Table 13.7
Predicted effect of strong copyright for interfaces.

directions, people who gave different ratings on the two questions were 3.5 times more likely to move in a more negative direction when predicting the industry effect. Particularly striking was the finding that 18 percent of respondents who expected to be unaffected in their own work if the current lawsuits established strong copyright for user interfaces, 69 percent expected a negative effect for the field.

THE EXTENT OF RESTRICTION PERCEIVED AT PRESENT

The survey also inquired about the extent of restriction the respondents currently felt about the use they could make of the latest research and design innovations which they saw or learned about at conferences such as CHI. Respondents were asked to select one of four statements that best described their views.

1. No restrictions: I can freely use anything learn about or see,
2. Some restrictions: I can't copy exactly, but I am allowed to reimplement or reverse engineer any interesting designs,
3. Significant restrictions: I can copy only general concepts or ideas at the research stage, or
4. Total restrictions: Once I see it at CHI, I know I can't copy it in any user interface design of my own.

Some 31 percent reported feeling "no restrictions" on use of innovations seen at CHI. Just under half of the respondents (48 percent) felt only "some restriction." One 1-in-5 respondents reported feeling "significantly" (19 percent) or "totally" (1 percent) restricted in their use of design innovations seen at CHI. (Here, there were some statistically significant responses among respondents by type of employer. Government employees felt least restricted, with 64 percent assuming no restrictions. However, even those who worked for computer manufacturers felt fewer constraints than one might have guessed, with 24 percent perceiving no restrictions, and another 50 percent reporting some restrictions.)

Not surprisingly, the fewer restrictions that people currently felt, the more likely they were to expect a negative effect on their own work if strong copyright protection was established by the current lawsuits about user interface issues. But even those who already feel significant restrictions predicted negative consequences if look and feel protection was established. with an average of 2.303 on the five point scale as to their own work, and 1.70 as to the industry/community effect. The average response of "no restriction" respondents was 1.464 for the industry/community effect.

HOW THE LEGAL DEBATE
AFFECTED RESPONDENTS' VIEWS

Perhaps the most dramatic finding from the survey was the fact that the more those in the user interface field learned about what copyright lawyers thought about copyright protection of user interface issues, the more likely they were to think copyright protection for user interfaces should be weaker, rather than stronger.

Attendees of the CHI legal debate came with some familiarity of the legal issues involved in the look and feel cases. Indeed, 64 percent of the respondents rated themselves a "moderately familiar" with the legal issues before the legal debate, and another 9 percent reported being "very familiar" with the issues. Given how much press attention the look and feel lawsuits have received, and given how important this community feels the legal issues to be to the health of their field, this result in itself is not surprising.

What was surprising was how people reacted to copyright protection for user interfaces after they had heard the legal debate. Half of the respondents indicated that attending the debate had caused them to change their opinion on copyright protection. Ten times as many changed their minds to thinking that copyright protection should be weaker than changed to thinking it should be stronger.

It was not the case that Jack Brown argued less persuasively than Thomas Hemnes, for Peter Lewis of the New York Times reported both sides of the legal debate to be equally persuasive (May 7, 1989). Moreover, a number of respondents praised Brown's skill in argumentation. The lawyers, quite appropriately, presented arguments based on the issues that copyright law regards as relevant to deciding legal disputes.

What then explains the strong shift toward thinking copyright protection should be weaker? We believe the CHI audience was not so much persuaded to one legal position or the other, but awakened to the nature of the legal debate and its implications for how they worked and for the field in which they worked. The comment of one survey respondent expressed well the authors' interpretation of the outcome of the legal debate: "The arguments and session made me very nervous because the arguments against strong protection were so compelling based on my knowledge of the field, but they may not be anywhere near as obvious to non-practitioners—and the courts are generally non-practitioners."

The respondents felt strongly enough about the predicted harm to their industry that 63 percent of those who expressed an opinion wanted SIGCHI to take an official position on the legal issues based on the results of this survey. Many who responded "no" to this question said they did so because they thought the entire SIGCHI membership should be polled before SIGCHI took an official position.

COMPARING THE CHI SURVEY
RESULTS TO LAW SCHOLARS' REPORT

In part because of some novel legal questions presented by the software copyright lawsuits, a group of 10 intellectual property scholars met last February at Arizona State University to try to reach consensus on the proper application of copyright law to the protection of computer programs. Among the questions they addressed was whether copyright protection was appropriate for the look and feel of computer program user interfaces. The conferees agreed it was not, saying that use of terms like look and feel "obscures rather than assists in the application of copyright principles to software interfaces" [1]. The conferees recognized that software user interfaces may be highly functional, and to the extent they are, that copyright protection is not available for them, nor for functionally optimal expression of them. In addition, the conferees recognized that user interface design may be constrained by technological considerations that may limit the range of viable "expressions," which would restrict the scope of copyright protection available to them.

The conferees found in traditional principles of copyright law: affirmation of the right to study and take unprotected elements from copyrighted programs and reimplement them in other products [1]. While accepting that intellectual property protection for computer programs should balance the needs of innovators and competitors so as to promote the health of industries such as that for software, the conferees regarded their aim to be a limited one of articulating how traditional copyright principles might be applied to computer programs, not to offer their judgment about whether the larger goal of intellectual property law can best be served by use of copyright law to protect computer programs.

The conferees, while agreeing with the user interface survey respondents that individual commands or even sets of commands should not be protected by copyright, were not able to reach consensus on whether a less than functionally optimal arrangement of commands (or icons) in a user interface would be protectable by copyright. Some conferees, like many in the CHI survey population, thought the benefits that would flow to users from standardization of such things as command names and command groupings in software user interfaces, as well as functional reasons that might exist for grouping certain kinds of commands together, made it generally inappropriate for copyright protection to attach to arrangements of commands. Other conferees thought that in view of the protection copyright law had traditionally afforded to compilations, the organization of a set of commands from one program, if original, might be protected by copyright from exact duplication in a competing program.

The conferees were also in agreement with those in the user interface field about some issues related to the protection of icons—that "adoption of a functional general purpose metaphor might limit the range of copyrightable expression" and when "the choice of icons is logically based upon the choice of an overarching metaphor (such as a desktop) or the icon itself has no fanciful characteristics, application of traditional principles would preclude copyright protection for the particular representation of the icon." However, the conferees also thought traditional principles of copyright law might provide protection for some more fanciful pictorial representation of icons. The CHI survey respondents, however, did not support copyright protection for icons, perhaps because they perceive user interface icons as not really having a fanciful character.

The CHI survey data suggests the user interface field has developed because people in the field come to conferences such as CHI to share their new user interface design ideas with others. When attendees see good design ideas and the research that stands behind them, they feel they can incorporate these designs into new products of their own, blending the ideas they have received from others with the ideas they have developed themselves. And they do not consider themselves thieves, plagiarists, or copyright infringers when they do so. Rather, they consider themselves scientists and engineers who are innovating on top of others' ideas in the kind of evolutionary fashion which has exemplified development in this field.

This evolutionary development seems to have brought about a considerable amount of innovation, improved designs which have made computers and software more accessible and usable by those with minimal or no technical training, and competition about performance, enhanced features, and price. If each software firm had to develop a different style of user interface to comply with copyright law, there is concern that copyright might impede how those in the user interface field do their work, might harm the health of the industry, and might make more difficult the achievement of the goal of making computers usable by ordinary people.

CONCLUSION

It is often stated, but nonetheless true, that a fundamental purpose of the intellectual property laws is to provide protection for innovations in order to give incentives for people to be creative, thereby promoting progress in various fields of endeavor. From this, it follows that where legal protection of some kinds of innovations is not needed to promote innovation in a field, no protective legislation is needed. Thus, it must surely be the case that where intellectual property protection would have a detrimental effect on innovation in a field, it should be withheld, especially in an area where the law does not as yet dictate the protection being sought.

In the case of user interfaces, the CHI survey clearly demonstrates that a significant segment of the leading designers and researchers in the user interface field are overwhelmingly opposed to strong copyright protection for user interfaces and regard such protection as likely to be harmful to the field, rather than helpful. These are the very people whom the copyright law is supposed to be encouraging to be creative. Given that copyright law has, as yet, not formed a firm position about protection of various aspects of user interfaces discussed in this column—and can be construed to support either side in the legal debate—judges in the current round of copyright look and feel cases should be receptive to considering the effect strong protection would have on the industry.

That the views of the technical community are largely consistent with views expressed by legal scholars [1] as to the application of copyright law to computer programs suggests that judges in look and feel cases could find an adequate basis in copyright doctrine to do what the user interface field thinks would be in the field's best interest.

Acknowledgments. The authors wish to thank Gary Perlman and Jonathan Grudin for reviewing a draft of the survey; Jonathan Grudin for his help in production of the survey; Jack Brown and Thomas Hemnes for their excellent legal presentations at the CHI legal debate; John Leggett and his army of student volunteers who distributed and collected the surveys at the CHI debate; Connie McFarland and Andrea Lynn for data entry and preliminary data analysis; Dan Sewell for statistical advice; Bill Curtis for encouraging the idea of the legal debate at CHI and the survey; and Mark Hall, editor-in-chief of the Jurimetrics Journal, for his editorial assistance with the article in [4], on which this column is based.

REFERENCES

1. Last frontier conference report on copyright protection for computer software. *Jurimetrics J. 30*, 13(Fall 1989).
2. Samuelson, P. Protecting user interfaces through copyright: the debate. *Proceedings of Conference on Human Factors in Computing Systems. 97* (1989).
3. Samuelson, P. Why the look and feel of software user interfaces should not be protected by copyright law. *Commun. of the ACM 32*, 563 (May 1989).
4. Samuelson, P., and Glushko, R. Comparing the views of lawyers and user interface designers on the software copyright look and feel lawsuits. *Jurimetrics J. 30*, 121 (Fall 1989).

READING QUESTIONS

1) Why would the CHI conference be a good group to survey on ownership issues. Is any group left out that is important?
2) "None of the factors characterizing the survey respondents were found to predict differences in answers concerning copyright." Why is this interesting?
3) What are the reasons that the respondents have for their rejection of "look and feel" copyright protection?
4) Does this mean the respondents were against any rules regarding intellectual property?
5) What effect did the legal debate have on respondents' views?
6) What effects on the industry did respondents think "look and feel" protection would produce? How does this square with the purpose of copyright law?
7) What is perfect appropriability, and why is it an invalid assumption about patent protection?
8) According to Levin, how does the semiconductor industry promote its returns on new technology?
9) What are the differences in opinion in different industries about the effectiveness of patent protection?
10) In terms of effectiveness, how was patent protection rated relative to other forms of protection?
11) What other purposes could patents be used for?
12) Under what circumstances does lengthening the term of patent protection help?

13) "If patent protection were inherently strong and imitation costs were high, then [substantial] restraints on licensees … might be viewed with disfavor [by public policy makers]." Explain.
14) Why would pursuing patent protection with other countries generate little benefit while costing a great deal?
15) Explain the method that Swinyard et al. used to get ratings of the "trade-off" between various kinds of pirating of software.
16) What differences were there between American and Singaporean students in knowledge of copyright law?
17) What differences were there in terms of the moral acceptability of copying software?

DISCUSSION QUESTIONS

1) The rule of thumb is that there is one illegal copy for every legal copy of any piece of microcomputer software. Check with the "self report" article in the section on computer crime to see if there are data that can validate this assumption. Are there better ways of determining the cost of piracy to software companies?
2) Is concern about intellectual property rights a cultural phenomenon (as Swinyard et al claim), or is it motivated primarily by the economic position of the parties involved? Are there concrete examples that might help make this discussion more clear?
3) Try the software copying case that Swinyard et al. present as a class exercise.
4) Identify the cultural differences evident in the Chapter 3 article by Anderson on codes of ethics. How are these disagreements similar to the ones suggested in the controversy over "look and feel" and over software piracy?

PRACTICING THE DESIGN ETHIC

1) Interview or survey at least 10 people (in your department, class, friends, family) who use a computer in some fashion. Tell each interviewee that his/her confidentiality will be protected. Determine the following information:
    • Have they ever made illegal copies of software? How many copies? Who did they give the copies to?
    • Why did (didn't) they make those copies?
    • Do they feel there are valid reasons for making copies of the software? If so, what are they?
    Summarize your data. Are there any patterns you see in the responses?
2) Do a survey similar to Samuelson & Glushko's. This would involve asking at least 10 researchers, designers, and developers questions similar to those in the survey reported here. Make sure to ask about the extent to which they borrow ideas from others in their field, and why they think this is acceptable or necessary.

CHAPTER

14

COMPUTING AND EDUCATIONAL REFORM

Like the coming revolution due to artificial intelligence (which has been "only 10 years away" for 40 years), the educational computing revolution has also sputtered. Despite continued promises that computing will change our classrooms, and regular increases in the number of computers in schools, the major changes in education have not been forthcoming. Both articles in this chapter argue that this is the "fault" not of the computer but of the expectations associated with the mere introduction of computers combined with the bureaucracy of the schools and social structure of the classroom.

Cuban compares the claims made for the computer with those made for earlier technologies and then asks a central question: "*Should* computers be used in the schools?" This provocative question focuses the attention on the models of learning that much educational computing assumes, its contrast with actual classroom experience, and the cost-effectiveness of providing enough computers to create the change the visionaries hope for. Cuban's conclusion is "a blinking yellow light." Use computers, he suggests, for those "outrageously conventional" things they are good for, and concentrate on less expensive reforms for the classroom.

Schofield provides an exquisitely detailed picture of the classroom structure that Cuban hints at. Her study of a large urban high school, involving detailed interviews and observation, gives us a picture of the day-to-day conflicts that face a teacher who wants to use technology in the classroom. She reviews the barriers in teacher beliefs, social organization of the classroom, lack of training and support, computer anxiety, etc., that stand in the way of even a concerted effort to involve computing in education. Her conclusion is that "with a few notable exceptions ... computers were actually used very little for instructional purposes ... even when they were readily available."

Both of these studies are pessimistic in tone. But they serve as useful cautionary tales to those who see great potential for educational computing. And they pointedly reveal the obstacles to achieving that potential. Again, the best efforts to use technology involve a thorough understanding of both the technology and the social situation in which it is used.

521

THE PROMISE OF THE COMPUTER[1]

Larry Cuban
Stanford University

There won't be schools in the future…I think the computer will blow up the school. That is, the school defined as something where there are classes, teachers running exams, people structured in groups by age, following a curriculum-all of that. The whole system is based on a set of structural concepts that are incompatible with the presence of the computer…But this will happen only in communities of children who have access to computers on a sufficient scale.   SEYM0UR PAPERT, 1984

Educational computing, like the Force, is with us. Microcomputers are proliferating in our schools and unless a lot of people are wrong they're here to stay. But the $64 question is whether these computers will make any difference in the education of our children. When my daughter graduates from high school in the year 2000, will she have received a better education with the help of computers than I did without them? DALE PETERSON, 1984[2]

In 1982 *Time* magazine put a computer on the cover of its issue heralding the editors' choice of "Man of the Year." In a special section headlined "Here Come the Microkids," *Time* added cutely that by "bits and bytes, the new generation spearheads an electronic revolution."[3] Predictions of the "information revolution" turn up in publication after publication. *Popular Computing* editors concluded that "schools are in the grip of a computer

---

[1] Reprinted by permission of the publisher from Cuban, L. (1986). The Promise of the Computer. Chap. 4 In *Teachers and Machines: The Classroom Use of Technology Since 1920*. Copyright © 1986 by Teachers College, Columbia University. All rights reserved.

[2] *Epigraph* sources: Seymour Papert, "Trying to Predict the Future," *Popular Computing*, October 1984, p. 38; Dale Peterson, "Nine Issues," *Popular Computing*, October 1984, p, 11. I selected these two epigraph quotes to demonstrate anew the ambitious claims of classroom computer advocates, as well as to suggest the skeptical note in their claims. Throughout this chapter, I will refer to "boosters," "enthusiasts," and "advocates" of classroom computers. While there is clearly a large number of supporters for instructional use of computers located in universities, school districts, corporate offices, and foundations, I do not suggest a monolithic view on how and why the machines are to be used. One wing of the advocates trace their origins back to enthusiasm for most forms of machine technology (e,g,, television, radio, films, language laboratories, CAI, etc.) as being far more efficient and effective in classrooms than teachers talking. The engineering orientation is most strong among the "ed techies." Another group of advocates is far more ambitious about the power of the computer and wishes to see the school, as it is currently organized, transformed into a learning environment anchored in computer technology. Yet another group sees the computerization of schools as necessary to their being relevant to society, but they also recognize that, while computer entry into schools may be slow and the uses of the machines may be unimaginative initially, this evolutionary pace is still worthwhile. Thus, while I will use such labels as "enthusiasts," readers should know that diverse views exist amidst the many who desire more instructional uses for computers.

[3] "Here Come the Microkids," *Time*, May 3, 1982, pp. 50-56.

mania."[4] Surveys report on the growing number of desk-top computers purchased by school districts. An editorial in *InfoWorld* cautions us about "Fighting the School Computer Fad."[5] Computer summer camps for children pop up like daisies every May. Two year olds in preschool sit in front of terminals, feet dangling eight inches off the floor, and punch in commands to machines. Workshops where teachers learn to program and use classroom computers are common. In the midst of fiscal retrenchment, parents raise thousands of dollars to buy microcomputers for their children's schools. As with film, radio, and instructional television, predictions of computers reshaping how schools will be organized, how teachers will teach, and how students will learn surface repeatedly. The unrelenting search for ever greater classroom productivity continues.

The usual cycle of predicting extraordinary changes in teacher practice. followed by academic studies of computers' classroom effectiveness, in turn followed by teacher reports about glitches in hardware, software, and logistics—all of this happened with computer-assisted instruction (CAI) almost two decades ago. With the advent of inexpensive desk-top machines and the promise of each student interacting with a personal computer, claims for a classroom revolution surfaced again.[6]

Yet how different is this current enthusiasm from the surge of interest in instructional television three decades ago or in classroom radio and motion pictures over a half century ago? The superficial similarities between periodic gushes in enthusiasm haunt conferences on educational technology like Marley's ghost. The similarities in claims, media interest, and investment are too vivid to simply brush aside as cynical mumblings from Neanderthal educators.

But there is, of course, a danger in viewing everything as a passing fad; recognizing a permanent and dramatic shift in practice becomes almost impossible when the metaphor of a pendulum or cycle dominates the conventional view of change in public schools. The earthquake is a change metaphor also. Did people seeing their first locomotive, telephone, automobile, and television set know instantaneously that society's tectonic plates had shifted, jolting their lives forever? Will computers in schools have as much impact on what happens as these technological inventions have had in creating new patterns of living? No one can say with any conviction. "It's hard to predict," physicist Niels Bohr was supposed to have said, "especially the future."[7]

---

[4]Editorial, *Popular Computing*, August 1983, p. 83.

[5]Joe Nathan, "Viewpoint," *InfoWorld*, July 25, 1983, p. 35.

[6]Burt Schorr, "Many Schools Buying Computers Find Problems with Using Them," *Wall Street Journal*, April 7, 1983, p. 1: Edward Fiske, "Computer Education: Update '83," *Popular Computing*, August 1983, pp. 86—96, 142—147.

[7]Edward Feigenbaum and Pamela McCorduck, *The Fifth Generation* (Boston: Addison-Wesley, 1983), p. 233.

As aids in probing the present enthusiasm for classroom computers, I offer the following set of questions. The first three are drawn from research on the spread of other technological innovations. The final question is seldom asked by policy makers or researchers, yet it is fundamental to the making of school and classroom policy.[8]

1. What is the nature of the innovation?
2. How is it being introduced?
3. Who are the users, and how much are the machines used?
4. Should computers be used in classrooms?

WHAT IS THE NATURE OF THE INNOVATION?

Advocates and observers have noted frequently the uniqueness of the computer, both in supplementing and transforming conventional classroom content and skills. Computers can display an electronic chalkboard that students can use for practicing essential skills. According to promoters, computers can lead children into understanding how the mind works in solving a problem. The process of writing and debugging a program, for example, breaks down problems into smaller, manageable chunks. Awareness of both logical and procedural thinking grows. Furthermore, there is the powerful tug that the machine has in capturing student interest—the pinball effect. Hooking children into learning with computers, boosters claim, also gives them a growing sense of self-esteem, a feeling of competence, even control, especially when students can teach adults how to use the machines. This sense of control over the machine, the argument goes, is vital to children acting independently.

The versatility of the machine's uses for drill, problem solving, motivation, and interaction suggest differences of such a magnitude as to dwarf comparisons with earlier classroom technologies that usually possessed only one or two of these characteristics. Policy makers and practitioners alike are lured by the promise of finally achieving the engineer's dream of individual instruction through a machine that has the capacity to drill and tutor each student swiftly and cheaply without regard to the pace of classmates, while simultaneously recording and reporting achievement.

Like radio, film, and video, however, there are hardware and software issues. As prices for microcomputers fall, accessibility to these machines increases. Manufacturers and reformers dream of the day when every student will have a desk-top computer. Stunning jumps in school-district purchases and corporate gift programs suggest student access to machines will expand beyond the current handful of computers for each school. Nonetheless, the

---

[8] See Rogers, chaps. 6, 7, 9, and 11. I chose these questions and not others because of the direction of my own research.

programs that run the machines continue to influence school use.[9] Inadequate software, especially in social studies, English, foreign languages, art, and music continues to weaken efforts to increase teacher use. Unsuitable programs persist since costs to produce improved software remain high. Even with these substantial issues, unquenched enthusiasm for computers in schools continues.[10]

HOW IS THE INNOVATION BEING INTRODUCED?

As with film, radio, and instructional television, cultural forces pressed schools to embrace computers. Growing concern for the United States losing its grip on markets that had U.S. stamped all over them (e.g., steel, autos, and high-tech industries) drove corporate officials to examine public schools and to join lawmakers in correcting what came to be viewed as a national problem: the inefficiency of U.S. schools in producing sufficient numbers of engineers, mathematicians, technicians, and workers flexible enough to survive in a rapidly changing workplace. Many states, for example, mandated stiffer graduation requirements, including a course in computer literacy.

Even before lawmakers wrote such language into bills, many parents, themselves touched by the computerization of the workplace, feared that their children lagged behind in college and job competition. Television commercials showed teachers suggesting to anxious parents the purchase of a home computer that would help their child do homework. Parents urged school boards to buy classroom computers. Active mothers and fathers went further and gave microcomputers to schools, a clear signal to the principal and teachers that the machines were to be used with children. Thus, much of the drumbeat for instructional use of computers came from outside schools.[11]

Not all administrators and teachers had to be drafted into the campaign for classroom use of the new machine. Substantial numbers of teachers promoted computers, and networks of computer buffs sprang up across the country. In visiting schools, for example, I frequently would meet at least one teacher or principal who believed deeply in the importance of students using computers. Championing the computer in that school or district, the practitioner and a small band of colleagues would lobby the central office for money and time to build a program. Sometimes inventive and entrepreneurial, such practitioners would beg foundations and local businesses for tax-sheltered gifts of microcomputers, just to launch a

---

[9]Milton Chen and William Paisley, "Children and the New Computer Technologies: Research Implications of the Second Electronic Revolution." in *Mass Communication Review Yearbook*, vol. 7 (Beverly Hills, CA: Sage, in press).
[10]Decker Walker, "Promise, Potential, and Pragmatism: Computers in High School," *IFG Policy Notes* (Summer 1984), p. 3. See also Decker Walker, "Reflections on the Educational Potential and Limitations of Microcomputers," *Kappan* 64 (October 1983), pp. 103—107.
[11]Fiske, p. 89.

program. They appeared, however, to be the exceptions. Most teachers and administrators seemed initially to be uninvolved in the hoopla.[12]

Once under way in a school or district, though, a growing clamor from policy makers increased pressure upon teachers to enlist in the movement. Other teachers joined regular users who saw early the rising tide and wanted their students to be part of the apparent information revolution. Already, there are some discernible patterns emerging.

Computers turn up in classes of willing users or teachers who are asked by the principal to take a workshop so they can teach a new computer course the following year. More often than not, teachers who may have a home computer and have expressed interest or see the connection with their subject (frequently math and science) volunteer. Programs for gifted students turn up as common reasons for introducing computers into elementary schools, with the machines located in the library. There has been much variety in which schools (i.e., urban, suburban, or rural) adopted micro-computers, and how they did so. This again highlights the external push for accelerated use of the machine and the intense internal uncertainty over the best use of the new technology.[13]

Note how previous efforts to install new technologies into schools also encountered initial enthusiasm from many school boards, superintendents, and groups of teachers. In those instances, the decision to adopt classroom radio programs or video lessons came from the top of the organization. Implementation directives flowed downward; that is, plans were drawn, money appropriated, equipment purchased, and guidelines distributed from district headquarters. The current embrace of the new computer technology, however, contains simultaneous top-down and bottom-up movement.[14]

Faced with uncertainty about computer use and the swift changes in the technology but still hearing a strong signal from parents and school boards to do something with computers, careful superintendents and principals, acting as gatekeepers for innovations entering their schools, have purchased some machines. For the principal, compliance with a school board's or superintendent's interest produces a few machines located in the library or the rooms of some teacher advocates. A few machines buy necessary

---

[12]In May and June of 1983, I visited seven high schools in California, Nevada, and Arizona that had been nominated as exemplary by the U.S. Department of Education, in a national effort to recognize effective secondary schools. My impressions are drawn from those schools' programs in beginning and sustaining computers in classrooms. Supplementing these impressions were my many visits to San Francisco and San Jose area schools.

[13]See Richard Shavelson et al., "Successful" Teachers' Patterns of Microcomputer-Based Mathematics and Science Instruction: A Rand Note (Santa Monica, CA: Rand Corp., 1984) Gail Meister, Successful Integration of Microcomputers in an Elementary School, Project Report No. 84-A13 (Stanford, CA: Institute for Research on Educational Finance and Governance, 1984).

[14]For a study that reveals some of the different approaches districts have taken to introducing and sustaining machine use in classrooms, see Karen Sheingold et al., "Microcomputer Use in Schools: Developing a Research Agenda," Harvard Educational Review 53 (November 1983), pp. 412—432.

insurance for withstanding criticism from parents and superiors for blocking the future. Such token adoption of an innovation, echoing earlier school responses to machines, not only insulates a principal (or superintendent) from static over the presence of modern technology in schools but also buffers unwilling or unconvinced teachers from the intrusive enthusiasm of boosters. Hence, the number of machines in schools grows, feeding researchers' appetites for statistics on number of machines per building. As with other innovations, however, such figures seldom bear a strong relationship to the frequency of teacher or student use.

WHO ARE THE USERS, AND HOW MUCH ARE THE MACHINES USED?

Teachers and administrators are the primary users. The computer's power to store, process, and retrieve information about attendance, scheduling, grades, inventories, and a host of other clerical tasks make it ideal for administrative uses both in the principal's office and the classroom. Other classroom uses fall into the visual workbook category, with simulations, writing, and machine tutoring among the less-used options. Teaching students to program computers appears to be increasing.

Elementary-school teachers use drill software in skill subjects, and the use of LOGO and programs for writing is reportedly growing. In secondary schools, the common pattern is to install a computer lab with twenty or more machines and schedule students for courses in programming or district-devised versions of computer literacy. Generally, math and science teachers use machines for classroom instruction more often than English, social studies, and foreign language teachers. Teachers, then, still control how much the classroom door opens to admit computers and how much they are used—provided, of course, that machines and appropriate software are accessible.[15]

The few statistics on classroom use underlines the uneven, limited penetration of machines into teachers' instructional repertoires. Determining what levels of teacher use now exist is like trying to snap a photograph of a speeding bicyclist. Every few months, a new survey on school computers announces increased purchases. One survey reports that the number of microcomputers available for instructional use tripled in 18 months (fall 1980 to spring 1982) to over 100,000 machines.[16] Two years later, that number climbed to 325,000. By 1984, of the 82,000 schools in the nation, 56,000 (or 68 percent) had at least one computer (either a terminal or micro), for an average of one machine for every 92 students.[17] In 1985, 92 percent of all secondary schools had at least one machine available for instruction; for

---

[15]See Walker, "Promise, Potential, and Pragmatism," pp. 3—4, and Sheingold article cited above.
[16]National Center of Educational Statistics, *Instructional Use of Computers in Public Schools* (Washington, D.C.: U.S. Department of Education, 1982), pp. 1—2.
[17]*Education Week*, April 18, 1984, pp. 1, 14.

elementary schools, it was 82 percent. The number of machines per school jumped sharply also. By 1984, the average elementary school had 5 machines, while the typical secondary school had just over 13.[18]

Such figures echo the results drawn from surveys on radio and television sets and film projectors. Although district purchases of equipment made machines accessible to schools, actual use of the earlier technologies by teachers and students was disappointing to promoters.

A 1981-1982 mid year survey of computer use, done by Johns Hopkins University researchers, calculated that almost 5 million students averaged nine hours each in front of a computer during the entire year. They reported that computers went unused more than half of the school day in three out of every four schools. Most schools used the computer (usually located in tightly secured labs, the library, math and science rooms, or the principal's office) about an hour a day. Student use varied between less than thirty minutes a week for three-quarters of lower-grade children to almost an hour a week for the same percentage of junior and senior high-school students.[19] Rand researchers studied sixty elementary- and secondary-school teachers identified as exemplary users of classroom computers in twenty-five California school districts. These regular and frequent users reported that students spent less than an hour a week receiving instruction via classroom computers.[20]

Even were those figures to double and triple in the next few years, it would still mean the typical elementary-school student would work a computer about 1.5 hours a week, while for upper-grade students the figure would be less than three hours a week. (Note that an instructional week typically runs between twenty-five to thirty hours.) None of these calculations, of course, considers how the curriculum would be reshaped to accommodate increased machine use, especially assuming that the amount of instructional time each week remains as it is. Nor do any of these calculations consider the differences in access to machines between male and female, white and nonwhite, and rich and poor students.[21]

And teacher use? In schools with computers, the Johns Hopkins University study found that only one or two teachers regularly used them. Researchers also found that computer use depended upon where in the building the machines were put. A National Education Association (NEA) questionnaire of its membership in 1982 also reported infrequent use. Teacher interest in using the machines ran high, according to the NEA survey, but only 6 percent said that they used the machines in their

---

[18]*Education Week*, March 27, 1985, p. 6.
[19]*Education Week*, July 27, 1983, p. 7.
[20]Shavelson et. al., pp. 33—49.
[21]Sheingold, pp. 426—427; Robert Hess and Irene Miura, "Access," *IFG Policy Notes* (Summer 1984), pp. 4—5.

classrooms. More than 80 percent said that they would like to take computer courses.[22]

Coming as they do in the beginning years of an enthusiasm of new technology aimed at altering classroom instruction, these surveys report a small but growing number of computers per building, limited student contact with the technology, few teachers with machines in their classrooms, and a growing cadre of energetic, willing colleagues using microcomputers as an adjunct to the core of instructional approaches.

Such results, again, echo familiar tones from earlier efforts to install innovations; however, patterns of infrequent film and video use were reported a decade or more after the technology was introduced, and microcomputers (excluding the twenty-year experience with CAI) are yet in their infancy. Low estimates of use may be due only to the common obstacles of inaccessible hardware, inappropriate software, and untrained teachers. I suspect, however, that, even if teacher use of machines and student contact triples, such levels of usage still would disappoint reformers and policy makers. Even then, most teachers still would be closing their doors to the technology, and the percentage of the instructional time each week devoted to desktop computers still would be slight. Were that to occur, I would expect that teachers, as in the past, would stand accused of resisting progress, of being neotroglodytes.

The temptation to blame teachers for the uneven penetration of computers into classrooms is, indeed, seductive. How infuriating it must be for true believers in the machine's liberating qualities and sheer productivity to find teachers blocking classroom doors, preventing the entry of this magical innovation, this panacea for the school's problems. If uncritical admirers of this electronic technology succumb to the temptation, they, like their forbears, will overlook the importance of settings in shaping instructional behavior. Limited teacher use of new technology may be due to organizational constraints built into classrooms and schools as workplaces.

Using one computer in the classroom as a student tutor, with a library of software available to the teacher, falls within well-known terrain: that is, the teacher uses the machine as a learning center for occasional student play when class members have completed their assigned work. Using the machine to drill a student in fractions or grammar or using it with proper software to enrich students' knowledge also falls well within the familiar. Such teaching practices resemble earlier uses of films, radio, and instructional television. Programming a microcomputer to reduce teachers' paperwork by preparing and marking tests, keeping attendance, and recording grades is also an appealing and certainly possible classroom use.

---

[22]Charles Euchner, "Teachers' Interest in Computers Is High, but Usage Is Low," *Education Week*, January 12, 1983, p. 5.

Gradually introducing computers into classrooms for such instructional and administrative tasks may succeed, since these limited uses respond to teacher-defined problems. Such solutions help teachers to cope with classroom issues. But for most teachers to instruct students in programming, to use the computer as a problem-solving tool, to learn procedural reasoning, and to encourage students to work alone with the machine in order to learn new content and skills violates what many informed observers and practitioners know to be the organizational realities. Transforming classroom practices through the computer stretch well beyond what many teachers view as possible, given the persistent imperatives tucked away in the DNA of classroom life.

That DNA is what I sketched out earlier as the implacable realities that policy makers institutionalized over a century ago: A teacher is required to face thirty or more students in a classroom for a set period of time, maintain order, and inspire the class to learn content and skills mandated by the community. Over the last century, teachers have adapted to this setting by generating a repertoire of practical methods that have come to be called teacher-centered instruction, classroom teaching, direct instruction, and so forth. School and classroom settings, as they have been and are presently organized, determine in large part the general direction that formal instruction takes.

Yet different models of teaching and learning with computers, suggested by Thomas Dwyer, Seymour Papert, and others, argue against this conventional version of teaching. In Dwyer's work with students in Pittsburgh, for example, he has constructed math settings where students control the technology and teachers act as "knowledgeable facilitators." Labs where teachers and students jointly become "discoverers of truths" permitted Dwyer to construct an environment where the new technology made learning math both natural and exhilarating. The customary classroom arrangement with the teacher in control gives way, according to Dwyer, to student-controlled computers and a world of experiences to be "lived in by both teacher and student." According to Dwyer, such labs do exist, but only in a small number of schools.[23]

Similarly, Seymour Papert's work in a few New York City schools where teachers have been trained to use fifteen or more machines with students suggests that at some future point the current teacher-student bond would be realigned into a mutual search for knowledge in real-life settings,. finally bringing into focus the dreams of John Dewey.[24]

---

[23]"Thomas Dwyer," in Robert Taylor (Ed.), *The Computer in the School: Tutor, Tool, Tutee* (New York: Teachers College Press,1980), pp. 96, 114.
[24]Seymour Papert, *Mindstorms: Children, Computers. and Powerful Ideas* (New York: Basic Books, 1980), pp. 177-187. Pat Suppes also predicted that teaching would change as computers penetrated schools in "The Uses of Computers in Education," *Scientific American* 215 (September 1966). pp. 218—219.

Left unsaid in their work with school districts is that while such arrangements are special, thus far they remain far outside the mainstream of public schooling. Most reports of school use of computers describe one or two machines in a classroom, or a room equipped with ten to twenty desk-top microcomputers where programming and literacy (however defined) are taught.

SHOULD COMPUTERS BE USED IN CLASSROOMS?

At this point, let me tilt the analysis slightly by questioning a basic assumption that thus far has directed the discussion of computers used for instruction. All of this analysis and speculation has assumed that the machine is a necessity and a boon to schooling. State and district policy makers, manufacturers, reformers, and most researchers seldom ask whether computers should be introduced into schools for instructional use. They ask only how computers should be used.

Because a machine can be used as a tutor, tool, or tutee or some creative mix of these, how it is used is uncertain. A computer can be programmed to teach subject matter and skills to students in CAI: it can be used by both teachers and administrators as a tool for keeping attendance, grades, inventories, and scheduling; it can be used by both teachers and students to create programs in which both machine and person learn from one another. Uncertain as to how the machine should be used, policy makers ask questions such as

1. Should we provide every student with access to a computer for a minimal time period, to insure some degree of literacy?
2. Should all students be exposed to programming languages? If so, which language? BASIC? LOGO? PASCAL?
3. Should we pursue CAI?
4. Should every school have ten to fifteen machines in a laboratory that is accessible to classes and individual students?
5. Should the number of machines differ for lower- and upper-grade schools?

Because no research evidence provides reliable guidelines and no consensus among professional educators yet exists for how machines should be used for instruction, such questions (and there are numerous others) have wildly different price tags attached to answers that experts offer to policy makers.[25]

In short, while the machine's versatility and promise for instruction exceeds the minuses of persistent hardware and software problems, knotty policy questions over how to computerize classrooms still puzzle decision makers. Few top officials, however, stop asking the "how" questions long

---

[25]Taylor. pp. 1—10. Also see experience of Scarsdale, New York, as reported in Charles Euchner, "A District Learns to 'Debug' Its Curriculum," *Education Week*, December 15, 1982, p. 6.

enough to reach the more fundamental issue: Should computers be used in classrooms?

Such a "should" question seems pointless, even anachronistic, in the rising tide of unrestrained glee for classroom computers. But unless debate occurs about the conditions under which computers may be used, I suspect that scorching criticism will be leveled once again at teachers and principals for blocking yet another innovative technology aimed at making classrooms productive. Tardy as this debate may be, open discussion is essential, if for no other reason than to map out the intellectual terrain that practitioners and noneducators must negotiate in dealing with computers in schools. Until recently, few scholars and policy makers considered this basic question. As gatekeepers to classrooms, teachers do ask the question of themselves and their colleagues. "The order of our questions is important," Harriet Cuffaro writes. "If *how* is asked before *why*, we will be building a shaky foundation."[26]

To ask this question of any technology, but especially about microcomputers, is to reopen inquiry into what the purposes of instruction are, what should be taught, and how children learn. These are tough and troubling points with which few policy makers wish to wrestle. I offer here three points of argument regarding whether or not teachers should use computers as a central or even substantial part of classroom instruction:

1. Cost-effectiveness of computers used in instruction
2. Increased mechanization of teaching
3. Impact upon children

Cost-Effectiveness of Computers Used in Instruction

In all of the enthusiasm for classroom computers, an assumption that has gone largely unchallenged is that these machines, with appropriate programs, could teach students knowledge and skills both efficiently and effectively. The inference in the shadow of the assumption is that the new technology could get students to learn better, faster, and more cheaply than any other instructional tactic.

Economist Henry Levin and his associates partially tested that assumption and inference.[27] They chose four common tools policy makers use to improve math and reading skills: reducing class size, increasing the amount of time devoted to skill instruction, tutoring, and computer-assisted instruction. The researchers collected all the studies done on these strategies and statistically analyzed their findings, especially how much effect each intervention had on student performance as measured by test scores. They

---

[26]Harriet Cuffaro. "Microcomputers in Education: Why Is Earlier Better?" *Teachers College Record* 85 (Summer 1984), p. 560.

[27] Henry Levin, Gene V. Glass, and Gail R. Meister, *Cost Effectiveness of Four Educational Interventions*, Project Report No. 84— A11 (Stanford, CA: Institute for Research on Educational Finance and Governance, 1984).

then priced what each component of the strategy would cost. Combining the known effects of each approach with its total costs, the researchers produced a cost-effectiveness ratio.[28]

What these researchers found is in some ways surprising. Students teaching students (peer tutoring) emerged as far more cost-effective than computer-assisted instruction. CAI was slightly more cost-effective than reducing class size from thirty-five to thirty or even to twenty students. Increasing the amount of time devoted to math and reading was by far the least cost effective.[29]

The researchers post a number of cautions about the study's limitations. For example, they used a popular CAI program concentrating on drill; other programs and computer uses might have been superior. Also, costs and results on an approach may vary in time from school to school.[30]

Aware of the study's limitations, I only note this research as simply one instance of applying two criteria favored by so many policy makers; efficiency and effectiveness. My point is not to convince anyone that hiring older students to coach younger ones is cheaper and better than stocking a lab with desk-top computers. Rather, I wish to underscore the flabbiness in the assumption that computerized instruction is automatically superior to other conventional classroom approaches in boosting academic performance. New machines stocked with flawless software may hook students' interest and improve their proficiencies, but the unit costs may be prohibitive compared to alternatives. Computerized instruction used as a tool, tutor, or tutee should not escape application of this criterion.

Increased Mechanization of Teaching

Converting teaching into a science historically has driven many reformers, researchers, and policy makers toward embracing numerous innovations that have promised precision harnessed to efficiency. Raymond Callahan documented how academics and administrators in the early decades of this century seized upon scientific management as both a philosophy and set of tools with which to transform American schools into productive businesses. The marriage of efficiency experts and educational administrators produced by the 1920s a mindset among scholars and practitioners that schools could be managed like corporations.[31]

Viewing schools as bureaucracies and teachers as technicians who execute in their classrooms mandates ordered by top-level managers is a perspective that has ebbed and flowed in popularity since the 1920s. Efforts to introduce systematic classroom procedures and rational teaching methods

---

[28]Ibid., pp. 3-4.
[29]Ibid.. p. 30.
[30]Ibid., pp. 30—31.
[31]Callahan, chaps. 4-5. See also Tyack, *The One Best System*. pp. 129—147, 182—216.

became especially faddish in the 1960s and 1970s with the growing awareness on the part of state and federal policy makers that many American children left school unfit to read, write, and calculate.

The surge of popular interest in making schools productive and accountable spurred efforts to train teachers to write precise objectives aimed at producing student results (e.g., "by June, 95 percent of my class will list correctly and in chronological order the wars that America fought since 1776"). Many teacher education institutions altered their curricula by breaking down the act of teaching into measurable behaviors that could be taught separately to prospective teachers (e.g., how to praise students, how to ask questions). States mandated testing programs that required teachers to concentrate on the skills that legislators believed were important (e.g., minimum competency tests, reading and math achievement exams). More recently, the Effective Schools reform movement, which gives special attention to improving low-income, minority students' test scores through a variety of school-based and district-directed strategies, has focused on certain teaching methods (e.g., monitoring student work, clarity in presenting information, question asking). Research has shown that these instructional practices yield improved test scores. Central to all of these efforts is the impulse to make teaching planned, systematic, and engineered.[32]

These and other developments, including the growth of unions and collective bargaining, have hardened the view that schools and classrooms are places where complex tasks can be broken apart, improved, and put back together to produce informed and skilled graduates. Teaching, according to this perspective, can be done by anyone who possesses the appropriate technical skills.

The periodic surges of interest in introducing video, film, radio, and computers overlap these larger efforts to bureaucratize schooling and rationalize teaching. Promoters believe that these machines give teachers additional tools for enhancing productivity. The unexamined assumption, of course, is that policy makers committed to viewing instruction as a technical process believe that student learning is mechanical; that is, what teachers do skillfully will cause predictable student outcomes. No persuasive body of evidence exists yet to confirm that belief.

Few of the various reform efforts have considered seriously the crucial nonrational elements of teaching. Some researchers have pointed out how highly teachers prize the emotional bonds with students, bonds that nourish learning. Others have found that teachers see student academic and emotional growth in holistic rather than narrow, fragmented terms. A few researchers have written how teachers see what they do as much closer to an art than a

---

[32]Arthur Wise, Legislated Learning (Berkeley, CA: University of California Press, 1979), chaps. 2-4; Larry Cuban, "Transforming the Frog into a Prince: Effective Schools Research, Policy, and Practice at the District Level," *Harvard Educational Review* 54 (May 1984), pp. 129—151.

science. Affection for speed, accuracy, detail, and efficiency—benchmarks for the engineer—are respected and at times even cultivated by teachers but clearly are of secondary importance to classroom learning. Such views embedded in how teachers see what they do slow the conversion of teaching into a technical process.[33]

Too often forgotten by policy makers intent upon transforming teaching practice is how much classroom learning is anchored in the emotional lives of thirty children and one teacher together for large chunks of time in a small, crowded space. What some have labeled "emotional rationality" only underlines how divorcing the mind from feelings and the senses robs children of learning about drama, music, art, nature, and relationships with responsible, caring adults. Even in the hard-core, cognitive skills of analysis, emotions fuel the drive for understanding and soften the abrasive edge of calculation.[34]

The complex relationships between teachers and students become uncertain in the face of microcomputers. What holds many teachers in classrooms for large portions of their lifetimes are the inner pleasures gained from contacts with young people. The keen satisfaction that comes from seeing an able student mature intellectually and emotionally rewards a teacher, regardless of whether the student or parent acknowledges the teacher's contribution. Teachers gain pleasure from the emotional circuitry wired into intense bonds that develop between them and certain students, often lasting for decades. The touches, smiles, warmth, and even the frowns, annoyance, and anger that pass between teacher and student cement ties that deepen learning and give gratification to teachers.[35]

I mean to portray no rhapsodic Winslow Homer scene of silver-haired teachers and laughing students alive to one another and their surroundings threatened by the golem of computerized learning. I mean only to say the obvious: Classrooms are steeped in emotions. In the fervent quest for precise rationality and technical efficiency, introducing to each classroom enough computers to tutor and drill children can dry up that emotional life, resulting in withered and uncertain relationships.

Students working with computers alone or in pairs for long periods of time lose time for direct and sustained contact with teachers. Bonds develop instead between students and machines. Information comes from the machine; the machine generates praise and nudges the student along programmed paths constructed to guide the user to further learning. Adult-

---

[33] Jackson, Life in Classrooms, chaps. 4—5: Elliot Eisner, "On the Uses of Educational Connoisseurship and Criticism for Evaluating Classroom Life," *Teachers College Record* 78 (Fall 1977), pp. 345—358.
[34] Douglas Sloan, "On Raising Critical Questions about the Computer in Education," *Teachers College Record* 85 (Summer 1984), pp. 539—545.
[35] Jackson, *Life in Classrooms*, chap. 4; Lortie, pp. 101—108.

child ties may unravel as a consequence of the newly developed child-machine liaison.[36]

While the argument can be carried to an extreme, making the classroom into a setting where few exchanges occur, that is not my intention. Some enthusiasts even argue that machines increase student-teacher interaction. The point I offer is simply that those advocates who push for a shift in the control of learning from teachers to students interacting with machines probably misunderstand how teacher communication, expectations, and feelings produce those very classroom features that give a human touch to instruction and generate those intense inner pleasures for teachers. Because so much of teaching is imagination, improvisation, and pacing combined with student rapport, shifting the center of gravity to machine-student exchanges lessens greatly the joys inherent to the art of teaching. At a deep level that often goes unspoken, I believe that many teachers may sense how the introduction of machines into classrooms endangers those intangible, highly prized rewards that count so heavily in why teachers decide to endure in a most difficult but intensely satisfying job.

These issues surely play a role in why the mechanization of teaching has proceeded so slowly over the last century. Efforts to introduce behavioral objectives, competency-based teacher education, and technology were seldom wholly or even partially successful in transforming classrooms into squeakless, efficient operations tended by teacher-mechanics. While there is much in classrooms that appears mechanical, such as lesson plans, rows of desks, worksheets, and textbook assignments, these practices do not constitute the core experiences or central aspects of most classroom life.

The major resistance to converting classrooms into technical enterprises, as I suggested, has come from the organizational realities of school and classroom life and the teacher's holistic perspective on what's important to young people. Without knowing exactly what the anticipated—much less the unanticipated—consequences of shipping machines into classrooms will be, prudence would suggest a yellow flashing light rather than a green one. Beyond whispering caution in policy makers' ears, however, here are some thoughts:

- Maybe the teacher's perspective about learning and children is correct. Perhaps learning is largely opportunistic, spontaneous, and unpredictable. In classrooms with a couple of desktop computers, teachers and students still can take advantage of those special moments. But computer-rich classrooms geared to machine-student interactions are very different settings that construct a very different role for the teacher.

---

[36]This issue of machine-student bonds is explored in Sherry Turkle. *The Second Self: Computers and the Human Spirit* (New York: Simon and Schuster, 1984), chaps. 1 and 3.

• Maybe the pedagogy (large- and small-group instruction, discussions, seatwork, textbook assignments, and so on) that teachers hold with great persistence (and that reformers label as archaic and inefficient) should be bolstered and improved upon. That pedagogy still provides an emotional foundation to cognitive growth and may need to be nourished, enhanced, and protected, but not satirized.

In a culture in love with swift change and big profit margins, yet reluctant to contain powerful social mechanisms that strongly influence children (e.g., television), no other public institution offers these basic but taken-for-granted occasions for continuous, measured intellectual and emotional growth of children. Without much evidence to support unrestrained entry of machines into classrooms, reopening policy discussions on both the how and the why seem to be in order. In that renewed policy discussion, both the merits of computers as classroom tools and the qualitative issues embedded in the act of teaching need to be considered seriously, especially because teaching is less susceptible to measurement but so profoundly important to the subjective, artistic side of instruction. As Philip Jackson says:

> People who are interested in the application of learning theory or the engineering point of view to teaching practice often have as their goal the transformation of teaching from something crudely resembling an art to something crudely resembling a science. But there is no good evidence to suggest that such a transformation is either possible or desirable. An equally reasonable goal . . is to seek an understanding of the teaching process as it is commonly performed before making an effort to change it. As we learn more about what goes on in these densely populated hives of educational activity it may turn out that we will seek to preserve, rather than to transform, whatever amount of artistry is contained in the teacher's work.[37]

Impact on Children

If the full influence, both positive and negative, of television watching on children continues to be debated three decades after its introduction, how can anyone assess the complexity of what happens to children using classroom computers? The image of five year olds pressing keys to create designs on a screen or learning to write or solve a problem feeds the enthusiasm of many parents and educators. But no one can answer with confidence the question of what impact continuous exposure to the surrogate reality called up on a computer screen has upon children.

---

[37]Jackson, *Life in Classrooms*, p. 175.

All we see in the media are the attractive, eye-catching pictures of small children working with machines. Concerns seldom are raised about negative or questionable influences. My concerns at this time concentrate on these three points:

1. No consensus exists among scholars and practitioners on how children should learn and how teachers should teach.
2. There is much uncertainty over what students can learn from computerized lessons.
3. Collateral learning may be more significant in children's lives than the formal lessons taught by machines.

Lack of Consensus on Learning Theories and Teaching Methods

Among teachers, administrators, and researchers, various theories of learning compete for attention. Operant conditioning, information processing, and social learning are three dominant ways of viewing how children learn. While practitioner vocabulary is often atheoretical (as in most practical arts), conceptual frameworks drawn from one or more of these theories exist in their minds, nonetheless. Teacher beliefs, for example, are working theoretical models that guide decision making regarding how to present content, how to teach skills, how to build student confidence, and a dozen other "hows" of teaching. Although few teachers would use the technical language favored by researchers, the basic core of concepts within each theory is familiar.

To cope with the awesome complexity of diversity in students and the unexpected in classroom life, practitioners develop expert knowledge of situations that arise in classes. In identifying any single learning episode, the experienced teacher chooses a strategy that fits the demands of that particular situation, tailoring instructional tactics to match the situation's inevitable uniqueness. What teachers select from their expert knowledge and apply to the singular setting is anchored in one or more theoretical constructs. No single theory of learning (or instruction) yet encompasses the uniqueness of classroom events or student differences.[38]

Computerized learning, however, is anchored in at least two of these theories: operant conditioning (drill) and information processing (programming). Teachers will use software that gets students to practice skills or remember knowledge—staples of teaching practice. Drill is common and considered by teachers as an important, if not tedious, instructional task. Already such software accounts for a substantial portion of machine use in classrooms. I see no problem here.

Where I see a potential issue is the growing popularity of LOGO, BASIC, and other programming languages. Formal languages appeal to

---

[38]For descriptions of theories, see N. L. Gage and David Berliner. *Educational Psychology* (Boston: Houghton Mifflin, 1984), chaps. 11—15.

advocates of classroom machines because they believe that children learning to program will develop analytic thinking skills and procedural reasoning that goes far beyond what teachers do in classrooms now. Drawing turtles and geometric figures on the screen and assembling programs, for example, teaches students to be aware of how both the machine and the human mind operate as information processors. The accelerating passion for LOGO as a means for teaching preschoolers to read and write accepts implicitly a cognitive learning theory that dwells upon such concepts as attention, memory, and retrieval of information. Both theoretical and practical questions arise from this constricted view of a growing child as an information processor.[39]

Adherents of the theories of Jean Piaget (including computer scientist Seymour Papert) stress the various developmental stages of thought that children pass through. But computer enthusiasts who advocate giving children a head start by getting them to think abstractly as soon as possible argue that seven year olds can leapfrog a developmental phase; that is, they can move from preoperational (ages 2—7) to formal operations (ages 11—16) without passing through concrete operating (ages 7—11). Critics suggest that this is a misreading of Piaget and is, at best, experimental. At worst, such a view perpetuates a narrow view of children as mere collections of cognitive abilities divorced from feeling and contact with stimulating surroundings.[40]

Furthermore, there is simply no persuasive body of evidence that children learning how to think procedurally or conceptually can transfer that learning to other settings. In a stinging rebuke of the notion of transfer, another computer scientist, Joseph Weizenbaum, responded this way to an interviewer's query about how computers improve children's problem-solving abilities: "If that were true, then computer professionals would lead better lives than the rest of the population. We know very well that isn't the case. There is, as far as I know, no more evidence programming is good for the mind than Latin is, as is sometimes claimed."[41]

The major point is that a heavy reliance upon classroom computers would draw heavily upon cognitive learning theory alone, forcibly narrowing teachers' repertoires enough to diminish the range of approaches skilled practitioners could use in classrooms. Moreover, such emphasis upon machines would be a terribly risky experiment, because researchers lack sufficient evidence that children exposed to machine interaction for long periods of time develop the full range of values, knowledge, and skills

---

[39]These quesions are raised in Hubert Dreyfus and Stuart Dreyfus. "Putting Computers in Their Proper Place: Analysis Versus Intuition in the Classroom," *Teachers College Record* 85 (Summer 1984), pp. 587—601.

[40]Papert. *Mindstorms.* pp. 173—176: Cuffaro. p. 560: John Davy "Mindstorms in the Lamplight," *Teachers College Record* 85 (Summer 1984), pp. 549—558.

[41]Joseph Weizenbaum, in an interview with Franz-Olivier Giesbert of *Le Nouvel Observoteur*, December 2, 1983, cited in *Harper's*, March 1984, p. 22.

expected by parents and the community. Just because researchers and visionary academics see computers as an inexorable tide engulfing this society is not sufficient justification for experimenting upon a captive and naive population.

What Can Students Learn from Computerized Lessons?

The claims that students acquire basic skills through CAI have been verified over the last two decades. CAI is effective in certain domains, under certain conditions. Whether it is cost-effective or enhances other instructional goals, of course, are separate and contestable issues.

Some claim that computers also will teach students more powerful ways of thinking than presently are taught. In the last section I mentioned the criticism of this assertion: beyond assertions and rebuttals, however, few studies have produced consistent findings that support either side of the exchange. Caution in purchasing equipment and software for this purpose seems appropriate, given the uncertainty, in both research and practice, over the quality and effectiveness of what is learned from computers.[42]

What Kinds of Learning Are Most Important to Children?

"Perhaps the greatest of all pedagogical fallacies," John Dewey wrote in *Experience and Education*, "is the notion that a person learns only the particular thing he is studying at the time."[43] Collateral learning—absorption of attitudes that accompany the formal lesson—often exceeds the importance of what is taught directly.

No body of evidence on collateral learning yet exists to persuade critics or advocates of classroom computers how much more is learned by students beyond the lesson on the screen. I include this point because such learning is observable, but its magnitude, pervasiveness, and persistence remain open to questions.

Harriet Cuffaro asks what a youngster learns when she presses the keyboard to call up cars and garages on a screen to figure out how to park a car in the garage. Eye-hand coordination? Perhaps. A sense of control? Not really, since the programmed instructions produce alternate paths from which the child chooses. She directs the car on the screen, unaware of the mysterious program as she presses the keys. Cuffaro then asks what occurs when the same girl parks a car when playing with blocks. Her eye-hand coordination now must deal with three dimensions, not just the two on the screen. The block that is the car must be maneuvered physically, by hand, to

---

[42]Walker, "Promise, Potential, and Pragmatism," p. 3: Mary Alice White, "Synthesis of Research on Electronic Learning," *Educational Leadership* (May 1983), pp. 13—15: Stanley Pogrow, "Linking Technology Use to School Improvement," in Allan Odden and L. Dean Webb (Eds.), *School Finance and School Improvement* (Cambridge, MA: Ballinger, 1983), pp. 133—135.
[43]Cited in Cuffaro, p. 567.

fit into a garage made of blocks. Cuffaro says, "The computer version of parking a car is action in a vacuum, motion without context, and with reality twice removed."[44]

She argues that the unanticipated lessons that children pick up informally when working with microcomputers should give educators pause before plunging ahead with the new technology.

> It is the presence of these collateral learnings—the distance and narrowing of physical reality, the magical quality of pressing keys, the "invisible" sharing of control, the oversimplification of process, the need for precision and timing—that merit great attention when thinking about young children's learning and the use of microcomputers.[45]

Cuffaro and others single out the computer's power to teach many significant, misleading, and unintentional lessons to children beyond the programmed ones. Few researchers can say with much confidence what the effect is, upon any given child, of sustained exposure to a two-dimensional reality displayed on a computer screen. Few scholars have investigated the computer learning environment, which John Davy calls "mentally rich" but "perceptually extremely impoverished."[46]

Even fewer researchers know what attitudes children carry away from prolonged contact with computerized lessons. Davy suggests in his critique of *Mindstorms* that if this technology is needed to introduce children to powerful ideas because teachers can't, as Seymour Papert argues, what does that teach children about where ideas come from? What, Davy asks rhetorically, is more cognitively powerful than people? If teachers do an inept job of presenting and generating ideas, "should we not be looking at how teachers work rather than selling them a prosthesis?"[47]

Skeptics like Davy make a fundamental point in their criticism of massive classroom use of computers;

> At the heart of real life is working with people. being with people, understanding people...As long as classrooms include real teachers, cognitive development cannot, in the nature of the situation, be divorced from emotional, social, and moral experience.[48]

Joseph Weizenbaum makes a similar point from a different angle. Because the programmer's thinking is linear, logical, and rule governed, that kind of technical, analytic thought (highly prized by engineers and policy makers) magnifies what he calls "instrumental reasoning." Such reasoning

---

[44]Cuffaro, p. 561.
[45]Ibid.
[46]Davy, p. 550.
[47]Ibid., p. 554.
[48]Ibid.

amplifies calculation, prizes numbers, and elevates scientific experts to social engineers; such reasoning, he says, has little to do with creativity, intuition, and feeling.[49]

What, then, is learned from computers? Davy, Weizenbaum, and others claim that computerized reasoning is essentially technical and nonemotional, divorced from the richness of human experience. The brain's cortex is not a whole human being; it is an important part but still a fragment. Computerized reasoning is but a sliver of the emotional rationality that constitutes thought. For students to view what they get out of machines as equivalent to human thought, the critics assert, is both inaccurate and, ultimately, dangerous.

Another collateral learning is the child-machine relationship. Media report stories about robot-child friendships and the personalizing of machines, such as with mechanical voices telling car owners to close the door. Art Buchwald's one-liner, "being a computer means never having to say you're sorry," underscores the uneasy ambiguity over what machines are.[50] Sherry Turkle's *Second Self* also explores this gray area in a six-year study of emerging computer culture, including children in a private school where "every child had almost unlimited access to personal computers." In this and other computer-rich elementary schools—unlike most public schools now—she found that child programmers saw "machines as 'sort of' alive because in these cultures it became taboo to kill them, to 'crash' them, to interrupt programs running on them."[51]

Turkle also found that, in young children, teenagers, and college students, interacting with machines generated varied notions of human-ness and machine-ness. Some students came to see themselves as machines, both as a working model and as "protection from feeling, invulnerability to the threat of being swallowed up."[52] But one can also turn to the machine for relationships. Turkle describes the school's computer culture and Henry, the awkward, rude and withdrawn boy at the private school who relaxed in front of the computer. Here he was in control, forging a relationship that meant a lot to him.[53]

I am uncertain what lessons to draw for public schools from computer-rich private schools and video game arcades. Turkle's plumbing of the computer culture does raise basic issues about what else is learned, beyond programming by hooked students. Such issues touch the very core of what the human mind is and what the dimensions are of child-machine bonds. I would like to see more policy makers attending to these subtle but profound

---

[49]Joseph Weizenbaum, *Computer Power and Human Reason* (San Francisco: W. H. Freeman, 1976), pp. 248—256.
[50]Art Buchwald, cited in Calendar of *Quotes*, 1984 (New York: Workman, 1983).
[51]Turkle, p. 59.
[52]Ibid., p. 135.
[53]Ibid., pp. 129—134.

issues, even though it means addressing difficult questions and challenging the popularity of classroom computers.

Summary

To what degree, then, and under what conditions—if at all—should computers be used in classrooms? The arguments presented here have raised questions about cost-effectiveness, further mechanization of teaching, and impact upon children if substantial numbers of classroom computers entered classrooms.

To question computer use in schools is to ask what schools are for, why teachers teach certain content, how they should teach, and how children learn. Unsettling questions as these probe the uneasy silence in public debate over the new technology's use in classrooms, a silence that helps no one who is truly concerned over the schooling offered to the next generation.

I fear, however, that basic questions such as these will go unasked and unanswered because researchers, reformers, and policy makers will discover how little teachers use the machines. I predict that most teachers will use computers as an aid, not unlike radio, film, and television. In elementary schools where favorable conditions exist, teacher use will increase but seldom exceed more than 10 percent of weekly instructional time. Pulling out students for a 30-to-45-minute period in a computer lab will, I suspect, gain increasing popularity in these schools. Where unfavorable conditions exist (i.e., limited principal and central office support, few machines, and so forth), teachers who are serious computer users will secure machines but schoolwide use will be spotty. In secondary schools, the dominant pattern of use will be to schedule students into one or more elective (rather than required) classes where a score of desk-top computers sit. Computer buffs on the staff will develop classroom schemes for using machines in instruction. In no event would I expect general student use of computers in secondary schools to exceed 5 percent of the weekly time set aside for instruction. I predict no great breakthrough in teacher use patterns at either level of schooling. The new technology, like its predecessors, will be tailored to fit the teacher's perspective and the tight contours of school and classroom settings.

If this is what will occur, and based upon my research and experience, I believe that it will, then the common complaints about educator conservatism, stubborn teachers, stifling bureaucracies, and so forth will surface again. The blinders that nonteachers wear once again will shut out any awareness of the teacher's universe and the substantial impact that existing organizational arrangements in schools and classrooms have upon how teachers teach. Teachers, again, will receive rebukes for closing the classroom door to the magic of another technology. Debates over whether computers should be used in classrooms, under what conditions, and to what degree—if at all—will be buried in the scorn heaped upon intransigent teachers.

Sadly, few teachers, principals, superintendents, and school boards raise important points about cost-effectiveness of computerized instruction, nourishing the artistry of teachers, and buffering the classroom from insistent efforts to make instruction mechanical. Nor do many educators acknowledge openly the emotional content of classrooms and question the narrow band of rationality prized in computer learning, or ask about what else is learned by students when they master LOGO and other languages. Because few educators raise these or similar questions or call attention to the powerful behavioral influences of the settings within which they work, nonteachers easily conclude that the problems of increasing the number of desk-top machines is one solely of technical implementation—get the hardware, develop the software, train the teachers, and shove those machines past that classroom door. But the issue of computers for instruction is far more complex, going to the very core of the purposes of schooling.

Thus, my answer whether or not computers should be used in classrooms is a cautious one. Given the current organizational settings, classroom computers should be used by teachers to cope with the routine, often tedious, student learning problems that machines can do patiently. Such use is neither sinister nor wasteful, as some computer boosters suggest. Such use meets a teacher-defined problem well. As unimaginative as drill, simulations, games, and enrichment software may strike reformers, these uses do fit well teachers' needs in adapting to the restless, unpredictable nature of classroom life.

These restricted uses of the new technology appear outrageously conventional. Yet unless existing classroom and school settings are altered substantially, much beyond the conventional will be tough to attain. No computer advocates that I have read or heard, for example, have suggested that schools should hire more teachers and adults to reduce the teaching load, bringing it closer to the college schedule than to the factory. No computer advocate urges increasing school district budgets by half to modify the existing school and classroom arrangements concerning class size, governance, training, and teacher collaboration. Their sole recommendation is to put money into classroom computers.[54]

Until there is far more research, far more public debate among academics, policy makers, and practitioners about why teachers teach the way they do; about the linkages between resources and classroom settings; and about the consequences of computer-rich schools, I would urge a moratoriam on more teaching of technical languages to students and heavy purchasing of interactive computers. Too many complex, interrelated policy

---

[54]While I am prepared to support the suggested reforms listed here, I use them not only to illustrate the constricted views that advocates of technology hold on school improvement. The notion that fundamental school changes would require enormous outlays in tax revenues is either beyond the pale for reformers imbued with visions of technological cures or secretly acknowledged but not explicitly voiced.

issues about the teacher's role, the act of teaching, collateral learning for students, and the purposes of schooling arise to press forward without questioning or anticipating consequences.

I will end this discussion by drawing a comparison to another public policy issue where a technological solution to a social problem went unexamined, the human consequences of which can be seen daily on city streets across America. In the 1950s and 1960s, the mentally ill were housed in institutions costing hundreds of millions of tax dollars. Researchers had begun to produce tranquilizers and other drugs that were billed as cures for psychoses, promising a revolution in the care of those in state institutions. Nationally, psychiatrists, researchers, political reformers, foundation executives, and professional organizations backed a policy of releasing the mentally ill from state facilities and letting community-based clinics handle them on an out patient basis, using the new miracle drugs. Studies that showed how well-staffed local clinics using drugs could treat patients in a much shorter time than state hospitals were used as ammunition by public officials anxious to shift heavy expenditures from state hospitals to other public ventures.

State after state legislated the release of mentally ill throughout the 1960s and 1970s. Federal legislation establishing community mental health centers spurred what came to be called the policy of de-institutionalization. What soon became apparent to many policy makers and local officials was that many severely ill patients had no business being released; drugs were insufficient to cope with many psychoses; and community health centers were inadequately staffed for dealing with schizophrenics and other psychotic clients. The sharp increase in homeless "street people" is simply one unanticipated consequence of the policy changes. Another is the long-term, undesirable effects of persistent drug use. The wholesale release of patients from state hospitals is generally regarded now as a failure in public policy.[55]

A former director of the National Institute of Mental Health and an advocate of this policy change recently thought back on those years:

> Many of those patients who left state hospitals never should have done so. We psychiatrists saw too much of the old snake pit, saw too many people who shouldn't have been there and we overreacted. The result is not what we intended, and perhaps we didn't ask the questions that should have been asked when developing a new concept, but psychiatrists are human, too, and we tried our damndest.[56]

---

[55]Richard Lyons, "How Mental Patients' Release Began," *New York Times*, October 30, 1984, sec. 3, p. 1.
[56]Ibid.

Other policy makers and reformers thought about how they "oversold community treatment" and how "the professional community made mistakes and was overly optimistic, but the political community wanted to save money." Over-promising the benefits of drugs and the capacities of community health centers emerges as the theme of the reflections of both academics and policy makers.[57]

I offer this example of a policy anchored in advances in medical technology, fueled by an impulse toward making public institutions more productive, and fed by a political hunger to save tax dollars to suggest only the seriousness of prematurely pushing a policy change that has potentially grave human consequences. The push for classroom computers is certainly not as dramatic or as wrenching as what happened to hospital patients sent to communities unprepared to deal with them, but the unexamined assumptions, unasked questions, and overselling bear much similarity to the present situation. In dealing with lives, young or old, patience and public reflection on both the anticipated and unanticipated consequences of policies are in order, rather than the headlong plunge into change followed by a heartfelt apology years later.

---

[57] Ibid.

BARRIERS TO COMPUTER USAGE IN SECONDARY SCHOOL[58]

Janet Schofield
University of Pittsburgh

Anyone with even the slightest familiarity with the American educational system in the last decade is well aware of the incredibly rapid proliferation of microcomputers in schools at both the elementary and the secondary level. The magnitude of this change is truly startling. For example, in the two-year period from the spring of 1983 to the spring of 1985 the number of computers in schools which had at least one in 1983 more than tripled. By the end of that period almost all secondary schools and five-sixths of all elementary schools in the U. S. had computers for use in instruction (Becker, 1986).

Although the remarkable rapidity with which microcomputers are being placed in schools is obvious, the effect of this change on teachers, students, and on school systems is not. In fact, opinions vary dramatically on what impact computers can or will have. At one extreme are those who see computers as having the capability to revolutionize education in absolutely fundamental ways. For example, Walker (1984, p. 3) makes the rather startling claim that "the potential of computers for improving education is greater than that of any prior invention, including books and writing." Others take quite a different stance, emphasizing the inherent conservatism of the teaching profession with regard to pedagogical change and the failure of other highly touted educational innovations to bring about far-reaching changes (Cohen, 1988; Cuban, 1984).

The very rapid acquisition of microcomputers by many school systems during the last decade means that many teachers now have available to them a tool with which they have little or no familiarity. The fact that computers have been acquired during a time period when many school systems have been feeling a financial pinch has led many systems to skimp on teacher training and support services. In addition, it seems apparent that school systems sometimes buy computers in response to parental pressures or because they want to gain prestige by being at the forefront of a new trend (Taylor & Johnson, 1986) rather than because they have a vision of the educational goals the computers will help them achieve or of how the change process can be handled in a way which maximizes the potential benefits of using microcomputers in instruction while minimizing negative effects.

---

[58]This article was written for inclusion in this text and will appear in revised form in a book-length treatment of the topic by Janet Schofield.

The goal of this paper is to highlight the fact that the presence of computers in schools does not automatically lead to their effective utilization and to shed light on some very important personal, social, and organizational factors which appear to inhibit the effective use of computer technology at the classroom level. Although relatively little is now known about interplay between microcomputer technology and social processes in the school and classroom, studies have begun to suggest that the school context is very important in determining if and how microcomputers will be utilized once they are available. For example, Becker (1984) found that the amount and type of microcomputer utilization in elementary school classrooms is related to the relative importance of different actors (teachers, principals, or other administrators) in the acquisition of those machines. A quite different study by Sheingold, Hawkins, and Char (1984) demonstrates that teachers' interpretations of their subject matter and of available software are critical to understanding if and how microcomputers are utilized. This chapter seeks to expand our current understanding of the link between social processes and microcomputer utilization in school settings through a close examination of this link in a school which is described below.

The Research Site

This paper grew out of an intensive two-year qualitative study of microcomputer usage in a large urban high school. The school, which will be called Whitmore High School, serves approximately 1,300 students from very varied socioeconomic backgrounds. Approximately 55 percent of the students are African-American, 40 percent are white, and 5 percent are from other, primarily Asian, ethnic groups. Although Whitmore was not the most highly regarded high school in the city, neither was it among the least well regarded. Rather it stood solidly somewhere in the broad middle range of schools which served the city's public school population. The school's faculty is about 80 percent white and roughly 55 percent male. The gender composition of different departments varies dramatically in ways that one might expect given traditional sex roles. For example, about 70 percent of the mathematics teachers are men, compared with about 30 percent of the English teachers.

Whitmore was selected for study for two reasons. First, it had computers available for an array of uses quite typical of those found in other high schools both locally and nationally. Thus, for example, its business and computer science classrooms had numerous computers, and single computers were available for use in a broad range of academic and vocational classes. In addition, Whitmore was the field test site for a state of the art intelligent computer-based geometry proofs tutor developed by John Anderson and Franklin Boyle at Carnegie Mellon University. Thus, this site let us examine numerous common present-day kinds of computer usage as well as their usage as intelligent tutors. Computers were concentrated in four areas in the school. One of these was the room in which ten Xerox Dandy Tiger computers, loaned to the school for the field test of the geometry proofs tutor, were located. The second main concentration of computers, in this case Tandy 1000s, was in the computer science lab. The third concentration of computers was a group of 12 Apple IIEs used by students in the school's gifted program. Fourth, in the study's second year, the business classes, which had formerly had only a small number of computers, received about 20 new ones. There were also a number of other classes (e.g., visual arts, home economics) with one computer available for use.

Data-Gathering Procedures

The two major methods of data gathering employed in this study were intensive and extensive classroom observation and repeated extended interviews with students and teachers. Administrators were also interviewed when appropriate. Classroom observers used the "full field note" method of data collection (Olson, 1976) which involves taking extensive handwritten notes during the events being observed. Shortly thereafter, these notes are dictated into a tape recorder and then transcribed. Observers made the field notes as factual and as concretely descriptive as possible to help avoid unwarranted inferences.

One clear problem with the use of such notes as a data base is what Smith and Geoffrey (1968) have termed the "two-realities problem"—the fact that the notes as recorded cannot possibly include literally everything that has actually transpired. Hence, a source of potential bias is the possibility of selective recording of certain types of events. Although this problem is impossible to surmount completely in qualitative observation, there are some steps that can be taken to minimize its negative effect. For example, we found it useful to have two researchers observe a single setting. Discussion of differences between the two observers' notes helped to point out individual biases and preconceptions. Another technique useful in reducing the effect of such biases is actively to seek out data that undercut one's developing assessment of a situation. These techniques plus a number of others discussed in recent books on qualitative research in educational settings (Bogdan & Biklen, 1982; Goetz & LeCompte, 1984) were employed to reduce the "two-realities problem." Fuller discussion of methodological details can be found in Schofield (1985, forthcoming).

An observational plan was developed for each year of the study which placed research team members in virtually all the classes in which computers were available for use. Thus, over the course of two years, we observed, in all, eight geometry classrooms which served as the field test site for the computer-tutor developed by Anderson, Boyle, and Yost (1985). In addition, over the two-year period we observed a total of four business classes taught by four different teachers. The Office Automation classes covered basic material on secretarial and clerical work ranging from how to answer a telephone in a businesslike manner to how to use word processors. The Business Computer Applications classes were intended to give students firsthand experience with using computers to perform a variety of business functions, such as entering various kinds of data into tables, computing payrolls, preparing taxes, and doing accounts. Computer Science classes were also observed intensively as was the computer lab for gifted students. Other sites in which computers were available, such as the library, visual arts classes, and vocational classes like Power and Energy were also studied. All in all, nearly 500 hours of observation were conducted by a team of four trained observers.

Observers, no matter how omnipresent or insightful, are at a great disadvantage if they do not test their emerging ideas through direct inquiry with those whom they are observing. Because interviews can be so useful in providing the participant's perspectives on events, both formal and informal interviews were the second major data-gathering technique utilized in the research. Thus, students from classes which were observed were formally interviewed, generally near both the beginning and the end of the school year. In some cases, such as the gifted lab and the classes using the artificially intelligent tutor, we interviewed all students. In others we selected a random sample of students, stratified by race and sex. The bulk of these semistructured interviews consisted of open-ended questions. All these interviews were taped and transcribed. Informal interviews were also conducted frequently with these students and others. Field notes based on these interviews were dictated for transcription immediately after they occurred.

Both formal and informal interviews were routinely conducted with the teachers whose classes were observed as well as with staff at both the school and district level who had experience with or responsibility for computer use at Whitmore. Finally, and very importantly, interviews were conducted with a sample of teachers who were selected for study precisely because they had access to microcomputers but used them rarely or not at all.

Although classroom observation and interviews were the primary data-gathering techniques utilized, other techniques were employed when appropriate. For example, archival material such as letters sent to parents about the computer-tutor, internal school memoranda and announcements, and copies of the student newspaper were carefully collected and analyzed. Similarly, close attention was paid to in-service training relating to computers, to teachers' conversations about computer use at lunch, and the like.

FINDINGS ON THE LEVEL OF UTILIZATION

This chapter focuses on one striking finding which emerged from the study of computer usage at Whitmore. With a few notable exceptions, such as the geometry classrooms and the computer science classrooms, computers were actually used very little for instructional purposes at Whitmore even when they were readily available. The purpose of this chapter is to explore the numerous intertwined factors which led to this situation. However, before turning to a discussion of why computers were so little used in most milieus in which they were available, it is necessary to lay out in some detail the evidence on which the conclusion that the computers were not heavily utilized rests.

This chapter discusses three particular situations in which the low level of utilization is particularly well illustrated—business classes, the library, and the computer lab for gifted students. However, a similarly low level of utilization was quite apparent in many other sites in the school as well. Of course, the claim that computers were not frequently utilized involves a comparison with some implicitly expected or desired level of use. It would hardly be reasonable to claim that textbooks are used infrequently merely because they are not in constant use in every class in which they are available. One might take a similar view of computer usage. However, there are at least two important differences between these cases. First, computers are, relatively speaking, quite expensive, so a low level of utilization means that the time during which the computers are being used must add something very significant to students' education to justify expenditures on them in an era in which many school districts are facing serious financial pressures. Second, at Whitmore, as is the case in many schools, computers, unlike textbooks, are used only during the school day. Thus the use which occurred during the day was the only use made of the machines, unlike textbooks, which are more likely to get at least some use outside of school hours. Although a few highly motivated students with computers at home sometimes took work back and forth from the machines at school to theirs at home, such behavior was very unusual. The rarity of this occurrence was undoubtedly not only a function of students' preferences about how to spend their time but also a reflection of the practical difficulties inherent in using machines which may not be completely compatible. Thus, although the conclusion that Whitmore's computers were used rather infrequently involves some judgments about what level of use one might expect, I believe the underutilization was a striking enough phenomenon that most individuals would agree that it was worthy of documentation and discussion.

It is certainly true that most of the teachers at Whitmore who were familiar with computers felt they were very definitely underutilized, as is apparent in the following excerpt from an interview with Mr. Edwards, a chemistry teacher who on his own initiative learned enough about computers that he ended up teaching computer science courses as well:

> Interviewer: How much would you say in general that computers are used for instructional purposes here at Whitmore, ignoring computer science classes for the moment?

> Mr. Edwards: Not anywhere near as much as they should be. Very little.

Office Automation and Business Computer Applications

As indicated above, in each of the two years during which data were gathered for this study, one class called Office Automation and another called Business Computer Applications were systematically observed. Computers were actually used quite rarely in Office Automation classes. For example, in one of the two classes observed, the computers were not used at all in the first semester. In the second semester the observer's best estimate was that the students used the computers roughly twice a month. This was consistent with the results of the student interviews in which 75 percent of the students said they used the computers infrequently. Although a few students reported using the machines two or three days a week, there were also a few students who claimed not to have used them more than once or twice during the entire year and one who insisted she had not used a computer even once in that class.

The low level of computer utilization in the Office Automation class may not be too surprising given the rather elementary nature of the material covered in the course and the wide variety of office machines to which students were exposed. However, a similar pattern also emerged in the Business Computer Applications course. For example, Ms. Parelli, whose class was observed during the first year of the study, usually taught in a very traditional manner the first three days of the week. Thus, these days were generally devoted to lectures, teacher-led question-and-answer periods, and written exercises in workbooks. Although Ms. Parelli planned to have students work on the computers at the end of these classes if there was time, very often there was not enough time left for students to do so.

The last two days of the week students worked individually or in small groups at their desks or on the computers. Desk work included inventory exercises in which students physically cut out pieces of paper which were then arranged in alphabetical or numerical order, vocabulary review, and the like. Computer work generally centered around the disks which came with the textbook. These covered a range of material including data entry and accounting exercises. Since there were only four computers and most of the exercises were designed to be done individually, students could not get a great deal of computer time even if the machines had been in constant use, which they were not. Specifically, even if the machines had been in constant use during the last two days of the week, students would have averaged less than 25 minutes each on the computers out of the roughly four hours they spent in their Business Computer Applications classes. Since the computers often sat idle and usage was not equally distributed among all students, a substantial number of students used them much less than this. Computer use was so infrequent for some students that they were observed asking peers for extremely rudimentary information, such as how to turn the machines on—in November after more than two full months into the course.

Usage in the other Business Computer Applications class was also very limited. Rather surprisingly, observers encountered not a single example of student computer use in this class during the entire first semester of the course. Rather, the class was observed spending its time learning about computers and in some cases performing by-hand tasks that could be easily automated, such as figuring payrolls based on information about wage rates and hours worked. The information about computers was conveyed through the textbook, which was not infrequently read aloud in class by students while the teacher inserted questions, clarifying comments, and additional explanations. Students spent their time learning basic material such as the name and function of the various parts of computer systems, how computers store and retrieve information, and the kinds of printers available and the functions for which they are most suited. The students also had a library project for which they selected a topic from a list presented to them by the teacher and prepared a brief report. Computer usage increased somewhat in the course's second semester after enough computers arrived that all students could work on them simultaneously. Then, the majority of students used the computers at least two or three times a week after an initial period of lower usage. However, many students had trouble making much progress because they used the computers little enough that they had to be constantly checking on basic information, which impeded their getting the software ready for use in the relatively short periods of time generally available for work on the computers.

The Library

The school library was another example of a situation in which the computer resources available were used very little. The librarian received a terminal which was connected to the BRS data base search system during the study's first year. Not only that, she was very strongly encouraged to use it by her supervisor. For reasons which will be discussed below, the librarian was very slow getting started using the system herself and in teaching students to use it. In fact, the lack of usage of the system became a real bone of contention between the librarian and her supervisor. As the librarian put it in an interview:

> I had been given a directive. "You WILL learn it. You WILL do the searching."

> It was almost like somebody had stock in BRS. [They insisted] you will USE it.

> ...My principal was receiving letters every month or so about my inability to push these searches here at this school.

The situation got so bad that the librarian at one point told researchers that she thought her job was in jeopardy because she was not able to get usage of the system's data base searching capability up to a level acceptable to her supervisor. In addition, the strong pressures for use combined with the difficulty the librarian had getting students to use the system led to cases in which she allowed the search system to be used very inefficiently or unproductively because that at least used up some of the budget allocated for the searches.

> Ms. Jackson: At each grade level there are online data bases that the librarian has to teach. Some teachers are library users and some are reluctant. . . . I have to sell it. It's like I'm selling it.

> Interviewer: When you said you have to spend the money, do you mean you are allotted a certain amount of connection time and then you are supposed to use it?

> Ms. Jackson: I think so. Yeah. That's what [they] want....One student...was doing a research paper on Buddhism. He went into a data base here—into the American Academic Encyclopedia [which the school library has]....He ran up a bill of two hundred something [dollars]. It was the full text. He sat there and he got his entire report off of that thing there [pointing to the terminal]....I let him....Even the student himself [said] "Mrs. Jackson this is costly. Why can't I just go and get it from the encyclopedia?"

The above might seem like an example of overuse rather than underuse since the terminal was used for something which could have been done at least as rapidly and at a fraction of the cost with the library's copy machine. However, it was clear from conversations with Mrs. Jackson that she allowed this overuse to occur because there were strong pressures for utilization of the terminal that she felt she could not meet.

The Gifted Computer Lab

The gifted computer lab was a room which contained 13 Apple IIE computers, 7 printers, and an expensive color plotter which was never actually hooked up to the other machines so it could be used. The equipment in the room arrived at the school in two or three small shipments over the two years preceding the start of this study. It was paid for by special state funds designated for use in the education of gifted children. Initially the computers had been placed individually in the classrooms of teachers who taught students in the gifted program. However, there was wide agreement that they were used very little when distributed that way.

As Mr. East, a chemistry teacher who was involved in the lab, explained in an interview:

> They were being underutilized....They were just sitting in the rooms and the teachers were not using them....[Some] had never even been turned on.

Mr. East's assertions were supported by the comments of Mr. Walters who initially served as the gifted program co-coordinator and as such was responsible for the computers purchased through this project. He characterized use of the machines during their first two years at the school as "very minimal." Interestingly, he reported that what little use there was of the machines was primarily for record keeping or basic word processing by teachers rather than for use in instruction.

The coordinators of the gifted program decided to place the computers together in a lab in the hope that they would be used more, although teachers who really wanted to keep one of the machines were allowed to do so. One of them explained the decision this way: "We [created] the computer lab because many people found the computer an inconvenient electronic device that they didn't have time for in the classroom." Only two teachers, Mr. East and Mr. Deppe, both male science teachers, elected to keep them. Mr. East kept his locked up most of the time, but occasionally used it for classroom demonstrations or individual student projects. Mr. Deppe kept his in the back of his room and used a rather extensive collection of disks he had for teaching various topics in biology. The other teachers relinquished their computers very readily. As a history teacher put it, "it was all right with me 'cause mine was just sitting there."

However, the creation of a lab did not do a great deal to increase the utilization of the computers. It did lead to their use during two lunch periods most days by roughly a dozen students who chose to come and spend that time playing educational games or word processing. However, with this one exception, the use of this lab remained extremely infrequent. In fact, our best estimate is that the lab was used on the average less than one of the remaining thirty class periods each week. The infrequency of use was made clear in an interview with Mr. East toward the end of the lab's second year of operation when he indicated that the two or three teachers who were the lab's heaviest users brought their classes there roughly two or three times a year. In addition, he asserted, consistent with our observations, that many teachers who were eligible to use the lab never did so even once.

The one obvious exception to the general tendency not to use computers in instruction outside of the GPTutor and computer science classes was their rather frequent utilization in special education classes. Mr. Pike used his computer on a daily basis in his SED (socially and emotionally disturbed) classes. Ms. Green also used a computer consistently to instruct her EMR (educable mentally retarded) students. Both of these teachers showed a degree of interest in using computers for instruction which contrasted very sharply with the general tendency to use them little or not at all. In fact, after trying to start out with a gerry-built system which included a TV screen and tape recorder he had scavenged from the school's audiovisual collection, Mr. Pike managed to put together a workable computer system through a serious personal effort which included persuading an acquaintance at the board of education to lend him a monitor and writing a small grant proposal to pay for a disk drive. Ms. Green also took the initiative to get her computer by going to Whitmore's principal and making the case that her students had the right to one of the computers originally placed in the CAS lab because those computers had been bought with funds for exceptional students, a category which included both gifted and EMR students.

BARRIERS TO COMPUTER USAGE

Belief that Computer Usage Will Add Little Value to Current Practice

The factors which appeared to inhibit computer use at Whitmore were many and complex. The contrast between the intensive use of computers in the field testing of the geometry tutor and in computer science and their infrequent use in most of the other locales in which computers were available at Whitmore makes one of these barriers clear. Quite sensibly, teachers will not use computers to any noticeable extent if they do not feel there is some educational purpose to be furthered by doing so. The developers of the GPTutor gave the teachers cooperating with them a clear rational for use of the machines. Specifically they pointed out that the constant monitoring and structuring of students' problem-solving attempts and the immediate feedback give the tutor the capability to provide important facilitators of learning which one teacher cannot hope to provide in a typical class of students (Anderson, Boyle, & Yost, 1985). The usefulness of using computers to teach programming in computer science classes is also quite readily apparent.

However, in general, Whitmore's teachers seemed to have little conception of what parts of the curriculum might best be taught using computers and of when and how they could be used for drill and practice, for simulations, for the graphic capabilities, and the like. As one teacher who did not use the computer he had been given for his gifted students put it, "it didn't do anything I couldn't do easier and cheaper on the blackboard." Another attributed his failure to use his computer with a gifted world cultures class to difficulty in finding appropriate software, saying, "I can't see teachers using computers unless they can see how it could be useful." A home economics teacher cited this issue as the crux of the matter stating, "If I could see a really good use for a computer, I would use one...but I have yet to think of anything I could do on a computer that I can't do by myself just as well." Similarly, Ms. Jackson, the librarian, attributed the low level of usage of the library's data base search capabilities at least partly to their lack of usefulness. Specifically, she said that students had little need to use the system because very few teachers assigned research papers that required the kind of intensive search of a variety of sources that data base searches supply. Further, she pointed out that many of the students could not read well enough to make use of the kinds of sources they were likely to locate when using many of the data bases available through the BRS search system.

It is worth noting that when teachers discussed whether or not they found computer use helpful in their classes, their emphasis was virtually always on how various pieces of software might fit into the already established curriculum. Thus the issues pertinent to them were the level of difficulty of the material, the precise subject material covered and the way the software meshed with their textbooks, as is evident in the following remarks of one of Whitmore's longtime faculty members:

> Implementation of all this [the gifted computer program] is not the way it should be. I never really understand how they [the central administration] never think through the program and its connection to the curriculum the way they ought to. It is just sort of pasted on top.

This emphasis on the fit between current practice and computer applications is also apparent in the following excerpt in an interview with Mr. Walters:

> Interviewer: If there were two or three things that somebody could do to make the computer a more useful tool for you what would they be?

> Mr. Walters: I think [locating] software that would be applicable to the curriculum. Second, developing lesson plans specifying step-by-step how this can be worked into the curriculum. Third, providing paid summer seminars on how to utilize it.

This emphasis on how computer applications fit into current curriculum is hardly surprising since teachers are, in fact, held responsible for covering certain material in their classes. Thus, innovations are likely to be judged on the basis of what they can contribute to the attainment of this goal. However, it is worth noting that this orientation differs dramatically from that of many proponents of computer utilization in schools, who see such usage as a vehicle for transforming education. For example, the developer of the widely used Logo software sees it as a way of increasing the emphasis on developing problem-solving skills and encouraging students to reflect on their own thinking processes in elementary schools (Papert, 1980). Others see the use of computers and related technology as a way of bringing the resources of the outside world into the classroom (Bossert, 1988), of fostering the development of inquiry skills (Groen, 1985; Lawler, 1984), of letting students follow their own interests more than they currently can in most school settings (Feurzeig, 1988), or of changing the current emphasis on didactic approaches to teaching to more collaborative, learner-centered ones (Collins, 1991). The point here is that many of the potential consequences of computer usage which are most exciting to those outside the schools are not given high priority by those working within that system. The latter tend to ask whether these applications can assist them with the more mundane task of doing their work, as they now understand it, better, quicker, or more easily.

The Disruption of the Classroom's
Traditional Social Organization

The common belief on the part of teachers that there was little software which was likely to work better in teaching their subject matter than current methods is a factor contributing to the lack of use of computers in many fields. However, it is not able to account for the relatively infrequent utilization of computers in a class like Business Computer Applications which was explicitly intended to give students a substantial amount of practical experience with computers. Teachers in these business classes spoke enthusiastically of the need for their students to learn to use computers.

Interviewer: What do you like best about teaching this course [Business Computer Applications]?

Ms. White: I think it is related to the world of work....Jobs are going to be white collar...working with computers, and I feel I'm making a contribution....Students [will] have the skills that they need to get jobs.

Yet, ironically, computers were used relatively little even in these teachers' classes, as discussed earlier. Two factors seemed to contribute to this situation. First, teachers were not able to easily solve the organizational problems posed by computer use when there were a great many more students than computers in their classrooms. Second, they were, generally speaking, not very knowledgeable about the computers or the software they were using. Although these two barriers stood out in clearest relief in Business Computer Application classrooms, they were also very real inhibitors of computer usage in other classrooms, as will become apparent.

The teachers in Business Computer Applications were much like their peers in the college preparatory courses in that they tended to use traditional "whole class" methods of instruction—that is, they lectured, conducted structured discussions, and had their students work on various kinds of written exercises. Given this format, it was not immediately apparent how to integrate computer use into normal classroom procedures when there were not enough computers to enable the entire class, or at least a large portion of it, to work on the computers simultaneously. The problem was, of course, that students working on the computers would miss the material covered in class during that time. Since different students would miss different portions of the material covered by their peers as they rotated in and out of the larger group, there was no quick or easy way for the teacher to help them make up what they had missed.

There were other, more prosaic kinds of problems as well. For example, the printers were noisy enough that it was distracting for students to use them while the teacher was trying to talk to their classmates. Thus, one of the teachers made it a rule that students could not use the printer when she was talking. Although this was reasonable given that one person's printing could disrupt the work of a dozen or more classmates, it led to inefficient use of the computers as students often sat at them waiting for an appropriate moment to print out their work. Another problem with detaching a few students from the class's main activity was that it meant the teacher was not likely to be readily available to help them when they needed help. If a problem arose for one of these students, the teacher either had to ignore it or shift her attention from the large group of students with whom she was working to the single individual who needed help. Both of these ways of handling the situation had serious drawbacks, thus putting the teacher under some pressure as she decided between the lesser of the two evils. Other possible mechanisms for handling this problem, such as having a particularly knowledgeable student serve as a kind of informal resource person, were occasionally used on an ad hoc basis. However, this solution did not always work well since its success depended on the knowledgeable students to be both willing to divert attention from their own academic and social concerns and able to communicate their knowledge to others.

Such organizational impediments to extensive computer use were not found only in Business Computer Applications. Teachers of a variety of classes ranging from history to home economics who had just one or two computers in their classrooms also spoke frequently of the organizational issues this raised for then,.

> Mr. Specter: Personally, I never got into using the computer at all. My experience with the software is that not a whole lot of it is very valuable or usable....And the other factor is how do you get kids, 30 or 25 or even 15 kids, to use one computer. The matter of scheduling...I was never willing to put the energy into answering those questions. Just too many other things to do.

Not too surprisingly, attempts to use one computer to teach an entire class simultaneously were both quite rare and generally rather unsuccessful. Mr. East occasionally used his computer for demonstrations in his gifted chemistry class, and Mrs. Jackson used hers in the library to demonstrate how to use the data base search system. But it was difficult to keep students' attention when one or two dozen of them were supposed to be attending to a standard-sized monitor that was often rather hard for those not right up in front to see clearly. A math teacher described his experience trying to use a computer for demonstrations as follows:

> Mr. Erie: I didn't find it very useful to have one terminal in the room. In the first place it was too small. It was about ten inches....Any demonstrations I could give, half the kids would have to gather round. [Then I would repeat it for the others]. I found I could put it on the board faster.

Mr. Powers, who taught a vocational course called Power and Energy, seemed to agree with his colleague, Mr. Erie, saying succinctly, "One machine in the classroom is not enough."

One French teacher, who did make the shift from a whole-class format to a format in which students rotated through a variety of work stations, including computers used for drill and practice and tape recorders for oral language practice, talked of the difficulty she had in making the adjustment to something other than a whole-class format. As her comments indicate, this shift is likely to mean not only that different students are working on different tasks, but that the classroom looks and sounds very different than it used to. Students are more likely to move around the classroom and to talk with one another. The teacher's role as lecturer becomes much less important, and his or her ability to juggle the competing needs of students working on different tasks becomes crucial.

> Ms. Wright: I'm for anything that will work. I had been on the committee that wrote the material for the gifted French classes. I had picked the book....I had ordered the stuff, including the computer software. So I was anxious to see what it would do and how it could be incorporated....It was a ninth grade class, and most of the kids in ninth grade have already worked in a class where a number of things are going on at a time, so it didn't bother them at all. IT DROVE ME CRAZY, but I could see it was benefiting them. I felt torn. I wanted to be with this [person]. I wanted to be with that group. It was just a question of convincing my soul that when there is noise and everybody is doing something different learning is taking place. It's difficult for me. My natural reaction to that is not good. I think you can train yourself to do that if you find it is valuable. I was learning to do that with anguish.

Ms. Wright's anguish was not an idiosyncratic reaction. Prior studies have suggested that many teachers attempting to use computer technology in instruction have similar difficulty adjusting to what may appear to be a noisy, even apparently disorderly, classroom (Sandholtz, Ringstaff, & Dwyer, 1990).

Many teachers, less motivated than Ms. Wright or less willing to experiment with classroom practices which were unfamiliar and initially uncomfortable, never made the transition from whole-class instruction toward formats more amenable to the incorporation of one or a small number of computers.

Lack of Familiarity with Computer Hardware and Software

The large majority of Whitmore's teachers, like the majority of teachers nationally, completed their formal education before the advent of the widespread use of personal computers. Thus, many of them never encountered computers in their training, or, if they did, their experience was with large and relatively inflexible mainframe machines. Thus their preteaching experience did not present them with creative models of how computers might be used to enrich the curriculum or of how to adjust traditional classroom procedures to make effective use of computers possible. Neither did it provide them with knowledge of how to use personal computers and the kind of software available for use.

This lack of knowledge on the part of teachers was a real impediment to utilization of computers in the classroom. Ms. Parelli freely admitted that she did not know enough about computers or about the software she was using to teach effectively in Business Computer Applications, saying things like, "I just plain don't know enough to teach some of the things I need to." When asked what she liked least about teaching the course, her reply was that she disliked feeling unprepared to teach it. Her lack of knowledge was readily apparent to students as evidenced by the following excerpt from field notes taken in her classroom when two of her students working on the computer encountered a problem they could not solve:

> Lauretta says, "Maybe we should ask Ms. Parelli for help." Janette replies, "Ms. Parelli doesn't know anything about computers. She won't be any help."

The girls decision not to consult their teacher may have been reasonable as suggested by the poor advice she gave some of her students a week or two earlier:

> Ms. Parelli leaves [after working with one of the students at a computer]. Lisa says to the boy sitting next to her, "She didn't help at all!" The boy replies, "Yeah, she spent one and a half weeks helping me to get started on the computer, but nothing worked..." [Later] Ralph is having trouble with his disk drive. The red light is on and he remembers that the teacher told him never to put a disk in when the disk drive light was on. He calls Ms. Parelli over and says, "What should I do now? I can't put the disk in." She replies, "Oh, go ahead and put it in anyway." He responds, "No, I'd better not because the disk drive is moving in there."

Ms. Parelli was not the only business teacher plagued by lack of thorough knowledge of the material she needed to teach. Another of the business teachers, Ms. Spring, explicitly told researchers that she avoided using the computers very much because she did not know how to teach students to use them very well.

This lack of real familiarity with computers was not restricted to the business teachers. In fact, because their jobs specifically included teaching students how to use computers, in general the business teachers appeared more familiar with computers than most other teachers. For example, Ms. Parelli spoke of several training sessions that were provided by the school system for business teachers, and Ms. Spring was one of the very few teachers who repeatedly checked books on computers out of the school library in order to increase her proficiency with them. With the exception of the computer science teachers and a few others, most teachers at Whitmore were even less familiar with computer technology than their peers in the business department. This posed a formidable barrier to utilization.

Threat to Teachers' Sense of Competence and Authority

Frequently coupled with the teachers' comments about their lack of knowledge about computers was a sense of concern that trying to use computers exposed teachers to potentially embarrassing situations which undermined either their sense of competence or their classroom authority, or both. For example, Mr. Trowbridge, a geometry teacher who indicated that he found it hard to "get the hang of computers," argued that because of their youth students could pick up on computers more quickly. Thus, by attempting to use computers with his class he reversed the usual situation in which he was more in command of the knowledge needed to perform well in class than were his students. Ms. Wright, the French teacher quoted earlier, made a similar point:

> I took a little bit of a course [on computers], just so I wouldn't be a total fool. When they first came even turning on the machine was a real trial....Something like this is always an opportunity to make a fool of yourself. When the computer first came to my room, even my dumbest student knew more about it than I did. If you are the kind of teacher who is frightened of making a fool of himself or herself, then that could be a real problem.... I'm a competent person, but sometimes I do things wrong and that doesn't bother me a lot. It doesn't bother me to say to the kids, "I can't turn this machine on. Will you turn it on for me? They will say, "You're dumb." I say, "I know, but I know lots of other things."

In spite of the fact that a few teachers like Ms. Wright appeared to tolerate knowing less than their students without too much discomfort, many were quite leery of putting themselves in such a situation. Ms. Green, who used a computer for a variety of purposes with her special education students, felt that this fear of looking incompetent or foolish was a major deterrent to others:

> Interviewer: Have any other teachers (aside from you and Mr. Lenno) in the special education department decided to use them [computers]?
>
> Ms. Green: No.
>
> Interviewer: Do you think they would like to?
>
> Ms Green: They may when they feel more comfortable with it themselves so that they don't feel like a fool in front of these kids trying to tell them how to use it. That's the fear I see.

One of the Business Computer Application teachers even contrasted her fear of the computer with the students' relaxed attitude, which she saw as conducive to their learning readily.

> Ms. White: They [the students] are very good at figuring things out. A lot of things they taught me, 'cause they're not afraid of it [the computer]. This is their thing, even the ones you wouldn't expect.

The teachers' concern about being or appearing to be less knowledgeable than their students is understandable. In the United States, the social structure of the classroom has traditionally been built around two complementary roles—those of teacher and student. An important part of the teacher's role is the exercise of authority, that is, legitimate power over the student (Bierstedt, 1970). The teacher's authority has a number of bases, but one of these is unquestionably his or her expertise and more specifically the gap between that expertise and the student's own (Benne, 1970). Although teachers have authority by virtue of the role they occupy, they must work to express and maintain that authority so it will not be eroded. In fact, Hughes (1959) has estimated on the basis of his research that 40 percent of teachers' actions are directed toward maintaining and displaying their authority.

Any change in the classroom which seriously undermines the teacher's image as a knowledgeable and competent individual has implications not only for the teacher's personal feelings of comfort and self-esteem but also for important aspects of classroom functioning related to the teacher's authority. In a high school with a very diverse student body concerns about maintaining authority are understandable and realistic. Many teachers felt that to display a lack of expertise would give students an opening to ridicule them that the students would be quick to take. This concern is clearly evident in the following excerpt from field notes of a conversation between a member of the research team and a physics teacher about why the teacher failed to use the computer he had in his classroom.

> Mr. Barber said that students are waiting to jump on teachers. He went on to say that many of the gifted students don't see teachers as really human. Rather they expect teachers to know everything and when teachers don't they react to it very negatively. He said, "There are a lot of opportunities to make a fool of yourself and the kids are just waiting for them."

In fact, cases did arise in which teachers were literally unable to perform some of their authority-linked functions because of the students' greater knowledge of computers. For example, one math teacher was unable to grade a project turned in to him by a gifted student because it was a computer program designed to perform various mathematical operations. Not knowing anything about programming, the teacher had to go to a colleague, who graded it for him. In two years of close observation at Whitmore, we found no case of one teacher asking another teacher to grade his or her students' class assignments which did not involve computer-based projects.

Although teachers most often mentioned a fear of looking stupid or foolish in front of their students, it was not uncommon for them to experience the same feelings when trying to improve their computer skills in both formal and informal training contexts in which students were not present. For example, Mr. Miller described his unsuccessful attempts to learn from a colleague, Mr. East, a chemistry teacher who was Whitmore High School's foremost "hacker."

> Mr. Miller: He's a computer whiz. He's way over my head.... A couple of times I've asked him to explain things to me, but it gets so complicated. He goes on and on and I just sit there and I say "I gotcha....I got it. I understand." But I don't understand a thing!

This sense of threat to one's sense of self as a competent professional was felt by some even in formal training. For example, the school librarian spoke frankly of the strain of trying to learn about computers in a training session which obviously did not take adequate account of the level of knowledge that she brought to it.

> Ms. Jackson: I went to an all-day training session....I didn't even know the basics of computers....At one point they were talking about a menu. I started wiping my glasses.... I kept cleaning my glasses looking for the word menu.

> Then I got upset, started running to the bathroom like a child because I don't know what is going on here. Finally I raised my hand timidly. [I said] "I don't see anything that looks like food...." It was overwhelming for me.... I was not computer literate.

Computer Anxiety

Although much of the teachers' trepidation about using computers in their classrooms appeared to stem from concern about how their relative lack of expertise would influence their position in the classroom, another factor also seemed to contribute to their reluctance. Many of the teachers felt quite anxious about the mere idea of having to learn to use an unfamiliar and rather intimidating machine. Teachers frequently used words like fear, anxiety, and phobia in discussing their own or others' reactions to the idea of learning to use a computer. The coordinator of the gifted program at the time the computers arrived observed this widespread reaction:

> Interviewer: How did you find the other teachers reacted that first year when you gave them one computer each?

> Mr. Deppe: I'll be honest with you. Everybody was afraid of them....

This reaction was by no means limited to the teachers of the gifted students. Many of their colleagues throughout the school evinced similar reactions. For example, a mathematics teacher gave the following reply to an open-ended question about what one thing the school system could do to help her decide whether and how she might be able to use a computer effectively in her classes:

> Ms. Baker: If I could have a few hours one-to-one with a really competent teacher that has used it—just let me ask questions—[about] what I'm afraid of about a computer, what I don't understand.

A computer science teacher, who arrived at Whitmore toward the end of the study, indicated that anxiety related to computers was not peculiar to Whitmore's faculty. She had encountered it in many teachers taking courses at a local university.

> Interviewer: What do you think would be the biggest impediment to utilization of computers [by teachers]? What sorts of barriers...?

> Ms. Patrick: I think it would be the teacher—how much they know and their fears and prejudices toward the computer....I was taking courses with a lot of teachers...and computers were a big topic. A lot of them seemed apprehensive....

PROBLEMS WITH TRAINING

In general, there appeared to be four types of training experiences available to teachers. First, over a period of several years, a few in-service training sessions related to computing were offered to teachers at Whitmore by knowledgeable colleagues. These sessions were typically no more than an hour or two long and the material covered was very rudimentary. For example, roughly once a year Mr. Brice, one of the computer science teachers, held a brief session on computers for interested teachers from all departments. Teachers asked him questions like, "Do computers ever make mistakes?" and "Should I buy a computer to do things like balance my checkbook?" In addition, Ms. Green once took her colleagues in the special education department to the gifted lab to familiarize them with the Apple computers there.

Another somewhat more extended kind of in-service training was offered to teachers at a Teachers' Center. All teachers in the school system were rotated through this center over a period of several years in a effort to provide a several week period during which, freed from their normal duties, they could select among a variety of seminars and training experiences designed to enhance their professional development. Several workshops on computer usage were offered to interested teachers. As part of this experience it was also possible for teachers to visit a software library at a local university.

A third kind of training was the workshops organized by the vendors of computer equipment in conjunction with the sale of equipment to the school district. These workshops varied from about one day to one week in length and tended to focus on very basic issues connected with how to operate computers and associated equipment such as printers. Finally, a few teachers reported availing themselves of opportunities to learn about computers during evening or summer courses at local institutions of higher education. Some of these teachers reported paying tuition for these courses themselves. Others indicated that the school district shared the tuition costs.

The inability of all but a few of Whitmore's teachers who had access to computers to effectively use them—or to use them at all for that matter—makes it clear that the training provided was not particularly effective. It is worth noting that other staff members also appeared not to get the training they needed to use computers readily. For example, Mr. East complained that the secretaries in the school's main office received such rudimentary training that they were unable to operate their newly arrived personal computers and that they had to learn in a very inefficient manner on their own.

> Interviewer: Did the school or the system provide you with any sort of training or incentive to help out in the gifted computer lab?

> Mr. East: No. This is a problem almost all the way across the board, not only in our program....The secretaries have a Burroughs terminal downstairs which is supposed to help them in their record keeping. None of them...They were given like a half hour [of training] quickly. [Like], "Here's the switch." They've learned it little by little on their own instead of [someone taking] a bit of time out and saying, "Let me show you what you can do with this." There's been nothing like that. It would make a good in-service program.

In addition, a new computerized systemwide procedure for recording grades and producing report cards operated so poorly that the start of summer school actually had to be delayed because students did not know whether they had failed courses in time to register to retake them in the summer. Although part of this problem stemmed from glitches in the software, some of the delay appeared to be attributable to the unfamiliarity of district employees with the required procedures. Thus, issues connected to training must be considered in any analysis of the barriers to effective computer use at Whitmore.

Timing

Policymakers at the district level were aware of the dangers of letting the pace of acquisition of computer hardware outstrip the development and implementation of appropriate training. In light of the problems described in this chapter, it is rather ironic that a high-evel administrator at the Board of Education had this to say about the district's policy:

> Mr. Petrella: Unfortunately a large number of districts consistently go out and lead with their face, for lack of a better phrase. They buy equipment and say, "Here you go," and everybody says, "No," and it sits in closets or is misused. The intent here is that nothing is

purchased until there is a relatively comprehensive plan that identified exactly what the outcomes are, what people will be doing with them, and how they will be trained before equipment is bought.

The process of computer acquisition and introduction at Whitmore did not appear to be as orderly and rational as one might expect from the preceding statement, as should be apparent from the earlier part of this chapter. Several factors may account for this. First, the school district decided to focus its major effort on encouraging computer use at the elementary level and was implementing a plan to introduce Logo into all of its elementary schools. Thus, much of the effort of central staff with responsibility for computer utilization was devoted to this project. In addition, a number of fairly innovative attempts to explore how computers might be effectively introduced and used at the middle and high school level were being made. So, for example, the district entered into an agreement with a local university and a foundation to field-test a program which gave relatively intensive computer training to middle school teachers with no prior computer experience in order to let them become expert enough to discover where and how such technology could enhance instruction in areas such as English, Social Studies, and Language Arts. Another program undertaken in cooperation with a different university gave a group of mathematics teachers considerable exposure to computer technology with the intention of having them serve as peer trainers in their home schools.

The problem was that while the district was concentrating on these many admittedly useful activities, computers were entering Whitmore and other high schools at a pace which exceeded the district's ability to ready teachers for the change. Various environmental forces contributed to this. For example, practices changed in the business world so rapidly in the 1980s that it became clear to district personnel that business students needed to learn to use computers rather than to focus on using typewriters as they traditionally had in many classes. Thus, a moratorium was placed on the purchase of new electronic typewriters and a decision was made to purchase various kinds of word processors and computers for business classrooms instead. In addition, in the years just preceding this study, the district found itself in serious danger of loosing state funding for its gifted program because of various deficiencies in it. The district knew as it drew up plans for revising the program that state funding for computers for gifted students was available. As a "free good" for which the state would pay, these computers were seen as desirable even though it is clear from the earlier part of this chapter that most teachers had relatively little idea what to do with them.

In fact, Mr. East suggested that merely possessing the computers was seen as valuable, whether or not they were used, since it allowed the school to show them off on parents' nights as part of their effort to keep talented students in the public school system who might otherwise go to private schools. He was not alone in his view of the situation as evidenced by the words of one of his colleagues:

It [having computers] is just another Band-Aid. Instead of suturing it into the system, we paste it on because we need it to look [good]. We need to bring people into the building or take them over there to the computer lab and say, "See this? Isn't this wonderful?" We need to bring in the press....

Thus, parents' belief that computers were the wave of the future and their desire to have their children prepared to live in a world in which computers are playing an increasingly important role also added pressure to acquire machines even when it was not clear exactly how they would be integrated with traditional policies and practices or what they would add to the students' education.

Coordination of the arrival of computer hardware and software with teacher training in its use was also a very real problem at Whitmore. From the teachers' perspective such coordination often appeared close to nonexistent. Teachers frequently reported either that a computer had just arrived in their classroom one day with virtually no advance warning or that they had expected the arrival of these machines months before the actual delivery was made. Some teachers reported receiving training in basic operational procedures and then waiting months for equipment to arrive in their classroom.

Ms. McDonald: We had...training 'cause we were going to get a computer, but it really did nothing for me...because I didn't have anything to come back and use....Plus it was on a different computer. Originally they ordered a TRS80 and they got one for use with no software. [Then] they realized...they don't have any software [for my subject]. Only Apple has Home Ec software. So they sold it to the Business Department and they reordered us new computers. So there was a lapse in there.

Frequently machines arrived in the middle of the semester and teachers ended up using valuable class time to familiarize themselves with new hardware or software. This even happened in computer science.

Carl tells me [the observer]...that students have been mainly playing games during the last two weeks [in his computer science class]. I asked him why and he said because Mr. Davidson still appears to have a lot to learn about the new computers [so] he hasn't been teaching very actively. [Instead, he has] allowed students to play games.

All in all it was clear that issues of timing and coordination constituted a real barrier to effective and efficient utilization of computers at Whitmore.

Matching Training to the Teacher's
Level of Knowledge and Instructional Concerns

Although most teachers at Whitmore were novices when it came to computer use, the precise level of knowledge and previous exposure varied quite widely. Many, like Ms. Jackson who was quoted earlier, had so little previous experience that words like "menu" or "disk" needed to be explained. A much smaller number, exemplified by Mr. East, were quite expert and enjoyed using the computer at home for recreational and other purposes. Some fell between these extremes. Thus, problems arose in matching the kind of training offered with the teacher's existing level of knowledge. Training that was too rudimentary in nature was obviously wasteful and boring for those with some expertise. Yet training experiences which presumed any knowledge of computers at all left many teachers floundering.

Many of the teachers who had access to one or more computers for instructional purposes could speak only vaguely of training sessions they remembered. For example, the comments of Ms. Prentiss, who volunteered to supervise the gifted computer lab after having seen her husband accomplish a lot on their personal computer at home, were quite typical.

Interviewer: How did you come to be in charge of the computer room here?

Ms. Prentiss: I volunteered....I didn't know much.

Interviewer: Did the school or the school system provide you with any training?

Ms. Prentiss (laughing): That one two-hour workshop at the Teachers' Center. That was it.

Interviewer: How long ago was that?

Ms. Prentiss: I have a hard time remembering. (Maybe three years ago)...Right after that a friend of mine, a nontechnocrat, got an Apple [computer]. The two of us figured it out over the summer. And I figured if I can teach her, I can teach anybody.

Those who could describe the training generally felt that it was inadequate. One of the characteristics of the training teachers were most likely to complain about was its restricted technical focus. Specifically, teachers tended to be critical of the fact that the training often focused primarily on issues such a how to operate the computer without giving them much advice or assistance with two fundamental issues discussed earlier— what software was available to assist in accomplishing their educational objectives and how to organize the class to make efficient and effective use of students' time when there were a small number of computers in the classroom. Mr. Powers explained his experience as follows:

Mr. Powers: I've had this thing (pointing to a personal computer) about two and one-half years. It came in the middle of the year. Nobody told us it was going to be part of the curriculum. Nobody told us what to do with them when they got here. They basically gave us the equipment and never said anything.... I actually had to teach myself how to work the computer.

Interviewer: Did you get any sort of in-service training?

Mr. Powers: Yeah. Included in the price of the computer they gave us six or eight hours of instruction...telling you how to turn it on, load the printer, stuff like that....It was very elementary.

Although most teachers needed training in basic operational procedures, they definitely needed much more than that to help them discover ways to use the computers effectively once they were turned on.

Lack of Concentrated Experiential Training

Training sessions tended to be relatively short and often covered a wide variety of issues. Thus, there was rarely time for teachers to become truly familiar with the machines and procedures they were learning. Rather, it was often a matter of hearing someone tell a class what command to use or seeing a demonstration in a training environment which did not encourage or even allow the kind of repeated practice that builds and consolidates skills. For example, a couple of individuals complained that the training sessions they had attended had more participants than computers. Therefore, they had not even been able to try out the procedures described to them because they did not have a computer on which to do so. Needless to say, they found this kind of experience extremely boring and felt that they had gained very little from it. A few of the teachers who were most interested in computers did arrange to borrow one from the school over the summer in order to develop their skills. This seemed to be very useful for those who were unusually motivated. The only problem was that occasionally teachers became so enamored of having a computer at home that they were quite dilatory in returning it to the school for students' use after the school year had begun.

Inertia and Resistance

It was clear that the training offered to Whitmore's teachers did not generally prepare them to use the computers available to them effectively. For training itself to be really effective, two things are necessary . First, of course, one needs carefully timed and structured training experiences which speak to the questions and concerns individuals have and build the skills they will need. Second, the individuals involved must want to learn. Many of the teachers at Whitmore indicated that they were at least mildly interested in learning about computers. However, it is important not to ignore the existence of a great deal of inertia and even some outright resistance on the part of other faculty members. Mr. Powers, who used a computer in some of his Power and Energy classes, highlighted this problem in an interview:

Interviewer: Do you think most teachers would be anxious to have more access to computers or not?

Mr. Powers: I think a lot of them that aren't familiar with them are going to be afraid of them.... They are opposed to any change. They don't want to roll with the technology.

The words of a geometry teacher suggest that Mr. Powers's assessment of the situation was quite accurate, at least with regard to some of his colleagues:

Interviewer: Have you had a chance to see the computer [tutor] which Mr. Adams and Mr. Brice...[are using]?

Mr. Carter: Yeah, but I'm not too fond with computers. I don't want any parts [sic] with computers. I'm the old-fashioned type. I don't want to learn anything new. Maybe that's my fault. I should go into learning computers...but I don't know. I just—after so many years, you build up a file on your subjects.... For me to go into teaching computers...I would have to start all over. I would have to actually sit down and work everything out, and it would require a lot more work on my part to run a class the way I want it run.... I suppose everybody gets lazy and...I just don't want to do it.... I'm doing what I'm doing. Don't want to change.

Thus, many teachers failed to take advantage of training that was available.

INFRASTRUCTURE PROBLEMS

For those teachers who were interested in discovering if and how their students' learning could be enriched through the use of computers, the lack of readily available, timely, pertinent training was not the only barrier to be overcome. Another serious problem was the lack of structural arrangements within the school to facilitate the achievement of this goal. For example, although Whitmore had a teacher who received release time from teaching to take care of the school's audio-visual equipment, this individual's responsibilities did not include computer equipment. Neither was there another individual or set of individuals at Whitmore responsible for helping teachers with computer hardware or software problems. Teachers generally struggled individually with problems they encountered in using various software packages, sometimes utilizing informal networks including computer-using teachers in other schools or knowledgeable peers at Whitmore to help with problems they could not resolve. Repairs which a teacher or those the teacher consulted could not perform were referred to commercial companies with which the school district had arranged service contracts.

These procedures were very inefficient since teachers often had to wait a substantial amount of time to get assistance with problems which a knowledgeable person on the spot could have solved almost instantly. For example, we observed one situation in which a computer in a business class was not used for some time as the teacher waited for a repair person to return her call. After finally receiving this call, the teacher, as instructed, checked the machine and discovered that the cause of the problem was that the computer was not plugged in. Ms. Prentiss described the difficulties she encountered before she persuaded Mr. East to help her out during his free period,which luckily coincided with part of the time the gifted lab was open:

> Ms. Prentiss: At first...it was terrible....I called my husband everyday at work [for advice]....I'd ask him all these questions. I was awful. I could just see this was not going to work....But having someone to talk over the problems with was invaluable.

Even with Ms. Prentiss and Mr. East doing their very best, the 6 to 12 students who usually came to the gifted computer lab at lunch time could not count on having machines and software operating smoothly as the following excerpt from our field notes indicates.

> The students...continue to have a lot of very nitty-gritty problems. Kathy can't get the printer going.... She's scowling and says in an annoyed tone of voice, "Please help me." Mr. East suggests several things, and after they try out four or five different approaches they finally get the paper to print out. Ms. Prentiss has been working with Sharon on word processing.... For the last 10 minutes cries like, "I don't believe it" and "Oh, no. Not again!" have been emanating from both of them.... Finally, Ms. Prentiss calls Mr. East over.... Sharon is clearly getting anxious, pacing around, picking her nails and the like. She takes her disk and inserts it in another computer hooked up to a different printer. She can't get this printer to work.... Ms. Prentiss rushes over to try to fix it saying, "I just don't believe it!!" Ms. Prentiss comes over to me [the observer] and says, "I feel like quitting this...." At this point Mark calls to Ms. Prentiss, "I need help...." Ms. Prentiss puts her head down on the desk briefly. She looks at me with what appears to be a mixture of mock and real despair and trudges over to Mark. [Later in the same period] Dan is trying to use a printer which Mr. East thought he had fixed. Dan's essay comes out quadruple-spaced. In addition, every single word is underlined. Ms. Prentiss looks at it and breaks into almost hysterical laughter. Dan looks annoyed. Ms. Prentiss says, "I'm sorry, this is just too much—too, too much!..." Mr. Adams and Mr. East are still working on the second malfunctioning printer. Mr. Adams says, "You know I have a trick. What I do with my Radio Shack computer

is just turn it on its side and hit it. Maybe that will work here...."
They turn it on its side and give it a whack as one of them holds the
tension on the paper feed. The machine begins to work.

The knowledge needed to make minor hardware repairs, to be able to
distinguish which problems one can fix and which require outside help, and
to operate specific pieces of software is only part of what is needed to utilize
computers effectively in teaching. Locating, trying out, and keeping abreast
of new and better software also take time and energy. Many of the teachers
interested in using their computers felt that they did not get adequate
assistance with this task.

> Mr. Powers: I've been ordering software out of catalogues because
> there's no person around the school board that's familiar with power
> and energy, that knows what software is available...[and] says,
> "Hey, this is a good program. Let's buy it." or "We want you to try
> this program or preview this program." It's basically look in the
> catalogue. If it looks like it has anything to do with the curriculum
> I'll order it....All the [Power and Energy] teachers got a computer at
> the same time. However, all of them are not using them in the same
> way because there is no standard set for this part of the curriculum.

Other teachers had the same kind of problems. Without a knowledgeable
person available for ready consultation, they failed to order software out of
inertia or a sense of uncertainty about whether it would be useful. Those who
did order it were frequently disappointed and reported that such
disappointments discouraged them from further similar expenditures. All this
is not to say that it was impossible for teachers to get useful information on
software. Whitmore was only four or five miles from a university-based
educational software library. Teachers reported that if and when they
attended professional conferences, sessions about educational software were
common. For some subject areas the school district did purchase software
and provided teachers with some opportunities to learn about it. However,
effective utilization of most of these avenues required some degree of extra
energy, initiative, or time. Some teachers just preferred not to add any extra
activities to what they perceived to be their already overburdened schedules.
Others were skeptical enough about the value of computing for their students
that they chose to invest their energies elsewhere. Peer norms among the
teachers clearly did not require teachers to go out of their way to give
students the opportunity to work with computers, as indicated by Ms.
Prentiss's following remarks:

> Interviewer: How have other teachers responded to your efforts to
> make computers available [by opening the gifted computer lab at
> lunch time]?

> Ms. Prentiss: Generally surprise. I'm a bit of an anomaly. Not that
> many women do these things and...just "Why?" "Why?" It's one

thing if you can do <u>YOUR OWN</u> work on it, but why would you [do the extra work]?...I've never been so isolated from teachers as I have this year. I don't even eat with them....So they...think I'm weird because I want to socialize with kids.

Without someone on hand to encourage and facilitate such efforts many teachers never really tried to explore what use they could make of computers in instruction, and those who did try often became discouraged.

OVERLOAD OF KNOWLEDGEABLE TEACHERS

Becker's (1984) work suggests that individual teachers very often play a major role in providing the impetus for a school's obtaining instructional computers. Although Becker reports a trend for administrators to become more involved in this process than was the case in earlier years, individual teachers still play a crucial role in the implementation stage with regard to issues such as deciding what software will be purchased and providing informal training for other teachers.

Such was certainly the case at Whitmore. For example, from all reports, if Ms. Prentiss had not volunteered to supervise the gifted computer lab at lunch time as her "duty" period instead of monitoring the halls, the lab would not have been used on a daily basis. Similarly, Mr. Adams often served as a resource for his colleagues at Whitmore. Since there was no individual or group of individuals at Whitmore with formal responsibility for helping teachers learn to use computers and assisting them with problems they encountered after they had learned enough to attempt to use the computers in their classroom, increased usage of computers within the school meant increased burdens on teachers like Mr. Adams, Mr. East, and Ms. Prentiss. This put knowledgeable teachers in a position of conflict when colleagues or students requested help because that help had to be taken from time that was either their own personal time or time from parts of the day officially allocated to other, more traditional uses, namely, teaching or preparing to teach.

Interviewer: What are the one or two major impediments to greater usage of the computers?

Ms. Prentiss: The time for some ONE person to coordinate the use of the room....What I didn't realize when we started is that a teacher who doesn't have complete control of the class...and know everything about the machines...could cause so much damage. They walk out of the room and who's got to deal with it? You know who....It's selfish, but I didn't bargain to... I've often given two periods a day and lots of extra time....One time that other teacher asked [to use the room]. I had to teach her class—make up the dittos [about using the computers]. Hey, I don't want word to get out I'm doing this. Then every...teacher...

THE LACK OF INCENTIVES AND
THE PRESENCE OF DISINCENTIVES

As has already been discussed, few teachers were drawn to devote energy to learning about the potential of the instructional use of computers out of an *a priori* conviction that computers have a lot to offer to their students. Incentives to entice them to try to make effective use of computers in instruction at Whitmore were few and far between. Disincentives were easier to find. In addition to the lack of really effective training and a supportive infrastructure, teachers often encountered difficulty in getting appropriate supplies when they did use computers in their classes, as indicated by the following excerpt from project field notes:

> Tammy tells me that Mr. Checkhov wants them to conserve the printer ribbons. There is only one left for the rest of the year (today is March 10). Students were urged to use the computer less according to Tammy.

On occasion teachers even reported bringing in computer-related supplies from home because they were unable to get them through the school.

> Interviewer: Are you able to get the supplies you need [for the computer], like paper or anything of that sort?
>
> Mr. Powers: I order one case of paper each semester which really isn't enough. I have to go and try to bum it from other departments. I've already brought some in from home.
>
> Interviewer: Is it just that it's hard [to get] or is it that you're not able to order as much as you need?
>
> Mr. Powers: When we order as much as we want...they start cutting things off the requisition. So I find that if I keep the orders low, at least I get that rather than nothing.

The disincentives for computer use were not all material. Teachers faced the risk of looking bad not only in front of their students, as discussed earlier, but also in front of administrators whose evaluations were important to them.

> Allen is working on a biology project [in the gifted computer lab today]. Steve is helping Ms. Prentiss load paper in a printer. Ms. Prentiss formally introduces Steve to the two vice-principals [who are visiting the lab today]. One of them says to Ms. Prentiss, "I thought this would be an organized lab...." After they tire of watching Allen, they go over to Ms. Prentiss. One of them says very audibly [to the other], "Boy, I don't see anyone doing anything... except for Ms. Prentiss." He [then] says to Ms. Prentiss, "You told us that you've got everything down to a T!" Then the vice-principals watch Ms. Prentiss try to print out something on the printer, but the printer wasn't cooperating. Dave...asks,..."Will you take the

computers away?" The vice-principal replies, "No, we'll take Ms. Prentiss away." Ms. Prentiss smiles somewhat nervously and says that she'll try to get the printer to work....At this point another vice-principal comes in. One of the vice principals who was there before him turns to him and says, "Ms. Prentiss is showing us how computers don't work today." Two of the vice-principals leave.

Given that the school system provided Ms. Prentiss with virtually no training and that she voluntarily gave up her lunch break to supervise the lab so that the computers would not sit idle, the rather unsupportive attitude of the vice-principals was quite striking.

Although there were many disincentives to computer use as discussed above, incentives were less numerous according to Whitmore's teachers. The partial payment of tuition for courses designed to build teachers' computer skills was one incentive to which a few of Whitmore's teachers responded. However, this was clearly not enough to induce most teachers to spend their own time and money in this way. A more obvious incentive would be to pay teachers to update their skills. Even Mr. Carter, whose fairly strong resistance to computer use was apparent in the interview excerpted earlier, might have been willing to explore the possibilities if paid to do so.

> Interviewer: Let me ask you a hypothetical question. Is there anything that the school or the school board could do if they wanted to entice teachers to see whether there was anything useful they could find in using computers? What would they have to do?

> Mr. Carter: They'd have to pay me money.

When asked a similar question, many of Whitmore's other teachers mentioned similar ideas such as paid summer workshops for teachers which would give them a reasonably extended time in which to explore the computer's possibilities. The problem with these suggestions is, of course, that they would be quite expensive. Furthermore, there is at least the possibility that some teachers who have little serious interest in actually using computers in their classrooms might see such workshops as a reasonably painless way to supplement their income, thus wasting money from the perspective of the school system.

One other possible incentive is suggested by the fact that a number of teachers reported that they had initially started using computers to create tests and to compute grades (e.g., in ways that made the administrative or clerical parts of their job easier or more efficiently performed). Some of these teachers then proceeded to experiment with ways in which they could use computers for instructional purposes. To the extent that the motivation to perform one's work in an easier or more efficient way is salient, it might be used to overcome the inertia and anxiety which kept some teachers from ever venturing to touch a computer in classroom settings. It is possible that familiarity with the technology gained through such usage might then lead at least a subset of teachers to venture further and see how and if they might use computers in their teaching.

SUMMARY AND CONCLUSIONS

In sum, computers available for instructional purposes were not utilized very much outside of computer science classes and the geometry classrooms which served as the field test site for the GPTutor. A wide variety of factors appeared to contribute to this situation. One factor of fundamental importance was the teachers' perception that much existing educational software does not have enough educational potential to make it worth using. Finally, many teachers found it difficult to envision how they could integrate the use of one or two computers into their rather traditional whole-class methods of instruction. Most teachers were quite unfamiliar with computers and with educational software. Inertia, concern about the impact of low levels of computer competence on their authority in the classroom, and anxiety about dealing with a new and unfamiliar machine all conspired to keep things this way. In addition, real problems with the training available to teachers and the fact that the school had neither an infrastructure to support teachers' attempts to learn nor many incentives designed to induce them to take the first steps toward increasing their knowledge in this domain contributed to the fact that many of the computers available for students' use at Whitmore were used quite infrequently.

REFERENCES

Anderson, J. R., Boyle, C. F., & Yost, G. (1985). The geometry tutor. *Proceedings of the 9th International Conference on Artificial Intelligence* (pp. 1-7), Los Angeles, CA.

Becker, H. J. (1984). School uses of microcomputers. reports from a national survey. *Center for Social Organization of Schools Newsletter*, Issue No. 4. The Johns Hopkins University, Baltimore, MD.

Becker, H. J. (1986). Instructional uses of school computers. *Reports from the 1985 National Survey*, Issue I. Center for Social Organization of Schools. The Johns Hopkins University, Baltimore, MD.

Benne, K. D. (1970). Authority in education. *Harvard Educational Review, 40(3)*, 385-410.

Bierstedt, R. (1970). *The Social Order.* New York: McGraw-Hill.

Bogdan, R. C., & Biklen, S. K. (1982). *Qualitative Research for Education: An Introduction to Theory and Methods.* New York: Allyn & Bacon.

Bossert, W. H. (1988). The use of technology to improve two key classroom relationships. In R. S. Nickerson & P. P. Zodhiates (eds.). *Technology in education: Looking toward 2020* (pp. 275-284). Hillsdale, NJ: Erlbaum.

Cohen, D. K. (1988). *Teaching Practice: Plus C Change.* East Lansing: National Center for Research on Teacher Education, Michigan State University.

Collins, A. (1991) The role of computer technology in restructuring schools, *Phi Delta Kappan, 73(1)*, 28-36.

Cuban, L. (1984). *How Teachers Taught.* New York: Longman.

Feurzeig, W. (1988). Apprentice tools: students as practitioners. In R. S. Nickerson & P. P. Zodhiates (eds). *Technology in Education: Looking toward 2020* (pp. 97-120). Hillsdale, NJ: Erlbaum.

Goetz, J. P., & LeCompte, M. D. (1984). *Ethnography and Qualitative Design in Education Research.* Orlando, FL: Academic Press.

Groen, G. J. (1985). The epistemics of computer-based microworlds. *Proceedings of the Second International Conference on Artificial Intelligence and Education.* United Kingdom: University of Exeter.

Hughes, M. (1959). *Development of the Means for the Assessment of the Quality of Teaching in Elementary Schools.* Salt Lake City, UT: University of Utah Press.

Lawler, B. (1984). Designing computer-based microworlds. In M. Yazdani (ed.). *New Horizons in Educational Computing.* Chichester, West Sussex: East Harwood.

Office of Technology Assessment (1988). *Power On! New Tools for Teaching and Learning.* Washington, DC: U.S. Government Printing Office.

Olson, S. (1976). *Ideas and Data: Process and Practice of Social Research.* Homewood, IL: The Dorsey Press.

Papert, S. (1980). *Mindstorms: Children, Computers, and Powerful Ideas.* New York: Basic Books, Inc.

Reichardt, C. S., & Cook, T. D. (1979). Beyond qualitative *versus* quantitative methods. In T. D. Cook & C. S. Reichardt (eds.). *Qualitative and Quantitative Methods in Evaluation Research.* Beverly Hills, CA: Sage.

Sandholtz, J. H., Ringstaff, C., & Dwyer, D. C. (1990). Classroom management: Teaching in high-tech environments: Classroom management revisited. *First-Fourth Year Findings, Apple Classrooms of Tomorrow Report No. 10.* Cupertino, CA: Apple Classrooms of Tomorrow, Advanced Technology Group, Apple Computer Inc.

Schofield, J. W. (1985). The impact of an intelligent computer-based tutor on classroom social processes: an ethnographic study. Unpublished manuscript, University of Pittsburgh, Learning Research and Development Center, Pittsburgh, PA.

Schofield, J. W., & Anderson, K. A. (1987). Combining quantitative and qualitative components of research on ethnic identity and intergroup relations. In J. S. Phinney & M. J. Rotheram (eds.). *Children's Ethnic Socialization: Pluralism and Development* (pp. 252-273). Newbury Park, CA: Sage.

Schofield, J W. (forthcoming). *Computers in the Classroom.* Monograph in preparation.

Sheingold, K., Hawkins, J., & Char, C. (1984). "I'm the thinkest, you're the typist": the interaction of technology and the social life of classrooms. *Journal of Social Issues, 40(3),* 49-62.

Smith, L. M., & Geoffrey, W. (1968). *The Complexities of an Urban Classroom.* New York: Holt, Rinehart & Winston.

Taylor, W. D., & Johnson, J. B. (1986). Some issues in the application of technology to education. In J. A. Culbertson & L. Cunningham (eds.). *Microcomputers and Education. Eighty-fifth Yearbook of the National Society for the Study of Education* (pp. 216-233).

Walker, D. (1984). Promise, potential and pragmatism: computers in high school. *Institute for Research in Educational Finance and Governance Policy Notes, 5(3),* 3-4.

READING QUESTIONS

1) What are the differences among those whom Cuban refers to as "boosters," "enthusiasts," and "advocates"?
2) Describe the "cycle of predicting extraordinary changes in teacher practice."
3) What are the advantages that advocates claim for the use of computers in education?
4) Where does much of the push for education reform using computers come from?
5) Who inside the schools adopted computers? How did most teachers and administrators respond to their introduction?
6) What are the "simultaneous top-down and bottom-up movements" Cuban refers to?
7) What is "token adoption"? What is its purpose?
8) Who are the primary users of computers in the schools?
9) Who controls access to computers in the schools?
10) How does the early adoption of computers echo—in its figures and its expectations—the early adoption of radio, television, and film?
11) When they were adopted, in what kinds of classes were computers used?
12) If figures triple from the time Cuban wrote this article (1986), how often will computers be used in the schools?
13) How might limited teacher use of new technology be due to "organizational constraints built into classroom and schools as workplaces"?
14) What are "teacher-defined problems"? What uses of computers respond to these problems?
15) Why is "should" a more basic question than "how"?
16) What is a "cost-effectiveness ratio"? How does computing compare with other major interventions in education in terms of cost-effectiveness?
17) What is the "schools can be managed like corporations" argument?
18) "Teaching can be done by anyone who possesses the appropriate technical skills." What assumption underlies this argument?
19) What is "emotional rationality," and how does it motivate teachers?
20) What is Cuban's argument for preserving teaching as an art?
21) Why is "transfer" an important notion in Cuban's argument?
22) What is "collateral learning"?
23) "If teachers do an inept job of presenting and generating ideas, should we not be looking at how teachers work rather than selling them a prosthesis?" Explain this argument.
24) What are Cuban's prediction for the future of educational computing, and what are his arguments for them?
25) How does overpromising of the benefits of drugs relate to the promises made about educational computing?
26) Why did Schofield select Whitmore for her analysis?
27) What "striking finding" did Schofield make about the use of computers at Whitmore?
28) How do you compare claims that computers are used "enough" with the claim that textbooks are used "enough"?
29) How much and in what way were the computers used in the Office Automation and Business Computer Applications classes?
30) Why did the librarian allow the search system to be used inefficiently?
31) Why were the computers for the gifted students moved into one lab?
32) What obvious exception (outside GPTutor and CS classes) was there to the lack of adoption?

33) Why does Schofield not find it surprising that teachers' emphasis was on how computers would fit into the current curriculum?
34) What organizational problems did computing pose in the classes at Whitmore?
35) "IT DROVE ME CRAZY." Why?
36) "Something like this is always an opportunity to make a fool of yourself." Explain why this concern is important to teachers.
37) What type of training was available to the teachers at Whitmore? What were the shortcoming of the training?
38) How was technical support a problem for the teachers at Whitmore?
39) In what way did the use of computing at Whitmore depend on volunteer labor?
40) What kinds of incentives and disincentives were present for those teachers who might want to adopt computing?

DISCUSSION QUESTIONS

1) Cuban claims that "adult-child ties may unravel as a consequence of the newly developed child-machine liaison." Sproull & Kiesler found that computing facilitated social interaction. Compare these competing observations about the effect of computing.
2) Is "we don't know enough yet" a good argument against educational computing?
3) Cuban asks that "technology advocates" push for basic support for higher pay, smaller classes, etc. If these reforms were undertaken, would they ease the introduction of computing into the classroom? Would the reforms by themselves produce better education than adding computing to the current situation?
4) Massive reforms usually ignore what Cuban calls "teacher-defined problems." How were computers used at Whitmore to solve teacher-defined problems? Is this "token adoption" or the verification of Cuban's predictions of the extent of the use of computing? How much support would be required to make adoption more extensive?

PRACTICING THE DESIGN ETHIC

1) Find at least three examples of the use of educational computing on your campus. By interviews with instructors or students, determine the extent to which this activity replaces others they might be doing in their class. Also ask about whether this activity isolates them or connects them to others. To what extent is the activity "teacher-defined"? In your report, discuss how each example fits with Cuban's portrait of educational computing. Make sure to address whether this approach would be successful if it were mandated for the entire school.
2) Design an interview form based on the kinds of computing support that Schofield lists as problematic in her article. Interview at least five instructors to determine whether these problems in support are evident at your school also.

CHAPTER

15

THE SOCIAL CONSEQUENCES OF EDUCATIONAL COMPUTING

In the last chapter, Cuban urged us not to think of education as simply a cognitive process. This is also a good reminder for educational computing. Both the articles in this chapter show how computing can have social and emotional effects on students who use it.

Sproull, Kiesler, and Zubrow undertook a detailed investigation of the consequences of entering a computing-intensive environment (Carnegie Mellon University). They use the concept of "culture shock" to explain the confusion and attempts to cope that accompany an introduction into a society where many of the rules and practices are unfamiliar. Coping with this confusion can be educational, but for at least some students, it leads to withdrawal from the computing culture—with the consequent risk that they will not return. Sproull et al.'s research suggests that instead of concentrating only on the technical issues of computing education, we should look to the social and cultural trappings that surround it. Not to do so risks alienating good students.

Hativa, Lesgold, and Swissa's study of two mathematical software packages in use in Israel supports this conclusion. This detailed study of an implementation shows that educational software can sometimes have unpredictable, even counterintuitive, effects. And the factors that control these effects have more to do with the classroom practice and social structure than with the technology itself.

581

ENCOUNTERING AN ALIEN CULTURE[1]

Lee Sproull
Sara Kiesler
David Zubrow
Carnegie Mellon University

Many organizations today are faced with the problem of introducing managers, secretaries, and other nontechnical people to computing. Previous investigations of this problem have generally not focused on organizational settings but have used a technical, instructional, or individual abilities perspective. Technical analyses usually investigate the relative ease or difficulty with which new users learn particular computer operations as a function of equipment or software variables (e.g., Bury, Boyle, Evey, & Neal, 1982: Black & Moran, 1982). Often these users are not new to computing itself, but rather are simply new to the particular operations being studied (e.g., Schneider, Nudelman, & Hirsh-Pasek, 1982; DeYoung, Kampen, & Topolski, 1982). Instructional analyses usually measure the accuracy with which people learn certain material, perhaps as a function of alliterative instructional techniques (e.g., Taylor, 1980). Analyses of individual abilities assume that more able students will have better experiences (e.g., Arndt, Feltes, & Hanak, 1983). In none of these perspectives does the investigator consider what the new person learns about such issues as: the context in which computing occurs, the status positions for those who compute, the kinds of people who compute, the social organization of computing, and the values placed on computing. These are cultural lessons and they constitute an important part of the newcomer's learning.

In this chapter we use a cultural perspective to try to understand people's initial encounters with computing. We begin by exploring some of the ways in which computing is embedded in a larger social order and suggest some of the ways in which it will be alien to newcomers. We then draw upon work in organizational socialization to suggest how newcomers will respond to it. Finally, we present a two-part study that investigates initial encounters with computing at CMU. The results of this study reveal that newcomers do indeed learn powerful cultural lessons about computing.

COMPUTING AS CULTURE

CULTURAL CONTEXT

In the early days of computing, few people outside the scientists and engineers directly involved in producing and using the new machines had any contact with computers (McCorduck, 1979). But today, ideas about computers, if not actual experience with them, permeate our society. Thus, in 1982 *Time* magazine named the computer, "Man of the Year"; computer magazines are found on newsstands; managerial publications such as *Fortune* and the *Harvard Business Review* publish numerous articles on managing computing; consultants are offering advice on how to overcome "fear of computing." Schools and universities are requiring their students to take programming courses or purchase microcomputers. Sales of machines to households are burgeoning. Computer camps are oversubscribed.

Cultural components of these phenomena include generally shared beliefs such as "everyone can benefit from computers, anyone can use a computer," and "the more powerful the computer, the better" (e.g., Ogdin, 1982). The use of terms like "novice," "user," and "wizard" signal cultural roles and values. *The Hackers Dictionary* (Steele et al., 1983) offers an irreverent description of the culture through definitions of many of its terms and phrases. The prevailing high evaluations of computing and its "ways of life," despite problems inevitably connected to the technology and its introduction into organizations and everyday life, indicates that norms of the culture are uncritically accepted by many people (Kling, 1980). Although a cultural perspective on computing is not commonly found in the scientific literature (see Turkle, 1980, & Kling, 1980, for two exceptions), the popular press frequently describes computing subcultures. See Zimbardo (1980) and Levy (1982) for a description of the hacker subculture at Stanford University. Kidder (1981) describes a similar culture in an industrial setting.

It would be difficult for a novice to sit down at a computer or terminal today without encountering the culture that surrounds computing. The novice will confront not merely neutral stimuli to which he may respond as desired, which he may regard as good or bad, right or wrong as immediate experience instructs. Most of the stimuli—hardware, software, manuals, the social and physical context—have already been judged by the social order and the novice's predecessors. In this sense any particular machine is an artifact of and embedded in the culture that produced it. Encounters with that artifact are also encounters with the culture and will lead to cultural lessons as well as to learning more narrowly focused on particular machines.

Certain organizational features found in research, development, and engineering divisions within the computer industry itself and college campuses foster development of a computer culture. One is that computers are used for many different purposes. On a typical college campus, for example, the same machine or machines may be used for research, administration, accounting, teaching, and text processing. Thus these machines tend to have operating systems and programming tools that make them relatively easy to use. Second, because these machines serve many purposes, many kinds of people have access to them. And furthermore, this access is relatively direct. That is, people have their own accounts; there need be no intermediaries between them and the machine. Third, many of the people with direct access are relatively smart, young, and they don't have enough to do. That is, they are students. They have few family or economic responsibilities, flexible schedules, and the stamina to stay up all night. Fourth, these organizations tend to be less bureaucratic and formal than most government, commercial, or manufacturing settings. In these cases, where smart understimulated people have direct access to flexible machines in non-bureaucratic settings, the culture of computing is nurtured and can flourish.

Every culture has values and norms, a status hierarchy, membership signs and boundaries to distinguish members from nonmembers, a language, and its own artifacts (Gamst & Horbeck, 1976). Although their specifics will differ from campus to campus, some of the general features of the culture of computing are quite widely shared. The culture is an adolescent one. Pranks, tricks, and games are benignly tolerated when not actually encouraged. People are often impolite and irreverent. Mild larceny is also tolerated, if not encouraged, through faking accounts, stealing time, copying proprietary software, and breaking codes. The culture is individualistic and idiosyncratic. Social cooperation or coordination is rarely necessary. There is competition to write the best, fastest, biggest program or to build the best, fastest, smallest hardware. The status hierarchy is revealed through assigning people to such categories as wizards, wheels, hackers, users, and losers. True members of the culture can be found at the terminal room or computer center at all hours of the day and night.

THE ALIEN NATURE OF COMPUTING

Despite its rapid intrusion into many areas of life, computing currently is not just something new. It is also strange. Its spatial and temporal characteristics, controllability, and nature of feedback are unlike those of other technologies. Consider a college student encountering a time-sharing system and some of the ways in which academic computing differs from all other course work. Computing differs in time and space characteristics from other academic activities. Whereas in other courses students are free to choose the time and space that suit them best to do their homework, students of computing are tied to a terminal room and a time at which a terminal is available. Computing also differs in reliability and controllability. When a student is reading a history book, the page never goes blank. When a student is writing a paper, if his pencil breaks he can sharpen it. But computer tools are not under a student's control. Computing also differs in speed and nature of feedback. If a student is doing a physics assignment, the first wrong digit he writes on the page does not generate an immediate cascade of error messages. In other courses, a student may stop after his exertions and imagine that the essay is good enough, or that he has worked enough math problems to demonstrate competence. In computing, there is no stopping until the program works—it either does or it doesn't.

In order for a novice actually to use a computer system, he must make his way through a host of arbitrary conventions that are unrelated to the science or theory of computing. New students are thrown into a sea of syntax, I/O devices, priority classes, programs, and system quirks with no conceptual life vest to keep them afloat. The stylized nature of person/computer interaction can be particularly alienating to these students. All new disciplines involve learning conventions, but it is humiliating to be at the mercy of so many seemingly trivial and arbitrary ones. These problems are compounded because computing is a scarce resource on almost every college campus; thus students can be forced to wait long periods of time just to gain access to the potentially frustrating machine.

As strange as these experiences may be, their strangeness is exacerbated by the fact that they occur within a social context with which other people are quite comfortable. This embedding of computing in the larger life of the organization distinguishes students' computing encounters from those of say, the physics laboratory. While the physics laboratory may also lead students to feel out of control, it is a very sheltered and isolated environment apart from the real business of physics or anything else. By contrast, the newly computing student must compete for terminal time and cycles with administrators who are managing accounting, secretaries who are typing manuscripts, faculty members who are doing research, students who are doing assignments, and "hackers."

PROCESSES OF ENCOUNTERING

One learns a culture through socialization into it. van Maanen and Schein (1979) describe organizational socialization as the "process by which an individual acquires the social knowledge and skills necessary to assume an organizational role" (p. 211). In the case of computing, the organizational role is that of "computer user." Once a person acquires that role in any organization, one then occupies a different status in all subsequent organizations.

If the culture is an alien one, then socialization will occur under conditions of strangeness. Strangeness or unfamiliarity means that the novices' habitual and therefore efficient models and means for learning will be neither useful nor appropriate. As a result, novices must learn how to learn as well as what to learn. They must develop new ways of assimilating information and a new framework for it. They must learn how to recognize and interpret cues, and whom to rely upon as informants. They must learn how to organize new bits and pieces of knowledge into coherent theories. In these processes the novice brings capabilities, prior experiences, and expectations to the new setting.

The initial interaction between a novice and a new culture inevitably produces reality shock for the novice. Reality shock is composed of changes, contrasts, and surprises (Louis, 1980). Changes are simply objective differences from the novice's prior situation, for example in title, workload, compensation, location, food preferences, social customs, and even facial expressions. Contrasts are differences in what is subjectively salient from that in the novice's former situation, for example in images of surroundings, pace, ethos and language (e.g., Smalley, 1963). Both changes and contrasts can be anticipated by the novice preparing to enter a new culture; through anticipatory socialization (Merton & Rossi, 1968), a novice can ease his transition to a new culture. Surprises, on the other hand, are unanticipated differences between expectations and reality. For example, technical assistants and management personnel sent overseas often experience role ambiguity and loss of personal status that are not at all what they anticipated (Byrnes, 1966; Higbee, 1969). Reality shock is important to the novice because it signals that prior instrumental behaviors are no longer appropriate and new ones must be learned. It is also important because it colors the early lessons learned in the new culture. The nature of the reality shock and how it is managed by the novice and the organization do much to define the process and outcomes of socialization (David, 1971; Church, 1982).

Reality shock leads the novice to experience confusion, both about self and the external environment (Oberg, 1966). Confusion about self leads the novice to feel overwhelmed and to question aspects of his or her self-identity or self-image. These questions can be of the form, "What am I doing?" and "Do I look foolish?" or "Maybe I'm not the person I thought I was." Confusion about the external environment leads the novice to question the capabilities and motivations of those around him. These questions can be of the form, "Do those people really know what they're doing?" or "Why can't they communicate clearly?"

Reality shock and confusion lead novices to try to establish control over the situation. In attempting to control the situation (for example, by explaining surprises) the individuals try to reduce discrepancies between the current state and reference values or standards in the situation (Kanfer & Hagerman, 1981; Bandura, 1977; Thompson, 1981; Carver & Scheier, 1982). These attempts can entail mental activity alone, for example constructing satisfying interpretations of the confusing events. They can also entail actions such as increased effort or talking with other people about the situation. In either case, aspects of the culture will play a part in the control attempts. They will provide sources of information for constructing interpretations and people who function as comparators or standards against which the novices can judge their behavior. If the control attempts are successful, the individual will be able to learn the values and skills necessary for the new role (i.e., to become socialized).

If the control attempts are not successful, anger or withdrawal will arise (Carver, Blaney, & Scheier, 1979; Brockner, 1979). Anger leads to intransigence and active rejection of the values of the socializing or enculturating agents (Goffman, 1961). Intransigence guarantees that the novice will remain an outsider but it allows the novice to maintain a positive self-image. The intransigent novice might say, "These people are so crazy that only an idiot would want to act like them." Withdrawal also precludes positive socialization, but does not contribute to a positive self-image. The withdrawing novice might say, "I'm no good at this and there's no sense in trying."

If computing does represent an alien culture, then we would expect that novices' first computing encounters would engender high reality shock caused by changes in amount of work, kind of work, place of work, timing of work, and surprises (differences between expectations and reality). Reality shock leads to confusion. We would expect that novices would be confused about their own capability and roles and that of the experts in their environment. The most likely responses to reality shock and confusion are attempts to exert control by using resources in the cultural setting. These resources might include other students or teachers who provide ideas and behavioral examples of control responses. If control attempts are successful, the person has gained the potential of becoming further socialized and a cultural recruit. If control attempts are unsuccessful, anger or withdrawal will ensue and the person is likely to become a cultural dropout.

In organizations, most novices will ultimately come to terms with the culture of computing. At an elementary level they will learn to work with computers, and some will become experts. But if the above framework is meaningful, novices will also learn much more in their initial encounters with computing. They will develop an image of "the computer," of the social organization surrounding it, and of their own degree of cultural competence. For the organization, these understandings are probably more important than any technical details of writing or using programs that can be conveyed to its nontechnical people in an introductory encounter because they determine a person's willingness to undergo further socialization.

OVERVIEW OF EMPIRICAL WORK

In the spring of 1982, we conducted a two-part study to explore the cultural perspective on computing and some hypotheses derived from the model described above. In part one, we conducted a survey of liberal arts freshmen to explore how their first encounters with computing might have differed from their first encounters with college generally (Feldman & Newcomb, 1969). This survey allowed us to rule out the possibility that college, not computing, was the alien culture by testing the predictions that reality shock and confusion will be stronger in computer programming courses than in other courses, and that there will be more control attempts and more failures of control attempts in computer programming courses than in other courses. Thus:

l. For nontechnical students, the computer programming course will be different from, and will violate expectations of, college work to a greater degree than other courses. This reality shock will be experienced as confusion about self and the environment.

2. Students will exert more control attempts in computer programming courses than they will in other courses by, for example, seeking out others and seeking explanation.

3. Students will have more difficulty finding constructive ways to exert control in programming courses than in other courses: they will exert more unconstructive control: and they will experience more unsuccessful outcomes as indicated by withdrawal and anger.

Part two of the study used interview data to explore these processes. We asked a group of liberal arts freshmen to talk with us about their initial experiences with computing to see if their descriptions revealed elements of the process we have described above. In addition, we were interested in whether the students' descriptions would reveal aspects of the culture of computing, its alien nature, and the cultural lessons learned that were not measured in the survey.

PART ONE

METHOD AND ANALYSIS

In order to compare computing to other kinds of college experiences, we administered a fixed-response questionnaire to 268 liberal arts freshmen during their required social science class in the spring of 1982. (This represents 95% of the freshman liberal arts class.) Students were asked to assess one of their English, social science, mathematics, and computer science (computer programming) courses on a number of dimensions using the scale:

l. false; not at all true
2. neither true nor false
3. true or very true of this course

The conceptual dependent variables were reality shock, confusion, control attempts, and outcomes (academic success, anger, and withdrawal). They were measured using the questionnaire items listed in Table 15.l. Statistical comparisons were made across courses to evaluate how similarly the students rated each course. These comparisons were conducted using repeated measures analyses of variance and t tests comparing courses and items within each factor. A "true or very true" response was set equal to "l" and any other response was set equal to "0". (When comparisons are made such that 1 = false or very false, 2 = neither true nor false, and 3 = true or very true, then the findings are stronger statistically but harder to interpret.)

The findings are based upon the responses of the 208 students who answered questions about one course in each of the four categories of courses we listed (English, social science, mathematics, computer programming).

Questions about socialization processes	My English course	My Social Science course	My Math course	My Computer Science course
Reality shock				
This course:				
Takes more time than I expected	28	19	17	78
Very different from other courses	22	40	19	82
My work habits in the course are very different	20	23	23	76
Confusion				
I feel I don't know what I am doing	11	8	20	59
I worry that I might look foolish	9	4	6	20
The course has a clear division of tasks	44	65	48	44
I feel like a different person when I am in class	14	11	12	24
I feel overwhelmed by the work	23	13	17	76
Control attempts				
1. Talking to people:				
I talk to friends about this course	68	66	61	87
I talk to my instructor	60	33	28	59
I talk to students who took the course in the past	38	45	41	70
I talk to other faculty about this course	9	5	9	21
I have talked to a counselor about this course	17	10	17	43
Class members help one another	32	52	57	71
2. Constructive attribution:				
I am highly motivated	29	28	29	24
I really want to understand	64	68	78	65
When I do well it is because I worked hard	72	69	65	72
When I do well it is because I had good ability	57	47	59	30
When I do well it is because the instructor was good	42	50	34	16
When I do poorly it is because I didn't work hard	52	50	51	44
3. Unconstructive attribution:				
When I do well it is because I had good luck	32	27	27	41
When I do well it is because the task was easy	26	30	40	27
When I do poorly it is because of poor ability	18	13	24	37

Table 15.1
Percentage of students answering "True or very true" to questionnaire items, by course. Continued on next page.

Questions about socialization processes	My English course	My Social Science course	My Math course	My Computer Science course
Outcomes:				
1. Academic success:				
My performance is better than I expected	19	15	27	21
I am learning valuable skills	36	44	46	50
I am acquiring knowledge	66	77	71	56
2. Anger				
I get the feeling my instructors don't know what they're doing	16	11	33	59
This course makes me angry	27	15	28	72
I complain	40	25	40	79
3. Withdrawal				
I want to do just enough to get by	16	10	16	41

Note: Repeated measures (courses by items) analyses of variance were performed on these data. All course main effects were significant $p = .05$ or better (F ranged from 3.6 to 123, df 3 and 276 to 312). Degrees of freedom varied because subjects who did not answer an item for four courses were dropped. A few course-by-item interactions were significant. We assume this to mean that some items discriminated among courses better than others, an essentially trivial finding.

Table 15.1 continued

The typical student in our sample was enrolled in a computer programming course at the time of the survey (nearly the end of second semester, freshman year), and was also enrolled in a literature course, an interdisciplinary social science course, and in calculus.

Approximately 60 students were excluded from the analysis because they had not yet taken a computing course (a few others were not freshmen or had not taken a course in one of the other categories). This introduces bias in our sample; however, we believe it is a bias that works against our hypotheses. According to some of the students in question, they postpone computer science because they have heard it is "terrible" and they want to have the summer (or the following year) to concentrate on it. Hence the students not included in the analyses are likely to be especially negative about the computing course.

RESULTS

Computing versus Other Courses

Table 15.1 presents the percentages of students who answered "true or very true" to questions about each course. These data indicate that students' experiences with computing are quite different from their encounters with other disciplines. For the three items related to reality shock, an average 79%

of the students answered "true or very true" for computing. In contrast, the average for the other three courses ranged from 20% to 27%. Confusion also was greater in the computing course, with three of the five variables having values at least three times the averages of the other courses. (The second most confusing course was English, which belies the idea that nontechnical students are generally more confused by quantitative courses.)

The control attempts that we investigated were talking with others about the course and making causal attributions about their good and poor performance in the course. Generally, more students in computer programming talked with others about the course. More than in other courses, they talked with friends, past students in the course, and counselors. The item "class members help one another" yielded a 71% true response in computing, but averaged only 47% in the other courses.

Overall, fewer students in the computing course made constructive attributions of performance (the greatest number were in English and mathematics). On three out of six positive attribution items, computing was lowest. Although students in computing just as frequently claimed to desire understanding and to be motivated as they did in other courses, they tended not to attribute their good performance to their ability. In addition, they made more unconstructive attributions. The data suggest that, when they were explaining their performance in their computing course, students externalized their successes and internalized their failures. Especially significant are the relatively high frequencies of, "When I did well it was because I had good luck" and "When I did poorly it was because I had poor ability."

The outcomes of the students' encounters with computing and other freshman courses, as reflected in our survey, were mixed. There were no overall statistical differences across courses in the percentages of students who indicated that academic success was being or had been achieved. Mathematics scored highest overall in numbers of students saying they performed "better than I expected." Social science was most frequently given credit for "acquiring knowledge." Computer science was most frequently cited for "learning valuable skills." On the other hand, the percentages of students who experienced anger and withdrawal were much greater in the computer programming course than in other courses. Forty-one percent said they wanted to "do just enough to get by" in computing versus an average of 14% in the other courses.

Comparing computer science to mathematics (usually calculus) tells us something about whether the problems students had with computing were due to its quantitative nature. Table 15.2 shows, contrary to that idea, that computing was a more shocking and confusing experience than mathematics was, that it precipitated more talking to others as well as more unconstructive attributions, and that negative outcomes anger and withdrawal were significantly higher.

	t	
	Reality Shock	
Computing vs. mathematics	15.60	114
Computing vs. other courses	16.03	101
	Confusion	
Computing vs. mathematics	9.44	113
Computing vs. other courses	9.49	100
	Talking to people	
Computing vs. mathematics	10.31	115
Computing vs. other courses	10.46	102
	Constructive attribution	
Computing vs. mathematics	-3.60	105
Computing vs. other courses	-2.28	92
	Unconstructive attribution	
Computing vs. mathematics	1.30	104
Computing vs. other courses	2.66	92
	Academic success	
Computing vs. mathematics	-1.10	113
Computing vs. other courses	0.23	100
	Anger	
Computing vs. mathematics	10.43	111
Computing vs. other courses	12.62	99
	Withdrawal	
Computing vs. mathematics	4.95	117
Computing vs. other courses	4.61	104

Note: The above statistical *t* tests were performed on the data presented in Table 15.1. For example, the first row shows that, for the three Reality Shock items, the mean frequency of "true or very true" answers was greater when students evaluated their computer science course than when they evaluated their mathematics course. "Other courses" refers to the mean frequency of "true or very true" answers for English, Social Science, and Mathematics. The critical value for this table is 2.10 ($\alpha = .05$, $k = 4$, $df = 60$) based on the adjustment recommended by Winer (1971, p. 202) for a set of comparisons sharing a common treatment (hence correlated responses).

Table 15.2
Comparison of computing with mathematics and with other courses.

Some effects of background

We investigated the influence of previous experience with computing and of gender on responses to the courses. Fewer students who had taken a previous course in computing (probably a high school course) experienced reality shock ($F = 3.0$, $p < .05$), but there were no other differences attributable to prior experience.

Gender differences were found for reality shock, confusion, and talking with others. Male students were more likely to experience reality shock in courses than were female students ($F = 4.34$, $p < .05$). However, female students were more confused by computer programming whereas the male students were more confused by mathematics, social science, and English ($F = 2.88$, $p < .05$). Consistent with these results, female students were more likely to talk with others about their computer-programming course whereas the male students were more likely to talk with others about their courses in mathematics, social science, and English($F = 4.94$, $p < .01$).

Classification of Students by Outcomes

We classified students as potential cultural recruits or dropouts according to their answers on the survey, and compared the resulting distributions for each course. This analysis, presented in Table 15.3, is consistent with our prediction that computer programming will produce more cultural dropouts and fewer cultural recruits than other freshman courses will. By our count, over one-third of the students in computer programming were potential cultural dropouts in that they reported no academic success at all (i.e., none of the three success items was checked as true). Only 8% of the students were potential cultural recruits who reported at least one academic success item as true and no anger or withdrawal. By contrast, the percentages of potential cultural recruits in other courses was much higher and, in those courses, potential recruits were a higher percentage than were potential dropouts.

PART TWO

METHOD

Twenty-five students, randomly selected from the liberal arts freshman class, were invited to talk with us about their experience with computing. This procedure yielded 23 interview subjects (two could not be found). Each interview, consisting of twenty-nine open-ended questions and lasting about half an hour, was conducted by one of three trained interviewers during two three-day periods in the spring of 1982. The questions (in addition to general background questions) centered on students' expectations about computing,

	Potential dropout: no academic success items reported	Mixed case: one or more success, and anger/withdrawal, items reported	Potential recruits: one or more success, and no anger/withdrawal, items reported
Course	(%)	(%)	(%)
English	28.3	34.0	37.7
Social Science	20.7	24.5	54.9
Mathematics	24.3	40.1	35.5
Computer Science	35.1	56.8	8.1

Table 15.3
Classification of students according to potential cultural outcomes.

their experiences with it, and their evaluation of it. For example: "Describe your first encounter with the computer [here]." "Where do (did) you do your computer work?" "Please describe some occasion when you felt especially proud (unusually discouraged) about something that happened to you in relation to the computer." All interviews were tape recorded; tape transcriptions were entered into computer text files for purposes of content analysis (Sproull & Sproull, 1982).

The data reported below are of two types: frequency data that suggest trends and direct quotations from students that illustrate the nature of those trends. Because of the open ended nature of many of the questions, it is not always appropriate to use the question as the unit of analysis in reporting frequencies; groups of questions, or even the interview as a whole, is sometimes the more appropriate unit. Unless otherwise noted, the quotations illustrate dominant or modal responses. At a minimum, the data demonstrate the existence of the phenomena we are interested in. More usefully, we believe, they can be viewed as a first step in specifying the determinants and consequences of the process of encountering an alien culture.

THE SAMPLE

The sample consisted of 12 males and 11 females. The two factors that predominated in their decision to come to this college were its general reputation (59%) and its liberal/professional and business majors (36%). Almost all of the students framed at least one of their principle objectives for this year in terms of grades (86%). But their stance toward grades was sharply differentiated: 54% said they want to "do well"; 41% said they want to "pass." An additional important objective is intellectual growth with 64% of the sample mentioning learning and discovering interests. Going into business (64%) or to professional school (34%) are the most prevalent post-graduation plans.

Half the students had some experience with computing before coming to the university; 36% had a course in high school. No student believed that his or her high school experience was directly relevant to computing at college; half of them acknowledged that it gave them some general familiarity. Sixty-eight percent of the sample took a computer science course (Pascal) during their freshman year. This compares with 77% for the freshman class as a whole. Students who had taken a high school course were more likely to take computing during their freshman year than were those who had no previous course. Students whose academic goal was to do well were no more or less likely to take computing during their freshman year than were those whose goal was to pass. For students who took computing, this course figured heavily in all of their comments about computing, as we shall see below. All of the remaining students had at least some direct encounter with computing during the year as in, for example, using a document formatting program to prepare letters, participating in a psychology experiment in which stimulus materials were presented on a computer terminal, doing logic problems in their philosophy course, and testing hypotheses about the French Revolution in their history course.

Prominent in student descriptions of their experiences were comments about how different computing is from other things they are used to and how it makes them feel out of control. These students did not dwell on how they attempted to regain control, but they did reveal some interesting lessons they learned as a result of their attempts.

RESULTS

Describing their Experience

Four elements predominated in students' descriptions of their experiences with computing and can be viewed as components of reality shock: time, the terminal room, actually working on the computer, and course-related factors such as lectures, homework, and exams.

Many students (68%) reported computing to be much more time-consuming than they had expected. They reported having to spend long hours at the computer center, often late at night, and having to schedule the rest of their life around the availability of computer time. As one student said (codes in parentheses are unique student identifiers),

> If a computer program is due that week, then the computer sign-up times range all over my entire schedule. I have to arrange everything else around that computer time. If I get computer time at 6:00, then I have to have everything else arranged around that. It just rearranges everything. If you work from 11:00 until 3:00 or from 1:00 until 2:00 or however you work, it arranges your time. It just totally re-does your schedule. (P16)

Another student explained that late at night is the only time for uninterrupted work.

> Last semester more than a couple times I got up at four o'clock to go to the computer room so you could get on the terminal and not be crowded out because there are so many people there. (R18)

Of the 8 students who did not find the time demands of computing remarkable, 4 had no course experience with computing, 3 still acknowledged having to schedule around the computer, and 1 had a terminal in his room. But this student is the exception. Late hours, long hours, and constrained scheduling characterize most students' encounters with computing and constitute one component of reality shock. The terminal room itself is a second component of reality shock. Most students (77%) find it somehow unpleasant, with the major complaints being about crowding and lack of privacy.

> There's so many people who want to use them. There're enough terminals but it's just that there's rush hours and you just can't get on

at all and then it will crash during that time and it takes even longer because people will wait for it to come back up. Plus privacy. It's kind of crowded and you can't set your books down cause there's not enough space between terminals. (I9)

Another student said about the terminal room:

I was surprised, really surprised at the people set up along the benches. There's no privacy. Where I was [in the Computer Science department], they had little stalls for each terminal. I thought that was a much better idea, just because I would think that working at a bench like that would be really distracting. It reminded me of a horse at a trough. (X24)

Four students had no complaints about the terminal room, but an equal number had extremely' negative reactions, One student said:

I feel like I'm in 1984, cells right next to each other. It's like Russia. You've got to just get as many people as you can, crammed in there...They're all white. And all they have are computer information on them. Maybe they could have a picture of Picasso. Anything just to break the monotony...All you see are computer geeks and computers and the xerox machines and white on the walls...(Q17)

Only 6 students had used a terminal anywhere other than the main terminal room. They all appreciated the quiet and privacy of terminal rooms in other campus buildings. One student occasionally worked in a fraternity house:

I was there until 4 o'clock in the morning. It was nice because the guys...I had a little tape on. There weren't all these people around bugging you...It was just nice to be away from everything and everybody. (K11)

Working on the computer itself produces a third component of reality shock. A striking instance of this is seen in how students described their first encounter with the computer at college. For example:

I sat down at this computer and started hitting the buttons and it started making all this noise and people kept looking at me. I didn't know what I was doing. I didn't even know if it was on. (C3)

And another student said,

And the first time it's like, "Wow, a computer! I've never used one of these before. I wonder how it works,...You didn't know what you were doing. I mean, you knew because the teacher told you what to do but you were just like, 'Oh, well, I type this, then I type that and I hope it works. Here goes...' (R18)

The fourth major component of student descriptions of their experiences with computing is course work lectures, assignments, exams. During the fall semester computing course, students' final grade was based entirely on a five-hour programming exam—the mastery exam—taken at the end of the semester. Although programming assignments were offered as homework, they were optional. During the spring semester, homework was mandatory and the mastery exam carried less weight.

Students' perceptions of the lectures had two features relevant to reality shock. The first had to do with their content; the second, with their relationship to homework and exams. A small number of students had expected the lectures would include more emphasis on the range of computer functions and applications. As one said:

> I did not expect I'd have to write out programs. I expected [to learn] here's how to use it to our advantage with economics and all sorts of fun courses like that. (Q17)

More students were surprised that the lectures seemed to have very little to do with writing programs or the mastery exam.

> I get the feeling from my computing teacher that he's just telling me half the story. That's all he is telling me because when I get to the computer I still don't know what I'm doing, even after listening to him in class...He explains procedures and functions and major things but he doesn't show us how to write a program. (L12)

Apparently there is a common tension in introductory programming courses between the principles of programming and the specifics of any programming assignment; it is common for professors to want to teach general principles and for students to want to be taught specific techniques. For the students in our sample, this tension manifests itself in beliefs that the lectures are irrelevant or not helpful. Three-quarters (73%) of the students who had taken or were taking a computing course evaluated the lectures negatively.

The fact that all (for fall semester) or a large part (for spring semester) of the student's final grade was based on a mastery exam was clearly an important way in which students were surprised by this course. Two-thirds (67%) of the students with course experience commented negatively on this feature of the course.

> That was the biggest change, when they told you everything was based on this one big final. All of a sudden, all of the pressure was on that one five hour test. (M13)

Reactions to Their Experience

Students described several ways that they feel out of control in their encounters with computing. Seventy-seven percent of the students reported such an experience. One common catalyst is ignorance:

It's frightening when everyone else is around You just typing in as fast as they can, and you don't even know what to do. (E5)

Another is system crashes:

I was almost finished with a program and it crashed. I didn't have a save. I didn't put save on. I had to start over. It was heartbreaking. (O15)

And a third is experts whose "help" simply emphasizes these students' fragile positions:

I was on the computer and something happened. I didn't know what was going on. I saw a guy sitting over there who looked like a real hacker. So I asked him, and he got up, and he started doing all of this stuff with my account without telling me what he was doing.

He started messing around. 'You need this. Let's see, I'll give you this file.' It's like, what are you doing? He wouldn't tell me. (W23)

These experiences appear to be engendered in part by students' comparing themselves with others more expert than they and in part by feeling victimized by others as well as by the machine.

In attempting to gain control over their situation, all but one of the students who had taken computing experienced some success. One-third were proud of their performance on the mastery; two-thirds were proud of getting a program to run, often after a great deal of work.

I was just euphoric. I was just...I was so glad. I remember that night I went running home and there were some kids in my room. I was just going crazy and they didn't know what for. It was probably just the most basic programs but I was just so psyched-up that I couldn't sit still. (C3)

Over half the students who hadn't yet taken a computing course also had found occasion for pride in an encounter with computing. The student who used text editing to type a letter thought it looked "very nice" (X24). One student took pride in logging in without help (N14). Another was proud of error free output in a history assignment:

It took me 20 minutes one night not to do a program but to get data from a program and run it. It came right out with no errors. It was perfect. I thought I did a good job. (O15)

Students also found occasion for discouragement: 82% reported some discouragement. Of those who had taken computing, one-third mentioned their performance on the mastery; almost two-thirds mentioned difficulty with trying to get a program to run. Other students reported discouragement with system crashes and a screen that scrolled too rapidly. On the whole, particularly for those students who took a computing course, the negative experiences out-weighed the positive ones. The combination of long hours, an unpleasant terminal room, confusing interactions with the machine, seemingly irrelevant lectures, a difficult mastery exam, discouraging times. and feeling out of control was oppressive.

Cultural Learning

In the aftermath of reality shock, confusion, and control attempts, students emerged having learned some cultural lessons. Newcomers commonly have a relatively undifferentiated view of a culture's social organization; these students were no exception. The students had only a rough idea of how the formal responsibility for computing on campus is managed. When asked to describe the major activities of the computation center, half the students had difficulty with the question. No single activity was mentioned by more than half the students. (Nine students said the computation center gives help; 5 said it maintains equipment; 3 said it writes programs.) One student, while admitting she had never thought of the computation center as an organization, was able to produce a helpful analogy for the computation center:

> I just thought of it more like a library: a place where you use things that you can't use anywhere else. And they're there to help you with your classes. If you stretch it a little, you can think of the user consultant as a librarian. Someone who advises you when you don't know what to do. (K11)

Only one other student was able to provide an analogy for the computation center, an analogy of a very different sort:

> They have little gnomes and they sit dawn in the basement in bug hot rooms, like the devil, and mess around with students and put errors in their programs. (J10)

The students' perceptions of the social organization of computing at the university were dominated by a we/they distinction: there are people who are competent in and committed to computing and there is the rest of the world. From the students' perspectives, people who use the terminal room are divided into two categories: "we" who do not know what we are doing and "they" who do. "They" are also differentiated by special names, characteristics, and behaviors. Two-thirds (68%) of the students made this distinction in their comments.

Within this dichotomous view of the world, students made both positive and negative assessments of "them," although people making negative assessments outweighed those making positive ones five to one. Positively, "they" are viewed as very smart and competent:

> The amount of more intelligent people I've met down there…What I did on the computer seems so amazing to me. Then I thought that some of the people around me were doing such more complicated things and how smart they must be. (C3)

Negatively, "they" are viewed as having strange personal habits and being very difficult to talk to.

> Some people just live and die with computers. They sleep there. They don't get any sleep because they sleep with computers...They can't relate to anything but the computer. They can't talk to a normal guy. Even when they talk, they talk computer language. It's like they've turned into a computer. (Q17)

In addition to learning the rudiments of role and subculture differentiation, students began to learn about the computer itself as a cultural artifact. This learning took the form of being able to use terminology properly, understanding that there are multiple computer functions and uses (and that this generality is valued), and not anthropomorphizing the computer. Employing terminology in their conversation is a sign of cultural learning. For example, one student, in describing an occasion that made him feel proud, said,

> I would say the first time I had a program actually work on the computer. It had taken some work to get through all the debugging. I call it debugging now. It's just correcting errors...(A1)

Some students demonstrated an understanding that there are multiple computer uses by distinguishing writing programs from using tools:

> It depends if I think about programming or if I think about using a computer. I don't like programming too much but when it comes to using a computer like the Minitab system that manipulates stuff for you, I like that kind of stuff where you use the computer to do stuff for you. But I don't like programming the computer to do the stuff. (K11)

Complexity in thinking about computers was, however, not typical of these students; only five students exhibited some sense of differentiated function in their comments about computers. Some students still anthropomorphized the machine. Five students said something like the following:

> I mean, sometimes I feel like the computer is out after me. You know, everybody gets that feeling that the computer's after them sometimes. (Q17)

Personal Outcomes

In forming their overall assessment of the effects of computers and computing, students distinguished between effects on themselves and effects on society. They are impressed with the capability and versatility of computers for society as a whole, believing they are the "wave of the future" (J10). But they were less positive about the effects of computers on themselves personally. In assessing the effects of the computer on their activities as students, 13 students listed more negative effects, 6 students listed more positive effects, 2 students listed equal numbers of positive and negative effects. One student who characterized the entire experience as "a fight," exemplifies an outcome of anger.

> The whole fact that you have to fight to get on, you the whole computer theory, everything about computing here is a fight to do it. It's something you don't want to do and you have to fight to get in there to do it. And you have to fight to sit down and do it. And you have to fight the system to stay up. And you have to fight your program to make it work. And the whole time you're fighting the clock. (110)

Another student, exemplifying withdrawal, said:

> Looking back, I'm really not afraid of computers, but I'm going to try to stay away from computers. I know I shouldn't, because it's probably the thing of the future. But I'm really kind of leery to get into any type of computing again. (C3)

This student of course does not speak for all freshmen. An opposite, but less common, view was offered by another student, who exemplifies success in her willingness for further socialization. When she learned that she would have to do a history assignment on the computer the semester following her computing course, she said,

> I was glad that we were doing it on the computer. I don't know why. I just thought, 'Oh neat, we get to use the computer again.' (K11)

DISCUSSION

We speculated that novice encounters with computing could be interpreted by considering computing as culture rather than simply as tool. In a series of open-ended interviews novices revealed reactions to computing which seem to have been influenced in part by the social order surrounding computing: by the attitudes and behaviors of people who are good at it, by the management of computing resources, and by the general perceived importance of computing in society and the organization. They also revealed different ways of trying to cope with the strangeness of computing, each associated with more or less success. We believe these interviews reveal reasons for the differences found in the first part of our study. There is nothing in the way electrons flow, operating systems work, or Pascal procedures are written that explains the reactions to computing and computer science courses we discovered. We believe they are explained, instead, by novice attempts to operate in and make sense of an alien culture.

People who know how rapidly computing technology is changing may claim that this research studies a non-problem in that soon the particular artifacts present in our study will be replaced by different computer systems or will be improved by better human factors engineering. Indeed by 1985, three years after the data reported in this chapter were collected, freshmen were less dependent on large mainframes and were using PCs much more. But the questions that we ask about culture, socialization, and control are independent of any particular computer system and are more tied to particular organizational settings. It is true that computer systems are always changing, but the social settings remain relatively stable. Indeed freshmen in 1985 found computing still to be different from their other courses, although the differences were somewhat diminished from 1982 (Sproull, 1986). Furthermore, the belief that things will get better in the future does not relieve us of the responsibility to understand them as they are today. This is not to deny that computers may serve long-term educational and organizational goals. The point is that whatever computer systems we happen to have now do result in short-run problems and it is precisely about the short run that people express concern.

This work highlights a nice irony in organizational socialization. CMU clearly values computing quite highly. But in their enthusiasm for computing, its managers and experts have created situations in which it is hard for novices to be enthusiastic. Like the overzealous tour guide who forces his charges to climb endless sets of steps for the perfect view, to eat sheep's eyeballs for the perfect culinary experience, and to sit through a five-hour native poetry reading, this organization can produce more cultural dropouts than recruits.

REFERENCES

Arndt. S., Feltes, J., & Hanak, J. (1983). Secretarial attitudes towards word processors as a function of familiarity and locus of control. *Behavior and Information Technology*, 2(1), 17—22.

Bandura, A. (1977). Self-efficacy: Toward a unifying theory of behavior change. *Psychological Bulletin*, 84, 191—215.

Black, J., & Moran, T. (1982). Learning and remembering command names. Paper presented at the Human Factors in Computer Systems meeting of the Association for Computing Machinery, Washington, D.C.

Brockner, J. (1979). The effects of self-esteem, success-failure, and self-consciousness on task performance. *Journal of Personality and Social Psychology*, 37,1732—1741.

Bury, K., Boyle, J., Evey, J., & Neal, A. (1982). Windowing vs. scrolling on a visual display terminal. Paper presented at the Human Factors in Computer Systems meeting of the Association for Computing Machinery. Washington, D.C.

Byrnes. F. C. (1966). Role shock: An occupational hazard of American technical assistants abroad. *The Annals, 368*, 95—108.

Carver, C. S.. Blaney, P. H., & Scheier, M. F. (1979). Reassertion and giving up: The interactive role of self-directed attention and outcome expectancy. *Journal of Personality and Social Psychology, 37*, 1859—1870.

Carver, C. S., & Scheier, M. F. (1982). Control theory: A useful conceptual framework for personality—social, clinical, and health psychology. *Psychological Bulletin*, 92, 111—135.

Church, A. T. (1982). Sojourner adjustment. *Psychological Bulletin, 91*, 540-572.

David, K. H. (1971). Culture shock and the development of self-awareness. *Journal of Contemporary Psychotherapy, 4*, 44-48.

DeYoung, G., Kampen, G., & Topolski,. J. (1982). Analyzer-generated and human-judged predictors of computer program readability. Paper presented at the Human Factors in Computer Systems meeting of the Association for Computing Machinery. Washington, D.C.

Feldman, K. A., & Newcomb, T. (1969). *The impact of college on students*. San Francisco: Jossey-Bass.

Gamst, F., & Horbeck, E. (Eds.) (1976). *Ideas of culture: Sources & uses*. New York: Holt, Rinehart & Winston.

Goffman, E. (1961). *Asylums*. Garden City, NY: Anchor Books.

Higbee, H. (1969). Role shock—A new concept. *International Educational and Cultural Exchange, 4*, 71—81.

Kanfer, F. H., & Hagerman, S. (1981). The role of self-regulation. In L. P. Rehm (Ed.), *Behavior therapy for depression: Present status and future directions*. New York: Academic Press.

Kidder, T. (1981). *The soul of a new machine*. New York: Avon Books.

Kling, R. (1980). Social analyses of computing: Theoretical perspectives in recent empirical research. *Computing Surveys, 12*, 61—110.

Levy, S. (1982, April). A beautiful obsession with the binary world. *Rolling Stone*, pp. 42—51.

Louis, M. (1980). Surprise and sense making: What newcomers experience in entering unfamiliar organizational settings. *Administrative Science Quarterly, 25*, 226-251.

McCorduck, P. (1979). *Machines who think*. San Francisco: N. H. Freeman.

Merton, R., & Rossi, A. (1968). Contributions to the theory of reference group behavior. In R. Merton (Ed.), *Social Theory and Social Structure* (pp. 279—334). New York: Free Press.

Oberg, K. (1966). Cultural shock: Adjustment to new cultural environments. *Practical Anthropology, 7*, 177—182.

Ogdin, C. A. (1982, November). The software ergonomics. Software Technique, Inc., Alexandria, VA.

Schneider, M. L., Nudelman, S., & Hirsh-Pasek, K. (1982). An analysis of line numbering strategies in text editors. Paper presented at the of Human Factors in Computer Systems Meeting of the Association for Computing Machinery. Washington, D.C.

Smalley, W. A. (1963). Culture shock, language shock, and the shock of self-discovery. *Practical Anthropology, 10*, 49—56.

Sproull, L. (1986). *Social aspects of computing at CMU*. Unpublished manuscript, Carnegie Mellon University, Pittsburgh.

Steele, G. L., Jr., Woods, D. R., Finkel, R. A., Crispin, M. R., Stallman, R. M., & Goodfellow, G. S. (1983). *The hackers dictionary*. New York: Harper & Row.

Taylor, R. P. (Ed.). (1980). *The computer in the school*. New York: Teachers College Press.

Thompson, S. C. (1981). Will it hurt less if I can control it? A complex answer to a simple question. *Psychological Bulletin. 90*, 89—101.

Turkle, S. (1980). Computer as Rorschach. *Society*, pp. 15—24.

van Maanen, J., & Schein, E. (1979). Toward a theory of organizational socialization. In Barry Staw (Ed.), *Research in organizational behavior, 1*, (pp. 209—264). Greenwich, CT: JAI Press.

Zimbardo, P. G. (Ed.). (1980, August). The hacker papers. *Psychology Today*, pp. 62—74.

COMPETITION IN INDIVIDUALIZED CAI[2]

Nira Hativa
Tel Aviv University

Alan Lesgold
University of Pittsburgh

Shimon Swissa
Tel Aviv University

When planning computer-based learning environments for school curriculum topics, the primary attention is given to cognitive learning. Although social factors such as social comparison and individual competition may substantially affect students' cognitive learning, issues related to these factors are seldom incorporated into the planning of CAI.

Competition in school occurs when "a participant consciously persists in attempts to achieve superiority, that is, a better relative position with regard to the goal than an opponent can achieve"... "Competition in school is the overall organization that enables and encourages a limited number of students to succeed at the highest level (however defined) while the majority do not". (Owens, 1985; p. 907). Social psychology literature explains competition as based on social comparison processes (Festinger, 1954; Toda, Shinotsuka, McClintock & Stech, 1978; Suls & Miller, 1977; Schofield, 1985). A large body of theory and research suggests that individuals are strongly motivated to compare their abilities with those of others in order to evaluate their own performance more accurately or to enhance their self-esteem. People compare themselves with others similar to them on a variety of classes of attributes, such as: attitudes, beliefs, emotions, aptitudes, and level of performance (Pepitone, 1972; 1980, Toda et al., 1978.)

DIFFERENTIAL EFFECTS OF AND ATTITUDES TOWARDS COMPETITION IN SCHOOL

Schools and classes within schools often provide environmental features that strongly encourage social comparisons and competition among children. Is competition a desirable factor in the learning of all students? Or is it non-beneficial to the learning of all students? Or could it have positive effects for

---

[2]From Hativa, N., Lesgold, A. & Swissa, S. (1993). Competition in individualized CAI. *Instructional Science*, *21*, 393-428. Reprinted by permission of Kluwer academic publishers, Dordrecht, The Netherlands. Copyright © 1992 Kluwer academic publishers.

some students and negative effects for others? Differential attitudes towards competition or effects of competition have been identified in relation to the cultural background, gender and level of achievement.

POSITIVE AND NEGATIVE EFFECTS OF COMPETITION

Competition accentuates the positive effect associated with success and the negative effect associated with failure (Ames & Ames, 1981). On the positive side, competitive activity is a powerful motive for stimulating effort and ambition both in school and outside; it is a source of self-confidence and self-esteem. Because comparative excellence is rewarded in society, students should begin experiencing it at school (Owens, 1985). In terms of cognitive gains, a review of studies that compared the effectiveness of learning through different goal structures in school found that very consistently, individual competition was superior to all other goal structures (Michaels, 1977). That is, learning that induced competition produced greater cognitive gains and achievement than non-competitive individualized or cooperative learning. However, other studies found cooperative learning to be superior to all other goal structures in terms of cognitive learning (e.g., Slavin, 1980, 1983; Sharan, 1980).

On the other hand, competition can result in the public humiliation of some students for the benefit of others, which is unethical. It can be a source of insecurity, self-doubt, and personal unhappiness for the large proportion of those who do not win. The positive effect of competition on increasing motivation is not experienced by many students—the only students motivated by competition are the relatively few who believe they have a chance of winning. Competition serves to increase the child's perception of ability and luck as factors accounting for win or loss (Ames, Ames & Felker, 1977; Lewis & Cooney, 1987), whereas we would like the child to perceive effort, rather than ability and luck, as important to achievement. Competition induces decreased or misleading communication among students; distrustful and negative attitudes toward each other; frequent misperceptions about each other's behavior; and a tendency to define conflicts as "win-lose" situations (Johnson, Johnson & Stanne, 1985). For some students, competition induces a continued state of high-level anxiety, which, in turn, significantly interferes with learning and may result in psychological damage (Johnson et al., 1985). Failure in competition leads to poorer performance in subsequent competitions (Ames & Ames, 1981). To avoid failure, students avoid attempting a task on which they are to be evaluated, especially when the probability of success is intermediate (Johnson & Johnson, 1975).

SES-RELATED DIFFERENCES

Systematic cultural differences in competitive behavior were identified by Toda et al., (1978). For example, Anglo-American children were found to be more competitive than other American children, e.g. Mexican-American and Afro-American children (Kagan & Madsen, 1971; Madsen & Shapira,

1970). Pepitone (1980) found that disadvantaged students placed in an environment with "privileged" students were forced to make unfavorable self evaluations.

GENDER-RELATED DIFFERENCES

Consistently across studies, boys appear to be more competitive than girls (Owens, 1985), and their attitudes towards competition have been found to be more positive (e.g., Ahlgren and Johnson, 1979). For example, a questionnaire answered by 247 elementary school students presented 14 options for liking to practice arithmetic with a particular CAI system and 13 options for disliking it. Of these 27 options, only two showed significant gender differences. Both these options presented the same item—competition induced by the CAI work—in both positive and negative statements (in order to examine the reliability of students' answers). Boys, significantly more than girls, liked the competition with classmates enforced by the CAI work, and girls, significantly more than boys, disliked this competition (Hativa, in press).

Gender differences in competition are also manifest in students' academic learning. Among elementary school students who practiced arithmetic through a CAI system and received feedback which encouraged competition, boys exhibited a significantly higher rate of progress than girls (Lewis & Cooney, 1987; Hativa 1988a). Johnson et al. (1985) also showed competition to have differential effects on males and females, with females exhibiting debilitated achievement and attitudes.

ACHIEVEMENT-RELATED DIFFERENCES

In most classrooms, fairly stable patterns of achievement exist so that the majority of students always "lose" and a few students always win (Johnson & Johnson, 1975). Because high achievers are the constant winners in class competition, they constantly experience its positive effects and usually prefer the individual competition goal structures. Gifted third- and fourth-grade students working competitively on math skills at the computer showed an increasing preference for more competition and less cooperation in their activities (Kanevsky, 1985). On the other hand, the low achievers in class frequently experience the negative effects of competition. Indeed, research has found that individual competition is ineffective particularly for initially low performers (Michaels, 1977). The social comparison process inherent in competition among students contributes to a self-defeating situation for the low achievers in the comparison group and therefore is detrimental particularly for them. Prolonged failure experiences of low achievers may result in a sense of worthlessness, inferiority, helplessness, and incompetence and in behaviors of avoiding failures by becoming less achievement oriented and attributing failure to lack of ability. All this may result in even lower levels of achievement (Lewis & Cooney, 1987; Johnson & Johnson 1975).

COMPETITION IN SCHOOL

Schools in the Western competitive society often transmit to students the culture of competitive striving as the key for future success in material terms (Owens, 1985). Indeed, research shows that a large amount of comparison behavior occurs in elementary classrooms (Pepitone, 1972), and that students perceive schools as encouraging competition amongst themselves (Johnson, Johnson & Bryant, 1973).

SCHOOL FACTORS THAT STIMULATE COMPETITION

Pepitone (1972) distinguishes several factors in schools that stimulate competition. These are:

Students' evaluations. Students are regularly compared, mostly through quizzes and examinations, to see who is superior and who is inferior (Johnson & Johnson, 1975). "Competitive motives are particularly likely to be evoked where evaluations of the other are involved, for in order to win over the other, relative positions of self and other must be established" (Pepitone, 1972, p. 49).

Cognitive unclarity about tasks. Children look to each other to reduce many sources of confusion. "Whenever at a loss for an answer, or unsure of the correctness of answers, pupils will turn to each other to gain cognitive clarity" (Pepitone, 1972, p. 47).

Similarity among tasks in which pupils are engaged. Assignments of the same problems as seat work for the whole class with each student working on the same problem by himself/herself, bring all students to a common level of comparison. "When pupils in one classroom are involved in the same learning activities at the same time, each child is offered a ready-made source of reducing his own uncertainties by reference to his neighbor's activities... comparison tendencies arise primarily under conditions where pupils are required to participate actively." (Pepitone, 1972, p. 47).

Similarity' of the reference group to the one making the comparison. As suggested above, students compare themselves to those similar to them. Comparisons are made on a variety of attributes such as behavior in class and achievement. Indeed, "Classmates who are daily present, and who continue on with each other throughout the grades, constitute a reference group" which is relevant for most school-related comparisons. The class is made still more relevant by the commonalties created in almost all public schools by grouping based on age and on homogeneity of ability, and, occasionally, interest. (Pepitone, 1972, p. 47).

REDUCING COMPETITION IN SCHOOL THROUGH INDIVIDUALIZED INSTRUCTION

Dissatisfaction with competition in school has led to the advocation of individualistic or cooperative goal structures (Johnson & Johnson, 1975). These two goal structures have been found in many studies (e.g., Owens,

1985; Johnson, Maruyama, Johnson, Nelson & Skon, 1981) to reduce competition and sometimes to increase learning. Because the study presented here concentrates on individualized work with computers, the following discussion excludes the cooperative goal structure.

Individualistic structures have been described as producing self-competition rather than competition with others (Ames & Felker, 1979; Johnson & Johnson, 1979). Individualistic goal structures eliminate or de-emphasize social comparison, encourage a focus on task mastery and result in effort attributions so that achievement is perceived as controllable through one's own effort (Lewis & Cooney, 1987). The increased focus on task-mastery in individualized non-competitive learning is expected to increase students' motivation and achievement (Lewis & Cooney, 1987).

REDUCING COMPETITION IN SCHOOL THROUGH CAI

Theoreticians suggest that the computer-based individualization of instruction will undercut one of the most obvious mechanisms for gaining social comparison information—attending to the performance of other students (Schofield, 1985). Osin & Nesher (1977) argue that individualized drill and practice through a CAI system can reduce or completely cancel competition among classmates because each student is the sole witness to his/her own successes, failures and advancement through the CAI curriculum material. Thus, one does not become anxious about being mocked by other students for low performance, or about dissatisfaction with the teachers' requirements. Hativa (1986), however, identified intensive competitions among students working with a CAI system for drill and practice in arithmetic. The competition observed was of benefit to some of the students but damaging to others. These contradicting views of CAI-related competition arise the questions: What factors in CAI encourage or discourage competition among students? What are the effects of competition in the CAI environment on different students? Thus, the objectives of the present study are:
(a) to identify factors in the software and the method of operation of two CAI systems that either encourage or discourage competition among students;
(b) to identify positive and negative effects of competition on children; and
(c) to identify SES-, achievement-level and gender differences in a variety of aspects of competition.

METHOD

To satisfy these objectives, we compare two CAI systems (called here System A and System B). Neither was designed to foster competition. Indeed, one (System A) was designed to minimize external competition while promoting a desire to achieve relative to one's current capabilities. The designers of the second system did not incorporate in their planning any considerations related to either competition or cooperation. These two CAI systems provide drill and practice in arithmetic, each to over 100,000 Israeli students. The basic assumption of the two systems is that the teacher presents new arithmetic concepts in the classroom and then students receive practice of these concepts in the computer lab. Thus, in both systems, students go to the computer lab regularly (usually twice a week) for approximately 40 through 60 minutes of weekly practice. However, the two systems differ in their hardware, software and other aspects of method of operation. Because of these differences, we believed that the two systems differed in the opportunities they offered for social comparisons and therefore would differ in producing individual competition in students. These differences would occur, not by design, but rather as unintended, but important, effects of system details.

Eight schools participated in the study—two schools of advantaged and two schools of disadvantaged population per CAI system. The study used two methods of inquiry—qualitative, to identify aspects of CAI systems that either encourage or discourage competition, and quantitative, to examine SES, achievement level and gender differences in the effects of competition induced by the CAI work.

THE QUALITATIVE STAGE

In each of the eight schools, several classes of grades 2 through 6 were observed while working in the computer lab over a six-month period. The observer was present in the computer lab for a full school day twice a week and recorded every event that related to competition or to social comparisons. Teachers and students were interviewed in relation to a variety of aspects of competition identified in these observations.

THE QUANTITATIVE STAGE

On the basis of the observations and interviews, a "competition questionnaire" was developed. Because of the differences in hardware, software and methods of operation, there were items that were relevant to only one of the two CAI systems. For this reason, two versions of the questionnaire were developed—one for each CAI system. The initial versions presented free-response questions related to objectives of this study. These versions were administered in several classes for each system. The students' answers to the initial versions served to form a variety of multiple-choice options for each question in the two final versions of the questionnaire. These latter versions went through several stages of administration in classes and of subsequent modifications based on the students' answers, to form the final versions. Most items on these questionnaires are presented in Tables 15.5 & 15.6.

Only fourth graders participated in the quantitative stage. For each of the eight schools in this study, students from two fourth grade classes who had not experienced the prior versions received the final versions of the questionnaire. Altogether, 457 students from 16 classes answered the questionnaire, each during one class session. The items were of two types:

yes/no questions and questions for which students were asked to check each applicable option from a list of options.

Feature	System A	System B
1. Numbering the levels (different types) of exercises		
(a) meaningful numbering within each single strand	**Yes**	No
(b) relationships of level numbering across strands	**Yes**	No
2. Fostering individualized work		
(a) table screens to separate computer stations	Yes	*No*
(b) timing of exercises	Yes	*No*
(c) computations on paper	No	*Yes*
(d) computer games	No	*Yes*
3. Screen feedback		
At the session's beginning		
(a) name of student	Yes	Yes
(b) Cumulative number of sessions	**Yes**	No
At the session's end		
(c) number of exercises presented in the session	**Yes**	No
(d) number of exercises solved correctly	**Yes**	No
(e) statements of commendation	**Yes**	No
Throughout the session		
(f) evaluation of each digit as typed in	Yes	No
(g) evaluation of only the final answer	No	Yes
(h) identification of type of error	No	No
(i) identification of level of the exercise presented	**Yes***	No
(j) statement of commendation on correct solution	**Yes**	**Yes**
(k) correct answer on failure to solve	Yes	Yes
4. Hard copy feedback (class report)		
Feedback related to each single student		
(a) current level of exercises for each strand	**Yes**	Yes
(b) current mean level of exercises across strands	**Yes**	No
Feedback related to the whole class	**Yes**	No
(c) current mean level across all students and all strands	**Yes**	No
(d) rank order of students on the basis of mean level	**Yes**	No
Clarity and usefulness of the report to teachers	**Yes**	No
Frequency of issuing the report to teachers	**Weekly**	Seldom

* Used to be presented explicitly until two years ago. Now it is encoded so that students are not able to decipher it.
Features that encourage competition are printed in **bold**. Features that encourage cooperation are printed in *italics*.

Table 15.4
Comparison of two CAI systems on features that affect social comparisons and competition.

ANALYSIS AND RESULTS

The following integrates findings from observations and interviews of students and teachers with analysis of students' answers to our questionnaire. The findings are summarized according to the three objectives of this study.

SOCIAL COMPARISON AND COMPETITION AMONG STUDENTS

Our observations suggested that System A included several features encouraging social comparison and competition that were not included in System B. Table 15.4 compares the two CAI systems with respect to these features. The features of each of the CAI systems are discussed separately.

SYSTEM A

Numbering the Levels of Exercises

Normative numbering within each strand. The System A curriculum in arithmetic is divided into 15 strands (different arithmetic topics). For each school year, the appropriate exercises within each strand are divided into ten "Levels" which are assigned normative numbers. Thus, an exercise of Level 43 represents the curriculum material designed for the third month of the fourth grade. The fact that each exercise is assigned a level-related number provides a basis for comparison among students.

Algorithm that relates the Levels of exercises across strands. A special algorithm provides each student with more exercises in the strands of which Levels he/she is low on, so that the discrepancy among the Levels in the different strands for a student is never large. This feature enables the level of CAI performance of each student to be presented by his/her computed mean Level across strands. The representation of each student's performance by a single number (the mean) promotes students' comparison behavior.

Fostering Individualized Work

The operators of System A take special measures to ensure proper solitary work and to cancel all opportunities for social comparisons. The system is operated centrally in Israel. The system is rented to schools as a package that includes hardware, software, teacher training, frequent communications with the school computer coordinator, and the furnishing of the computer lab. A computer coordinator in each school receives instructions from the central office as to how to operate the system.

Table screens that separate the computer stations. Each of the many dozens of System A computer labs looks almost the same. Forty terminals are placed on tables with screens between them so that a separate carrel is formed for each student. This arrangement was introduced by the system's designers to make it difficult for a student to see a neighbor's computer screen while sitting in front of his/her own terminal.

Timing of exercises. The rationale for the time limitation was to avoid students' procrastination while working with the computer and thus improve their time on task. However, this feature serves unintentionally to foster solitary work and to reduce cooperation among students. The timing of exercises discourages students from leaving their seat to go to another student's stand because exceeding the time limit is recorded as an erroneous solution. If several exercises are recorded as wrong, the student is "punished" by being demoted in the CAI Levels. The timing of exercises reduces also the extent and amount of help that the teacher can provide to the students while on line. In the computer lab, there is only a single teacher to supervise 30 through 40 students in the advantaged population and 20 through 30 students in disadvantaged schools. When the teacher helps one student in the CAI work, other students who face problems cannot wait until the teacher becomes available to help them, because the particular exercise in question is recorded as wrong and is replaced by another exercise when the time is over.

Prohibition of doing computations on paper. Students come to the computer lab empty handed, with no paper, pen or pencil. Although the rationale is to save students' time (copying from the computer to paper and back), this arrangement makes it difficult for students to provide written solutions to other students or to work cooperatively on solving a particular problem.

Screen Feedback

At the session's beginning, the name of the student and the cumulative number of CAI sessions (starting from the beginning of the school year) are displayed on the screen.

At the session's end, a summary of the student's performance during that session is printed on the screen. The summary includes the total number of exercises presented (affected by the level of difficulty of exercises, and by the speed of the student's typing in the solutions); the number of exercises solved correctly at the first trial, and the number of those solved correctly only after more than one trial. An algorithm provides special positive statements in cases of improved performance in the present session as compared with the last three sessions. These statements are of several degrees of excellence, such as: "You have done well"; "You have advanced very well"; "Extraordinary"; and the like. The highest commendation appears on the screen in flashing type.

Throughout the session, students receive positive and negative statements as feedback for the solution of each particular exercise (whether it is correct or not). Other verbal statements relate to maintaining the time limit in the solution to exercises. During the first ten years of System A's operation, the screen presentation of each exercise included the identification of its "Level." Our observations showed that students were extremely conscious of these Levels. A regular feature of computer sessions was that students boasted loudly of the high level of exercises that they were receiving ("I am in Level

57...". Other students were not indifferent to these proclamations and several would respond loudly describing their Levels ("Big deal, 1 was at that Level a long time ago.." or "I'm now in Level ..."). When the system A operators became aware that screen presentation of the normative level of each exercise encouraged comparison behavior and competition, they canceled the presentation of this number (in fact, it remained on the screen in an encoded form so that students could not identify the Level). This change was initiated only at the beginning of the school year in which our questionnaire was implemented. This meant that our fourth graders had experienced the screen presentation of Levels during the two previous years.

All the numbers and verbal statements displayed on the screen serve for students as a source for comparison with their classmates.

Hard Copy Feedback—The Weekly Class CAI Report

A CAI class report is printed upon the teacher's request, usually once a week. It provides teachers with information about the mean performance of each student in each strand that is "active" for him/her, and across all strands. It also identifies the types of exercises on which the student is encountering problems in the CAI practice. In addition, the report presents the mean performance of all students in the class. At the teacher's request, the report may be printed in decreasing rank order of mean performance rather than alphabetically. The school principal receives a copy of reports of all classes and these reports are kept where every teacher who is interested can examine them. The fact that the class CAI arithmetic performance is exposed to "outsiders" puts pressure on some of the teachers and leads to a subtle competition among teachers. Generally, this type of teachers' competition is positive for students. It prompts teachers to invest time and effort in facilitating individual students' advancement and keeps them alert to students' problems (Hativa, 1966). On the other hand, in a considerable number of observations, we identified less desirable teacher behavior: several of the observed teachers acted in ways that contradicted the policy of the System A designers and the principles of individualized learning. In order to increase students' motivation to advance fast in the system's levels, these teachers read out to the whole class the mean Level of each student from the weekly computer reports, or they posted these reports for all students to see. The information in these reports, when available to students, provides a major source of comparisons among students and exposes the failures of weak students. The CAI report fosters comparisons even more intensely than the knowledge of the regular teacher's grades, because the successes and failures of students are quantified as normative Level measures. The discrepancy between high- and low-achieving students of the same class may amount to 4-5 grade levels, and low-achieving students are often mocked for their below grade-level performance (Hativa, 1986, 1988).

BEHAVIOR AND ATTITUDES

Table 15.5 presents the frequency of students' choices of items that present issues related to the particular features of System A, those that do not have counterparts in System B's questionnaire. The discussion below refers to the particular features in Table 15.5.

Fostering individualized work. Although System A was designed to foster individualized work, our observations showed students frequently compared themselves to others during System A computer sessions. Students succeed resourcefully in overcoming the obstacles to social comparison inherent in System A. Many students moved their chairs to one end of their carrel or left their chairs to watch another student's screen, or leaned over the table screen to watch the computer of the student sitting on the opposite side of the table, etc. The purpose of watching the computer screen of other students was to identify their level of practice. When the Level number was not displayed on the screen, students still were able to evaluate other students' standing. In their interviews, students explained that if the other student received an exercise of a type familiar to the observing student, that meant that the other student was at a lower level whereas an unfamiliar type suggested that the other student was more advanced. The timing of exercises, although reducing the opportunities for social comparison, did not eliminate this phenomenon, and comparison behavior was evident in almost every class that was observed.

Several items in the questionnaire examined students' attitudes towards the arrangement of terminals in the computer lab and the extent of students' knowledge of the CAI Levels of other students—information that was not supposed to be available to students. Because these questions are relevant also to System B, they are discussed in the section comparing students in both CAI systems (Items 8 through 15 in Table 15.6).

Screen feedback. When the change in presenting the normative level of each exercise was first implemented, we heard several students complaining about the disappearance from the screen of the Level of exercises. Item 1 in our questionnaire asked students whether they preferred screen presentation of the Level (as in the previous years). The majority (two thirds) preferred the previous screen presentation of Level of exercises. Most of those who preferred the level to be displayed explained that it was important and helpful for them to get comparison information. Few students admit that the knowledge of the Level enables them to boast to their friends. Those who prefer that the Level not be shown want to avoid the shame and humiliation of those who are low achievers.

So far as other features of the screen feedback are concerned, our observations and interviews show that students tend to compare everything that is comparable in their computer work, even if it is totally irrelevant to their arithmetic knowledge or to their performance in that session. For example, many times we recorded students comparing the number of sessions that was displayed on the screen at the beginning of the session (Hey—I'm in

	All	SES advantaged	SES dis-advantaged	χ2	Sex Boys	Sex Girls	χ2	Achievement Low	Achievement High	χ2
1. Do you prefer the CAI level to appear on screen?										
Yes	67	66	67	0	66	67	0	65	69	.2
If yes, why?										
a. I like to know my level	43	46	50	.4	49	48	0	40	56	.2
b. it helps me to progress quickly	34	33	35	0	31	38	1.2	28	47	3.1
c. it enables me to boast	6	4	8	1.1	8	2	4.3*	8	11	.3
3. If no, why?										
So that:										
a. weaker pupils will not be hurt	11	9	13	1.3	11	10	.1	10	11	0
b. other pupils will not know my level	10	8	13	1.8	9	12	.6	13	0	4.8*
c. pupils will not mock others	8	4	13	7.7**	8	8	0	0	17	7.2**
d. other pupils will not mock me	7	2	14	12.7***	9	5	1.4	13	3	2.5
4. What do you compare with other pupils during the computer session?										
a. # of correct/incorrect responses	41	47	35	3.7*	43	39	1.3	13	69	25.7***
b. feedback statements of excellence	40	33	50	7.0**	41	39	.2	25	50	5.1
c. # of the computer session	33	35	31	.5	32	36	.5	15	39	5.6*
d. difficulty of the exercise	16	17	14	.4	16	16	0	10	25	2.0
e. type of exercise solved successfully	17	15	19	.6	17	16	.1	10	22	2.1
f. type of exercise solved unsuccessfully	12	14	9	2.3	14	9	2.0	10	9	0
g. negative feedback	10	6	14	4.0**	12	7	1.5	5	11	1.0
5. Do you like the teacher to read the computer report to the class?										
Yes	28	19	35	8.2**	32	16	8.4**	15	37	5.4
6. If yes, why?										
a. to know my level	19	14	26	6.2**	24	12	5.6	10	33	6.2**
b. to know who is good and who is not	9	9	9	0	12	5	3.3	5	17	2.8
c. to know who is weak and needs help	8	7	9	.4	10	6	1.1	3	17	4.5*
d. to know the level of all the pupils	6	4	8	1.8	9	2	5.0*	3	14	3.4
7. If no, why?										
a. it hurts the weaker pupils	33	36	29	1.2	29	39	2.6	15	36	4.5*
b. pupils will not mock me or others	25	25	25	0	23	29	1.2	25	20	.3
c. there are pupils who are ashamed	24	28	20	2.2	24	25	0	20	28	.6
d. pupils in other classes won't mock us	12	11	12	0	14	9	1.3	3	14	3.4

*p < .05; **p < .01; ***p < .001

Table 15.5
Pupil's attitudes towards competition-fostering features specific to System A.

Session 73!!!). Most of the loud comparisons are done when the session is over. Many proclaim aloud the displayed information about the number of exercises attempted and those solved correctly. Students who receive special printed commendation of their performance usually take particular care that most other students and the teacher learn of their success. Very often they announce loudly any positive statements printed on their computer screen, and they call on the teacher and friends to see it. If the degree of commendation is the highest, several students will accumulate around that screen to watch the flashing statement, and that particular student becomes the subject of much admiration and prestige.

One item in the questionnaire (#4) asks the students what is compared during and immediately after the computer session. Students most often chose the number of exercises presented and the number solved correctly. It should be noted that these are absolute numbers and in many cases do not at all reflect the student's level of performance. For example, the better students advance in their CAI practice far beyond the grade level and receive difficult exercises that they have not yet learned. Thus, they need to invest more time in thinking than many medium and low achievers who receive more familiar or easier exercises. Consequently, the better students may get fewer exercises and solve fewer exercises correctly in a session than lower-achieving students. It can also happen that a student does not take the care to solve an exercise correctly and just types in any answer quickly. Even if this student has a low proportion of correct answers, the absolute number may be larger than that of other students who do make efforts to produce correct solutions. As a result, that student may boast of receiving and of solving large numbers of exercises.

Students' next most commonly compared positive feedback statements—an appropriate measure of quality of performance. However, the third most common choice—the cumulative number of sessions—chosen by one third of the students, is totally irrelevant to the students' level of performance. These students' answers reinforce the findings of our observations that students tend to compare every detail that is comparable—regardless of relevance to good performance.

Hard-copy feedback. Three items in the questionnaire investigated students' attitudes towards publicizing the information in the computer reports. Only 28% of the students like this behavior; 58% dislike it. The large proportion of students (86%) who answered this question provides evidence that teachers frequently make known students' CAI standings. Students who like to hear the report want it for purposes of social comparison. Students' who do not like to hear the report want to avoid hurting the low achievers.

SYSTEM B

Our observations in System B identified several features that seemed to encourage cooperation among students and to discourage individualized competition. These were:

Numbering of the Levels of exercises

Non-meaningful numbering of Levels within each strand. As in System A, the System B curriculum arranged the exercises in strands. However, rather than numbering the different types of exercises (Levels) within a particular strand with normative numbers, as done in system A, the System B Levels start with the same number for each strand, no matter what the class level of the first exercise. Exercises with the same number, therefore, may belong to curriculum topics that are taught in different months or even in different years at school. Consequently, no meaningful average score across all strands can be assigned.

No relationships of levels across strands. Advancement in Levels (numbered exercises) of a particular strand is almost unrelated to advancement in the other strands. Consequently, the Levels of the exercises given a student in the different strands are only loosely related. This fact also contributes to the lack of meaning of the mean score across strands.

Fostering Relaxed Work and Cooperation among Students

No table screens. In the computer laboratories of System B there are no table screens to separate the computers, so that students can easily watch one another's work.

Untimed exercises. The exercises presented to students in System B are not timed, so students are not penalized if they quit their computer in the middle of a solution and go to work with other students or to wait for the teacher until she is available to help. Our observations show that, because the single teacher in the computer lab is not able to help all the students who ask for help without making them wait for a long time, the teacher assigns or encourages the better students to help those who need help.

Encouragement of paper-and-pencil computations while on line. Students carry their notebooks with pen or pencil with them to the computer lab. They are encouraged by the software and the teachers to use these for making intermediate computations. While the software in System A evaluates each digit as it is typed, requiring the student to type in all intermediate steps of the solution in a particular prespecified order, the software in System B evaluates only the final answer for each exercise, leaving all intermediate steps to be done on paper.

Incorporation of computer games. System B provides each student with arithmetic games (usually unrelated to the current practice) after the student is presented with a certain fixed number of exercises. These games contribute to a relaxed environment in the computer work. Nobody rushes to get more and more exercises in order to advance fast in the levels of practice, as the System A students do.

Total absence of screen feedback

There is almost no reference on the screen to the particular student, except for the display of the student's name at the beginning of a session. No numbers related to the individual student are displayed on the screen either at the beginning of the session or at its end. Nor are there any screen printouts of the Levels of exercises or any verbal statements to summarize the student's performance when the session is over. The sole individualized feedback relates to the correctness or incorrectness of each solution. The absence of verbal statements or scores to evaluate each student's work eliminates an important factor for comparison behavior.

Useless computer reports

We have found the computer class reports in System B to be very unclear and complicated; it is difficult to gain any beneficial information from them. It is complicated to use these reports to compare the performance of the different students in the same class because each student may be at completely different Levels in the different strands and the report does not indicate the mean performance of each student (or of a class) across all strands as in the System A report. Teachers of System B seldom ask for a printout of the report, and they almost never use it to compare the performance of different students or classes, nor are they pressed by the principal to show better CAI results for their classes. Consequently, the teachers in System B do not press their students to work hard nor to invest much effort in solving exercises, as some of the System A teachers do.

All these particular features of the hardware, software, and method of operation of System B seem to foster a relaxed work environment and to encourage students' cooperation in solving problematic exercises and in helping one another when encountering problems. Indeed, a regular feature observed in System B computer laboratories is the peer help. The complete absence from the computer screen in System B of a student's evaluation and of any information related to the individual student's performance reduces the opportunities for social comparisons dramatically. However, students in System B were observed frequently to watch one another's screen and exclaim aloud if they detected that the other student received "easier" exercises.

To summarize, our observations reveal inherent differences in the method of operation of the two CAI systems in spite of the similarity in objectives. The students' work with System B seems to be relaxed and to encourage peer help, whereas work with System A puts a good deal of pressure on both teachers and students, discourages cooperation, and attempts to foster concentration and strictly individual work. We should emphasize here that we do not have any measurement of differential gains in learning of arithmetic through using the two CAI systems.

COMPARISONS OF STUDENTS' ANSWERS TO IDENTICAL ITEMS IN BOTH SYSTEMS

Table 15.6 compares the answers of students of the two systems on items that are common and relevant to both systems. Chi-square tests identify items for which the differences between the groups are statistically significant.

The first two items in Table 15.6 (Items 8 & 9) deal with the physical arrangement of computers in the lab. The students who work with System B seem to be significantly more content with the current arrangement than the System A students. Students' choices of beneficial aspects in the

	Frequency in Percentages		
	System A n=247	System B n=210	χ^2
8. Are you satisfied with the organization of the computers in the lab?			
Yes	58	75	15.2***
9. What is important to you in the organization of the computers in the lab?			
a. it must be comfortable	57	58	.1
b. it should enable me to concentrate	26	17	5.7*
c. it should be easy for the teacher to help everyone	21	36	12.9***
d. I don't like to work alone	18	27	4.7*
e. that other people cannot see another's computer	17	5	19.8***
f. that there will not be noise to disturb me	10	11	.1
g. that other pupils won't mock me	9	6	2.6
h. that my mistakes cannot be seen	9	3	5.9*
i. that my friends can help me	7	12	4.0*
j. that I can help other pupils	5	20	22.2***
k. that I can compare with friends and can learn from them	4	13	13.3***
10. Do you know which are the most advanced pupils on the computer?			
Yes	76	66	7.5*
11. How do you know?			
a. according to who is good in arithmetic in class	28	39	6.8**
b. according to pupils who receive feedback statements of excellence	26	14	11.3**
c. the teacher announces the names of the good pupils	19	9	8.8**
d. you look at the computers of other pupils	14	11	.8
e. the pupils say that they are the most advanced	8	8	0
12 Do you know which are the weakest pupils on the computer?			
Yes	54	53	.1
13. How do you know?			
a. according to who is weak in arithmetic in class	30	31	.9
b. they receive easier exercises	16	16	.1
c. you look at the computers of other pupils	8	12	.4
d the teacher announces their names	11	7	.2
14. Do you discuss the CAI exercises that you receive with your friends?			
Yes	60	76	7.0**
15. If yes, what is the reason?			
a. when I receive a difficult exercise	36	36	1.2
b. to learn from friends	26	23	.3
c. to know if they are better or worse	22	12	7.6**
d. to help them	21	26	1.4
e. that they will help me	12	18	4.4
f. that they will know that I am at a high level	10	10	.1

$*p < .05; **p < .01; ***p < .001$

Table 15.6
Comparison of the two CAI systems on common items. Continued on next page

	System A	System B	χ^2
16. What do your friends tell you?			
a. that they receive statements of excellence	46	41	1.0
b. that they do not know how to solve certain exercises	24	27	1.3
c. they brag that they receive difficult exercises	24	15	8.0*
d. they teach me how to solve new exercises	22	28	2.0
e. they brag that they have progressed the most	17	15	1.2
17. How do you feel when the computer tells you that your solution is wrong?			
a. that I need to make more of an effort	45	49	.7
b. that it happened because I was not concentrating on the solution	25	22	.4
c. I get cross with myself	25	16	4.8*
d. I don't feel good because pupils see that I erred	21	24	4
e. content because the computer showed me my mistakes	20	37	16.3***
f. cross with the computer	13	5	7.6**
g. I don't feel like continuing	13	6	6.0**
h. I don't care	12	19	4.0**
i. Sad	11	9	.4
18. What do you do when your solution is wrong?			
a. use the second option for solution (try again)	55	69	9.4**
b. put more into the solution	45	25	19.4***
c. continue trying until I succeed	28	12	16.7***
d. call the teacher for help	24	20	.9
e. try and solve it at home	20	11	6.8**
f. ask for a classmate's help	9	14	.3
19. Do you like the competition in computer work?			
Yes	20	31	15.6***
20. If yes, why?			
a. I want to be amongst the most advanced	11	22	11.0***
b. in order to show that I am clever	5	10	4.5*
c. I want to brag about my high level	4	2	1.0
d. because I am good on the computer	4	11	7.2**
e. it is a strong incentive for learning	7	1	7.3**
21. If no, why?			
a. because competition makes it hard to concentrate	48	36	6.8**
b. everyone learns according to his/her ability	32	29	.3
c. competition does not reflect knowledge	30	28	.3
d. in order not to make many mistakes	25	20	2.0
e. it is unpleasant to fail	17	8	8.6**
f. in order not to feel like a bragger	11	11	0
g. in order not to be mocked	9	2	9.5**
22. Do you know of incidences of mockery or insulting of pupils who do not succeed with the computer exercises?			
Yes	46	44	2.0
23. If yes, how?			
a. Pupils are mocked because they receive easy exercises	29	21	3.5
b. Pupils are mocked because they are at a low level	24	26	.5
c. Pupils are insulted and called names	15	17	1.3

$*p < .05; **p < .01; ***p < .001$

Table 15.6 continued.

arrangements of computers in the lab indicate that System A students emphasize aspects of learning conditions (e.g., concentration) and the avoidance of social comparison (e.g., "That other pupils cannot see another's computer") significantly more; System B students emphasize the cooperation in solving exercises (e.g., "That I can compare with friends and learn from them") and the teacher's help (e.g., "It should be easy for the teacher to help everyone") significantly more. These findings are very intriguing. They suggest that students adapt their attitudes and expectations to those fostered by the learning environment, in order to achieve optimal success in learning in this environment.

Seven items (Items 10 through 16) investigate the extent to which students gain information regarding the CAI performance of other students and the sources for such information. That is, these items investigate the extent and sources of social comparison related to the CAI work. Approximately 70% of the students indicate that they know which students are the most advanced in the CAI work and approximately 50% know who are the least advanced students.

Students attribute their information about other students' standings in CAI work from several sources. One is the level of performance in class arithmetic, which many students believe to be the same as in the CAI work. Another is the screen performance of the other students. Many students indicate that they watch other students' screen displays to read the verbal-statement feedback or the Level number displayed on the screen or to compare the level of difficulty of the exercises of the other students with their own. A third source is the teacher. Indeed, our observations identified teachers who publicly complimented the students who advanced the most, or who publicly named those students who performed at the lowest Level. Finally, students furnish information about themselves. Our observations show that many students announce aloud their receipt of feedback that indicates their good performance, or their receipt of difficult exercises, indicating high level of work.

Table 15.6 indicates that significantly more System A students than System B students know who are the better students in the class. However, there is no difference in the proportion of those in the two systems who can identify the weak students. This suggests that the particular features of System A—the normative Levels, the elaborated feedback on the screen, etc.—encourage the recognition of excellence either by the teacher or by the high achievers themselves. In support of these interpretations, the answers to items 11 & 13 indicate that the System A students gain comparison information from the positive statements printed on the computer screen and from the class teacher significantly more often than the System B students. System A students also reveal significantly more desire for social comparison (e.g., "To know if the other students are better or worse") and for showing off their successes and superiority over other students in the CAI work (e.g., "My friends brag that they receive difficult exercises"). The System B students put more emphasis on helping other students, that is, the cooperative work.

Two additional items (Items 17, 18) ask how the student feels when his/her solution of an exercise is incorrect. The choices of System A students indicate significantly more negative feelings resulting from failure to solve correctly (e.g., "I get cross with myself"). The students in System B react to failure in a much more relaxed manner (e.g., "I am content because the computer showed me my mistakes," and "I don't care").

MEASURES OF COMPETITION

So far, the analysis of students' answers to our questionnaire provide support for our findings from observations—that the two CAI systems involved are very different in features that encourage comparison behavior and competition. On the basis of these differences we expected that students in the two systems would differ in their attitudes towards social comparisons and towards competition, so that System B students would reveal less competitive behavior than the other students. To examine this hypothesis, we asked students directly about their attitudes towards competing with other students in the CAI arithmetic work. Surprisingly, contrary to our expectations, the System B students show significantly more positive attitudes towards competition in CAI than the System A students. Students' answers to this question (Item 19) reveal that the majority of the students (80% in System A and 69% in System B) do not like competition in CAI work. However, these numbers show that a lower proportion of System B students than the other students resist that competition. In addition, the System B students who admit to liking the competition explain their attitudes (Item 20) significantly more than the other students in terms of a variety of types of competitive behaviors (e.g., "in order to show that I am clever"). We see here, again, that the students of System A emphasize more the negative experiences of failure (e.g., "In order not to be mocked"). We will try to explain these unexpected results in the discussion below.

In order to compare the overall competitive behavior of students in both CAI systems, we defined a measure of competitive behavior, using Owens' (1985) definition of "competition as behavior" (pp. 907-908):

> Competitive behavior is a composite of three types of action. The first is a stated intention to achieve superiority over an opponent...the second is persistence in striving during the complete period of time allocated to the contest, even in the face of discouragement or wariness. The third is the experience (and possibly display) of a positive emotion such as pleasure at a successful outcome... or some degree of dismay at an unsuccessful outcome.

We sorted all the items in our questionnaire that we judged to be relevant to competition into three groups. The first two categories correspond broadly to the first two categories suggested by Owens. These are: (1) intention to achieve superiority; and (2) persistence in striving for success even in the face of discouragement. We were not able, however, to represent Owens' third category ("pleasure at a successful outcome"), because our observations and findings both from a previous questionnaire (Hativa, In press) and from the present questionnaire indicate that all the students without exception very much enjoy the positive feedback from the computer. All are happy to get the "very good" statement when an exercise is solved correctly. Instead of Owens' third category we substituted (3) self-report of competitiveness.

Intention to achieve superiority. This measure is composed of responses to six items common to both systems. Two additional items have been included only in the System A questionnaire. In these responses, students either expressed their intentions to make public their successes with the CAI work or described efforts to achieve a standing superior to that of other students in the class (e.g., Item 2c in Table 15.5; Item 15f in Table 15.6).

Persistence in striving for success even in the face of discouragement. This measure is composed of three items describing students' behavior investing effort and persistence when the students do not know how to solve a particular exercise (e.g., Item 1 8b in Table 15.6).

Self report of competitiveness. Five items in the questionnaire ask students directly whether they like or dislike competition and then to explain why (e.g., Items 19 and 20 in Table 15.6).

We have defined a student's score on each of these three categories of competition to be the number of items chosen out of all items included in that category. This number cannot be used to compare a student's scores on the different categories, partly because of the different number of items in each category. It is used here solely for purposes of comparing two populations on the same category.

The measure of competition. We define this measure as the sum of the scores of the three categories of competition, that is, the number of choices of items related to all aspects of competition in our questionnaire. This procedure assigns equal weight to each answer that relates to competition. We have not used for this definition the weighted mean of the three categories that constitute our definition of competition because using the weighted mean would have assumed that the three categories make equal contributions to the measure of competition.

So far, we have defined the more direct measures of competition and its components. However, students' open answers in the preliminary stages of the questionnaire development revealed other themes related to either cooperation or competition in CAI work in addition to those already presented. These are:

Self report of making social comparisons. In five items (13 altogether for System A students) of this group, students directly state that they compare their own CAI performance to that of their classmates (e.g., all options of Item 4 in Table 15.5).

Evidence of social comparison made by other students. Nine items describe how other students look at each other's screen or compare their CAI performance in other ways (e.g., Item 9e in Table 15.6).

Teacher Effect on Students' Competitive Behavior. Our observations show that not only the students but also the teachers are attuned to the "actual" objectives, those that come from the particular method of operation of the CAI system. To maximize their students' success, they encourage their students to behave in accordance with the conditions of the system they use. Thus, a substantial proportion of the System A teachers we observed read to their classes the Levels of all students or otherwise provided information about students' standings in the CAI work. By making this information available to all students in the class, these teachers encouraged social comparison and competition. In contrast, System B teachers were not able to provide this type of information and rather than that, they encouraged cooperation and peer work. Our questionnaire includes three common items (eight altogether for System A students) that describe how teachers make the CAI performance information available to students (e.g., Item 11 c in Table 15.6).

Student Effort to Advance in Level. Nine items in the questionnaire describe the effort students make in order to advance in the levels of practice faster than their classmates (e.g., Items 17a,b in Table 15.6).

The students of System B choose more items that show positive attitudes toward competition and willingness to compete than the System A students (see Tables 15.7 & 15.8). This result is completely contrary to our expectations that, because System A includes features that encourage competition, the students of that system will report competitive behavior significantly more than the students of System B. The contradiction between our expectations and these results are discussed below.

On the other hand, the students of System A perceive their teachers as encouraging competition significantly more than System B students whereas the latter group of students indicate a significantly higher measure of helping other students in CAI work than System A students. These results are in complete agreement with the findings of our observations.

POSITIVE AND NEGATIVE EFFECTS OF COMPETITION

Although the questionnaire does not include items that relate directly to gaining pleasure from competition or from its results, our observations give ample evidence of students' favorable reactions to the positive feedback that they receive from the computer. On the other hand, we have also encountered in our observations many cases of students' expressing negative feelings because of failure in the CAI work. Two major themes emerged from students' answers to relevant items.

Self evidence of negative feelings following failure in the CAI work. In seven items for both groups and two additional ones for the System A group students express their own negative feelings such as shame, sadness, anger,

	System A						
				SES			
	All		advantaged		dis-advantaged		
			n=140		n=107		
	Mean	SD	Mean	SD	Mean	SD	t
1. Intention to achieve superiority	.4	(.7)	.3	(.7)	.5	(1.0)	1.5
2. Persistence in striving for success despite discouragement	1.4	(1.0)	1.4	(1.0)	1.4	(1.0)	0
3. Self evidence of competitiveness	.7	(1.1)	.6	(1.1)	.8	(1.2)	1.5
4. Competitiveness	2.5	(2.1)	2.3	(2.0)	2.7	(2.2)	1.5
5. Self evidence of making social comparisons	1.0	(1.2)	1.0	(1.1)	1.2	(1.2)	1.7
6. Evidence of social comparison made by other students	2.8	(1.7)	2.7	(1.7)	2.8	(1.7)	.6
7. The teacher's role in encouraging or discouraging competition	.4	(.7)	.4	(.3)	.3	(.6)	1.1
8. Self evidence of helping others	.3	(.5)	.3	(.5)	.2	(.4)	2.7**
9. Self evidence of negative feelings	.7	(1.0)	.5	(1.0)	1.0	(1.1)	3.5***
10. General evidence for negative behavior towards students who fail in CAI work by other students	1.1	(1.3)	1.0	(1.3)	1.5	(1.5)	2.0
	System B						
			n=128		n=82		
1. Intention to achieve superiority	.5	(.9)	.6	(1.0)	.5	(.7)	1.1
2. Persistence in striving for success despite discouragement	1.5	(1.0)	1.6	(1.0)	1.4	(1.1)	1.1
3. Self evidence of competitiveness	1.0	(1.3)	1.0	(1.3)	1.0	(1.2)	.2
4. Competitiveness	3.1	(2.2)	3.2	(2.3)	3.0	(1.9)	1.0
5. Self evidence of making social comparisons	1.2	(1.0)	1.3	(1.1)	1.0	(.9)	.8
6. Evidence of social comparison made by other students	2.5	(1.6)	2.4	(1.5)	2.5	(1.7)	.5
7. The teacher's role in encouraging or discouraging competition	.2	(.6)	.1	(.3)	.4	(.7)	4.6***
8. Self evidence of helping others	.5	(.6)	.5	(.7)	.3	(.6)	2.5**
9. Self evidence of negative feelings	.7	(1.0)	.7	(1.0)	.6	(.9)	.6
10. General evidence for negative behavior towards students who fail in CAI work by other students	1.1	(1.3)	1.1	(1.4)	1.1	(1.3)	.3

$*p < .05; **p < .01; ***p < .001$

Table 15.7
Comparison on SES, sex, and achievement on composite items related to competition, for each system. Continued on next page.

	Sex					Achievement					
System A	Boys n=146		Girls n=101			Low n=41		High n=35			
	Mean	SD	Mean	SD	t	Mean	SD	Mean	SD	t	F
1. Intention to achieve superiority	.5	(1.0)	.2	(.5)	3.1**	.4	(.6)	.7	(1.4)	1.5	4.2**
2. Persistence in striving for success despite discouragement	1.4	(1.0)	1.5	(.9)	.2	1.2	(1.0)	1.7	(1.0)	2.3*	1.9
3. Self evidence of competitiveness	.8	(1.2)	.5	(1.0)	1.7	.8	(1.1)	1.0	(1.5)	.9	2.2
4. Competitiveness	2.7	(2.3)	2.2	(1.3)	2.1*	2.4	(1.9)	3.4	(2.9)	2.1*	4.3**
5. Self evidence of making social comparisons	1.1	(1.3)	1.1	(1.0)	0	1.9	(1.0)	1.5	(1.4)	2.6**	4.5**
6. Evidence of social comparison made by other students	2.3	(1.7)	2.7	(1.3)	.5	2.6	(1.6)	3.3	(1.9)	2.0*	3.2*
7. The teacher's role in encouraging or discouraging competition	.5	(.3)	.3	(.6)	2.0*	.5	(.8)	.2	(.5)	2.0*	3.2*
8. Self evidence of helping others	.2	(.5)	.3	(.5)	1.3	.2	(.5)	.3	(.5)	1.8	1.2
9. Self evidence of negative feelings	.8	(1.1)	.6	(.9)	1.6	1.0	(1.2)	.7	(.9)	1.5	1.6
10. General evidence for negative behavior towards students who fail in CAI work by other students	1.2	(1.3)	1.0	(1.3)	1.0	.8	(1.3)	1.2	(1.4)	1.4	3.1*
System B	n=112		n=98			n=60		n=46			
1. Intention to achieve superiority	.7	(1.0)	.4	(.7)	2.8**	.7	(1.1)	.4	(.8)	1.3	.7
2. Persistence in striving for success despite discouragement	1.4	(1.1)	1.7	(1.0)	2.4*	1.5	(1.0)	1.5	(.8)	.2	.4
3. Self evidence of competitiveness	1.2	(1.2)	.9	(1.3)	1.9	1.1	(1.2)	.8	(1.2)	1.0	.4
4. Competitiveness	3.3	(2.3)	2.9	(2.0)	1.0	3.2	(2.0)	2.8	(1.9)	1.1	.6
5. Self evidence of making social comparisons	1.1	(1.0)	1.2	(1.0)	.5	1.2	(1.0)	1.0	(1.2)	.7	.5
6. Evidence of social comparison made by other students	2.4	(1.6)	2.5	(1.5)	.3	2.3	(1.3)	2.5	(1.6)	.9	.7
7. The teacher's role in encouraging or discouraging competition	.2	(.6)	.2	(.5)	.4	.2	(.5)	.2	(.6)	.4	.1
8. Self evidence of helping others	.4	(.6)	.5	(.7)	1.2	.4	(.6)	.5	(.7)	1.4	.7
9. Self evidence of negative feelings	.6	(.9)	.8	(.9)	1.5	.8	(.9)	.4	(.7)	2.6	2.0
10. General evidence for negative behavior towards students who fail in CAI work by other students	1.2	(1.3)	1.0	(1.3)	1.2	1.2	(1.4)	1.1	(1.3)	.6	.1

$*p < .05; **p < .01; ***p < .001$

Table 15.7 continued.

decrease in motivation to pursue the CAI work further, anxiety at the prospect of being mocked, and the like. These negative feelings are explained in students' answers as resulting from the exposure of their failures when other students watch the student's computer screen or when the teacher makes information about standings available to the whole class (e.g., items 17d,f,g in Table 15.6).

General evidence for negative behavior towards students who fail. Four items of this category (with an additional six for the System A group) reflect either: (a) students' awareness of cases that other students are being mocked or being called names because of low CAI performance; and (b) students' behavior designed to prevent other students from treating the low achievers negatively (e.g., Items 23 a,b & c in Table 15.6).

	Main Effects				2-way interaction		
	CS	SES	Sex	Ach	CS x SES	CS x Sex	CS x Ach
1. Intention to achieve superiority	4.4**	0	15.5***	1.8	1.5	0	2.7*
2. Persistence in striving for success despite discouragement	9.4**	1.0	5.9*	.4	.1	.1	1.7
3. Self evidence of competitiveness	.7	.5	3.0	1.0	1.1	2.8	1.1
4. Competitiveness	8.9**	.1	4.6*	1.1	1.4	.4	3.2
5. Self evidence of making social comparisons	.5	0	.1	2.0	2.2	.2	3.0*
6. Evidence of social comparison made by other students	3.3	.4	0	1.9	.2	.1	2.0
7. The teacher's role in encouraging or discouraging competition	8.5**	2.2	3.0	2.1	14.6***	.8	1.8
8. Self evidence of helping others	12.6***	12.2***	2.6	1.6	.4	.4	.3
9. Self evidence of negative feelings	.6	5.3*	0	2.6*	8.6**	3.4	.6
10. General evidence for negative behavior towards students who fail in CAI work by other students	0	1.6	2.2	1.5	2.3	.2	1.5

CS = Computer System (A vs. B), SES = Socio-Economic Status, Ach = Achievement

$*p < .05; **p < .01; ***p < .001$

Table 15.8
F-values in ANOVA for comparisons on SES, sex, system, and achievement on composite items related to competition.

Results of the analysis of these items, summarized in Tables 15.6 & 15.7, reveal no difference between students of the two CAI systems. This is contrary to our expectation that the high degree of competition shown to exist in the System A environment would inflict negative feelings of failure to a higher degree than System B.

SES, GENDER AND ACHIEVEMENT-LEVEL DIFFERENCES IN ASPECTS OF COMPETITION

SES Differences

Statistical tests to establish differences between the advantaged and disadvantaged students (Chi Square as presented in Table 15.5, F-tests in Tables 15.7 & 15.9 and ANOVA in Table 15.8) show that the disadvantaged students in System A, significantly more than the advantaged students, are sensitive to the mocking of students as the result of their poor performance in CAI work, and to positive as well as negative feedback statements. They are also more interested than advantaged students in receiving information that helps to make comparisons of performance with the other students in the class. Out of the ten measures included, only two show a main effect of SES (Table 15.8). These are students' self-report of negative feelings following failure in the CAI work, and students' self-report of helping others. In both CAI systems, advantaged students say that they help other students in the

	All		SES advantaged n=140		SES disadvantaged n=107		
	Mean	SD	Mean	SD	Mean	SD	t
1. Intention to achieve superiority	.5	(1.0)	.4	(.8)	.6	(1.2)	1.9
4. Competitiveness	2.6	(2.2)	2.4	(2.1)	2.9	(2.4)	1.6
5. Self evidence of making social comparisons	3.0	(2.2)	2.8	(2.1)	3.3	(2.3)	1.7
7. The teacher's role in encouraging or discouraging competition	.8	(1.1)	.8	(1.1)	.8	(1.1)	.6
9. Self evidence of negative feelings	1.0	(1.2)	.8	(1.1)	1.4	(1.3)	3.7***
10. General evidence for negative behavior towards students who fail in CAI work by other students	2.1	(1.9)	1.9	(1.7)	2.3	(2.1)	1.5

	Sex					Achievement					
	Boys n=146		Girls n=101			Low n=41		High n=35			
	Mean	SD	Mean	SD	t	Mean	SD	Mean	SD	t	F
1. Intention to achieve superiority	.6	(1.4)	.2	(.7)	3.3***	.3	(.6)	.8	(1.7)	1.7	2.0
4. Competitiveness	2.8	(2.4)	2.2	(1.9)	2.2*	1.3	(1.4)	3.8	(3.0)	3.5***	9.9***
5. Self evidence of making social comparisons	3.2	(2.4)	2.7	(.7)	1.9	1.7	(1.6)	4.3	(2.7)	5.2***	10.7** *
7. The teacher's role in encouraging or discouraging competition	1.0	(1.2)	.5	(.8)	3.3***	.7	(.9)	1.0	(1.3)	1.0	.5
9. Self evidence of negative feelings	1.1	(1.2)	.9	(1.2)	1.1	1.1	(1.1)	.8	(1.4)	.8	2.1
10. General evidence for negative behavior towards students who fail in CAI work by other students	2.1	(1.9)	2.0	(2.0)	.4	1.4	(1.1)	2.6	(2.3)	2.9**	2.3*

*$p < .05$; **$p < .01$; ***$p < .001$

Table 15.9
Comparison on SES, sex, and achievement on composite items related to competition that are particular to System A.

CAI work more than disadvantaged students (Table 15.7). However, with respect to negative feelings that result from failure, there is a computer-system x SES interaction: in System A disadvantaged students feel more negative about their failures than advantaged students whereas in System B the trend is opposite, though students' choices are very close on both SES groups.

Gender Differences

The same statistical tests for differences on SES were used to identify gender differences in students' answers. Only a few statistically significant differences between the answers of boys and girls are evident in Table 15.5. More boys than girls in System A are interested in receiving information about theirs and others' CAI performance so that they can compare themselves to others' Levels of practice. Significantly more boys than girls state that they like to boast about their successes in CAI work. This is also true for System B. Table 15.7 reveals that in both groups boys state their intention to achieve superiority significantly more often than girls. In System

A boys are significantly "higher" than girls on the measure of competitiveness. Indeed, Table 15.8 indicates that the only two significant main effects of gender are the intention to achieve superiority and competitiveness. However, an interesting finding from Table 15.7 is that girls state that they are more persistent than boys in striving for success in CAI work. For System B, this gender difference is even statistically significant. No significant interactions of CAI-system x gender are evident on any of the ten measures.

Level-of-Achievement Differences

We derived the students' achievement level from two sources. For purposes of comparisons between the systems (Tables 15.7 & 15.8), we used teachers' class grades in arithmetic. However, we believe that the CAI report was a better measure of students' achievement in CAI work in arithmetic than the teachers' grades. Therefore, we used students' CAI Levels on the computer reports for purposes of comparisons within System A, the system for which the reports were available (Tables 15.5 & 15.9).

Using these measures, we sorted the students in each class into four achievement levels, with reference to the class mean and standard deviation. The highest achievement group included all students whose achievement level (either in CAI or in teacher's assigned grade) was greater than the sum of the mean and the standard deviation of the class achievement level. The lowest achievement group included all students whose achievement level was below the difference of the class mean and the standard deviation . The other two groups were those within one standard deviation from the class mean.

In Table 15.5 we present statistical tests (t-test) between the two extreme achievement groups . In Table 15.8 we use all four groups of achievement in order not to omit students from the ANOVA. Because we use Table 15.7 as an interpretation of the findings of Table 15.8, we have included in Table 15.7 both t-values for the two extreme groups of achievement and F-values for the four achievement groups. Table 15.9 also presents the results of both tests.

As expected, high achievers in System A are not bothered at all by other students getting to know their CAI Level (Table 15.5). Low achievers are more concerned about this matter. The high achievers show more interest in social comparison. They compare almost any information that can be compared during the computer session. On the other hand, high achievers seem to empathize with lower-achieving students when they are being mocked or hurt as a result of low CAI performance.

Table 15.7 reveals a very interesting phenomenon. Although seven out of the ten measures for System A show achievement-related statistically significant differences, there is not even one achievement-related difference for System B students that is statistically significant. The competitiveness-evoking nature of System A apparently produces differential effects on students with different aptitudes whereas the non-competitive nature of System B does not.

We found no main effect of achievement on competitiveness or any of its components (Table 15.8). However, there are significant interactions between achievement and competition, intention to achieve superiority, and self report of making social comparisons. System A students show achievement-related differences and System B students do not. The only main effect of achievement is students' self-report of negative feelings following failure in the CAI work. As expected, in each of the systems low achievers report more negative feelings as the result of failure to solve correctly than high achievers do.

SUMMARY AND DISCUSSION

This study shows that in actual operation, students' competitive or cooperative behavior in two CAI systems diverges from the intentions of the respective systems' designers. Computer systems such as those we studied do not cause dysfunctional competition. We believe that competition is rooted in the social and content structure of schooling. Because the value of the tasks assigned to students is often not obvious, they search for ways to validate that their performances are "good" by some standard. Often, the most salient standard is normative. When teachers can find no better standard, they may encourage normative self-evaluation by announcing scores or by more subtle means. System A was designed to be an environment in which this would not happen. Indeed, its designers, more than others, provide teacher training and consulting aimed at minimizing dysfunctional social comparisons. However, the system does make data on student performance available, at least in teacher reports and implicitly, in things a student experiences and might talk about. Some teachers use this information to foster competition, against the suggestions of the system designers, and many students manage to make profound social comparisons while working with this system and to strongly compete with one another.

On the other hand, the designers of System B did not entertain any considerations of cooperation versus competition in their planning (personal communication). However, our results show that the features of this system minimize social comparisons and competition among students, induce a relaxed working environment, and foster student cooperation and peer help in CAI work. These features also prompt the teachers in this system to help students and to encourage student cooperation and peer help.

We should note here that we do not compare here students' cognitive gains from work with the two CAI systems neither do we judge cooperation or competition to be desired or undesired goal structures. We join Malone & Lepper's (1987, pp. 242-243) position that "Often, cooperation has been assumed to be *good* and competition has been assumed to be *bad*...both can provide powerful motivations for learning, and both can be employed in ways that have detrimental effects and in ways that have beneficial effects."

Our findings of differences between what is designed and what actually happens in CAI work add to the accumulating evidence that the preparation of learning material and the design of learning environment is very complex and may produce unpredictable results, at times results that even contradict the objectives of the designers of these materials. For example, the Sesame Street program, designed primarily to benefit disadvantaged young children, was found in a study (Cook, Appleton, Conner, Shaffer, Tamkin and Weber, 1975) to benefit much more students of advantaged families. Another example is a CAI system designed to benefit the low achievers which was found in research to benefit primarily the better students (Hativa, 1986; 1988).

In addition to the main findings of the study, the following is a summary of several interesting CAI-induced effects of competition and cooperation identified here:

SES effects. Advantaged and disadvantaged students do not show any significant difference on the measure of competitiveness or on its components. However, disadvantaged students choose, significantly more than advantaged students, items that point to their tendency to help others in the computer lab and they suffer significantly more than advantaged students from negative feelings as the result of failure or low CAI performance. Moreover, the more competitive CAI system (System A) evokes significantly more failure-related negative feelings with disadvantaged students than with the other students.

Gender effects. In complete agreement with the research literature, boys appear to be more competitive than girls in each of the two CAI systems examined in this study. Girls appear to perceive themselves as being persistent in their CAI work significantly more than boys. There are no CAI-system related differences related to aspects of competition between boys and girls.

Level-of-achievement effects. In both CAI systems, low achievers, significantly more than the high achievers, express negative feelings from their low performance or their failures in the CAI work. Another interesting finding is that the particular features of a CAI system foster aptitude-related differences among students. The competition-evoking CAI system (System A) encourages the high achievers, significantly more than the low achievers, to show a variety of features of competitive behavior whereas the non-competitive nature of the other CAI system cancels aptitude-related differences in competitive behavior.

Effects of system features on the students' behavior. The students seem to adapt their objectives in the CAI work and their behavior during this work to the objectives inherent in the method of operation of the CAI system. The students using the competition evoking system (System A) stress the importance of aspects of good learning conditions and of avoidance of social comparisons whereas the students using the other CAI system stress the importance of teacher's and of peer help and of cooperation in the CAI work.

Effects of system features on teacher behavior. Teachers, as perceived by the students who answered the questionnaire, seem to adapt their behavior to the particular CAI system's features. In the more competitive CAI environment they encourage social comparison and competition among students and in the other CAI environment they encourage cooperative work and peer help.

Positive attitudes towards competition. An unexpected finding of this study, one that totally contradicted our initial expectations, was the significantly more positive attitudes and higher competitive tendencies that were self-reported by the students of the non competition-evoking system (System B) than by the students of the more competition-evoking system (System A). These results may be explained by the fact that the students of System B do not experience the unpleasant features of a strict competitive environment as do the students of System A. Because the slight competition that the System B students experience is of a pleasant nature, they are much more positive towards its existence and features than are the other students.

Our discussion implies that aspects of social comparison and competition may have significant impact on students' learning, for all types of learning conditions. Lepper & Chabay (1985, p. 217) argue that "Motivational factors may often exert as great an influence on children's achievement as do cognitive factors...; yet over the past 20 years, such motivational influences have received but token research attention." We argue here that the same is true for social factors. Researchers and designers of learning environments, particularly of computer-based learning systems, often overlook social aspects of students' behavior. Therefore, findings of this study should alert educational researchers and instructional designers of CAI systems to take into their planning considerations that either encourage or discourage social comparisons and competition. Additional suggestions for methods to encourage cooperation or competition in CAI work are discussed by Malone & Lepper (1987).

The question raised by the results of this study is whether the inherent difficulties children have in valuing practice performance require a more radical approach. Perhaps new approaches are needed, such as assigning tasks to groups or making practice tasks authentically valuable by assuring that, at least part of the time, there is a use for the results of mathematical computations students are asked to perform. These are important questions and research is needed to provide some answers. We suggest also that research investigates further a variety of features of competitiveness and social comparison behaviors in CAI work identified in this study. Particularly, we need to learn more about the positive and negative effects of competitive versus cooperative CAI environments on students' motivation and cognitive learning, and on features of the hardware, software, and method of operation that may affect social comparison and competition among students.

REFERENCES

Ahlgren, A. & Johnson, D.W. (1979). Sex differences in cooperative and competitive attitudes from the 2nd through the 12th grades. Developmental Psychology, 15, 45-49.

Ames, C., Ames, R. & Felker, D. (1977). Effects of competitive reward structure and valence of outcome on children's achievement attributions. Journal of Educational Psychology, 69, 1-8.

Ames, C. & Felker, D. (1979). An examination of children's attributions and achievement-related evaluations in competitive, cooperative, and individualistic reward structures. Journal of Educational Psychology, 71, 413-420.

Ames, C. & Ames, R. (1981) Competitive versus individualistic goal structures: the salience of past performance information for causal attributions and affect. Journal of Educational Psychology, 73(3), 411-418.

Cook T.K., Appleton, H., Conner, R.F., Shaffer, A., Tamkin, G. & Weber, S.J. (1975). "Sesame Street" revisited. New York: Russell Sage Foundation.

Festinger, L. (1954). A theory of social comparison processes. Human Relations, 7,117-140.

Hativa, N. (1986). Computer-based practice in arithmetic (TOAM): Dreams and realities—an ethnographic study. The Pinchas Sapir Center for Development, Discussion Paper No. 7-86.

Hativa, N. & Shorer, D. (1988). SES, aptitude, and gender differences in CAI. The Unit for Communication & Computer Research in Education, Tel Aviv University. Report No. 18.

Hativa, N. (1988). Computer-based drill and practice in arithmetic—widening the gap between high and low achieving students. The American Educational Research Journal, 25(3) 366-397.

Hativa, N. (In press). Students' conceptions of and attitudes towards specific features of a CAI system. The Journal of Computer-Based Instruction.

Johnson, D.W. & Johnson, R.T. (1975). Learning together and alone. Prentice Hall , Inc., Englewood Cliffs, New Jersey, 29-53.

Johnson, D.W. & Johnson, R.T. (1979). Cooperation. competition and individualization. In H. Walberg (Ed.), Educational Environments and effects. Berkeley, Ca.: McCutchan.

Johnson, R.T., Johnson, D.W. & Bryant, 19. (1973). Cooperation and competition in the classroom: perceptions and preferences as related to students' feelings of personal control. Elementary School Journal, 73, 306-313.

Johnson, R.T., Johnson, D.W., & Stanne, M.19. (1985) Effects of cooperative, competitive and individualistic goal structure on computer-assisted instruction. Journal of Educational Psychology, 77(6), 668-677.

Johnson, D.W., Maruyama, R., Johnson, R. Nelson, D. & Skon, L. (1981). Effects of cooperative, competitive and individualistic goal structures on achievement: meta-analysis. Psychological Bulletin, 89(1), 47-62.

Kagan, S. & Madsen, M.C. (1971). Cooperation and competition of Mexican, Mexican-American, and Anglo-American children of two ages under four instructional sets. Developmental Psychology, 5, 32-39.

Kanevsky, L. (1985). Computer-based math for gifted students: comparison of cooperative and competitive strategies. Journal for the Education of the Gifted, 8(4), 239-255.

Lepper, M.R. & Chabay, R.W. (1985). Intrinsic motivation and instruction: conflicting views on the role of motivational processes in computer-based education. Educational Psychologist, 20(4), 217-230.

Lewis, M.A. & Cooney, J.B. (1987). Attributional and performance effects of competitive and individualistic feedback in computer-assisted mathematics instruction. Computers in Human Behavior, 3(1), 1-13.

Madsen, M.C. & Shapira, A. (1970) Cooperative and competitive behavior of urban Afro American, Anglo-American, and Mexican village children. Developmental Psychology, 3, 16-20.

Malone, T.W. & Lepper, M.R. (1987). Making learning fun: a taxonomy of intrinsic motivations for learning. In Snow, R.E. & Farr, M.J. (Eds.) Aptitude. learning. and instruction Volume 3: conative and affective process analyses. Hillsdale, New Jersey: Laurence Erlbaum Associates.

Michaels, J.W. (1977). Classroom reward structures and academic performance. Review of Educational Research, 47(1), 87-98.

Osin, L., & Nesher, P. (1977). Computer-aided teaching of arithmetic in the elementary school. Iunim Bechinuch, 24, 93-108 (Hebrew).

Owens, L. (1985). Competition in the classroom. International Encyclopedia of Education. Pergamon Press, (2), 906-910.

Pepitone, E. A. (1972). Comparison behavior in elementary school children. American Educational Research Journal, 9(1), 45-63.

Pepitone, E. A. (1980). Children in cooperation and competition. Lexington, Mass : Lexington Books, D.C. Heath and Company.

Schofield, J.W. (1985). The impact of an intelligent computer-based tutor on classroom social processes: An ethnographic study. Learning Research and Development Center, University of Pittsburgh.

Sharan, S. (1980). Cooperative learning in teams: recent methods and effects on achievement, attitudes, and ethnic relations. Review of Educational Research, 50(2), 241-272.

Slavin, R. (1983). Cooperative Learning. New York, Longman.

Slavin, R. (1983). When does cooperative learning mean student achievement. Psychological Bulletin, 94, 429-445.

Suls, J.M. & Miller, R.L. (Eds.) (1977). Social comparison processes: Theoretical and empirical perspectives. Washington, DC.

Toda, M., Shinotsuka, H., McClintock, C.G. & Stech, F.J. (1978). Development of competitive behavior as a function of culture, age, and social comparison. Journal of Personality and Social Psychology, 36, 825-829.

READING QUESTIONS

1) How is a students' experience with a computer "culturally embedded"?
2) Name several ways that the computing culture is "alien."
3) Why must novices "learn how to learn as well as what to learn"?
4) What is "reality shock"? Why is it important?
5) What determines the difference between successful socialization, active rejection, and withdrawal?
6) In initial encounters, why is knowledge about the culture surrounding computers more important than technical knowledge?
7) How are students' experiences with computing different from their experiences with other disciplines?
8) How did student reactions to computing compare with their reactions to other technical courses?
9) What is the difference between a cultural recruit and a dropout?
10) What four items of reality shock were most apparent in students' reactions?

11) How did the students categorize the inhabitants of the computing culture?
12) What cultural lessons did students learn?
13) What "irony of organizational socialization" was highlighted by the reality shock the students experienced?
14) What are some of the potential positive and negative effects of competition in educational settings?
15) How might these effects differ depending upon SES, gender, and achievement-related differences?
16) How do schools encourage competition?
17) What is "self-competition," and how might it be different from competition with others?
18) How does the timing of answers in System A discourage cooperative work?
19) Why did the designers of System A change the system during the study?
20) How does the sharing among teachers of CAI grades put pressure on teachers (and thereby students)?
21) Were the goals of the designers of System A achieved?
22) What kinds of information from System A did students compare among themselves?
23) Why was it "good" that the reports from System B were complicated and difficult to use?
24) What design differences were there between the two systems?
25) What differences were there in the classroom environment between the two systems?
26) How did the students who use the two systems differ in their attitudes about learning?
27) How did the students who use the two systems differ in their knowledge of who were the "best" students?
28) Why might a System A student like competition less?
29) How did students of the two systems feel following failure feedback?
30) Why might disadvantaged students be more sensitive to mocking? Why did this occur only with System A?
31) Why would System B "cancel" the aptitude-related differences in competitive behavior?

DISCUSSION QUESTIONS

1) What were the goals of the designers of System A? What characteristics did they include in System A to produce that effect? How did those characteristics enhance competition? How did they resolve these differences between design intention and actuality?
2) In both papers, students are placed in a computer-intensive environment that has some unintended effects. Did the *computers* cause the problems? If not, how did the problems come about?

PRACTICING THE DESIGN ETHIC

1) Identify the computing culture on your campus or in your business. You might do this by spending some time in the computer room, taking notes on the computer about what you see. Be sure to include the physical layout, the temporal changes in activity, and the interactions and interaction styles of the participants. To what extent is this computer culture a "conscious" creation of the administration (managers), faculty, and students (workers)? That is, is it intended?

2) What are your own feelings about competition and cooperation in the classroom? What was your experience in the past? Is one approach better than another, or is there a mix that you feel best addresses the classroom environment? How can computers be used to foster your view? Design a small computer program (on paper) that would provide the "right mix" of competition and cooperation and that addresses some of the issues mentioned in the Hativa et al. paper. How could your program be implemented in a way that would reverse its intended effect?

CHAPTER
16

SOCIAL ISOLATION AND COMPUTERS

The popular press accounts of unwashed "hackers" spending untold hours in front of glowing computer screens are now legend. They have been immortalized in fiction and film, and popular opinion is split: They are either virtuosi artists or sick and dangerous people.

In her now classic chapter on hacking, Sherry Turkle claims that "both sides sell the hackers short by saying either that they are just like everyone else or that they are like nobody else except perhaps junkies or poets." On the basis of a series of extensive interviews, Turkle creates a picture of the hacker and hacker culture at Massachusetts Institute of Technology. Her detailed outline shows real people with an intimate relation to the machine who have created their own society. Still, Turkle's impression leaves us slightly uncomfortable with the implications for these individuals' growth.

If Turkle is ambivalent about the prospects for the hacker, Shotton is clearly optimistic. Her study of "computer dependents" is the most extensive and thorough one available, and leads her to conclude that "intensive interest in computers differs little from dedication to many other activities." In this excerpt from the final chapter of her book, she attempts to understand why "computer dependency" has been perceived as such a problem, and suggests that the root is a generalized fear our society has for things computational. In line with many other exhortations from this text, Shotton suggests that those who are concerned about "computer dependents" focus their energies on the social and psychological pressures that produce individuals who receive more satisfaction from interaction with objects than from social interaction. But, she warns, this sort of social engineering may be misguided, since devotion to a pursuit like computing may be of great value to society.

HACKERS: LOVING THE MACHINE FOR ITSELF[1]

Sherry Turkle
Massachusetts Institute of Technology

Every spring, MIT students hold an unusual contest. It has the form of a beauty pageant, but it is a contest to choose "the Ugliest Man on Campus." For several weeks, the students who think of themselves as most ugly parade around the main corridors of the Institute, wearing placards that announce their candidacy. They flaunt their pimples, their pasty complexions, their knobby knees, their thin undeveloped bodies. They collect funds to support their campaigns. There is a vote. The proceeds of the campaign collections go to charity.

I spoke with the ex-student, now a professor at another university, who began the contest more than twenty years ago. He is proud of his contribution to MIT culture. "Everyone knows that engineers are ugly. To be at Harvard is to be a gentleman, to be sexy, to be desired. To be at MIT is to be a tool, a nerd, a person without a body. The contest just makes irony of the obvious."

Today's MIT students echo his words. They feel comfortable with a ritual that celebrates a denial of the body, yet at the same time some are upset by the contest. "It hits too close to home. I'm not ugly enough to compete, but I'm not pretty enough to be normal, to have a girlfriend, to know what to do at a party." Some are angry about it, and angry at me for noticing it. "I hate that goddamn contest. It gives the whole place a bad name. It makes me ashamed to be around." Some deny the importance of the whole thing. Others reproach me for being just a "humanist type," oversensitive. Don't I know it's "just a joke"? They point out that good-looking people sometimes compete "trying to look ugly for a good cause." But most feel that although the contest is a joke it nevertheless expresses a truth. Some might call it the "social construction" of the engineer. These students see it more simply: an engineer is ugly in the eyes of the world, an alien to the sensual. [2]

---

[1] Turkle, S. (1984). Hackers: loving the machine for itself. Chapter 6 in *The Second Self*. New York, Simon and Schuster. Copyright 1984 by Sherry Turkle. Reprinted by permission.

[2] In this chapter I owe a great debt to my student Justin Marble, who did a series of interviews with student hackers. This chapter situates the hacker within the MIT engineering culture. Other social and psychological studies of this surrounding culture provide useful background. See, for example, Benson Snyder, *The Hidden Curriculum* (Cambridge, Mass.: MIT Press, 1971) and Kenneth Keniston, "The Unpracticed Heart: Youth and High Technology," Invited address to the American Psyciatric Association, Toronto, Ontario, May 19, 1982. Keniston divides MIT engineering students into two categories: "the craftsman engineer" and "the passionate engineer." The hackers I describe here belong to this second category, characterized by Keniston as the engineer who "becomes" his project.

THE SOCIAL CONSTRUCTION OF THE ENGINEER

I probably do not have to say the obvious, that many MIT men are involved with and proud of the body and its pleasures. But there is, too, a widespread presence of what has to be described as self-loathing. This is more than the symptom of an individual malady; the illness is social. Our society accepts and defensively asserts the need for a severed connection between science and sensuality, between people who are good at dealing with things and people who are good at dealing with people.

This split in our culture has many social costs, of which the first and most poignant is paid by children, particularly the suffering of many gifted adolescents. MIT students talk about growing up in "all-American" schools. For example, Ron, a junior majoring in astronomy:

> I've always thought of myself as ugly, inept. All of the boys who had friends and were popular were into sports and didn't care about school. Or if they cared about school they were sort of good more or less at everything. But there I was. All alone, fixing used ham-radio equipment. And all of the other kids I knew who were into ham-radio stuff felt just as ugly as I did. We had a club in sixth grade. And we called it "the Gross Club." I'm not kidding. So don't expect me to be surprised to come to MIT and find that all the other loners, doing their math and science and thinking of themselves as losers, make themselves an ugly man contest.

Ron's sense of himself as ugly is not supported in any way by his physical inheritance, although it is well supported by his grooming and gait. Muscles eventually take their form from the habitual posture of the body and set of the face. Ron's muscles express ambivalence, long felt, toward his body. He sees the power of his mind as a gift that brought him mastery over technology, but for which he has had to pay with shame and misery in the world of people.

The sense of a polarization between science and sensuality is made explicit by Burt, a sophomore majoring in chemical engineering:

> I think of the world as divided between flesh things and machine things. The flesh things have feelings, need you to know how to love them, to take risks, to let yourself go. You never know what to expect of them. And all the things that I was into when I was growing up, well, they were not those kinds of things. Math, you could get it perfect. Chemistry, you could get exactly the right values when you did your experiments. No risks. I guess I like perfection. I stay away from the flesh things. I think this makes me sort of a nonperson. I often don't feel like a flesh thing myself. I hang around machines, but I hate myself a lot of the time. In a way it's like masturbating. You can always satisfy your self to perfection. With another person, who knows what might happen? You might get

rejected. You might do it wrong. Too much risk. You can see why I'm not too pleased with the way my personality turned out.

The chances are that Ron and Burt will make an adaptation. They will emerge one day with diplomas and good job offers to be used as steppingstones to well-paid careers, to a sense of belonging in a social world that contains wives and children and the fabric of a supportive culture. But the transition from pariah to social integration is not easy; getting there is a struggle. Many feel the presence of a choice that can be put off, but that is always there. You are constantly coming to the fork in the road.

One path leads to what many MIT students call the "real world." The other leads to what Ron sees as a continuation of the Gross Club—an ever deeper commitment to ways of thinking and living that keep one apart from it. Those who take the second path flaunt their rejection of "normal" society by declaring, "We are the ugly men. You can keep your hypocrisy, your superficial values, your empty sense of achievement. We have something better and purer.

The struggle of the choice is described by Burt, who feels that he and his roommate are choosing opposite branches of the fork:

> For me, MIT isn't the real world. It's sort of a joke around here, to talk of the Institute and to talk of the "real world." But it's not funny. I mean I think of it as a struggle. But my roommate—for him there was no struggle. All there was for him was the ninth floor of Technology Square. I mean where they keep the computers. No struggle at all. Intellectually, I mean when I tried to feel normal about it I always came back to feeling that he had a perfect right to live in any world he wanted to, but when I would see him—and I hardly ever saw him, because he more or less lived there, all nerdy and talking about "foobar. bletch, meta-bletch"—I really hated him. I mean I pitied him. But I can get like that myself. I was like that in high school. I hated him for giving up. I think that if you become obsessed with computers it makes it easy to give up trying to be a real person.

Burt's anger is not merely a feeling of the moment. It is persistent. He uses his roommate as a foil for his own struggle. It is a struggle to create a bridge between a world of things and a world of people. Like other students who talk about a split between their "people selves" and their "technology selves," Burt is trying to put things together. He wants to believe that intense relationships with technical things need not keep him from productive relationships with the larger culture and caring relationships with other people. In short, Burt wants to be an engineer and live in the real world.

Within every culture, even a culture that wears a collective badge of self-denigration, there is a hierarchy. At MIT, some science is uglier than other science. Some engineering is uglier than other engineering. Some kinds of self-absorption are more unsavory, perhaps even more dangerous than others. And contact with some machines is more contaminating than with others.

THE IMAGE OF THE HACKER

In the MIT culture it is computer science that occupies the role of the "out group," the ostracized of the ostracized.[3] Computer science becomes a projective screen for the insecurities and self-hate of others in the community. And many of the computer science students accept this reflection of themselves as archetypal nerds, loners, and losers. On the MIT computer system that is considered to be the most advanced, the most state-of-the-art, the users are referred to as the "lusers." When you "log in," on the system to activate your account, you are given a "luser number" that identifies you to the computer and you are told how many other lusers are working along with you. How many other ugliest men.

Why are the computer-science students seen as the ugliest men or, when they are women, women who are somehow suspect? The self-image of engineering students is already low. Already they fear that quietly, insistently, in a way they do not understand but through paths they dimly suspect, the world of machines has cut them off from people, that they are the "kind of people" who demand perfection and are compelled by the controllable. The formal mechanical and mathematical systems they play with are the externalization of their taste. In the "computer person" they find someone who seems to have taken their taste and carried it to an extreme, someone who has taken their taste, already a source of tension, and transformed it into a perversion.

A fear about oneself is projected onto the perceived excesses of another. Such processes proceed by stereotyping, by mythologizing. In the case of seeing computation as ugly, as perversion, it is carried by taking a special community within the computer-science world and constructing the image of the "computer person" around it. At MIT, that community is known as "computer hackers." Elsewhere they are known as "computer wizards," "computer wheels," "computer freaks," or "computer addicts." Whatever the label, they are people for whom computers have become more than a job or an object of study, they have become a way of life.[4]

---

[3]This is true although it is also the case that increasing numbers of MIT students want to major in electrical engineering and computer science. And the self-denigration of the computer scientists coexists with their sense of being a privileged elite. The situation I am describing is nothing if not paridoxical.

[4]My field research on the hacker culture included participant observation within the MIT hacker community, reading two years of "science-fiction-lovers mail," "human-nets mail," and system messages as well as interviewing twenty-seven people who identified themselves as hackers, ex-hackers, and "on the way to becoming hackers." The hacker study also used a data collection strategy made possible by the computer itself. When I began to study the world of programmers and hackers, I sent out a message describing my project on a nation-wide computer net and said I would like to talk to anyone who was interested. On the computer system I was using, people could respond to my message when I was "off-line," that is, they could leave electronic mail for me in a "mailbox" file or they could wait until I was "on-

Engineers rationalize, indeed sometimes apologize for, the overintensity of their relationships with machines by describing them as tools, even as they express their identification by describing themselves as tools as well. The image of the machine as tool is reassuring because it defines a means—ends relationship. With our tools we forge things that can be used by other people. What is different for many hackers is that the means—ends relationship is dropped. The fascination is with the machine itself. Contact with the tool is its own reward. Most hackers are young men for whom at a very early age mastery became highly charged, emotional, colored by a particular desire for perfection, and focused on triumph over things. Their pleasure is in manipulating and mastering their chosen object, in proving themselves with it. It is not hard to understand why these few who "flaunt" the pleasures of the thing-in-itself become the objects for the projection of the nervousness of the many.

We saw the engineering student living with ambivalence, with the sense of being at a fork in the road. One direction leads to engineering being integrated into the everyday flow of relationships with people; the other leads to isolation and ever deeper immersion in the world of machines. Engineering students place great value on those things—books, movies, ideas—that connect their concerns with something larger. Star Wars was loved for the way it offered a bridge, even if superficial, between high technology and a romantic humanism. Robert Pirsig's *Zen and the Art of Motorcycle Maintenance* and Samuel Florman's *The Existential Pleasures of Engineering* are held in great regard.[5] These works achieved cult status because they describe how intense relationships with technical objects can lead to reflections on the philosophical concerns of the larger culture. They give courage to people like Burt that it is possible to be an engineer and live in the real world as well. By contrast, the hacker crystallizes an image of getting lost in the thing-in-itself.

One of the ways groups mark and protect their boundaries is through the use of language. Engineers develop a language of their own, a jargon. It is a source of pleasure, but also of alienation from nonengineers: "I try not to use it [the jargon] in "mixed company," if you know what I mean," says one student. The hacker, however, is lost in the jargon of his machine and its programs. His machine is "intelligent." His machine is "psychological." It offers a language easily applied to people. He uses it in mixed company, and his refusal to talk of other things enrages his engineering colleagues who are struggling to assimilate, to find a language for moving into the real world. This rage helps to set the hacker off as so ugly that the others feel beautiful,

---

line," working at my terminal. The system has a feature which allows someone who wants to "speak" with another on-line user to flash a message onto his or her screen. Both parties can type at each other, sending messages back and forth. Over the several years of working with this medium I received hundreds of letters and had many more brief and not-so-brief electronic correspondences.

[5] Robert Pirsig, *Zen and the Art of Motorcycle Maintenance* (New York: Bantam, 1975). Robert Florman, *The Exsitential Pleasures of Engineering* (New York: St. Martin's Press, 1976).

at least for the moment, by comparison. The hacker is a threat because he comes to stand for cultural isolation in the enterprise of engineering.

PASSION IN VIRTUOSITY

With the computer young people can find channels to a certain kind of virtuosity without passing through the filter of formal education. And a large research environment can benefit from an almost unlimited quantity of this virtuosity. Over the years at MIT there developed what was perceived by both sides as a fair trade. The hackers would supply virtuosity; in return they would be left free to construct their own way of life around one of the most powerful computer systems in the world. To understand what hackers do and how they do it, let us take a case in point: how the MIT hackers built the operating system that controls the computer on which the final draft of this book was typed.

When a company buys a computer, the machine comes with a large collection of programs called the operating system. These are the tools that enable the company's programmers to write special-purpose applications programs with vastly less effort and technical knowledge than would be necessary if they had to work with a bare machine. A simple example of what an operating system does is time-sharing, which allows many users to be served by the same computer in a way that seems to them to be simultaneous. In fact the computer is giving each user a quantum of time so short that he or she does not even notice and become jealous of the attention being paid to the others. This idea is simple, but bringing it about needs so much work that the job of making a time-sharing system of the professional quality of those supplied by a major manufacturer has probably not been carried out as many as a hundred times in the history of computation. The operating system is standard, and may not be optimal from the individual purchaser's point of view, but the purchaser of a computer has little choice but to accept the operating system offered on it. This system would have been constructed by a team of dozens or even hundreds of professionals and would represent the investment of many millions of dollars. To repeat the work and construct an operating system "to one's taste" is unthinkable.

When the Artificial Intelligence Laboratory at MIT obtained its first large computer it did the unthinkable almost without thinking. There had already grown up a community of gifted and totally dedicated young men, many of whom had dropped out of MIT academic programs in computer science in order to devote themselves more exclusively to computers. They were prepared to be on the job sixteen or eighteen hours a day, seven days a week; they lived and breathed and thought computers. More important for the story of the operating system they developed they lived and breathed and thought the one computer that the lab had purchased. In record time they built what many considered to be the world's most advanced time-sharing operating system, and one to their taste: ITS. The letters stand for Incompatible Time Sharing, a joking reference to contrast it with the operating system that another, more professionally structured MIT laboratory had recently installed, the Compatible Time Sharing System, CTSS. CTSS was compatible with systems outside MIT to make it easier to run programs written by outsiders. CTSS was practical, but some felt that the system had achieved its practical advantage by compromising its power. ITS was written by people who loved the machine-in-itself. It sacrificed nothing.

ITS was built with little planning and certainly with no formal decisions about the "specs" of the system. It cost a fraction of what it would have cost to make such a system under "industry" conditions. Its development became a model for a mode of production different from the standard, a mode of production built on a passionate involvement with the object being produced. Loyalty was to the project, not to the management; there was no rigid hierarchy, no respect for power other than the power that someone could exert over the computer.

This hacker-style work is not confined to university settings. Industries have learned to profit from intense relationships with computers—some have become quite expert at capitalizing on in-house cultures of passionate virtuosity.

In *The Soul of a Machine*, Tracy Kidder tells the story of how a new computer, the Eagle, was designed and built by people with uncommon devotion within the Data General Corporation. The book is written as an adventure story, indeed as a "cowboy tale" of a distinctly American variety. There are the "good guys"—the ones who are trying to build the machine. There are the "bad guys"—their rivals working on a competing machine in North Carolina. There is the struggle of the individual to "get back at" the authority of a corporation tempted to take the straight and conservative path when genius and vision offer another.

The word "Soul" in the title of the book is well chosen. It is what the group who created the machine devoted to the task. For the period of production they lived an almost monastic life. Other worldly cares and responsibilities dropped away. A religious leitmotif runs through Kidder's story of their dedicated labors where personal ego and personal reward had no place. What was important was winning. But this is a story in the real world. When the machine goes "out the door" to be marketed, the reality of that dedication is denied.

The day after the formal announcement, Data General's famous sales force had been introduced to the computer in New York and elsewhere. At the end of the presentation for the sales personnel in New York, the regional sales manager got up and gave his troops a pep talk, "What motivates people?" he asked, He answered his own question, saying, "Ego and the money to buy things that they and their families want," It was a different game now. Clearly, the machine no longer belonged to its makers. [6]

---

[6]Tracy Kidder, *The Soul of a New Machine* (Boston: Little Brown, 1981), p. 291.

The Data General hackers created a successful new machine. The MIT hackers associated with ITS also wrote other influential programs and became an integral part of the intellectual life of the MIT Artificial Intelligence Laboratory. In short, hackers play a significant although controversial role in the history of computation. What sets them apart is that they work for the joy of the process, not for the product.

THE HACKER CONTROVERSIES

The roommate who so angered Burt by spending all his time on the ninth floor of Technology Square is following in the footsteps of the senior hackers, most of whom have gone on to other things, some of whom are still around, all of whom are mythologized. As the earlier hackers did in their time, Burt's roommate is finding that the computer allows him rapidly to attain a level of virtuosity that will make him indispensable. And as he moves closer to the center of hacker culture he is moving farther away from academic values, from acceptance of hierarchy, from the "day life" of most of the rest of the world. It is not surprising that he upsets a lot of people.

Indeed, hackers have become objects of criticism and controversy both within and outside the computer community. Their existence challenges assumptions about human motivation ("ego and money") somehow more forcefully because they are technologists than does the existence of priests or poets. People seem ready to accept that artists play with paint or clay, brush or chisel, with a certain disinterest in the final product. However, when an engineer adopts this stance toward his tools, it evokes anxieties about intellectual masturbation. Tools are made to be used, not played with. They should belong to work life, not to intimate life. Public controversies about hackers are fueled by the fact that hackers externalize widespread fears about machines and the dangers of too intimate relationships with them.

Many people first became aware of the existence of hackers in 1976 with the publication of Joseph Weizenbaum's *Computer Power and Human Reason*. The book's description of hollow-eyed young men glued to computer terminals is reminiscent of descriptions of Opium addicts and compulsive gamblers:

> Wherever computer centers have become established, that is to say, in countless places in the United States, as well as in virtually all other industrial regions of the world, bright young men of disheveled appearance, often with sunken glowing eyes, can be seen sitting at computer consoles, their arms tensed, and waiting to fire, their fingers already poised to strike at the buttons and keys on which their attention seems to be as riveted as a gambler's on the rolling dice. When not so transfixed, they often sit at tables strewn with computer printouts over which they pore like possessed students of a cabalistic text. They work until they nearly drop, twenty, thirty hours at a time. Their food, if they arrange it, is brought to them: coffee, cokes,

sandwiches. If possible they sleep on cots near the computer. But only for a few hours—then back to the console or the printouts. Their rumpled clothes, their unwashed and unshaven faces, and their uncombed hair all testify that they are oblivious to their bodies and to the world in which they move. They exist, at least when so engaged, only through and for the computers. These are computer bums, compulsive programmers. They are an international phenomenon. [7]

Hackers have been the centerpiece of numerous articles in the popular press expressing grave concern about the dangers of "computer addiction." The nature of this concern varies. There are fears that young people will fall victim to a new kind of addiction with druglike effects: withdrawal from society, narrowing of focus and life purpose, inability to function without a fix. Others fear the spread, via the computer, of characteristics of the "hacker mind." And hackers are almost universally represented as having a very undesirable frame of mind: they prefer machines to sex, they don't care about being productive.

Several years ago *Psychology Today* published an interchange called "The Hacker Papers."[8] It was a warning on the part of some, including some hackers, that hacking was dangerous and depleting, and a defense on the part of others that hacking was a creative outlet like any other. The article prompted a flood of electronic mail debating the question. Artificial intelligence scientist Marvin Minsky presented the strongest defense of the hackers. They are no different from other people seriously devoted to their work, he said. "Like poets and artists they are devoted to developing tools and techniques." And as for their alleged ineptness at social relationships, Minsky said that the hackers are superior to the psychologists who trivialize human beings in their rush to stereotype and classify.

In this polemical form the debate is, to say the least, flat and oversimplified. Hackers are caught up with their computers, often to the point where other things in their lives do drop out. But the metaphor of addiction evokes an image of a deadened mind, which does injustice to the hackers' experience of their work as alive and exciting. Minsky is right that hackers are intellectually serious people. But, on the other hand, Minsky contributes to flattening the issue by refusing to allow any difference between hackers, poets, and artists. There are differences between hackers and most poets. Indeed, Minsky might well be betraying the side of himself that is closest to the hacker when he tells us that he sees the essence of the work of a poet as developing tools and techniques. This might be true in some cases. But in many, perhaps most, the work of the poet includes exploring the complexities

---

[7] Joseph Wiezenbaum, *Computer Power and Human Reason: From Judgment to Calculation* (San Franscisco: W. H. Freeman, 1976), p. 116.
[8] "The Hacker Papers," *Psychology Today*, August 1980, pp. 62-69.

and ambiguities of areas of feeling where, we shall see, the hackers seek simplicities.

Both sides sell the hackers short by saying either that they are just like everyone else or that they are like nobody else except perhaps junkies or poets. A better understanding requires a closer look at hackers as individuals and as part of a culture that expresses and supports the psychological needs they bring to their relationships with computation.

Hackers live a paradox: this is a culture of "lusers" who see themselves as an elite. They are the holders of an esoteric knowledge, defenders of the purity of computation seen not as a means to an end but as an artist's material whose internal aesthetic must be protected. Most paradoxically, they live with a self-image as "lusers" at the same time as they define their relationship with the machine in terms of "winning." They are caught up in an intense need to master—to master perfectly—their medium. In this they are like the virtuoso pianist or the sculptor possessed by his or her materials. Hackers too are "inhabited" by their medium. They give themselves over to it and see it as the most complex, the most plastic, the most elusive and challenging of all. To win over computation is to win. Period.

PERFECT MASTERY

The issue of mastery has an important role in the development of each individual. For the developing child, there is a point, usually at the start of the school years, when mastery takes on a privileged, central role. It becomes the key to autonomy, to the growth of confidence in one's ability to move beyond the world of parents to the world of peers. Later, when adolescence begins, with new sexual pressures and new social demands from peers and parents, mastery can provide respite. The safe microworlds the child master has built—the microworlds of sports, chess, cars, literature, or mathematical expertise—can become places of escape. Most children use these havens as platforms from which to test the difficult waters of adolescence. They move out at their own pace. But for some the issues that arise during adolescence are so threatening that the safe place is never abandoned. Sexuality is too threatening to be embraced. Intimacy with other people is unpredictable to the point of being intolerable. As we grow up, we forge our identities by building on the last place in psychological development where we felt safe. As a result, many people come to define themselves in terms of competence, in terms of what they can control.

Pride in one's ability to master a medium is a positive thing. But if the sense of self becomes defined in terms of those things over which one can exert perfect control, the world of safe things becomes severely limited— because those things tend to be things, not people. Mastery can cease to be a growing force in individual development and take on another face. It becomes a way of masking fears about the self and the complexities of the world beyond. People can become trapped.

The computer supports growth and personal development. It also supports entrapment. Computers are not the only thing that can serve this role; people got "stuck" long before computers ever came on the scene. But computers do have some special qualities that make them particularly liable to become traps.

The adolescents who got stuck on ham-radio or fixing cars or playing chess could only with great difficulty take these worlds with them into adult careers. There was room for just so many radio repairmen or auto mechanics or chess masters. Parents, teachers, the educational system didn't support these hobbies—there was pressure to move beyond them, to "grow up." Not so for computer worlds: the gifted high-school programmer can go on to a college major in computer science and on again to lucrative adult work. Other factors in the computer's seduction, and these are the more important ones, have to do with the specificity of the computer as a medium to support the desire, the needs and in extreme cases the obsession for "perfect mastery."

With the computer you can set your own goals. Joe is twenty- three; he dropped out of computer science at Stanford in order to devote himself more fully to computers. The course work was not challenging enough; Joe needed to set his own goals in order to be able to continually surpass them. Now he is part of the support staff for one of MIT's large computer systems. His "official" job is rather undefined. He defines it as continually improving the system by adding features to it (improvements on its editor and mail and message programs) that test the limits of his knowledge. Joe describes himself as "stuck on winning" before he met computers. As a freshman at Stanford, he was stuck on the violin.

> I tried to do the same thing with the violin that I am doing now with the computers. But it really couldn't be the same thing, with a musical instrument, you are continually confronting the physical thing. The violin can only do so much, and your fingers can only do so much. You can work for years and not feel that you are making a real breakthrough. And you are constantly under the pressure of knowing your own limitations. I mean I knew I was not great. I was obsessed—but I was not great. With programming, whatever you think of—and you are always thinking of something—it can be immediately translated into a challenge. That same night. You can set yourself up to do it in some really esoteric, unusual way. And you can make a deal with yourself that you won't be satisfied, that you won't eat or go out or do anything until you get it right. And then you can just do it. It's like a fix. I couldn't get that kind of fix with the violin. 1 could be obsessed, but I couldn't get the high.

With the computer as your medium there is no limit to how much you can flirt with losing in your pursuit of winning. There is no limit to the violence of the test.

In *The Right Stuff* Tom Wolfe tells the story of the Air Force test pilots who were chosen to be the first generation of astronauts.[9] As gripping as the story of Project Mercury is what the narrative reveals of the psychology of the test pilot. It is a psychology that demands that one constantly test the limits of the physically possible, push "the outer edge of the envelope": flying aircraft higher than they were designed to be flown, pushing them beyond their maximum intended speeds, pulling out of a dive with more acceleration than they were designed to tolerate. Always pushing, playing with the limits until the system failed, the limits of the technology were reached, and only having "the right stuff" could save a man's life. This is the stuff that lets you function as a superhuman when you have pushed yourself beyond the edge of the humanly and technically possible. Belief in "the right stuff" allowed a man to feel in control in situations that were set up in advance as situations where control would be lost.

The test pilots didn't put their psychologies away when they left the airfield, when they left their jobs. None of us does. Pushing the "outer edge of the envelope" was translated into rituals of "drinking and driving." They would drink until they were almost out of control and then race cars at speeds almost out of control. And when they survived, they would have further proof that they were the magical few who had the right stuff—which is what they needed to have the courage to go on.

People are not "addicted" to test piloting or race-car driving or computer programming. They are addicted to playing with the issue of control. And playing with it means constantly walking that narrow line between having it and losing it. Computer programming offers this kind of play, and it is a part of the hacker culture. MIT hackers call this "sport death"—pushing mind and body beyond their limits, punishing the body until it call barely support mind and then demanding more of the mind than you believe it could possibly deliver. Anthony, twenty years old, an MIT senior, is a computer hacker who is very aware of the pleasure and the perversion of sport death.

> Computer hacking is kind of masochistic. You see how far you can push your mind and body ...women tend to be less selfdestructive... hackers are somewhat self-destructive. They don't take care of their bodies and are in general flunking out. Burnout is common. Women are not so sport death; they are more balanced in their priorities. The essence of sport death is to see how far you can push things, to see how much you can get away with. I generally wait until I have to put in my maximum effort and then just totally burnout.

There are few women hackers. This is a male world. Though hackers would deny that theirs is a macho culture, the preoccupation with winning and of subjecting oneself to increasingly violent tests makes their world

---

[9]Tom Wolfe, *The Right Stuff* (New York: Bantam, 1980).

peculiarly male in spirit, particularly unfriendly to women. There is, too, a flight from relationship with people to relationship with the machine—a defensive maneuver more common to men than to women. The computer that is the partner in this relationship offers a particularly seductive refuge to someone who is having trouble dealing with people. It is active, reactive, it talks back. Many hackers first sought out such a refuge during early adolescence, when other people, their feelings, their demands, seemed particularly frightening. They found a refuge in the computer and never moved beyond. Alex is one of these.

Alex spends fifteen hours a day on the computer. "At least fifteen, maybe three for eating, usually a big pancake breakfast with the other guys after a night of hacking. Or sometimes we'll do a dinner in Chinatown at about one in the morning. Six for sleeping. I sleep from about nine in the morning to three, when I go over to the computer center."

> If you look at it from the outside, it looks like I spend most of my time alone. But that is not really true. First of all. there are the other hackers. We eat together a lot, we talk about the system. And then I spend a lot of time, I mean *a lot of time*, on electronic mail. Sometimes I think that electronic mail is more of an addiction for me than the computer is. I talk to people all over the country. When you type mail into the computer you feel you can say anything. A lot of it is just about the system, but sometimes it gets pretty personal. When you type into the machine you can go really fast. The touch is very sensitive. I don't even feel that I am typing. It feels much more like one of those Vulcan mind melds, you know, that Mr. Spock does on *Star Trek*. I am thinking it, and then there it is on the screen. I would say that I have a perfect interface with the machine...perfect for me. I feel totally telepathic with the computer. And it sort of generalizes so that I feel telepathic with the people I am sending mail to. I am glad I don't have to see them face to face. I wouldn't be as personal about myself. And the telepathy with the computer-well, I certainly don't think of it as a person there, but that doesn't mean that I don't feel it as a person there. Particularly since I have personalized my interface with the system to suit myself. So it's like being with another person but not a strange person. Someone who knows just how I like things done.

The image of computer telepathy comes up often and not just among hackers. It is an important aspect of the holding power of the machine. And it is another reason why people who know computers come to fear them, why, as one architecture student put it, "I swore to myself that this semester I wouldn't touch the machine. It's like making a novena. Promising to give up something for God. But in this case I have promised myself to give it up for myself." He describes himself as "very involved with my work," but "I like to think of my work as 'out there.' And I am 'in here.' The thing with the computer is that you start to lose track of the ins and the outs."

The experience of losing track is captured by Alex's description of the computer as transparent to his thoughts. So much so that he is aware only of a flow of ideas from him to the machine. Programming can be a Zen-like experience. We have seen this quality as the power of the transitional object—the object that is felt as belonging simultaneously to the self and to the outside world. Such objects can evoke an "oceanic feeling" of fusion and oneness. And for Alex, the computer is this kind of object.

> Some people don't program straight from their mind. They still have to consciously think about all the intermediate steps between a thought and its expression on a computer in a computer language. I have basically assimilated the process to the point that the computer is like an extension of my mind. Maybe of my body. I see it but I don't consciously think about using it. I think about the design, not implementation. Once I know in my mind exactly what I want to do, I can express it on a computer without much further conscious effort.

> I usually don't even hear in my mind the words that I am typing. I think and type ideas expressed in LISP. My hands know which way to go. I think of an idea that I want to express and then I listen to how my hands are saying it. My hands are a really important source of feedback.

Alex's comments evoke the power of the transitional object. His remarks about when he eats and sleeps, about electronic mail, pancakes, and Chinese food touch on something else that makes getting stuck on computers much easier than getting stuck on mathematics or physics, the two things that hackers are most likely to suggest they would have done if they hadn't met the computer. This is the power of belonging to a group, in this case a cohesive and self-protecting computer culture. Most of these young men grew up as loners. Many of them describe a sense, as long as they call remember, of a difference between themselves and other people. Finally, they feel that they belong. Alex is very clear about this: "I always knew I was weird. I mean I didn't know why I was weird, but you could see from how other kids treated me that I must have had a big sign on me saying: "Weird One—Fold, Bend, Spindle, and Mutilate this One."

LONELINESS AND SAFETY

Hackers don't live only with computers; they live in a culture that grows up around computers. The mathematics world that hackers might have joined would have left them alone much of the time. Of course, mathematicians get together, talk about their work, hold departmental colloquia and professional meetings, but the culture of mathematics is a culture of relative isolation. The hacker culture is a culture of loners who are never alone.

It is a culture of people who leave each other a great deal of psychological space. It is a culture of people who have grown up thinking of themselves as different, apart, and who have a commitment to what one hacker described as "an ethic of total toleration for anything that in the real world would be considered strange. Dress, personal appearance, personal hygiene, when you sleep and when you wake, what you eat, where you live, whom you frequent—there are no rules. But there is company."

The people who want to impose rules, the inhabitants of the "real world," are devalued, as is the "straight" computer-science community. They are in a means—end relationship with the computer. They want it to "run" their data, facilitate their experiments. The "straights" control the resources and pay the salaries, but they do not share a true allegiance to the machine. In academic departments, research laboratories, and industries where communities of scientists, engineers, and policy analysts become dependent on complex computer systems and thus on the hackers who maintain them, there is skirmish after skirmish. The hackers are always trying to "improve" the system. This can make the system less reliable as a tool for getting things done, because it is always changing. The hackers also make the system more complex, more "elegant" according to their aesthetic, which often makes it more difficult for other people to use. But the hackers have to keep changing and improving the system. They have built a cult of prowess that defines itself in terms of winning over ever more complex systems.

In most of these settings there is a standoff based on mutual dependency and a measure of mutual distrust. The researchers and administrators can push things only so far, because if the hackers don't get what they want, they will leave. The hacker wants to work on the best systems, but even if he has access to the most state-of-the-art computer he will remain in a work environment only if he feels it is a safe place, that is, an environment where he can work with relative autonomy.

David is a hacker at Stanford. He has moved around a lot looking for safety.

> I only really feel good around the computers at night. It used to be that the night culture got going because that was the time when the turnaround time on the system was fastest. Now the systems are so powerful that you hardly ever get that feeling of slowdown. If anything, you sometimes get it at night when all the hackers are on. But the night culture remains. Because that is when you are on the machine with your friends, with other people like you. Then it is a secure place where nobody can tell you what to do. And if somebody tries to, you can out-hack them—screw up their programs so that they are kept real busy trying to sort out what hit them. Then they come running to you asking for help and are not exactly in a position to boss you around.

> At night there is security. I feel safe from people who think they are smarter than me and from those who want to tell me what to do.

By the standards of the outside world, the hacker culture is tolerant. But it has its own codes and rituals; it provides a framework for living. For Nick, an MIT senior, it is home.

> Hacking is a safe lifestyle, but it's a lifestyle that once you're in it, it's hard to get out of it again. Your whole life is amazingly clear. You hack, you talk to other people who hack, etc. There's a society associated with it, there's a culture associated with it, and there's a lifestyle associated with it. It's a whole world. It's always a retreat. There's always things to do, you're never alone.

> Deli-Haus, IHOP [a twenty-four-hour-service International House of Pancakes], eating Chinese food at one of the "officially certified" Chinese restaurants—all of these are good, all-American things to do if you're a computer person. The lifestyle grew up from the things hackers did. They stayed up all night, so they always seemed to see the same people, ate at the same open-all-night-type places, they engaged in the same leisure activities, and they grew together, since they always lived together. New comers fall into it as if it were natural.

BEING SPECIAL

Hackers do fall into the life as though it were natural. Its routines reassure. But it is set up to leave maximum room for people who have defined themselves for a long time, for as long as most of them can remember, as different. Alex makes this point very clear. "Since I was different, different enough so that I wasn't exactly going to fit in with "the guys," I guess I decided that I was really going to be different. Really different. I have always wanted to be very special. And when I hack, it is very important to me to have my own territory. I think true hackers all feel this way."

A large computer system is a complicated thing. It leaves plenty of room for territoriality, plenty of room for people who feel that carving out their own terrain and winning at what they are good at might be their only chance of being loved ("I certainly am not going to be loved for being the same as everybody else," Richard says as he points to his hair, a wild Afro that reaches down past his shoulders). And so the hacker culture is held together by mutual tolerance and respect for radical individualism. You can't be a real winner if you are the same as everybody else. Even on the computer system, only difference can make you indispensable. Indispensable means that "they" cannot get rid of you. And indispensable is at least a stand-in for love, as Nick explained:

I feel a very strong need to be different. I have spent all my life set apart and have been taught that this is the right way to live. My dream, what I want to do, is to be a person that does something, discovers something, creates something, so that people will look at me and say, "Wow, this guy is really something special, let's love this guy." That is all I ever wanted. To be loved by everybody in the whole world.

Hacking. . . it's another world. It was a place where I could make a name for myself because it was stuff that I was good at, something I could do, something that makes me different—sets me apart. There are programs on the system right now that can't be fixed without my help, and that makes me happy. I don't know why I need this so bad.

His friend Anthony hacks on the same system, and shares his values. Nick talks about being unique in terms of being loved. For Anthony, being unique is the only way to give life meaning and purpose.

One thing that bugs me the most whenever I fly home: I look down and see all those houses and all those people who have never done anything that could not have been done by anyone else. That's a terrible thing. I would never want to be like that. It is important not to be common because if you are your existence is meaningless because it makes no difference if you exist or not. So you must do something out of the ordinary like computer hacking to leave something behind you maybe even more than having kids will.

Computer hackers try to distinguish themselves both from the rest of the world and among themselves. A hacker comes in and he makes sure his personality is different from every other hacker's personality as much as possible even if it means becoming something he's not. Computer hackers have a great fear of drowning in the sea of humanity—all those blank faces. So they set themselves apart.

SEX AND ROMANCE: GETTING BURNED

The hacker culture appears to be made up of people who need to avoid complicated social situations, who for one reason or another got frightened off or hurt too badly by the risks and complexities of relationships. This impression comes in part from talking to hackers about their experiences growing up—of being misunderstood and even terrorized by other children, particularly in early adolescence. And it is something that hackers tell you if you ask, "What do you get out of hacking?" They talk about the high of working on complex machines, of being the best, of winning, of the companionship of the culture. And then there is an almost inevitable turn to a theme best summed up by the word "safety." First, there is safety from painful isolation. Most people escape isolation through relationships with other people. But if having control is always a necessity, this can seem too risky. Hacking is a way out of isolation without what many hackers refer to as "complicated" relationships with other people. "Complicated" can mean several things. It can be synonymous with "unpredictable," it can be synonymous with "risky." Hackers talk a lot about getting burned. And if you need to feel in total control, "getting burned" is one of the worst things that can possibly happen to you.

Anthony has "tried out" having girlfriends:

> Hacking is easy and safe and secure. I used to get into relationships that usually led to me getting burned in some way. It is easy to go out with people who are only interested in hacking because it is a safe and secure environment. It is safe from rejection if rejection is the act that is going to cause anguish. It is safe from getting involved.

> With a computer you can take nice little steps and you don't have to worry, because there is always someplace to come back to. With anything else you are less sure and you won't know if you like it before you try it. With a computer you know what is going on and you know everything is going to work out. So with computers you have confidence in yourself, and that is enough. With social interactions you have to have confidence that the rest of the world will be nice to you. You can't control how the rest of the world is going to react to you. But with computers you are in complete control, the rest of the world cannot affect you.

There is no such thing as the "average" way twenty-year-olds talk about romance. Most are struggling with establishing intimate relationships, efforts that bring painful rejections as well as pleasures. Certain themes do recur: self-doubt, realization that their knowledge of themselves and empathy with others need further development, worries about how much they are able to let go and get close to another person.

Most people talk about relationships by comparing them to other relationships, real or fantasized. Anthony compares relationships to the sense of accomplishment and control that you can get from a machine. This does not mean that he sees machines as a "substitute" for women. A better way to hear Anthony is by keeping in mind that his quest is for what can be controlled and mastered. He judges everything he meets according to this standard. He knows he is not getting a "substitute." But he is not sure that he can function in the worlds where you can get burned.

Sex and romance are desirable, but they are risky. "Sport death" is risky, too, but it is a special kind of risk where you assume all the risk yourself and are the only one responsible for saving the day. It is "safe risk." Anthony sees sex and romance as another, more disturbing kind.

> I haven't figured this sex thing out, but I don't think the important issue is control. It's bizarre. I don't understand it. A lot of the drives that cause hacking and sex are the same. They are both risk-taking

activities and they both lend a sense of accomplishment. But hacking is safe in that you are in complete control of your computer world, and sex and relationships are risky in that the rest of the world has control.

Hacking and sex do not fill the same needs. I think every hacker feels he is missing out on life. They say, "Oh, God, if only I could get a girlfriend I wouldn't be so miserable all the time." It's really a matter of time. If you want to do something to make yourself feel good and you want to share that with some people, hacking is a lot more of a sure bet than if you ask some one out on a date. There's a chance the other person doesn't have the same thing as you in mind, whereas the machine always has the same thing in mind. Sometimes I think I spend too much time with computers, because they might be pushing out other parts of my life like relationships. But I'm not sure yet....A romance is a very controlling thing. It pushes computer hacking and a lot of other things I like to do out. I think computer hackers tend to get very strongly involved in relationships. This is because they are used to having this very close, clear, intimate relationship with the computer and they expect to have the same kind of relationship with a girl. They expect to understand the other person more than it is possible; they expect more control over the other person than is reasonable. People just don't work like computers.

Computer hacking tends to be incompatible with romance. It's just that when you do something a lot you don't have much time for other things and you also get into this computer mind-set that is hard to break out of. Romance is not a safe kind of thing. Computer hacking is almost pure pleasure with very little risk. But it is not as fulfilling, because in the end you have just made a few lights blink. You only have so much energy. You can either spend it on computers or you can spend it on people.

It is poignant that Anthony begins by admitting that as far as sexual relationships go, control probably isn't the most important thing, but then he goes on to talk about sexual relationships almost entirely in terms of control. Anthony prefers the mysteries of complex systems because he can get to work decoding them. People, especially women, are a different matter.

Along with the fear of getting burned there is another, perhaps more fundamental issue at the heart of the hacker's relationship with sexuality: the insistent antisensuality of the hacker culture.

ANTISENSUALITY

Hackers are not alone in denying the sensual. But it is fair to say that the hacker culture crystallizes something problematic in engineers' relationships with what Burt called "the flesh things."

The sensual goes beyond the overtly sexual. There is sensuality in music, literature, art, and there are sensual relationships with the world of things: the musician caresses his or her instrument; its shape, its tonality its touch, can be pleasing and exciting. But the prototypical hacker's taste in each of these realms tends not toward a sensual caress but toward all intellectual contact.

There is a strong music culture within the hacker community. Yet it is one where preference rarely moves out of the Baroque. The hacker's computational aesthetic with its emphasis on intricacy of structure carries over to musical taste. Musical hackers are intrigued by the contrapuntal complexity many see as "mathematical," by the purity of compositional forms that depend less obviously on tonal color and drama for their effect. Peter, a systems programmer at Carnegie Mellon University, says, "Beethoven is too emotional. He really didn't get into what you could create with the mathematics of the scale." Peter is passionate about music, but in his own way. He spends a lot of time playing an out-of-tune piano, practicing a technically excellent Bach.

Bill is a systems hacker in California who has invited me to see the harpsichord he is building. He shows me the half-finished product, and I ask to stay and watch him work on it. I am interested in how he goes about it and how he feels as he puts things together. I sit with him for many hours. He does not work in silence. Bach fugues are playing in the background. The record is scratchy, to me painfully so. The record player is a stereo, but Bill casually mentions that "every once in a while the left speaker sort of conks out" and the stereo is "transformed into a hi-fi—you know, circa 1956." To me, there is no high in the poor and painful fidelity of the sound. But Bill is not listening to the sound, he is listening to the "sense." He has analyzed these fugues before, has read Douglas Hofstadter's *Godel, Escher, Bach*, and is listening for "recursive phenomena." The sound quality is irrelevant. This is an exercise in composition, structure, technique.

As I watch Bill work, my mind goes back to the only other person I knew who built a harpsichord. I met him many years before, a fellow graduate student who explained that he wanted to "get a feel for the texture of the medium" in which Bach worked. He was a friend. I wasn't interviewing him. I was simply drinking tea and reading as he worked on his harpsichord, but I remembered the expression "texture of the medium." Bill is making his harpsichord in a state of equal reverence for Bach, but his comments don't have to do with texture, they are about the intricacies of a system. "Bach wrote programs, you know—his structures are every bit as complicated as a really complex program. And this was his machine." Bach is a hacker colleague, and, to put it most flatly, Bill is checking out Bach's computer.

Bill's sensibility is not unusual in the computer world, where the preference for the formal extends from music to art. Escher was a favorite among computer people before *Godel, Escher, Bach* captured a longstanding computer-culture aesthetic by making the point well known to programmers, that Escher's prints of hands drawing each other or of stairs that continue to rise until they reach their starting point are recursive. These are "strange loops" whose power originates from the fact that they refer to themselves. When Bill makes a visit to Cambridge I interview him in my office. On the wall are several Japanese prints, line drawings with blushes of color, mere suggestions of place and feeling, and reproductions of two Monet paintings. Bill visits several times, and on the third visit he brings me an Escher print. "I thought you might like this," he tells me. "It gives you things to think about." I thank him for the gift wondering to myself if he is giving me an "object-to-think-with" for my study of the hacker culture. This is not the case. Bill's gift is not that selfconscious. "I don't like your art," he tells me. "It doesn't have ideas.''

Curt is a stranger to MIT who spends a term visiting the computer-science laboratory. He is a linguist who is interested in music. At first, he is excited by all the "music talk" in the laboratory, excited by the intensity of the interest, pleased that music is a bridge between himself and "technical" people he always thought of as so different. After a few months we speak again. Curt is frustrated and disappointed. The divide has not disappeared; it seems deeper than ever because it is no longer sustained by stereotypes about "humanists" and "engineers." Now it is connected to something concrete and important to him: his music.

> Of course I am held by the "form" of music. It's fundamental. But I also have the sense sometimes of becoming the music. Sometimes a note or a phrase will make a color or a feeling happen, some kind of knowledge that makes me feel close to the composer. Sometimes I hear instruments in different parts of my body, like feeling cellos in my chest. But I don't think that this kind of thing is what people around here are responding to. It's not that they don't talk about the "content" of music. It's that, in some very fundamental sense, I think they're not connecting to what I experience in the content and that makes me feel pretty strange. I mean, their interest is so formal, but not in a musical sense. They want to "hack" counterpoint. They want to know the algorithm. But I don't think they want to know the music

On another occasion, Curt talks more about his life inside the computer culture.

> The other night I invited some people over, some people from the lab and some of my other friends: a philosophy graduate student, a psychologist. The next day I was talking to them, and one of then said that he thought the lab people were amazingly smart, but had I ever noticed how few words they use? It's true. Everything is precise and nothing is left unspecified, but not much vocabulary. I was talking about this with another friend, and she said that Virginia Woolf had said that the only worth while conversations were those where no sentence was ever finished and everyone knew what was

meant. That has to do with empathy, with a shared sense of understanding. And to me, it's a lack around here.

Curt's comments about language, precision and intuition bring us to another aesthetic domain: literature. Engineers are devoted readers of science fiction. Why shouldn't they be? They feel participant. They are the ones who will design the spacecraft. In this computer culture, science fiction has a special place.

A science-fiction story is a microworld, isolated from all the assumptions of everyday reality, including assumptions about sexuality. In Barbarella's world, people make love by taking "transcendence pills." In Woody Allen's vision of the robotized future, people take sex breaks by jumping in and out of little ecstasy boxes. I distribute a questionnaire to a programming course for computer-science majors. One of the questions is: "What are some of your favorite books and can you say why?" A student answers: "Winning science fiction. In science fiction you can start from scratch. It's like writing a program. Even in Logo programming, children can create worlds that operate by Aristotelian principles instead of Newtonian ones. No physical constraints. Make a whole new world with its own rules." As in the case of writing a program, the only imperative in science fiction is consistency. Once you write a microworld, in computer code or between the covers of a book, you have to obey its constraints. Hackers are drawn to making microworlds. They provide safety, elegance, controlled fantasy. Science fiction operates by their code. Another student answering the same question writes, "I like science fiction. I like watching the author making up rules and sticking to them. Even when it gets really hard to stay with them. It's a very disciplined form of writing."

Science fiction gets its complexity from the invention of worlds rather than the definition of character. While most traditional fiction takes everyday reality as its backdrop and develops its interest in the complexity of its human characters, science fiction characters tend to be more one-dimensional. They often are representative types with a stock "psychology. " Mr. Spock will always be logical; Captain Kirk will always be smug and philosophical, the engineer Scotty will always be plodding and loyal. All of this is reassuring if you have a strong taste for consistency.

The Arpanet is a communication system that links all of the major computer centers in the United States. When the net was designed, the idea was that instantaneous mail and message-passing facilities would foster collaborative work among scholars at different centers. In fact things worked out differently. The Arpanet is mostly used for sending mail and messages. The messages can be sent "person to person" or they can be sent to many members of a community of people who declare themselves to have an interest in common. This community constitutes a "mailing list," a forum for ongoing conversations.

One of the largest of such mailing lists is the "science-fiction-lovers" list to which most hackers belong. Some of the conversations on it are technical.

For example, there were long correspondences discussing engineering inconsistencies in the design of the set for the starship Enterprise in the first Star Trek movie. These discussed the incompatibility of the Enterprise's docking system with the ship's overall structure and the foolishness of using round screens for the crew's video monitors. (It may have looked futuristic, but it was far from optimal: too much information would be lost.) But many of the interchanges are not about technical matters but about metaphysical ones. For example, what are the implications in Star Trek of "beaming down" crew members to the planets they wish to visit? The molecules that "reconstitute" them on the planet's surface are not the same ones that made them up originally. What new definitions of personhood would be required in a world where technology could make a copy of a person? If I can create a second me, which one of them is "I"? Are we both Sherry Turkle? And what if the second Sherry sets off on her own and has her own set of experiences, her own travels, her own friendships. Is "she" still "me"? Do I have proprietary rights over her by virtue of being her "nonartificial" originator?

Through these descriptions emerge the large outlines of the hacker culture: a culture of mastery, individualism, nonsensuality. It values complexity and risk in relationships with things, and seeks simplicity and safety in relationships with people. It delights in ambiguities in the technological domain—where most nonscientists expect to find things totally straightforward. On the other side, hackers try to avoid ambiguity in dealing with people, where the larger culture finds meaning in the half-defined and the merely suggested.

Something important is missing in this description: what it feels like to hack. If you are not an expert programmer, there is no way to share it directly. For me, two discoveries led to a better understanding of the hacker's experience.

THE GAME OF ADVENTURE

During my interview with Ron I expressed frustration at not knowing the "feel" of hacking. He came back with a plan of action, the same that was suggested to Tracy Kidder in the basement of Data General when he waited to experience what draws someone into becoming a "Midnight Programmer". Ron typed some commands at my terminal and set me to playing the game of Adventure.

In Adventure the computer creates a complex underground world. You are in a clearing in the forest, standing before a house. It is up to you to find the grate which, if you open it correctly, will put you into Colossal Cave. The computer will move you through this world in response to the commands you type on the keyboard. Each time you move, a new message appears on the screen telling you where you are (a room, a dark tunnel, a maze, a passageway) and what objects and beings are there with you. At each point you must convey a two-word instruction saying what you want to do next. You can choose direction and you can pick up things, drop things, open things, close things. in principle, you are trying to get the treasure, but even after months of playing, drawing maps, struggling with strategies, few players arrive. Most have been permanently stalled by dragons, trolls, snakes, hatchet-hurling dwarfs. Each of these adversaries can be conquered, but only through complicated strategies. The program will let you carry only so many things at a time, so if you face a rusty door you will probably decide to drop the water you are carrying, which might be useful later, but now will only make rust rustier, and go back to retrieve the oil can that you passed on the trail fourteen moves ago. On your way back to the oil, a path you can find only if you have been making a map as you proceed, you may be outwitted if you forget to bring something to carry it in. Finally, perhaps several hours later, if you are not skillful, you will have retraced your steps back to the rusty door.

Adventure is a window onto a way of experiencing the computer. The experience it gave me was of a far different order from that I had gotten from a beginning course in computer programming. There I learned to write simple instructions and got to watch the computer following them. Like most people, I came out of this with a vision of the machine and of programming as simple, controllable, linear. "The machine is dumb, just a giant calculator," the professor had said. "Programming is a straightforward act of mechanical regurgitation. Garbage in garbage out."

Adventure has nothing in common with writing a simple program in an introductory course. But this just means that the course fails to give its students a sense of what programming is to its virtuosi. When systems get complex they become worlds that you can live in.

Imagine yourself at the computer. You are a systems programmer. A truly peculiar piece of behavior—a bug—has been reported by a fellow hacker. You have printed out the program on a stack of folded paper. It has twenty thousand lines of code. Somewhere in all that is the cause of the bug. How will you find it? It is like being lost in Colossal Cave. You come to a "place" in the cave. You don't see what you are looking for, but you see something that might be relevant later if you can remember where it was and find your way back to it. You debug your game by developing the skill of getting through the maze.

Cultures take their central experiences and play with them through fantasy, ritual, and art. When "winning" is at the center of cultural life, a game takes on this role. For the hacker, where what is most central is mastery over complexity, the game takes the form of a labyrinth.

THE HACK

Adventure is a window onto the phenomenology of hacking, but the hacking experience has another component that goes beyond mastery of the labyrinth.

Remember Howard, whose magician's gesture symbolized his fantasy of walking up to any program and bending it to his will with a few deft strokes at the keyboard. I came to understand what he was looking for as a central organizing theme in the hacker culture. It is "The Hack." It is the holy grail. It is a concept that exists independently of the computer and can best be presented through an example using another technology complex enough to support its own version of hacking—and hackers.

In the 1960s, telephone hackers were called "phone freaks." One of the most famous was known as Captain Crunch, who took his name from a breakfast cereal. In every box there was a toy whistle, like the prize in Cracker Jacks. The whistle produced a 2600-cycle tone. A young man just entering the Air Force as a radio technician, Crunch was fascinated with electronics, circuitry, and wiring. He was a hacker without a computer. He discovered that the Crunch whistle was a lock pick to one of the most complex closed systems ever designed. First you dial a long-distance telephone number. Then you blow the Crunch whistle. This disconnected the dialed conversation but kept the trunk open without further toll charge. From that point on any number of calls could be dialed free.

Crunch experimented with the whistle for several years. His feats became more and more extraordinary, more and more legendary. His most mythologized "hack" became known as "the call around the world." Crunch sat in a room in California with two telephones. Using the whistle and his knowledge of international telephone circuitry and codes, he picked up the first phone and dialed the number of the second phone. The call started in California, went through Tokyo, India, Greece, Pretoria, London, New York, and back to California. The second telephone rang. He talked into phone number one and heard himself twenty seconds later on phone number two. Even this became boring and needed more embroidery. Winning means making the system and the challenge ever more complex. Finally there were four phones, and he called himself simultaneously around the world in two directions.

The hack became a myth and its replication a challenge. During my junior year in college I attended an open house at one of the undergraduate dorms at MIT, and several of the students boasted that they had set up something extraordinary on the third floor. They called it "Phineas Fogg." A small troop of technologically naive Radcliffe students climbed up to the third floor and watched the by-now "classic" around-the-world demonstration by this time done not with whistles but with "blue boxes" of circuitry. The demonstrators explained that the hack was not new, but that the size and reliability of the box was. Their achievement had been to miniaturize the hack. The telephone switching system was as complicated as any computer. It had taken them months to master it. The diagrams that covered their walls were not unlike the maps for the game of Adventure that would be covering those same walls ten years later. Intricate tunnels, unexpected connections. A world unto itself. They had been on a collective adventure: the exploration of a labyrinth. They had won out over complex mysteries.

Appreciating what made the call around the world a great hack is an exercise in hacker aesthetics. It has the quality of Howard's magician's gesture: a truly surprising result produced with a ridiculously simple means. Equally important: Crunch had not simply stumbled on a curiosity. The trick worked because Crunch had acquired an impressive amount of expertise about the telephone system. This is what made the trick a great hack, otherwise it would have been a very minor one. Mastery is of the essence everywhere within hacker culture. Third, the expertise was acquired unofficially and at the expense of a big system. The hacker is a person outside the system who is never excluded by its rules.

Great hacks, telephonic or computational are mythologized much as Crunch was. The early hackers at MIT made an attempt to publish some of their most powerful techniques in a document called *Hackmem*. In a different culture this might have been the beginning of a journal but it is not in the nature of the hacker culture to do anything so official or academic. Great hacks are passed along in more direct ways: as things you are shown, as something done to you. What did happen to the document was that it itself became part of myth. We catch a glimpse of it in a piece of hacker literature.

"Software Wars," by Stanford hacker Mark Crispin was "published" on the science-fiction mailing list. Crispin takes the *Star Wars* plot, a battle between good and evil and transforms it into a battle between good and evil computer cultures. The good is the hacker culture; the evil is the culture of the "straights," the administrators and "computer-as-tool" programmers who do not respect the magic of the machine. In "Software Wars" the two cultures are symbolized by their taste in programming languages. In principle you can "say," the same things in different programming languages just as you can say the same things in French and in German, but the structure of the programming languages, like that of the natural languages, encourages different ways of thinking. To the eyes of the hacker, business languages, for example the IBM languages FORTRAN and COBOL and the "scientific" language PASCAL have come to represent the uniformity of mass culture that buries the individual in the crowd. In "Software Wars" these appear as the languages appropriate to the totalitarian rule of "the Empire." LISP is a language of pleasure, of individuality that facilitates a way of thinking where, as Douglas Hofstadter once remarked to me, "It is easy to live in the world of *Godel, Escher, Bach*. These MIT hackers lived inside of my book before I ever wrote it." For the hacker, the beauty of LISP is that it is fully recursive and self-referential, higher levels are built up from their own elements, like Escher's endlessly rising staircases and Bach's "endlessly rising fugue" that keeps going to a higher key until seemingly inexplicably, it ends up exactly where it began.

The moral struggle in "Software Wars" centers around evildoers known as PASCALS, and the forces of good, the hackers, energized by the software equivalent of "The Force." This is The Hack, a magical flow of power and computer wizardry that turns the computer from a tool into an artistic medium.

As in *Star Wars*, "Software Wars" begins with the memory of a golden age. In this case it was a time when hackers weren't regimented by computer bureaucrats and engineers.

> Long ago and far away, the data processing galaxy was ruled by the sinister forces of the PASCAL Empire. Years ago, it had been the Hacking Republic, where all programming languages and programmers lived together in peace and harmony. The land of the Republic was patrolled by the Wizards, skilled in all forms of magic, who daily unveiled new miracles for the wonder of the citizens of the Republic. They drew their mystical powers from THE HACK, which was their succor in any difficulty.

The villain who put all end to all this was Daemon Feature. His name plays on several programming "puns," as does his method of doing evil, the entrapment of wizards on "fencepost errors," a common programming bug.

> But the day's of the Republic were numbered, for one of the wizards, Daemon Feature, fell in with the PASCALS, who brought in crooks and bletcherousness to the beleaguered Republic. Using methods both sinister and cunning, he managed to entrap most of the loyal wizards in a fencepost error, where they were ruthlessly slaughtered. At last the Republic was proclaimed to have ended, and the Empire was established with Record Structure, the leader of the PASCALS, proclaimed Emperor. And the lot of programmers was unhappy.

Of course the programmers are unhappy. Their aesthetic has been submerged. When hackers are inspired and in creative telepathy with the machine, it is as if they are inhabited by the medium, inspired by the muse. Their minds must be free to fly, to invent, to surpass the limits. "Records" and "Structure" are spiritual death. It is time for the forces of life to enter: the hacker as rebel enemy of the establishment and conformity, defender of idiosyncrasy, individuality, genius, and the cult of the individual.

Who can be the hero of a software soap opera? It must be someone who is trapped in a false identity. Someone who will, through confrontation with a force greater than himself, The Hack, find his true measure as a man. In "Software Wars," it is Fluke Software Specialist. Fluke has been raised by his aunt and uncle, who "over the years had established a prosperous, if unpretentious business, supplying COBOL utilities for many of the settlements in this galaxy." Fluke does not know his true origins. The hacker-to-be is doing the most "losing" spirit-deadening thing that a hacker—born to be inspired by the interactive, breathing presence of a computer beneath his fingers—could possibly do: he writes COBOL programs on cards, on pieces of paper that he feeds into the machine. Although Fluke's aunt and uncle have raised him as their own, when he receives a message addressed to the mythologized hacker hero, Moby Foobar, they realize that his destiny is elsewhere and that they must let him go. His aunt understands: "You know, we can't keep him forever. He's just not destined for COBOL. There's too much of his father in him." But his uncle fears destiny: "Yes, that's what I'm worried about. For him. I'm afraid he'll get involved in hacking like his father did."

"Software Wars" gets played out as the dramatic projection of loves and hates, supports and threats to the hacker's universe. There is a feared tribe of "users," the professors and graduate students who believe the machine to be theirs (because their research funds pay for it), and who try to keep the hackers under their boot. There is the power of The Hack, and its "darker side." This is the aspect of hacking that has gripped Daemon Feature, who has the power but uses it for evil.

And, of course, "Software Wars" has its reference to *Hackmem.* Fluke finds Moby Foobar, who tells him of better days, speaks to him of his father, and of The Hack.

> Moby... paused. searching his memory, back to a time long ago,"... Your father left me something to give to you." He reached into the piles of paper and old, dusty manuals on the table, and withdrew a single Binder. "This is HAKMEM, an elegant programming tool of a more civilized age. With it, one skilled in The Hack could perform programming miracles, get better response time, and be invited to all the good parties. Here." He handed the HAKMEM to Fluke.

> Fluke took it, and looked at its first page intently; strange it seemed, yet a feeling grew on him, as if he were looking at something far greater than he could comprehend. He was considered a good programmer, one of the best in the quadrant; but the HAKMEM took his breath away. "What is The Hack?" he asked finally.

> "The Hack is that which is nearest and dearest to the hearts of all the Wizards. It is what gives the Wizard his power. The Hack is everywhere and is part of everything. Without The Hack, only crocks remain.

> "The Hack!" gasped Fluke. He then pondered these words in silence. A whole new vision was before him; he saw things of beauty and elegance that he could not yet put into words.

Fluke captures enemy base by using the special magic power of LISP. When the time comes, he is inspired:

> Fluke, remember The Hack. The Hack, Fluke. He could almost hear Moby's voice repeating this to him. But what could he do? He turned around to face his approaching foe, and attacked. LISP has base ROMAN to read and print Roman numerals.

The blow that Fluke has struck is recursive, a feature that uses itself to build itself. The ultimate weapon in this hacker tale is one that uses the same

image of generation through self-generation that got Douglas Hofstadter to
the weaving of his *Godel, Escher, Bach* "Golden Braid."

The rebels had succeeded! And all the users tried the new operating
system and pronounced it a winner. Instantly everything was
converted to run on it. Almost immediately, a flood of new software
appeared...and the universe was again winning.

Mythologized in an elaborate oral and written tradition the ideal of the
hack suffuses the hacker culture. It embodies shared values and passions.
And, of course, it is the centerpiece of hacker rituals.

RITES OF PASSAGE

Rituals of initiation bring novices, defined as being on the "outside" of a
culture, and subject them to experiences designed to alter their identity. The
novices emerge on the other side as different people, full members of the
group. In some societies, rituals of initiation take the form of large collective
festivals. In the hacker culture, the principal relationship is dyadic, between
the individual and the computer. So the rites tend to be more private,
although they are often followed by some collective expression: a Chinese
banquet, a pancake breakfast. Certain experiences of an individual with a
computer are invested by the group with the consequence of a passage.

Initiations into the hack are through mastery games that stand somewhere
between playing Adventure and "phone freaking." For example, you log into
the computer. Instead of finding your files you find yourself in another
world. The challenge is to recover your files by finding your way through the
computer's labyrinth. What you need to triumph is the force of "The Hack."

At MIT, hackers speak of a moment when they would accept someone
new into their fellowship. It would be when an individual had developed
enough mastery of the system to figure out how to triumph over one of
several "hacker harassment" programs. For example, there is the "Cookie
Monster" program. An experienced hacker sends a little beasty into the
program of the novice. The recipient of the cookie invader finds a small
creature starting to chomp away at the text written on his terminal's screen.
He becomes a hacker when he can successfully battle the encroachment of
the Cookie Monster.

The hacker culture has a code. These games are for testing the mettle of
the novice or for playing among master hackers. They are not pranks to be
played on others. This would be aggression, unfair play. When this happens
(and sometimes it does), one or a group of the system masters sets traps for
the aggressor, who is likely to find his or her own files garbled or chomped
or hidden. An MIT hacker told me the tale of how many years ago he began
to "hack" the files of a graduate student he had a crush on. To win her
attention he set it up so that whenever she logged in and asked for a file, the
Weizenbaum ELIZA program would be summoned in its stead.

Let's say she would ask for the file "foobar.3." The program would say to her, "Tell me more about why you feel that way about foobar.3." And if she typed ":help" (the standard way of asking for instructions to get you out of trouble on the system), instead of getting a menu of helping instructions, the machine would just come back with "Why do you feel you need help?" or "You seem to have a lot of strong feelings about help." I thought it was sort of funny. I guess I was pretty immature. But I got paid back, and in kind. I spent two weeks of nights at the lab trying to ungarble my files..

LOCKED DOORS

The mastery games and initiations test the ability to win over complexity and break out of confining situations. And we saw that hackers are drawn not only to winning over computers. Other complex systems have a similar appeal.

Many hackers are expert lock-pickers and carry their "picks" around with them on their key chains. Their pleasure is in "beating" the lock. They break, they enter, and then they leave. They are not after material goods, but after the thrill of triumph. Richard, an MIT hacker, had a summer job working at a large computer company with a conservative, corporate environment. At night, every desk and file drawer was locked. Every office door was locked. This was the kind of computer culture where people work nine to five. Richard, of course, was from another culture, where nothing is private and people work all night. At MIT, he had worked out a detailed time schedule for himself. "I discovered that I work best on a thirty-six-hour cycle. So I get myself into a thirty-six-hour cycle—twenty-four hours awake, twelve hours asleep. This is what maximizes my efficiency." Over the summer, largely to avoid overlap with the members of the day culture. whom he found alien in spirit, Richard went back onto "standard hacker time," sleeping during the day and working at night. And every night, alone in the building, he unlocked every office door. "They changed the locks. I opened them again. They changed the locks again. I never took anything. I'm not a thief. I just don't like a locked door."

A closed system is a challenge. A safe is there to be cracked. A mystery is there to be solved. It is the hacker's variant on the more widely understood cliché that Mount Everest is there to be climbed.

If you can't tolerate a locked door on a computer system, you are going to be an enemy of what is usually called "system security." "Security" comprises all of the features of a computer system that protect the information within the system and the privacy of its authorized users. A first level of protection simply controls access. To gain entrance to most computer systems, you need to be given an account, which means that the system will receive you if you log in with your name. And then you need to be given a password. When I log in as Turkle on the MIT MULTICS system, the computer asks me for my password. When I type it in, no characters appear on my screen. My secret name prevents outsiders from entering the system by using my name. But this is only the first-level protection. Most computer systems control what files within the system I can have access to, and what I can do with them if I am allowed to see them.

Many different issues are tied up in the question of system security. In an academic computer facility, where computer power is being used for research and writing, keeping people out is justified most often by the claim that a little knowledge is a dangerous thing. If I can wander around a computer system I can do a lot of inadvertent damage. Second, there is the issue of privacy. On the ITS system at MIT I can look at, manipulate, and print any file of any user. I can also run a program called "SPY" to look in on what any other user of the system is doing at any moment. SPY was designed by hackers who don't believe in locked doors.

In nonacademic computer systems, security issues go beyond the fear of accidental damage and personal privacy. Files may contain confidential information about people, products, institutions, and events. The locked rooms that Richard broke open contained data that, from most people's point of view, deserved to be protected: corporate secrets and personnel files. But for Richard the fact that a door is locked is justification enough to open it.

Most assaults on computer-system security are not done by members of the culture of hackers I have been discussing. Indeed, the systems programmers I interviewed expressed dismay that their vocation has been tainted with the image of "computer crime." "It gives hacking a bad name." But the break-ins are often done by people who share the hacker's style of relating to the machine as a puzzle and who share their glorification of "the win." Many are done by high-school and college students who talk about the exercise the way they would about a good game of Dungeons and Dragons. They see the labyrinth. And they see the opportunity for something else. After they enter, they leave their mark, a trace that they were there. Usually this is a message to taunt the system's authorities who have tried to keep them out. They make the point that the system is not secure and sometimes add that they would be happy to be hired as consultants to work on the problem. Captain Crunch and several of his associates did end up working for the telephone company. The pattern of hack the system, leave a trace, get a little famous, and be recognized by the big guys has become part of the Hacker myth.

For example, a group of four thirteen-year-old students at the Dalton School, an exclusive preparatory school on the Upper East Side of Manhattan, carried on an elaborate security-breaking hack through which they electronically entered the computer systems of twenty-one organizations in the United States and Canada. At one point, when their "victims" began to install new protection devices, the students became frustrated and decided to see how far they could go. They went quite far. One of their victims claimed they had erased about a fifth of its computer files. "This looks like what we used to do as kids—ring someone's doorbell and run around the block. Only it's a more sophisticated doorbell and a longer block."[10]

The media often portrayed the computer expert who breaks system security, if not as a hero, then at least as a genius. Many people are intimidated by computers. And don't like them much. When they hear about teenage boys who broke into a large computer system, turned it off for an hour, and left a message of triumph, they know that they have probably broken the law, but they are sympathetic.

The Dalton students had broken the law. But for many people, something about the sophistication of the doorbell, the length of the block, and the havoc they caused made the "Dalton Four" seem like heroes. In the two weeks after their story hit the newspapers, I interviewed a diverse group of New Yorkers on how they saw what had happened. A common reaction was to soften all criticism of the students with a heavy dose of admiration. One high school science teacher commented, "They were just out to beat the system. We all are, in a way. It's natural." A businessman did not side with the companies that had lost money because of the hack, but with the students: "myself, I hate those lousy computers. If a bunch of kids can get the better of them, so much the better." And another teacher felt that in some way the students were acting in her behalf: "Somebody's gotta demystify those computers. It looks like it'll be through a children's crusade."

People are deeply ambivalent toward computers. For many, they have replaced Ma Bell or ITT, or even the CIA as the symbol of things too big, too complex, too impersonal. People use computerized bank tellers, find them convenient, but resent them as well. Going to the bank used to involve a relationship with a person who said hello, knew your name and sometimes did you a favor. This is gone. People are also becoming increasingly aware that everytime they use their credit card they are leaving an electronic trace of where they have been of what they were doing. Computers are perceived as the medium for all automated intrusiveness and violation of privacy, and they are perceived as a medium of mystery.

In the hacker, people see someone who holds a key to the mysteries and is willing to defy the establishment to open them: there is the fantasy of an electronic Robin Hood.

BUILDING STRAIGHT FROM YOUR MIND

Anthony, the MIT student who hacks for sport death, also hacks to build. As a child, Anthony took clocks apart and "tried to put them back together in new ways—to make new kinds of clocks." There are limits to how far you

---

[10]Cited in Don B. Parker, *Fighting Computer Crime* (New York: Charles Scribner's Sons, 1983), p. 146. Parker's book contains a section on system hackers. It is important to note that the hackers I describe in this chapter have committed no crimes. This does not mean, however, that understanding their relationship to the machine "as puzzle" does not illuminate the motives of those who do.

can make the materials of a clock into something new, but programming presents no such limits. The rules need not respect the physical laws that constrain the real world. "When you are programming," Anthony tells me, "you just build straight from your mind." Anthony makes an association with parenting.

> Men can't have babies, and so they go have them on the machine. Women don't need the computer, they have them the other way. Why do you think people call ideas brainchildren? They are something you create that is entirely your own. I definitely feel paternal towards the programs I write. I defend them and want them to do good for the world. They are like little pieces of my mind. A chip off the old block. But the computer doesn't act like a kid, so the effect is limited.

The image of paternity is widespread among hackers. Nick hopes to leave behind some monuments.

> If you are a computer scientist, all your monuments, all the things you are proud of, are computer things. You protect your monuments. The computer is your world, your reality. When someone screws around with this they are messing with your universe.

> Hacking computers is not just intellectual, there are emotions. But the delicate emotions like empathy or sadness or loneliness have no place, because there is no application for them. The primitive emotions exist, like anger or fear. You get mad at the undefinable "they" who are sticking it to you.

Nick expresses love, intellectual excitement, and pride of authorship. He also expresses sadness. a sense of loss, the fears of young men that the fork in the road no longer exists for them. Richard goes on a thirty-six-hour day. Anthony pushes himself to the limit of his physical strength. They justify these acts in the service of "maximization" but what is being maximized?

When Weizenbaum's description of the hollow-eyed programmer became a *cause celebre*, many hackers rose to their own defense: they were artists, they were masters, they were not different from other people intensely involved with their work. But there was another reaction as well: self-recognition. Many hackers are worried. They feel in the grip of something powerful. They know they can control the computer, but they are less sure that they control themselves.

Anthony is afraid: "I have devoted so much of myself to the computer that all the humanity has drained out of me. You're just a device. I am afraid that by hacking I am draining myself of something I need to live—humanity or something."

There is fear as well as joy in fusion with the machine. Some people can't break away. "When you hack on a computer you are taking this risk that you won't finish for three days and you will forget about. everything else that you have to do. You are taking a risk... only if you finish your project fast are you out, because you can't stop before your project is finished. You are trapped."

Artists become inhabited by their medium. The poet "makes" a poem, but the poem also "makes," and sometimes haunts, the poet. There is no question that hackers are the artists of their medium. They too are possessed.

> *I control you.*
> *You're inside me.*
> *Might as well obey me*
> *Or I'll make you go away.*

This poem by a hacker is called "Punk Sollipsist." The poem also speaks of "No more talking/No more thinking," and of other things that were left behind: "No more kneeling down to idols/No more feeling suicidal." The computer is there to wall out the pain of being with other people. You control and internalize it. It is you and not-you. Your anger at not being able to control yourself is transferred onto the machine.

In *The Empty Fortress*, Bruno Bettelheim tells the story of "Joey the Mechanical Boy," an autistic child who thought of himself as a machine run by other machines as a defense against the unpredictability of people. Bettelheim comments that Joey was particularly hard to work with, not because the child was more "difficult" than others at the Orthogenic School but because Bettelheim and his colleagues were so uneasy around Joey—an expression of their feelings and fears about machines. In the Middle Ages, Bettelheim says,

> even Lucifer was viewed as a person though a distorted one. What is entirely new in the machine age is that often neither savior nor destroyer is cast in man's image any more. The typical modern delusion is of being run by an influencing machine.... Just as the angels and saints of a deeply religious age help us to fathom what were man's greatest hopes at that time. and the devils which he trembled at most, so man's delusions in a machine world seem to be tokens of both our hopes and our fears of what machines may do for us, or to us.[11]

Bettelheim and his colleagues had a hard time getting close to Joey. "His delusions had an impact which we, accustomed to living with autistic

---

[11]Bruno Bettelheim, *The Empty Fortress: Infantile Autism and the Birth of the Self* (New York: The Free Press, 1967), p. 234. For a classic discussion of the machine and psychotic process, see Victor Tausk, "The Influencing machine," in Robert Fliess, ed., *The Psychoanalytic Reader* (New York: International Universities Press, 1973), pp. 31-64.

children had experienced with no other child. Our fascination was morbid, instead of the vital one so needed to reach him."[12]

Marvin Minsky's response to the popular fascination with hackers was to put the burden on the other side, on the "people hackers" who categorize others with psychological labels. For him, attempts to characterize the hacker are ill-intentioned. But for me these attempts are symptoms of a profound unease. I think that what was true of Bettelheim as he faced Joey is true of most of us as we try to comprehend the hacker in his relationship with the computer.

We are surrounded by machines. We depend on them. We are frightened by how powerful they have become. Our nuclear machines have the power to destroy the world. We are suspicious of the new "psychological machines" and fear the hacker's intimate relationship with his object. Its control over him is disturbing because we too feel controlled. We fear his sense of becoming a "device" because most of us, to one extent or another, have had that feeling. We fear his use of the machine as a safe companion because we, too, can feel its seduction.

Intimate involvements and identification with machines pose what Bettelheim calls "the unspoken anxiety of our age": "Do machines still serve our human purpose or are they cranking away by now without purpose? Even more unnerving: are they working away for their own ends which we no longer know or control?"[13]

---

[12]Bettelheim, *The Empty Fortress*, p. 234.
[13]*Ibid.*, p. 238.

SHOULD COMPUTER DEPENDENCY BE CONSIDERED A SERIOUS PROBLEM?[14]

Margaret A. Shotton
University of Nottingham

This research was undertaken in order to determine whether and why computer dependency occurs, to examine its effects, and to ascertain whether the fears and anxieties shown towards this syndrome have any foundation.

The results from this exploratory study revealed that although computer dependency did occur for a small proportion of computer users, the effects arising from it were not as dire as suggested in the literature. Furthermore there were logical reasons why some people chose to turn to an interaction with inanimate artifacts for the satisfaction of their needs. What was less clear was why the cognoscenti should have voiced their fears so forcefully, and why alarm was expressed for those who used computers intensively when dedication to other activities was often encouraged.

The discussion within the first part of this chapter puts forward the theory that computer dependency was only one of a multitude of computer-related anxieties current at the time this research was initiated, many of which had been well-publicized in the press although not all were necessarily well-substantiated. It is posited therefore that the fear that some people would become socially and psychologically dependent upon computers was merely one of many fears attributed to computer usage and was not atypical of what one might expect. The introduction of this new technology appeared to have created a climate of apprehension about computers in general, and any overt behavior patterns associated with their use were perhaps seen as suspect.

That these worries occurred was not in dispute, but they were found to differ little from the anxieties which surrounded the introduction of many other technologies over the centuries. This is not to suggest that such misgivings should be ignored or dismissed, but they have been shown to occur with a certain regularity when people do not fully understand the ramifications of a new technology. The discussion in the following section suggests that anxieties about technology have been ever-present, and that time and greater understanding and experience tend to allay them somewhat as the artifacts themselves become commonplace.

Much of the remainder of the chapter deals with specific suspected concerns related to computer dependency, including effects upon the working environment, upon children and upon the wider population.

---

[14]From Shotton, M.A. (1989). *Computer Addiction?* London: Taylor & Francis. Chapter 11, Should computer dependency be considered a serious problem? This is an excerpt from the final chapter. Copyright © 1989 by Taylor and Francis. Reprinted by permission. All rights reserved.

An attempt is made to deduce why many authors had believed that extensive computer use could be damaging to the individual concerned and why computer dependency had been singled out for their attention. It is suggested that intensive interest in computers differs little from dedication to many other activities. 'Dependency' upon one particular pastime was not shown to be unusual, and other devotees were found to show very similar characteristics to those observed within the computer dependent population; the difference appeared to lie in the attitudes of others towards what were considered to be acceptable pursuits.

ANXIETIES ASSOCIATED WITH NEW TECHNOLOGY

The introduction of computers into our society occurred with great rapidity with the development and widespread use of the microchip, and was often poorly executed without adequate information being given to those who were expected to use them. This lack of knowledge and understanding appeared to some extent to have been influential in the development of many and diverse anxieties being associated with the use of new technology. Many within the population were extremely sceptical, if not specifically fearful, of computers; therefore any people who showed a serious interest in new technology were viewed as atypical and perhaps somewhat suspect, especially if they were the type who were generally not well-understood by others. It is suggested that the anxieties associated with computer dependency and the effects arising from it may be no more unusual than many others which have been attributed to new technology.

The 'computer revolution', although developing slowly during the last two decades, exploded in Great Britain in 1980 with the introduction of the first mass-produced microcomputer, the *Sinclair ZX80*. Until that time the computer had remained within the domain of industry, science, academia and the serious electronics hobbyist; now it was available to all, at a price less than that of a colour television. The domestic market accelerated at an astounding rate as did the installation of terminals and microcomputers in the workplace, but along with the computer came many fears and suspicion.

The introduction of any new technology may be considered cyclical; from the development of the science and its application, to the mass production and widespread dissemination of the machinery. This appears to be followed quickly by concern about the possible negative results flowing from its use; concern about the environment, society and the individual. However, most older technologies only directly affected a few people at their inception, and most systems were well accepted for their benefits before they became the common property of society. This appears not to be so with computers; their introduction was extremely rapid and seemed to affect the lives of those who have never directly used or even seen them. They were held responsible for faulty wage packets and invoices, endless delays, and even serious accidents. Despite the thought that the computer was 'intelligent' it was also believed to be uncontrollable and to have no conscience or morals, as humans seemed unwilling to take responsibility for any faults in its output.

Computers affect most western people, thousands of whom have to work with them, many of whom remain suspicious. Quite regularly the press bring computer-centered scares to our notice and few can be thoroughly disproved to the satisfaction of society. Each nation (and one may probably link this to the influence of the press) seems to develop its own local computer 'health hazard'. In Australia computer users seem to be particularly susceptible to the crippling physical condition of tenosynovitis (Ferguson, 1987), in the USA cataracts are thought to be caused by the radiation emitted by VDU screens (Zarat, 1984), the Scandinavians suffer from facial rashes (Tjonn, 1984) whilst Europeans seem more concerned with postural effects (Grandjean and Vigliani, 1980).

In Great Britain various documents, especially from within trades unions, echo these fears by suggesting that the use of computers could be responsible for such physical problems as visual discomfort, ocular damage, postural fatigue, tenosynovitis, facial rashes, epilepsy, and even miscarriages and birth defects. (See the *ASTMS Guide to Health Hazards of Visual Display Units,* 1979; the APEX document, *New Technology: A Health and Safety Report,* 1985; the *TUC Guidelines on VDUs,* 1986; and the *NALGO Health and Safety Briefing,* 1986.)

Fears often develop through suspicion and lack of knowledge, and although some of these anxieties may be ill-founded the response from ergonomists confirms the fact that these claims are being taken seriously and are under rigorous investigation. For a review of these issues see Berqvist (1984), Cakir *et al.,* (1980), Grandjean (1984) and Ong *et al.* (1 988).

The new, unknown technology is frequently seen as more threatening than older mechanisms which have been proven to be dangerous but are now familiar. Ergonomists, consulted in order to reduce the 'health hazards' associated with computerization, often encounter dichotomous situations.

> "I have walked through factories full of noise, dust, and noxious fumes, past unsecured ladders and dangerous equipment to reach an office in a corner. Here it is relatively quiet, and has a pleasant thermal environment where workers sit at comfortable desks using keyboards. I have been called into these offices because they are worried about the health hazards of *VDUs.*" Stewart (1984)

This quotation sums up much of the apparent irrationality of the fears expressed towards the new technology. Our lives are normally surrounded by risks and hazards. The high death toll on our roads will not lead to a governmental ban on motor vehicles nor to the majority of people becoming fearful of driving their cars. Although the medical hazards of smoking are well documented, many continue to smoke and new smokers perpetuate the habit. The risks are clear and obvious, we make choices from the available information and take the gamble that we will be safe. The same applies within factories and upon farms and building sites; the hazards are well understood and obvious. Acts of Parliament have made industrial and agricultural work much safer, but still there are deaths. Productivity is the important issue, and further precautions arc not taken because of the financial and political implications which would occur through loss of revenue.

However, unlike the machinery of heavy industry, the risks of working with computers are neither obvious nor well-understood. Manufacturers assure us that the radiation levels are well within the safety limits, but the setting of these limits could be seen to be arbitrary and is of little comfort to the pregnant VDU user who is worried about the health of her child. One cannot see radiation, as one can the traffic on the road or the pool of oil on the factory floor, and the mystery of the computer remains hidden from the majority. To those for whom it does not, they themselves become mysterious and incomprehensible and seem unable to communicate in laymen's terms in order to allay the public's fears.

Any potential psychological effects are less tangible, and therefore more disturbing than the more obvious accusations of physiological damage caused by computerization. Anxieties and stress-related reactions towards working with new technology have already led to the coining of the term 'cyberphobia' by Weinberg (1982); a condition he describes as exhibiting the characteristics of rapid heart beat, nausea, diarrohea, sweating, and so on. Generalized fears seem to concentrate upon the belief that new technology strips people of their freedom and privacy. Thimbleby (1979) saw the potential for irreversible totalitarianism and oppression caused by the concentration of power in the hands of the few, and cites the example of police databases. Many believe that the computer professionals, whose programs are able to create such situations, are ill-equipped to perform their functions adequately. They are seen as lacking humanitarian concern, centering solely upon the capabilities of the computer rather than on the societal effects (Rothery, 1971).

Computers have been accused of causing such psychological and sociological effects as the de-skilling of labour (Tuckman, 1984), job stress, redundancy and unemployment, social isolation, powerlessness (Mendelson, 1983) and alienation (Sprandel, 1982). Further, the use of computers has been charged with altering personalities (Weinberg, 1971), with changing the socially gregarious into recluses and destroying relationships, and Simons (1985) even speculates that if:

> " . . . the computer proves to be a quite sufficient companion, then
> the seeds of anthrophobia (fear of other human beings) may develop
> in the obsessive programmer, the hacker . . . the computer is clearly a
> potentially fertile source of phobic conditions."

Papert (1980) also saw the possibility that computers could damage human relationships and create social differentiation between the cognoscenti and the 'computer illiterates', exacerbating the existing class distinctions rather than reducing them. Although personally believing in an optimistic computerized future he also believed that use of the computer could alter the way people think, reason and react:

> "If the medium is an interactive system that takes in words and speaks back like a person, it is easy to get the message that machines are like people and that people are like machines. What this might do to the development of values and self-image in growing children is hard to assess. But it is not hard to see reasons for worry."

Weizenbaum (1976) even described new technology and some of its applications as potentially 'obscene', 'morally repugnant' and 'dangerous', and attacked the dehumanizing aspect of computerization and its impact upon society. 'I'm coming close to believing that the computer is inherently anti-human—an invention of the devil.' One might believe that he is attributing anthropomorphic, super-human characteristics to a mere electronic tool. If such mistrust and apprehension occur to those who have spent years working closely with computers, who understand them and can 'control' them, what chance have the rest of the population to believe in the worth and goodness of the machine?

The fears cited appear not unrelated to the new anxiety, that certain people seem to become 'addicted' to their interaction with the computer. Especially when children are affected in this way, the machine appears to be seen as a potential source of danger and subversion. Children seem to be less suspicious of new technology than older generations, with many quickly learning the jargon of the professionals and showing little reluctance to use computers. This in itself can cause problems. Parents become concerned when their children appear to cut themselves off from social activities in order to 'play' with the computer for hours at a time. This differs little from the fears expressed thirty years ago with the advent of another revolutionary technology into the home, the television. The television was accused of affecting children in very much the same way that the computer is today, to the extent that various research programmes were established to investigate its influence over young minds. As suggested by Weizenbaum (1976) with respect to computer games, the common fear expressed with particular reference to children and television was that they were being adversely influenced and affected by violence on the screen. It was thought that children could be directly influenced, to the extent that they would imitate the actions seen, and become inured and habituated to it. Although disputed by Halloran (1964), research by McIntyre and Teevan (1971) and the Report on the Future of Broadcasting (1977) (known as the Annan Report) seemed to confirm these beliefs, and the potentially damaging influence of television is still being debated (see Howitt and Cumberbatch, 1975 and Cullingford 1984).

A more pervading fear lay with the fact that many people seemed to be cutting themselves off from other forms of recreation by watching television excessively, and once again children were thought to be especially susceptible. Himmelweit et *al.* (1958), undertook a special study to investigate the young 'television addict' and hypothesized that:

> "Emotional insecurity or inadequate facilities at home cause the child to become a heavy viewer. In this way he restricts his outside contacts and so reduces still further his opportunities to mix. With escape through television so readily available, other sources of companionship may demand too much effort and offer too little promise of success."

Although some people still remain concerned about the levels of violence and even sex and 'bad language' on television, the general population no longer seems to consider television watching to be overtly damaging. Television viewing has become one of the most popular forms of recreation in Britain, and a recent survey showed that the 'average viewer' watched 27.8 hours of television per week (Miller, 1988). This is more than the average time spent computing at home by the Dependents in this study of 22.4 hours per week. One would assume that any activity, which could provide the benefits and advantages listed by the Dependents in Chapter 10 as flowing from their interactive computing experiences, would be seen as preferable to somnolent evenings spent in front of the television set. However, few have recognized these advantages (see Greenfield, 1984 and Nicholson, 1984) and most remain suspicious; even those who have professional knowledge of computer systems, such as Boden (1977):

> "The socially isolating influence often attributed to television is as nothing to the alientation and loneliness that might result from over-enthusiastic reliance on the home terminal and associated gadgetry."

Although a computer scientist, or perhaps because of it, Weizenbaum (1984) expressed more doubts and fears than most and was very concerned about the influence of science in general, and computers in particular:

> "All thinking, dreaming, feeling, indeed all outer sources of insight have already been deligitimated. The indoctrination of our children's minds with simplistic and uninformed computer idolatry, and that is almost certainly what most of computer instruction is and will be, is a pandemic phenomenon."

Although apparently extreme, the fears directed towards the computer were not entirely new and differed little from those expressed towards television. Further research was able to show that such negative reactions had been expressed for centuries with reference to the introduction of other older technologies, and for this reason such reactions could have been anticipated.

CONCLUSIONS

From a study such as this it is difficult to propose firm, proven conclusions. The research had to be exploratory as so little of a factual nature was known about the syndrome of computer dependency, and for this reason some areas could only be examined somewhat rudimentarily. Not all of the Dependents who agreed to be interviewed could be, because of limitations upon the resources of time and money, and for the same reason none of the control group members were visited. The majority of the information therefore had to be obtained through the use of questionnaires and scales which, although providing ideal results from which statistical analyses could be carried out, did reduce much of the data to that which was easily measurable. There had been little guidance within the previous literature as to which areas to explore, since the authors seemed only to have described the activities undertaken at the keyboard or the effects arising from computer dependency. Any suggested causal relationship seemed to concentrate upon the features of the computer and rarely mentioned the individuals, other than to describe them as introverted. There was an obvious need to try to determine why this syndrome had actually occurred for some people who used computers.

That computer dependency occurred was established as far as was possible. The people who responded to the publicity and their partners all recognized and described the same syndrome as found in the literature. The Dependents devoted the vast majority of their spare time to computing, and for many most of what they did was only of intrinsic interest, done for intellectual stimulation and to learn about new technology. Most of the Dependents were not producing workable code, but were playing with the system hands-on and enjoying the resultant debugging. They differed from the control group of Owners in this respect but conformed to the image given to them by the press and the literature. What had not been anticipated was that there was more than one type of computer dependency. Although the majority of the interviewees were Explorers, as just described, some had graduated from this type of computing either to networking activities or to using the computer for work-related purposes. However, there was no difference between the groups for the effects that this had on others or for the time they devoted to their chosen activities; more important, irrespective of the group from which they came, both they and their spouses still considered them to be computer dependent.

The results from this study demonstrated that computer dependent people were not drawn from a cross-section of the population, nor were they typical socially or psychologically. These differences had been observed by some previous authors, but as most had made little attempt to try to understand why the syndrome had occurred one could only assume that their motives were not to offer assistance or personal advice if they felt it was required. However, most seemed to feel that such activities with a computer were detrimental, either directly to the individual or indirectly to computer systems, and as such should be prevented.

As the results from this research suggested that the Dependents had exhibited object-centredness and schizoid personality tendencies early in life, 'cures' offered in adulthood would have little positive effect even if one should wish to prevent the continuation of this condition. Merely altering behaviour patterns by weaning people away from computers could be very counter-productive. The computer was adopted because it offered the ideal interaction for those who had traditionally found great difficulties with personal relationships; computing was a fulfilment of needs, not an illness. For some it was a recognized escape from problems, but it was also seen more positively, as a substitute for something lacking in the outside world. Reducing the time spent on the computer would not solve the Dependents' problems and might in fact do more damage to the individual and the family than if the dependency continued. One man at least admitted that he had been cured from gambling by the advent of the computer in his life, and there were some suggestions of previous alcohol and drug 'abuse' by others. Few would suggest that the replacement of these would not be beneficial. Perhaps all who show personality traits similar to those exhibited by the Dependents need an object-centered, intellectual activity to give purpose, stability and control to their lives.

As suggested by Turkle (1984), we are perhaps all looking for an 'idealized person' with whom to share our lives, and some find it in a relationship with a computer. For the Dependents it was able to satisfy what we all hunger for, perfect acceptance and security. Others no doubt never find it at all and remain distressed and unhappy. If we are truly concerned about the Dependents and the thought that many more children will become like them as the computer becomes more widespread, we need to look at what is happening within the home during the pre-school years of the child, and especially within the middle-class home.

Although physical violence was occasionally mentioned as occurring within some families, the overriding picture which remained after the interviews was of people who, as children, had been well cared for in the physical sense but who had never been sure that they were loved. Follow-up interviews would have been necessary in order to explore this area more fully, but the distress created and the difficulty felt when describing their family backgrounds must be considered as highly significant for the development of the Dependents' subsequent interests. Whether rejected or neglected when young, they found acceptance through the performance of tasks and the achievement of goals and did not feel that they were loved unconditionally for being the child of the parents. The insecurities with which they were then left remained throughout their lives, only to be appeased by the manipulation of the trustworthy and reliable *inanimata*.

It is perhaps not surprising in a culture which appears not to like children that this situation should occur. No doubt many of the Dependents' own parents had received a similar upbringing and were therefore unable either to break out of the mould or to see any damage which could be caused by their methods. Such an upbringing was perhaps seen as advantageous, by ensuring that the children became independent early in life. It certainly appeared to have been successful in that respect; however, not only did it encourage them to be independent from their parents but also from almost all other human beings. 'Dependency will out' should perhaps be the main conclusion drawn from this research. All need to feel secure and of use in this world, and the hopelessness which was felt by some of the Dependents early in life was replaced by a dependency upon objects which would not hurt them.

In a society which is prepared to spend millions of pounds upon child abuse after the event has taken place, but offers so little in the way of marriage guidance, let alone lessons in parenthood and marriage while at school, it seems unlikely that things will change. The noble district nurse would notice nothing abnormal about the family and would therefore never suggest that help and advice should be given. It is perhaps the middle-classs mother who is less likely to take employment while her children are young, thereby keeping her children with her and out of nursery schools, and less likely to have an extended family around her to offer additional carers to the child, other than the occasional *au pair*. If so, such situations will probably be perpetuated.

The family members would probably be unaware of any difficulties, and it may be the child's first teacher who notices a reclusiveness, an avoidance of contact with other children, and an aloofness from adult caring. By this stage it may be too late. The size of classes may inhibit the teacher from giving sufficient personal attention to the child, and a child who will quite happily play alone will not demand the same attention as would the more boisterous and gregarious children. The child would be allowed to continue in its object-centered activities, and will be shunned by other children if showing interest in the more academic activities. This will be perpetuated throughout life, as even within secondary and tertiary education the studious tend to be derided and have to pretend that they do as little work as possible if they are to be acceptable to others.

Thus one can only advise all parents, who must desire the best for their children, to make positive efforts to show overt, physical signs of affection towards them when they are very young. It is not sufficient to offer them the best of material goods and the best schooling; children's needs are more basic if they are to grow up to be secure, happy and well-rounded adults.

Sex differences are also apparent in this issue, as the large proportion of male Dependents indicated. Cursory observation suggests that it is the male who is more likely to concentrate upon one particular subject or activity in order to perfect it, while females tend to be more eclectic in their interests and are more likely to be content to be the 'jack-of-all-trades' and know a little about a lot of things. This can be seen reflected in the contents of magazines aimed either at the male or the female markets. The 'male' magazines will, for example, concentrate almost exclusively upon one topic, whether it be fishing, football, cars, motorbikes, chess, pornography, or of course computers; invariably they centre upon one object-centered activity. Women's magazines are less exclusive, and even the few which may appear to centre upon one topic (such as fitness) will probably all contain articles about food, clothes, hair, exercise, kitchens and houses in general, as well as stories about people, and personal relationships and their attendant problems.

Some may suggest that women have no time to specialize in one particular subject due to family commitments, but the schoolgirl and the single women with similar diversity show that this is not the reason. Our early socialization must form one of the major causes, leading the majority of boys to exclusivity and the majority of girls to diversity and interactions with people. In babyhood it tends to be the female child who is praised just for being; being pretty, clean, smiling, quiet, etc, and for expressing emotions. Malatesta (1985) demonstrated that mothers would often ignore the emotional expressions of boys but encourage and respond favourably to those of girls. Boys on the other hand are encouraged to be physically active and to 'do things'.

These tendencies continue. While at school boys are encouraged to struggle with the difficult 'masculine' subjects, moulding them to the desired image, while girls are allowed to opt out. But those who have repressed their emotions through such early conditioning, usually males, are not given extra lessons in feeling and caring, and this research has demonstrated that they are often the ones to be actively encouraged to attain inaminate goals. Even in these days of sexual equality, girls are allowed to explore their psyches and emotions at will, and are still eased into the caring professions to exploit their strengths, while often allowing the mathematical and scientific sides of their characters to remain undeveloped. Both sexes are losing a great deal, and it should be of little surprise that communication between them is often unsatisfactory. In spite of the worthy work of the Equal Opportunities Commission, among others, there is still a long way to go before boys and girls are seriously encouraged to develop not only their strengths but their weaknesses; weaknesses which have been instilled since they were infants, because one sex is more highly favoured if it expresses emotions and an interest in others and the other if it does not.

The childhood difficulties experienced by the Dependents were often ameliorated to a great extent by marriage, which brought them the security they so desired. In some cases, however, as their problems diminished so the problems of their partners increased. The impression was gained that some of the wives of the Dependents had little knowledge of their partners' backgrounds, or an understanding of the effect it could have upon them. There were also suggestions that some of the wives' backgrounds were not entirely free from trauma and abuse of some sort, and for this reason they may have turned to a partner who so obviously needed them, perpetuating any problems. The need for wives to love those who seem unable to love in return is discussed by Norwood (1986), mainly with reference to wives of alcoholics. She describes the early experiences of such women as being:

"either very lonely and isolated, or rejected, or overburdened with inappropriately heavy responsibilities and so became overly nurturing and self-sacrificing… Inevitably, she will involve herself with a man who is irresponsible in at least some important areas of his life because he clearly needs her help, her nurturing, and her control. Then begins her struggle to try to change him through the power of persuasion of her love."

This was shown to be true within some of the Dependents' relationships, as was the fact that the wives were usually unable to change the behaviour of their husbands. Their lives depended upon the care of their man and upon his control. One wife, a psychologist, was well aware of the very traumatized childhood of her husband and was prepared to indulge his needs to help ease the pain, the cause of which the husband seemed unable to recognize. However, although she seemed to have managed to convince her husband of her love for him, to the extent that his dependency upon her was almost total, she was not able fully to replace his long established interests by her own needs.

How can such marriages be helped? To summarize the advice given by Norwood, she suggests that wives have to admit that they are helpless to stop the dependency and need to start to take charge of their own lives, by focusing upon themselves and their feelings using the support of others. This may help the woman, but as it is not a shared experience of the couple it may not save the relationship. From the basis of this research, additional assistance could also be suggested. As the relationships which showed the greatest problems were not always those where the wives were reluctant to use computers, perhaps one could suggest that the very medium at the centre of their difficulties could be utilized to help them. One feels that there would be scope for some computer software which would enable the partners to explore each others' needs and personalities in more depth than previously.

Someone commented that they had observed two 'junkies' communicating with one another via the networks, whilst sitting only a few feet apart. To those with good social skills this may seem bizarre, but this type of interaction successfully removes the non-verbal cues from conversation which can cause distraction and distress to some; the very things which give life to conversation to most people can be torment to others who cannot read the signs accurately. Exasperation, boredom, anger and frustration are not readily apparent on the networks, even if felt. A question mark appearing on the screen is a helpful indication that something has not been entirely understood and is far less distressing than to be told 'I don't know what you are talking about' or 'Forget it, it doesn't matter'. On the networks, one is not interrupted and nor are one's sentences completed inaccurately by the other person, for example, and this method of interaction seems perfectly to suit the Dependents' logical, precise modes of thinking and reasoning.

Face-to-face interaction was often difficult for the Dependents especially when talking about their feelings and backgrounds. Perhaps they were rarely understood by their partners because they so rarely explained themselves to others. A program which allowed each person to question the other and to express their opinions somewhat privately, without the problems of non-verbal communication and outward emotion so apparent within the couple's interactions, might prove of great benefit to both. Neither the Dependents nor their partners were insensitive creatures who wished to hurt the other, and as both were invariably committed to their relationships such a program, using a medium considered unthreatening to the Dependents, may have some success.

It was not difficult to empathize with both parties during the interviews but their lack of communication, at a level which both could appreciate and understand, inhibited successful adaptations being made to their behaviours. I found it somewhat disturbing to be told by some of the Dependents that I now knew more about their histories and family backgrounds than did their partners. I obviously offered no threat, was impartial and non-judgmental, and perhaps the computer could act as a similar intermediary. One felt that if both had been able to share their needs, interests and insecurities with one another then greater understanding would have been achieved.

Males in particular will need help to express themselves, and from an early age if they are to realize their self-worth as human beings, not just as the performers of tasks. The interviewed men often felt totally innocent of the charges of neglect laid before them by their partners; they were at home, not in the pub, were stimulating their intellects and not wasting time, and had often through their interests increased the family income considerably. What more did women want, and why? The use of the computer as a device for communication may help them to discover the answers, and help the wives to understand their partners' difficulties.

From the results obtained, it did seem somewhat strange to discover that this group had been singled out for special attention, to an extent which had inspired this research. The interviews revealed the Dependents on the whole to be a group of middle-class, young, intelligent and well-educated people who were happy with their lot, and invariably very successful if this may be measured by the status of their jobs. It was therefore somewhat difficult to see how they were not merely conforming to the images presented as desirable today.

The philosophies of the current age positively cultivate the fulfilment of one's own ends regardless of others; the welfare state in Britain appears to be in the process of being dismantled and it is 'each man for himself. The desire for success, prestige, status, money, and to be at the forefront of technology are all encouraged, within our schools and universities, by the press and the government. Interdependence is not fashionable; there are no common causes, and a sense of belonging to a society is no longer encouraged; science is worshipped, art relegated. Western culture is now object- and task-centered, the nurturing, caring society seems all but to have disappeared and the present political influences are apparent even within the student population, traditionally the site of radicalism and social reform. Self-need and individuality are fostered at the expense of the group. Life becomes work-centered and many people have no time for others, not even their families. Personal fulfilment has become paramount; there is no longer the need to make an effort to belong, or to be concerned about the welfare of others. This could be described as a 'schizoid' era, with the Dependents merely conforming to this image.

In the society within which we live, especially for the employed middle-classes, basic needs are taken care of; there are no wars to fight nor national goals to strive for. It is not difficult to clothe, feed and house oneself, and to achieve self-actualization and fulfilment individuals have to create their own personal challenges and excitement. This the Dependents had done very successfully, but they differed from others in the fact that they were not necessarily achieving anything tangible from their labours. Most were not getting paid for the many hours they devoted to their activities at home; it was done for sheer pleasure and enjoyment, and perhaps this marked them out as different.

As a conclusion to this study, I offer therefore no list of predisposing factors one should look for in a child so that computer dependency may be recognized and prevented; after all the child may instead grow up to be a famous sculptor, racing driver or high-technology innovator. What I would like to suggest is that perhaps our society needs people such as this; perhaps a diversity of extroverts and introverts is healthy and to the benefit of us all. Perhaps we need 'thinkers' and 'doers' if we are to make progress. From the work of Rosner and Abt (1970), when describing the creative experience from interviews with some of the most famous scientists of the day, one could easily see that backgrounds similar to the Dependents, full of shyness and isolation, may lead to the development of wondrous inventions and ideas. Why then, one might ask, were the Dependents not achieving such heights? Give them a little more time and perhaps they will.

REFERENCES

APEX. (1985). *New technology: a health and safety report.* (London: APEX).

ASTMS. (1979). *Guide to health hazards of visual display units.* ASTMS Policy Document, London.

Berqvist, U. (1984). Video display terminals and health. *Scandinaivian Journal of Work, Environment and Health, 10*, supplement 2.

Boden, M. A. (1981). The meeting of man and the machine. In *The design of information systems for human beings*, edited by K. P. Jones and II. Taylor (London: ASLIB).

Bowden, Lord, B. V. (1965). *New Scientist*, 30th September, 849.

Brod, C. (1984). *Technostress: the human cost of the computer revolution.* (Reading, MA: Addison-Wesley).

Cakir, A., IIart, D. J. and Stewart, T. F. M. (1980). *Visual display terminals.* (Chichester: John Wiley).

Carlyle, T. (1829). Signs of the times. In R. Williams (1967). *Culture and society 1780-1950.* (London: Chatto and Windus).

Catt, I. (1971). *Computer worship.* (London: Pitman).

Cullingford, C. (1984). *Children and television.* (Aldershot: Gower).

Duncan, A. M. (1986). *The splitting of the culture.* Unpublished, Loughborough University.

Eisele, J. E. (1981). Computers in the schools: now that we have them...? *Educational Technology, 21,* 10, 24—27.

Ferguson, D. A. (1987). 'RSI': Putting the epidemic to rest. *Medical Journal of Australia, 117,* 213—214.

Firschein, O., Fischler, M. A., Coles, L. S. and Tenenbaum, J. M. (1973). Forecasting and assessing the impact of artificial intelligence on society. In *3 rd International Conference on Artificial Intelligence,* 105—120.

Fitter, M. J. (1978). *Towards more natural interactive systems.* MRC Memo 253, Sheffield.

Frude, N. (1983). *The intimate machine: close encounters with new computers.* (London: Century Publishing).

Grandjean, E. and Vigliani, E. (Eds.) (1980). *Ergonomic aspects of visual display terminals.* (London: Taylor arid Francis).

Greenfield, P. M. (1984). *Mind and media.* (London: Fontana).

Halloran,J. D. (1964). Television and violence. *Twentieth Century,* Winter, 61—77.

Himmelweit, II. T., Oppenheim, A. N. and Vince, P. (1958). *Television and the child.* (Oxford: Oxford University Press).

Hollands,J. (1985). *Silicon Syndrome: How to survive a high-tech relationship.* (New York: Bantam Books).

Howitt, D. and Cumberbatch, G. (1975). *Mass media, violence and society.* (London: Elek Science).

Hoyle, F. (1968). *Physics Today. 21,* 4,148.

Kidder, T. (1981). *The soul of a new machine.* (London: Allen Lane).

Laurie, P. (1980). *The micro revolution: A change for the better or for the worse?* (New York: Futura Publications).

Levy, S. (1984). *Hackers: heroes of the computer revolution.* (New York: Anchor Press/Doubleday).

Malatesta, C. Z. (1985). Developmental course of emotion expression in the human infant. In *The development of expressive behaviour,* edited by G. Zivin, (New York: Academic Press).

Mclntyre, J. J. and Teevan, J. J. (1972). Television violence and deviant behaviour. In *Television and adolescent aggression,* Vol. 3, edited by G. A. Comstock and E. A. Rubenstein, (Washington, DC: US Government Printing Office).

Meek, B. (1972). Computers and education. In *Computers and the year 2000,* edited by Lord Avebury, R. Coverson,J. Humphries and B. Meek, (Manchester: NCC Publications).

Mendelson, L. (1983). U.S. prepare to combat the electronic sweatshop image. *Computing,* 2lst July, 17.

Miller, J. (1988). ITV's shows turn off the audience. *The Sunday Times,* 16th May,C6.

NALGO Health and Safety Briefing. (1986). (London: NALGO).

Nicholson, J. (1984). *Video games-threat or challenge? A preliminary report.* Unpublished, University of London.

Ong, C. N., Koh D. and Phoon, W. O. (1988). Review and reappraisal ofhealth hazards of display terminals. *Display,* 9, 1.

Papert, S. (1980). *Mindstorms: children, computers and powerful ideas.* (Brighton: Harvester Press).

Pateman, T. (1981). Communicating with computer programs. *Language and Comunication, 1,* 3—12.

Pearce, B. G. (1983). *Ergonomics and the terminaljunkie.* (Loughborough: HUSAT Research Centre).

Pearce, B. G. (1983). True ergonomic design for users: more than just furniture. *Ergonomics, 25*, 5, 6—8.

Pile, S. (1980). *The book of heroic failures.* (London: Futura).

Plum, T. (1977). Fooling the user of a programming language. *Software Practice and Experience, 7*, 215—222.

Poulson, D. F., (1983). *An investigation of cognitive factors relating to the way that people respond to the use of computers.* Unpublished PhD thesis, Loughborough University.

Report on the future of broadcasting (Lord Annan, chairman). (1977). Cmnd. 6753; 6753-1 vi. (London: HMSO).

Rosner, S. and Abt, L. E. (1970). *The creative experience.* (New York: Dell Publishing Inc).

Rothery, B. (1971). *The myth of the computer.* (London: Business Books Ltd).

Russell, C. A. (1976). *Science and the rise of technology since 1800.* Unit 4, O.U. AST 281. (Milton Keynes: Open University Press).

Schiebe, K. E. and Erwin, M. (1979). The computer as alter. *Journal of Social Psychology.* 108, 103-109.

Schwartz, M. D. (1983). The impact of computer mediated work on individuals and organizations. *Computing, Psychiatry and Psychology* U.S.A. 5, 6—8.

Simons, G. (1985). *Silicon shock.- the menace of the computer invasion.* (Oxford: Basil Blackwell).

Simons, G. (1985). *The biology of computer life: survival, emotion and free will.* (Brighton: The Harvester Press).

Simpson, B. (1983). Why kids love chips. *The Guardian*, 15th December.

Sprandel, G. (1982). A call to action—psychological impacts ofcomputer usage. *Computers and Society* (USA), 12, 2, 12-13.

Stewart, T. F. M. (1984). More practical experiences in solving VDU ergonomic problems. In *Health hazards of VDTs?* edited by B.G. Pearce (Chichester: John Wiley).

Surtees,J. (1988). Memories are made of this. *The Sunday Times*, 31st July, C11.

Thimbleby, II. (1979). Computers and human consciousness. *Computers and Education*, 3, 241-243.

Tjonn, II. II. (1984). Report of facial rashes among VDU operators in Norway. In *Health hazards of VDTs?*, edited by B. G. Pearce, (Chichester: John Wiley).

Toffler, A. (1971). *Future Shock.* (London: Pan Books).

TUC Guidelines on VDUs. (1986). (London: Trades Union Congress).

Tuckman, B. W. (1984). Thinking out loud—Why (and why not) teach computer usage. *Educational Technology*, February, 35.

Turkle, S. (1984). *The second self computers and the human spirit.* (London: Granada).

Vallee, J. (1984). *The network revolution: confessions of a computer scientist.* (Harmondsworth: Penguin).

Waddilove, K. (1984). The case for cost effective chalk. *The Guardian*, 20th March, 11.

Weeks, D. J. (1988). *Eccentrics: the scientific investigation.* (Stirling: Stirling University Press).

Weinberg, G. M. (1971). *The psychology of conputer programming.* (New York: Van Nostrand Reinhold).

Weinberg, S. (1982), cited by R. Wrege in High (Tech) Anxiety. *Popular Computing.* January, 46-52.

Weizenbaum, J. (1976). *Computer power and human reason.* (San Francisco, CA: W. II. Freeman and Company).

Weizenbaum, J. (1984). *Computer power and human reason.* (Harmondsworth: Penguin).

Zarat, M. M. (1984). Cataracts and visual display teriilinals. In *Health hazards of VDTs?*, edited by B. G. Pearce, (Chichester: John Wiley).

READING QUESTIONS

1) What "split in our culture" does Turkle refer to?
2) How is the stereotyping of computing carried out?
3) In what way is the hacker a "threat"?
4) What "fair trade" was negotiated between hackers and administrators at MIT?
5) How did ITS become a "model for a mode of production"?
6) Why might hackers challenge our society more than priests or poets?
7) What is the simple form of the debate over hackers?
8) "As we grow up, we forge our identities by building on the last place in psychological development where we felt safe." How does Turkle think this applies to hackers?
9) What "special qualities" do computers have that make them "particularly liable to become traps"?
10) Hackers are "addicted to playing with the issue of control." Why does Turkle claim this?
11) What is "sport death," and how does it fit into hacker culture?
12) Why is the hacker world peculiarly male?
13) How is the "power of belonging to a group" important in hacker life?
14) Describe the conflicts between "straights" and hackers.
15) In what way is the hacker culture "safe"?
16) What is a "safe risk"? Why is sex and romance not one?
17) In what way is hacker culture "antisensual"?
18) How is hacking like playing "Adventure"?
19) Why must a great hack involve mastery?
20) What "rites of passage" are there in the hacker culture? What rules are there about these rites?
21) Why does "winning" conflict with system security?
22) "People are deeply ambivalent toward computers." How does this ambivalence contribute to sympathy for those who break into computer systems?
23) Why does Shotton think people are worried about computer dependency?
24) Is computer dependency "unusual" in comparison with dependency on other pastimes?
25) What was it about computers that made people afraid of them?
26) How are those fears expressed?
27) Why does Shotton call these fears about computers "irrational"?
28) Why is it that the "psychological effects" of computers might be more disturbing than their physical effects?
29) In what way is "hacker fear" similar to "television fear"?
30) What different "types" of computer dependency did Shotton find in her study?
31) Are computer dependents "typical" socially or psychologically?
32) Were the computers the "cause" of computer dependency?
33) Would reducing the time spent on computers "solve" the problems that computer dependents have?
34) If we are concerned about computer dependency, where does Shotton suggest we look for the causes of it?

35) "Dependency will out." Explain.
36) What is Shotton's advice to parents who are concerned about computer dependency?
37) How does Shotton explain the gender imbalances in the number of computer dependents?
38) How was the dependency of the computer dependents modified by marriage?
39) What does Shotton suggest to help dependents communicate with other people?
40) Why did the male dependents feel "totally innocent" of the charges of neglect that their spouses made?
41) Why was it "somewhat strange" that this group had been singled out for concern?
42) How might computer dependents be merely conforming to the image of the era?
43) Shotton says she "offer[s] therefore no list of predisposing factors one should look for in a child so that computer dependency may be prevented." Why?

DISCUSSION QUESTIONS

1) If computer dependency is not really much different from other forms of dependency, why has our culture been so seriously frightened by it? How might we allay fears that computers will destroy the lives of children?
2) In an earlier chapter, Cuban claims that the admission of computers to schools may reduce the attachment of children to their teachers and make them dependent on computers. How do his claims compare with Turkle's and Shotton's?
3) If you could "offer [a] list of predisposing factors one should look for in a child so that computer dependency may be prevented," would you? Why?

PRACTICING THE DESIGN ETHIC

1) Schedule a short interview with a teacher in the psychology department on campus, or with a local psychiatrist/psychologist. During the interview, determine the following:
   - What are his or her opinions about dependency (alcohol, drugs, etc.)? Is it a real problem? Has he or she noticed any patterns in the dependent patients?
   - Does your interviewee feel that people can become dependent on technology (computers, TV, telephone)? Why or why not?
   - Does your interviewee feel that certain technologies can improve/harm social skills development? Why?
   - How would the doctor address the problem of computer dependency if he or she ran across it?
   - How would the doctor suggest technology designers do things differently to reduce the chances for dependency?

   Get together in small groups and discuss your findings. Are there differences in doctors' opinions? If so, why do you think this is so? Determine if there are any patterns concerning how the doctors would handle the issue of computer dependency.
2) What kind of program does your school have to deal with computer dependents? Using the information from these two articles, either evaluate the current program or design a new one.

CHAPTER

17

TOWARD A DESIGN ETHIC FOR COMPUTING PROFESSIONALS

Chuck Huff
St. Olaf College

Bruce Jawer
IBM Rochester, Minnesota

If concern for the social effects of computing is to be anything more than a laudable diversion (like consulting for a local charity), it needs to affect the way computing systems are designed and the way computing professionals go about their tasks. This final chapter is intended to suggest some ways that you, as a computer professional, might do this. Our suggestions are based on our conviction that ethical concern, social awareness, and quality design are intricately linked to form what we call a *design ethic*. We hope that by the time you are finished reading this chapter you will be convinced that these are three interdependent legs of a tripod.

WHY A DESIGN ETHIC?

We expect that the previous chapters in this book have convinced you that computing technology changes the way people work, play, and educate themselves (among other things). It should also have convinced you that the design and implementation of the technology is influenced in turn by our conceptions of how work, play, and education are done.

There are clear areas where society and computing do not influence each other. It is largely a matter of mathematics that makes one sorting algorithm faster than another for a particular task (though social concerns might influence which one is finally chosen for a product). It is simply a matter of physics that makes silicon a more suitable material for chip manufacture than, say, aluminum.

A pattern of reciprocal influence between computing technology and society is really too basic and pervasive a phenomenon to doubt. If it is true that (a) computing technology affects society and that (b) some choices in computing design are not completely constrained by mathematics, physics, chemistry, etc., then it is clear that (c) designers, implementers, and managers of technology make choices that affect society.

This simple syllogism should make it obvious that those who work with technology make choices that affect others in their society. We can, if we wish, choose not to think about the clear effects of the technology we design and implement. But we can no longer say that we are merely doing technology in a vacuum. In fact, we already *have* a design ethic, whether or not it is carefully thought out. Our plea in this chapter is that we look more carefully at the design ethics we already have, and that we realize that they affect the design of our products and services, the ethical responsibilities we claim, and the society we inhabit.

The design ethic we present is a framework for your own thinking. It is not a prescriptive program. There is still within it plenty of room for disagreement on many (perhaps most) issues, practices, and choices. Its primary aim is to illuminate the interdependencies of good design, ethical concern, and social awareness. We will present each leg of the design ethic individually, but it will soon become evident that the links among them are numerous. Since most of the readers of this text will be considering careers as computer professionals, we will start with the most obvious leg: quality design.

QUALITY DESIGN

THE TRADITIONAL APPROACH AND ITS SHORTCOMINGS

The tradition of computing design has been that of smart and capable people designing, by themselves, systems that *they* think will be good to use and then giving or selling those systems to others (Borenstein, 1991; Bauer, Collar, & Tang, 1992). Certainly this has resulted in some exceptional systems. Most systems have been designed this way (that is, after all, what "traditional" means), and many of them have been widely successful. But as in most industries that depend on innovation, widespread success can obscure widespread failure.

For example, in 1985-1986, IBM was developing a new midrange system code named Fort Knox. The older, fairly successful versions of the IBM midrange line (Systems 36 and 38) were losing market share in the competition, partly because the various machines in the IBM midrange line were not compatible with one another (and in fact sometimes openly competed with one another). The idea was to take the various machines and consolidate them into a single line that would both do the different jobs of the earlier machines and represent a significant technical advance over them. But as IBM technical teams began squabbling with one another over the feasibility of the system, it became apparent that they were building the wrong system for the wrong reasons.

It was the wrong system because it attempted to be all things to all people: replacing all the functions of all the earlier systems, while adding innovations that would make the new machine a technical standout. This resulted in specifications that disagreed with one another, and in a machine that looked on paper more like one of Dr. Seuss's creations than an integrated, purposeful product.

It was the wrong system primarily because it was built for the wrong reasons. IBM was concerned about consolidating its product line, about making technical advances on its machine, and, in short, about making a machine that designers at IBM would like. IBM had the problems of traditional computing design in spades. Fort Knox ended up getting canned because IBM could never agree on which internal group the design was supposed to satisfy.

The misadventures with Fort Knox were understandable. The work of large organizations is so complex that specialization is necessary. And in the computer industry, the technical challenges are so enormous that one can only survive by hiring highly specialized, technically proficient people. As you organize these specialists into divisions and into subgroups in divisions, they speak to each other less and rarely if ever see the actual users of the machines they build. This isolation makes it easy to think that your concerns are the concerns of everyone. So it is easy to understand how IBM became preoccupied with its own machine (as opposed to its customers' machines) and could squabble internally about which divisions' conception of its machine was the correct one.

QUALITY DESIGN AS AN ANSWER

The cancellation of Fort Knox was as clear a wakeup call as a business is likely to get, short of bankruptcy. A postmortem of the Fort Knox project could have led IBM Rochester to decide that it should just get out of the midrange computer business (something outside business analysts had been whispering). Under the direction of a new director of development, IBM Rochester drew a different lesson: The failure of Fort Knox was due to a lack of cooperation and communication both internally (that is, within and between divisions) and externally (with its customers). This led IBM to change from the traditional and isolating "we will build a good machine" mentality to "we will build the right machine for our customers." Making this transition required an approach that emphasized a few basic principles: teamwork, quality control, market analysis, and cooperation with the customer.[1]

---

[1] The book *SilverLake* (Bauer et al. 1992) breaks these out into 10 principles and provides much more detail on how they were implemented. Most of these ideas are not novel. Many companies are now

The outcome was the Silverlake project, which resulted in the AS400 line of minicomputers, the resurgence of IBM Rochester, and the award of the 1990 Malcolm Baldrige National Quality Award to IBM Rochester. The outcome was not just a marketing success (over 200,000 systems sold in its first 4 1/2 years), or just a technical achievement (though patents from IBM Rochester did increase 100 percent) but was also a major change in the process of design, manufacture, sales, and support of a computer. Much of the change stems from the way IBM organized the Rochester lab and incorporated the customer into the design process.

Market analysis

An aphorism that aptly sums up this principle is "know thy customer." A business that builds a computer for itself (see the traditional approach above) will have itself as its best customer—and other customers will be left to chance. IBM conducted a careful analysis of the market for their mid-range computer and found not only the types of customers who were likely to purchase their machines but the applications for which they intended to use them. On a narrow analysis, this allowed IBM to target its sales efforts, and it did so very effectively. But at least as crucial, it allowed IBM Rochester to identify potential users so that they could incorporate them into the design process.

Quality control

Quality control is all the rage today, but it is often thought of as merely testing products after they come off the line and then rejecting the bad ones. Good quality control starts with the design of the product, continues through prototyping and testing, and extends through manufacturing, delivery, and support. It involves people from all stages, not by merely making sure they do the right thing but by asking them what the right thing to do is. For instance, manufacturing was involved in producing the prototypes for the AS400, and they introduced innovations that made it easier to manufacture reliably. In addition, this teamwork with manufacturing made it possible to get more than one prototype, and allowed Rochester to share prototypes with customers and get their recommendations and reactions.

Market analysis and quality control (at least in their rudimentary states) are relatively standard news in industry today. But as Tom Peters (Peters, 1992) has observed, the heart of the new approach at IBM Rochester was the openness both within the company and between the company and its customers. This openness allowed the market analysis to be used by more than just the marketing department, and made quality control more than

---

moving away from narrow compartmentalization in favor of the team approach to design, production, and implementation. Quality circles (where production teams meet regularly to monitor quality) and Total Quality Management are becoming recognized and respected management approaches. But in the oddly conservative world of the major computing companies, and in the mid-1980s, these ideas were new and exciting.

merely culling out the bad items on a line. It had its most profound effect in opening lines of cooperation and communication across divisions and between IBM and its customers.

Teamwork

The central concept in teamwork is shared responsibility for the final product. This runs counter to the traditional "divide and conquer" approach to computing design. And it provides precisely what the traditional approach leaves out: coherence, perspective, and integration. For instance, customer complaints often get lost between divisions of a company and bounce around until the customer leaves in exasperation. One response to this is to create yet another division to deal with these complaints. IBM Rochester established a cross-functional team, consisting of people from marketing, planning, manufacturing, engineering, and service to handle these complaints. The buck stopped there, and the broad-based group had the perspective to diagnose problems that crossed traditional divisional boundaries. This made people from engineering responsible for the entire product, as were people from manufacturing, and from the other divisions.

Cooperation with the customer

When Fort Knox was canceled, IBM Rochester completely redesigned the proposed new system and, this time, asked, "Why don't we get some customers to come in here and ask them what they want us to do?" The customers were involved in planning, specification, analysis and design, development, building and testing, and support of the project.

The IBM development team in Rochester, Minnesota, made it a fundamental part of the design process to include the user in the design process to develop new systems. Developers also spent several days at customer sites to better understand how the system was actually being used. Customer advisory councils were run that allowed users to hear about plans and decide if those plans met their future needs. And feedback from these councils actually made a difference in the design of the AS400. Customers were gratified and astonished that their opinions mattered. This approach of involving users in all phases of the development process has helped make IBM Rochester one of the most successful development sites in IBM (Bauer et al. 1992).

THE PLACE OF QUALITY DESIGN IN THE DESIGN ETHIC

As you can see from the example above, quality design done right encompasses more than technical proficiency. It requires taking into account the business, personal, and social expectations of both your colleagues and your customers. It means understanding how the machine you design is used in the businesses that purchase it, and understanding the problems that customers are trying to solve. And as you bring the customer more into the design process, you become more aware of the social settings in which your product is used.

In fact, the entire purpose of openness in quality design is to allow other perspectives to inform your design. If you build an information system for an insurance company, knowing how managers and workers will use it will help you design a better system (see Grant et al. in Chapter 12). If you build hardware or software for medical radiation equipment, knowing the actual conditions under which technicians use the equipment will help you make it safer (see Kling in Chapter 2 or Reason in Chapter 5). If you build systems to support communication and cooperative work, knowing how people work together will help you tailor your system to the real needs of your customers (see Allen in Chapter 2). Even if you are building general purpose computing equipment (like the AS400), knowing the ways it is used by your customers will help you make a better machine for your customer.

Your technical expertise is crucial, but it needs to encompass an understanding of the social systems in which your product will be used— because it is these social systems and organizational imperatives that will constrain the ways your product will be used. Thus, you need to find out the concerns and issues that motivate users of your product. In the attempt you will find out the (sometimes surprising) ways your product is used. In addition, you find out how your own organization thinks about its product. Clearly, the heart of quality design involves being aware of the environments in which your products are produced and used.

The final leg of the design ethic tripod, ethical concern, is also intimately connected to quality design. Clearly, a dedication to a reliable product, a commitment to open dealing with clients, and a concern for including customers and employees in the design process are parts of both the ACM ethics code and of quality design. These values are at the heart of the profession (Johnson, 1991), and it should not be surprising that they are woven into quality design and the need for social awareness.

Unfortunately, an abstract commitment to ethical ideals can too easily seem disconnected from issues of design. Surely we are all "for" safe products, we all support honesty in product claims, and we all think workers have rights to decent job conditions. We may even have taken an ethics class in which we had to defend and challenge these ideals. But the connection of these ideals to quality design comes in when they are taken out of the classroom and applied to specific products and their specific uses.

A concern for privacy rights can lead you to ask questions about the amount of monitoring a system does. A concern for equal access can lead you to design an interface that includes options for the handicapped. A concern for honesty in product claims can lead you to make close inquiries into how a system will be used before making guarantees about performance. And each of these ethical concerns can be approached in a way that enhances the quality of the product you build or the service you offer.

ETHICAL CONCERN

Because computer professionals have special knowledge about computer systems, they also have a special responsibility to "take care" of those that might be affected by those systems. As Deborah Johnson says, there is a "value at the heart of the profession" to build prudent and safe goods for society. Johnson suggests that a guiding principle for engineering and computer professionals is that they "direct their professional skills to projects they deem, on balance, to be of positive value to humanity and should refuse to work on projects that put people at risk, unless information about such projects is made generally available" (Johnson, 1991).

Becoming aware of, and actively engaging, these issues are a fundamental part of every computer professional's job, in the same way that it is part of the medical doctor's job. This is because, just like medical doctors, computer professionals are agents of change in people's lives. We often think of ourselves as simply technicians (programmers, analysts, designers, managers). But every chapter of this book provides examples of ways that computing technology changes the lives of those who use it. We are changing the world and have some ethical responsibility for the changes we create. But this responsibility is complicated because our position as workers in an industry diffuses moral agency.

Most computer professionals do work defined by their employers. This makes it difficult to determine where the "moral agency" for the outcomes of the work is located. Is it that computer professionals simply do whatever work is asked of them by the employer and the boss takes the credit or blame?

This confusion is heightened by the fact that organizations usually compartmentalize their functions. Each department specializes in one function of a larger system. In addition, individuals within each department further specialize, and focus on only small parts of the department's function. We have already argued that this specialization can reduce the quality of the product—and it reduces the responsibility each worker feels for the larger system to which he or she contributes. When one focuses on just a small part of the whole, the consequences of the larger system can easily be missed.

Specialization and compartmentalization, while designed for efficiency, can hide the social consequences of the system. If I'm just focusing on database design, I might ask myself how that has any social impact on others. Only by seeing how the entire system will be used (including "my piece" of the puzzle) can I make judgments about the social and ethical aspects of my piece. In short, compartmentalization limits the knowledge you need to make an ethical evaluation of the work you are doing. Thus, a side effect of specialization is to limit your responsibility to technical matters. But as we (and others in this book) have argued, the technical matters are too intertwined with the social and ethical matters to be separated so easily.

A drastic example of the difficulties of denying responsibility for technical work is provided by Albert Speer, the Nazis' minister of armaments. In talking about the Nazi use of technology, he said, "I exploited the phenomenon of the technician's often blind devotion to his task. Because of what appeared to be the moral neutrality of technology, these people were without any scruples about their activities." Note that Speer's argument is that work on technology only appears to be morally neutral.

It is precisely because technical matters are difficult to separate from social and ethical ones that courts of law, moral philosophers, and even the military code agree that moral agency is not the sort of thing you can check at the door. Computer professionals are, in fact, *always* moral agents; the responsibility for ethical decision making is never suspended. Being asked to do unethical work to make a quick buck is similar to being asked to do shoddy work to make a quick buck.

We agree that most computer professionals are not trained ethicists or sociologists. Many technical professionals entered their field expecting to concentrate on technical matters and not to be saviors or crusaders. We are not suggesting that a computer professional's core responsibility is anything other than being the best technician he or she can be. However, we are suggesting that computer professionals should recognize that *part* of their job includes these larger issues of social responsibility, both because of the values in the profession and because this concern will likely make their work of higher quality.

But what, in practical terms, can we do now that we are aware of the social and ethical issues raised by computing? For simplicity's sake we will divide the action into two camps: global and local. The global perspective includes understanding the broader issues involved with the social consequences of our work and working with national and international organizations to further their ends. The local perspective involves the things we can do as professionals when we design, build, or implement systems.

GLOBAL ACTION

From a global perspective, the professional can join and become an active participant in organizations and causes that take this broader view of the computer professional's role. By joining these organizations computer professionals can learn about, and get some training in, the issues they have to handle at a local level. Furthermore, by participating in these national organizations, professionals can help create the standards and awareness necessary to do their job at the local level.

Organizations like the ACM's special interest group on Computers and Society (SIGCAS), the Electronic Frontier Foundation (EFF), and Computer Professionals for Social Responsibility (CPSR) are at the forefront of many issues facing our profession and society. Many of these organizations also hold annual conferences on topics discussed in this book. The conferences are excellent opportunities to learn more about these topics, and to meet and discuss these issues with others in the profession. (A list of some these organizations can be found at the end of this paper.) Computer professionals can also become active in learning about the issues related to computer ethics, and become more aware of the various computer professional's codes of ethics (some organizations listed at the end, like the ACM SIGCAS group, were involved in drafting the ACM's code of ethics).

In addition, most other computing organizations touch on ethical issues relevant to their specialty. For instance, issues of reliability are closely followed by several ACM special interest groups, and access for the handicapped is a part of the agenda of ACM's special interest groups on Computer-Human Interaction and on Computers and the Physically Handicapped. More generally, your dues to ACM or IEEE or other national organizations provide support for groups working in these areas and also support outreach and educational programs like the ACM-sponsored television special "The Machine That Changed the World."

Participating in organizations and activities at the professional level provides a conduit for you to take action on social and ethical issues that concern you. It also provides you with a larger voice in decisions that are made at the national level. And finally, it helps you stay abreast of current problems and issues that face the profession. The information and training you receive from these organizations can help in your local work.

LOCAL ACTION

Computing professionals can act locally by carrying out their own version of a design ethic in their work. This ethic involves a commitment to quality work, a knowledge of the connection between the technology and the social environment in which it is used, and a recognition of the responsibility to consider the social consequences of that work.

This design ethic recognizes computer professionals' broader responsibilities and links them closely to the quality of the product itself. Inherent in this design ethic is the view that the designer's responsibility does not end with a focus on the technology itself. Responsibility extends to a consideration of the user (human-computer interaction), organization (organizational computing), and the community (social implications of computing) (Kling, Chapter 2; Winograd, 1990). Furthermore, the design process can be viewed as a collective inquiry and search by all affected parties. The designer is part of a larger team of users, who work together to find system solutions (Greenbaum & Kyng, 1991). This pattern of responsibility links a quality product to a more open method of design.

Frederick Brooks, in *The Mythical Man-Month*, suggests that software design should be handled by a "small surgical team"(also known as the chief programmer team) who support one another to get the job done. We suggest that this is the level at which the social issues arising in design should be considered. It is not a side show (nor is it the main event), but consideration of social issues is important enough to be considered at the highest levels in design. Methods for the team to use in considering the social issues are suggested later in this paper, but they could range from simple interviews to a participatory design team that includes technicians, users, and management. No matter what methods are used, it is the team's responsibility to encourage an "inquiring attitude" into the consequences, risks, and benefits of a system. "Simply getting relevant decision-makers to think about various outcomes can be....mind-stretching, forcing people to consider different applications, time frames, and uses from those that come readily to mind. When [those who will be affected by a decision] have been forced to explore consequences, they are less likely to forget or ignore them" (Westrum, 1991).

However, we must be careful about oversimplifying what is meant by understanding the social issues that arise from the technology we design. As Terry Winograd has pointed out, "this is not just a matter of sensitivities about 'listening to users.' To understand what will really work we need to go beyond the superficial aspects of 'user friendly' and 'seamless' and pursue a deeper analysis of what people are doing in larger human and organizational contexts, and how this is influenced by the use of computers" (Winograd, 1990). We must ask tougher questions. The questions must begin with: *why* are we building this system?

Often, when we view our responsibilities as limited to technical issues, the only question we ask is: "*How* can we build this better?" We must start with the questions related to *whether* we need to build the system at all. This is the level of questioning that the Fort Knox project lead IBM Rochester to engage in. It involved a drastic rethinking about who the users of the system were and what it was they wanted. It required a drastic departure from traditional design procedures, bringing in customers and users to help make crucial decisions. But it produced a machine that was more useful to the customers, and thus a better product.

We also need to ask other questions: In selecting a particular system or solution, what kind of world are we seeking to create? Who will benefit from the new system? Who are the forgotten, the invisible? Who are the decision makers on this project, and are they the right people to be making the decisions regarding this system?

Obviously, people will have differing opinions in answer to these questions. As Langdon Winner says, "it is no easy matter to set about clarifying the basic notions that ought to guide the development and use of our technical means. People have widely different understandings about the meaning and proper application of terms like freedom, justice, security, human rights, well-being, public good, and other key concepts. But it is crucial that such ideas be continually discussed and debated throughout our deliberations about key technical choices. If we do not do this, ideas about 'how' begin to compromise the whole of our thinking" (Winner, 1991a).

So how do we begin the process of asking these questions? We considered (and even made several attempts) to compile a list of issues that should be considered as a system is designed, produced, implemented, and updated. We finally decided not to include it—partly because the list became formidable if we tried to cover a variety of situations, implementations, and social settings, and partly because when we cut items to "representative" or "core" ones, we felt uncomfortable leaving out some issues. Our final recommendation is more a process than a checklist. If you stay informed on the issues by joining one of the organizations we mentioned, consider the multiple perspectives of the people in the organizations that use your product or service, and carefully seek to understand how the technology is actually used, you will be in a much better position than we to assess which issues are relevant.

This difficulty in determining the "right" issues to consider in any instance underlines our contention that this is, in the final analysis, a judgment for each professional to make in each situation. So how does one decide which items to pursue? One answer comes in the section below: The decision comes after finding out what you can about how the product will be used. But in the end, even with good information to support the decision, it is a judgment call. It is, after all, your job as a computer professional to decide which items are relevant to the project at hand, which are important enough to spend time on, and which can be done within the time limits of the project.

SOCIAL AWARENESS

Ben Shneiderman has suggested that computer professionals prepare a *social impact statement* (SIS) at the start of every system project. He suggests that it be patterned after the Environmental Impact Statement, and that it "identify user communities, establish training requirements, specify potential negative side-effects (health, safety, privacy, financial, etc.), and indicate monitoring procedures for the project's lifetime" (Shneiderman, 1990).

This may sound like a great deal of work to add to an already full agenda—isn't every schedule already too compressed? But what an SIS should do is merely make the process of implementing a system more rational (Westrum, 1991). As we have argued before, the difficult technical tasks involved in computing often leave one thinking that when those problems are solved, the system is ready to go. The process of designing a system for the needs of users is a constant struggle between wanting to finish the implementation of the system and wanting to react to the concerns of the market and the system's potential users (Borenstein, 1991). Issues of ethics and social concern often get lost in the shuffle. There are already methods in systems design and interface design that involve users and other constituents in the design and implementation of a system (Greenbaum & Kyng, 1991). And these inclusive methods are becoming the standards by which good design is judged (Shneiderman, 1992).

Including an SIS in the cycle of design, implementation, maintenance, and revision of a system ensures that the design team is paying attention to a wider world than the technical one. It begins the process of becoming aware of the influence and importance of nontechnical issues. For instance, as a result of user complaints, IBM Rochester redesigned the user interface to the AS400. But this time, instead of doing the design in isolation, IBM brought customers to the lab to try prototypes, looked at how customers used the interface in the field, and asked customers to assist in the design of the interface. We would have been better off incorporating customers into the user interface design the first time through, but we did get it right the second time. If we had done even a rudimentary SIS, these interface issues might have shown up earlier.

The SIS not only keeps us in touch with the technical needs of the customer but also makes more explicit our choices in designing a system. This is what we mean when we say that an SIS makes system design more rational: it makes us aware of the choices we are making and helps us avoid making a choice out of sheer habit. There are a variety of choices that an SIS will make more explicit in the design process:

Reality versus Preconception

We can only design the system that *we* think is needed, but we can be wrong about what *is* needed. In a study of the design of educational software, for instance, Huff & Cooper (1987) asked a group of teachers to design software for boys, girls, or students (gender unspecified). Those who designed software for boys made games (lots of action, competitive and aggressive themes, timed performance); those who designed for girls made "learning tools" (cooperative, slower-paced, controlled by the student). But those who designed for students made software that looked just like the software for boys. Thus, software for the regular "student" was really "boy" software. The teacher's preconceptions showed through in the design of the software and left out half the students in the classroom. The teachers in this study frequently expressed a concern about gender bias in software—showing that good intentions and even close acquaintance with the users can still result in a design that is guided by preconception. The earlier example about the AS/400 system is also relevant here. We were surprised by what our businesses thought a good midrange computer was—but we had to *ask* before we could be surprised. And asking made the surprise a more pleasant one.

Openness versus Groupthink

Groupthink is a phenomenon identified by Janis (1982) in his analyses of government decision-making teams (for example, the decision to invade Cuba during the Kennedy administration). Its primary determinant is a decision-making group that has lost touch with the environment around it. People engaging in groupthink *believe* they are open to outside influence. But in a variety of subtle ways, all outside influence is either blocked, filtered, or denigrated. This produces a group of decision makers who think they have the right answer, but who have effectively foreclosed any disagreement with them. Only luck or low standards can keep a process like this from failing.

All the recommendations that have been made to avoid this precarious position involve opening up the discussion to other people and ideas: assigning a "devil's advocate" to help foresee trouble; having alternate teams working on the same problems; open leadership that discourages "yea-saying"; and searching for alternatives without premature evaluation (there are more—see Janis, 1982). These are precisely the sort of strategies that an SIS encourages and that are already included in some models of system design. Using these strategies to investigate the social and ethical issues surrounding an implementation can help reduce the unfounded confidence that "we know what they want."

Actual versus Idealized Practice

In 1938, a paint chemist at California Ink in Berkeley was introduced to the difficulties of putting new technology to work. He was in charge of varnish production. The varnish was cooked in 250-gallon open kettles at 600 degrees, and careful temperature control was essential to assure good quality. The previous chemist had established a rigorous quality control procedure, but quality of the varnish declined steadily. When the new chemist took over, his first step was to inquire among the workers about the reason for the trouble. As it turned out, the quality control was the reason.

Vern "Pappy" Maynard was the supervisor of the workers and was officially classified as an "unskilled" worker. Before the "quality control" had been implemented, he had been able to correct for vagaries in the thermometer readings by spitting in the kettles. The noise the spit made when it hit the varnish allowed him to tell the temperature of the varnish within 5 degrees. Chicken feathers, according to Pappy, were even more accurate: the color they turned when dipped in the varnish was the indicator (Westrum, 1991).

There are innumerable tales of this sort of divergence in actual versus ideal practice—and many of them have been recounted in the preceding chapters. The fact that a system is designed to be used one way often has little influence on those who eventually have to run it. You need to ask the right questions of the right people to find out how the work you are automating is *really* done. Errors like these are not mere slips. With critical systems they can endanger lives; with business systems they can produce large financial losses.

Sponsors and Participants

Often the people who will be affected by a system are hidden from the view of the technical people who design the system. Even if a company builds a system specifically for a client, the technical people may not get to meet the client, much less the employees and customers of the client's organization or the other people affected by the system that are still more remote. For instance, in designing a database system for tracking criminal offenses, the police department or the state government may be the immediate client. Employees who have a stake in the system's design include data entry operators, dispatchers, and other employees who use the system. More "remote" but still important are the criminals whose records are being kept and the citizens who are innocent of crimes but who may appear in the database because of entry errors or faulty design. And they need not be thought of as simply the citizens within the client's jurisdiction: states, counties, and cities share criminal data continually, and thus people on the other side of the continent can be affected by a poorly designed database system in one county (see the article by Clarke in Chapter 11).

An SIS encourages the designers to identify all the people who are affected by a system and to take into account all their concerns, resulting in a better-planned system. Again, this is not entirely new to system and interface design methods. For example, the IBM AS/400 was advertised as an easy-to-use system, as easy to use as one of its predecessor systems (the IBM System/36). However, in some areas, it was harder to operate than the System/36. The AS/400 interface had largely been designed without direct involvement of the end users of the system. After customers complained, IBM decided to spend time with customers and business partners to determine exactly what kind of interface would better meet their requirements. IBM's business partners helped design the new screens, including the wording on some of the screens. Two years after the AS/400 system was released, IBM introduced the Operational Assistant, a new interface for the AS/400. Operational Assistant was designed, to a large extent, by IBM customers and business partners who used the system. The new interface got rave reviews, but some people asked why IBM didn't create the interface when the system was first released.

Values and agendas

It is inevitable (and directly to the point of an SIS) that when we identify the various sponsors of and participants in a system, we will be confronted with people who value different aspects of that system or who have agendas for how the system should be used that differ from our own. Often, when we hear and understand others' values and agendas, they seem reasonable—but again, we need the chance to hear them. When their values and agendas differ from ours, or when various people who will be using the system disagree with each other, we need at least to identify these differences and perhaps attempt to resolve them.

The choices posed by these disagreements can be difficult. Clearly it is awkward to tell an efficiency-oriented client that the employees value the chance to talk with one another and that they do not want a system that alienates them. It makes it easier if one can make the argument that this interaction helps productivity by encouraging joint problem solving (see the article by Kraut in Chapter 9). It is difficult to tell a cost-conscious government office that redundant (and possibly expensive) accuracy checks and update reminders need to be put into a database. It makes it easier if you can argue that the cost outweighs the risk of false-arrest lawsuits (see Clarke in Chapter 11). These choices are seldom as clear as they might seem in a textbook and often involve risk. But it is better to know that these choices are there than to assume that they are not.

SUGGESTIONS FOR DOING AN SIS

Contrary to popular belief, most of the benefits of an SIS can be gained by a targeted and relatively modest investment of time. If they are done right, even a one-day field trip, a half-day meeting with a user panel, or the construction of a day-in-the-life scenario can provide the careful designer with surprises. And after all, what you are looking for are surprises: Finding them now is better than finding them after the product has shipped or the system has been implemented.

An SIS should not be a graven-in-stone algorithm but a set of topics, decisions, and techniques that a project leader can select from so that the team does the "right amount" of work on an SIS for the project at hand. Some projects will require a larger amount of work than others, and the managers involved are the only ones who can make the decisions. They will need to determine (or get someone to determine) the appropriate topics for consideration, the people to include in the SIS, and the appropriate techniques to use to gather information.

Each project is different, as is each client and each product and each design team. Thus we cannot recommend any single method for doing an SIS that would be helpful to everyone. The individual project manager will need to customize the SIS for each particular instance. Some projects may not even need an SIS. The ethical and social implications of a faster sorting algorithm are likely (but not certain) to be minor and diffuse—and thus an SIS is likely to be a waste of time.

We can give some general suggestions for implementing an SIS. Not surprisingly, many of these suggestions are borrowed from the literature on Systems Design and Human-Computer Interaction. We will first mention some general considerations that should be included in any SIS. Then we will provide some suggestions about when an SIS might be appropriate. And finally, we will briefly present some methods that you might consider when doing an SIS.

Initial Considerations

Incorporate the SIS into the entire cycle of design, testing, implementation, maintenance, and revision of your system. You will do these stages anyway, and social and ethical issues can arise and be addressed in any of them. The social issues and risks associated with a system stem not just from the product but from the use of that product in a particular situation. So a problem with, say, privacy, might arise later as a system is used in an organization. You might not have been able to foresee this problem, but if you look, it may show up during maintenance and revision. Just as technical issues must be confronted throughout the life cycle of a product, the social and ethical issues are present throughout the life cycle as well.

Don't take it for granted that the "obvious" issues are the only ones that matter in implementing your system. It is a common cognitive failing to stop searching when a single instance has been found, but there are no guarantees that the issue you have identified is the only one—or even the most important one. Again, it will require a balancing of the available time and resources with the cost of missing an important issue.

When to Do a Social Impact Study

Just as technical and personnel requirements differ among projects, the requirements for a social impact study will differ from project to project. Not every system change requires a complete SIS, so the project manager must decide whether to do an SIS and how complete it should be. This judgment will require a balancing of the costs of the SIS with the risks of being ignorant of the information the SIS could provide.

Costs

Certainly there are direct costs for doing an SIS. The person-hours required and the incidental expenses (paper, travel, etc.) are perhaps the easiest part of this cost to estimate. There are, however, other costs that are much more difficult to estimate. To the extent that an SIS uncovers problems that require redesign, the additional time and materials required for the redesign is a cost (knowing what to redesign is also a benefit, but this is the cost section). This makes it clear that the tighter the schedule for a product, the more costly an SIS will become. This is when the project manager must choose among the various techniques listed below with an eye toward time savings. Some time savings can be achieved by running the SIS in parallel with other design work, but as design gets further along, redesign based on the outcome of an SIS becomes more costly.

Remember that the audience for an SIS is really your own design team (and perhaps the client). You are not producing publishable social science research; you just want to get a reasonable idea of the social and ethical issues associated with your project. Even major research projects often have difficulty predicting the actual path of technology change (Westrum, 1991; Rapp, 1991), so you should not expect to exceed their success rates. What you can do is alert yourself to the issues that your project is likely to raise, and thus be forearmed against problems associated with them. Remembering that your goal is merely to be forewarned can save you from costly investment in an elaborate SIS when only a quick look would have done.

Benefits

Much of this article has been an apology for the benefits of doing an SIS, but a few specific points should be made here. First, if your product is likely to be part of a critical system, you will certainly want the benefit of knowing the various ways that system might fail (there are always more than a first glance suggests). You may know (and should certainly ask!) the extent to which your product will be a part of a critical system or the single-point-of-failure in a system. Since components are often used in a variety of systems and since the social system surrounding a technology often changes, you cannot always know these things. An SIS can increase your chances of finding the failure points and can thus be a very valuable tool.

Second, it should be noted that whether an organization is buying or building their software, an SIS can provide the benefits of bringing to light the social and ethical issues associated with the use of the technology. Finally, the benefits you look for may not be associated with any changes in the design of the product but with changes in the process of implementation (e.g., training, distribution, documentation, support) or in your relationship with the client.

Thus, the basic question becomes: Will the effort we spend on an SIS pay off in changes to the design of the product or the process of implementation? If, as the project manager, you think this is likely, then an SIS, even in a limited form, is worth doing.

Some Useful Methods

For extremely small projects, the standard armchair method of inquiry may do fine. But even a group of concerned people cannot be sure to foresee all the issues a project might raise (see groupthink, above). There really is no substitute for looking for yourself.

The following methods are a selection of those that may be useful to you. Unless you are involved in a very large project, you are unlikely to use all of them. But using even one can help avoid nasty surprises when a system is finally implemented.

Field Observation

This involves taking time out from design to go to an organization that may be using your product and seeing how they do their tasks currently. If you use a field observation method, the extent of the system you are designing will determine the extent of the observation. A useful short observation may involve anywhere from 4 hours of time walking around asking questions and watching to a full day, or even several days. You may spend your time in 30-60 minute blocks, but even for very small jobs don't spend less than 4 hours total. Even (perhaps especially) those who know their jobs thoroughly may forget the "special cases" that will make your system founder. And people often describe their jobs in a way that leaves out significant portions. You can only catch this by paying special attention to what people do on their desks or with one another—these may be crucial to the job but left out of the design if they go unnoticed. Also be sure to choose times and places that represent the variety of jobs that individuals do. The less total time you spend, the more critical it is to choose representative (or nonrepresentative but crucial) times to observe.

Participatory Design

The best known models of participatory design teams are the Scandinavian models. These models propose (and have implemented) design processes where users, and other affected parties, take an active role in the design of the applications. Active user participation starts at the very beginning of the cycle and continues through the entire development life cycle. Several projects in Scandinavia have involved users, including UTOPIA, DEMOS, hospital information systems, and hotel information systems. For a good, short introduction to these procedures, see the book by Greenbaum & Kyng (1991) and the special issue of *Communications of the ACM* (Muller & Kuhn, 1993).

User Panels

A user panel can be a one-time event or a panel that is reconvened regularly throughout the life of the project. These panels can comment on how the system is used in their organization and how they currently do their job. They can also be involved in testing prototypes of the systems. Be sure your user panels are composed of both management and rank-and-file workers (if both types will be using the system). Be sure the users focus on how the system will work back at their organization—and not how it works in the lab. Finally, be sure to take their comments seriously. If user recommendations are ignored or, worse, belittled, then the reaction may be worse than if they were never sought at all. If you decide not to implement some suggestion (and you *will* have to decide this with every project), you should explain your decision in clear and respectful terms.

Specialized Team Members

Design teams often include specialized members recruited to deal with specific problems in a design. If your project is likely to have a great deal of impact on the social system in an organization or is likely to be in critical systems, you may consider including a sociologist or psychologist who is conversant with applications in your area. Alternatively, you may want to assign these duties to one of the team members who might then consult with others on these issues. The team member responsible for Computer-Human Interaction issues might be best suited for this assignment (Shneiderman, 1992). The presence of someone whose explicit duty is to consider these issues assures that they will get the consideration they need.

Questionnaires

If you need to find out the opinions of a large number of people about a few items, then a questionnaire is a reasonable way of going about it. But this method can also have serious pitfalls. Remember that most organizations (and most people, for that matter) are oversurveyed and that low return rates on your survey can seriously damage its usefulness. (Did just the people who hate your system reply? Just those who love it?) Questionnaires are particularly vulnerable to the tendency of people to report that they do a job in one way when they actually act quite differently. And there is no way to check on this except by doing some observation in addition to the questionnaire. In addition, the wording of a question can change the answers drastically, and wording effects can only be checked by having alternate wordings on the questionnaire. Finally, respondents to questionnaires may be trying to influence your decisions by slanting their answers in a way that distorts their true opinion or the realities of their job. So despite their apparent ease and objectivity, questionnaires are a tricky way to find out what opinions are in an organization.

If you still think you should use a questionnaire, consult with a professional in the area before spending much time on one. But it is better to think of some sort of observation that you can do (see Field Observation and Day-in-the-Life) that is less subject to the biases in questionnaires. If you need to do your own questionnaire, Fowler (1988), Miller (1991), and Shneiderman (1992) provide good, short introductions to the practical considerations in questionnaire design.

Day-in-the-Life

Building a day-in-the-life scenario is a good way to make sure that you have not overlooked what your clients really do with their time. Builders of a system are focused on the system they build (and rightly so). But this focus can blind them to other ways their system might be used—or misused. A day-in-the-life scenario forces you to look at the entire job of a client, again providing an opportunity for surprises about how the work your system is meant to do is actually done. The basic data for these scenarios can be gathered with panels, with interviews, with questionnaires, or with field observation (or with all these techniques). The scenario should account for *all* the time in a typical day, from arrival to departure, and should include as many "unusual" events as the participants can muster. These unusual events (incomplete data, power failures, etc.) can help to point out flaws in the system. The scenario need not concentrate on the day of a person, but might be a day-in-the-life of a program, or of some data. See Shneiderman (1992) for more in depth suggestions on the day-in-the-life approach.

Interviews

The interview is a good way to get some standard information from several people while including the possibility of in-depth information gathering. To make sure that at least some of the information in interviews is comparable across people, the interviews should have some portions of them standardized. Whenever possible, ask concrete questions (like "What is the first thing you usually do when you come in in the morning?" rather than "How do you spend your day?"). Shneiderman (1992) and Miller (1991) have good advice for designing interviews.

APPROPRIATE MODESTY AND THE DESIGN ETHIC

The technology we design is no longer being used just by other "computer people." It is being used in a wide range of complex situations, by a wide range of people and organizations. And this diversity and complexity demand our attention if we plan to design, build, and implement systems in the real world.

On a practical level, we think the examples from this book are convincing evidence that a system designed without considering larger social issues is a system in jeopardy of failure. Educational software can, because of its design and unknown to the designer, change the class dynamics for the better or the worse (see the article by Hativa et al. in Chapter 15). Components designed to be reasonably reliable individually can fail when combined with others or when not properly maintained (see the article by Reason in Chapter 5). Systems designed to increase the reliability of data entry can focus workers' attention on productivity, which may decrease the reliability of data entry (see the article by Grant et al. in Chapter 12). Thus, even if you do not want to build "prudent and safe" goods for society, you will still need to think about the social issues that your system brings to the fore. Or if you primarily care about a good system, on time, within budget, you will still have to take into account the social systems within which your computing system will be used. These two reasons for concerning yourself with social issues are woven together throughout this book.

In this chapter we have been emphasizing the similarities between the goals and values of the three legs of the design ethic. We have presented them as three mutually reinforcing pillars of our design ethic. And it is clear that they are connected and interdependent.

But our argument is not a naive proposition that ethical concern will always lead to better design, or to more satisfied customers. Or that quality products cannot be designed without social awareness. And within the limited time and budget for a system, there are surely cases where these are in conflict. Employees who have to make decisions about "whistle blowing" (Bok, 1983) know that the choices are not easy. If there is an outstanding concern about an issue (say, of reliability) and there is time pressure to produce the product, the system designer will have to make difficult choices.

Disagreements over these choices may lead to a designer deciding to blow the whistle, but people of goodwill can disagree on these decisions.

There are legitimate differences of opinion on many of the issues presented in this book. For instance, one designer may feel that extensive monitoring of work is both ethical and good for business, while another may feel that only limited monitoring is allowable. But both designers, if they care about producing a quality product, will want to know how monitoring affects workers and will want to think carefully about the ethical implications of the system they are designing. This example makes it clear that the design ethic is not a monolithic structure. There is no algorithm that resolves the differences in opinion that arise in system design, production, implementation, support, and maintenance. This is where your informed professional judgment comes in, and where you earn your salary.

An unwavering insistence on perfection in any of the three legs of the design ethic will destroy your chances of completing a project on time and within budget. But so, too, will an unreasoned commitment to technical excellence. The death of the Fort Knox project mentioned earlier was assured by the disagreements among technicians about what kind of, and what degree of, technical excellence was called for in the product. There are trade-offs to be made, and balancing things is your job.

For this reason, we do not care to pronounce absolute principles about ethical or moral imperatives. Systems design and technological innovation are, after all, not religions but practical undertakings. And in any practical undertaking, modesty about what we can really accomplish within the time allowed us is a helpful antidote to inflexibility. The design ethic we propose—and that we hope you will practice—will not make all systems always safe, or equitable, or ethical. It may not even make most systems attain these goals. But it will help us remember these goals, and provide some practical suggestions about how to reach them.

REFERENCES

Bauer, R., Collar, E., & Tang, V. (1992). *The Silverlake Project: Transformation at IBM*. New York: Oxford University Press.

Bok, S. (1983). *Secrets: On the Ethics of Concealment and Revelation.* New York: Random House.

Borenstein, N. S. (1991). *Programming as if People Mattered.* Princeton, NJ: Princeton University Press.

Brooks, F. (1975). *The Mythical Man-Month.* Reading, MA: Addison-Wesley.

Fowler, F. J. (1988). *Survey Research Methods.* Newbury Park, CA: Sage.

Greenbaum, J., & Kyng, M. (1991). *Design at Work : Cooperative Design of Computer Systems.* Hillsdale, NJ: Erlbaum.

Huff, C. W., & Cooper, J. (1987). Sex bias in educational software: the effects of designers' stereotypes on the software they design. *Journal of Applied Social Psychology, 17,* 519-532.

Janis, I. L. (1982). *Groupthink,* 2d ed. Boston: Houghton Mifflin.

Johnson, D. (1990). The social responsibility of computer professionals. *The Journal of Computing and Society, 1(2).* 107-118.

Johnson, D. (ed.) (1991). *Ethical Issues in Engineering*. Englewood Cliffs, NJ: Prentice Hall.

Miller, D. C. (1991). *Handbook of Research Design and Social Measurement*. Newbury Park, CA: Sage.

Muller, M. J., & Kuhn, S. (eds.) (1993). Special issue: participatory design. *Communications of the ACM, 36(4)*.

Peters, T. (1992). Foreword to Bauer, R., Collar, E., & Tang, V. (1992). *The Silverlake Project: Transformation at IBM*. New York: Oxford University Press.

Petroski, H. (1992, March-April) Making sure. *American Scientist, 80*, 121-124.

Rapp, F. (1991). The limited promise of technology assessment. In Paul Durbin (ed.). *Europe, America, and Technology: Philosophical Perspectives*, Boston: Kluwer Academic, 157-173.

Shneiderman, B. (1990, October). Human Values and the Future of Technology: A Declaration of Empowerment. *Computers & Society, 20(3)*, 1-6.

Shneiderman, B. (1992). *Designing the User Interface*. Reading, MA: Addison-Wesley.

Westrum, R. (1991). *Technologies & Society*. Belmont, CA: Wadsworth Publishing.

Winograd, T. (1990, April). What can we teach about human-computer interaction? *Empowering People: CHI'90 Conference Proceedings*, 443-449.

ORGANIZATIONS

Computer Professionals for Social Responsibility (CPSR). P.O. Box 717, Palo Alto, CA 94302. Focused on a number of computers and society issues, including the relatively new 21st Century Project, which is going to try to address the issues of environmental neglect, global cooperative development, and citizen participation in technical decision making.

EDUCOM. Suite 600, 1112 Sixteenth Street NW, Washington, DC 20036. One of the organizations focused on computing in higher education.

Electronic Frontier Foundation (EFF). 155 Second Street, Cambridge, MA 02141. Founded by Mitchell Kapor, one of the original founders of Lotus (of Lotus 1-2-3 fame). Focused on privacy, security, and property issues.

Research Center on Computing and Society. Southern Connecticut State University, 501 Crescent Street, New Haven, CT 06515. Sponsored the National Conference on Computing and Values (NCCV). The proceedings from that conference are well worth the investment.

Society on Social Implications of Technology (SSIT). IEEE, 345 East 47th Street, New York, NY 10017. This is IEEE's special group on technology and society. Interesting magazine published for members.

Special Interest Group in Computers and Society (SIGCAS). ACM, 11 West 42d Street, New York, NY 10036. This is ACM's special interest group on computers and society. This group sponsors or cosponsors a number of important conferences on computers and society, and computer ethics.

International Society for Technology in Education. 1787 Agate Street, Eugene, Oregon 97403-1923. This group sponsors conferences on technology in education at all grade levels and publishes books and journals.

In addition to the organizations mentioned above, there are several conferencing disk and bulletin boards that focus on computers and society issues. Among them are: The WELL (California), CompuServe, EcoNet, and PeaceNet.

READING QUESTIONS

1) Does the syllogism the authors lay out imply the conclusion they claim?
2) What has "traditional computing design" been like? What are the authors' complaints about this approach?
3) Why was Fort Knox the wrong system?
4) Why does isolation make it easy to think your concerns are the concerns of everyone?
5) What lesson did IBM Rochester draw from the failure of Fort Knox? How was it a change from the traditional approach?
6) Why was market analysis crucial to the success of AS400?
7) How is quality control more than "making sure [people] do the right thing"?
8) Why are cross-functional teams a response to isolation?
9) How does quality design connect with social awareness and ethical concern?
10) How do technical expertise and social systems interact to determine the design of a product?
11) How does the position of most designers in an industry diffuse their moral agency?
12) How does participating in organizations connect to ethical concern?
13) Why is a quality product linked with a more open method of design?
14) Why should we ask, "Why are we building this system?"?
15) Why is it difficult to determine the "right" issues to pursue when working on any particular system?
16) What is an SIS, and why might it be useful?
17) How does an SIS make the process of design "more rational"?
18) Why was the software designed for students really software for boys?
19) Why don't good intentions help to catch this bias in design?
20) What is groupthink? Why is it a danger in traditional design?
21) What is the difference between actual and idealized practice? How does one determine it?
22) Why is it important to identify "remote clients"?
23) Why should an SIS be incorporated into the entire life cycle of a product?
24) What "common cognitive failing" should we be concerned about when doing an SIS?
25) Who is the audience for the SIS, and how does that determine the rigor of methods?
26) What are the costs and benefits of doing an SIS?
27) What are some useful methods for doing an SIS, and how are they related to avoiding groupthink?
28) Why should the minimum field observation still be fairly long?
29) "If you primarily care about a good system, on time, within budget, you will still have to take into account the social systems...." Why?

DISCUSSION QUESTIONS

1) Do the three parts of the design ethic hang together? Under what kinds of circumstances might they conflict?
2) Look back at Anderson's article (in Chapter 2) on the ACM ethics code and on computer professionals. Try out various "core values" to see how they work with both the statements of the code and Anderson's claims about what a "profession" is. For instance, "make as much money as possible for my employer," "make the most advanced technology possible," "follow my obligation to my employer," etc. What light can this exercise shed on whether the design ethic proposed here hangs together?

GLOSSARY

active error: A term used when discussing the human contribution to system disasters. This type of error is most often associated with front-line operators like pilots, air traffic controllers, etc. The effects of this type of error are felt almost immediately. Contrast with *latent error*.

adaptive computer technology: An application of computer technology that provides to people with disabilities new resources for bridging educational and employment gaps.

address vectors: An internal table in DEC computers that allows the software to link up correctly with the hardware.

aggregate demand: Total desired purchases of an economy's output by all the buyers.

algorithm: A series of instructions or a prescribed set of steps for solving a problem.

algorithmic programs: A program with a series of instructions or a prescribed set of steps for solving a problem.

analog computer: A computer that measures infinitely varying conditions, such as temperature and pressure, and converts them to quantities.

analyses of variance : See *ANOVA*.

ANOVA (Analysis of Variance): A statistical technique that is used to compare the differences between two or more groups in order to decide whether or not there is a difference between the groups on the measured variable.

ARPANET (Advanced Research Projects Agency NETwork): A resource-sharing computer network that links government offices, research centers, and other host computers around the world.

artificial intelligence (also AI): A branch of computer science that studies machines that exhibit humanlike behavior and intelligence. AI also studies how "smart" a machine can be.

AS/400 (Application System/400): A series of computers introduced in 1988 by IBM.

ASCII (American Standard Code for Information Interchange): A code for data used to facilitate interchange of data among various types of computer equipment.

backward chaining: One of two strategies used by a control structure to manipulate the knowledge-base rules in an expert system. The other strategy is called *forward chaining*. Of the two, backward chaining is by far the more popular.

bandwidth: Measurement of the transmission capacity of a computer or communications channel. Expressed in bits per second or baud.

BASIC (Beginners' All-purpose Symbolic Instruction Code): A simple programming language that has been implemented on all sizes of computers.

batch production system: A technique of processing computer data wherein the transactions are collected in one "batch" and then processed as a single unit, instead of as they arrive. (compare with *time-sharing system*)

Beta-weights: See *regression coefficients*.

bit-mapped graphics: An area of memory that represents a graphic image. Each pixel corresponds to one or more bits in memory.

bivariate analysis: Any statistical analysis that uses two varibles, usually to compare them or to determine the extent to which they influence each other.

bootlegged software: Software that has been in some way illegally obtained, stolen, or not properly licensed.

bootstrapping: (1) starting the computer or (2) when clinicians are replaced by the regression equation that models what they do.

bug: An unwanted, unintended property of computer software or hardware that causes a computer operation to malfunction, or to function unexpectedly.

bulletin boards: BBS Bulletin Board System. A collection of information that is stored on a computer network and available to anyone using a modem who dials the number over the public phone system.

CAD (Computer Aided Design) *system:* A process which uses a computer system to assist in the creation, modification, and display of a design.

CAI (Computer Assisted Instruction): The use of computers to aid in or support the education and training of individuals. Allows students to proceed at their own pace.

capital costs: The costs associated with all things needed to produce goods and services.

carpal tunnel syndrome: Condition characterized by attacks of pain and tingling in the first three or four fingers of one or both hands, which usually occur at night.

CD-ROM: (Compact Disk–Read Only Memory): The same size as a music compact disk but used instead to store data to be read by a computer. This form of storage is read only.

Chi-square: A common statistical test used in psychological research to help one make a decision about whether the items being counted are proportionally distributed among the groups.

chips: See *Microchips.*

clinical psychologist: A psychologist trained in the diagnosis and treatment of emotional or behavioral problems and mental disorders.

COBOL (Common Business-Oriented Language): A high-level programming language developed in 1960 for business data processing applications.

command-driven: A program that relies on the typed-in phrases of the user in order to run. Compare with *menu-driven.*

commercial information systems: Information systems accessible via the internet that one must pay to use.

compiler: A program that translates high-level language statements readable by humans (e.g., BASIC, COBOL, C) into a machine code form used by the computer.

component: One element of a computer system or a part of an application.

Computer Supported Cooperative Work (CSCW): The domain of the study of individuals working together using computer technology to improve or aid in the work they do together. *Groupware* is a subfield of this domain.

computer conferences: The interacting of individuals at various locations through the use of computer terminals.

computer-mail system: See *electronic mail.*

computer-matching or matching: Comparing separate electronically stored records of individuals in a way that allows one to check for matches or mismatches in the information. Often used to detect fraud or misuse of funds.

configuration: (1) The mix, connection, and layout of a network. If the network is running through satellites, more than one path is possible for the data being transmitted to follow. The picking of the shortest route, done by computers, is called the configuration. (2) The mix, connection, and layout of components in a computer system. (3) Using an expert system to translate a customer's need into a complete computer system.

control structure: The part of an expert system that consists of metarules and manipulates the rules that make up the knowledge base.

correlation: A statistical technique that determines the relationship between two variables.

correlation analysis: Statistical analysis to determine if two variables vary together; e.g. taller people have longer arms.

coupling: Defines the way in which a computer system is tied together. *Tight coupling* means that the events in the system are very dependent on one another, processes happen very fast, and they cannot be stopped or turned off since one interaction leads directly to the next. Therefore, if a system is tightly coupled and an accident occurs, recovery is almost impossible. *Loose coupling* means that the events in the system occur independently of one another and use their own logic to run. In this case, the system can incur shocks and failures without taking down the entire system.

CPMCS (Computerized Performance Monitoring and Control Systems): A computerized monitoring mechanism that records and reports computer-driven activity in an organizational setting.

CPU (Central Processing Unit): The central part of a computer containing the internal storage (memory), control unit, and arithmetic unit.

Cray supercomputer: Considered the first computer in the *supercomputer* class. It has, for many years, held the title of the fastest production computer in the world.

cyberspace: A very broad term used to define the space "out there" where we all connect when communicating via computers.

database : A large file of data organized so that various programs can access and update the information.

dataveillance: The use of personal data systems to investigate or monitor the communications or actions of one or more individuals.

deadlock (also deadly embrace): A situation that occurs when two or more processes on a single computer are competing for the same resources and each is waiting for the other to release control of the resources the other needs to complete the task.

debugging: The detection, location, and correction of errors (also called *bugs*) in hardware or software.

DEC (Digital Equipment Corporation): An established computer hardware and software manufacturer known for the VAX systems and recently for the Alpha computer chip.

decision support system: System used to gather, analyse, and present data to aid in making a decision. Compare with *persuasion support system*.

dependent variable: A factor in an experimental setting that depends on (usually meaning: is caused by) the action of the independent variable.

deskilling: A perspective on the impact of new information technologies. Deskilling suggests that computerization strips a job of its conceptual (and rewarding) characteristics. Contrast with *upgrading*.

digital circuits: An electronic circuit that responds to digital signals and produces digital signals as its output.

digital computer: A computer that manipulates data presented as binary numbers.

discriminant analysis: A statistical technique that attempts to determine if two or more groups are different from each other by combining several variables to predict those differences.

DRAM: Random Access Memory that is readable and writable.

economic dualism: An economic system separated into two main parts, the core and the peripheral economies. The core consists chiefly of large, well-capitalized organizations, whereas the periphery tends to be small companies with less technological sophistication.

editor: Computer programs designed for reviewing and altering files or programs interactively.

electromechanics: A branch of electrical engineering that deals with machines operated by or producing electric currents.

electromyography: A method of recording the electrical currents generated in an active muscle.

electronic communication: See *electronic mail.*

electronic mail (E-mail): The use of electronic communications media to send, receive, store, and forward messages by means of a computer network. The messages can be sent either to one person or broadcast to many recipients.

electronic surveillance: Surveillance of one or more individuals using both physical surveillance, such as microphones and bugs, and communications surveillance, such as telephone taps.

end-user: Anyone who uses a computer system at an application level. Most technical personnel are not thought of as end-users when working in a professional capacity with computers.

epicondylitis: Infection or inflammation of a projection from a long bone near a joint.

exogenous variables: Variables that are not affected by other variables under consideration in a study. However, an exogenous variable may affect a variable in the study.

expert system (ES): An artificial intelligence application that has been designed to assist the user by making intelligent choices. The computer makes a decision based on what the user has input. All this is done with limited user interaction. Expert systems are highly specialized and sophisticated *knowledge-based* computer programs.

file analysis: The application of dataveillance techniques to existing records on an individual.

flaming: A term used for behavior on the internet where one person attacks another with sarcastic comments, using extreme opinions.

floppy disk: A magnetic disk that can store computer data; relatively inexpensive.

fly-by-wire control system: A control system that is operated entirely or mainly by electronic devices rather than by mechanical or hydraulic ones.

FORTRAN (FORmula TRANslator): Fortran was the first high-level programming language. It was developed in 1954 by IBM and is used to perform mathematical, scientific, and engineering computations.

forward-chaining: One of two strategies used by a control structure to manipulate the knowledge-base rules in an expert system. The other strategy is *backward-chaining.*

front-end audit: Broad form of personal dataveillance that uses the occasion of the detection of an exceptional transaction as an opportunity to further investigate other matters relating to the individual.

front-end verification: A personal dataveillance technique for verifying and testing transactions that involves the collection of data from other personal-data systems.

ftp (File Transfer Protocol): Transferring a file from one computer to another over a network. Also the standard and the program used to do this operation.

fundamental attribution error: Term used for the blaming of outcomes on the individual and ignoring or underestimating situational factors that are beyond an individual's control.

fundamental surprise: Reveals a profound difference between an individual's view of the world and reality. A major reassessment is required from the individual. Compare with *situational surprise.*

gate-array: Basic gates found on one computer chip that are arranged in a geometric pattern.

graphic interface: An interface similar to a Macintosh that uses graphics as its base; for instance, icons, mouse, and pull-down menus.

groupthink: A phenomenon in which a decision-making group loses touch with the environment around it, yet thinks it is still receptive to outside influence. All outside influence is, however, filtered, blocked, or denigrated.

groupware: Software that is developed for use on a network in order to allow different members of a group to cooperate and work jointly on a project.

hacker: Originally, a person who is experienced in using computers and is totally engrossed in programming and technology; now used more to refer to someone who intentionally invades or generally misuses computers.

hardware: The physical, tangible equipment that makes up a computer system. Contrast with *software*.

horizontal fragmentation: Process of industrial development by which an organization, specifically a computer company, is transformed into self-standing companies separate from the parent company. The parent company is left standing alone with not much room for growth.

Human Computer Interaction (HCI or, sometimes, CHI, for Computer Human Interaction): The study of the interaction of humans with all aspects of computing.

human supervisory control: Retaining humans (called operators) in a highly complex system in order to handle possible failures that the system designers did not foresee and the computers have no ability to deal with.

human system interface: See *interface*.

human-interactive system (HIS): Part of a computer system that intercedes between the human operator and the lower-level controllers, called the task-interactive systems (TIS). The HIS is an "intelligent" computer that controls the TIS, is capable of communicating the state of the system to the operator through its displays, and can also receive commands from the operator. Compare with *task-interactive system*.

IF...THEN statements: One of the basic building blocks of programming languages that permits the choosing between two alternatives, depending on the answer given.

ILS (Integrated Learning Systems): Connected sets of computer programs that are used to teach a series of lessons or several related lessons to students.

information processing capacity: A measure of the impact an expert system has on an organization. The information processing capacity of an organization captures the changes in input and output of a target task.

information processing: The creation, storage, retrieval, communication, and evaluation of information in organizations or the economy as a whole.

information system: A computer-based system integrated into an organization whose primary purpose is to collect, record, store, and retrieve information to support decision making and control.

information technology: Any software, hardware, or techniques associated with moving, collecting, storing, or accessing the commodity of information.

input: Data that are ready for entry, or have been entered, into a computer.

input fraud: A form of computer crime that involves the manipulation of information fed into a computer; probably the most widespread as well as the most often reported computer crime.

input/output analysis: A form of economic analysis that examines the links between factors of production (e.g., labor, capital), intermediate goods (e.g., chips for computers), and final goods (e.g., the computer itself).

Intel: A semiconductor manufacturer that has produced the 8088, 80286, 80386, and 80486 microprocessors, which are installed in well over 70 million computers worldwide.

intercorrelation: The correlation of a variable with each of the other variables in a group.

interface: The connections and interrelationships among hardware, software, and the user. For instance, user interfaces include the keyboards, mice, and menus used to communicate to the computer.

internet: (1) a group of smaller connected networks. (2) The worldwide network consisting of smaller government and academic networks.

interoccupational change: A manifestation of *deskilling* in which the number of people in less-skilled jobs increases and the number of people in skilled jobs decreases. Could also mean that the skill required for a particular job decreases over time.

IRC (Internet Relay Chat): A program that allows two or more individuals to type messages to each other that appear on the other person's screen as they are typed.

knowledge-based system: An artificial intelligence application that is most often found in expert systems. The knowledge base could represent the knowledge and experience of an expert in the field in which the application is being used.

labor productivity: A factor of production consisting of all physical and mental efforts provided by individuals.

latent error: A term used when discussing the human contribution to system disasters. This type of error is most often associated with "behind the scenes" individuals, i.e., program or equipment designers. The adverse effects of this type of error may not be felt immediately since they can be present yet unnoticed in a computer system for a long time.

life course socialization: A school of sociological thought that emphasizes the importance of social expectations and their influence on the individual over an entire life span.

Likert scale: A method for scaling items usually found in survey format where, for instance, (5) may be strongly agree and (1) may be strongly disagree.

line editor: A simple, rudimentary text editing program that permits text to be changed a single line at a time.

linear system: The structure of a computer wherein items are organized in terms of strict rules of precedence. This type of structure is very simple and comprehensible because it is the expected and familiar sequence of events. Contrast with *nonlinear system*.

LISP (LISt Processing): A programming language primarily designed for use in AI research that manipulates nonnumeric data.

local area network (LAN): A network of software, hardware, and servers within a certain geographical area that allows sharing of data and other resources.

LOGO: A high-level programming language that was developed in the 1960s for use in teaching children. It is highly interactive and has been widely used in business and industry for graphic reports.

Macintosh: A series of popular microcomputers from Apple Computer, Inc., introduced in 1984.

macroeconomic: The study of economic aggregates, such as total output, total employment, the price level, and the rate of economic growth.

macroethical: Ethical issues in an organization that confront members of a profession as a group in their relation to society. Contrast with *microethical*.

mainframe: A class of computer decided upon by speed, capability, and price. The meaning of the word has changed over time because of the ever-increasing power and speed of computers.

mass surveillance: Surveillance of groups of people, usually large groups. Usually the reason for the investigation or monitoring is to identify individuals in the group who are of interest to the surveillance organization.

mean: A measure of central tendency; an average of a set of scores.

mechatronics: The combination of mechanical and computer technologies.

median nerve: Nerve in the the forearm, innervating most of the forearm flexor muscles, the short muscles of the thumb, hand joints, skin on the hand, elbow joint, pulp under nails.

memory: The form of storage on a computer where information can be read and written and held for later use.

menu-driven: A program that presents all commands in a series of menus from which the user selects options from a list. Compare with *command-driven*.

microchips: A single device consisting of components that form the central processor of a computer.

microcomputer: The smallest and least expensive classification of computers available. The entire computer system is integrated on one circuit called a microprocessor. It functions similar to a larger computer, but is aimed at one user.

microelectronics: The entire body of electronics that is connected with or applied to electronic systems from extremely small electronic parts.

microethical: Ethical issues in an organization that concern the personal relationships between individuals. Examples include the ordinary notions of civility, honesty, respect, and decency. Contrast with *macroethical.*

microprocessors (also called processors): Central control device of a microcomputer that holds the portion that executes instructions for the rest of the computer to follow.

MIS (Management Information System): A system that helps managers with their planning, monitoring, and controlling functions in an organization; can also refer to all of the computing systems in an organization that support management.

modem: A device that sends computer data over telephone circuits.

module: A specific part of a hardware or software component. Hardware modules are a smaller part of the larger computer system, and software modules handle a specific task in a computer program.

MS-DOS (Microsoft Disk Operating System): Standard operating system for PC-compatible computers.

multiple regression: A statistical technique that allows predictions to be made about the performance of one variable based on performance of two or more other variables.

multivariate analysis: Any statistical technique that looks at the relationship between three or more variables.

multivariate correlation: A statistical technique that can be used to determine the relationship between two sets of variables.

musculoskeletal: Pertaining to the muscles and skeleton.

negative somatic effects: Negative effects relating to the body (soma = body).

network: An arrangement of interconnected workstations that ties users together.

network protocols: A set of rules used to govern the exchange of information over a communication medium.

neurologist: A physician who studies the treatment and diagnosis of nervous system diseases.

nodes: Servers and workstations or other types of devices connected to a network.

nonlinear system (also called complex interactions): The structure of a computer in which the interaction of events happens outside the normal linear pattern. This type of structure is unexpected and not easily comprehensible. Contrast with *linear system.*

nonvolatile memory: Memory that keeps its information even during the removal of operating power.

occupational overuse syndrome: See *repetitive strain injury.*

oligopoly: A market structure in which few sellers dominate the sales of a product and the entrance of new sellers is difficult or impossible.

operating system (also called OS): The master control program for a computer that runs the overall operation of the computer. All programs used must be written so that they "talk to" the specific operating system.

optical storage technology: The storage of data or images by optical means.

organization information: The entire information system of an organization, including the gossip about other individuals and the information about organizational goals.

organizational informatics: A broad field which studies very diverse aspects of computation, including the development and use of computerized information systems and communication systems in organizations as well as in many different social settings.

organizational norms: Standard, accepted forms of behavior in an organization, including dress, punctuality, and productivity.

output: End result of data that have been generated by a computer. Contrast with *input*.

output-oriented crime: A technique of computer fraud that involves the manipulation and misappropriation of computer output. Compare with *input fraud*.

packet switching systems: A method of transmitting messages where the connection through a communications network occupies a channel only for the duration of the transmission of one packet.

parallel computing (also called multiprocessing or parallel processing):   An architecture in a computer that enables it to simultaneously perform more than one operation at the same time. For instance, one operation could be performed on many sets of data, or multiple computers could process a job together.

parallel port: An external connector on a computer where parallel devices are plugged in, such as a printer.

parallel processing: See *parallel computing*.

PASCAL: A high-level programming language that was developed in the 1970s. Used in both applications programming and system development.

PDP-11 (Programmed Data Processor): A family of computers manufactured by Digital Equipment Corporation. The first PDP-11 was introduced in 1959, and eventually led to the development of the VAX computers.

performance program: A measure of the impact an expert system has on an organization. A performance program is all the mechanisms used within an organization to make decisions and to carry out work.

personal computer: A class of computer that has storage and processing capabilities while able to sit upon a desk. Generally the smallest and slowest of all the classes of computers.

personal dataveillance: Surveillance of an identified person using personal data systems to monitor or investigate his or her communications and actions.

personal surveillance: Surveillance of an identified person. Usually a specific reason exists for the monitoring or investigation.

persuasion support system: System used to gather data to persuade others that the decision which has already been made is the correct one. The actual decision itself has nothing to do with the support system. Compare with *decision support system*.

principle components analysis: A multivariate statistical technique that analyzes the relationships among a large number of variables, allowing the user to describe these relationships in terms of a smaller set of constructed variables. If this is successful, the new "components" can be thought of as describing the structure of the original data set.

profiling: A technique used to make a judgment about an individual on the basis of past behavior of other individuals who appear similar.

programmable logic chips: Microchips that can be programmed or altered by the user after they are manufactured.

programming language: A sequence of commands, functions, and statements used by programmers to write instructions for a computer to follow. Hundreds of different programming languages exist.

psychomotor: Combined physical and mental activity.

psychophysiological: A psychological factor affecting physical condition.

psychosocial: Any situation where both psychological and social factors are assumed to play a role.

public domain software: Software available for free distribution to anyone who wants to use it.

RAM (Random Access Memory): The primary memory of a computer. Data are temporarily stored here for processing but erased when the computer is shut off.

regression coefficients: Numbers in a regression equation that represent the amount that one variable contributes to the prediction of another variable.

regression equation: A statistical technique in model building concerned with defining a dependent variable in terms of a set of independent variables.

reliability: The degree to which results are consistent and reproducible in an experiment. Compare with *validity*.

reliability coefficient: A measure of reliability that describes the degree of relationship between two sets of scores.

remote terminal: Computer that is physically separated from the mainframe.

Repetitive Strain Injury (RSI): A computer-related health epidemic thought to be caused by rapid, repetitive movement of the arms or hands. (Also *occupational overuse syndrome*)

RISC (Reduced-Instruction-Set Chip): A microprocessor made under the philosophy of streamlining the internal workings of the computer. It reduces the number of instructions the processor can do, thus making it faster than the traditional CISC (Complex-Instruction-Set chip).

segmented institutionalist: Makes the assumption about computing in organizations that goals are ambiguous and resources inadequate and problematic. Further, groups may seriously conflict within and between organizations. Computerization is viewed as much more problematic than a *systems rationalist* would. Compare with *systems rationalist*.

semiconductor: An electronic device made of semiconductor materials, such as silicon, that provides insulation inside a computer.

serial port: An external port on a computer where serial devices, such as a modem, are plugged in.

server: A high-speed machine that holds programs and data shared by all users in a computer network

Silicon Valley: The area in northern California around Sunnyvale that has attracted most semiconductor manufacturers.

silicon: A chemical element that serves as a semiconductor in microelectronics.

simulation: The imitation of the behavior of some existing or intended system or process on a machine that will act as if it were the system itself.

situational surprise: Specific events that require the solution of individual problems. There is no change of the individual's actual perception of the world or reality. Compare with *fundamental surprise*.

snoopware: Using groupware to monitor all employees' work, sometimes even threatening to shut down computers or cut off budgets if enough progress isn't seen.

social control: Efforts to define and bring about "correct" behaviors or statuses. Social control enables organizations to exclude inappropriate individuals from things to which they are not entitled and to take coercive action against those whose behavior is considered threatening.

social psychology: A branch of psychology that concentrates on aspects of human behavior as it relates to relationships with other persons, groups, social institutions, and society as a whole.

social stratification: The segmentation of people into groups in a society. Usually refers to segmentation based on economic status

software piracy: The illegal copying of commercial software.

software: The programs designed to run on a computer system. Contrast with *hardware*.

spreadsheet: Any program with a wide range of business uses that arranges formulas and data into a matrix of rows and columns called cells. The worksheet can have thousands of horizontal and vertical cells.

standard deviation (sometimes written s.d., sd or SD) A statistical technique measuring the variability of a sample of scores from the mean of a sample.

supercomputer: The largest, fastest classification of computers available. They are very expensive and are typically used for only the most difficult or time-consuming computational tasks.

surveillance: Investigation or monitoring of the communications or actions of one of more individuals.

systems rationalist: Makes the assumption about computing that emphasizes the positive roles computers play in life. Assumes further that organizational goals are clear, resources are ample, and participants are generally very cooperative.

t-test: A common statistical test used in psychological research that allows one to tell if differences between two groups are reliable.

task-interactive system (TIS): Part of a computer system which separates the human operator from the processes he or she controls. A TIS is the lowest level of interaction. It controls the various detailed aspects of the operation, like propellers, engines, pumps, and switches. The TIS is incapable of adjusting these things, but instead brings them to predetermined set points. Compare with *human-interactive system*.

TCP/IP (Transmission Control Protocol/Internet Protocol):   Communications protocols that internetwork different types of systems.

telecom networks: The equipment (wiring, routers, computers) and software that are used to transport signals involved in telecommunications, i.e., voice, data and computer communications from one point to another.

telecommunications: All types of systems that convert and transmit information between two points, one of those points usually being a computer.

telecommuting: The use of computers and telecommunication networks to perform the tasks of your job while being away from the "office."

teleconferencing : Simultaneous meeting of people over one network, allowing them to communicate over some distance.

telework: Working at a location other than the typical office setting (usually at home) and communicating with the office via telecommunications.

tenosynovitis: Inflammation of a tendon.

terminal: A general term used for the collection of hardware, such as keyboards and screens, that provide access to the network.

text editing: Making additions, deletions, or any other changes to words, sentences, or paragraphs in electronically stored data.

text editor: Programs which allow changes to be made in electronically stored data.

text formatting: The laying out of a document. Includes the font type, point size, numbers of columns, etc.

time-sharing system: A technique for sharing the time of a computer among several users for different purposes at the same time. The computer serves each user in sequence, but the high speed allows the transactions to appear simultaneously. Compare with *batch production system.*

Turing machine: A simplified imaginary computing machine that is used for the theoretical study of computer algorithms.

type one error: An error made when one believes there are differences in an experimental group because of the independent variables, when in fact the differences were the result of chance.

type two error: An error made when one believes there are no differences between experimental groups, when in fact the independent variable did have an influence.

ulnar nerve: Nerve that runs along the forearm next to the ulna—one of the forearm bones that run from the elbow to the wrist—and innervates the muscles of the hand, elbow, wrist and hand joints, and the skin of the palm of the hand.

univariate data: Data that consist of only one variable.

UNIX: Operating system, designed in 1971 by AT&T Bell Laboratories, that runs on a wide range of computer systems, from microcomputers to mainframes.

upgrading: A perspective on the impact of new information technologies that believes computerization removes the mundane aspects of jobs which are basically repetitious.

USENET: A large, decentralized bulletin board system that is supported mainly by UNIX machines.

user: Any individual who utilizes a computer at the application level. Usually, programmers or others involved in computers at the professional level are not considered users.

user-friendly: Software or hardware that is easy to learn and use.

validity: Accuracy of ideas and research. To be valid, a measurement must reflect the true score within certain limits. Compare with *reliability.*

vascular electrodiagnosis: Determining the nature of a disease relating to blood vessels through observation of changes in electrical activity.

VAX (Virtual Address Extension): A family of computers, ranging from desktop computers to large-scale mainframes, introduced in 1977 by Digital Equipment Corporation.

vertical fragmentation: Process of industrial development by which an organization, specifically a computer company, is broken down into several independent entities, each operating in its own best interest.

virtual reality: Three-dimensional space generated by the computer that the user can interact with using all the senses.

wideband net: A network that can carry a lot of information. It can, for instance, transport many messages at one time.

word processor: Computer programs designed for the creation, management, and manipulation of text documents.

working memory: The portion of the computer the CPU uses for storage while running programs. It is not considered permanent and is cleared when power is removed.

workstation: An input/output station connected to a network that can access other workstations and shared resources.

XSEL: An expert system that helps a salesperson translate a customer's business needs into specific parts and computers.

zero-order correlation matrix: A set of correlations, each item of which represents the relationship between two variables. All possible pairwise correlations between variables are included in the matrix. Three variables would produce a correlation matrix of three items; four variables would produce a correlation matrix of six items, etc.